Museum Law

NOTE TO THE READER

"This publication is designed to provide accurate and authoritative information in regard to the subject matter covered. It is sold with the understanding that the publisher is not engaged in rendering legal, accounting, or other professional service. If legal advice or other expert assistance is required, the services of a competent professional person should be sought." —*From a Declaration of Principles Adopted Jointly by a Committee of the American Bar Association and a Committee of Publishers*

Museum Law

A GUIDE FOR OFFICERS, DIRECTORS, AND COUNSEL

FOURTH EDITION

Marilyn E. Phelan

ROWMAN & LITTLEFIELD
Lanham • Boulder • New York • Toronto • Plymouth, UK

Published by Rowman & Littlefield
4501 Forbes Boulevard, Suite 200, Lanham, Maryland 20706
www.rowman.com

10 Thornbury Road, Plymouth PL6 7PP, United Kingdom

British Library Cataloguing in Publication Information Available

Library of Congress Cataloging-in-Publication Data

Phelan, Marilyn E., author.
Museum law : a guide for officers, directors, and counsel / Marilyn E. Phelan.—Fourth Edition.
pages cm
Includes bibliographical references and index.
ISBN 978-0-7591-2434-9 (cloth : alk. paper)—ISBN 978-0-7591-2435-6 (electronic) 1. Museums—Law and legislation—United States. I. Title.
KF4305.P54 2014
344.73'093—dc23 2014003636

∞™ The paper used in this publication meets the minimum requirements of American National Standard for Information Sciences—Permanence of Paper for Printed Library Materials, ANSI/NISO Z39.48-1992.

Printed in the United States of America

To Harold; our children, Pat, Scott, and Kim; their spouses, Cara, Laura, and Robert; and the inspirations for us all: Ryan, Katherine, Claire, Grace, Michael, Rachel, Reece, and Sydney.

CONTENTS

PART II: MUSEUM COLLECTIONS

TABLE OF SELECTED CASES

PREFACE

The Congress of the United States, in establishing the National Foundation on Arts & Humanities in 1965 (Pub. L. 89-209, 20 U.S.C. § 951), declared that an "advanced civilization must not limit its efforts to science and technology alone, but must give full value and support to other great branches of scholarly and cultural activity in order to achieve a better understanding of the past, a better analysis of the present, and a better view to the future." In acknowledging that "democracy demands wisdom and vision in its citizens," Congress determined that it was necessary that the federal government "foster and support a form of education, and access to the arts and the humanities, designed to make people of all backgrounds and wherever located masters of their technology and not its unthinking servants." Congress acknowledged that the "arts and humanities belong to all the people of the United States" and found that "to fulfill its educational mission, achieve an orderly continuation of free society, and to provide models of excellence to the American people, the Federal Government must transmit the achievement and values of civilization from the past via the present to the future."

Museums serve as depositories of the world's treasures, and as such, must carry out a special mission to preserve and protect these treasures and to assist Congress in transmitting "the achievement and values of civilization from the past via the present to the future." In possessing the resources and the knowledge through their professionals to fulfill their special mission, museums must form mutually beneficial relationships with the art world and with individuals and countries that play major roles in the protection and preservation of the natural and cultural heritage. A museum's unique kinship with "great branches" of artistic, scholarly, and cultural activity, and each museum's special mission to protect the natural and cultural heritage, mandate that museum officials and personnel possess a knowledge of laws and regulations protecting the arts and humanities and the world's natural resources and cultural property. The role of museums in promoting and advancing the arts dictates that museum personnel be knowledgeable of laws that protect artistic collections. Further, in protecting and preserving the natural and cultural heritage, museum personnel must be aware of the growing and distinct body of national and international cultural property laws that expound on the ownership, preservation, and protection of cultural property and that protect wildlife and natural resources. This text provides a comprehensive summary of those laws.

Museum professionals often are respected artists, archaeologists, and anthropologists. They generally have reputations in the sciences, humanities, and arts. However, their exceptional expertise in these fields does not prepare them for the complicated, recurring, sometimes mundane, and often multitudinous legal, tax, and governance issues that will confront them in their role of managing and operating a museum. Museum professionals must make daily decisions that will have significant legal and tax consequences, but in failing to recognize a legal or tax issue, a museum professional may not address a problem sufficiently and in advance to avoid unintended and often harmful results. When museum professionals do seek counsel, they may discover the problem can no longer be solved in a favorable manner. In addition, the lawyer may not be familiar with laws that are particularly relevant to museum operations. Thus, the museum director may find it difficult to communicate with counsel and may find that solutions to their problems are not readily available. Museum professionals also must monitor the daily activities of a museum to avoid jeopardizing the museum's tax exempt status, but most would not recognize a tax problem. In addition, these professionals frequently find themselves ill-equipped to deal with the difficult personnel problems related to supervising museum employees. The purpose of this text is to furnish museum professionals and personnel with a guide to recognizing, addressing, and preventing legal and tax complications. The book provides a comprehensive coverage of the laws and tax provisions that affect museum operations through a simple and concise discussion of these laws as well as a practical application of the laws to specific situations through examples and case studies taken from actual events.

Part I (Chapters 1–4) provides museum officials and personnel with an understanding of the laws, regulations, and tax provisions that affect museum operations on a daily basis. Although the reader may find material in these chapters to be less interesting than, and not as piquant as, the discussions in Parts II and III, the chapters in Part I may prove to be the most useful because they furnish museum personnel with the valuable guidance they need to meet daily, recurring governance issues. By supplying a basic understanding of the legal principles that apply to the different types of museums, a comprehensive study of the first four chapters will provide a substantial working knowledge of the legal and tax principles needed to operate a museum properly. These chapters should bring about a recognition and understanding of basic governance principles that will provide a foundation to address concepts and problems in the later chapters. For example, the first four chapters include a discussion of legal and ethical standards governing the roles and responsibilities of directors and trustees of nonprofit organizations. One chapter considers conflict of interest transactions. Another chapter discusses laws relating to personnel as well as possible liability for the tortious actions and activities of employees, guards, and volunteers. Two chapters cover rules and procedures to obtain and maintain tax exempt status; the tax provisions relating to donations to museum collections; a summary of accounting rules to provide an understanding of accounting records and reports; and a discussion of funding opportunities and the unrelated business taxable income concept, to include the tax treatment of revenue generated from museum gift shops, snack bars and cafeterias, travel tours and advertising, and investments, such as rental income, royalty income from licensing agreements, sales of mailing lists, and affinity credit card arrangements. The tax chapters are lengthy and cover somewhat complex tax issues; thus, they are not easy reading. Still, a museum professional must recognize basic tax issues to assure the museum maintains its tax exempt status. Although a museum would not owe any income taxes as a tax exempt entity (unless it has unrelated business taxable income), the federal government will have substantial controls over its activities because it is tax exempt. The museum professional must keep and preserve substantial information and records to demonstrate the museum's financial accountability as well as to maintain its tax exempt status.

Part II (Chapters 5–8) provides guidance in managing and protecting collections. It includes a discussion of legal issues relating to acquisitions, such as the possibility of unauthentic and stolen or illegally exported objects in a collection and laws relating to collections on loan and through donations. It summarizes the statutes that exempt loaned collections from seizure and the issues relating to the deaccessioning of acquisitions. One chapter sets out current case law relating to stolen and illegally exported cultural property. The chapters include a discussion of rights of artists in their works and a review of copyright laws as they pertain to museum collections as well as other laws affecting collections, to include the right of privacy and the right of publicity.

Part III (Chapters 9–11) sets out conventions, laws, and regulations, both national and international, that have been enacted to govern and to provide guidance in the protection and preservation of the natural and cultural heritage. One chapter discusses the international treaty that protects the natural heritage (Convention on International Trade in Endangered Species of Wild Fauna and Flora) and summarizes federal statutes protecting our wildlife, to include, among others, the Migratory Bird Treaty Act, the Marine Mammal Protection Act, the Endangered Species Act, and the Bald and Golden Eagle Protection Act. Another chapter covers laws protecting the cultural heritage, including the federal antiquities laws, the National Historical Preservation Act, and the Archaeological Resources Protection Act. This chapter details legal issues related to sunken treasures and summarizes issues relating to the preservation of Native American artifacts. It includes a discussion of the American Indian Religious Freedom Act and the Native American Grave Protection and Repatriation Act, as well as the cases construing these acts. One chapter summarizes provisions of the 1954 Hague Convention for the Protection of Cultural Property in the Event of Armed Conflict; the 1970 UNESCO Convention on the Means of Prohibiting and Preventing the Illicit Import, Export and Transfer of Ownership of Cultural Property; the 1972 UNESCO Convention for the Protection of the World Cultural and Natural Heritage; the 1995 UNIDROIT Convention on Stolen or Illegally Exported Cultural Objects; and the 2001 Convention for the Protection of the Underwater Cultural Heritage.

The Appendix contains sample documents to provide practical applications of the legal principles discussed in the text.

A few caveats and disclaimers are in order. Although it would be difficult and impractical to have a more complete and in-depth coverage of some subjects beyond that covered in the text, it was thought there should be more expansive coverage of some topics. Thus, some issues are discussed in more detail than others. I caution that while the information in this book is about legal issues of relevance to museums, it is not legal advice; the book is not intended to be a substitute for good legal advice. Although the book should give the reader a basic understanding of the laws affecting museums and does illustrate the application of these laws to many specific transactions and actual cases, it cannot provide a solution to every particular problem. A problem discussed in the text may be somewhat similar to one encountered by the reader, but the solution, or the outcome as decided by a particular court, may differ when the facts are changed somewhat. In addition, laws differ in the different states. (This is very evident in the discussion of laws applicable to stolen art that are discussed in Chapter 6.) Further, when federal law applies, the various federal circuit courts of appeal will have differing interpretations of that law. (The reader should observe the differences in judicial interpretations of the law by noting the court that decided the particular issue discussed in each of the examples in the text. The examples set out the court in which a particular case arose and was decided.) In addition to the problem that laws and regulations may differ in the various states, new laws are enacted and legal developments occur daily; thus, this book may contain some outdated material. The sample legal documents in this book can be very useful documents, but they must be used with caution. These also should not be substituted for good legal advice. Specific clauses may not apply in certain situations and, in some instances, may not cover a particular transaction. State law should be consulted to determine the applicability of the forms in that state and to determine whether certain clauses should be added or deleted.

Despite some limitations, this text can serve as a valuable guide for museum officials and counsel in recognizing, working through, and securing some understanding of the myriad of laws that are applicable to museum operations. With the general knowledge of the law provided in this book, which is illustrated through real-life examples, the museum professional should recognize a legal problem (as well as a possible solution) and can confer better with an attorney. In addition, a general knowledge of the law may preclude legal problems from happening as the museum professional, in some instances, can prevent a problem occurring by recognizing in advance major issues or concerns.

I welcome your comments, questions, and feedback and encourage readers to contact me at marilyn_phelan@yahoo.com.

ACKNOWLEDGMENTS

I acknowledge and thank Ed and Roxie Smith at Kalos Kapp Press for the assistance and encouragement they provided in producing the first three editions of the books I prepared earlier on laws of interest and relevance to museum officials and for their granting permission to use portions of the third edition. I also thank Thomson Reuters for granting permission earlier to reprint portions of Marilyn Phelan, *Nonprofit Organizations: Law and Taxation*. I refer readers to this three-volume treatise for a comprehensive treatment of laws applicable to nonprofit and tax exempt organizations generally. I especially thank Charles Harmon, Julia Loy, Piper Wallis, and staff members at Rowman & Littlefield for their support and help in producing this fourth edition of *Museum Law: A Guide for Officers, Directors, and Counsel.*

PART I

OPERATIONS

CHAPTER 1

MUSEUM GOVERNANCE
Laws and Principles

How does one measure the success of a museum?

PAUL GETTY

A museum, as defined in the International Council of Museums Code of Ethics for Museums,[1] is a "non-profit making permanent institution in the service of society and of its development, open to the public, which acquires, conserves, researches, communicates and exhibits, for purposes of study, education and enjoyment, the tangible and intangible evidence of people and their environment."[2] Directors and trustees of museums must act with integrity and in accordance with strict ethical principles, as well as the highest standards of objectivity, to ensure the museums they represent fulfill their special service to society through the communication and exhibition of the tangible and intangible evidence of people and their environment.

In recent years, the public has demanded increased accountability from trustees and directors of all charitable organizations. The legal duties of trustees and directors of charitable organizations are owed to the public at large. These legal duties, as well as ethical standards, apply especially to museum professionals. Serving on a museum-governing body, as well as employment by a museum, has been characterized as a "public trust," one that requires a strict duty of care and loyalty. This public trust (noted further below) should require museum professionals to be knowledgeable of the laws and regulations, tax provisions and requirements, and accounting and governance principles which are reviewed in Part I of this text. The need of museum officials to understand and to fulfill their particular museum's special commission for the protection, preservation, and exhibition of society's heritage, given the important position of museums as guardians of societal treasures, mandate that museum officials also have knowledge of laws and regulations protecting the arts and humanities, the natural resources, and the world's cultural property. This text serves to provide a knowledge of these laws to assist museum officials and personnel in carrying out their service to society.

The purpose of this first chapter is to provide a better understanding of the organizational structures of museums and an appreciation of certain guiding governance principles that can assist in managing and directing a museum. Subsequent chapters in Part I review laws and regulations, tax provisions, and accounting principles that daily affect museum activities and operations. Parts II and III set out additional laws, regulations, and conventions that impact museum governance to provide further direction for museum professionals in fulfilling their public duties and responsibilities.

A. ORGANIZATIONAL STRUCTURE OF A MUSEUM

Museums in the United States are either public or private whereas museums in other countries generally are only public and, for the most part, are state controlled. This book focuses on the privately governed, and the unique organizational structure of, museums in the United States where even public museums are somewhat private actors (in comparison to the mostly governmentally controlled, public actor status of museums in other countries).

Public museums in the United States include federal and state museums,[3] those that are created by local governments, such as a city or county, and those that are part of a state university system.[4] Federal museums include the Smithsonian Institution[5] and those that are a part of the Departments of the Navy, the Army, and the Air Force.

The most common example of a federal museum in the United States is the Smithsonian Institution, which is a system of museums.[6] The Smithsonian was created by Congress to increase knowledge and to protect cultural property of national interest.[7] All objects of art and of foreign and curious research and all objects of natural history, plants, and geological and mineralogical specimens belonging to the United States must be delivered to the Board of Regents of the Smithsonian for examination and study.[8]

Example 1. In Crowley v. Smithsonian Institution, 636 F.2d 738 (D.C. Cir. 1980), the District of Columbia Circuit Court of Appeals ruled that the action of the Smithsonian's Museum of Natural History in presenting exhibits containing references to the theory of evolution fell within the language creating the Smithsonian—"to increase and diffuse knowledge among men."[9]

Example 2. In State of California v. Smithsonian Institution, 618 F.2d 618 (9th Cir. 1980), the Ninth Circuit Court of Appeals recognized the special status of the Smithsonian as a depository of objects of interest found on federal property. A 6,070-pound meteorite was found on federal land in the Old Woman Mountain Range in southern California. State officials in California removed the meteorite and placed it on public exhibition in the Los Angeles County Museum of Natural History. State officials then applied for a permit under the Antiquities Act of 1906 (discussed in Chapter 10) to retain the meteorite. However, the Department of the Interior issued a permit to the Smithsonian to place the meteorite in the Smithsonian. The Department of the Interior and the Bureau of Land Management consulted with the Smithsonian to determine procedures to be followed to transfer the meteorite to the Smithsonian. Officials of the State of California filed a lawsuit to enjoin removal of the meteorite and to void the permit issued to the Smithsonian. The Ninth Circuit ruled that officials of the Department of the Interior had not violated the Antiquities Act when they contacted the Smithsonian. Although the Smithsonian had not filed an application in compliance with federal regulations, the Ninth Circuit decided that permits "may" be granted to institutions that officials of the Department of the Interior deem properly qualified. The Ninth Circuit ruled that the Secretary of the Interior is not limited in ability to act in absence of an application. It also ruled that because the Smithsonian serves as a depository for federal resources, the meteorite should be transferred to the Smithsonian.

Several states in the United States have established public museums to serve as depositories of the historical and archaeological resources of the state.[10] State statutes generally also provide for the establishment and operation of local museums subject to control by a city or county.[11] For example, in California, the legislative body of a city could establish a public museum of natural and historical objects.[12] In addition, the board of supervisors of a county could construct a historical museum in the county.[13] In New York, any county, city, or town could establish a museum by a majority vote of the electors and could appropriate money raised by taxes to maintain and equip the museum.[14] In Texas, a city or county could acquire lands and buildings for the establishment of a historical museum.[15] Condemnation proceedings could be used for acquisitions if it was necessary to prevent destruction or deterioration of a historical site, building, or structure. Arizona had a statute providing that the board of supervisors of a county could appropriate money from the general fund to operate an arts organization, whether it was operated by a city or county or by a private entity established for the benefit of the public as a nonprofit § 501(c)(3)corporation.[16] In Wisconsin, any city of the first class could establish and maintain, for the free use of its inhabitants, a public museum for the exhibition of objects in natural history, anthropology, and history.[17]

Private museums in the United States generally have nonprofit status and are tax exempt as § 501(c)(3) organizations (discussion of tax exempt status in Chapter 3). Many museums, those that are funded by members of a family or by a few donors, are classified as private operating foundations for tax purposes (also discussed in Chapter 3).

Knowledge of the legal structure of a museum is important for several reasons. Public institutions are subject to governmental control and regulation. Private institutions are subject to some governmental regulation, particularly with reference to their operation as a tax exempt organization, but they are controlled by their boards or sometimes by their members. State and federal museums are subject to statutory law, federal and/or state, regarding their creation and their operation. Legal constraints regarding funding, policies, and programs of public institutions vary from state to state and by type of institution. Management and supervision of public museums will differ in the several states, with some states having few provisions regulating management and others having extensive statutory regulations. As noted previously, museums in other countries usually are state museums and are governmentally controlled.

With respect to nongovernmental museums in the United States, the government does not exert much more influence over these private museums than it does over private businesses. (There are exceptions because private museums will have tax exempt status as charitable organizations. The federal government can, and often does, exert some control through its tax regulations to assure each museum has satisfied, and continues to meet, the requirements for § 501(c)(3) status [discussed in detail in Chapter 3]. Further, private museums that are incorporated are subject to a state's nonprofit corporation statutes [discussed below].) The unusually private positions of most museums in the United States, which sometimes includes the public museums, causes museum governance and organizational structures for most museums in the United

States to differ, sometimes significantly, from that of the governmentally controlled museums in other countries.

Private museums in the United States, as nonprofit charitable organizations, will have one of three forms—trust, association, or corporation. Museums with some private autonomy in other countries generally are established as associations or foundations. Because the legal concept of a trust does not exist in most civil law countries (only in common law systems, such as that in the United Kingdom and the United States), museums would not be organized as a trust in most other countries.

1. Charitable Trust

Nonprofit charitable organizations sometimes are established as charitable trusts in the United States. (As noted above, trust law is not a part of most civil law jurisdictions; thus, museums would not be organized as charitable trusts in most countries.)

State statutes relating to trusts, the common law of trusts, and the provisions of the trust instrument govern the operation of a trust. Statutory provisions for charitable trusts are limited; however, the powers, duties, and liabilities of trustees of unincorporated charitable trusts are basically the same as in the case of private trusts.[18] A charitable trust differs from a private trust in the purposes for which it was created and in the character of its beneficiaries. While a private trust must have definite beneficiaries, the essence of a charitable trust is the indefiniteness of its beneficiaries.[19] The public, whether limited to a few or the public in general, is the beneficiary of a charitable trust.

The concept of a "public trust," which is a carryover from the charitable trust structure, has been integrated into governance principles for museums. The American Alliance of Museums (AAM) Code of Ethics for Museums states that museum governance in its various forms is a "public trust" responsible for the institution's service to society.

To establish a charitable trust, a grantor must execute a declaration of trust specifying how the trust is to operate (or establish the trust through a will or by will but from an existing instrument properly incorporated by reference in the will).[20] The grantor of a trust must convey property to the named trustee or trustees who administer the trust property in accordance with the trust instrument. The grantor may specify that a charitable corporation must be formed to be the trustee or that named trustees will govern the trust property as an unincorporated charitable trust.

A charitable trust can have no element of profit-making for individuals or for noncharitable organizations. Trust income must be distributed solely for the public benefit. However, charitable trusts can produce profits; the prohibition is only that any profits obtained may not be used for the benefit of the founders, managers, or other individuals.[21]

A charitable trust is managed by a trustee or trustees. The grantor of a trust vests title in one or more trustees. Trustees of charitable trusts have full power to invest, collect income, and distribute net proceeds directly for the public benefit. The entire responsibility is placed upon the trustees. Charitable trustees are usually joint tenants; they generally act by majority vote.[22] A nonprofit organization in the form of a charitable trust would not have officers. Trustees of a trust, over whom the beneficiaries have no control, are not employees.[23] Further, a trust is under a duty not to delegate the performance of acts which the trustee can reasonably be required personally to perform.[24]

While a trustee has no power to change the purpose of a charitable trust, if the charitable objective or restriction prescribed by the donor becomes impractical or impossible of fulfillment, the trustee may apply to the court for a change in that purpose under the cy pres power of the court (discussion of cy pres doctrine in Chapter 5). As noted in Chapter 5, pursuant to this power, a court can alter the purpose of the trust by substituting another trust purpose which it deems to be similar to that of the donor.[25] The basic premise for application of the cy pres doctrine is to defeat the failure of the charitable donation. The cy pres power is the power of the court; a charitable organization may not receive a gift for one purpose and use it for another unless the court, applying the cy pres doctrine, so approves or commands.[26]

A museum organized as an unincorporated charitable trust would not have the flexibility or the legal guidelines affecting its operations as would a museum organized as a nonprofit corporation; thus, a museum director would find burdensome the operation of a museum organized as a charitable trust. However, for those museums that have supporting foundations, which simply hold property to benefit the museum, museum officials may find the trust to be an acceptable form of organization for these foundations. Because the trust is not a statutory organization, reporting to the state is not required.[27] Thus, a foundation in the form of a trust may have more privacy than one in the form of a nonprofit corporation.

2. Association

Some nonprofit organizations in the United States, particularly those with few assets, are established as associations. An association is an unincorporated organization acting without a charter but upon the methods and forms used by incorporated bodies. An association refers to a group of persons organized for a nonprofit purpose; it is not, however, a legal entity separate from the persons who compose it. As a general rule and if a state has not adopted the Uniform Unincorporated Nonprofit Association Act, associations in the United States, unlike corporations, have no power of perpetual duration, cannot contract, and cannot hold title to property.[28]

The associational structure differs in many other countries. For example, in some countries, forming groups to further mutual interests has been prohibited.[29] However, in many countries, wherein associational status is permitted, an association that is registered with the government generally will have entity status.

Because the unincorporated association is not a legal entity in the United States (unless the association is located in a state that has adopted the Uniform Unincorporated Nonprofit Association Act), the rights and obligations of the association are the cumulative rights and obligations of its members. Associations may enact provisions governing admission of members and may prescribe the necessary qualifications of its members.[30] Members of an association that is not deemed to be a legal entity by state law may be held personally liable for contracts of the association and may be held personally liable for tortious actions committed by an individual acting in her capacity as an association member.

For an unincorporated association, members of the association elect officers informally.[31] If the association has articles of association and bylaws, these should specify the manner in which officers are elected.[32]

3. Nonprofit Corporation

Most private museums in the United States have corporate status. The law relating to corporations is more defined than that for charitable trusts or unincorporated associations, and, as a general rule, provides more flexibility in terms of operational guidelines for a museum. Incorporation provides a nonprofit organization with limited liability for its members, centralized management, and perpetual duration.[33] Other countries may not provide for similar corporate status; thus, museums in other countries, which at any rate generally are governmentally controlled, would not have this particular organizational structure.

The United States Supreme Court defined a corporation in a very early decision, as "an artificial being, invisible, intangible, and existing only in contemplation of law."[34] The Supreme Court ruled two centuries ago that being a creature of law, a corporation possesses only those powers granted it by law.[35] In addition, because it is a creature of law, courts later determined that a corporation cannot be created by agreement of interested parties or members, that it requires authority from a sovereign power, either express or implied. This means that a corporation, including a nonprofit corporation, can be created and corporate powers granted only by constitutional provisions or by or under authority of an act of the legislature.[36] Thus, the legislature of the state, as the state sovereignty, has inherent power to create both for-profit and nonprofit corporations, to determine the procedure for incorporation, the purposes for which a corporation can be created, and the powers to be conferred upon a corporation.

Corporations can be private, public, quasi-public, profit, or nonprofit. Public corporations are those corporations that are connected with the administration of the government and that are created for public purposes only. Private corporations are created for private purposes; the fact that a private corporation serves a public interest does not make it a public corporation.[37] Thus, a nonprofit corporation created by individuals is a private corporation even though it was created for charitable purposes.[38] Corporations are classified as profit or nonprofit. Profit corporations are business corporations organized to benefit their shareholders. Nonprofit corporations are devoted to charitable or other purposes whereby profits may not be distributed to the members or the corporate directors or used in any manner for private benefit.

State statutes in the United States prescribe the procedures by which persons may form corporations. These statutes generally provide that a charter or a certificate of incorporation authorizing the entity to do business, or engage in activities within a state, will issue upon compliance with the provisions of the state statute. In most states, the first step is the filing of articles of incorporation with the Secretary of State.[39] While the initial requirements for organizing a corporation are substantially the same whether the corporation is for profit or not for profit, the statutes of each individual state must be consulted to ascertain whether any special provisions may be applicable.

The contents of the articles of incorporation are determined by the statutes of the state of incorporation. The articles generally include the corporate name; the street address of the corporation's initial registered office and the name of the initial registered agent (person who can receive official documents for the corporation); the name and address of each incorporator; a statement whether or not the corporation will have members; any provisions not inconsistent with law regarding the distribution of assets on dissolution; the purpose for which the corporation is organized; and the names and addresses of the individuals who will serve as the initial directors. If a nonprofit corporation seeks federal tax exempt status under § 501(c)(3) of the Internal Revenue Code, its articles of incorporation must limit the purposes of the corporation to one or more charitable purposes. In addition, the articles must dedicate the corporate assets to an exempt purpose. The articles must provide that, upon dissolution, all assets of the corporation will be distributed for one or more exempt purposes, or to the federal government, or to a state or local government, for a public purpose.[40] The articles, or the law of the state in which the organization is created, cannot permit assets of the nonprofit corporation to be distributed upon dissolution to members or shareholders.[41] The articles of incorporation for a charitable corporation that is a private foundation must include provisions that require officials of the corporation to act or to refrain from acting in a manner that would cause the corporation to become liable for penalty taxes imposed by § § 4941–45 of the Internal Revenue Code (discussed in Chapter 3).

If the Secretary of State of the state of incorporation finds that the articles comply with the law, the Secretary shall, upon receipt of the proper incorporation fees, file one of the duplicate originals in the office of the Secretary and attach the other to a certificate of incorporation which is returned to the incorporators. Upon issuance of the certificate of incorporation, the corporate existence begins.

Bylaws are continuing rules for the governance of a corporation. The bylaws of a corporation determine the rights and duties of directors, officers, and members with reference to the internal governance of the corporation and the management of its affairs. A bylaw is an agreement or contract between the corporation and its officials and members to conduct corporate affairs. It includes all regulations of the corporation. A corporation's board of directors adopts the initial bylaws of a corporation. The power to alter, amend, or repeal the bylaws or to adopt new bylaws is vested in the board of directors unless otherwise provided in the articles of incorporation or in the bylaws. The bylaws may contain provisions for the regulation and management of the affairs of the corporation that are not inconsistent with the law or with the articles of incorporation. The power to amend bylaws resides in the corporate body, either the corporate directors or the corporate members.

a. Members

A nonprofit corporation may have one or more classes of members or it may have no members.[42] If the corporation has members, the designation of the class of membership, the manner of election or appointment, and the qualifications and rights of the members of each class must be set out in the articles of incorporation or in the bylaws. If the corporation has no members, that fact must also be stated in the articles or in the bylaws.[43]

Although a nonprofit membership corporation is a corporate entity, courts have held that members in membership nonprofit corporations nonetheless are treated much the same as members in unincorporated associations. As a general rule, the same rules concerning members apply to both. Consequently, a member of a nonprofit corporation does not acquire a severable right to any of the property or funds of the corporation, but rather merely a right to the joint use and enjoyment of the corporate property so long as she continues to be a member. Termination of a member's interest generally must be by voluntary act of the member or by act of the organization pursuant to authority granted it by the bylaws. However, waiver or abandonment also terminates a member's interest.[44] Some states permit corporations to become members of nonprofit corporations;[45] consequently, control through holding companies can occur. While issuance of shares of stock are forbidden in most states, some states do permit nonprofit corporations to issue shares of stock.[46]

Meetings of members generally are held at the place designated in the bylaws. However, if the bylaws have no provision as to place of meetings of members, the meetings should be held at the registered office of the corporation.[47] The annual meeting of the members must be held at the time provided for in the bylaws.[48] However, failure to hold an annual meeting does not cause a forfeiture or dissolution of the corporation.[49] Special meetings may be called by the president or by the board of directors. Special meetings also may be called by the corporate officers or by the number or proportion of members as provided in the articles of incorporation or in the bylaws.[50] Should the board of directors fail to call the annual meeting at the designated time, some state statutes provide that any member may make demand that a meeting be held within a reasonable time. If the annual meeting is not called after a demand is made, a member may compel the holding of the annual meeting by legal action directed against the board.[51]

At least one general meeting of members should be held annually to elect directors and to approve the annual reports. Meetings are required when the approval of members is necessary to enter into a particular transaction or to adopt, or to amend, the bylaws. Meetings generally must be held to elect directors; to adopt or amend bylaws; to amend the articles of incorporation; to sell, lease, or mortgage property; to merge with another corporation; or to dissolve the corporation.

A quorum is the number of members required to be present at a meeting to make binding upon the corporation any action taken at the meeting. Generally this is a majority of the members; however, it may be a majority of the voting members present at a particular meeting.[52] The bylaws should specify the number of members constituting a quorum. Some state statutes specify the number of members required to enter into a particular transaction. If this is the case, a quorum cannot be set at a lesser number.

Written notice stating the place, day, and hour of a meeting of the members must be delivered to the members within a certain period of time before the date of the meeting. The Model Nonprofit Corporation Act specifies that notice should be delivered to the members not less than ten or more than fifty days before the date of the meeting.[53] If the meeting is a special meeting, the purpose or purposes for which the meeting is called should be a part of the notice.[54]

The right of members to vote may be limited, enlarged, or denied to the extent provided for in the articles of incorporation or in the bylaws.[55] However, unless limited, each member, regardless of class, is entitled to one vote on each matter submitted to a vote of the members.[56] If the corporation provides that no members may vote, the directors have the sole voting power.[57]

While the right to vote has been considered a property right for a shareholder of a business corporation, it is generally not a vested right for a member of a nonprofit corporation. Courts have stated that the right of a member of a nonprofit corporation to vote is not constitutionally protected because a member of a nonprofit corporation does not have an interest in property of the corporation.[58]

Some states provide members of a nonprofit corporation with the right to bring a member's derivative action.[59] A member's derivative suit permits a member of a nonprofit corporation to institute a lawsuit for the corporation to secure a judgment in favor of the corporation for restoration of corporate property or for compensation to the corporation for losses suffered.

Most state statutes do not have provisions relating to the removal of members of a nonprofit corporation.[60] The power to expel is limited; one's membership in a nonprofit membership corporation generally may be terminated only by voluntary act of the member or by an act of the organization pursuant to authority granted it by the charter or the bylaws. While the right of expulsion of a member as a penalty for an infraction or disobedience of the laws of the organization is well settled, there is nonetheless a presumption against the power to expel because it is in the nature of a forfeiture.[61] Where grounds and procedures for expulsion are prescribed in the bylaws, expulsion procedures must conform to the provisions of the bylaws. Courts are reluctant to interfere with the internal affairs of a membership corporation in regard to its disciplinary proceedings; thus, a court generally will look to the record to see whether the member's proceeding has been in accordance with the charter and bylaws of the organization, whether the charges were substantial, and whether the member had fair notice and opportunity to be heard. If so, a court will not ordinarily substitute its judgment for that of the organization.

b. Directors

The affairs of a nonprofit corporation are managed by a board of directors.[62] The Model Nonprofit Corporation Act provides that directors need not be residents of the state of incorporation unless the articles of incorporation or the bylaws provide otherwise.[63]

The Model Nonprofit Corporation Act[64] requires that there should be at least three directors of a nonprofit corporation, and most states have this requirement. The number of directors is fixed by the bylaws (with the exception of the first board of directors where the number is fixed by the articles of incorporation).[65] The number of directors can be changed by amending the bylaws (unless the articles of incorporation provide that a change in the number can only be made by amending the articles).[66]

Generally the term of office of a director is one year.[67] The first board of directors, which is named in the articles of incorporation, holds office until the first annual election of directors or for the time as prescribed in the articles of incorporation or in the bylaws. Thereafter, directors are elected or appointed in the manner stated in the articles or in the bylaws.[68] Terms of office of directors need not be uniform. Each director holds office until the director's successor is elected or appointed.[69]

A majority of the number of directors fixed by the bylaws or by the articles of incorporation generally constitutes a quorum for the transaction of business.[70] The Model Nonprofit Corporation Act provides that the articles of incorporation or the bylaws can provide otherwise but in no event can a quorum be less than one-third of the number of directors.[71] An act of the majority of the directors present at a meeting at which a quorum is present constitutes an act of the board of directors unless the articles or bylaws provide for a greater number.[72]

Directors are elected or appointed in the manner and for the terms provided in the articles of incorporation or in the bylaws.[73] A vacancy occurring in the board of directors is generally filled by vote of a majority of the remaining directors (unless the articles or bylaws provide for some other method). A director elected or appointed to fill a vacancy is elected or appointed for the unexpired term of his predecessor.[74]

The Model Nonprofit Corporation Act provides that any directorship to be filled by reason of an increase in the number of directors may be filled by vote of a majority of the remaining directors.[75] Some states have not followed this provision. Some state statutes provide instead that a directorship must be filled by election at either an annual meeting or a special meeting of members of the corporation. If the corporation has no members, or no members having a right to vote, the directorship should be filled as provided for in the articles of incorporation or in the bylaws.

Meetings of the board of directors, whether regular or special meetings, may be held within or without the state of incorporation.[76] Attendance of a director at any meeting constitutes a waiver of notice of the meeting except when a director attends a meeting for the express purpose of objecting to the transaction of any business because the meeting was not lawfully called or convened.[77] Some states provide that regular meetings of the board of directors may be held without notice. Special meetings are held upon notice as is prescribed in the bylaws.

Except for actions that the articles of incorporation or the bylaws require to be approved by members of the corporation, as well as certain inherent powers in the members, the activities and affairs of a nonprofit corporation are conducted, and all corporate powers are exercised, under direction of the board of directors.[78] Courts have stated that bylaw provisions vesting in the board of directors of a nonprofit corporation the right to manage the corporation affairs and even to control the election of successors to the board do not infringe upon any property or other enforceable right of the members. It is not unlawful, arbitrary, or unreasonable for the board of directors of a nonprofit corporation to be granted these powers.

As a general rule, the board of directors may delegate the management of activities of the corporation to committees, but all activities and affairs of the corporation must be managed, and all corporate power exercised, under the ultimate direction of the board. The Model Nonprofit Corporation Act provides that committees may be designated and appointed by the board if the articles or the bylaws so provide and if the board appoints the committees by resolution adopted by a majority of the directors.[79] The Model Act also provides that these committees may not exercise extraordinary powers, such as appointing or removing members; altering bylaws; amending or restating the articles of incorporation; selling, purchasing, leasing or mortgaging property; or adopting a plan of merger, consolidation, or corporate dissolution.[80]

All corporate action to be taken by the board of directors generally requires action at a meeting of the board. The vote of a majority of the directors present at the time of the vote, if a quorum is present at that time, is the act of the board. Directors acting separately and not collectively as a board cannot bind the corporation. State statutes, or the articles or bylaws, may provide that any action required or permitted to be taken by the board of directors can be taken without a meeting if all members of the board consent in writing to the adoption of a resolution authorizing the action. A resolution to that effect and the written consents by members of the board must be filed with the minutes of the proceedings of the board. The articles or bylaws may provide that participation in a meeting of the board may be by means of a conference telephone, or similar communications equipment, permitting all persons participating in the meeting to hear each other at the same time. If so, participation by these means constitutes presence in person at a meeting.

Generally a director may be removed from office pursuant to any procedure provided for in the articles of incorporation.[81] The Revised Model Nonprofit Corporation Act provides that members of a nonprofit corporation may remove without cause a director elected by them.[82] A director generally may be removed only if the number of votes cast to remove the director would be sufficient to elect the director. An entire board of directors may be removed without cause if sufficient votes to elect the board are cast. A special meeting must be called for these purposes, and notice of the meeting must state the purpose. A board of directors generally may remove a director without cause if the director was elected by a vote of the directors then in office.[83] Those states that have adopted the Revised Model Nonprofit Act would permit a director to be removed by a court in a proceeding commenced either by the corporation, its members holding at least ten percent of the voting power, or the Attorney General in the case of a charitable corporation, if the court finds that the director engaged in fraudulent conduct or grossly abused her authority or discretion.[84]

Members of the board of directors of museums often are called trustees. This is a misnomer. They are directors. They are referred to as "trustees" following the concept that a museum is a "public trust" and because the principal officer of the museum generally is referred to as the "director." This also is a misnomer, however. The title for the person corresponding to the museum director in other corporations is "president." The president is the chief officer of a corporation as discussed below.

c. Officers

Officers of a nonprofit corporation should be a president, a secretary, a treasurer, and other officers as are appointed by the board.[85] Each officer is elected or appointed at the time and in the manner prescribed in the articles of incorporation or in the bylaws.[86] The term of office should be set out in the articles of incorporation or in the bylaws.[87] If the articles of incorporation or bylaws do not provide for the election or appointment of officers, the board of directors should elect or appoint officers annually.[88]

The same person generally can hold any two offices, except in some instances, the offices of president and secretary.[89] The articles of incorporation or bylaws may provide that any one or more officers of the nonprofit corporation will be ex officio members of the board of directors.[90]

The duties of the officers of nonprofit corporations parallel the duties of corporate officers generally. Officers are agents of the corporation and have whatever authority the board of directors delegates to them to execute and administer policies determined by the board.[91] As delegates of the board of directors, officers are fiduciaries of the corporation and, within the scope of their delegated management functions, are subject to the same fiduciary duties as are directors (discussed below).[92]

The president of a corporation normally is recognized to be the general manager of the corporation.[93] The board of directors may grant the president authority to act as the chief executive officer of the corporation. Often, as noted above, in a nonprofit corporation the person designated as the general manager of the corporation is called a "director," rather than "president." In this case, the "director" should be distinguished from a director who is a member of the board of directors.

A vice-president has no authority by virtue of the office.[94] However, in the event of the disability or absence of the president, a vice-president may exercise whatever authority the president has.[95] The secretary and treasurer also have no authority by virtue of their office to bind the corporation.[96] The secretary is a ministerial officer who keeps the minutes of meetings of members and of the board of directors. The secretary gives notices, prepares certified copies of corporate records, and keeps and attests the corporate seal.[97]

The authority of the officers of nonprofit corporations is essentially the same as that of corporate officers generally. While the vice-president, secretary, and treasurer of a corporation normally have no authority by virtue of their offices to bind the corporation, the president, as general manager of the corporation, may bind the corporation through contracts that are necessary, proper, or usual to be made in the ordinary course of corporate affairs.[98] Though traditionally the president of a corporation presided at meetings and played no active part in management, the preferable present rule is that a president is head of the corporation, subject to the control of the board of directors, but with power to bind the corporation in regard to contracts involved in the everyday activities of the corporation. Because a corporation is a fictitious entity and can act only through human instrumentality, individuals must exercise its corporate power and its actions. While the board of directors may exercise management powers, the everyday affairs of the corporation cannot await periodical meetings of the board but must be handled by officers and agents of the corporation. The officer on whom such responsibility naturally falls is the president.

Officers of a corporation are agents of the corporation. The authority of an officer or agent of a corporation need not necessarily be express. It may be implied from the circumstances. The law of agency provides that the general manager of a business has implied authority to make contracts and to perform other acts necessary to operate the business.[99] Even though state statutes stipulate that the board of directors manages the affairs of a corporation, should the corporation indicate to third persons that an officer of the corporation may act for the corporation, the officer may have "apparent authority" to act.[100] If a third person relies on the apparent authority of the officer, the corporation will be bound by any action on the part of the officer, assuming the reliance was reasonable and there would otherwise be detriment to the third party. Consequently, the fact that a corporate president is considered to be the general manager of the corporation can cause the president to have authority to bind the corporation as to its ordinary transactions by virtue of the office.

d. Employees

There are distinctions between corporate officers and the regular employees of a corporation, including a nonprofit corporation. The articles of incorporation or the bylaws create the duties of corporate officers. In addition, either the board of directors or members of the corporation elect officers. An employee, on the other hand, is employed by the managing officer of the corporation and normally occupies no office. While officers are in a quasi-fiduciary relationship to members of the corporation, employees are not. Employees are under the control of the corporate officers while the officers exercise management powers under the policies or direction of the board. Generally an officer is not required to work under any specific schedule of hours because an officer devotes whatever time and effort is necessary to accomplish the affairs of the corporation. Consequently, officers are not paid overtime as are employees.

Even though an officer occupies a management position in a corporation, the Internal Revenue Service (IRS) nonetheless treats an officer as an employee. A corporate officer is subject to withholding for income tax and Social Security purposes just as are regular employees.[101] On the other hand, the IRS does not consider a corporate director to be an employee. The IRS treats directors' fees as self-employment income.[102]

B. GOVERNANCE PRINCIPLES FOR MUSEUM OFFICIALS

The trustees, board members, and officers of a museum have a duty to manage affairs of the museum they represent so that property entrusted to the museum will be used for public purposes. Museum officials must be concerned that their actions reflect the highest level of ethical standards; thus, they should be knowledgeable of the fiduciary duties imposed upon them. In addition, there are substantial penalty taxes for museum professionals in the United States imposed by two sections in the Internal Revenue Code, § § 4958 and 4941 (discussed below), as well as potential legal liability imposed by state laws for managers of nonprofit organizations if they engage in certain prohibited acts or failures to act. Thus, it is imperative that those who represent museums be cognizant of laws regulating conduct of trustees, directors, and officers of nonprofit organizations.

Currently some level of ethical conduct for managers of nonprofit organizations is secured by imposing certain legal constraints and reporting standards upon executives of nonprofits. Both the federal and state governments impose legal standards on managers of nonprofit organizations to ensure at least a minimum level of ethical performance. While some members of the public have expressed concern that legal fiduciary standards have not promoted ethical behavior, others have become apprehensive that these legal standards, as well as too-exacting governmental regulation, eventually may suppress philanthropic efforts and volunteerism.

1. Standards of Conduct for Trustees and Directors

Trustees and directors of nonprofit organizations are fiduciaries. As such, they must act in good faith and display complete loyalty to the interests of their beneficiaries, in this instance the public. They also must exercise some degree of skill, prudence, and diligence. Fiduciaries are liable for negligence in the performance of their duties, but whether or not a fiduciary has been negligent often depends upon the facts and circumstances of a particular case. The Revised Model Nonprofit Corporation Act[103] provides standards of conduct for officers of nonprofit corporations that require an officer to discharge the officer's duties in good faith and with the care an ordinarily prudent person in a like position would exercise under similar circumstances and in a manner the officer believes to be in the best interests of the corporation. The Revised Model Nonprofit Corporation Act provides that an officer may rely on information, opinions, reports, or other statements, including financial statements, prepared by one or more officers or employees of the corporation whom the corporate officers reasonably believe to be reliable and competent in the matters presented, or on legal counsel or public accountants.[104]

Trustees and directors of nonprofit organizations can be liable for losses caused by their negligent management of property and investments. However, in judging whether negligence occurred, the standard and degree of care required may vary in the several states. Further, pursuant to the common law, there has been a higher standard of care and loyalty required of a trustee than for a corporate director.

Both trustees and corporate directors are subject to a duty of loyalty and a duty of care, but the duties of directors are less exacting in most states than those required of trustees. Less stringent standards have been applied to the corporate director based upon the theory that corporate directors have more areas of responsibility than trustees, and directors can delegate their management duties to committees and officers whereas the common law provided that trustees could not delegate duties.[105]

To apply fiduciary standards to directors and trustees of nonprofit enterprises involves an analysis of the type of nonprofit organization. A charitable trust generally is subject to trust standards. The nonprofit corporation that is not charitable in nature is governed by corporate standards. However, the charitable nonprofit corporation is somewhat of an enigma because it is much the same as the charitable trust. The charitable organization does not fit neatly into the established common law categories of corporation or trust; thus, the standard that should be applicable to the director of a charitable nonprofit corporation was not clearly established. Because the charitable nonprofit corporation is much the same as a charitable trust, there had been uncertainty as to whether the common law trust standard or the corporate standard should apply.

The trend now is to apply corporate rather than common law trust principles in determining the legal liability of directors of charitable corporations based on the perception by some that their functions are virtually indistinguishable from those of their for-profit corporate counterparts and the concern of many that fear of liability from use of the common law trustee standard could have a debilitating effect upon members of a governing board of a nonprofit corporation, most of whom would be "uncompensated public minded citizens."[106]

A sample conflict of interest policy for a museum is included in the Appendix. It is suggested that museum board members adopt a conflict of interest policy and introduce and explain the policy at a meeting of all newly appointed or elected board members. Alerting new board members to conflict of interest problems that can arise and making them aware of their duties and responsibilities initially rather than pointing them out after the fact may deflect future problems that otherwise would be difficult to address and resolve.

a. Duty of Care

A trustee has been subject to a very rigid duty of care. The common law duty of care for a trustee required a trustee, in administering a trust, to exercise the care and skill a person of ordinary prudence would exercise in dealing with his own property. This common law standard caused a trustee to be liable for acts of simple negligence.

A corporate director (member of a corporation board of directors) also is subject to a duty of care. The duty of care requires that a director exercise reasonable skill in the exercise of her responsibilities. A director should exercise the same care and skill that an ordinary prudent person would exercise under similar circumstances in the director's own personal affairs. While this duty is similar to the common law duty of care of a trustee, a corporate director has had broader discretion than does a trustee. A corporate director may delegate to officers or to committees the operation of the corporation. Further, courts have ruled that while directors are liable for negligence in the performance of their duties, they are not insurers and, thus, are not liable for errors of judgment or for mistakes so long as they act with reasonable skill and prudence. This "business judgment" rule (or "fair judgment" rule for a director of a nonprofit corporation), in effect, relieves a corporate director of liability unless the director was grossly negligent. Directors will not be excused because of their lack of experience or ability, but they are not responsible for mere errors of judgment or want of care short of clear and gross negligence. The business judgment rule dictates that directors or officers of a corporation will not be held liable for errors or mistakes in judgment pertaining to law or fact if they acted on a matter calling for the exercise of their judgment or discretion and they acted in good faith in using their best judgment.[107]

Example 3. In Spitzer v. Grasso, 893 N.E.2d 105 (N.Y. Ct. App. 2008), a State Attorney General brought an action charging that compensation the New York Stock Exchange (NYSE) paid its chairperson and chief executive was excessive. The NYSE chairperson was paid a base salary of roughly $1.4 million from 1995 through 2002, but his bonus awards escalated from $900,000 in 1995 to $10.6 million in 2002. A 2003 agreement provided him an immediate lump sum payment of $139.5 million and an additional $48 million payable over four years in compensation for past and future work. The New York Court of Appeals decided that an action against the NYSE chairperson would override New York's Not-for-Profit Corporation Law, which is fault-based and which grants directors and officers protections of the business judgment rule. The New York appellate court ruled that the Attorney General's claims would require the Attorney General to overcome a business judgment defense and affirmed the lower court's dismissal of claims against the NYSE chairperson. The case illustrates the far-reaching effects of the business judgment rule to prevent officers and directors from liability for what members of the public clearly would view as an abuse of power. [There is a question whether the IRS would have been successful in imposing a conflict of interest penalty tax against the NYSE chairperson pursuant to § 4958 of the Internal Revenue Code (discussed below).]

Board members of a nonprofit organization are negligent and violate the standard of care if the board fails to invest a nonprofit's funds in a prudent manner. To invest funds judiciously, a board may require investment counselors. Still, there has been a question in some states whether a director or trustee could delegate investment decisions.[108]

A number of states had adopted the Uniform Management of Institutional Funds Act that provided a standard of business care and prudence in the investment of funds of certain nonprofit organizations. The act authorized the delegation of investment decisions and provided for the expenditure of the appreciation of invested funds. The act required governing boards to exercise "ordinary business care and prudence" considering the facts and circumstances existing at the time of their action. The standard of care was that of a reasonable and prudent director of a nonprofit corporation—similar to that of a director of a business corporation. Drafters of the act adopted corporate standards based upon their assumption that corporate standards are more appropriate than trustee standards. Several states had adopted the Uniform Prudent Investor Act, which provided that the standard of care applicable to investments should be directed toward the investment portfolio as a whole, and as part of an overall investment strategy, rather than to any particular investment. The act directed a trustee of funds to invest and manage assets prudently by considering the purposes, distribution requirements, and other circumstances of the entity. A trustee generally had a duty to diversify investments. Circumstances appropriate to consider in investing and managing funds included general economic conditions, effects of inflation and deflation, the role that each investment or course of action plays within the overall portfolio, and the entity's needs for liquidity, regularity of income, and preservation or appreciation of capital.

The Uniform Laws Commission replaced the Uniform Management of Institutional Funds Act and the Uniform Prudent Investor Act with the Uniform Prudent Management of Institutional Funds Act. This act combines the two prior acts and also updates provisions of the acts to make investment decision making rules of the Prudent Investor Act applicable to nonprofit corporations as well as to trusts. It also provides that in addition to identifying facts a charity must consider in making management and investment decisions, including the general requirement to diversify investments[109] and to make decisions about each asset in the context of the portfolio of investments, those who manage and invest charitable funds must give primary consideration to donor intent as expressed in a gift instrument, must incur only reasonable costs in investing and managing charitable funds, must dispose of unsuitable assets, and, in general, must develop an investment strategy appropriate for the fund and the charity.

b. Duty of Loyalty

The fiduciary relationship between a trustee and the beneficiaries of a trust dictates an especially exacting and strict standard. The most fundamental duty owed by a trustee to beneficiaries of a trust is the duty of loyalty. The common law required a trustee to administer a trust solely in the interest of the beneficiaries; the trustee could not place himself in a position where it would be for the trustee's own benefit to violate the duty of loyalty. When a trustee's personal interest came into conflict with the trustee's duty to beneficiaries of the trust, the trustee's interest had to yield to that of the beneficiaries. In this regard, a transaction involving the trustee personally that was in all respects fair and reasonable might be enforceable if the trustee dealt directly with the beneficiaries, made full disclosure, and did not take advantage of the trustee's position. However, should the trustee act without consent of the beneficiaries, the transaction would be set aside even though it was otherwise fair and reasonable. A purchase of trust property by a trustee individually, or a sale to the trust of the trustee's individual property, can be set aside under statutes in some states no matter how fair the sale may have been.[110]

Currently legal standards applicable to a corporate director are stated in less exacting but similar phraseology. The duty of loyalty for a corporate director requires that a director not exploit corporate opportunities or misuse inside information. Only reasonable salaries may be paid board members, and often directors serve without compensation. A board member must account to the corporation for any profits received as a result of the directorship. A corporate director should not cast a vote upon a matter in which the director has an adverse interest. However, there has been some support for the possibility that a vote of an interested director, while not necessarily valid, may be counted in favor of a transaction between the director and the corporation if the transaction appears to be fair and is characterized in good faith.

> Example 4. A New York court [In re Estate of Rothko, 372 N.E.2d 291 (N.Y. 1977)] found a conflict of interest for two trustees/executors of the Mark Rothko Foundation and the estate of Mark Rothko. The two trustees were named as executors of the estate of the artist upon his death. The principal asset of the estate consisted of 798 paintings of tremendous value. The artist's will left the paintings to the foundation. The trustees/executors entered into a contract of sale with an art gallery whereby the gallery had the exclusive right to sell all the estate paintings for a period of twelve years. The art gallery received a fifty percent commission on each painting sold. One executor was a director and the secretary of the art gallery. The other benefited from the contract in his status as an artist. The New York court also found a third executor liable because the court determined he knew his coexecutors were committing breaches of trust but did nothing to prevent their activities. (Discussion below of self-dealing penalty taxes imposed on the trustees/executors. The trustees/executors also were subjected to substantial self-dealing penalties, set out in the Internal Revenue Code, in their role as directors of the Mark Rothko Foundation.)

A corporate director is under a fiduciary obligation not to divert a corporate business opportunity for the director's own personal gain. This so-called doctrine of corporate opportunity is a species of the duty of a fiduciary to act with undivided loyalty to the corporation. The doctrine charges any interest acquired by the director with a trust for the benefit of the corporation. The theory is that an insider should not use an inside position to benefit the insider by seizing an investment opportunity available to and suitable for the corporation. It operates because the corporation was not given the opportunity to engage in the transaction. A corporate opportunity covers an opportunity that accrues to the fiduciary as a result of the fiduciary's position within the corporation. Once a corporation demonstrates that an opportunity is a corporate opportunity, it must show either that the director did not offer the opportunity to the corporation or that the corporation did not reject the opportunity properly. If the corporate board did not reject a corporate opportunity by a vote of disinterested directors after full disclosure, the interested director may defend her actions by demonstrating that the director's taking of the opportunity was fair to the corporation. Still, if the director failed to offer the opportunity at all, then the director may not defend on the basis that the failure to offer the opportunity was fair.

Example 5. In Northeast Harbor Golf Club, Inc. v. Harris, 725 A.2d 1018 (Me. 1999), the Maine Supreme Court ruled that even if an opportunity to engage in an activity, in which an officer or director becomes involved, is not discovered through the officer or director's connection to the activity, an opportunity still may be considered a corporate opportunity if the officer or director knew it was closely related to an activity in which the corporation was engaged or expected to engage. The court noted a strict requirement of full disclosure prior to taking advantage of any corporate opportunity. It commented that full disclosure likewise is important to prevent individual directors and officers from using their own "unfettered judgment" to determine whether an opportunity is related to the corporation's activities and whether it would be in the corporate interest to take advantage of the opportunity.

Example 6. A member of the board of directors of an art museum discovers an exceptionally good bargain on a valuable art collection while he is representing the museum at a particular function. The director buys the collection for himself. The director may be charged with a trust for the benefit of the museum with respect to the art collection. If the director has diverted a "corporate opportunity" of the museum, he may be required to sell the collection at cost to the museum. Thus, if the museum wants the art collection, it could obtain it legally from the director at the director's cost.

Example 7. If the board of directors of the art museum, discussed in Example 6, is not interested in acquiring the art collection for the museum, the board member has not acted illegally in obtaining the collection for himself.

The law relating to a corporate director's use of inside information is not well defined. Under some state laws and under federal law, it is a higher duty, resembling the duty of a trustee. For profit corporations, a federal statute provided that directors and shareholders with at least a ten percent ownership must return to the corporation all profits derived from sales and purchases (or purchases and sales) of equity securities of the corporation within a six-month period.[111] Liability is attached regardless of the intention of the insider. While this rule generally is not a part of state law, some states have adopted the concept.

Example 8. In Diamond v. Oreamuno, 24 N.Y.2d 494, 248 N.E.2d 910 (1969), a New York court held that insider information of a corporate officer or director is an asset of the corporation, acquired by the insider as a fiduciary of the company. The court held that a misappropriation of this information is a violation of that trust. The New York court quoted the well-established rule that a person who acquires special knowledge or information by virtue of her fiduciary relationship with another is not free to exploit that knowledge or information for her own personal benefit but must account to the person's principal for any profits derived therefrom. The court then likened a corporate director to a trustee in this regard and stated that "just as a trustee has no right to retain for himself the profits yielded by property placed in his possession but must account to his beneficiaries, a corporate fiduciary, who is entrusted with potentially valuable information, may not appropriate that asset for his use even though, in so doing, he causes no injury to the corporation."

Example 9. A member of the board of directors of an art museum is a collector and dealer in fine art. The board member obtains inside information about good prices on artworks in the art market. He purchases an artwork as a result of information obtained as a trustee of the art museum and sells it to a third party at a substantial profit. The board member has exploited inside information of the art museum. Based on the federal law, the board member should be required to give his profit on the sale to the museum. Though the law in most states would not require the board member to give the museum his profit, there is a definite ethical problem relating to his purchase and sale.

The code of ethics adopted by the International Council of Museums (ICOM)[112] states that members of the museum profession should not compete with their institution either in the acquisition of objects or in any personal collecting activity and that "an agreement between the museum professional and the governing body concerning any private collecting must be formulated and scrupulously followed." The ICOM Code of Ethics further states that "while members of a profession are entitled to a measure of personal independence, they must realize that no private business or professional interest can be wholly separated from that of their employing institution."[113]

2. Disposition of Assets upon Dissolution

A nonprofit organization may dissolve if provisions of state statutes are followed. However, both state statutes and federal tax provisions restrict the manner in which assets of a nonprofit corporation can be distributed. Assets held in trust, or upon certain conditions, must be returned, transferred, or conveyed in accordance with requirements of conditions imposed on the assets. Assets held for charitable, religious, eleemosynary, benevolent, educational, or similar purposes, but not held upon a condition requiring return, transfer, or conveyance by reason of a dissolution, must be transferred or conveyed to one or more nonprofit organizations engaged in activities substantially similar to those of the dissolving corporation. Treasury Regulations[114] require that upon dissolution of a § 501(c)(3) organization, all assets must be distributed for one or more exempt purposes, or to the federal government, or to a state or local government, for public purposes.

Other assets must be distributed in accordance with provisions of the articles of incorporation or bylaws to the extent the articles or bylaws determine the distribution rights of members or provide for distribution to others. Any remaining assets may be distributed to those persons, societies, or organizations, whether profit or nonprofit, as the plan of distribution specifies.

The cy pres doctrine (discussed in Chapter 5) may be applicable in dissolution proceedings to determine the distribution of assets. Pursuant to its cy pres power, a court can alter the purpose of a trust by substituting another trust purpose the court deems to be similar to that of the donor. A modified cy pres, called the doctrine of approximation, permits a court to direct application of property to some charitable purpose that falls within the general purpose of the donor when it has become impossible or illegal to carry out the particular purpose and when the donor has manifested a more general intention to devote the property to charitable purposes. If the subsequent failure of a gift after vesting is because of the dissolution of a charitable corporation, there may be no necessity for an independent cy pres proceeding; state dissolution statutes, which normally provide for the transfer of charitable assets to other charitable organizations, generally will suffice.

> Example 10. A New York court ruled [In re Friends for Long Island's Heritage, 80 A.D.3d 223, 911 N.Y.S.2d 412 (S. Ct., App. Div., 2nd Dept., N.Y., 2010)] that in a judicial dissolution proceeding, a court could order that assets held for a limited purpose cannot be used to pay creditors. The court confirmed that New York's long-standing policy honoring donors' restrictions on the use of donated property has greater weight than the claims of creditors. The court stated that the New York Not-for-Profit Corporation Law[115] emphasizes the view that the public places greater importance on limitations on the use of a donated asset than the entity which actually holds it. The court decided that even in dissolution, the limitations on donated assets must be honored and not necessarily to the lesser extent of cy pres. The court pointed out that items in a museum collection could be lost to the public forever if they could be used to pay debts during liquidation. According to the court, to permit assets held for a specific purpose to be liquidated to pay claims of creditors would extinguish the purpose behind the gift. The court ruled that, with respect to a special collection and consistent with the doctrine of cy pres, the court could provide for sale as a single collection to an entity engaged in activities substantially similar to those of the entity in liquidation. A condition of sale would be that the purchasing entity agree to be bound by the collection's gift agreement.

3. Enforcement of Fiduciary Obligations

Because of limitations in the law, discussed below, relating to the enforcement of fiduciary obligations, the public has almost no power to control activities of nonprofit directors. Members of the public generally lack any authority to prevent a director of a nonprofit corporation from abusing her power. Although beneficiaries of a charitable enterprise are members of the public, the courts generally have held that the public has no standing to sue (discussed below) to correct abuses in nonprofit enterprises.

a. Immunity from Liability

Initially it was assumed that the potential liability a director could experience for the director's negligence provided sufficient incentive for a director to administer the assets of a nonprofit organization in accordance with the director's role as a public trustee. Thus, state statutes imposing director liability for negligent conduct are deemed to be necessary to ensure ethical behavior on the part of nonprofit directors. Recently, however, some states became concerned that those directors who are volunteers would refuse to provide their services to nonprofits if they could encounter liability for their acts. Thus, some state legislatures adopted statutes granting volunteers some immunity from liability.[116] The rationale is the concern that persons will no longer volunteer for service on nonprofit boards if a high standard of care is imposed upon volunteer philanthropists.

Those states that have enacted statutes providing for immunity from liability for directors of nonprofit corporations who serve on a volunteer basis generally provide that these directors will not be liable unless they engage in "willful" or "wanton" misconduct or are "grossly" negligent. Some provide that a director will not be liable for the acts of other directors, officers, or employees of the organization.

Congress enacted the Federal Volunteer Protection Act in 1997[117] to provide additional protection from liability for volunteers in the performance of services for nonprofit organizations. Congress had become concerned that many nonprofit public and private organizations and governmental entitles had been affected adversely by the withdrawal of volunteers from boards and from service in other capacities. The Federal Volunteer Protection Act provides that no volunteer of a nonprofit organization or governmental entity will be liable for harm caused by an act or omission of the volunteer on behalf of the organization or entity if (1) the volunteer was acting within the scope of his responsibilities in the nonprofit or governmental entity at the time of the act or omission; (2) the volunteer was properly licensed, certified, or authorized (if appropriate or required) by the appropriate authorities for the activities or practice in the state in which the harm occurred; (3) the harm was not caused by willful or criminal misconduct, gross negligence, reckless misconduct, or a conscious, flagrant indifference to the rights or safety of the individual harmed by the volunteer; and (4) the harm was not caused by the volunteer operating a motor vehicle, vessel, aircraft, or other vehicle for which the state required an operator's license or insurance.

The federal immunity statute preempts the laws of any state to the extent state laws are inconsistent. Thus, if a state does not have an immunity statute, volunteers can look to the federal immunity statute for possible immunity from liability. Further, the federal immunity statute defines a "volunteer" to include an individual who serves as a director, officer, trustee, or direct service volunteer. If a state has an immunity statute that excludes directors, officers, and trustees from its provisions, these persons nonetheless can look to the federal immunity statute for immunity from liability if they serve without compensation.

b. Standing (Right) to Sue

It is difficult for members of the general public to challenge the actions of non-profit enterprises. While the public has an interest in enforcement of a charitable trust, generally the Attorney General is the representative of the general public in compelling the trustees to perform their duties properly. In most states, the Attorney General alone has power to maintain suits for enforcement of charitable trusts. A person who has no interest in performance of a trust other than as a member of the community cannot maintain a suit for enforcement.

> Example 11. An Illinois court [In re Estate of Stern, 240 Ill. App. 3d 834, 608 N.E.2d 534 (1992)] stated that the Attorney General is the sole officer authorized to represent the people of the state in any litigation in which the people are the real party in interest absent a contrary constitutional directive. The court ruled that funds, which have been appropriated for the benefit of society at large, are considered to be held in a charitable trust over which the Attorney General has regulatory authority.

With respect to suits in federal court, Article III of the U.S. Constitution confines the federal courts to adjudicating actual cases and controversies. The Supreme Court[118] has emphasized that Article III requires a federal court to act only to redress injury that fairly can be traced to the challenged action of the offender and not injury that results from the independent action of some third party not before the court. Article III requires a party seeking to invoke a federal court's jurisdiction to demonstrate that (1) she personally has suffered some actual or threatened injury as a result of the putatively illegal conduct of the offender, (2) the injury fairly can be traced to the challenged action, and (3) the injury is likely to be redressed by a favorable decision. These limitations prevent members of the public from having standing to challenge alleged wrongful conduct on the part of officials of nonprofit organizations.

With respect to a donor, the common law rule is that a donor who has made a completed gift to a charity has no standing to bring an action to enforce the terms of the gift, including any conditions or restrictions on the gift, unless the donor expressly reserved the right to do so (discussion and examples in Chapter 5).

c. Indemnification of Directors

Because there is no common law right of indemnification for corporate directors, some states have added provisions providing for indemnification for directors for liability for damages and for expenses to defend an action brought against the director. While the expenditure of a reasonable amount to defend a suit brought against a nonprofit corporation has been held to be an expenditure for the carrying on of the ordinary activities of the organization, a court may determine that the payment of attorney's fees to defend directors, prior to a determination that the directors were not guilty of negligence or misconduct in the performance of their duties, is an unauthorized transfer of funds of the nonprofit and is not in conformity with the nonprofit's purposes. A nonprofit organization might consider adopting a bylaw to provide indemnification for its officers and directors. In compliance with the bylaw, the board of directors may purchase errors and omission insurance to protect directors should they be sued for breach of their duties.

> Example 12. In Armenian Assembly of America v. Caresjian, 924 F. Supp. 2d 204 (DDC 2013), the court ruled that a museum's status as a private foundation for tax purposes (discussion of private foundation status in Chapter 3) did not preclude the museum from indemnifying former trustees for legal fees they incurred in defending claims brought against them in their capacities as former officers of the museum. The museum's bylaws contained an indemnification provision. The provision stated, however, that no payment would be made if the payment constituted self-dealing under § 4941 of the Internal Revenue Code (discussion of § 4941 below). The legal fees were incurred in the former trustees' efforts to enforce their reversionary rights in a grant agreement. The return of grant properties that had increased in value was the most consequential aspect

of the litigation. The court found that the legal fees, which a magistrate awarded in the amount of $1.461 million, were necessarily incurred. The court referred to a provision in § 4941(d), which states that self-dealing provisions of § 4941 do not apply to a private foundation's indemnification of a foundation manager with respect to the manager's defense in a civil proceeding if the manager reasonably incurred the expenses in connection with the proceeding and the manager had not acted willfully and without reasonable cause with respect to the act or failure to act that led to the proceeding.

4. Federal Regulation

The United States Congress, through conditions it has imposed upon tax exempt organizations and their managers, demands a stricter accountability than do most state legislatures from those directors of nonprofit corporations who receive compensation for their services and/or who engage in conflict of interest transactions with the nonprofits they govern. A nonprofit organization can lose its tax exempt status if any part of its net earnings inure to the benefit of private individuals. In addition, directors and officers of these tax exempts can find themselves subjected to substantial penalty taxes if they are the beneficiaries of the inurement.

The payment of excessive salaries or excessive rents and the use of the facilities of a nonprofit organization to serve a private interest constitute inurement. The policy underpinnings of the noninurement rule derive from the common law belief that charities should promote the public good rather than provide a private benefit. In addition, the IRS takes the position that, to the extent personnel or other private individuals, particularly a select few, materially benefit from a nonprofit organization's activities, the sincerity of the claimed nonprofit purposes may be called into question. If a particular individual or a few individuals reap commercial benefits from the operation of a nonprofit organization, though they do not do so by direct acquisition or payment over to them of its earnings, the earnings may nevertheless inure to their benefit within the intendment of this phrasing so as to destroy the tax exempt status of the organization.[119]

a. Self-Dealing—§ 4941 of the Internal Revenue Code

Those charitable § 501(c)(3) organizations that do not qualify for public charity status under § 509 of the Internal Revenue Code and, as a result, are classified for tax purposes as private foundations are subject to substantial limitations and reporting requirements as well as to substantial penalty taxes for failure to comply with certain Code provisions. (As noted, Chapter 3 defines and discusses the public charity and private foundation tax status applicable to charitable organizations.) Private foundations are those charitable organizations that receive most of their support from a small number of contributors and, thus, cannot qualify for public charity status under § 509 of the Internal Revenue Code. Private foundations generally are controlled by their founders or substantial donors. Because these charitable organizations often are responsive to private groups rather than to the public, the IRS closely supervises their operations to make certain there are no abuses relating to their tax exempt status and as to the tax benefits their donors receive for contributions to the organizations. (Refer to discussion of rules and procedures related to public charities and private foundations in Chapter 3.)

Section 4941 imposes a penalty tax on any act of self-dealing between a private foundation and a "disqualified person," i.e., a substantial donor or a person in control of the foundation. The penalty tax on self-dealing is imposed on the self-dealer, not the foundation. Acts of self-dealing include sales or exchanges of property, leases, and loans between a private foundation and the foundation's substantial donors or managers; the providing of goods, services, or facilities by a private foundation to these persons; and the payment of unreasonable or unearned compensation to the foundation's substantial donors, officers, directors, or trustees. The initial penalty tax under § 4941 is ten percent of the "amount involved." The tax is increased to a second-tier penalty tax of two hundred percent if the self-dealing is not corrected. This tax is imposed on the individual, the "self-dealer," not on the nonprofit organization.

A director's participation in a conflict of interest transaction would be an act of self-dealing regardless of whether the transaction was fair to the private foundation. A person taking part in a conflict of interest transaction, and possibly the foundation manager, would be subject to substantial penalty taxes even though the Revised Model Nonprofit Corporation Act and many state statutes provide that no liability is attached to a conflict of interest transaction if it is fair to the corporation. The Internal Revenue Code, in effect, imposes trustee standards upon persons administering those charitable organizations that are classified as private foundations for tax purposes. When states adhere to the lesser corporate standards, directors of nonprofit corporations may misconstrue their level of accountability and their possible liability for involvement in conflict of interest transactions.

Example 13. Mark Rothko, an internationally recognized artist, bequeathed paintings in his estate to a foundation the artist created during his lifetime. Oscar Reis was one of the executors of the artist's estate and was also a director of the artist's foundation. As executor of the artist's estate, Reis entered into contracts on behalf of the estate with a gallery in which Reis was a director and an employee. The contract provided that the artist's paintings could be sold only by the gallery for a period of twelve years and at a commission to the gallery of fifty percent of sales proceeds. The artist's surviving family members sued in a state court to set aside the twelve-year exclusive sales contract and to remove Reis as executor of the estate. Most of the legal relief sought by the family was granted. The IRS then audited the Mark Rothko Foundation and determined that Reis was liable for self-dealing taxes in excess of $18 million pursuant to § 4941 of the Internal Revenue Code. Reis contended that assets of the estate were separate and distinct from assets of the foundation; therefore, improper conduct that occurred in administering the assets of the estate would not also constitute self-dealing in the use of the assets of the foundation. Reis also contended that he was not involved in self-dealing because assets of the foundation were not used for his benefit or transferred to him. In Estate of Reis v. Comm., 87 T.C. 1016 (1986), the court, however, agreed with the IRS that because the foundation was a beneficiary under Mark Rothko's will, the foundation had a vested beneficial interest in the property of the estate. The court did give Reis the opportunity to demonstrate in a trial on the merits that he had no substantial benefit from the transaction. In Stamos v. Comm., 87 T.C. 1451 (1987), the court held Stamos, another of the executors of the Mark Rothko estate, liable for self-dealing excise taxes in excess of $19 million because of the exclusive contract the executors entered into on behalf of the estate. Stamos also served as a director of the Mark Rothko Foundation.

b. Excess Benefit Transactions—§ 4958 of the Internal Revenue Code

Until 1995, only officers and directors of § 501(c)(3) organizations that were classified as private foundations for federal income tax purposes were subject to self-dealing penalties. Section 4958 was added to the Internal Revenue Code in 1995, effective in 1996, to subject officers and directors of the § 501(c)(3) organizations that qualify as public charities and § 501(c)(4) social welfare organizations to a penalty tax on "excess benefit transactions." An "excess benefit transaction" is any transaction in which the covered organization provides an economic benefit directly or indirectly to or for the use of any disqualified person (donors, officers, directors, and trustees) if the value of the economic benefit provided exceeds the value of the consideration (including the performance of services) received for providing the benefit.[120] Excess benefit transactions include any financial and non-fair-market value transactions that benefit individuals.

The tax on an excess benefit transaction is twenty-five percent of the excess benefit and is imposed on the disqualified person. If the excess benefit is not corrected within a "taxable period,"[121] a tax of two hundred percent of the excess benefit is imposed on the disqualified person. The penalty tax is imposed on the disqualified person, not the public charity. A tax of ten percent of the excess benefit, maximum of $20,000, is imposed on the organization's manager if the manager participated in the transaction knowing the transaction was an excess benefit transaction unless the manager can show that the manager's participation was not willful and was due to reasonable cause. An excess benefit transaction is corrected by undoing the excess benefit to the extent possible and taking any additional measures necessary to place the organization in a financial position not worse than that in which it would be if the disqualified person were dealing under the highest fiduciary standards.

The payment of any "unreasonable" compensation clearly is an excess benefit transaction.[122] Still, a person may rely on the reasonableness of compensation if a compensation arrangement was approved by a board or committee (1) that was composed entirely of individuals who were unrelated to, and not subject to control by, the disqualified person involved in the arrangement; (2) that obtained and relied upon appropriate data as to comparability; and (3) that documented adequately the basis for its determination.[123] If all three criterion are satisfied, penalty taxes will be imposed only if the IRS develops sufficient contrary evidence to rebut the probative value of evidence established by parties to the transaction. For example, the IRS could show that compensation data relied on was not for a functionally comparable position or that the disqualified person did not, in fact, perform substantially the responsibilities of the position.[124]

Sales or other transfers to a disqualified person are subject to a similar rebuttable presumption if the sale or transfer was approved by an independent board that used appropriate comparability data and documented adequately its determination.[125]

Example 14. The salary of a museum director is increased and the director is given a current annual compensation package of $400,000. The IRS successfully contends that a "reasonable salary" for the director should be limited to $200,000 per year. The director could be subjected to an initial penalty tax of $50,000 [$400,000 (current compensation) - $200,000 (reasonable salary) = $200,000; $200,000 x 25% = $50,000]. If the director does not return the excessive portion of his salary ($200,000) to the museum, he will be subjected to an additional penalty tax of $400,000 ($200,000 x 200%).

Example 15. A member of the board of directors of an art museum periodically takes valuable paintings from the museum collection and hangs them at her private residence or at her office. If the museum is a private operating foundation for tax purposes (discussion of private operating foundation, as noted previously, in Chapter 3), this is self-dealing and will subject the board member to the substantial tax penalties noted above.[126] If the museum is a public charity for tax purposes (discussion of public charity also in Chapter 3), the board member would be liable for a penalty tax of twenty-five percent on the value of the benefit the board member receives from having the painting in her home. (Although the board member may be subject to penalty taxes as provided for in the Internal Revenue Code, there likely are no state statutes prohibiting her from hanging the paintings temporarily in her home or office. The practice probably is not illegal under state law. Nonetheless, there are ethical considerations in approving such a practice.)

Example 16. A member of the board of directors of a museum has a proprietary interest in a firm which does business with the museum. The museum awards contracts to the board member's firm at a substantial profit to the firm. If the museum is a private foundation for tax purposes, this is an act of self-dealing and will subject the board member to the substantial tax penalties noted above and set out in § 4941 of the Internal Revenue Code. If the museum is a public charity for tax purposes, the board member may have received an excess benefit, which will subject the board member to the significant penalty tax set out in § 4958 of the Code. Further, awarding the contract to the board member's firm may be inurement (discussion of inurement in Chapter 3) that could cause the museum to lose its tax exempt status. In addition, if the museum were a trust, the board member, as a trustee, would violate the trust standard of loyalty and may subject the trustee to damages for breach of loyalty in a state court proceeding. The board member may be liable in damages for breach of loyalty even as a corporate director if the transaction was not "fair" with respect to the museum.

Example 17. A member of the board of directors of a museum sells artifacts from the museum's collection to a dealer at prices advantageous to the dealer in return for discounts on the board member's private purchases from that same dealer. For tax purposes, the sales are self-dealing if the museum is a private foundation for tax purposes and excess benefit transactions if the museum is a public charity for tax purposes. The agreement would be a conflict-of-interest transaction and clearly would violate the trust standard of loyalty. If the museum is incorporated, there may be a violation of the corporate standard of loyalty.

C. ACCOUNTING FOR MUSEUMS

A museum director has a duty to manage wisely and in accordance with the charitable purposes of the organization in obtaining funds received from governmental entities and from the public. Adequate accounting records are essential for a museum director to substantiate that the museum has operated in a manner consistent with its charitable purposes and that the museum director has fulfilled stewardship requirements. It is imperative that a museum director have some knowledge of accounting principles and a basic understanding of the financial statements that should be prepared for a museum and its supporting foundations. The following discussion provides a very basic knowledge of accounting records and statements for a nonprofit organization and for a museum in particular.

For business enterprises, financial statements must be prepared in accordance with "generally accepted accounting principles."[127] An auditor who attests to a firm's financial statements must call attention to any departure from these principles and must qualify its audit opinion should there be a departure. Because user reaction to a qualified opinion is serious, publicly owned businesses generally do not publish financial statements if they are not prepared in accordance with generally accepted accounting principles. In the past, there had not been a set of generally accepted accounting principles for nonprofit organizations. Now, however, both the American Institute of Certified Public Accountants (AICPA) and the Financial Accounting Standards Board (FASB) have developed guidelines for preparing financial statements designed to communicate to users of statements of nonprofit organizations the manner in which resources of these organizations have been used to carry out the organizations' objectives.[128] A complete set of financial statements of a nonprofit enterprise are a Statement of Financial Position (Balance Sheet), Statement of Activity (or Statement of Revenue and Expenses), Statement of Changes in Net Assets or Fund Balance, and Statement of Cash Flows, including accompanying notes to statements.

Because of certain distinguishing characteristics of nonprofit organizations, financial statements for nonprofit organizations have somewhat different reporting objectives than those for profit organizations. As the FASB noted, nonprofit organizations have receipts of significant amounts of resources from resource providers who do not expect to receive either repayment or economic benefits proportionate to resources provided.[129] In addition, nonprofit organizations have operating purposes other than to provide goods or services at a profit or profit equivalent. They do not have defined ownership interests that can be sold, transferred, or redeemed or that provide a property interest in resources of the organization. As the FASB stated, these characteristics result in certain types of transactions that are largely absent in business enterprises, such as contributions and grants. There is an absence of transactions with owners, such as stock transactions and the payment of dividends.[130]

The FASB has determined that financial statements for nonprofit organizations should provide the user with information needed to make rational decisions concerning allocation of resources of a nonprofit organization and should inform the user of the organization's total resources available to perform various program services and activities, as well as the use made of those resources. The information furnished should be useful to those interested in a nonprofit organization's present and future capacity to render service and to achieve operating goals. The financial statements should report the nature and amount of resources and change in net assets (assets less liabilities) during an accounting period. They also should identify an organization's principal programs and their costs.

1. Statement of Financial Position

The statement of financial position (balance sheet) for a nonprofit organization presents the financial position of the organization as of the end of a reporting period. It summarizes assets, liabilities, and net assets (fund balances, which represent assets less liabilities) of a nonprofit organization. A statement of financial position must report the amounts for each of three classes of net assets—permanently restricted net assets, temporarily restricted assets, and unrestricted net assets—based on the existence or absence of donor-imposed restrictions.

The statement of financial position must disclose limitations on the use of assets, such as those that may be used only for charitable purposes and that must be transferred to another nonprofit organization upon dissolution of the organization, or that must be returned to the donor upon dissolution. Assets of a nonprofit organization are recorded in the organization's financial records at cost if purchased and at fair value if acquired by donation. All long-lived assets, except rare works of art and historical treasures (if the holder takes steps to protect and preserve the works and limits their use to display), should be depreciated (and the amount of the deprecation charged against income of the organization).[131]

2. Statement of Activity

The statement of activity (statement of revenue and expenses) reports results of operations of a nonprofit organization. The difference between revenues, gains, and other support, and expenses of the organization, represents the change in the organization's net assets.[132] Although nonprofit organizations do not have a purpose to make "profits," nonprofit entities can survive only if they have support, revenue, and other asset additions equal to or in excess of their expenses. The statement of activity, then, is an important statement to users as an indicator of the financial health of a nonprofit organization.

The statement of activity focuses on the nonprofit organization as a whole and reports the amount of change in net assets (assets minus liabilities) for the period. It must report the amount of change in permanently restricted net assets, temporarily restricted net assets, and unrestricted net assets for the period. The statement must report revenues as increases in unrestricted net assets unless use of the assets received is limited by donor-imposed restrictions.[133] The bottom line excess of revenues over expenses (or excess of expenses over revenues), which corresponds to the net income or net loss of a for-profit entity, ties the fund balance (or net assets) of a nonprofit organization for the prior year to the current year. The fund balance (or net assets) of the prior year plus the excess of revenues over expenses (or less the excess of expenses over revenues) equals the fund balance (or net assets) of the current year.

Expenses are reported on the statement of activity on a functional basis. The FASB has concluded that information about expenses by function, such as major programs or services and major classes of supporting services, is necessary to an understanding of a nonprofit organization's service efforts.[134] Thus, the FASB requires that a set of financial statements include that information. The information may be communicated either in the statement of activity or in notes to financial statements. The functional classifications should include specific program services that describe the organization's service activities and supporting services, such as fund-raising and administration. Program activities are those activities directly related to the exempt purposes of the organization, while supporting activities include fund-raising and management and general expenses that do not relate directly to the organization's exempt purposes. Cost of each significant program and supporting activity should be separately presented.

3. Statement of Cash Flows

The statement of cash flows provides the user with information about changes in the cash account. It sets out the cash receipts and cash payments during a period and shows their origin.

4. Fund Accounting

Many restrictions are placed on resources donated to a nonprofit organization that prohibit use of resources either directly or indirectly for operating purposes. Observance of these limitations may require separate accountability. This separate accountability often is accomplished by use of fund accounting in which resources are classified for accounting and reporting purposes into funds associated with specified activities or objectives. Each fund is a separate accounting entity with a self-balancing set of accounts for assets, liabilities, net assets (fund balance), and changes in net assets (or fund balances). Funds most commonly used are: current unrestricted (operating) fund, temporarily restricted (or current restricted) fund, permanently restricted (or endowment) fund, and plant fund.

The unrestricted fund represents the net amount of resources available without restriction for performing the organization's objectives. The only limits on use of unrestricted net assets are the broad limits resulting from the nature of the organization and the purposes stated in the articles of incorporation or bylaws.[135] Many nonprofit organizations have only unrestricted funds. The temporary restricted fund includes resources restricted as to use by the resource provider. (Current resources restricted for future acquisition of fixed assets can be reported in the balance sheet as deferred revenue until restrictions are met.) Some assets are donated with stipulations that they be invested to provide a permanent source of income. These result from gifts and bequests that create permanent endowment funds. Endowment funds are restricted resources in which donated principal remains intact. Only income from the fund may be spent. Many organizations use a separate fund to account for investment in operating plant, art collections, rare books and manuscripts, and similar items. A plant fund may be reported separately or may be combined with either the unrestricted or restricted funds.

Fund accounting is not required but reporting on a fund accounting basis may be helpful to segregate unrestricted from restricted resources. If a museum elects not to report on a fund accounting basis, the financial statements should disclose all material restrictions and observe other requirements, such as grouping similar accounts.

5. Museum Collections

Originally, the AICPA had concluded that it was generally impracticable to determine a value for inexhaustible collections of museums and, thus, that these assets need not be recorded in the financial statements.[136] Based upon studies that determined these collections should be recorded in the financial statements (but not depreciated) as their values usually represented the largest assets of nonprofit organizations such as museums, the AICPA later decided it was desirable to catalogue and control collections. If records and values do exist for the collections, the cost of these assets, if purchased, and fair value, if acquired by donation, should be recorded on the organization's financial statements.

The current practice and position is that the nature and cost, or contributed value of, and the nature of, and proceeds from, current period accessions and deaccessions should be disclosed in financial statements of a museum. Further, collections that are exhaustible, such as exhibits with a limited display life, and that have been recorded in the accounting records and financial statements, should be amortized (charged against the museum's income) over their useful lives.

6. Donated Services and Materials

The nature and extent of donated or contributed services received by nonprofit organizations vary and range from limited participation of many individuals in fund-raising activities to active participation in a nonprofit organization's service program. The AICPA has concluded that it is difficult to place a monetary value on these services and, thus, their values usually are not recorded. Still, if significant in amount, donated materials and facilities should be recorded at their fair value provided the organization has a clearly measurable and objective basis for determining value.[137]

7. Governmental Reporting Requirements

Tax exempt nonprofit organizations must file annual return forms with the IRS. Many states also require that reports be filed with an appropriate designated state official, generally the Attorney General or the state comptroller of the state. Officials of the National Association of Attorneys General and the National Association of State Charities worked with the IRS to develop a uniform approach to annual reporting for regulatory purposes. Form 990, which is the annual return form that must be filed annually with the IRS for most tax exempt organizations, was revised in 1981 and became the nationwide uniform annual report for nonprofit organizations. With the broadening of Form 990 in 1981, many states permitted its use as the required statement nonprofit organizations must file with the state.

Form 990 was redesigned in 2008 to provide for more uniform and complete reporting by a growing exempt sector. Form 990 requires the same complete accounting information prescribed by the AICPA and the FASB for financial reporting purposes. Form 990 requires completion of a Statement of Financial Position (Balance Sheet), a Statement of Revenue and Expenses (Statement of Activity), and a Statement of Changes in Net Assets (or Fund Balances). A museum that is classified as a private operating foundation for tax purposes must file annually with the IRS using Form 990PF. Form 990PF also requires completion of a Statement of Financial Position and a Statement of Activity (referred to in Form 990PF as Analysis of Revenue and Expenses). Thus, a museum would report assets, liabilities, revenue, and expense on either the annual Form 990 or Form 990PF in much the same manner as required for state reporting purposes.

A museum that has unrelated business taxable income in excess of $1,000 in a year (discussion in Chapter 4) also must file Form 990T and pay tax on its unrelated business income in the same manner as a for-profit entity.

NOTES

1. The International Council of Museums (ICOM) Code of Professional Ethics was adopted unanimously by the General Assembly of the International Council of Museums

in 1986. It was amended in 2001 and, in 2004, was retitled ICOM Code of Ethics for Museums.

2. ICOM Code of Ethics, Glossary, http://icom.museum/the-vision/code-of-ethics/glossary/.

3. Example of a state museum is the Maine State Museum (27 MRSA § 81).

4. An example is the Texas Memorial Museum, which is an integral part of the University of Texas at Austin (Tex. Educ. Code § 67.23). The Board of Regents of the University of Texas has management and control of the museum.

5. The Smithsonian Institution is subject to statutory provisions set out in 20 U.S.C. §§ 41–85, which has been cited as the National Museum Act of 1966.

6. The Smithsonian Institution controls and directs, among others, the Air and Space Museum, the African American History and Culture Museum, the American Indian Museum, the Hirshhorn Museum and Sculpture Garden, the National History Museum, the National Zoo, the Portrait Gallery, the American Art Museum, the Renwick Gallery, the Postal Museum, the Sackler Gallery, and the African Art Museum.

7. The Smithsonian Institution was created in 1846 when James Smithson of London made a bequest to the United States to be used for the establishment of an institution, to be located in Washington, D.C., and to be known under the name of "Smithsonian Institution," for the "increase and diffusion of knowledge among men." (Smithson's will stated the purpose of the Smithsonian was for the "increase and diffusion of knowledge among men.")

8. 20 U.S.C. § 50. The Smithsonian is governed by a board of regents composed of the vice president, the Chief Justice of the United States, three members of the Senate, three members of the House of Representatives, and nine other persons. Id. at § 42. A member of the board of regents is elected as chancellor and is the presiding officer of the board of regents. Id. at § 44.

9. The language tracks the provision in Smithson's will and is set out in 20 U.S.C. § 41.

10. See, as examples, museums in Illinois (70 ILCS 1105/17) and Maine (27 MRSA §§ 81–86-A).

11. See, as examples, Cal. Gov't. Code §§ 37541 and 25351 and Pa. Stat. Ann. tit. 16, § 7925.

12. Cal. Gov't. Code § 37541. The legislative body of a city would establish a museum in the city upon receiving a petition signed by one-third of the city electors.

13. Cal. Gov't. Code § 25351.

14. N.Y. Educ. Code §§ 253, 255–258. The trustees of the museum applied to the regents within the state board of education for a charter and the state board of education supervised the museum.

15. Tex. Local Gov't. Code Ann § 331.001. These local governments could enter into joint agreements to provide for museum services (Tex. Local Gov't. Code Ann. § 331.008). A city with a population in excess of 40,000 could create a park board of trustees to acquire or improve lands or buildings to be used for historical museums (Tex. Local Gov't. Code Ann § 306.031).

16. Ariz. Rev. Stat. Ann. § 11–262. Discussion of § 501(c)(3) organizations in Chapter 3.

17. Wis. Stat. § 229.11. A museum could receive and manage bequests, donations, and loans for the establishment, increase, or maintenance of the museum. A public museum was administered by a board of ten trustees. Wis. Stat § 229.12. The trustees would have control of the receipt, selection, arrangement, and disposition of specimens and objects pertaining to the museum. Wis. Stat. § 229.13.

18. Discussion in Bogert & Bogert, Trusts and Trustees § 391.

19. Id. at § 362.

20. Restatement, Trusts, §§ 349(b), 358.

21. Discussion in Bogert & Bogert, cited in note 18, at § 364.

22. Id. at §§ 391, 394.

23. See Scott, Law of Trusts, § 8 (3d ed.).

24. Id. at § 224.2.

25. Discussion in Bogert & Bogert, cited in note 18 at § 394. The Uniform Prudent Management of Institutional Funds Act, which was adopted by the Uniform Laws Commission in 2006 and has been enacted by most states, provides that upon application by a charitable institution, a court may modify a restriction in a gift instrument if the restriction has become impracticable or wasteful or impairs management or investment of the fund or, because of circumstances not anticipated by the donor, modification would further the purposes of the fund. The act requires the institution to notify the Attorney General of the state and give the Attorney General an opportunity to be heard.

26. The Uniform Prudent Management of Institutional Funds Act provides that if an institution determines restrictions in a gift instrument, which created a fund that is less than $25,000 and that has been in existence for a certain specified number of years, are unlawful, impracticable, impossible to achieve, or are wasteful, and the institution notifies the Attorney General of the state, the institution itself may release or modify the restrictions if it then uses assets of the fund consistent with the charitable purposes of the fund.

27. However, those charitable trusts that are classified as private foundations for federal income tax purposes must file copies of their annual tax returns (Form 990PF) with the Attorney General of the state in which the foundation is located. Discussion in Chapter 3.

28. In those states that have adopted the Uniform Unincorporated Nonprofit Association Act, an unincorporated association has almost the same rights and status as a nonprofit corporation.

29. An example referred to by Salli Swartz, an attorney who practices in Paris, is the Napoleonic Code, which originally did not provide for a right to form associations in France. (Discussion in Marilyn Phelan and Robert J. Desiderio, *Nonprofit Organization: Law and Taxation*, 3d ed. [2010], pp. 52–57), As Swartz noted, Articles 291–94 of the Napoleonic code made the association a crime. As she stated, associations were prohibited in France until the enactment of the "Association Law" in July of 1901. Swartz mentioned that the Association Law did not create a legal entity specific to associations; rather it provided for an association that represented an agreement by which two or more persons mutually and permanently made available to themselves their knowledge and activities for a purpose other than making a profit.

30. These rules were established early in cases that included Martin v. Curran, 303 N.Y. 276, 101 N.E.2d 683 (1951); and Evans v. Southside Place Park Ass'n, 154 S.W.2d 914 (Tex. Civ. App. 1941).

31. See Uniform Unincorporated Nonprofit Association Act (1996).

32. See Uniform Unincorporated Nonprofit Association Act (2008).

33. The laws governing nonprofit corporations will be set out in a state's nonprofit corporation act. The management and activities of a nonprofit corporation are determined by state law and each individual state's nonprofit corporation acts. A few states do not have a separate corporate act for nonprofit corporations; in these states, nonprofit corporations are governed by the state statute relating to for-profit corporations. These statutes will have a few separate provisions that address special problems or issues relating to nonprofit corporations.

34. Trustees of Dartmouth College v. Woodward, 17 U.S. 518 (1819).

35. Bank of United States v. Deveaux, 5 Cranch (9 U.S.) 61, 3 L. Ed. 38 (1809).

36. United States v. State Tax Commission of State of Mississippi, 505 F.2d 633 (5th Cir. 1974)

37. York County Fair Ass'n v. South Carolina Tax Commission, 154 S.E.2d 361 (S.C. 1967).

38. Trustees of Dartmouth College v. Woodward, discussed in note 34.

39. In Texas, "Certificate of Formation" has been substituted for "Articles of Incorporation" (Tex. Bus. Org. Code § 1.002(6)).

40. Treas. Reg. § 1.503(c)(3)-1(b)(4). Discussion in Chapter 3.

41. Id.

42. See Mod. Nonprofit Corp. Act § 11 (1964) and Rev. Mod. Nonprofit Corp. Act §§ 6.03 and 6.10 (1987). (Most state nonprofit corporate statutes are taken from the provisions of one of these Model acts. The American Bar Association completed a Third Edition Model Nonprofit Corporation Act in 2008, but because most of the state nonprofit corporate statutes have provisions from either the 1964 Model Act or the 1987 Revised Act, this text refers to provisions of these acts.)

Nonprofit corporations in California have no members unless the articles of incorporation or the bylaws provide otherwise. If the corporation has no members, approval of the board is required of transactions otherwise requiring approval of the members. Cal. Corp. Code §§ 5310, 7310. If corporations have members, no person may hold more than one membership. Cal. Corp. Code §§ 5312, 7312.

43. Mod. Nonprofit Corp. Act §11 (1964) and Rev. Mod. Nonprofit Corp. Act § 6.10 (1987).

44. Discussion in Raulston v. Everett, 561 S.W.2d 635 (Tex. Civ. App. 1978) and Schroeder v. Meridian Improvement Club, 36 Wash. 2d 925, 221 P. 2d 544 (1950).

45. See N.Y. Not-for-Profit Corp Law § 601. See N.J. Rev. Stat § 15A:5-13, which provided that if memberships are controlled by a corporate member, any memberships held by that corporation cannot be voted at any meeting.

46. See, e.g., Pa. Stat. Ann. tit. 15, § 5752.

47. Mod. Nonprofit Corp. Act § 13 (1964).

48. Id. and Rev. Mod. Nonprofit Corp. Act § 7.01 (1987).

49. Mod. Nonprofit Corp. Act § 13 (1964).

50. Id.

51. See Rev. Mod. Nonprofit Corp. Act § 7.03 (1987).

52. An amendment in 2012 to the Third Edition Model Nonprofit Corporation Act § 7.24(c) states that the articles or bylaws may provide that when a meeting, which has been adjourned for lack of a quorum, is reconvened, those members present, although less than a quorum, nonetheless constitute a quorum if the original notice of the meeting, or a notice of the adjourned meeting, states that those members who attend a meeting adjourned for lack of a quorum will constitute a quorum even though they are less than a quorum. The reason for this amendment was that many nonprofit corporations have low member turnout and need a low quorum to hold meetings of the members. To protect against the possibility that a few members may plan to take over an annual or regular meeting and vote on matters that were not noticed, § 7.24(a) of the Third Edition Model Act prohibits members from voting on a matter that was not noticed unless one-third or more of the voting power is present.

53. Mod. Nonprofit Corp. Act § 14. The Revised Model Nonprofit Corporation Act § 7.05 provided for fair and reasonable notice. It provided that notice is fair and reasonable if it is delivered no fewer than ten but not more than sixty days prior to the meeting.

54. Mod. Nonprofit Corp. Act § 14. The notice of meeting could be delivered personally, by mail, facsimile, or electronic message and should be delivered at the direction of the president, the secretary, or the officers or persons calling the meeting. If the notice was delivered by mail, it was deemed delivered when it was deposited in the United States mail addressed to the member at the address on the corporate records. Notice of a meeting need not be given to a member who submitted a signed waiver of notice, in person or by proxy, either before or after the meeting. The attendance of a member at a meeting, in person or proxy, without protesting prior to the conclusion of the meeting of a lack of notice of the meeting, constituted a waiver of notice by that member. The Revised Model Nonprofit Corporation Act, § 7.06(b), provided that a member's attendance at a meeting waived objection unless the member, at the beginning of the meeting, objected to the holding of the meeting or to the transacting of business at the meeting.

55. Mod. Nonprofit Corp. Act § 15.

56. Id.

57. Id.

58. Discussion in Westlake Hospital Ass'n v. Blix, 13 Ill. 2d 183, 148 N.E.2d 471 (1958); Harris v. Board of Directors of Community Hospital of Evanston, 55 Ill. App. 3d 392, 370 N.E.2d 1121(1977) and Petition of Sousa, 26 Misc. 2d 474, 203 N.Y.S.2d 3, 5 (1960).

59. See N.Y. Not-for-Profit Corp Law § 623; Cal. Corp. Code §§ 5710, 7710.

The Revised Model Nonprofit Corporation Act provided for this right in any member having five percent or more of the voting power or by fifty members, whichever was less, or by any director. Rev. Mod. Nonprofit Corp. Act § 6.30.

In Moore v. Christ's Christian Fellowship Church, Inc., 172 Ohio App.3d 398, 875 N.E.2d 121 (5th Dist. Fairfield County 2007), some church members filed a derivative action against the directors and trustees of a church corporation in which they contended the directors and trustees committed financial misconduct, refused to provide an accounting, improperly converted corporate property, and interfered with the church's ability to function as a religious entity. The court noted that members of the corporation were not defined nor were any requirements set forth for membership. It ruled that absent any specific definition of membership qualifications, the trustees were the sole members of the church corporation as they were named in the church's articles of incorporation as the corporation's sole members. The court stated that a right to file a derivative claim was a right conferred solely on corporate members or shareholders.

60. The Model Nonprofit Corporation Act does not have a provision relating to the removal of a member. The Revised Model Nonprofit Corporation Act, § 6.21, provided that a member of a nonprofit corporation could not be expelled or suspended except pursuant to a fair and reasonable procedure carried out in good faith. The Revised Model Act sets out a "fair and reasonable" procedure.

61. In Bartley v. Augusta Country Club, Inc., 254 Ga. 144, 326 S.E.2d 442 (1985), the Supreme Court of Georgia ruled that disciplinary matters taken by a private social club against a member were not matters of constitutional law. The court stated that the rights of a member, if any, were governed by the bylaws of the club. The bylaws constituted an agreement between the club and its members.

62. Mod. Nonprofit Corp. Act § 17 and Rev. Mod. Nonprofit Corp. Act § 8.01(b).

63. Id.

64. Mod. Nonprofit Corp. Act § 18.

65. Id.

66. Id.
67. Id.
68. Id.
69. Id.
70. Id. at § 20.
71. Id.
72. Id.
73. Id. at § 18 and Rev. Mod. Nonprofit Corp. Act § 8.05.
74. Mod. Nonprofit Corp. Act § 19.
75. Id.
76. Id. at § 22 and Rev. Mod. Nonprofit Corp. Act § 8.20(b).
77. Mod. Nonprofit Corp. Act § 22. The Revised Model Nonprofit Corporation Act, § 8.23(b), provided that a director's attendance at or participation in a meeting waived any required notice of the meeting unless the director objected to lack of notice and did not thereafter vote for or assent to the objected to action.
78. Mod. Nonprofit Corp. Act § 17. The Revised Model Nonprofit Corporation Act, § 8.01(c), provided that the articles could authorize a person or persons to exercise some or all of the powers that would otherwise be exercised by a board. The acts provided that this person or persons would have the duties and responsibilities of the directors. The Revised Model Act provided that the directors would be relieved to that extent from these duties and responsibilities.
79. Mod. Nonprofit Corp. Act § 21; Rev. Mod. Nonprofit Corp. Act § 8.25. The Uniform Prudent Management of Institutional Funds Act, which has been adopted by a number of states, specifically authorizes boards of nonprofit organizations to delegate to committees, officers or employees, or to outside agents, including investment counsel, the authority to act in place of the board in investment and reinvestment of institutional funds.
80. Mod. Nonprofit Corp. Act § 21.
81. Id. at § 18.
82. Rev. Mod. Nonprofit Corp. Act § 8.08.
83. Id. at § 8:08(h).
84. Id. at § 8:10.
85. Id. at § 8:40.
86. Mod. Nonprofit Corp. Act § 23.
87. Id.
88. Id.
89. Id.
90. Id.
91. See Henn & Alexander, Laws of Corporations, § 217 (3d ed.).
92. Fletcher Cyc. Corp. § 838 (Perm. ed.).
93. Id. at § 553.
94. Id. at § 627.
95. Id.
96. Id. at §§ 637, 645.
97. Henn & Alexander, Laws of Corporations, § 225 (3d ed.).
98. Id.
99. Restatement (2d) Agency, § 73.

100. See Henn & Alexander, Laws of Corporations § 226; Fletcher Cyc. Corp. §§ 442, 742.

101. Rev. Rul. 57-246, 1957-1 CB 338.

102. Id.

103. Rev. Mod. Nonprofit Corp. Act § 8.42.

104. Id.

105. Delegation of a trustee's duties is not permitted under the common law. Although the Uniform Trust Act, § 807, provides that a trustee may delegate duties, several states have not adopted this act. The Uniform Prudent Management of Institutional Funds Act, § 5, which has been adopted in most of the states, permits a trustee to delegate management and investment of institutional funds. The Uniform Trust Entity Act, which was adopted by the Uniform Laws Commission in 2009 and which is used chiefly as a model for business organizations, also permits trustees to delegate their duties and powers (§ 511).

106. Discussion in Louisiana World Exposition v. Federal Ins. Co., 864 F.2d 1147 (5th Cir. 1989); Midatlantic National Bank v. Frank G. Thompson Foundation, 405 A.2d 866 (N.J. Super. Ch. 1979); and Stern v. Lucy Webb Hayes Nat. Training School for Deaconesses & Missionaries, 381 F. Supp. 1003 (D.D.C. 1974).

107. Discussion in Financial Industrial Fund, Inc. v. McDonnell Douglas Corp., 474 F.2d 514 (10th Cir, 1973). In Oberbillig v. West Grand Towers Condominium Ass'n, 807 N.W.2d 143 (Iowa, 2011), the Iowa court stated that the "heart of the business judgment rule" is "judicial deference to business decisions by corporate directors."

108. Refer to discussion in note 105. Delegation of a trustee's duties is not permitted under the common law. The law can be unclear in many of the states, most of which have not adopted the Uniform Trust Act, which now permits a trustee to delegate duties. However, most states have adopted the Uniform Prudent Management of Institutional Funds, which permits trustees to delegate investment decisions (§ 5 of the act).

109. The Prudent Management of Institutional Funds Act, § 3(4), states that a charitable institution should diversify unless it determines that because of special circumstances, the purposes of the fund are better served without diversification.

110. Under a prior provision in the Uniform Trust Act, § 5, a trustee was prohibited from directly or indirectly buying or selling any property from the trust, from or to himself, or from or to any relative, employee, partner, or other business associate. The Uniform Trust Act, § 802, now provides that a trust transaction involving the trustee is "voidable" unless it was authorized by the trust instrument, was approved by a court, or was consented to or ratified by the beneficiary(ies).

111. 15 U.S.C. § 78p(b); 17 C.F.R. § 240.16b-6.

112. ICOM Code of Ethics, 8.14.

113. Id. at 8.9.

114. Treas. Reg. § 1.501(c)(3)-1(a)(4).

115. § 1002-a(c)(1).

116. See, e.g., Ark. Stat. Ann. § 16-120-102; Minn. Stat. §§ 317A.251, 317A.361; Tex. Civ. Prac. & Rem. Code §§ 64.001–64.008; Wis. Stat. § 181.287.

117. 42 U.S.C. §§ 14501–5.

118. Allen v. Wright, 468 U.S. 737 (1984).

119. Discussion in Harding Hospital v. United States, 505 F.2d 1068 (6th Cir. 1974). Discussion also in Chapter 3.

120. I.R.C. § 4958(c).

121. The "taxable period" is the period beginning with the date on which the transaction occurs and ending on the earliest of (1) the date of the mailing of a notice of deficiency with respect to the initial tax, or (2) the date on which the initial tax is imposed. I.R.C. § 4958(f)(5). If a disqualified person makes a payment of less than the full correction amount, the two hundred percent penalty is imposed only on the unpaid portion of the correction amount. Treas. Reg. § 53.4958-1(c)(2).

122. Treas. Reg. § 53.4958-4(h)(3).

123. Id. at § 53.4958-6.

124. HR 104-506, 104th Cong. 2d Sess. 54 (1996).

125. Treas. Reg. § 53.4958-4(b)(3)(i).

126. In Rev. Rul. 74-600, 1974-2 C.B. 385, the IRS ruled that placing a foundation's paintings in a substantial contributor's residence was self-dealing even though the collection occasionally was open to the public.

127. "Generally accepted accounting principles" are a common set of accounting theories and procedures that serve as a general guide for the accounting profession in financial reporting. They are accounting principles that have substantial authoritative support.

128. See Financial Accounting Standards Board, *Statement of Financial Accounting Standards No. 117* (Norwalk, Conn: FASB, 1993), which is referred to as FASB Statement No. 117; American Institute of Certified Public Accountants, *Accounting Standards Division Statement of Position 78-10, Accounting Principles and Reporting Practices for certain Nonprofit Organizations* (New York: AICPA, 1978), referred to as Statement of Position 78-10; and American Institute of Certified Public Accountants, *Audits of Certain Nonprofit Organizations* (New York: AICPA, 1981).

129. Financial Accounting Standards Board, *Statement of Financial Accounting Concepts No. 4, Objectives of Financial Reporting by Nonbusiness Organizations* (Norwalk, Conn: FASB, 1980), p. 3.

130. *Statement of Financial Accounting Concepts No. 4,* cited in note 129.

131. FASB Statement No. 93, para. 36. Originally the AICPA's position was that depreciation need not be recorded "for assets that were not exhaustible, such as landmarks, monuments, cathedrals, or historical treasures" (AICPA Statement of Position 78-10, former para. 108). After the FASB issued Statement No. 93, requiring depreciation of all long-lived assets (except rare works of art and historical treasures if the holder takes steps to protect and preserve the works and limits their use to display), the AICPA modified its position. It then concluded that exhaustible fixed assets should be depreciated over their useful lives.

132. FASB Statement No. 117.

133. Id.

134. Id.

135. See FASB Statement No. 117, pp. 5–6.

136. AICPA Statement of Position 78-10, para. 113.

137. Id. at paras. 67 and 85.

CHAPTER 2

MUSEUM PERSONNEL

> Museums are becoming gathering places for the community.
>
> ED ABLE

This chapter summarizes the laws that impact museum personnel and a museum's employment practices. While employees are subject to control by their museum employer and an employer generally is unrestricted in its ability to hire and fire, there are federal and state laws that limit an employer's control. The chapter provides guidelines for museum officials in establishing employment policies that comply with legal requirements. The chapter also considers the possible liability of a museum for proscribed actions of its employees. A museum can incur liability when museum personnel are involved in, or fail to engage in, certain activities. For example, a museum may become liable in damages to another party if one of its employees impinges upon a legally created right of the other party.

Chapter 7 considers rights of artists but also sets out some of the intentional torts (civil wrongs) that can occur and can present problems for museum officials. This chapter includes a discussion of other tortious actions as they involve employees, which not only can cause liability for a museum but can also generate public disfavor. Museum officials should be knowledgeable of the laws relating to, and the possible means to prevent, tortious conduct.

Some museums may have museum employees who are union members so that officials of these museums will be required to engage in collective bargaining. This chapter also has a brief summary of provisions of the National Labor Relations Act, which permits unionization of museum employees.

A. EMPLOYMENT LAWS AND PRINCIPLES

Corporate bylaws generally vest the power of a nonprofit corporation to appoint and discharge its officials and employees in the governing board (for museum officials) and in the corporate president (for museum employees). As a general rule, there are no restrictions on the right to hire and fire. Museum officials and employees are subject to control by their museum employer regarding performance of work. However, a museum may be subject to certain federal statutes relating to discriminatory practices in employment. The relevant federal statutes prohibiting discrimination in employment are the Civil Rights Act of 1964[1] (commonly referred to as Title VII); the Equal Pay Act;[2] the Age Discrimination in Employment Act;[3] the Employment of Individuals with Disabilities and the Vocational Rehabilitation Act;[4] the Veterans Employment Emphasis under Federal Contracts Act;[5] and the Americans with Disabilities Act.[6] The Fourteenth Amendment and the Fifth Amendment to the Constitution provide further restrictions upon those museums that are state or federally controlled. The extent of coverage of employment statutes for a particular museum depends in part at least on the museum's legal status.

1. At-Will Employment Doctrine

The law has not required that employment be rational, wise, or well-considered. Generally, in the absence of a contract to the contrary, an employer has sole discretion in hiring and has the authority to discharge an employee with or without cause.[7] This so-called employment at-will doctrine is the rule in most states.[8] However, the general rule has been limited by nondiscrimination provisions of both state and federal statutes.[9]

> Example 1. The Supreme Court of Texas carved out a very narrow exception to the employment at-will doctrine in Sabine Pilot Service, Inc. v. Hauck, 687 S.W.2d 733 (Tex. 1985). The exception covers only the discharge of an employee for refusing to perform an illegal act, one that carries a criminal penalty for performance of the illegal act.

> Example 2. In Wagner v. City of Globe, 722 P.2d 250 (Ariz. 1986), the Supreme Court of Arizona listed three exceptions to the at-will employment doctrine that were applicable in Arizona. One was an implied contract exception wherein there is an implied promise of continued employment. Another was a public policy exception wherein an employer

has undermined an important public policy. The Court noted that the public policy exception protected an employee who refused to participate in illegal behavior. The Court cited whistle-blowing activity as one that served a public purpose and should be protected. The third exception was a good faith and fair dealing exception which protected employees from termination for bad cause. The Court stated that whether the parties intended to modify their at-will contract by use of a personnel manual was a question of fact.

Example 3. In Johnson v. McDonnell Douglas Corp., 745 S.W.2d 661 (Mo. 1988), the Supreme Court of Missouri ruled that there was no handbook exception to the at-will employment doctrine in Missouri. The court stated that the unilateral act of publishing a handbook for employees was not a contractual offer to employees. The handbook was merely an informational statement of self-imposed policies, which provided a nonexclusive list of acts for which an employee might be subject to discipline.

Example 4. In Demasse v. ITT Corp., 984 P.2d 1138 (Ariz. 1999), the Arizona Supreme Court ruled that an employee handbook created a contract only as to provisions a reasonable employee would conclude were contractual in nature.

2. Civil Rights Act of 1964 (Title VII)

Nonprofit organizations that are engaged in activities affecting commerce and that have fifteen or more employees on each working day in each of twenty or more calendar weeks in the current or preceding year are subject to the Civil Rights Act of 1964,[10] which is referred to as Title VII. Title VII makes it an unlawful employment practice for an employer to fail or refuse to hire or discharge any individual, or otherwise to discriminate against an individual with respect to compensation, terms, conditions, or privileges of employment, because of an individual's race, color, religion, sex, or national origin.[11] The act also prohibits an employer from limiting, segregating, or classifying employees, or applicants for employment, in any manner that would deprive, or tend to deprive, any individual of employment opportunities or would otherwise affect his status as an employee, because of the individual's race, color, religion, sex, or national origin.[12] The act is enforced by the Equal Employment Opportunity Commission.

The appropriate starting point for evaluation of a personal claim of employment discrimination under Title VII is the Supreme Court's ruling in McDonnell Douglas Corp. v. Green.[13] The Supreme Court declared in McDonnell Douglas that a complainant in a Title VII case must carry the initial burden of establishing a prima facie of racial or sex discrimination by showing that she is a member of a minority, that she applied, and was qualified for, a position for which the institution was seeking applicants, that despite proper qualifications the applicant was rejected and that, after the rejection, the position remained open and the institution continued to seek applicants from persons with the complainant's qualifications. The complainant also may demonstrate that despite proper qualifications, the applicant was rejected and a non-minority was hired. The burden then shifts to the institution to articulate some legitimate, nondiscriminatory reason for the applicant's rejection. If the institution can sustain its burden, the burden shifts back to the complainant to demonstrate that the institution's stated reason for the complainant's rejection was in fact pretext.

> Example 5. In Price Waterhouse v. Hopkins, 490 U.S. 228 (1989), the Supreme Court ruled that an employer who has permitted a discriminatory motive to play a part in an employment decision must prove by a preponderance of the evidence that it would have made the same decision in the absence of discrimination. The Court stated that once a claimant in a Title VII case shows that gender played a motivating part in an employment decision, the employer may avoid a finding of liability only by proving that it would have made the same decision even if it had not allowed gender to play such a role. According to the Court, this balance of burdens is the direct result of Title VII's balance of rights. In O'Louglin v. Procon, Inc., 627 F. Supp. 675 (E.D. Tex. 1986), the court held that an employer's stated reason for termination of an employee is pretextual only if the reason camouflages a discriminatory decision.

An employee can demonstrate a claim of employment discrimination under a theory of either disparate impact or disparate treatment. Discriminatory motive is critical in proving disparate treatment, but this motive may be inferred from the mere fact of differences in treatment.[14] Disparate impact is used to attack employment practices that are facially neutral but that fall more harshly on a protected class of employees. The disparate impact model requires proof of a causal connection between a challenged employment practice and the composition of the workforce. Aptitude tests, height and weight requirements, and similar selection criteria all may be shown to affect one class of employees more harshly than another.[15] Still, absent proof that the disparate impact is caused by one or more of the challenged employment practices, a court will not require an employer to justify the legitimacy of any (or all) of its employment practices. In addition, while disproportionate impact might cause further inquiry, an inference of discrimination nonetheless may be negated by an employer's affirmative efforts to recruit minorities.

Example 6. In Watson v. Fort Worth Bank & Trust, 487 U.S. 977 (1988), the Supreme Court determined that disparate impact analysis could be applied to cases in which subjective criteria are used to make employment decisions, that disparate impact analysis is not limited to cases in which employment decisions are based on tests, verbal skills, or height and weight requirements. The Court stated that if disparate impact analysis were limited to "objective" criteria, an employer could refrain from making standardized criteria absolutely determinative by simply including brief interviews with the candidates. A claimant must begin by identifying the specific employment practice challenged. Once the employment practice at issue has been identified, causation must be proved, i.e., the claimant must offer statistical evidence of a kind and degree sufficient to show that the practice in question caused the exclusion of applicants for jobs or promotions because of their membership in a protected group. Statistical disparities must be sufficiently substantial to raise an inference of causation. The employer then can present countervailing evidence to show that there are fallacies or deficiencies in the statistical data offered by the claimant. The employer may endeavor to impeach the reliability of the statistical evidence or may offer rebutting evidence to demonstrate the probative weight the claimant's evidence should be accorded. The Court noted that the ultimate burden of proving that discrimination against a protected group has been caused by a specific employment practice remains at all times with the claimant.

Example 7. In Lewis v. NLRB, 750 F.2d 1266 (5th Cir. 1985), the Fifth Circuit Court of Appeals ruled that the claimant's challenge to an employer's promotion practices was subject to disparate treatment rather than disparate impact. Under this analysis, the court held that the employer must have had a discriminatory intent. Nonetheless the court stated that racial discrimination may be inferred if gross statistical disparities are shown in an analysis of the relevant statistics. In determining intent, the court noted that a trial court may examine "history of the employer's practices, anecdotal evidence of class members, and the degree of opportunity to treat employees unfairly in the appraisal process."

To dispel an adverse inference from a prima facie showing of employment discrimination, an employer only need articulate some legitimate, nondiscriminatory reason for the applicant's rejection.[16] Statistical proof that the workforce was racially or sexually imbalanced or contained a disproportionately higher percentage of minority employees could be considered in determining motivation, but courts will not require different business practices for an employer until a violation of the Civil Rights Act has been demonstrated.[17] If there is this showing, the burden that shifts to the employer is to prove that its employment decision was based on a legitimate consideration and not an illegitimate one, such as race or gender. There is no requirement that an employer hire a minority or female applicant whenever that person's objective qualifications are equal to those of a white male applicant.[18]

The purpose of Title VII is to achieve equality of employment opportunities and to remove barriers that have operated in the past to favor an identifiable group of white employees over other employees. Still, discriminatory preference for any group, minority or majority, is precisely and only what Congress has proscribed. Employers have faced loss of substantial federal contracts and liability to minorities for refusing to initiate affirmative action as a remedy for past discrimination. On the other hand, they also have faced liability to non-minorities for any voluntary preferences accorded minorities. Because of the dilemma facing employers, courts have been reluctant to discourage implementation of bona fide affirmative action plans.[19] Thus, a claimant in a reverse discrimination case must present evidence that would demonstrate some reason other than a remedial one motivated an employer in implementing an affirmative action plan or that the plan adopted unreasonably exceeded its remedial purpose.

Example 8. In Johnson v. Transportation Agency, Santa Clara County, California, 480 U.S. 616 (1987), the Supreme Court ruled that consideration of gender as one factor in promoting a female employee over male employees under a voluntary affirmative action plan did not violate Title VII.

Example 9. In Setser v. Novack Inv. Co., 675 F.2d 962 (8th Cir. 1981), the Eighth Circuit Court of Appeals ruled that an employer's plan is a bona fide one if it is reasonably related to its remedial purpose. The court held that once an employer has produced evidence that its treatment of a person was a direct consequence of its implementation of a bona fide affirmative action plan, the employer is entitled to judgment as a matter of law unless the person shows that the purpose of the employer's affirmative action program was not remedial.

It is not an unlawful employment practice to apply different standards of compensation, or different terms, conditions, or privileges of employment pursuant to a bona fide seniority system, provided these differences are not the result of an intention to discriminate because of race, color, religion, sex, or national origin.[20] It *is* an unlawful employment practice under Title VII to condone a workplace that consists of sexual or racial harassment.

Example 10. In Harris v. Forklift Systems, Inc., 510 U.S. 17 (1993), the Supreme Court ruled that sexual harassment is actionable if it is "sufficiently severe or pervasive to alter the conditions of employment and create an abusive work environment."

Example 11. In Burns v. MacGregor Electronic Industries, Inc., 989 F.2d 959 (8th Cir. 1993), the Eighth Circuit Court of Appeals ruled that in hostile environment litigation, the appropriate standard is that of a "reasonable woman" under similar circumstances, rather than the "reasonable person" standard.

Example 12. In Oncale v. Sundowner Offshore Services, Inc., 523 U.S. 75 (1998), the Supreme Court ruled that workplace harassment violates Title VII's prohibition against discrimination even when the harasser and the harassed employee are of the same sex. It commented that Title VII protects men as well as women. In a same-sex harassment case, the inquiry would require a careful consideration of the social context in which the behavior occurred and how the target victim experienced it.

Example 13. In Faragher v. City of Boca Raton, 524 U.S. 775 (1998), the Supreme Court ruled that an employer is liable vicariously for a supervisory employee's sexual harassment of a subordinate, but that the employer is subject to an affirmative defense taking into account the reasonableness of the employer's conduct as well as that of a victim.

Example 14. In Pennsylvania State Police v. Suders, 542 U.S. 129 (2004), the Supreme Court stated that to establish a hostile work environment, an injured party must show harassing behavior "sufficiently severe or pervasive to alter the conditions" of employment. The Court ruled that to establish "constructive discharge," an injured party must make a further showing that the abusive working environment became so intolerable that her resignation qualified as a fitting response. An employer may defend against a claim by showing both (1) that it had installed a readily accessible and effective policy for reporting and resolving complaints of sexual harassment, and (2) that the injured party unreasonably failed to avail herself of the employer-provided preventive or remedial apparatus. This defense is not available to the employer, however, if the injured party quit in reasonable response to an employer-sanctioned adverse action officially changing her employment status or situation, such as a humiliating demotion, an extreme cut in pay, or a transfer to a position in which the injured party would face unbearable working conditions.

Example 15. In Vance v. Ball State University, 133 S. Ct. 2434 (2013), an African American state university employee brought Title VII hostile work environment and retaliation claims based on the employee's racial harassment complaints. The Supreme Court ruled that an employer's liability for workplace harassment may depend on the status of the harasser. If the harassing employee is the victim's coworker, the employer is liable only if it was negligent in controlling working conditions. If the harasser is a "supervisor," different rules apply. The Court decided that an employee is a "supervisor" only if the employee is empowered by the employer to take tangible employment actions against a victim. If a supervisor's harassment culminates in a tangible employment action, which is a significant change in employment status, such as hiring, firing, failing to promote, reassignment with significantly different responsibilities, or a decision causing a significant change in benefits, the employer is strictly liable. However if no tangible employment action is taken, the employer may escape liability by establishing as an affirmative defense (1) that the employer exercised reasonable care to prevent and correct any harassing behavior and (2) that the injured party unreasonably failed to take advantage of the preventive or corrective opportunities the employer provided. The Court ruled in Ball State University that a university was not vicariously liable for an employee's actions toward the injured party because the employee was not a supervisor and, thus, could not take tangible employment actions against the injured party.

3. Equal Pay Act

An employer may not pay different wages to employees of opposite sexes for equal work on jobs the performance of which requires equal skill, effort, and responsibility and which are performed under similar working conditions unless payment is made pursuant to (1) a seniority system, (2) a merit system, (3) a system that measures earnings by quantity or quality of production, or (4) a differential based on any factor other than sex.[21] The Equal Pay Act is administered by the Equal Employment Opportunity Commission.

A person alleging unequal pay need not show discriminatory intent. The Equal Pay Act creates a type of strict liability; no intent to discriminate need be shown.[22] A person establishes a prima facie case by a showing of payment of different wages to employees of opposite sexes for equal work on the job. Although job titles are entitled to some weight in the assessment of comparative responsibility, the controlling factor under the Equal Pay Act is job content—the actual duties the respective employees are called upon to perform.

Example 16. In Grigoletti v. Ortho Pharmaceutical Corp. 470 A.2d 903 (N.J. 1990), the Supreme Court of New Jersey ruled that to establish a prima facie case under the Equal Pay Act, a claimant must show that her employer paid her a lower salary than that paid to employees of the opposite sex for equal work on jobs the performance of which required equal skill, effort, and responsibility, and which were performed under similar working conditions. The court noted that an equal-work comparison should focus on whether the jobs have a "common core" of tasks. Factors to be considered include quantity and quality of production, education, relevant prior work experience, conduct, and skill. If, in the aggregate, the jobs require substantially similar skills, efforts, and responsibilities, the work should be adjudged equal despite minor variations.

Example 17. In Odomes v. Nucare Inc., 653 F.2d 246 (6th Cir. 1981), the Sixth Circuit Court of Appeals stated that the issue of whether jobs are substantially the same is resolved by an overall comparison of the work, not its individual segments. As the Ninth Circuit Court of Appeals ruled in Spaulding v. University of Washington, 740 F.2d 686 (9th Cir. 1984), "substantially equal" does not necessarily mean identical, and jobs from different academic disciplines can be substantially equal.

Once a prima facie case of unequal pay has been established, the employer has the four affirmative defenses noted above. The employer must prove that any wage disparity was the result of a seniority system, a merit system, a system that measures earnings by quantity or quality of production, or that the differential was based on any other factor than gender.[23]

A violation of the Equal Pay Act also is a violation of Title VII. The only justifiable pay differentials under Title VII are those attributable to the four affirmative defenses under the Equal Pay Act.[24]

4. Age Discrimination in Employment Act

An employer engaged in an industry affecting commerce with twenty or more employees for each working day in each of twenty or more calendar weeks in the current or preceding calendar year may not fail or refuse to hire or to discharge any individual or otherwise discriminate against any individual because of the individual's age pursuant to the Age Discrimination Employment Act.[25] The act is limited to persons who are at least forty years of age.[26]

The purpose of the Age Discrimination in Employment Act is to promote employment of older persons based on their ability rather than on age, to prohibit arbitrary age discrimination in employment, and to help employers and workers find methods of meeting problems arising from the impact of age on employment. The act was not intended to prevent employers from changing the job responsibilities of employees over forty years of age.

Example 18. In Frazer v. KFC Nat. Management Co., 491 F. Supp. 1099 (M.D. Ga. 1980), the court stated that the act was not intended to give employees the right to walk off their jobs and sue their employer because they disliked their changed job responsibilities. If the employees walk out, the court said they can complain of discharge only if the offered or altered working conditions would have been so difficult or unpleasant that a reasonable person in the employee's circumstances would have felt compelled to resign.

Title VII standards are applied to charges of age discrimination. The purposes and structure of the acts are similar. Still, Title VII standards are not applied automatically in age discrimination cases. An employer can establish a bona fide occupational qualification as a defense to a charge of age discrimination. A business necessity test, not a business convenience test, is used.

Example 19. In Tribble v. Westinghouse Elec. Corp., 669 F.2d 1193 (8th Cir. 1982), the Eighth Circuit Court of Appeals ruled that a claimant established a prima facie case of age discrimination by showing the claimant was in the protected class, that during the period involved the claimant was confronted by his employer with the alternative of early retirement or termination, that the claimant took early retirement under protest, and that after discharge and after claimant's application for other positions for which he was qualified, the position remained open and the employer continued to seek applications from persons with similar qualifications. The court found that the employer's offer of a legitimate nondiscriminatory reason for discharging the claimant—that the claimant elected to take early retirement due to an intracompany reorganization that eliminated the claimant's job—was pretextual.

Example 20. In Trans World Airlines, Inc. v. Thurston, 469 U.S. 111 (1985), the Supreme Court held that the policy of Trans World Airlines of transferring its captains who were sixty years of age to flight engineers only on a bid basis when other captains were transferred automatically, violated the Age Discrimination in Employment Act. Age was not a bona fide occupational qualification for flight engineers.

Example 21. In Western Air Lines, Inc. v. Criswell, 472 U.S. 400 (1985), the Supreme Court held that the bona fide occupational qualification defense is an extremely narrow exception. The defense is available only if the job qualification is reasonably necessary to the overriding interest in public safety and if the employer is compelled to rely on age as a proxy for a safety-related job qualification.

Example 22. In EEOC v. Tennessee Wildlife Resources, 859 F.2d 24 (6th Cir. 1988), the Sixth Circuit Court of Appeals held that Tennessee's mandatory retirement age of fifty-five for wildlife officers violated the Age Discrimination Act. The court noted that the employer did not demonstrate that physical and coronary fitness was reasonably necessary to the job of serving as a wildlife officer. There was no evidence that persons over fifty-five who had been permitted to continue to work had proved to be unsatisfactory. In addition, there was no provision for testing whether officers either under or over fifty-five were physically fit for service. Evidence showed that some persons over the age of fifty-five had been retained for political and economic reasons.

Example 23. In Hodgson v. Greyhound, Inc., 499 F.2d 859 (7th Cir. 1974), the employer successfully demonstrated that its maximum hiring age policy was founded upon a good-faith judgment concerning the safety needs of its passengers and others and that its hiring policy was not the result of an arbitrary belief lacking in objective reason or rationale.

5. Vocational Rehabilitation Act

The Vocational Rehabilitation Act[27] provides the sole remedy for federal employees alleging employment discrimination based on a disability. It requires federal agencies, including the Smithsonian Institution, to submit to the Interagency Committee on Employees who are Individuals with Disabilities, which is an affirmative action program plan for the hiring, placement, and advancement of individuals with disabilities in federal agencies. The plan must include a description of the extent to which, and methods whereby, the special needs of employees with disabilities are being met.

Example 24. In Rivera v. Heyman, 157 F.3d 101 (2nd Cir. 1998), a long-time employee of the Smithsonian brought a discrimination claim, by reason of his disability, against the Smithsonian. The Second Circuit Court of Appeals noted that, as a federal employee, Rivera had no remedy for employment discrimination under the American with Disabilities Act (discussed below). The employee's only remedy was to file a claim under the Rehabilitation Act. The Second Circuit decided that there is a private right of action to enforce the Rehabilitation Act.[28]

The Rehabilitation Act requires persons or firms having contracts with the federal government in excess of $10,000 to take affirmative action to employ and advance qualified individuals with disabilities.[29] Reasonable allowances must be made for an employee's handicaps unless doing so would impose an undue hardship on the conduct of the employer's business.

Some courts have ruled that the Rehabilitation Act does not give injured parties a private right of action to challenge employment discrimination.[30] Enforcement of the act is through the Department of Labor. If a handicapped individual believes a federal contractor has failed to comply with the act, the individual may file a complaint with the Department of Labor. Upon a finding of a failure of compliance, the Department of Labor may withhold payments or terminate the contract with the employer.

6. Veterans' Employment Emphasis under Federal Contracts Act

Any organization having a contract in the amount of $100,000 or more with the federal government must take affirmative action to employ and advance in employment qualified disabled veterans.[31] An aggrieved party may file a complaint with the Secretary of Labor. Some courts earlier ruled that there is no private right of action to enforce provisions of the act.[32]

7. Americans with Disabilities Act

The Americans with Disabilities Act (ADA)[33] represented what some thought was a "long-delayed but very necessary step to welcome individuals with disabilities fully into the mainstream of American society." The purposes of the act are (1) to provide a clear and comprehensive national mandate for elimination of discrimination against individuals with disabilities; (2) to provide clear, strong, consistent, and enforceable standards addressing discrimination against individuals with disabilities; (3) to ensure that the federal government will play a central role in enforcing standards established on behalf of individuals with disabilities; and (4) to invoke congressional authority, including power to enforce the Fourteenth Amendment and to regulate commerce, in order to address major areas of discrimination faced daily by persons with disabilities.

The ADA prohibits a covered entity from discriminating against a "qualified individual with a disability" because of the individual's disability with regard to job application procedures; hiring, advancement, or discharge of employees; employee compensation; job training; and other terms, conditions, and privileges of employment.[34] A "covered entity" is an employer engaged in an industry affecting commerce that has fifteen or more employees for each working day of twenty or more calendar weeks in the current or preceding calendar year and any agent of the employer.[35] The federal government and Indian tribes are not covered by the act,[36] but nonprofit organizations are covered. The act designates museums, libraries, galleries, parks, zoos, amusement parks, and other places of recreation, among others, as being public accommodations that are covered by the act.[37] The term "qualified individual with a disability" means an individual with a disability who, with reasonable accommodation, can perform the essential functions of an employment position the individual holds or desires.[38] Consideration is given to the employer's judgment as to what functions of a job are essential, and if an employer has prepared a written description before advertising or interviewing applicants for the job, the description is considered evidence of the essential functions of the job.

The term "disability" means, with respect to an individual, a physical or mental impairment that substantially limits one or more of the major life activities of the individual and a record of the impairment.[39] A "qualified individual with a disability" does not include any employee or applicant who currently is engaging in the illegal use of drugs, when a covered entity acts on the basis of drug usage.[40] An individual who has completed successfully a supervised drug rehabilitation program and is no longer engaging in the illegal use of drugs is not excluded from being a qualified individual with a disability. A covered entity must post notices in an accessible format to applicants, employees, and other persons describing provisions of the ADA.[41]

A covered entity is deemed to have discriminated against a qualified individual with a disability if the employer does not make reasonable accommodations to the nonphysical or mental limitations of an otherwise qualified individual with a disability who is an applicant or employee unless the covered entity can demonstrate the accommodation would impose an undue hardship on the entity's business.[42] A covered entity also discriminates against a disabled individual if the entity denies employment opportunities to a job applicant or employee who is an otherwise qualified individual with a disability based on the need of the entity to make reasonable accommodation to the physical or mental impairments of the employee or applicant. The term "reasonable accommodation" may include making existing facilities used by employees readily accessible to and usable by individuals with disabilities; job restructuring such as part-time or modified work schedules; reassignment to a vacant position; acquisition or modification of equipment, or devices; appropriate adjustment or modifications of examinations, training materials, or policies; provision of qualified readers or interpreters; and other similar accommodations for individuals' disabilities.[43] No qualified individual with a disability can be excluded from participation in, or be denied the benefits of, services, programs, or activities of a public entity.

An undue hardship means any action requiring significant difficulty or expense when considered in light of the following factors: (1) the nature and cost of the accommodation; (2) the overall financial resources of the facility or facilities involved in provision of the reasonable accommodation;

number of persons employed at the facility; effect on expenses and resources, or impact otherwise of the accommodation upon operation of the facility; (3) the overall financial resources of the covered entity; overall size of the business of the covered entity with respect to number of its employees; and the number, type, and location of facilities; and (4) the type of operation or operations of the covered entity, including composition, structure, and functions of the workforce of the entity, geographic separateness, and the administrative or fiscal relationship of the facility or facilities in question to the covered entity.[44]

The ADA incorporates by reference enforcement provisions of Title VII including injunctive relief and back pay.[45] The ADA provides an employer with a defense to a charge of discrimination if the employer can demonstrate that application of its qualification standards, tests, or selection criteria to screen out or tend to screen out, or otherwise deny a job or benefit to an individual with a disability, is job-related and consistent with business necessity and that performance cannot be accomplished by the reasonable accommodations required by the act.[46] The term "qualification standards" may include a requirement that an individual not pose a direct threat to the health or safety of other individuals in the workplace.

An employer may prohibit the illegal use of drugs and the use of alcohol at the workplace by all employees. It also may hold an employee who engages in the illegal use of drugs or who is an alcoholic to the same qualification standards for employment or job performance and behavior that it holds for other employees even if any unsatisfactory performance or behavior is related to drug use or alcoholism of the employee.

8. Fifth and Fourteenth Amendment Requirements

Those museums controlled by the federal or state governments are subject to the requirements of the Fifth and Fourteenth Amendments to the United States Constitution. The Fifth Amendment provides that the federal government shall not deprive a person of life, liberty, or property without due process of law, while the Fourteenth Amendment provides that no state government shall deprive a person of life, liberty, or property without due process of law. If the museum is federally or state controlled and a museum employee can demonstrate a "property" or "liberty" interest in reemployment, the museum must give the employee notice and a "for cause" hearing before termination. (In the absence of a "property" or "liberty" interest, no due process protections attach to a termination.)

a. Property Interest

A "property" interest in employment is a "legitimate claim of entitlement."[47] A person must have more than a unilateral expectation of reemployment to have this interest, but if one is found to exist by reason of some independent source, the Fifth and Fourteenth Amendments protect it. Property interests are not created by the Constitution; rather, they are created, and the dimensions are defined, by existing rules or understandings. A person with tenure has a property right and cannot be terminated without a hearing based on cause. A nontenured employee, on the other hand, has no right to reemployment except to the extent of any contractual rights,[48] and the employer need not provide the employee with a hearing prior to termination.

b. Liberty Interest

A "liberty" interest is violated if a governmental entity brings charges against an employee that impose a stigma or other disability, foreclosing the employee's freedom to take advantage of other employment opportunities.[49] This suggests that liberty interests are implicated when an employer makes a charge regarding an individual's honesty or morality. Still, a charge must be made public before a termination will infringe an individual's liberty interest.

An employer does not infringe an employee's liberty interest by the mere presence of derogatory information in confidential files.[50] The employer infringes a "liberty" interest when it perpetuates untrue charges about an employee; thus, an employee must demonstrate that the employer made public its decision not to renew employment. The mere fact of nonretention is not sufficiently stigmatizing to implicate a liberty interest. The embarrassment and reflection on professional competence that usually accompany a denial of tenure and subsequent termination are not sufficient to implicate a liberty interest.[51] The fact that an employee is unsuccessful in seeking other employment is immaterial.

> Example 25. In Goffer v. Marbury, 956 F.2d 1045 (11th Cir. 1992), the Eleventh Circuit Court of Appeals ruled that a university published stigmatizing references in an exit termination form, which described a university employee as "untruthful, unethical, subversive," and one who demonstrated poor judgment, when it placed the form in the employee's file and when it repeated comments on the form to city employees who called seeking information about the employee as a possible job applicant.

Example 26. In Bishop v. Wood, 426 U.S. 341 (1976), the Supreme Court ruled that a liberty interest was not violated when a policeman was terminated for reasons privately communicated to him. The Supreme Court stated that even if reasons for termination were not well founded, the fact that the communication was not made public offered no basis for a claim that the policeman's interest in his "good name," reputation, honor, or integrity was thereby impaired.

c. Procedural Due Process

A governmental entity may not deprive a person of "property" or "liberty" without "due process of law." The concept of "due process" in this context relates to a right of an individual to have a hearing preceding an employer's deprivation of the individual's property or liberty interest, which gives the individual the opportunity to be heard at a meaningful time and in a meaningful manner.[52]

The pretermination hearing need not be elaborate. The formality and procedural requisites for the hearing can vary, depending upon the importance of the interests involved and the nature of subsequent proceedings. Something less than a full evidentiary hearing is sufficient because the hearing is just an initial check against mistaken decisions.[53] The Supreme Court has listed the essential requirements of due process to be oral or written notice of the charges against the individual, an explanation of the employer's evidence, and an opportunity for the individual to present his side of the story.[54]

9. Safety Requirements

Congress adopted the Occupational Safety and Health Act[55] "to assure so far as possible for every working man and woman in the Nation safe and healthful working conditions." Nonprofit and charitable organizations are covered by the act.[56] The United States and any state or political subdivision of a state are not included, however.[57] Any entity created directly by the state so as to constitute an arm of the government or one administered by individuals who are controlled by public officials or the general electorate would be excluded from the act. Except for government-controlled museums, then, museums are covered by the act.[58]

Congress delegated broad authority to the Secretary of Labor to promulgate standards to ensure safe and healthful working conditions for workers.[59] The act authorized the Occupational Safety and Health Administration

(OSHA) to promulgate "start-up" standards on an expedited basis without public hearing or comment, based on "national consensus" or "established Federal standards" that improve employee safety or health. The act provided for two mechanisms to update the standards.[60] There must be a finding that workplaces in question are not safe. OSHA is not entitled to regulate any risk, only those that present a significant risk of material health impairment.

Example 27. In Industrial Union v. American Petroleum, 448 U.S. 607 (1980), the Supreme Court limited the otherwise extensive powers of the Secretary of Labor to promulgate voluminous standards. The Supreme Court concluded that "safe" is not the equivalent of "risk-free." The Court decided that a workplace "can hardly be considered 'unsafe' unless it threatens the worker with a significant risk of harm." Thus, the Court ruled that before the Secretary may promulgate any permanent health or safety standard, the Secretary must make a threshold finding that the place of employment is unsafe in that significant risks are present which can be eliminated or lessened by a change in practices.

To enforce provisions of the act, the Secretary of Labor is empowered to inspect at reasonable times any place of employment covered by the act.[61] Although a search warrant is not required under the act, the Supreme Court has held that a search warrant or its equivalent is constitutionally necessary for nonconsensual workplace inspections as discussed in Example 28 below. Thus, nonconsensual administrative searches must comply with the probable cause requirement of the Fourth Amendment.

Example 28. In Marshal v. Barlow's, Inc., 436 U.S. 307 (1978), the Supreme Court ruled that inspection without a warrant of a commercial enterprise violates the Fourth Amendment to the Constitution. The Court stated that the Fourth Amendment protects commercial buildings as well as private homes from unwarranted searches by government officials. The Court commented that the owner of a business has not, by the necessary utilization of employees in its operation, thrown open areas where employees alone are permitted to "warrantless scrutiny of government agents." According to the Court, the fact that an employee is free to report, and the government is free to use, any evidence of noncompliance with the act that an employee observes, furnishes no justification for federal agents to enter a place of business from which the public is restricted "to conduct their own warrantless search."

Example 29. In Matter of Midwest Instruments Co., 900 F.2d 1150 (7th Cir. 1990), the Seventh Circuit Court of Appeals ruled that probable cause in the usual, criminal sense is not required of administrative warrants. Probable cause will support an OSHA warrant if the warrant application supports a "reasonable belief" or leads to a "reasonable suspicion" that the act or its regulations have been violated. According to the Seventh Circuit, an OSHA warrant application at least must inform a magistrate of the substance of the employee complaints to enable the magistrate to exercise independent judgment as to whether an inspection is justified. The court decided that a complaint which described the employees who were being injured, where they were being injured, the types of injuries, the number of injuries, and the believed cause of the injuries was sufficient to support a reasonable belief that OSHA was implicated and that an inspection was warranted.

Example 30. In Martin v. Intern. Matex Tank Terminals, 928 F.2d 614 (3rd Cir. 1991), the Third Circuit Court of Appeals ruled that because a magistrate had "ample specific evidence, including the first-hand observations of the compliance officer, to show a 'plausible basis' for believing that violations were likely to be found, a wall-to-wall warrant was supported by administrative probable cause to inspect" and was not overly broad.

B. EMPLOYEE'S TORTIOUS CONDUCT

A museum can incur liability from a "tort" violation. A tort is a violation of a duty fixed by law independent of a contract, though it sometimes may relate to obligations growing out of, or coincident with, a contract. Tort liability stems from a legal right possessed by one party, a corresponding duty or obligation on the part of another party, and a breach of, or failure to perform the duty, or discharge the obligation, by the other party. There are three elements of every tort action: (1) the existence of a legal duty from the one party to the other, (2) a breach of that duty, and (3) damages as a proximate result of the breach. A legal duty is that which the law requires to be done or forborne to a determinable person, or to the public at large. The general area of torts is divided into three parts: (1) intent to interfere with a person's interest or right, (2) negligence, and (3) strict liability, wherein a party is held liable in the absence of intent or negligence, very often for policy reasons. Those torts involving intent, called intentional torts, involve wrongs perpetrated by a person who intends to perform an act which the law has declared wrong, as contrasted with "negligence," in which a person fails to exercise a certain degree of care in doing what is otherwise permissible. Intentional torts include, among others, assault, libel and slander (discussed in Chapter 6), malicious prosecution, false imprisonment, and trespass.

1. Negligence

Liability for negligence most likely would be imposed upon a museum because of negligence, or fault, on the part of its officials or employees. Negligence is conduct that falls below a standard established by law for the protection of others. It is composed of the following elements: (1) a duty, or obligation, recognized by the law, requiring an individual or organization to conform to a certain standard of conduct for the protection of others against unreasonable risks; (2) a failure on the part of the individual or organization to conform to the required standard; (3) a reasonably close causal connection between the conduct and the resulting injury, called "proximate cause"; and (4) actual loss or damage resulting to the interest of another.[62]

The standard of conduct is measured by the conduct of a reasonable person under similar circumstances. Professional persons and those who are engaged in occupations or activities requiring special skills are required not only to exercise reasonable care but also to possess a minimum of special knowledge and ability. For example, a physician is required to exercise that care and/or skill that an ordinarily prudent physician would exercise under the same or similar circumstances. If the physician is a specialist, the level of care or skill required would increase because the physician's conduct then would be measured against that of a reasonably prudent specialist. A museum director would be held to that care of skill that an ordinarily prudent museum director would exercise under similar circumstances. If the director's conduct does not meet this standard, the director would be negligent.

> Example 31. A visitor to a museum falls on a stairway because some chewing gum was lodged on a step. The museum will be liable for injuries to the visitor if museum personnel knew or should have known of the condition and failed to act within a reasonable time to remove the gum. The mere fact that the gum was lodged on one of the steps will not render the museum liable if its employees have not had sufficient time to discover its existence.

> Example 32. A visitor to a museum slips and falls on the sidewalk outside the museum because it was covered with snow and ice. Museum

personnel have the duty to use reasonable care to maintain areas over which the museum has control. The sidewalk leading into the museum must be cleared. Still, the mere accumulation of snow does not cause the museum to be liable immediately. Its personnel must be given a reasonable time after the storm has ceased to remove the accumulation of snow or ice or to take those measures that will make the area reasonably safe from hazards arising from the condition.

There are degrees of negligence. For example, if danger from a particular event is present, an individual or organization is required to exert more caution. The degree of care required increases as the danger increases. Further, one's actions may be deemed "gross negligence," which is the lack of even the slightest care. There is also a "willful, wanton, or reckless" action that differs in quality rather than in degree from ordinary lack of care but which is, for the most part, the same as gross negligence. A statute may prescribe a standard of conduct, deviation from which is negligence.

2. Museum's Vicarious Liability

A museum will become liable indirectly for the tortious acts of its officials or employees through the doctrine of "vicarious liability." Liability is based upon the ancient doctrine called "respondeat superior," which originated in a business context and which means that a master is liable for the torts of a servant that occur in the course of employment.[63] The loss caused by the torts of employees, which as a practical matter are certain to occur in the conduct of business, are placed upon the organization as a required cost of doing business. The theory is that by placing the loss upon the employer, rather than upon the innocent injured party, the employer will distribute the loss through prices, rates, or liability insurance, to the public and so will shift them to society, or the community at large. In addition, an employer should instruct and supervise its employees to make certain transactions are conducted safely. The doctrine of vicarious liability currently is applicable to nonprofit organizations to cause these organizations also to be liable for the tortious actions or conduct of their employees.

If an employer-employee relationship exists, the employer, whether a for-profit or a nonprofit entity, becomes subject to vicarious liability for its employee's torts. Still, vicarious liability only extends to conduct "within the course of employment." Many factors determine what occurs "within the course of employment." These include[64] time, place, and purpose of the action;

its similarity to authorized conduct; whether it is an act commonly performed by employees; the extent of departure from normal methods; previous relations between the parties; and whether the employer had reason to expect that a tortious act would be performed. Expressly forbidding an act of an employee does not necessarily remove it from "course of employment."

> Example 33. A museum presented a series of lectures on historical objects within the museum to some schoolchildren. A museum employee was instructed to use his car to give several children rides home. After delivering the children to their homes, the employee was driving at an excessive rate of speed to his home. He failed to stop for a red light and collided with another automobile. Several parties in the other automobile were injured seriously. These parties want to bring suit against the museum on the theory that the employee's reckless conduct occurred during the course of employment. The museum's defense would be that the employee ceased to work for the museum after he delivered the children to their homes. Given the time, place, and purpose of the employee's act, i.e., driving himself home, he was not acting within the course of employment.

> Example 34. If the employee had the accident while driving the children home, the museum probably would be vicariously liable (unless it had a defense as discussed below).

If an individual performing services for an organization is an independent contractor, rather than an employee, the employer ordinarily is not liable vicariously for that individual's torts. The reason is that the employer has no right to control the manner in which an independent contractor performs an act. The contractor is, in fact, engaged in her own business and should be the one charged with the responsibility of preventing accidents. Whether a hired party is an employee or an independent contractor is determined by considering the hiring party's right to control the manner and means by which an assignment is accomplished. Other relevant factors to the inquiry include the location of the work, the duration of the relationship between the parties, whether the hiring party has the right to assign additional projects to the hired party, the extent of the hired party's discretion over when and how long to work, the method of payment, and the tax treatment of the hired party. An independent contractor may be an agent of the employer, however, in which case the employer may or may not become liable vicariously for the contractor's torts.

An employer could be liable personally for other reasons even though an independent contractor is performing the service. An employer is required to exercise reasonable care in selecting a competent and careful contractor and is required to keep the premises safe.

3. Defenses

A defense to a negligence claim includes demonstrating the injured party has not shown a museum representative's duty to act; the injured party has not demonstrated a proximate cause between the museum representative's act, or failure to act, and the harm to the injured party; or the injured party cannot confirm that the museum representative failed to meet the required standard of care. There are also affirmative defenses which can defeat a claim. These include contributory negligence, which in many states has been replaced with a comparative negligence theory, and/or assumption of the risk. For some museums, governmental or charitable immunity may apply.

In some cases, a negligent museum representative would be excused from liability if the injured party also was negligent and the injured party's negligence was a proximate cause of the injury. An injured party also must act as a reasonably prudent person, but the museum representative has a greater duty toward the injured party than the injured party has toward herself. Most states have abolished the contributory negligence rule and have adopted a comparative negligence theory. Comparative negligence can mean that an injured party may recover regardless of her own negligence but only as to the museum representative's negligence. Some states use comparative negligence to mean that an injured party can recover even though the museum representative is negligent so long as the injured party is not as negligent as the museum representative. Under this application of the theory, an injured party could not recover if her negligence was fifty percent or more.

> Example 35. A person is injured while visiting a museum. The injured party recovers a jury verdict against the museum in which the jury assesses damages of $100,000. The injured party was thirty percent negligent and the museum representative was seventy percent negligent. The injured party can recover $70,000 from the museum. If the injured party was sixty percent negligent and the museum was only forty percent negligent, in some states, the injured party could recover $40,000, but in others, the injured party could not recover because the injured party was more negligent than the museum representative.

Assumption of the risk is another defense in a negligence action. If an injured party assumes the risk of an actor's negligence, the actor is relieved from liability. Assumption of the risk is a form of consent on the part of the injured party, while contributory negligence involves conduct of the injured party. A victim's assumption of the risk of the another's negligence may be express or implied. Express assumption occurs in the form of a release, or agreement to hold (the actor) harmless. (A sample hold harmless agreement is included in the Appendix.) Still, a court may or may not accept such a release as a defense. Clearly a release must be made voluntarily. It will not be enforced in the event of gross negligence or willful negligence, nor will it be enforced if the party executing such an agreement is at an obvious disadvantage. Assumption of the risk may be implied if the injured party fully understood the risk to himself and voluntarily chose to be subject to the risk.[65]

> Example 36. A museum employee has arranged a tour of several historical sites. The employee required all participants to sign a release holding the museum harmless from any injury that might occur to the participants. In exploring some dangerous caverns, one of the participants falls into a pit and is seriously injured. If the tour guide is held to have been grossly negligent in supervising the exploration in the dangerous area, a court may rule that the release is ineffective to release the museum from liability. A release of this type generally does not prevent liability for gross negligence. Nonetheless, the museum employee always should secure a release from each participant before conducting a tour. (The release may provide the defense of assumption of the risk for ordinary negligence and also may deter a person from bringing a lawsuit should an accident occur.)

Some states have abolished the doctrine of assumption of the risk. It may have little application in a state that has adopted the doctrine of comparative negligence. Still, even in those states, the doctrine may be applicable to strict liability suits and to instances in which an injured party knowingly consents, either orally or in writing, to a dangerous activity or condition.

4. Immunity from Liability

In a few states charitable organizations may have some immunity from liability. The concept of vicarious liability of an employer for the torts of its employees is based on the concept that losses should be borne by the entity, as a cost of business, rather than by the injured party. Theoretically this concept should not apply to an organization that is not operating a business for profit. Immunity from tort liability evolved for certain governmental and charitable organizations. These organizations historically had been given special protection, at the expense of an injured party, in the form of an immunity from liability. An immunity admits that a wrong has been committed but provides a complete defense for the protected class.

The concept of governmental immunity is predicated on the theory that "the King can do no wrong." Originally, an injured party had to obtain consent to sue the United States prior to filing an action. Currently, except to the extent that the federal government consents both to suit and to tort liability, it and its agencies are immune from liability. In addition, states and their governmental agencies are not subject to suit without the consent of the state.

The United States did later waive its immunity from liability for some tort actions when Congress passed the Federal Tort Claims Act.[66] Many states likewise have a tort claims act similar to the Federal Torts Claims Act, waiving immunity from liability for many torts. The extent of waiver of immunity varies from state to state. For suits in federal courts, the Eleventh Amendment to the Constitution grants immunity to a state from suit by a private citizen in a federal court. If a museum is either an agency of the federal government or of a state government, it may have governmental immunity for the torts of its employees or officials.

Political subdivisions of the state or local governmental entities have not enjoyed the immunity given the state. Local governments have had a more limited form of immunity. A local government generally is immune from tort liability for acts and omissions constituting the exercise of a legislative or judicial function and the exercise of an administrative function involving the determination of fundamental governmental policy.[67]

Charities also share in the defense of immunity from liability. The doctrine of "charitable immunity" evolved from an old English case which held that trust funds in the hands of a charity could not be subjected to the payment of tort claims because the funds would be diverted from the purpose intended by the donor.[68] The charitable immunity doctrine has diminished considerably in importance in most states. If there is a danger of dissipation of a charity's assets, insurance is available to guard against it, and prudent management should provide the protection. Although the doctrine of charitable immunity has been abrogated in many states, some states provide for a qualified immunity.[69]

5. Strict Liability

In some instances an individual or an entity may be held liable when there has been no departure from a standard of care. Strict liability is imposed in instances wherein there are abnormally dangerous conditions or activities, and an entity employee has engaged voluntarily in, or permitted, these conditions or activities. An entity employee can act "at his peril" and can be an insurer against the consequences of his conduct.

The keeping of vicious animals is an example of an instance where courts have applied strict liability. If a vicious animal should attack or otherwise harm someone, the person in charge of the animal may be liable even if she was not negligent.

> Example 37. A museum has vicious animals on its premises as part of a display. Though properly caged, one of the animals injured a visitor to the museum who placed his hand in the cage. The museum may be liable, even though it was not negligent, under the doctrine of strict liability. (Assumption of the risk may or may not be a defense.)

In some states, a manufacturer is held strictly liable to the consumer for defective food or drink. Strict liability also applies to the manufacturer of other products and, in some states, to retail sales as well. In most states, the supplier of a defective product, which was unreasonably dangerous at the time the supplier surrendered possession, can incur liability without proof of negligence for all those whose injuries were likely to result from the defect. For liability to attach, a court must find a product was defective as marketed. The defective condition must exist when the manufacturer surrenders control (unless change can occur with respect to the product, creating a dangerous condition).

> Example 38. A visitor to a museum buys a soft drink from a vending machine in the museum. The bottle explodes, causing injury to the visitor. Should the visitor sue the manufacturer, alleging strict liability on the part of the manufacturer, the visitor must show the bottle was defective when it left the manufacturer's possession and control. A defect in the product at the time of the accident is not by itself sufficient to render the manufacturer strictly liable.

> Example 39. The visitor to the museum discovers an insect in the soft drink. The manufacturer undoubtedly will be held liable in that it breached its duty to prevent injurious foreign substances in the product.

The principal statutory application of the doctrine of strict liability is workers' compensation acts, which are based upon the theory that the burden of employment-related accidents should fall on the employer. Presumably, the employer is in a better position, through insurance, to bear the cost. Workers' compensation statutes provide that an employer is liable for injuries to workers arising during employment regardless of the employee's negligence. The employer has no common law defense, such as contributory negligence and assumption of risk.

All states require a covered organization, including nonprofit organizations, to carry workers' compensation insurance. Through this type of insurance, an employee automatically is entitled to limited compensation if she suffers an injury by an accident arising out of and in the course of employment. Thus, in exchange for a more modest but assured benefit (generally a percentage of a weekly wage and medical expenses), employees relinquish their common law right to sue their employer. The employee files a claim with an administrative agency that will determine the award.

Workers' compensation insurance is compulsory for all employers in some states. Other states require this type insurance only for employers employing more than a stated number of employees. It is elective for those employing fewer. Some states permit self-insurance and private insurance. Some provide insurance through state funds. If an employer is required to carry workers' compensation but fails to do so, the employer will be liable for full damages and will have no defenses.

> Example 40. A museum has sixty employees. Although it is required by state law to carry workers' compensation insurance because of the number of its employees, it does not do so. One of its employees is injured while working in the museum. Even though the employee was negligent in causing his injury, the museum probably will be liable for the employee's injuries. Because the museum failed to carry workers' compensation, it has no defenses such as contributory negligence or assumption of the risk.

6. Special Liability Rules for Owners of Land

As an owner and occupier of land, a museum is required to exercise reasonable care to assure that its premises and its activities are safe for persons who are on its property. Liability for failure to maintain safe premises, or to carry on activities in a safe manner, may fall into one of three categories: it may rest upon intent; it may be based upon negligence in the creation of an unreasonable risk;

or there may be strict liability. The concept of duty becomes especially relevant as to persons who are on the premises. Those who enter upon one's "land" have been divided into three categories: trespassers, licensees, and invitees.[70]

a. Trespasser

A trespasser is one who enters another's property without consent. An owner of property owes no duty to a trespasser except to make the premises reasonably safe and not to engage in activities on the premises that might endanger a trespasser. A trespasser cannot expect ordinary care for her safety.

b. Trespassing Children

Most states require that a possessor of land exercise care with respect to trespassing children. The doctrine of "attractive nuisance" exists in many states. Under this principle, a possessor of land who has an artificial condition upon the possessor's land is liable to trespassing children if the condition is such that the possessor knows, or has reason to know, children are likely to trespass, and the condition is one of which the possessor knows, or has reason to know, involves an unreasonable risk of injury to children.[71] The possessor need not have created the condition. The possessor can be liable if the possessor permits the condition to exist. Generally, the doctrine applies only to artificial conditions, such as swimming pools, equipment, or excavations, and not to natural formations. There is no duty to inspect the premises, but the possessor is charged with conditions the possessor actually knows, or should know, exist.

> Example 41. A reflector pool is located in front of a museum building. There also are several sculptures in an outdoor court at the museum. The sculptures are located on a rock surface. One is a sculpture of an animal. A young child climbs on the animal for "a ride." The child falls from the animal onto the rock surface and suffers head injuries. Another child falls in the pool and suffers injuries. The museum has a notice posted that children may not be on its premises unless supervised by an adult. Even though the children were trespassers, the museum may be liable under the "attractive nuisance" doctrine. The notice is ineffective with respect to small children, many of whom cannot read and certainly do not understand any possible dangers or the need to be cautious.

> Example 42. A museum employee was escorting a group of elementary school children during the summer months. An old barn was located

at the rear of the museum as part of a display of an old farm site. One of the children climbed onto the hay loft of the barn and fell when a board broke. There was a sign prominently displayed stating that no one was permitted to climb on any part of the buildings or other displays in the museum. The museum may be liable for injuries to the child despite the sign prohibiting persons from climbing in the barn. The barn is an "attractive nuisance" to the trespassing school children.

Example 43. A small child is playing on the lawn in front of a historical museum. There is a sculpture of longhorn cattle on the front lawn. Would the museum be liable for injuries to the child should the child neglectfully fall on the display and become impaled on the very sharp horn of one of the cows?

c. Licensee

A licensee is one who has a privilege to enter upon another's "land" but who has not been specifically invited. The duty owed a licensee is like that owed a trespasser. There is no general duty to exercise ordinary care. The premises must be reasonably safe and free of dangerous traps, but there is no express or implied duty to a licensee except for active operations of the landowner.

d. Invitee

An invitee is in a special category because he has been invited by the possessor of land to enter or remain upon the land for the purpose for which the land is held open to the public. A customer in a gift shop on museum premises would be an invitee. A visitor to museum collections also would be an invitee. Employees and independent contractors are invitees. The possessor of land owes a duty to exercise reasonable care for the safety of an invitee. The premises must be in a reasonably safe condition, and the invitee must be given adequate and timely notice of concealed or latent perils known to the possessor. Still, the possessor is not a guarantor of the invitee's safety.

e. Abolition of Categories

Some states have abolished the distinctions between trespasser, licensee, and invitees and have imposed on the possessor of land a common duty of care and an obligation of ordinary care to all three categories of persons who enter upon the possessor's property.

7. Need for Insurance

Proper sympathy and concern for anyone injured improves public relationships and can lessen the chances that a lawsuit will occur. Still, a museum director should take certain other precautions to avoid extremely negative consequences from accidents as well as certain acts and omissions. A good protection against liability is procuring adequate insurance.

Liability insurance is a form of indemnity whereby an insurer undertakes to indemnify the insured against loss the insured may sustain by becoming itself legally liable to a third person. This becomes a matter of contract (the insurance policy) between the insurer and the insured. Liability on the part of the insurance company is based upon liability on the part of the insured.

A liability insurance policy not only pays damages to an injured party. It also protects the insured against the expense and inconvenience of litigation based on claims of negligence or other tort actions. The investigation of a person's claim, negotiation with the claimant, defense of the action brought against the insured, and payment of attorney's fees and other expenses, including payment of medical expenses for the injured person, become the responsibility of the insurer.

A museum director should purchase adequate general comprehensive liability coverage that would cover automobile accidents and premises defects. Still, insurance coverage may fail if the museum does not give notice of an accident, does not cooperate with the insurance company, or misrepresents the facts. If an accident occurs on the premises of the museum, the director should obtain a report at the time of the occurrence.

If a museum rents its premises temporarily, it should endorse the lessee onto its insurance policy for the time of the activity or should make certain the lessee has adequate insurance that covers the particular activity as well as the museum. There should be a written agreement between the museum and the lessee in which any latent defects on the property are pointed out to the lessee. If the museum director is aware of activities of the lessee which might subject others to harm, the director should require proper precautions on the part of the lessee.

A museum that has a snack bar or a museum shop may be strictly liable for defective food or products as noted above. Liability insurance may be needed. If a museum supervises tours, it should provide travel insurance and should check particularly the territorial limitations of the insurance. A travel agency engaged to conduct the tour should supply proper evidence of insurance. The museum director should obtain a release from all travelers even though a court might later decide the release was not sufficient to protect the museum from liability. (A sample copy of release is included in the Appendix.) A museum director should purchase workers' compensation insurance to cover injuries to museum employees.

C. USE OF GUARDS

Although the use of security guards is mandatory in museums with priceless collections, any action on the part of a guard to detain a person suspected of theft can cause a museum to be liable for false imprisonment. False imprisonment is the unlawful restraint by one person of the physical liberty of another. The essential elements are a willful detention of a person without consent of the person detained and a detention without authority of law.[72] One who restrains an individual in his movement can be liable in damages to the restrained party.

Restraint upon a person's freedom may be imposed by assertion of legal authority. If the person submits, there probably has been an arrest. If the arrest is without proper legal authority, there is a false arrest and, thus, false imprisonment.[73] A private person generally is privileged to arrest another without a warrant if the other person committed a felony (generally a crime the punishment of which is imprisonment in a penitentiary) for which that person was arrested, or if an act or omission constituting a felony was committed and the actor reasonably suspects the other has committed the act or omission.[74] A peace officer may arrest without a warrant on the same grounds but in addition may arrest without a warrant if, although no act or omission constituting a felony has been committed, the officer reasonably suspects that the act of omission was committed and that the other person committed it. Generally, a peace officer may justify the arrest and is not liable for false imprisonment upon a showing of satisfactory proof that a felony crime was committed within his presence or within view, or as to a person found in a suspicious place and under circumstances that reasonably indicate the person has been guilty of some felony. Ordinarily, in the absence of a statute to the contrary, neither a peace officer nor a private person may make an arrest without a warrant for a misdemeanor (a lesser crime than a felony for which the punishment is a fine or imprisonment in a jail) except for a breach of peace. Some states have extended the power of an officer to make an arrest for a misdemeanor if the misdemeanor was committed in the presence of the officer.[75] Although the original detention of one suspected of having committed a felony may have been lawful, circumstances may be such that a continued detention becomes unlawful. When a peace officer rightfully makes an arrest without a warrant, it is her duty to take the arrested person immediately to a magistrate for examination.

If a person voluntarily submits to detention and voluntarily accompanies another, there is no detention and consequently no false imprisonment. One who voluntarily submits to law enforcement officers for questioning concerning a crime is not restrained illegally.

The measure of damages for false imprisonment is the amount that would afford reasonable compensation to the injured party. The injured party can be compensated for physical and mental suffering and for injury to reputation. Consequently, all questioning of one detained should be done in a tactful manner. The person detained should be questioned outside the presence of other persons.

> Example 44. A security guard employed by a museum believes a visitor to the museum has one of the artifacts in the museum's collection in his possession with the intent of stealing the artifact. The guard did not see the visitor take the artifact. The guard wants to detain the visitor and question him. The guard should request that the visitor accompany her to another room outside the presence of other museum visitors and should question the visitor in a tactful manner. If the guard is mistaken in her belief that the visitor has the artifact, the visitor probably has not been damaged under these circumstances (he has not been publicly ridiculed), so that an action for false imprisonment would not render the museum liable.

A museum should adopt a training program for its guards to instruct them in the law in the particular state regarding liability for false imprisonment and false arrest so as to discourage and prevent guards from making reckless accusations. Museum officials should prepare manuals that set out the authority of a museum's floor supervisor or security guards to detain visitors. Museum officials should formulate rules based on applicable state law regarding measures that guards can take to prevent theft. These rules should be made a part of the manual.

D. USE OF VOLUNTEERS

The volunteer status of a person who commits a tort while performing services for a museum does not preclude liability on the part of the museum. A person who volunteers services even though for no expectation of compensation or reward nonetheless may be the "servant" of the entity accepting such services. The so-called master-servant relationship ordinarily exists between a volunteer and a museum.[76] A museum generally would be liable for negligent acts of an unpaid docent if the museum engaged and controlled the docent and if the negligent act or acts occurred while the docent was acting within the scope of "employment"—while performing services for the museum.

Courts characteristically ruled that a charity must have the right to control the activities of a volunteer before the charity would be liable for the volunteer's torts.[77] Various facts are considered to determine if a requisite right of control exists. Some of these factors are the solicitation of volunteers, the right of control over the mode of performance of a volunteer's work, the retention of a list of volunteers or other documentation indicating a quasi-employee status for the volunteers, the certification or accreditation of volunteer help, the investigation of the qualifications of the volunteer, and the providing of instruction on how to perform the volunteer's duties. The degree to which a museum controls the specific actions of a volunteer, both before and after a tort is committed, is the most crucial factor. If a volunteer regularly offers his services, the volunteer's relationship to the museum probably will be considered evidence of a right of control.

Volunteers should not be placed in situations requiring skills beyond their capabilities or be asked to perform duties that are somewhat risky. While supervision of the volunteer's activities indicates a master-servant relationship, failure to supervise a volunteer placed in a situation requiring skills beyond her ability may cause liability for failure to supervise. A museum can be liable because it placed volunteers in positions requiring skill but failed to train the volunteers properly or to control their activities. Thus, liability can occur even though the museum does not control a volunteer sufficiently to create a master-servant relationship.

D. UNIONIZATION OF MUSEUM EMPLOYEES

Museums not under governmental control with an operating budget of at least $1 million a year are subject to the National Labor Relations Act (NLRA).[78] As a result, a museum director may find that museum employees are union members, in which case the director may be required to engage in collective bargaining. Even if a museum's budget does not meet federal guidelines, the museum still may face unionization under state law. When employees designate a labor representative, their employer must bargain with the labor representative with respect to the employees' rates of pay and conditions of employment. Thus, a museum director should have some knowledge of laws regulating labor disputes.

I. Selection of a Labor Representative

The first step in established collective bargaining for a group of employees is the designation or selection of the employees' labor representative. The NLRA provides that representatives designated or selected for the purposes of collective bargaining by a majority of the employees in a unit appropriate for these purposes are the exclusive representatives of all the employees in that unit for the purpose of collective bargaining with respect to rates of pay, wages, hours of employment, or other conditions of employment.[79] An employer must recognize and bargain collectively with representatives chosen by a majority of the workers in a bargaining unit.[80] An employer may not bargain with any other representative or representatives.[81]

A labor organization wishing to be certified as the exclusive bargaining unit must acquire authorization from a majority of the employees of that unit. Union organizers often seek to enlist a majority of the workers of a particular bargaining unit through solicitation on the employer's premises. The Supreme Court has ruled that while an employer may not restrict its employees' right to discuss self-organization among themselves, it may prevent nonemployee organizers from using the employer's property to distribute union literature when other means are readily available.[82]

Example 45. In National Labor Relations Board v. Babcock & Wilcox Co., 351 U.S. 105 (1956), the Supreme Court decided that the private property rights of an owner prevailed over the intrusion of nonemployee organizers. However, if the locations of the place of business and the living quarters of the employees place the employees beyond the reach of reasonable union efforts to communicate with the workers, the employer then must permit the union to approach its employees on the employer's property. Where these conditions do not exist, an employer validly may post its property against nonemployee distribution of union literature.

Example 46. In Lechmere, Inc. v. National Labor Relations Board, 502 U.S. 527 (1992), the Supreme Court ruled that an employer did not commit an unfair labor practice by barring nonemployee union organizers from its property. The Court held that the fact the employees lived in a

> large metropolitan area did not render them "inaccessible." The Court decided that, because the union did not establish the existence of any "unique obstacles" that frustrated access to the employees, the NLRB erred in concluding that the employer committed an unfair labor practice by barring the nonemployee organizers from its property.

If a union can satisfy an employer that it represents a majority of the employees within a bargaining unit, the employer may recognize the union voluntarily. However, the employer may, and probably should, require an election conducted by secret ballot or may insist that the question of representation be settled by a National Labor Relations Board (NLRB) election.[83]

Before an employer agrees to meet with a union, the employer should determine that the union, in fact, does represent a majority of the employees in the bargaining unit.[84] The employer need not accept authorization cards from a union that indicate the union represents a majority of the employees. In fact, the employer may refuse to accept any evidence of the union's majority status other than the results of a board election. Further, in the absence of any agreement to permit majority status to be determined by means other than a board election, a union has the burden of taking the next step in invoking the board's election procedures.[85]

The employer, any person, or a labor organization acting on behalf of a substantial number of employees (at least thirty percent of the workers of a particular unit) may initiate a petition to the NLRB for investigation of the question as to whether a union represents a majority of an appropriate grouping of employees.[86] Upon receipt of a petition regarding the question of union representation, the NLRB will conduct an investigation to determine (1) whether the board has jurisdiction, (2) whether there is an appropriate unit of employees for the purposes of collective bargaining, (3) whether the election would reflect the free choice of employees in the appropriate unit, and (4) whether, if the petitioner is a labor organization, there is a sufficient probability that the employees have selected it to represent them. (This requires a designation by thirty percent of the employees.)

The NLRB makes available to the parties two types of informal consent procedures through which representative issues can be resolved without recourse to formal procedures. These informal arrangements are referred to as consent election agreements. A board agent will arrange the details incident to the mechanics and conduct of the election. Board agents conduct and supervise the actual polling on the employer's premises.

If there is a certified or currently recognized labor representative, any employee or groups of employees or any labor organization may file decertification proceedings with the NLRB to test the question of whether the certified union still represents the employees. A person seeking decertification must have the signatures of at least thirty percent of the employees covered by an expiring bargaining agreement in the petition.[87]

2. Duty to Bargain in Good Faith

Once a union has been established as the representative of a bargaining unit, the employer must bargain collectively with that representative of its employees. Collective bargaining is the performance of a mutual obligation on the part of the employer and the employee representative to meet at reasonable times and confer in good faith with respect to wages, hours, and other terms and conditions of employment. An employer is not required to make concessions or to yield any position fairly maintained, but it is under an obligation to make sincere, serious efforts to adjust differences and to reach an acceptable common ground. There is no duty on the employer to reach an agreement, but there is a duty to negotiate with a spirit of sincerity and cooperation.

The duty to bargain in good faith assumes that the parties will meet at mutually convenient places and will be willing to devote a reasonable amount of time to the bargaining process. The parties must be represented by someone who has authority to speak for the principals. The parties must reply to each other's proposals within a reasonable period of time, and they must not impose unfair conditions upon bargaining, such as settlement of outstanding grievances or unfair labor practice charges. The parties must not bypass each other's designated representatives and must supply each other with any reasonable information required to bargain effectively.

3. Subject Matter of Bargaining

Labor and management are required to bargain as to terms and conditions of employment, such as wages, hours, and other terms and conditions of employment, and the negotiation of an agreement regarding such matters.[88] Other matters are permissive. A mandatory subject of bargaining is one that materially or significantly affects the terms or conditions of employment.

Neither party is required to bargain on permissive subjects. Illegal subjects are not subjects of bargaining and an agreement on these subjects is unenforceable.

4. Unfair Labor Practices

Certain practices on the part of management and labor are unfair labor practices. The NLRB is empowered to prevent both labor and management from engaging in unfair labor practices.[89] The NLRA lists the following as unfair labor practices of employers: (1) interfering with, restraining, or coercing employees in the exercise of their right of self-organization and to bargain collectively; (2) dominating or interfering with the formation or administration of any labor organization; (3) discriminating in regard to hire or tenure of employment, or any term or condition of employment, to encourage or discourage membership in a labor organization; (4) discriminating against an employee because the employee has filed charges or given testimony with the NLRB; and (5) refusing to bargain collectively with the labor representative.

The act[90] lists the following, among others, as unfair labor practices for a labor organization or its agents: (1) restraining or coercing employees in the exercise of their right to self-organization and to bargain collectively through representatives of their own choosing, or their right to refrain from any of these activities; (2) causing or attempting to cause an employer to discriminate against an employee in violation of the act; (3) refusing to bargain collectively with an employer; (4) charging excessive fees; (5) engaging in featherbedding (attempting to exact a payment from an employer for services that will not be performed); and (6) engaging in recognition picketing.

If either management or labor is aggrieved by an unfair labor practice of the other, it may file a complaint with the NLRB.[91]

5. Strikes

Employees have the right to strike.[92] In addition, unions may take disciplinary action against a union member who refuses to engage in protected activity that will not jeopardize the union member's job. Lawful strikes are of two types: economic strikes and unfair labor practices strikes. An economic strike generally occurs when employees cease work to achieve a labor objective classed as a mandatory subject of bargaining. These strikes most often occur after negotiations for an initial or renewal labor agreement have deadlocked. Strikes also occur to protest alleged employer unfair labor practices.

The principal distinction in the two types of strikes is the reinstatement rights of the striking employees. An economic striker is entitled to reemployment after the termination of the strike if a vacancy exists for which the striker is qualified; however, an employer is permitted to replace economic strikers permanently by employing new workers. On the other hand, employees who strike because management has committed an unfair labor practice are protected with respect to their reemployment even if the employer has hired replacements. These strikers are entitled to unconditional reinstatement with back pay.

On-the-job slowdowns designed to place economic pressure on the employer are partial economic strikes. These strikers may be terminated in instances where their activities breach the employer's work rules. As a result, even though a union may properly adopt rules disciplining members who refuse to engage in a full economic strike in which the members must refuse to work for the employer, a union may not force its members to engage in this type of unprotected activity.

An economic strike may become an unfair labor practices strike. A strike to secure an initial labor agreement generally does not require notice to the employer or to governmental agencies. Should the employer refuse to continue to bargain with the union over mandatory subjects during the strike, the strike will be transformed from an economic strike into an unfair labor practice strike in which management's prerogatives will be limited.

If a striker has violated an employee unfair labor practice, the striker may be discharged from employment lawfully on a nondiscriminatory basis. In addition, an employee who engages in an illegal strike—a strike for an unlawful purpose or one that is an unfair labor practice on the part of the union—may be denied reinstatement. An employer who is subjected to an unlawful strike may sue the union for damages, may file an unfair labor practice charge with the NLRB, and may seek an injunction to prohibit the strike.[93]

Striking employees have the right to establish a picket line, to use arguments in support of their position, and to attempt by proper means to induce other persons not to work at jobs which they vacated by striking or not to patronize the establishment.[94] On the other hand, the employer and other employees have a right to be free from the harassment of illegal picketing. Those who exceed the permissible scope of picket activity forfeit their right to reinstatement. In addition, an employer may be able to recover damages against the union when it engages in unlawful mass picketing.

6. Agency or Union Shops and Right to Work Laws

The NLRA[95] permits individual states and territories to exempt themselves from the provisions of the NLRA permitting union or agency shops.[96] A union shop agreement provides that no one will be employed who does not join the union within a short time after being hired. An agency shop agreement provides that while employees are not required to join the union, they are required—usually after thirty days—to pay the union a sum equal to the union initiation fee and are obligated to make periodic payments to the union equal to the union dues. (These are distinguished from a closed shop agreement, which is banned by the NLRB,[97] prohibiting employers from hiring anyone who is not a member of the union at the time of hiring.) The concern of Congress in permitting union and agency shop agreements was that employees should not be entitled to the benefit of union representation without paying for it.

Example 47. In Chicago Teachers Union, Local No. 1 v. Hudson, 475 U.S. 292 (1986), the Supreme Court held that procedural safeguards are necessary to prevent compulsory subsidization of ideological activity by nonunion employees who object to this activity, while at the same time not restricting a union's ability to require any employee to contribute to the cost of collective bargaining activities through an agency shop agreement.

Example 48. In Davenport v. Washington Educ. Ass'n, 551 U.S. 177 (2007), the Supreme Court ruled that a state does not violate the First Amendment when it requires its public-sector labor unions to receive affirmative authorization from a nonmember before spending that nonmember's agency shop fees for election-related purposes.

Example 49. In Knox v. Service Employees Intern. Union, Local 1000, 132 S. Ct. 2277 (2012), the Supreme Court ruled that the First Amendment prevents a public-sector union from requiring objecting nonmembers to pay a special fee for the purpose of financing a union's political and ideological activities.

While the NLRB permits compulsory unionism, any state may adopt so-called right-to-work laws that prohibit the union and agency shop agreements.[98] With or without right-to-work laws, most employers are free to hire whomever they choose. The concern is principally over workers' rights—whether or not a majority of workers should have the right to compel an unwilling minority to join a union after the employee has been hired.

7. How Labor Laws Affect a Museum

A museum that is covered by the NLRA must recognize the right of its workers to organize. Under nonunion conditions, a museum director unilaterally establishes the rules on wages and other labor matters (with the exception of certain antidiscrimination requirements imposed by other federal statutes, as noted above). These rules may be largely implicit. Under union conditions, the rules typically are written down in explicit terms and result from negotiation with a union through collective bargaining. An organization that has established rules providing for grievance procedures for employees and that prohibits arbitrary dismissal often provides employee satisfaction that discourages employees from desiring union representation. Dissatisfied employees generally cause unionization.

What should museum management do when a union is beginning to organize museum employees? A policy of trying to prevent a union from organizing employees is not unrealistic, but it does require that the museum director handle himself with great care. Management interference with employees in the exercise of their right to self-organization is an unfair labor practice, as noted above. Management may not counter a union drive with threats or discrimination or promises of benefit. At the early stages of a union drive, union organization generally is conducted secretly, with the union contacting employees who might join the union. Only after a number of employees have shown an active interest will the organization normally conduct its campaign for members in the open. The law restricts the use of picketing by unions as a means of persuading employers to grant recognition in those instances where federal or state labor relations statutes are applicable. In addition, nonemployee union members can be prevented from soliciting employees to join a union on company property so long as the employees are reasonably accessible to union organizers at their homes after work.

Assuming that a majority of museum employees want a union to represent them in collective bargaining and assuming that the union can satisfy a museum director that it does represent a majority of the employees within a bargaining unit, the museum director may recognize the union voluntarily. If the director is not satisfied that the union represents a majority of the employees within the bargaining unit, the director may require an election conducted by secret ballot or may insist that the question of representation be settled by an NLRB election. Once management is required to "recognize" the union as the bargaining agent for the employees (this occurring voluntarily if the museum director is satisfied that the union represents a majority of employees within the bargaining unit, otherwise by election), museum management is required to negotiate in good faith with the union regarding those mandatory subjects of bargaining.

Those museums which are subject to the NLRA should articulate job descriptions carefully. Supervisors and managerial employees are not covered by the act; these employees may be denied union membership. Supervisors or managerial employees would include curators, the editor of a museum publication, its publicity director, its librarian, and its coordinators.

A museum director generally should exercise her discretion to refrain from bargaining on permissive subjects so as not to lose management prerogatives regarding these subjects. Bargaining is required only for mandatory subjects.

Those museums which are controlled by a state, or a political subdivision thereof, are not subject to the act, and unless there is a state labor relations act that covers public employees, will not be required to bargain with labor representatives. Employees of federal museums are covered by federal collective bargaining provisions.

NOTES

1. 42 U.S.C. § 2000e et. seq.
2. 29 U.S.C. § 206(d).
3. 29 U.S.C. § 621 et. seq.
4. 29 U.S.C. §§ 791–93.
5. 38 U.S.C. § 4212.
6. 42 U.S.C. § 12101 et. seq.
7. See Powell v. Syracuse University, 580 F.2d 1150 (2nd Cir. 1978), and Phillips v. Goodyear Tire & Rubber Co., 651 F.2d 1051 (5th Cir. 1981).
8. See, e.g., Maine Human Rights Commission v. Canadian Pacific Ltd., 458 A.2d 1225 (Me. 1983); Allen v. Southeastern Michigan Transp. Authority (Mich. App. 1984); Sabine Pilot Service, Inc. v. Hauch, 687 S.W.2d 733 (Tex. 1985), and Weiss v. Opportunities for Cortland County, Inc., 40 A.2d 890, 337 N.Y.S.2d 409 (1972).
9. State statutes on employment discrimination vary. Some states have established civil rights commissions to receive, investigate, and conduct hearings regarding charges of discrimination in hiring and firing.
10. Cited in note 1.
11. 42 U.S.C. § 2000e-2. In University of Pennsylvania v. EEOC, 493 U.S. 182 (1990), the Supreme Court ruled that peer review materials that are allegedly relevant to charges of racial or sexual discrimination in tenure decisions are discoverable.
12. Id.
13. 411 U.S. 792 (1973).
14. Bryant v. International Schools Services, Inc., 675 F.2d 562 (3rd Cir. 1982).
15. Pouncy v. Prudential Ins. Co. of America, 668 F.2d 795 (5th Cir. 1982); Griggs v. Duke Power Co., 401 U.S. 424 (1971).

16. Furnco Const. Corp. v. Waters, 438 U.S. 567 (1978).

17. In Griffin v. Carlin, 755 F.2d 1516 (11th Cir. 1985), the Eleventh Circuit Court of Appeals held that a prima facie case of disparate treatment may be established by statistics alone if they are sufficiently compelling.

18. See Texas Dept. of Community Affairs. v. Burdine, 450 U.S. 248 (1978).

19. See Setser v. Novack Inv. Co., 675 F.2d 962 (8th Cir. 1981).

20. 42 U.S.C. § 2000e-2(h).

21. 29 U.S.C. § 206(d). Nonprofit organizations are subject to the Equal Pay Act.

22. Strecker v. Grand Forks County Social Service Board, 640 F.2d 96 (8th Cir. 1980).

23. Id.

24. Futran v. Ring Radio Co., 501 F. Supp. 734 (N.D. Ga. 1980). If an employee demonstrates a violation of the Equal Pay Act, the employee is entitled under Title VII to the difference between what the employee would have earned and what the employee actually earned.

25. 20 U.S.C. §§ 623, 630(b).

26. 29 U.S.C. § 631. Persons over 65, who for two years prior to retirement were employed in executive or high policy-making positions, are not subject to the act if those persons were entitled to an immediate annual nonforfeitable retirement benefit equivalent to $44,000 or more.

27. 29 U.S.C. § 791.

28. See 29 U.S.C. § 794a(a)(1).

29. Id. at § 793(b).

30. See Roberts v. Frito Lay, Inc., 611 F.2d 1074 (5th Cir. 1980); Meyerson v. State of Arizona, 709 F.2d 1235 (1st Cir. 1983); Painter v. Horne Bros., Inc., 710 F.2d 143 (4th Cir. 1983). But see Davis v. Modine Mfg. Co., 426 F. Supp. 943 (D. Kan. 1981), wherein the court ruled that the requirement of including an affirmative action clause in all covered contracts provided a private right of action.

31. 38 U.S.C. § 4212.

32. See Butler v. McDonnell-Douglas Saudi Arabia Corp., 93 F.R.D. 384 (S.D.Ohio 1981) and De Leon Cruz v. Loubriel, 539 F. Supp. 250 (D. PR. 1982).

33. 42 U.S.C. § 12101 et. seq.

34. Id. at § 12112.

35. Id. at § 12111(5).

36. Id.

37. Id. at § 12181.

38. Id. at § 12111(8).

39. Id. at § 12102(2). The term "disability" does not include transvestism, transsexualism, pedophilia, exhibitionism, voyeurism, gender identity disorders not resulting from physical impairments or other sexual behavior disorders, compulsive gambling, kleptomania, pyromania, or psychoactive-substance-use disorders resulting from illegal drug use.

40. Id. at § 12114.

41. Id. at § 12115.

42. Id. at § 12112(b)(5).

43. Id. at § 12111(9).

44. Id. at § 12111(10).

45. Id. at § 12117. No person may discriminate against an individual because the individual opposed any act or practice made unlawful by the ADA or because the individual

made a charge, testified, or participated in any manner in an investigation, proceeding, or hearing pursuant to the act. Id. at § 12203.

46. Id. at § 12113(a).

47. Board of Regents v. Roth, 408 U.S. 564 (1972), and Perry v. Sindermann, 408 U.S. 725 (1972).

48. Perry v. Sindermann, 408 U.S. 593 (1972). In this context, the usual practices surrounding a contractual relationship, such as the hiring policies and practices of a museum as embodied in its employment regulations, can become the contractual obligation.

49. Board of Regents v. Roth, cited in note 47.

50. Ortwein v. Mackey, 511 F.2d 697 (5th Cir. 1975).

51. Haimowitz v. University of Nevada, 579 F.2d 516 (9th Cir. 1978), and Davis v. Oregon State University, 591 F.2d 493 (9th Cir. 1978).

52. Moore v. Warwick Public School Dist., 794 F.2d 322 (8th Cir. 1986).

53. Cleveland Board of Education v. Loudermill, 470 U.S. 532 (1985). The court ruled that the pretermination hearing should involve a determination of whether there are reasonable grounds to believe that the charges against the individual are true and support the proposed action.

54. Id.

55. 29 U.S.C. §§ 651–71.

56. 29 C.F.R. § 1975.4(4).

57. See 29 U.S.C. § 652(5).

58. A museum that has received a citation for a serious violation of the requirements of the Occupational Safety and Health Act or of any standard, rule, or order of the act or the regulations, may be subject to a civil penalty of as much as $7,000 for each violation. Id. at § 666. An employer who willfully or repeatedly violates the act, or any standard, rule or order, may be subject to a penalty of as much as $70,000 for each violation.

59. Id. at § 655.

60. Id. at § 655(b). This section sets out procedural and substantive criteria that standards must meet. In promulgating standards, OSHA officials must provide notice of proposed rulemaking, give interested parties an opportunity to comment, and hold a public hearing if requested. OSHA officials also may issue emergency temporary standards when it determines that employees are exposed to "grave danger from exposure" to toxic substances. Once OSHA officials have published an emergency standard, proceedings must commence for issuance of a regular standard.

In AFL-CIO v. OSHA, 965 F.2d 962 (11th Cir. 1992), the Eleventh Circuit Court of Appeals ruled that, in setting an element of a standard, OSHA must demonstrate substantial evidence for all matters of determinable fact, must explain the relevant considerations on which it relied, and must explain its reasons for rejecting alternate views. It noted that the validity of an agency's determination must be judged on the basis of the agency's stated reasons for making the determination.

61. Id. at § 657(a). An inspection may be made pursuant to an employee complaint. Id. at § 657(f).

62. Restatement (2d) Torts § 328A.

63. Liability also is based on an agency theory. One party, the agent, is authorized to act for another party, the principal. When a person acts through an agent, the agent is a representative of the principal for conduct of the transaction. Acts performed by the agent, whenever they are within the scope of the agent's actual or apparent authority, are binding

on the principal. A principal will be held liable in damages for all tortious acts committed by his agent when the agent is acting in the course of the principal's business and in furtherance of the principal's interest. Still, if the agent's tort is committed during the pursuit of the agent's individual interests and not in furtherance of the principal's business, the principal will not be held responsible. Prosser and Keeton on Torts, § 69, 5th ed., p. 500.

64. Prosser and Keeton § 70.

65. Restatement (2d) Torts § 496C.

66. 28 U.S.C. §§ 1346, 1402, 1504, 2110, 2402, 2671–80. This act makes the federal government liable for tortious acts of federal employees acting within the scope of their employment. There are some exceptions to tort liability on the part of the federal government. Except for federal investigation or law enforcement officers, it is not liable for assault or battery, false imprisonment, false arrest, malicious prosecution, abuse of process, libel, slander, misrepresentation, deceit, or interference with contract rights [28 U.S.C. § 2680(h)]. In addition, the federal government is not liable for acts done with due care in the execution of a statute or regulation, even though the statute is invalid [28 U.S.C. § 2680(a)].

67. Discussion in Restatement (2d) Torts § 895C.

68. Feofees of Heriot's Hospital v. Ross, 12 Clark & Fin. 507, 513, 8 Eng. Reprint 1508 (1846). The theory was based on dictum of Lord Cottenham. However, this dictum was later repudiated by the English courts [Docks Trustees v. Gibbs, LR 1 HJ 93 (1866) and Foreman v. Mayor of Canterbury, LR 6 QB 214 (1871)]. Still Massachusetts and Maryland adopted the doctrine apparently unaware of the English reversal [Perry v. House of Refuge, 63 Md. 20, 52 Am. Rep. 495 (1885) and McDonald v. Massachusetts General Hospital, 120 Mass. 432, 21 Am. Rep. 529 (1876)].

69. The concept has been reinstated in some states through the enactment of charitable immunity statutes, which place a cap on the amount of damages that can be awarded against a charity.

70. Restatement (2d) Torts §§ 329, 330, 332.

71. Restatement of Torts (2d), § 339. Generally recovery has been limited to children under the age of twelve or, in some jurisdictions, fourteen. The doctrine first was applied only to "young" children.

72. Wal-Mart Stores, Inc. v. Resendez, 962 S.W.2d 539 (Tex. 1998). According to the Restatement of Torts, Restatement (2d), Torts, § 41, a person is subject to liability to another for false imprisonment if that person acts intending to confine another within boundaries fixed by that person and the act directly or indirectly results in confinement of another when the other party is conscious of the confinement or is harmed by it.

73. Restatement (2d) Torts § 41.

74. Restatement (2d) Torts § 119.

75. Restatement (2d) Torts, § 121; Prosser and Keeton on Torts, § 26, 5th ed. The fact that neither a peace officer nor a private person can arrest someone who has committed a misdemeanor has caused problems for merchants. Thefts by shoplifters are often of merchandise of relatively small values. Some states have recognized this problem and have granted shopkeepers immunity for the detention of suspected shoplifters but only if the detention is for a reasonable time and is handled in a reasonable manner. See Prosser and Keeton on Torts, § 26. The Restatement of Torts (§ 120A) provides that one who reasonably believes another has taken her property can detain that person without arresting the suspected thief for the time necessary for a reasonable investigation of the facts.

A majority of the states have expanded a merchant's immunity from liability for false imprisonment by enacting shoplifting legislation. These statutes typically contain limitations in that the shopkeepers must act with probable cause to believe the person detained has committed a theft. Mere suspicion is not enough to constitute probable cause. Thus, though a merchant may have some immunity, she still is limited in a right to apprehend and arrest suspects. These restrictions are based upon the rationale that the rights of the customer to maintain her personal dignity and reputation outweigh the property rights of the merchant. See Prosser and Keeton on Torts, §§ 11 and 26. See also Wal-Mart Stores, Inc. v. Resendez, 962 S.W.2d 539 (Tex. 1998).

Shoplifting statutes generally have little relevance for museum guards, however. Museum artifacts have great value; theft of these objects would be a felony. Still, thefts of items from a museum gift shop may involve items of small value and shoplifting legislation may be relevant as to these thefts.

76. Discussion in Baxter v. Morningside, Inc., 521 P.2d 946 (Wash. App. 1974), in which the court held that consideration or monetary compensation is not necessary to create a master-servant relationship between a volunteer and a charitable organization.

77. In Malloy v. Fong, 232 P.2d 241 (Cal.1951), the court ruled that the existence of a right of control establishes the existence of an agency relationship. The court held a church liable for an injury caused by the negligent driving of an unpaid volunteer who was transporting children attending the church's vacation Bible school from a Bible class to the playground.

In Garcia v. Herald Tribune Fresh Air Fund, Inc., 51 App. Div. 2d 897, 380 N.Y.S.2d 676 (1976), the court found a principal-agent relationship to exist when one has control over another. The court held a charity—which provided volunteers to place children in summer homes in a rural environment—liable when one of the children staying at a volunteer's home drowned. The court decided that the charity's providing of instructions to the volunteers on how to handle an emergency situation was sufficient control over the volunteer.

78. 29 U.S.C. §§ 151–69. Federal museums are subject to provisions regulating collective bargaining among federal employees. See 5 U.S.C. §§ 7101–7901.

79. 29 U.S.C. § 158(a)(5).

80. Id.

81. Id. at § 159(a).

82. National Labor Relations Board v. Babcock & Wilcox Co., 351 U.S. 105 (1956).

83. See National Labor Relations Board v. Lyon & Ryan Ford Inc., 647 F.2d 745 (7th Cir. 1981), cert. denied, 454 U.S. 894 (1981). Once the employer recognizes the union, no matter how informally, the employer loses the right to require an election.

84. See 29 U.S.C. § 159. Representatives of a majority of the employees in the unit are the exclusive representatives.

85. Linder Lumber Division v. National Labor Relations Board, 419 U.S. 301 (1974).

86. 29 U.S.C. § 159.

87. 29 C.F.R. §§ 101.26 and 101.27.

88. Mandatory subjects of bargaining are those listed in 29 U.S.C. § 158(d).

89. 29 U.S.C. §§ 158, 160.

90. Id. at § 158(b.

91. Id. at § 160(b). The charge is filed with the regional director for the region in which the alleged violation occurred. A staff member of the NLRB will investigate the charges.

After investigation, the case may be disposed of through informal methods such as withdrawal, dismissal, and settlement. If efforts to dispose of the charge through informal methods fails, the regional director will issue a notice of a hearing. Following the hearing, a formal decision and recommendations are filed by the hearing judge. Either party may file exceptions to the judge's finding with the board at its Washington, D.C., office. The final decision of the board may be appealed to the U.S. court of appeals in the circuit where the unfair labor practice in question is alleged to have occurred. See 29 C.F.R. § 101. If the board's decision is not appealed, the board will seek enforcement of its order, in court if required. Courts can enforce, modify, or set aside an order of the board. However, findings of fact by the board are conclusive if supported by substantial evidence on the record considered as a whole.

92. Id. at § 163. However, because public (governmental) employees are not covered by the act, they do not have the right to strike unless a state statute so provides.

93. 29 U.S.C. §§ 185, 187.

94. 29 U.S.C. § 158(g).

95. Id. at § 164(b).

96. Id. at § 158(a)(3). The provision permitting the union or agency shop is § 8(a)(3) of the Taft-Hartley Act, 80th Cong., 1st Sess., 6 (1947).

97. Id. at § 158(a)(3). Under the Wagner Act, enacted in 1935, closed shops, union shops, and agency shops all were permitted. However, the Taft-Hartley Act, enacted in 1947, banned closed shops though still permitting union and agency shops. See S. Rep. No. 105, 80th Cong., 1st Sess, 6, Legislative History of the Labor Management Relations Act (1947).

98. Id. at § 164(b).

CHAPTER 3

OBTAINING AND MAINTAINING TAX EXEMPT STATUS

Tax complexity itself is a kind of tax.

MAX BAUCUS

A museum qualifies for exemption from federal income taxes as a charitable organization under § 501(c)(3) of the Internal Revenue Code; however, tax exempt status is not automatic unless the museum is a governmental agency. A museum that is not a governmental agency, as well as any separate trust or nonprofit corporation established to fund a museum, must apply to the Internal Revenue Service (IRS) for recognition of federal tax exempt status. The Internal Revenue Code, in §§ 501, 521, 527, and 528, grants exempt status to several types of nonprofit organizations. These include the following, among others: charitable organizations; civic and social welfare organizations; labor, agricultural, and horticultural organizations; business leagues, chambers of commerce, and real estate boards; social clubs; credit unions; war veterans' organizations; farmers' cooperatives; homeowners' associations; and political organizations. Exempt organizations are referred to by their Internal Revenue Code classification. For example, charitable organizations (those operated exclusively for religious, charitable, scientific, public-safety testing, literary, or educational purposes; for fostering national or international amateur sports competition [if no part of the activities involves provisions of athletic facilities or equipment]; or for the prevention of cruelty to children or animals) are described in § 501(c)(3) of the Internal Revenue Code and are referred to as § 501(c)(3) organizations. Social welfare organizations, a category that would include civic associations and organizations similar to the Sierra Club and League of Women Voters, are referred to as § 501(c)(4) organizations. Social clubs are § 501(c)(7) organizations, while war veterans' organizations are § 501(c)(19) organizations. Political organizations are exempt under § 527 of the Code and are referred to as 527 organizations.

It is important that a museum director understands the tax categorization of a museum, as well as that of a museum's supporting organization(s), and the tax consequences of the differing classifications. Rules and benefits differ for each categorization. For example, as discussed below and in Chapter 4, a museum that obtains § 501(c)(3) tax exempt status and that, as such, qualifies as a public charity or as a private operating foundation, provides its donors with more favorable charitable contribution deductions than does a supporting organization classified for tax purposes as a private nonoperating foundation. (Donors may claim a charitable contribution deduction for donations to a § 501(c)(3) organization whereas donors may not claim a charitable contribution deduction for donations to most other tax exempt organizations.[1])

Although a museum and any of its supporting organizations must apply for tax exempt classification to qualify as a charitable organization under § 501(c)(3), a museum that is a governmental agency need not apply for exempt status. Governmental agencies are automatically exempt from taxation under § 115 of the Internal Revenue Code. Further, donations to governmental entities made exclusively for public purposes provide donors with charitable contributions deductions pursuant to § 170(c)(1) of the Code. Qualification as a § 501(c)(3) organization then is not necessary.

As discussed below, an organization that qualifies as a § 501(c)(3) organization for tax purposes and that can also qualify under § 509 of the Code is designated as a public charity. One that cannot qualify for public charity status because of its lack of public support is a private foundation for tax purposes. A museum that has few donors and, as a result, is classified as a private foundation for tax purposes, generally can qualify for more beneficial tax treatment as a private "operating" foundation (discussed below).

This chapter sets out the requirements to obtain and maintain § 501(c)(3) status and explains the public charity and private foundation classifications as well as the tax consequences of each classification. It includes a discussion of the requirements under § 509 for obtaining and maintaining public charity status but also reviews requirements for private "operating" foundation status for those museums with few donors that are classified as private foundations for tax purposes.

A. SECTION 501(C)(3) STATUS

Section 501(c)(3) organizations must be established and operated exclusively for charitable purposes. Thus, a § 501(c)(3) organization must meet two tests—an organizational test and an operational test. To meet the organizational and operational tests and, thus, to be entitled to tax exempt status as a § 501(c)(3) organization, a museum must be organized and operated exclusively for charitable purposes. No part of its earnings may inure to the benefit of any private shareholder or individual. Further, no substantial part of its activities can be devoted to attempts to influence legislation, and no part of its activities can include the intervention or participation in a political campaign on behalf of, or in opposition to, a candidate for public office.

The organizational test for qualification as a charitable organization requires that the articles of incorporation, articles of association, or declaration of trust limit the organization to one or more charitable purposes. A charitable organization may not be permitted to engage in activities not in furtherance of its exempt purposes (other than as an insubstantial part of its activities). The requirement that the articles of organization or the trust indenture limit the organization's purpose and powers to charitable ones is not satisfied if the limitation is contained only in bylaws or other operating rules. It also is not satisfied by statements of officers that they intend to operate only for exempt purposes. A museum (and any of its supporting organizations) must have its assets dedicated to an exempt purpose in order to meet the organization test. Upon dissolution, all assets of the organization must be distributed to a charitable entity for one or more exempt purposes, to the federal government, or to a state or local government, for a public purpose.[2] Articles of incorporation for an organization seeking § 501(c)(3) status must contain provisions indicating that the above requirements have been met.

The operational test requires that a nonprofit organization be "operated exclusively" for one or more exempt purposes. An organization must engage primarily in activities that accomplish one or more of the exempt purposes specified in § 501(c)(3). None of the earnings of a charitable organization may inure in whole or in part for benefit of private individuals or entities. If a substantial part of an organization's activities is attempting to influence legislation, the organization will be deemed an "action" organization, and unless it complies with certain Code requirements, will not meet the operational test. The presence of a single nonexempt purpose, if substantial in nature, will destroy the museum's tax exemption regardless of the number or importance of the museum's truly exempt purposes.[3] A museum director, then, must monitor a museum's activities closely to make certain the museum is not involved in ventures that could threaten its tax exempt status.

Example 1. The IRS challenged the § 501(c)(3) tax exempt status of an organization whose principal asset was a historic plantation and that limited the general public access to the plantation. The IRS ruled that, to maintain tax exempt status, the organization was required to open the plantation home to the public during specific hours and the organization had to make public tours available.[4]

1. Inurement

To retain tax exempt status, no part of the net earnings of a museum may inure to the benefit of private individuals or entities. The payment of excessive salaries or excessive rents and the use of a museum's facilities to serve a private interest constitute inurement. The policy underpinnings of the noninurement rule derive from the belief that charities should promote the public good rather than provide a private benefit. In addition, to the extent that personnel or other private individuals, particularly a select few, materially benefit from a nonprofit organization's activities, the sincerity of the claimed nonprofit purposes may be called into question.[5]

Example 2. In Spokane Motorcycle Club v. United States, 222 F. Supp. 151 (E.D. Wash. 1963), the court ruled that an organization which furnished refreshments, goods, and services to its members from its net profits provided benefits that inured to the individual members and did not qualify for tax exempt status.

Example 3. In Bubbling Well Church of Universal Love, Inc. v. Comm., 670 F.2d 104 (9th Cir. 1981), the Ninth Circuit Court of Appeals commented that the potential for abuse is created by a person's control of a tax exempt organization.

Example 4. In Anclote Psychiatric Center, Inc. v. Comm., TC Memo 1998-273, the Tax Court agreed with the IRS that the tax exempt status of a § 501(c)(3) organization should be revoked because sale of the organization's assets for less than the fair market value resulted in inurement to the purchaser's private shareholders who also were directors of the § 501(c)(3).

As illustrated in the above examples, an organization's net earnings may inure to the benefit of private individuals in ways other than by actual distribution of profits or payment of excessive salaries. If a second organization is created to serve to funnel income to an individual who controls a purportedly exempt organization and if the income exceeds a reasonable salary, income inures to the benefit of a private person.[6] If a particular individual or a limited number of individuals reap commercial benefits from the operation of a nonprofit organization, though they do not do so by direct acquisition or payment over to them of its earnings, the earnings nevertheless may inure to their benefit within the intendment of this phrasing so as to destroy the tax exempt status of the organization.[7]

2. Commercial Activities

The requirement that a tax exempt organization be organized and operated exclusively for its specific exempt purposes presupposes that the organization will not engage in activities of a commercial nature that are unrelated to the tax exempt purpose of the organization. However, a tax exempt organization is regarded as being operated exclusively for its exempt purposes if its activities are primarily those that are carried on to accomplish one or more of its exempt purposes and if not more than an "insubstantial" part of its activities furthers a nonexempt purpose.[8] Thus, an "insubstantial" amount of nonexempt, or commercial, activity will not disqualify a museum for tax exempt status.

Example 5. As the Third Circuit Court of Appeals noted in Presbyterian & Reformed Pub. Co. v. Comm., 743 F.2d 148 (3rd Cir. 1984), courts have focused on the manner in which activities of a tax exempt organization are carried on, implicitly reasoning that an end can be inferred from the chosen means. Should an organization's management decisions replicate those of a commercial enterprise, there is an inference that at least one purpose of the organization is commercial and hence nonexempt. Should the nonexempt goal be substantial, tax exempt status may be denied or revoked. The Third Circuit commented that an organization may be forced to choose between expanding its commercial activities and influence on the one hand and maintaining its tax exempt status on the other.

There are no definitive guidelines as to how much commercial activity is "substantial" and, thus, could jeopardize the tax exempt status of an organization. Courts have established the following factors to be considered in determining whether an organization's nonexempt activities exceed the "benchmark of insubstantiality": (a) the manner in which the organization's activities are conducted, (b) the commercial hue of the nonexempt activities, and (c) the existence and amount of profit from the activities.[9] The facts and circumstances of a particular activity determines whether tax exempt status is in jeopardy.

Example 6. In Associated Master Barbers & Beauticians of America, Inc. v. Comm., 69 T.C. 53 (1977), the court revoked an organization's tax exemption where approximately thirty percent of its revenues were derived from nonexempt activity.

A museum is taxed on activities that are unrelated to its exempt educational purposes (discussion of the unrelated business income tax in Chapter 4). It is assumed that involvement in unrelated activities is insubstantial because increased and substantial involvement in a commercial activity would raise questions of whether a museum is entitled to tax exempt status. If a museum increases its involvement in commercial activities, an inquiry may be made of the purpose for which the increased business activity is directed. Still, success in certain business activities does not, in and of itself, jeopardize the tax exempt status of an organization if the organization remains true to its stated exempt purpose goals.

Example 7. In Orange County Agr. Soc., Inc. v. Comm., 893 F.2d 529 (2nd Cir. 1990), the Second Circuit Court of Appeals stated that a non-profit organization which has substantial nonexempt activities cannot avoid revocation of its tax exempt status simply by paying an unrelated business income tax on its nonexempt activities.

The source, and not the destination, of funds is considered in determining whether activities are unrelated to an organization's exempt purposes and, thus, subject to tax. Still, the ultimate use or destination of the funds, as well as the extent of involvement in an unrelated commercial activity, has relevance in judging whether involvement in the unrelated business jeopardizes the organization's tax exempt status.[10]

Example 8. In Church by Mail, Inc. v. Comm., 765 F.2d 1387 (9th Cir. 1985), the Ninth Circuit Court of Appeals commented that the objective or purpose to which the income of a charity is devoted is the ultimate test in determining whether the organization is operated exclusively for an exempt purpose. Although substantial profits are made from certain activities, an organization can nonetheless remain tax exempt if all the profits realized are used exclusively for the organization's exempt purposes.

3. Involvement in a Partnership

Charitable organizations have utilized the limited partnership arrangement to accomplish various commercial objectives.[11] Although the participation of a charitable organization in a partnership arrangement will not per se result in the denial of tax exempt status, a partnership arrangement must be scrutinized closely to assure that any obligations imposed on the tax exempt partner do not conflict with the exempt organization's ability to pursue its charitable goals. In all limited partnership arrangements, the initial focus is on whether the tax exempt organization is serving a charitable purpose. Once charitability has been established, the partnership arrangement must be examined to determine whether the arrangement permits the tax exempt organization to function exclusively in furtherance of its tax exempt purpose or purposes. The tax exempt partner cannot operate for the benefit of the nonexempt partners. Because the tax exempt organization must be in control of partnership projects so that the projects are administered for a nonprofit purpose, the tax exempt partner must be the general partner. In addition, benefits received by the limited partners must be incidental to the public purpose served by the partnership.[12]

Example 9. In Redlands Surgical Services v. Comm., 113 TC 47 (1999), the Tax Court ruled that a § 501(c)(3) surgical corporation, which was a general partner with a for-profit corporation in a partnership formed to acquire a majority interest in an outpatient surgical center, did not qualify for tax exempt status when it gave control to its for-profit partner.

If a museum is a partner in a commercial venture, it must be insulated sufficiently from serving the private interests of the partnership or the other, nonexempt, partners. If the limited partners are present, or were past, members of the museum's board of directors, a conflict may arise between partnership obligations and tax exempt objectives. As a result, involvement in the partnership could jeopardize the museum's tax exempt status.[13] (One means to alleviate this problem is the establishment of an independent committee, composed of individuals who are not members of the museum's board of directors and who are not limited partners, to monitor and oversee the museum's activities as the general partner.)

4. Shareholder in a For-Profit Corporation

If a museum's commercial activities become substantial, a separate for-profit corporation should be established. The assets that were used for commercial activities would be transferred to the for-profit corporation to prevent the museum from jeopardizing its tax exempt status. Activities of a separately incorporated subsidiary will not be attributed to the parent corporation unless there is clear and convincing evidence that the subsidiary is, in reality, an arm, agent, or integral part of the parent corporation.[14] A parent corporation and its subsidiary are separate entities for tax purposes as long as the purposes for which the subsidiary was incorporated are the equivalent of business activities or the subsidiary subsequently carries on business activities. Thus, if a museum organizes a subsidiary corporation with the intention that it will have some real and substantial business function, its existence generally would not be disregarded for tax purposes. However, the museum should not so control the affairs of the subsidiary that the subsidiary is merely an instrumentality of the museum parent.[15]

As noted previously, the fact that a tax exempt organization maintains a controlling interest in a subsidiary for-profit corporation will not cause the commercial activities of the for-profit corporation to be attributed to the tax exempt parent if the separate for-profit subsidiary is not an arm or an agent of the parent and provided the subsidiary is organized for some bona fide purpose of its own. The parent tax exempt organization must not be so involved in, or in control of, the day-to-day operations of the subsidiary that the relationship between the parent and the subsidiary assumes the characteristics of a principal-agent relationship. Control through ownership of stock or power to appoint the board of directors of the subsidiary, of itself, will not cause attribution of the subsidiary's activities to the parent. The fact that board members of a subsidiary for-profit corporation consist solely of directors or staff employees of the parent tax exempt organization will not cause the subsidiary corporation to be viewed as an instrumentality of the parent as long as the subsidiary's board members are independent and self-governing and the board members conduct all transactions between the parent and the subsidiary at arm's length. Problems will arise if the for-profit subsidiary is operated as another division of the tax exempt parent.[16] Should funds of the tax exempt organization pass through the subsidiary organization to individuals so that funds of the tax exempt organization inure to private individuals, the funds will be deemed to have originated from the tax exempt organization and the parent may be disqualified for tax exempt status.

Control of more than fifty percent of the stock, by vote or value, of a for-profit subsidiary will cause a portion of the interest, rents, royalties, and annuities distributed to the tax exempt parent to be taxed (discussion in Chapter 4).[17] However, dividends distributed to the tax exempt parent are not taxed even though the parent has control of one hundred percent of the subsidiary stock.[18]

5. Lobbying Activities

A § 501(c)(3) organization will not meet the operational test (which requires the organization to operate exclusively for exempt purposes) if it engages in substantial lobbying activities or if it is a qualifying electing organization under § 501(h) of the Internal Revenue Code (discussion below) and its lobbying expenditures exceed 150 percent of the permitted amounts as set out in § 4911 of the Internal Revenue Code (discussed below). In addition, a § 501(c)(3) organization will be disqualified for tax exempt status if it engages in *any* political activities involving the participation in, or intervention in, any political campaign on behalf of (or in opposition to) any candidate for public office. Charitable entities, whether electing or nonelecting organizations, must annually report to the IRS the amount of their lobbying expenditure amounts. Section 501(c)(3) organizations that are private foundations for tax purposes may not engage in any lobbying activities. For a private foundation, lobbying expenditures constitute taxable expenditures (discussion below).

The Lobbying Disclosure Act[19] requires tax exempt organizations that engage in substantial lobbying (lobbying expenditures in excess of $10,000) to register with the Secretary of the Senate and the Clerk of the House of Representatives. The act requires an organization that has employees who are paid to lobby and who spend more than twenty percent of their time engaged in lobbying activities to register within forty-five days after an employee who is a lobbyist makes a "lobbying contact." The act applies only to federal lobbying activities. It does not include attempts to influence legislation by any state legislature or by any local governing body. Still, an organization may use the federal tax definition of lobbying in determining whether an individual has made a "lobbying contact."

a. Definition of Lobbying

Lobbying is an attempt to influence legislation by propaganda or otherwise. An organization is regarded as attempting to influence legislation if the organization contacts, or urges the public to contact, members of a legislative body for the purpose of proposing or supporting legislation, or if it advocates the adoption or rejection of legislation. The term "legislation" is defined as any action by Congress, by any state legislature, by any local council or similar governing body, or by the public in a referendum, initiative, constitutional amendment, or similar procedure.[20]

b. Electing Organization

A museum, or its supporting organizations, may elect under § 501(h) of the Internal Revenue Code to engage in some specifically defined amount of lobbying.[21] For an electing organization, permissible lobbying expenditures are as follows: (1) twenty percent of exempt purpose expenditures up to $500,000; (2) $100,000, plus fifteen percent of the excess of exempt purpose expenditures over $500,000 and up to $1 million; (3) $175,000, plus ten percent of the excess exempt purpose expenditures over $1 million up to $1.5 million; or (4) $225,000, plus five percent of excess purpose expenditures over $1.5 million. In no event may the permitted level exceed $1 million for any one year.[22]

Lobbying for electing organizations is defined as any attempt to influence legislation through communication with any member or employee of a legislative body, or with any government official or employee who may participate in the formulation of the legislation.[23] Lobbying for electing § 501(c)(3) organizations is divided into "direct" lobbying and "grassroots" lobbying communications. The amount of grassroots lobbying permissible expenditures is twenty-five percent of the lobbying permissible expenditures. An electing organization must keep a record of its lobbying and grassroots lobbying expenditures made during each year.

"Direct" lobbying communication is any attempt to influence legislation through communication with (1) any member or employee of a legislative body, or (2) any government official or employee, other than a member or employee of a legislative body, who may participate in the formulation of the legislation, but only if the principal purpose of the communication is to influence legislation.[24] A communication with a legislator or government official will be lobbying only if the communication refers to specific legislation and reflects a view on the legislation.

"Grassroots" lobbying is the influencing of legislation through any attempt to affect the opinions of the general public. A communication will be treated as grassroots lobbying communication only if the communication (1) refers to specific legislation, (2) reflects a view on the legislation, and (3) encourages the recipient of the communication to take action with respect to the legislation.[25] Communication encourages a recipient to take action with respect to legislation if the communication (1) states that the recipient should contact a legislator or an employee of a legislative body, or should contact any other government official or employee who may participate in the formulation of legislation (but only if the principal purpose of urging contact with the government official or employee is to influence legislation); (2) states the address, telephone number, or similar information of a legislator or an employee of a legislative body; (3) provides a petition, tear-off postcard, or similar material for the recipient to communicate his views to a legislator or an employee of a legislative body, or to any other government official or employee who may participate in the formulation of legislation (but only if the principal purpose of so facilitating contact with the government official or employee is to influence legislation; or (4) specifically identifies one or more legislators who will vote on the legislation as opposing the communication's view with respect to the legislation, being undecided with respect to the legislation, being the recipient's representative in the legislature, or being a member of the legislative committee that will consider the legislation.

Example 10. The definition of grassroots lobbying is a three-part definition: it requires that communication contain a reference to specific legislation, that it reflect a view with respect to the legislation, and that it encourage the recipient to take action. Thus, grassroots communication may advocate or oppose legislation and still not be lobbying if it does not encourage the recipient to take action with respect to the legislation.[26]

An expenditure made for a communication that has both a lobbying and a bona fide nonlobbying purpose must be allocated between the lobbying and the nonlobbying purposes.[27] A communication that is both a direct lobbying communication and a grassroots lobbying communication will be treated as a grassroots lobbying communication except to the extent the organization can demonstrate the communication was made primarily for direct lobbying purposes. If the organization can demonstrate the communication was made primarily for direct lobbying purposes, the organization then can make a reasonable allocation between the direct and the grassroots lobbying purpose served by the communication.

If two or more § 501(c)(3) organizations are members of an affiliated group of organizations and the organizations have elected under § 501(h) of the Code, the organizations are treated as one for purposes of determining whether the organizations have made excess lobbying expenditures.[28]

If an electing § 501(c)(3) organization exceeds the permissible amount, it is subject to a penalty tax of twenty-five percent of the excess amount.

> Example 11. A museum expends $400,000 expenditures in the current year to accomplish its exempt purposes. Its permissible lobbying expenditures for the year would be $80,000 (twenty percent of $400,000). Its permissible grassroots lobbying expenditures would be $20,000 (twenty-five percent of $80,000). Assume the organization spends $100,000 for lobbying, $30,000 of which is grassroots lobbying. The organization would be subject to a penalty of $5,000 [25% x ($100,000 - $80,000)]. The penalty for excess grassroots lobbying would be $2,500 [25% x ($30,000 - $20,000)]. The penalty tax would be the greater amount.

> Example 12. Assume the museum in Example 11 expends $130,000 for lobbying expenditures in the current year. The museum's lobbying expenditures would exceed one hundred and fifty percent of the permissible amount; thus, the museum would be subject to losing its exempt status.

c. Nonelecting Organization

A § 501(c)(3) organization that does not elect under § 501(h) of the Internal Revenue Code is subject to a subjective test. A nonelecting charitable organization will lose its tax exempt status if it engages in "substantial" lobbying activities,[29] but the term "substantial" is not defined. The election under § 501(h) removes the uncertainty of judging whether an organization has met the subjective "substantial" test.

> Example 13. In Seasongood v. Comm., 227 F.2d 907 (6th Cir. 1955), the Sixth Circuit Court of Appeals determined that if no more than five percent of the time and effort of an organization was devoted to lobbying, the lobbying was not "substantial." In Haswell v. United States, 500 F.2d 1133 (Ct. Cl. 1974), the court compared the lobbying activities of a

§ 501(c)(3) organization with its other activities and determined that the organization was engaged in substantial efforts to influence legislation and, thus, was disqualified for tax exempt status. The lobbying expenditures were twenty percent of the organization's total expenditures for the year. This court ruled that the lobbying activities of an organization must be balanced in the context of the objectives and circumstances of the organization to determine whether a substantial part of the activities are to influence, or to attempt to influence, legislation.

d. Exceptions to Lobbying

A communication is not a direct or grassroots lobbying communication if the communication falls within one of the following exceptions: (1) nonpartisan analysis, study, or research, including making the results available to the public; (2) examinations and discussions of broad social, economic, and similar problems; (3) requests for technical advice; and (4) communications pertaining to self-defense by the organization.[30] "Nonpartisan analysis, study, or research" is the independent and objective explanation of a particular subject matter, including any activity that is "educational." The term "educational" refers to the instruction or training of an individual in order to improve or develop the individual's capabilities, or the instruction of the public on subjects useful to the individual and beneficial to the community.[31]

"Nonpartisan analysis, study, or research" may advocate a particular position or perspective so long as the presentation is a sufficiently complete and objective critique of the pertinent facts to permit an individual or the public to form an independent opinion or conclusion. The mere presentation of unsupported opinion does not qualify as nonpartisan analysis, study, or research.

Lobbying does not include public discussion, or communication with members of legislative bodies or governmental employees, even if the general subject is legislation, if the discussion does not address itself to the merits of a specific legislative proposal. Thus, expenditures for examinations and discussions of broad social, economic, and similar problems are not lobbying expenditures even though the problems are of the type with which the government would be expected to deal ultimately.

e. Penalty Taxes

A museum can be liable for penalty taxes for involvement in lobbying and political campaign activities. Although a § 501(c)(3) organization that pays or incurs any amount for participating or intervening in any political campaign on behalf of, or in opposition to, any candidate for public office cannot qualify for § 501(c)(3) status, small and often unintentional political campaign expenditures, which could cause the IRS to hesitate to revoke tax exempt status, will nonetheless subject the organization to a penalty tax under § 4955 of the Internal Revenue Code.[32] Section 4955 was added to the Code to provide for intermediate sanctions for a § 501(c)(3) organization that has minor or inadvertent involvement in a political campaign. Without the intermediate sanctions, the only penalty was loss of exempt status.

A museum that is a private foundation for tax purposes is subject to a penalty tax on all lobbying expenditures under § 4945 of the Code (discussion below). A § 501(c)(3) organization that loses its tax exempt status because of substantial lobbying expenditures is subject to a penalty tax under § 4912 of the Code.[33]

B. STANDING (RIGHT) OF THE PUBLIC TO CHALLENGE TAX EXEMPT STATUS

It is difficult for members of the general public to challenge the actions of nonprofit enterprises. For example, as noted in Chapter 1, while the community has an interest in the enforcement of a charitable trust, the Attorney General of a state is the representative of the general public in compelling trustees and directors to perform their duties properly. Generally the Attorney General alone has power to maintain suits for the enforcement of charitable trusts. In most states a person who has no interest in the performance of the trust other than as a member of the community cannot maintain a suit for enforcement.

Some members of the public have sought to invalidate the tax exempt status of organizations that allegedly have failed to meet the requirements of tax exempt status.[34] Based upon decisions of the Supreme Court,[35] it is questionable whether a person whose own tax liability was not affected would ever have standing to litigate the federal tax liability of another. As one court[36] pointed out, the statutory scheme created by Congress is inconsistent with, if not preclusive of, third-party litigation of tax exempt status.

> Example 14. In Abortion Rights Mobilization, Inc. v. Baker, 885 F.2d 1020 (2nd Cir. 1989), cert. den., 495 U.S. 918 (1990), the Second Circuit Court of Appeals ruled that organizations and groups of individuals who were advocates of a woman's right to an abortion did not have standing

to challenge the tax exempt status of the Catholic Church. (The Catholic Church allegedly was involved in political campaigns on behalf of candidates who supported the church's views on abortions.) The Second Circuit pointed to the decision of the Supreme Court in Allen v. Wright, 468 U.S. 737 (1984), in which the Court ruled that to have standing a person must show that the person has suffered an injury in fact that is both concrete in nature and particularized to that person. The court found no particularized injury in the Abortion Rights case.

Example 15. In a concurring opinion in Simon v. Eastern Kentucky Welfare Rights Organization, 426 U.S. 26 (1976), Justice Stewart pointed out the special problems attendant upon the establishment of standing (right to sue) in tax cases when a litigant seeks to attack the tax status of a third party.

C. MUSEUM WITH PUBLIC CHARITY STATUS FOR TAX PURPOSES

As noted above, an organization that qualifies as a § 501(c)(3) organization for tax purposes also is classified either as a public charity or as a private foundation. Public charities include religious organizations, schools, hospitals, and other charitable nonprofit organizations that have broad public support or that actively function in a supporting relationship to other public charities. A private foundation is a charitable organization that is supported, and often controlled, by one or a few donors. Because private foundations are controlled by a few individuals, they are supervised more closely by the IRS and are subject to substantial penalties for engaging in certain prohibited acts (discussed below). In addition, donations to private nonoperating foundations receive less favorable tax treatment than do contributions to public charities and private operating foundations. Although most museums and their supporting organizations can qualify either as a public charity or as a private operating foundation, it is imperative that a museum director be cognizant of the requirements to obtain and maintain such status. Loss of tax exempt status and/or public charity or private operating foundation status will bring about costly consequences.

A § 501(c)(3) organization is presumed to be a private foundation unless it notifies and verifies to the IRS that it qualifies as a public charity.[37] To avoid private foundation status and, thus, be classified as a public charity, an organization must fall into one of the categories specifically excluded from private foundation status under § 509(a) of the Internal Revenue Code. Section 509 defines a private foundation as a § 501(c)(3) organization other than an organization described in §§ 509(a)(1–4). This means that public charities are either § 509(a)(1), (2), (3), or (4) organizations. Because a § 509(a)(4) organization includes only organizations that test for public safety, a museum and its supporting organizations would qualify for public charity status under either § 509(a)(1), (2), or (3) of the Internal Revenue Code. A museum, or a supporting foundation, that qualifies for public charity status, then, would be a § 501(c)(3) organization as well as a either a § 509(a)(1), (2), or (3) organization. The requirements for, and the consequences of, each of the three classifications under § 509 [§ 509(a)(1), § 509(a)(2), and § 509(a)(3)] are discussed below.

1. Disqualified Person Characterization

Whether a museum, or any of its supporting organizations, is a public charity or a private foundation, the director must be aware of the tax consequences attributed to individuals and entities that are "disqualified persons" to the organization. The amount of donations from "disqualified persons" is a determining factor in whether a museum or its supporting organizations can qualify as a public charity. "Disqualified persons" include the following: (1) all substantial contributors to a charitable organization (a person or entity that contributed an aggregate amount of more than $5,000 during a year if that amount is more than two percent of the total contributions and bequests received by the organization during that year); (2) all managers of the organization; (3) an owner of more than twenty percent of a corporation, partnership, or trust if the corporation, partnership, or trust contributed more than $5,000 to the organization, and provided that amount was more than two percent of total contributions received by the organization during the year; (4) a corporation, partnership, trust, or estate wherein any of the persons noted above has more than a thirty-five percent interest; and (5) the family of a substantial contributor, but including only spouse, ancestors, lineal descendants, and spouses of lineal descendants.

2. Section 509(a)(1) Public Charity

A museum, or any of its supporting organizations, can qualify for public charity status under § 509(a)(1) of the Internal Revenue Code if it obtains most of its funding from the general public rather than from "disqualified persons." The § 509(a)(1) organization is one that receives most of its support from charitable contributions or from donations from governmental units. The requirements to be "publicly supported" are set out in § 170(b)(1)(A)(vi) of the Internal Revenue Code and in the Treasury Regulations pursuant to that Code section.

Section 170(b)(1)(A) of the Code becomes relevant with respect to a § 509(a)(1) public charity because it sets out the charitable organizations with the most favorable treatment for purposes of the charitable contribution deduction. Section 509(a)(1) of the Code simply refers back to this Code section, § 170(b)(1)(A), to classify the organizations that qualify for § 509(a)(1) status. To understand the requirements for § 509(a)(1) status then, one must consider qualifications, and identify the organization, under § 170(b)(1)(A). The classifications pursuant to § 170(b)(1)(A) for § 509(a)(1) organizations are: § 170(b)(1)(A)(i)—churches; § 170(b)(1)(A)(ii)—schools; § 170(b)(1)(A)(iii)—hospital and medical research organizations; § 170(b)(1)(A)(iv)—organizations for the benefit of state and municipal colleges and universities; § 170(b)(1)(A)(v)—governmental units; and § 170(b)(1)(A)(vi)—publicly supported organizations. A museum, as well as any of its supporting organizations, would qualify only under § 170(b)(1)(A)(vi). A public charity under § 509(a)(1) that qualifies as a public charity because of its substantial support from the general public then also is referred to as a § 170(b)(1)(A)(vi) organization; thus a museum would be a § 501(c)(3) organization under §§ 509(a)(1) and 170(b)(1)(A)(vi).

As set out in the Code and Regulations, a charitable organization is "publicly supported" if the total amount of support the organization normally receives (as an average over a five-year period) from governmental units or from the general public is at least thirty-three and one-third percent of total support. For these purposes, support does not include amounts received for services rendered (gross receipts).[38] Further, if support from services rendered is substantial, the organization cannot qualify as a § 509(a)(1) public charity. It must seek public charity status under § 509(a)(2), discussed below.

a. Support Test

Public support for a § 509(a)(1) public charity, which is qualified under § 170(b)(1)(A)(vi), is measured by a fraction; the numerator of the fraction is the amount of support from governmental units and from the general public, and the denominator is total support reduced by amounts received for services performed by the organization (including admission fees). The determination of public support is set out (and the support fraction determined) on

Schedule A to Form 990. The IRS reviews the information regarding public support provided on Schedule A to determine on an annual basis if the organization continues to qualify as a public charity.

Donations from "disqualified persons" are counted in full in the denominator of the one-third support fraction, but these donations are counted in the numerator of the fraction only to the extent of two percent of total support. In this manner, then, the support fraction requires the elimination of most of the support from substantial contributors in the numerator to determine whether a charitable organization is "publicly supported." This is to assure that support will be, in fact, from the general public rather than from a few substantial donors.

The one-third support test is computed for the five-year period including the current year and the four years immediately preceding the current year as described in the following example.

Example 16. A museum received support of $1,200,000 from the following sources in the current year and previous four years:

Contributions	$440,000
Governmental Unit (City)	80,000
United Fund	80,000
Investment Income	600,000
	$1,200,000

Of the $440,000 contributions, six contributors, who gave a total of $340,000, gave in excess of $24,000, or two percent of total support. To satisfy the support test, the numerator of the fraction must be $400,000, or one-third of total support of $1,200,000. The numerator for the fraction is $404,000, determined as follows:

Support from governmental units	$80,000
Indirect contributions from the general public (United Fund)	80,000
Contributions by various donors—no one in excess of two percent of total support) [$440,000 - $340,000 (contributions from disqualified persons)]	100,000

Six contributions (each in excess of $24,000 or two percent of total support), 6 x $24,000	144,000
	$404,000

The museum "normally" received in excess of thirty-three and one-third of its support from governmental units and from the general public, and the museum qualifies as a public charity under § 509(a)(1) of the Code.

Example 17. Assume an individual gave $800,000 to the museum in Example 16 in Year 5. Total support would then be $2 million ($1.2 million set out in Example 16 plus the $800,000 gift from the individual). To meet the one-third support test, $666,666 must be received from governmental units and the general public ($2 million divided by one-third). Assume the six substantial contributors noted in Example 16 each gave in excess of $40,000, or two percent of total support of $2 million. As noted previously, contributions from disqualified persons count in the numerator only to the extent of two percent of total support; thus, each of the six contributions from the disqualified persons count in the numerator up to $40,000 (which is two percent of $2 million). For six contributors, $240,000 ($40,000 x 6) will be included in the numerator. In addition, $40,000 of the $800,000 gift can be counted in the numerator. Thus, $280,000 of the contributions from disqualified persons can be counted in the numerator of the one-third support fraction. The numerator of the one-third support fraction is computed as follows:

Support from governmental units	$ 80,000
Indirect contributions from the general public (United Fund)	80,000
Contributions by various donors (no one in excess of two percent of total support, or $40,000)	100,000
Seven contributions (each in excess of $40,000 or two percent of total support); $40,000 x 7	280,000
	$540,000

The $540,000 is less than one-third of total support of $2 million. (The organization needed $666,666 to meet the one-third support test [$2 million divided by one-third].) Thus, the museum will not meet the one-third support test.

Only $40,000 of the gift from the individual can be included in the numerator of the one-third support test. Thus, because of the large gift from the individual, the museum would not meet the one-third support test. The above example illustrates the problem when a museum is given a large donation in one year. Still, there is a possibility that the museum can qualify under some other test for public charity status to avoid being classified as a private foundation. The museum in Example 17 still may be able to qualify as a publicly supported charity under § 509(a)(1) if it can meet an alternative facts and circumstances test available under § 509(a)(1) (discussed below) or can exclude the individual's large gift from both the numerator and the denominator of the support fraction as an unusual and unexpected gift (discussion of unusual grants below). However, if the museum fails to meet the alternative facts and circumstances test and if it cannot exclude the gift as an unusual gift, it would not qualify as a public supported charity under § 509(a)(1).

The substantial contribution from the individual in Example 17 presented a dilemma for the museum. The museum would want to accept the contribution but would not want acceptance of the gift to cause it to lose its public charity status. Although the museum would attempt to qualify the gift as an unusual gift, if the museum is organized and operated in a manner that would permit the museum to meet the facts and circumstances test discussed below, it would not encounter the problem of having to reject large gifts to sustain its public charity status.

b. Facts and Circumstances Test

Even though an organization fails to meet the one-third support test, it still can qualify as a publicly supported charity status under §§ 509(a)(1) and 170(b)(1)(A)(vi) if it normally receives a substantial part of its support from governmental units and from direct or indirect contributions from the general public and if it meets certain other requirements.[39]

The percentage of support required for these purposes is at least ten percent of total support "normally" received.[40] "Facts and circumstances" to be considered in addition to the support requirement relate to the type of support received and the manner in which a nonprofit entity is organized. An entity must be organized and operated to attract new and additional public or governmental support on a continuous basis. This requirement is met if an organization maintains a continuous and bona fide program for solicitation of funds from the general public, community, or membership group involved, or if it carries on activities designed to attract support from governmental units or other charitable organizations. Consideration is given to the scope of an organization's fund-raising activities.

Five factors, in addition to the ten percent support test, are taken into consideration in determining an organization's public status under the facts and circumstances test. While an organization is not required to satisfy all of the five factors, the number required to satisfy the test and the weight accorded to each depends upon the nature and purpose of the organization. The factors are

(1) Percentage of support received by an organization from public or governmental sources. The higher the percentage of support above the ten percent requirement, the lesser the burden of establishing the publicly supported nature of the organization through other factors, while the lower the percentage, the greater the burden. If the percentage is low, the source of endowment funds is noted. If the funds originally were contributed by a few individuals or by members of their families, the burden on the organization to establish compliance with other factors is increased.

(2) Sources of support. Consideration is given to whether support is from a representative number of persons or almost all from members of a single family.

(3) Representative governing body. The fact that an organization has a governing body that represents broad interests of the public, rather than personal or private interests of a limited number of donors, will be given weight in determining whether an organization is publicly supported. An organization has a "representative governing body" if its governing body is comprised of (a) public officials acting in their official capacities, (b) individuals selected by public officials, (c) persons having special knowledge or expertise in the particular field or discipline in which the organization is operating, (d) community leaders, or (e) a broadly based membership (for membership organizations).

(4) Availability of public facilities or services and public participation in programs or policies. The fact that an organization is of the type that generally provides facilities or services directly for the benefit of the general public on a continuing basis, such as a museum, is evidence that an organization is publicly supported. Other facts, such as members of the public participating in or sponsoring programs of the organization, an organization's use of a definitive program to accomplish its charitable work in the community, and

an organization's receipt of a significant part of its funds from a public charity or governmental agency to which it is in some manner held accountable as a condition of the grant also are considered evidence that an organization is publicly supported.

(5) Additional factors. Other facts to be considered include whether solicitation for dues-paying members is designed to enroll a substantial number of persons in the community or area; whether membership dues for individual members have been fixed at rates designed to make membership available to a broad cross-section of the interested public; and whether activities of the organization likely will appeal to persons having some broad common interest or purpose.

3. Unusual Grants

Unusual grants affect both § 509(a)(1) and § 509(a)(2) organizations in their attempts to meet the publicly supported tests. If a large gift or grant can qualify as an unusual grant, it can be excluded from both the numerator and the denominator of the fractions and, thus, lessen substantially the adverse effect of such a contribution on the publicly supported status of the organization.[41]

An unusual grant, which is excluded from an organization's support fraction, is a substantial contribution or bequest from a disinterested party that was attracted by reason of an organization's publicly supported nature, that is unusual or unexpected as to its amount, and that would, by reason of its size, adversely affect the status of an organization as a public charity. In determining whether a particular contribution can qualify as an unusual grant, all relevant facts and circumstances are considered. No single factor is determinative.[42]

A grant may be categorized as an unusual grant without a formal ruling from the IRS if the grant meets the requirements noted above and also the following conditions: (1) the grant or contribution is not made by a person (or related person) who created the organization or who was a substantial contributor prior to the grant; (2) the grant is not made by a person in a position of authority such as a foundation manager, someone else who can exercise control over the organization, or a person who assumes a position of authority as a result of the grant; (3) the grant or contribution is in the form of cash, readily marketable securities, or assets that directly further the organization's exempt purpose; (4) the organization has met the required publicly supported test before the year of the grant; and (5) the grantor has not imposed any material restrictions upon the organization in connection with the grant.[43]

4. Section 509(a)(2) Public Charity

A charitable organization that receives support from the general public in the form of receipts for services rendered or for other activities related to the organization's exempt functions may qualify as a public charity under § 509(a)(2) of the Internal Revenue Code. A museum that obtains a substantial amount of its receipts from admission fees would be in this category. As previously noted, a charitable organization that receives a substantial amount of its support from gross receipts (in performing its exempt function activities) cannot qualify as a public charity under §§ 509(a)(1) and 170(b)(1)(A)(vi) of the Code. It may qualify, however, as a § 509(a)(2) public charity.

A § 509(a)(2) charity must meet two tests—a one-third support and a not more than one-third gross investment test. The one-third support test is similar to the one-third support test for § 509(a)(1) public charities except that gifts from disqualified persons cannot be included at all in the numerator of the support fraction (they are counted in full in the denominator), and gross receipts from the organization's exempt functions are included in both the numerator and the denominator. A § 509(a)(2) public charity cannot receive more than one-third of its support from gross investment income. (This is not a limitation for a § 509(a)(1) charity; however, substantial investment income also is a problem for a § 509(a)(1) charity. The total amount of investment income is included in the denominator of the organization's one-third support test but is not included at all in the numerator. A substantial amount of investment income then can cause the organization difficulty in meeting the one-third publicly supported test.)

a. Support Test

An organization seeking public charity status under § 509(a)(2) of the Internal Revenue Code will meet the one-third test if it "normally" (as an average over a five-year period) receives more than one-third of its total support from any combination of gifts, grants, contributions, membership fees, and gross receipts from admissions, sales of merchandise, performance of services, or furnishing of facilities (unless any of these activities constitute an unrelated trade or business [discussion of unrelated trade or business in Chapter 4]). Funds from governmental units, from § 509(a)(1) public charities, and from persons other than disqualified persons also are permitted sources for this test.

There are limitations on the amount of gross receipts from an individual or entity that can be included in the numerator of the support fraction to assure that receipts are derived, in fact, from the general public rather than from a few persons or entities. Gross receipts from related activities received from a person, or from a bureau or similar agency of a governmental unit, are included in the numerator of the one-third support test for any year only to the extent the gross receipts from the person or entity do not exceed the greater of $5,000 or one percent of the organization's support in that year.

Example 18. In the current year, a museum received $200,000 support from the following sources:

Governmental bureau, for services rendered	$50,000
An individual, for services rendered	50,000
General public, for services rendered	40,000
Gross investment income	30,000
Contributions from individual substantial contributors (disqualified persons)	30,000
	$200,000

Because the $50,000 received from the governmental bureau and from the individual is more than the greater of $5,000 or one percent of the museum's support for the year (one percent of $200,000, or $2,000), each amount is included in the numerator of the one-third support fraction only to the extent of $5,000. Contributions from disqualified persons cannot be included at all in the numerator of the fraction. The numerator of the support fraction, then, is $50,000, computed, as follows:

Governmental bureau	$5,000
Individual	5,000
General public	40,000
	$50,000

> Because the denominator of the fraction is $200,000, the one-third support test is not met for the year. Still, qualification is determined over a five-year period. While amount of gross receipts from any one individual or governmental unit is limited to the greater of $5,000 or one percent support on an annual basis, determination of whether an organization meets the support test to qualify as a § 509(a)(2) charity is made on a five-year basis. If the test is not met based on data for a five-year period, the organization will not qualify as § 509(a)(2) public charity. (The alternative facts and circumstances test is not available for a § 509(a)(2) organization.)

As set out in the above example, gross receipts from any individual or entity in excess of the greater of $5,000 or one percent of total support for a year are excluded from the numerator of the support fraction. This requirement limits § 509(a)(2) public charity status to those nonprofit organizations that provide services to the general public rather than to only a few individuals or entities. (A § 509(a)(1) public charity, on the other hand, qualifies for public charity status because it receives "contributions" from the general public rather than from only a few donors.)

b. Investment Income Test

A § 509(a)(2) organization may not receive more than one-third of its support in any year from gross investment income and from the excess of its unrelated business taxable income over the tax imposed upon that income. Gross investment income is the gross amount of income from interest, dividends, rents, and royalties.

> Example 19. The gross investment test was met in Example 18 above. The museum did not receive more than one-third of its support from gross investment income. The museum's investment income was fifteen percent of its total support ($30,000 [gross investment income] divided by $200,000 [total support for the year]).

5. Section 509(a)(3) Public Charity

An organization that receives little, if any, support from the general public can qualify as a public charity if it supports a qualified § 509(a)(1) or (2) public charity. Supporting organizations operated exclusively for the benefit of, and that are controlled by, § 509(a)(1) and (2) organizations qualify for public charity status under § 509(a)(3) of the Internal Revenue Code. An advantage to § 509(a)(3) status is that, unlike a § 509(a)(1) or (2) public charity, a § 509(a)(3) organization need not be concerned with annual fund drives (or providing services to the general public) to ensure substantial public support.

A publicly supported organization qualifies for public charity status under § 509(a)(1) or (2) whereas a § 509(a)(3) organization is one that has established a specified relationship with, and in support of, a § 509(a)(1) or (2) public charity. Even though a single donor or only a few donors may fund such an organization, the organization nonetheless may qualify as a public charity if it has limited purposes and activities and if it relinquishes a substantial degree of independence. Private foundations that wish to obtain public charity status can obtain this status more easily by electing to qualify under § 509(a)(3).

An entity qualifies for § 509(a)(3) status by meeting three tests set out in Treasury Regulations relating to the entity's organization and operation and its relationship with a § 509(a)(1) or (2) charity (or charities). A supporting entity under § 509(a)(3) may not be controlled directly or indirectly by one or more disqualified persons other than foundation managers and other than one or more publicly supported organizations.[44]

a. Organizational Test

A § 509(a)(3) organization must be organized exclusively for the benefit of, to perform functions of, or to carry out purposes of, one or more specified publicly supported charities.[45] The supporting organization's articles of incorporation must so limit its purposes and must not empower it expressly to engage in activities that are not in furtherance of those purposes. The articles must state the publicly supported organization(s) on whose behalf the supporting organization is operated and must not expressly empower the supporting organization to operate or benefit any other organization.

b. Operational Test

A § 509(a)(3) organization must engage in activities that support or benefit its specified publicly supported charity (or charities). Its activities may include making payments for use of, or providing services or facilities for, members of the charitable class benefited by its specified publicly supported charity (or charities).

c. Relationship with Publicly Supported Charities

A supporting organization under § 509(a)(3) must be responsive to the needs and demand of a public charity and must constitute an integral part of, or maintain a significant involvement in, operations of its supported charity (or charities).[46] The relationship between the supporting organization and its supported charity (or charities) requires either the presence of a substantial degree of direction by the supported charity over conduct of the supporting organization, the presence of common supervision or control among governing bodies of all organizations involved, or a supporting organization responsive to, and significantly involved in, operation of the supported charity (or charities).

To meet the relationship test, one of three types of relationships must exist between the supporting organization and its supported charity (or charities). A supporting organization must either be (1) operated, supervised, or controlled by one or more publicly supported charities; (2) supervised or controlled in connection with one or more publicly supported charities; or (3) operated in connection with one or more publicly supported charities. Although these three relationships are somewhat alike, there are distinctions.

I. Type 1—Operated, Supervised, or Controlled By

The distinguishing feature of this type of relationship is the existence of a substantial degree of direction by the publicly supported charity over conduct of the supporting organization. Each of the terms—"operated by," "supervised by," and "controlled by"—presupposes a substantial degree of direction over the policies, programs, and activities of a supporting organization by a publicly supported charity. The relationship is comparable to that of a parent corporation and its subsidiary. The relationship is established by the fact that a majority of officers, directors, or trustees of the supporting organization are appointed or elected by members of the governing body, officers acting in their official capacity, or the membership of the publicly supported charity.

II. Type 2—Supervised or Controlled in Connection With

The distinguishing feature of this relationship is the presence of common supervision or control among governing bodies of all organizations involved, such as the presence of common directors. There must be common supervision or control by persons supervising or controlling both the supporting organization and the publicly supported charity to ensure the supporting organization will be responsive to the needs and requirements of the publicly supported charity. Thus, control or management of the supporting organization must be vested in the same persons who control or manage the publicly supported charity (or charities).

III. Type 3—Operated in Connection With

The distinguishing feature of this relationship is that the supporting organization is responsive to, and significantly involved in operations of, the publicly supported charity. A supporting organization is "operated in connection with" a public charity if it meets two tests: the responsiveness test and the integral part test.

The responsiveness test requires that a supporting organization be responsive to the needs and demands of the designated publicly supported charity. To meet this test, at least one of the officers, directors, or trustees of the supporting organization must be elected or appointed by officers, directors, trustees, or members of the supported public charity. In addition, at least one of the members of the governing body of the publicly supported charity must hold some important office in the supporting organization. Finally, there must be a close and continuous working relationship between officers, directors, or trustees of the supporting organization and the supported public charity. Officers and directors of the supported public charity must have a significant voice in affairs of the supporting organization. If the supporting organization is a charitable trust, each specified publicly supported charity must be a named beneficiary under the trust's governing instrument, and the beneficiary organization must have power to enforce the trust and compel an accounting under state law.

The integral part test requires that a supporting organization maintain a significant involvement in the operations of a publicly supported charity and that the designated publicly supported charity be dependent upon the supporting organization for the type of support it provides. This test requires that the supporting organization either be engaged in activities that the public charity would be required to undertake but for involvement of the supporting organization or that the supporting organization make payments of substantially all its income in a sufficient amount to ensure that the public charity will be attentive to operations of the supporting organization. The amount of support received by a publicly supported charity must represent a sufficient part of the charity's total support so as to ensure attentiveness.

6. Procedures to Obtain Public Charity Status

A charitable organization seeks to obtain public charity status at the same time it applies for tax exempt status—by filing Form 1023 with the IRS. Form 1023 serves both as an application for exempt status and also as a notification to the IRS that the organization is or is not a private foundation.

A museum claiming public charity status must designate itself on Form 1023 as a § 509(a)(1) organization, with its classification under § 170(b)(1)(A),[47] or as a § 509(a)(2) or (3) organization. The IRS will analyze information provided on the form to determine whether the organization meets the one-third support test and the not more than one-third investment income test for § 509(a)(2) organizations, and either the one-third or the ten percent support test for § 509(a)(1) organizations under § 170(b)(1)(A)(vi). The museum would demonstrate its continuing public charity status by providing information regarding its support annually on a separate schedule (Schedule A) to the annual reporting Form 990.

7. Annual Reporting Requirements

A charitable organization qualifying as a public charity must file an annual information return on Form 990 specifying receipts and expenditures and indicating current financial status as well as providing the IRS with considerable additional information about the organization.[48] The annual return forms for public charities must be made available for public inspection for a period of three years after the date the returns are filed.[49]

8. Involvement in Excess Benefit Transactions

As discussed in Chapter 1, certain "disqualified persons" are subject to a penalty tax on their involvement in "excess benefit transactions" with a public charity.[50] Further, as noted in Chapter 1, an "excess benefit transaction" is any transaction in which an economic benefit is provided by a public charity directly or indirectly to or for the use of a disqualified person if the value of the economic benefit provided exceeds the value of the consideration (including the performance of services) received by the charity for the benefit. The penalty tax on an "excess benefit transaction" is twenty-five percent of the excess benefit and is imposed on the disqualified person. If the excess benefit is not corrected within a "taxable period,"[51] a tax of two hundred percent of the excess benefit is imposed on the disqualified person. A tax of ten percent of the excess benefit is imposed on the organization's manager[52] if the manager participated in the transaction knowing the transaction was an excess benefit transaction unless the manager can show her participation was not willful and was due to reasonable cause.[53]

a. Disqualified Persons under Section 4958

A "disqualified person" under § 4958 is any person who has substantial influence over a charity during a five-year period ending on the date of a transaction with the charity. The definition of a "disqualified person" for purposes of § 4958 is not the same as the definition for the "disqualified person" discussed above whose support for a public charity is limited in determining whether the organization meets the one-third support test. The following are included in the definition of a disqualified person for purposes of § 4958: (1) members of the governing body who are entitled to vote; (2) presidents, chief executive officers, or chief operating officers;[54] and (3) treasurers and chief financial officers.[55] A person who has managerial control over a discrete segment of a charity may be in a position to exercise substantial influence over the entire charity and, thus, may be a disqualified person. Some persons are deemed not to have substantial influence. They include employees who receive benefits from a public charity of less than a designated amount ($100,000 in 2012) and are not substantial contributors to the charity.[56]

> Example 20. An artist works part time at a museum. The first year the museum employed the artist, it paid him a modest salary and provided no additional benefits except free admission to the museum, which is a benefit the museum provides all its employees and volunteers. The second year of the artist's employment, the museum purchased one of the artist's paintings for $90,000. The total economic benefits the museum provided the artist in that year exceeded the amount of compensation the artist can receive to be deemed not to have substantial influence over the museum. Whether the artist will be deemed to have substantial influence, and, thus, be a disqualified person, will depend upon all relevant facts and circumstances.[57]

b. Excess Benefit Transaction

An "excess benefit transaction" is one in which a public charity provides a benefit to a "disqualified person" in excess of the consideration received for the benefit. It includes any financial and non-fair-market-value transaction that benefits an individual. Excessive compensation paid to a director or employee of a public charity is an "excess benefit transaction." Compensation paid may not exceed what is reasonable under all circumstances. Compensation is reasonable if it is no more than an amount that ordinarily would be paid for like services by like enterprises under like circumstances.[58]

There is a rebuttable presumption that compensation is reasonable if a compensation arrangement was approved by a board or committee which (1) was composed entirely of individuals who were unrelated to and not subject to control of the disqualified person involved in the arrangement, (2) obtained and relied upon appropriate data as to comparability,[59] and (3) documented adequately the basis for its determination.[60] If all three criteria are satisfied, penalty taxes are imposed only if the IRS develops sufficient contrary evidence to rebut the probative value of evidence established by the charity. For property sold or otherwise transferred by a public charity, there is a similar rebuttable presumption if the sale or transfer was approved by an independent board that used appropriate comparability data and documented adequately its determination.[61]

A decision of a governing board is documented adequately if written or electronic records note (1) the terms of the transaction that was approved and the date it was approved, (2) members of the governing body or committee who were present during the debate on the transaction or arrangement that was approved and those who voted for it, (3) the comparability data obtained and relied upon by the committee and how the data was obtained, and (4) actions taken with respect to consideration of the transaction by anyone who is otherwise a member of the governing body or committee but who had a conflict of interest with respect to the transaction or arrangement.

If a governing body or committee determines that reasonable compensation for a specific arrangement or fair market value in a specific transaction is higher or lower than the range of comparable data obtained, the governing body or committee must record the basis for its determination. For a decision to be documented concurrently, records must be prepared by the next meeting of the governing body or committee occurring after the final action or actions are taken. The records must be reviewed and approved by the governing body or committee as reasonable, accurate, and complete within a reasonable time thereafter.

Example 21. The person employed as the director of Art History Museum has a substantial salary plus a home and automobile. The home and automobile are part of the director's compensation package. As a result, the director is the highest paid museum director in the state. It may be a problem for the director that she is the highest paid director. The board could not point to a higher paid director in its comparability data. If the IRS can contend successfully that the director's compensation package is excessive, the director will be subject to a twenty-five percent tax initially on the amount deemed excessive. Assume the IRS proves the director's compensation is excessive in the amount of $100,000. The director would be subject to a penalty tax of $25,000 (twenty-five percent of $100,000). The director then would be required to repay the $100,000 to Art History Museum or be subjected to a penalty tax of $200,000 (two hundred percent of $100,000).[62]

D. MUSEUM WITH PRIVATE FOUNDATION STATUS FOR TAX PURPOSES

A § 501(c)(3) organization that cannot meet the requirements of public charity status is a private foundation. A private foundation is subject to substantial restrictions and reporting requirements as well as to an excise tax on net investment income and penalty taxes for failure to comply with certain Internal Revenue Code provisions. Private foundations receive most of their support from a small number of contributors and generally are controlled by their founders or substantial donors. Because these organizations may be responsive to private individuals rather than to the general public, the IRS closely supervises their operations to make certain there are no abuses relating to their tax exempt status and with respect to the tax benefits the donors receive for donations to the organizations. A director of a museum established and funded by only a few donors must be aware of the private foundation status of the museum and also of any supporting organizations, which cannot qualify as public charities, and of the consequences of this status.

1. Classification as a Private Foundation

A private foundation, like a public charity, is a § 501(c)(3) organization.[63] A museum that is classified as a private foundation continues to be treated as a private foundation until its status is terminated in accordance with § 507 of the Internal Revenue Code (discussed below). Generally, notice of termination must be given to the IRS. Failure to terminate a private foundation in the manner prescribed in § 507 of the Code will subject the foundation to substantial penalty taxes as noted below.

Private foundations are subject to five two-tier excise taxes for engaging in certain prohibited acts or for failing to perform certain required acts. Some of the taxes are imposed on foundation managers and other disqualified persons (the charity's substantial contributors) who engage in these acts rather than on the private foundation. The prohibited acts, or failures to act (discussed below), are (1) self-dealing, (2) failure to distribute income (to a public charity or to an "operating" foundation), (3) having excess business holdings, (4) making investments that jeopardize the charitable purpose of the foundation, and (5) making certain improper, taxable expenditures. There is an initial, first-tier penalty tax for engaging in these prohibited acts or failures to act, and an additional, second-tier tax if the prohibited act or failure to act is not "corrected" within a designated period of time.

The governing instrument of a private foundation must contain special provisions that prohibit it from acting, or refraining from acting, in a manner that would make the foundation liable for the above noted penalty taxes unless state law has these prohibitions with respect to nonprofit entities organized in the state.

a. Charitable Contribution Deduction

Gifts to private "nonoperating" foundations receive less favorable income tax treatment than do gifts to public charities and to private "operating" foundations. A donor may deduct gifts of appreciated long-term capital gain property to private nonoperating foundations only to the extent of the property's tax basis (which generally is the donor's cost less depreciation).[64] On the other hand, gifts to public charities (and to private operating foundations) of appreciated property that would produce a long-term capital gain if sold are generally deductible in the amount of the property's fair market value.[65]

A private operating foundation is treated as a public charity for purposes of determining the charitable contributions deduction for donors. As a general rule, a museum can qualify as a private operating foundation (discussion of private operating foundations below).[66]

b. Excise Tax

A private foundation is subject to an excise tax of two percent of its net investment income.[67] Net investment income, which is subject to the excise tax, is the amount by which the sum of the organization's gross investment income exceeds ordinary and necessary expenses paid or incurred for production or collection of gross investment income or for the management, conservation, or maintenance of property held for production of investment income.[68] A private foundation may deduct only those expenses relating to its investment activities in computing its net investment income.[69]

c. Self-Dealing

Each act of self-dealing between a disqualified person and a private foundation is subject to an excise tax under § 4941 of the Internal Revenue Code. (This penalty tax was discussed in Chapter 1.) The tax is imposed upon the disqualified person who participated in the act (rather than on the private foundation) and applies regardless of whether the disqualified person was aware the act was one of self-dealing under § 4941. The penalty tax on self-dealing is ten percent of the "amount involved" for each year but is two hundred percent of the amount involved if the act is not corrected.[70]

The term "self-dealing" refers to transactions, whether direct or indirect, between a private foundation and a disqualified person. It includes sales or exchanges of property, leases, and loans between a private foundation and a disqualified person; the provision of goods, services, or facilities by a private foundation to a disqualified person (unless the goods were made available to the general public on at least as favorable a basis as they were made available to the disqualified person); a disqualified person's use of a private foundation's income or assets; a private foundation's payment of compensation to a disqualified person (unless the payment is a reasonable amount for the performance of personal services that are reasonable and necessary to perform the foundation's exempt purposes); and payment of money or property to a government official.[71] Self-dealing can occur even though the disqualified person who participated in a prohibited act received nonpecuniary benefits.

> Example 22. A museum that is a private foundation pays a fixed commission to its officers and directors for arranging sales of the museum's artworks. In the absence of special circumstances, payment of any of the commission would be an act of self-dealing. In PLR 9011050 the IRS ruled that the payment of a fixed commission to the officers and directors of a private foundation for arranging sales of the foundation's artworks would not be an act of self-dealing if the commissions constituted reasonable compensation for services rendered. The foundation would use comparability factors to determine reasonable compensation. The factors would be (1) commissions charged by nondisqualified persons for selling

the artist's work, (2) commissions paid by the artist during his lifetime to persons who were not then disqualified persons and to others, (3) commissions agents charge to sell art of the same school as the artist, and (4) commissions received by agents who sell art generally in the foundation's geographic area.

Example 23. In Estate of Reis v. Comm., 87 T.C. 1016 (1986), which was discussed in Chapter 1, Reis, who was the executor of the Mark Rothko estate and also a director of the Mark Rothko Foundation (a private foundation), was found liable for self-dealing penalty taxes under § 4941 in excess of $18 million. The executors of the Mark Rothko estate entered into contracts on behalf of the estate with a gallery in which Reis was a director and an employee. The contracts provided that the paintings of Mark Rothko could be sold only by the gallery for a period of twelve years and at a commission to the gallery of fifty percent of proceeds from the sales. Surviving members of Mark Rothko's family filed a lawsuit in New York state courts to set aside the twelve-year exclusive sales contract and to remove Reis as executor of the estate. Most of the relief sought by the family was granted. The IRS audited the foundation and determined that Reis was involved in self-dealing. Reis contended that assets of the estate were separate and distinct from assets of the foundation and that assets of the foundation were not used for his benefit or transferred to him. The court agreed with the IRS that because the foundation was a beneficiary under Mark Rothko's will, the foundation had a vested beneficial interest in property of the estate. Thus, property of the estate was treated as an asset of the private foundation. The court did rule that a disqualified person who receives only tenuous benefits from his use of an asset of a private foundation will not be subject to self-dealing taxes. Thus, it granted Reis the opportunity to demonstrate in a trial on the merits that he had no substantial benefit from the transaction. In Stamos v. Comm., 87 T.C. 1451 (1987), the court held Stamos, another of the executors of the Mark Rothko estate, liable for self-dealing excise taxes in excess of $19 million because of the exclusive contract the executors entered into on behalf of the estate. Stamos also served as a director of the Mark Rothko private foundation.

Example 24. A museum that is a private foundation furnishes living quarters to its executive director. Furnishing of the living quarters will not be self-dealing only if the value of the quarters is not excessive. The director's salary and the value of the quarters is added to determine whether the director is being paid excessive compensation.

Example 25. A private foundation furnishes living quarters to its curator/director and her immediate family in a manor house on the plantation owned by the private foundation. The curator/director lives in the manor house to secure the house and the surrounding property against theft and to maintain daily upkeep and care. In PLR 9646002, the IRS ruled that because the director's constant presence on the foundation premises was needed for security or other purpose, furnishing of the living quarters to the curator/director was not an act of self-dealing. However, the IRS stated the manor house must be open to the public.

Example 26. Historical Museum, which was housed in a replica of a European castle situated behind the mansion of its founder, was established as a charitable private foundation. It had a collection of medieval arms and armor suits, as well as various art relics, as its collection. The founder of Historical Museum directed in his will that the collection be maintained; he left all the property in his estate to the museum for use in operating the museum. Directors of the museum kept the collection on display until the founder's death, at which time the directors of the museum moved the collection to another building. One of the directors used $250,000 of the estate left to the museum to acquire stock in a bank in which he, and other directors of the museum, were receiving salaries. The museum also paid rent on an office used by a director as a law office. The state filed suit against Historical Museum and its directors, alleging the directors were mismanaging the museum. The court ordered that the museum collection be transferred to Art Institute of Chicago and that the museum's liquid assets be placed under court administration. The IRS learned of the proceedings and sought to terminate the museum's status as a tax exempt charitable organization. During the proceedings, attorneys for directors of Historical Museum submitted a statement to the court, requesting that the court pay from the museum's funds their fees, in excess of $1 million, for representing the directors. The IRS contended that the museum's indemnification of the directors for willful breach of their fiduciary duties would be a dissipation of the charity's assets, that payment of the attorney's fees would be an indemnification, and that payment would be subject to substantial excise taxes for self-dealing. In George F. Harding Museum v. United States, 674 F. Supp. 1323 (N.D.

Ill. 1987), the court agreed with the IRS, but refused to place a jeopardy assessment on the museum's assets.

The transfer of real or personal property by a disqualified person to a private foundation is treated as a sale or exchange if the property is subject to a mortgage or similar lien which the foundation assumes or if it is subject to a mortgage or similar lien which a disqualified person placed on the property within the ten-year period ending on the date of the transfer. A disqualified person can lend money to a private foundation only if the loan is without interest or other charge and only if the proceeds of the loan are used exclusively for the organization's exempt purposes. A disqualified person's use of a private foundation's income or assets ordinarily is self-dealing.

Example 27. A major contributor to a museum purchased property with a cash down payment and the execution of a note and deed of trust for the balance of the purchase price. The donor then transferred the property to the museum. The museum paid interest and principal on the note for one year and then conveyed the property to the seller of the property (the holder of the note and deed of trust) in full payment of the note. Because the property was subject to a lien that the donor, a disqualified person to the museum, had placed on the property within ten years of the date of the transfer, the transfer of the property to the museum was an act of self-dealing. The amount of the self-dealing was the fair market value of the property on the date of the transfer. Although the note was fully paid by the conveyance of the property back to the holder of the note, the donor (the disqualified person) must repay the museum the funds the museum paid as interest and principal on the note, plus a fair rate of interest on those amounts, in order to correct the act of self-dealing.

There are limited exceptions to the rule that transactions between a private foundation and a disqualified person are acts of self-dealing. A transaction between a private foundation and a corporation, which is a disqualified person, pursuant to a liquidation, merger, redemption, or other corporate adjustment, is not an act of self-dealing if all securities the foundation received, which are of the same class as those held by the foundation prior to the transaction, are subject to the same terms and the terms provide for receipt by the foundation of no less than fair market value. A person can lease property to a private foundation but only if the lease is without charge.[72] Performing trust functions and general banking services by a bank or trust company that is a disqualified person is not an act of self-dealing if services are reasonable and necessary in performing the exempt purposes of the foundation and compensation paid the bank or trust company is not excessive.

> Example 28. A museum that is a private foundation wants to undertake a restoration program to restore personal property of one of its substantial contributors. The substantial contributor, who is advanced in age, has transferred ownership of the property to the museum subject to her retaining the property until she dies. The restoration program would not be an act of self-dealing only if any benefits to the donor from the restoration program were incidental. In PLR 8704046, the IRS ruled that, given the advanced age and poor health of the disqualified person, any benefits to her from the restoration program would be incidental or tenuous.

Other acts of self-dealing involving trustees, directors, and officials of museums were discussed in Chapter 1 in reference to governance of a museum.

d. Failure to Distribute Income

A private nonoperating foundation must distribute its income to public charities or to private operating foundations. Section 4942 of the Internal Revenue Code subjects a private nonoperating foundation that does not distribute the net income it received during a year, by the end of the following year, to a penalty tax of thirty percent of any "undistributed income." There is an additional tax of one hundred percent of any undistributed income remaining at the end of a correction period.[73]

Undistributed income subject to the penalty tax is a "distributable amount" reduced by "qualifying distributions," the net investment income excise tax, and any regular taxes paid by the foundation.[74] Distributable amount is an amount equal to the "minimum investment return" of the foundation (discussed below) reduced by the sum of any regular taxes imposed on the foundation and the net investment income excise tax. Qualifying distributions are expenditures for charitable purposes, for reasonable administrative expenses, and for amounts "set aside" for charitable projects.

Qualifying distributions include amounts paid for charitable purposes, contributions to public charities and to private operating foundations to be used by the recipient charity for charitable purposes, amounts paid to acquire assets to be used directly to carry out a charitable or other public purpose, and any qualifying amounts set aside for charitable purposes. Program-related investments and reasonable and necessary administrative expenses are qualifying distributions.[75]

A foundation's minimum investment return is five percent of the fair market value of all the foundation assets not used for charitable purposes less any acquisition indebtedness on the property. Assets used by a foundation for its exempt purposes and any assets used in a functionally related business are not included in the computation.[76]

Example 29. The Supreme Court of Pennsylvania [In re Estate of Hermann v. Board of Trustees of John Hermann Memorial Art Museum, 312 A.2d 16 (Pa. 1973)] considered the effect of the penalty tax under § 4942 shortly after that section was added to the Internal Revenue Code. A trust fund that was a private foundation for tax purposes was set up to distribute its earnings to a museum, which was also a private foundation. The museum had qualified in the past as an operating foundation, but had lost its operating status because it had made substantial investments and, as a result, was not using enough of its property for its exempt purposes. The court ruled the trust would be required to distribute its funds to the museum even though the museum had ceased to qualify as an operating foundation. (As a private nonoperating foundation, the trust's distributions to the museum would not be qualifying distributions and would subject the trust to the penalty tax under § 4942.) The court held that the mere fact the trust would be required to pay a tax on its distributions to the museum did not justify the trustees in refusing to make further distributions to the museum. Consequently, the trustees of the trust fund could not decide the trust funds must lapse based upon their decision that it was no longer possible to administer the trust. The court had reservations should the distributions result in the imposition of the one hundred percent penalty tax but noted that the museum had not ceased to exist. The court determined that conditions placed upon the gift property, that it was to be used to maintain the museum, had not become impossible to accomplish.

Example 30. A trust classified as a private nonoperating foundation for tax purposes was established to provide operating funds for a museum classified as a private operating foundation for tax purposes. The trust acquired by bequest a ranch worth $5 million. There were no liabilities on the ranch. The trust received $100,000 as net rental income from the ranch during the current year. Pursuant to § 4942 of the Internal Revenue Code, the trust is required to distribute to the museum at least $250,000 (five percent of $5 million) by the end of the next year.[77] If the trust does not distribute this amount by the end of the next year, it will be subject to the excise tax, initially thirty percent, of the undistributed amount. If the undistributed amount is not distributed by the end of the correction period, the penalty tax will be one hundred percent of the undistributed amount. Considering that the amount of rental income the trust received from the ranch is less than the required amount the trust must distribute to the museum each year, the trust may be forced to sell the ranch. Retention of the ranch could cause the ranch to pay tax penalties of as much as $150,000. (Five percent of $5 million is $250,000. This amount must be distributed. The trust had income of $100,000 and can distribute this amount. The undistributed income of $150,000 is undistributed and will be subject to a penalty initially of thirty percent of this amount. If not corrected, the penalty is one hundred percent.) Problems discussed in this example should cause an organization classified as a private nonoperating foundation for tax purposes to reconsider accepting a donation of property that is not bringing in annual net income at least five percent of the value of the property unless the foundation intends to sell the property immediately.

A private nonoperating foundation can set aside amounts for a specific charitable project and have the amounts treated as qualifying distributions if the charity engaged in the project will complete the proposed project in five years and the private foundation can better accomplish needs of the project by set-aside funds than by an immediate payment of funds.[78]

Because a private nonoperating foundation must distribute its income to public charities or to private operating foundations to avoid the one hundred percent penalty, a museum official should consider applying for grants from these private nonoperating foundations. As noted below, a private foundation must file Form 990PF annually to report its activities for the year. A private nonoperating foundation must provide information about its grant program on Form 990PF. It must indicate how a charity applies for a grant—the form it must use, how a proposal must be submitted, any deadlines for proposals, and the person to whom a grant proposal must be submitted and that person's address. A copy of Form 990PF must be filed with the state's Office of the Attorney General at the same time it is filed with the IRS (by the fifteenth day of the fifth month following the close of the foundation's tax year) so that these forms are easily accessible.[79]

e. Excess Business Holdings

The combined holdings of a private foundation and all its disqualified persons may not exceed twenty percent of the voting stock (or profits interest in a partnership or joint venture) of a business enterprise.[80] If control of a business enterprise is in persons other than disqualified persons, permitted holdings can be as much as thirty-five percent.

If a private foundation's business holdings exceed the permissible amount, the foundation will be subject to an initial penalty tax of ten percent of the value of the foundation's excess holdings. If the foundation continues to have excess holdings after the end of a correction period,[81] the foundation is subject to a second-tier penalty tax of two hundred percent of the excess holdings. The amount of excess holdings is determined as of the day during the year when the foundation's holdings in any business are the greatest.

f. Jeopardizing Investments

A private foundation is subject to an excise tax on investments that could jeopardize performance of its exempt purposes. Section 4944 of the Internal Revenue Code imposes an initial tax of ten percent of an amount invested in a jeopardizing investment. If the foundation does not remove its investment from jeopardy,[82] an additional penalty tax of twenty-five percent of the amount of the investment is imposed.[83]

The jeopardizing effect of each investment is determined on an individual basis, considering the foundation's portfolio as a whole. No category of investment is treated as per se jeopardizing.[84] Although program-related investments are not jeopardizing investments, investments will not qualify as program-related if the primary purpose for making the investment is the production of income or for appreciation of the property rather than to accomplish a foundation's exempt purposes.

g. Taxable Expenditures

A private foundation is subject to a two-tier penalty tax on any "taxable expenditures." Section 4945 of the Internal Revenue Code imposes an initial penalty tax of twenty percent of the amount involved in a taxable expenditure. Taxable expenditures include amounts expended for the following purposes: (1) to carry on propaganda or to attempt to influence legislation; (2) to influence the outcome of any specific public election or to carry on any voter registration drive; (3) to make a grant to an individual for travel, study, or other similar purposes unless certain requirements noted below are satisfied; (4) to make a grant to an organization other than a public charity unless expenditures responsibility is exercised; and (5) to carry out any purpose other than a charitable one (as defined in § 501(c)(3) of the Code).

If expenditures are not corrected within the taxable period,[85] a second-tier tax of one hundred percent of the amount of expenditures is imposed.[86] A foundation corrects a taxable expenditures by recovering part or all of the expenditure to the extent possible.

Taxable expenditures include amounts paid to influence legislation. Attempts to influence legislation relate to communications with a member or employee of a legislative body, or with an official of the executive department of a government, or efforts to affect the opinion of the general public with respect to legislation being considered by a legislative body. Amounts paid to provide technical advice or assistance to a governmental body, a governmental committee, or a subdivision of either in response to a written request by that body of committee is not a taxable expenditure. Further, engaging in nonpartisan analysis, study, or research and making results of the work available to the public is not an attempt to influence legislation. Amounts paid to appear before, or to communicate with, any legislative body with respect to a possible decision of that body which affects the existence of a private foundation, its powers and duties, its tax exempt status, or the deductibility of contributions to the foundation is not a taxable expenditure.

Grants to individuals and to organizations can be taxable expenditures. A grant, scholarship, fellowship, internship, prize, or award to an individual for travel, study, or some other similar purpose will be a taxable expenditure unless the following requirements are met: (1) the foundation awards grants on an objective and nondiscriminatory basis and pursuant to a procedure the IRS approved in advance,[87] and (2) the foundation demonstrates to the IRS that the grant qualifies as a scholarship and will be used at an educational institution, or the purpose of the grant was to achieve a specific exempt charitable purpose.

A private foundation must exercise "expenditure responsibility" for grants to organizations unless a recipient organization is a public charity (or is a private operating foundation that is exempt from the excise tax on net investment income; discussion below).[88] A private foundation exercises expenditure responsibility by exerting all reasonable efforts, and establishing adequate procedures, to make certain all grants are spent solely for purposes for which they were made.[89]

A taxable expenditure includes any amount paid or incurred by a private foundation for a purpose other than a charitable one. Expenditures for unreasonable administrative expenses, including compensation, consultant fees, and other fees for services rendered, will be taxable expenditures unless the foundation can demonstrate the expenses were paid or incurred in the good-faith belief they were reasonable and payment was consistent with ordinary business care and prudence.

2. Private Operating Foundation

A museum that is a private foundation because it was organized and is funded by only a few donors should seek private operating foundation status. Donations to private operating foundations receive identical tax treatment as donations to public charities. In addition, a private operating foundation may be the recipient of qualifying distributions from a private nonoperating foundation (if the donor foundation does not control the operating foundation).

Private operating foundations are subject to the same restrictions and penalty taxes as are nonoperating foundation with the exception of the tax on failure to distribute income. Except for "exempt operating foundations," a private operating foundation must pay the excise tax on net investment income.

An exempt operating foundation is not required to pay the excise tax on net investment income.[90] An exempt operating foundation is one that has been supported publicly for at least ten years, has a governing body that at all times during the year consisted of individuals at least seventy-five percent of whom were not disqualified individuals, and is broadly representative of the general public. None of the foundation officers can be a disqualified person.

To be classified as a private operating foundation, an entity must meet an income test and must satisfy either an assets test, an endowment test, or a support test.

a. Income Test

The income test requires a foundation to make "qualifying distributions" *directly* for the active conduct of activities constituting its exempt purposes equal in value to substantially all of the lesser of its "adjusted net income" or its "minimum investment return."[91] Adjusted net income is the excess of a foundation's gross income for the year over its deductions. Gross income does not include gifts, grants, or contributions but does include income from a functionally related business.[92] Minimum investment return is five percent of the foundation's total assets not used for charitable purposes less the acquisition indebtedness on those assets. Qualifying distributions are those expenditures used by a foundation "directly" in furtherance of its exempt purposes.[93]

Amounts paid to acquire or maintain assets that are used directly in the conduct of a foundation's exempt activities, such as operating assets of a museum, are considered to be direct expenditures for the active conduct of the foundation's exempt activities. Administrative expenses and other operating costs necessary to conduct the foundation's exempt activities also are treated as qualifying distributions "directly" expended for the active conduct of the foundation's exempt activities so long as the amounts are reasonable.[94]

Because a private operating foundation need only make qualifying distributions equal in value to eighty-five percent of the lesser of its adjusted net income or its minimum investment return, a foundation that is a museum, which would have only a few assets that are used for nonexempt purposes, can qualify easily as an operating foundation. A museum with only a few assets that it does not use for exempt purposes generally would have no difficulty in meeting the income test and either the assets or the endowment test.

b. Assets Test

A private foundation will meet the assets test if sixty-five percent or more of its assets are devoted directly to the active conduct of activities constituting the foundation's exempt purposes, to functionally related businesses, or to any combination thereof. Assets must be actually used directly in the active conduct of exempt activities. Assets held for the production of income or for investment are not devoted directly to the active conduct of a foundation's exempt activities even though income from the assets is used to perform exempt activities.

c. Endowment Test

A private foundation will meet the endowment test if it makes qualifying distributions directly for the active conduct of activities constituting its exempt purpose in an amount that is not less than two-thirds of its minimum investment return.

d. Support Test

A foundation will meet the support test if eighty-five percent of its support (other than gross investment income) is received normally from the general public and from five or more exempt organizations. A foundation cannot receive more than twenty-five percent of its support from any one exempt organization and cannot receive more than half its support from gross investment income.[95]

Example 31. An art museum was established by one donor. It receives no support from the general public; thus, it cannot qualify as a public charity. It should attempt to be classified as an operating foundation. Its income for the year was $1 million. Its expenses relating to the production of its income were $250,000. Reasonable expenses of managing the museum were $300,000. The museum purchased artifacts costing $400,000 during the year. The museum building and its contents, along with other assets used in activities directly to perform the museum's exempt purposes, are valued at $10 million. The museum has other assets not related to its exempt purposes valued at $3 million. The art museum would qualify as an operating foundation. Its adjusted net income is $750,000 ($1,000,000 - $250,000) and its minimum investment return is $150,000 ($3,000,000 x 5%). Qualifying distributions total $700,000 ($300,000 + $400,000). The qualifying distributions were more than, but definitely at least eighty-five percent of, the lesser of adjusted net income or minimum investment return; thus, the income test is satisfied. In addition, the assets test is satisfied in that almost seventy-seven percent of the museum's assets ($10,000,000 [assets used for exempt purposes] divided by $13,000,000 [total assets]) are devoted directly to the active conduct of the art museum's exempt purposes.

3. Termination of Private Foundation Status

Unless and until a private foundation affirmatively performs functions required to terminate voluntarily its private foundation status, it will remain subject to the tax provisions discussed above—§§ 4940–45 of the Internal Revenue Code. A private foundation can terminate its status either by transferring all its net assets to one or more public charities organized under § 509(a)(1) of the Code or by itself converting to public charity status. The IRS of its own volition can terminate the existence of a private foundation if the foundation has engaged in willful and repeated acts (or failures to act) that are subject to any of the penalty taxes set out in §§ 4941–45 of the Code.[96]

a. Termination Tax

A private foundation is subjected to a substantial penalty tax if it is terminated involuntarily. The termination tax is the lesser of (1) the total amount of all tax benefits (income, estate, and gift) derived by all substantial contributors since the foundation's inception plus the increase in taxes that would have been imposed on the foundation had it been a taxable organization, or (2) the value of the net assets of the foundation. (The termination tax, then, generally will cause a foundation to transfer all its assets to the federal government.)

There is no termination penalty tax imposed on a voluntary termination if the termination follows procedures set out in § 507 of the Internal Revenue Code.

b. Voluntary Termination

Section 507 of the Code provides that a private foundation may terminate voluntarily its status as a private foundation in one of the two following methods: (1) transfer all its net assets to one or more public charities that have qualified under § 509(a)(1) of the Code for at least sixty months immediately preceding the transfer or (2) qualify itself as a public charity under either § 509(a)(1), (2), or (3) of the Code for a continuous sixty-month period after it has given the IRS notice of intent to terminate.

If a private foundation chooses to terminate voluntarily by transferring its assets to a public charity, it must make certain the public charity is one described in § 509(a)(1) of the Code and that it has qualified under § 509(a)(1) for at least sixty months immediately preceding the distribution. Section 509(a)(2) and (3) public charities may not be transferee organizations for this purpose.

A private foundation may terminate its status by itself meeting the Code requirements of either § 509(a)(1), (2), or (3) for a continuous sixty-month period. The foundation must notify the IRS before commencement of the period that it is terminating its private foundation status.[97] If a museum has only a few donors, it should seek qualification under § 509(a)(3) of the Code (discussed above) as a supporting organization of a § 509(a)(1) or (2) public charity.

4. Annual Returns

As noted previously, a private foundation files Form 990PF annually with the IRS to set out its activities during the preceding year and to demonstrate it continues to qualify for § 501(c)(3) status. Both private nonoperating foundations and private operating foundations file Form 990PF. A private foundation must file a copy of Form 990PF with the Attorney General of the state in which it has residence at the same time it files the form with the IRS. The private foundation also must make the form available for a three-year period to anyone requesting a copy.[98]

NOTES

1. A charitable contribution deduction also is available for § 501(c)(13) organizations, which are nonprofit cemetery organizations, and for § 501(c)(19) war veterans' organizations.

2. Treas. Reg. § 1.501(c)(3)-1(b)(4).

3. See Better Business Bureau v. United States, 326 U.S. 279 (1945) and Steven Bros. Foundation, Inc. v. Comm., 324 F.2d 633 (10th Cir. 1963).

4. PLR 9646002.

5. Discussion in Presbyterian & Reformed Pub. Co. v. Comm., 743 F.2d 148 (3rd Cir. 1984).

6. Hall v. Comm., 729 F.2d 632 (9th Cir. 1984). The unaccounted for diversion of resources by one who has complete and unfettered control can constitute inurement. Parker v. Comm., 365 F.2d 792 (8th Cir. 1966).

7. Harding Hospital v. United States, 505 F.2d 1068 (6th Cir. 1974).

8. Treas. Reg. § 1.501(c)(3)-1(c)(1). The regulation states that an organization must engage "primarily" in activities that accomplish one or more of its exempt activities. The regulations further provide that an organization will not be operated exclusively for exempt purposes if more than an "insubstantial" part of its activities are not in furtherance of an exempt purpose.

9. See Better Business Bureau v. United States, cited in note 3, and American Institute for Economic Research v. United States, 302 F.2d 936 (Ct. Cl. 1962).

10. Church by Mail, Inc. v. Comm., 765 F.2d 1387 (9th Cir. 1985).

11. In Plumstead Theater Soc., Inc. v. Comm., 74 T.C. 1324 (1980), aff'd, 675 F.2d 244 (9th Cir. 1982), a nonprofit corporation established to promote the performing arts created a limited partnership to obtain financing for production of a play. The court ruled that the involvement of the tax exempt § 501(c)(3) organization as the general partner in a limited partnership was not indicative of private interest and was not a prohibitive activity.

12. GCM 39444 (1985).

13. Id.

14. Moline Properties, Inc. v. Comm., 319 U.S. 436 (1943).

15. If the subsidiary were so controlled, its corporate entity status may be disregarded. See PLR 8706012.

16. Id.

17. If the subsidiary corporation is a nonstock corporation, the income will be taxed if representatives of the tax exempt parent comprise more than fifty percent of the directors or trustees of the subsidiary. Treas. Reg. § 1.512(b)-1(k)(4).

18. I.R.C. § 512(b)(3).

19. 2 U.S.C. § 1601 et. seq. Failure to comply with requirements of the act will subject a tax exempt organization to a fine of up to $200,000. 2 U.S.C. § 1606.

20. Treas. Reg. §§ 1.501(c)(3)-1(c)(3) and 56.4911-2(e)(1). The term "action" is limited to the introduction, amendment, enactment, defeat, or repeal of acts, bills, resolutions, or similar items.

21. The election currently is made by filing Form 5768. The form must be signed and postmarked within the first day of the year to which it applies. The election, once made, is effective until revoked. A museum or a supporting organization that is a private foundation for tax purposes cannot make this election. I.R.C. § 501(h)(4).

22. I.R.C. § 4911(c). Although the expenditure limitations for an electing organization may seem to permit excessive lobbying activities at first glance, the limitations are much more limited than initially assumed. The limitations are based on an organization's exempt "expenditures" rather than on the organization's revenues.

23. Treas. Reg. § 56.4911-2(e). The term "legislative body" does not include executive, judicial, or administrative bodies. An "administrative body" includes a school board, a housing authority, a sewer and water district, a zoning board, and other similar federal, state, or local special-purpose bodies, whether elective or appointive.

24. Treas. Reg. § 56.4911-2(e). "Specific legislation" includes both legislation that already has been introduced in a legislative body and a specific legislative proposal that the organization either supports or opposes.

25. Treas. Reg. § 56.4911-3(b)(2).

26. Treas. Reg. § 56.4911-2(b). With one exception, the three-part grassroots lobbying definition is applicable to mass media communications. To be grassroots lobbying, mass media communication must contain a reference to the specific legislation, must reflect a view with respect to the legislation, and must encourage the recipient to take action. However, for a communication in the mass media that is made within two weeks before a vote by a legislative body, or by a legislative committee, on a highly publicized piece of legislation, the communication will be presumed to be grassroots lobbying if the communication reflects a view on the general subject of the legislation or encourages the public to communicate with legislators on the general subject of the legislation. However, the organization can rebut the presumption by demonstrating that the communication is a type of communication regularly made by the organization in the mass media without regard to the timing of legislation or that timing of the communication was unrelated to the upcoming legislative action. Treas. Reg. § 56.4911-2(b)(5).

27. Treas. Reg. § 56.4911-3. The organization has not made a reasonable allocation if it includes as the lobbying expenditures only the amount expended for the specific sentence or sentences that encourage the recipient to take action with response to legislation.

28. I.R.C. § 4911(f)(1)(A). An organization is a member of an affiliated group if (1) the governing instrument of the organization requires it to be bound by decisions of another organization on legislative issues, or (2) the governing board of one organization includes persons who are designated specifically as representatives of another organization or are members of the governing board, officers, or paid executive staff members of the other organization and, if by aggregating their votes, the above noted persons have sufficient voting power to cause or prevent action on legislative issues by the first organization. Thus, two organizations are affiliated if one organization can control action on legislative issues by the other by reason of interlocking governing boards or by reason of provisions of the governing instruments of the controlled organization. The ability of one organization to control action on legislative matters of another organization is sufficient to cause the organizations to be affiliated. It is not necessary that control be exercised. Treas. Reg. § 56.4911-7(a).

29. Section 501(c)(3) of the Internal Revenue Code states that to qualify for § 501(c)(3) status, no substantial part of the organization's activities may constitute attempts to influence legislation or to carry on propaganda.

30. Treas. Reg. § 56.4911-2(b)(3), 2(c)(1).

31. Treas. Reg. § 53.4945-2(d).

32. The initial, first-tier tax is ten percent of the amount involved. Section 4955 provides that if a political expenditure is not corrected within a specified period as set out in § 4955, an additional tax of one hundred percent of the expenditure is imposed on the organization. A political expenditure is corrected if all or a part of the expenditure, to the extent possible, is recovered and safeguards are established to prevent the organization from making future political expenditures. The correction period begins on the date the political expenditure is made and ends on the earlier of the date of mailing of a notice of deficiency for the first-tier tax or the date on which the first-tier tax is assessed.

If the organization's manager agreed to the expenditure when the manager was aware the expenditure was a political expenditure, the manager is subject to a penalty tax of 2.5 percent of the amount of the expenditure unless the agreement was not willful and was due to reasonable cause. If the manager does not agree to a correction of the expenditure, an additional tax of fifty percent of the amount of the political expenditure is imposed on the manager.

33. The tax is five percent of the amount of lobbying expenditures incurred during any year in which the organization has ceased to qualify for tax exempt status. Section 4912 imposes a penalty tax of five percent of the amount of the lobbying expenditures on the organization's manager if the manager agreed to the making of the expenditures knowing that the expenditures would likely result in the organization losing its tax exempt status.

34. In Allen v. Wright, 468 U.S. 737 (1984), the Supreme Court held that parents of African American public school children had no standing to challenge IRS regulations governing the tax exempt status of private schools. See also Fulani v. Brady, 935 F.2d 1324 (D.C. Cir. 1991) and Abortion Rights Mobilization, Inc. v. Baker, 885 F.2d 1020 (2nd Cir. 1989).

35. Allen v. Wright, cited in note 34, and Simon v. Eastern Kentucky Welfare Rights Organization, 426 U.S. 26 (1976).

36. Fulani v. Brady, 955 F.2d 1324 (D.C. Cir. 1991).

37. A charitable organization gives notice to the IRS that it qualifies for public charity status under one of the provisions of § 509 at the same time it seeks tax exempt status, by filing Form 1023 for both purposes [to obtain § 501(c)(3) tax exempt status and to classify itself either as a private foundation or as a public charity (and the provision under § 509 that qualifies it for public charity status)]. Form 1023 is available on the IRS website. A charitable organization must file Form 1023 with the IRS within 27 months after the organization is established for the IRS to recognize exempt status from the organization's inception. If the organization does not file Form 1023 within 27 months after its creation, the IRS will recognize exempt status only from the date the IRS receives the application. Treas. Reg. § 1.508-1(a)(2).

38. Amounts received for services rendered are excluded from both the numerator and the denominator of the support fraction. However, an organization that depends primarily on gross receipts for its support cannot qualify as a § 509(a)(1) public charity. This type of organization should seek public charity status under § 509(a)(2) of the Code.

39. Treas. Reg. § 1.170A-9(e)(3).

40. Treas. Reg. § 1.170A-9(e). "Normally" is the average over the current year and a four-year period immediately preceding the current year.

41. Treas. Reg. § 1.170A-9(e)(6).

42. Treas. Reg. § 1.509(a)-3(c)(4).

43. Id. If an organization has doubt as to whether a grant or contribution may be excluded as an unusual grant, it should request a revenue ruling from the IRS. (See Rev. Proc. 2014-4 for procedures to be following in obtaining a revenue ruling.) Additional facts that the IRS may consider include (1) whether the contribution was a bequest (a bequest is given more favorable consideration than a contribution made during the donor's life); (2) whether the organization was able to attract a significant amount of public support; (3) whether the organization may reasonably be expected to attract a significant amount of public support after the gift; and (4) whether the organization has a representative governing body.

44. Treas. Reg. § 1.509(a)-4(j). An organization is "controlled" if disqualified persons, by aggregating their votes or positions of authority, may require the organization to perform any act that significantly affects its operations, or may prevent the organization from performing these acts. A supporting organization will be controlled if voting power of disqualified persons is fifty percent or more of total voting power of the organization's governing body or if one or more of these persons has the right to exercise veto power over actions of the organization.

45. Treas. Reg. § 1.509(a)-4(a).

46. Id. at § 1.509(a)-4(f).

47. As noted previously, for a museum, the Code section would be § 170(b)(1)(A)(vi); the museum would be designated as a § 501(c)(3) organization with public charity status under §§ 509(a)(1) and 170(b)(1)(A)(vi).

48. Form 990 and its currently sixteen schedules are available on the IRS website. Schedule A to Form 990 requires information about an organization's support over a five-year period to provide the IRS with information needed to determine whether the organization can continue to be classified as a public charity. If a museum, or its supporting organization, elects to be subject to lobbying expenditure limitations, it must provide information on a separate schedule, currently Schedule C, which the IRS reviews to determine whether the organization exceeded the limitations. Even though a public charity does not elect to be subject to the limitations, it still must list lobbying expenditures it paid or incurred during the year on Schedule C. An organization that fails to file a return or that fails to include the required information on the return is subject to a penalty of $20 per day not to exceed $10,000 for any one return. I.R.C. § 6652(c). If an organization has gross receipts exceeding $1 million for any year, the penalty is increased from $20 to $100 and the maximum penalty from $10,000 to $50,000.

49. I.R.C. § 6104. There is a penalty of $5,000 for willful failure to permit public inspection of the returns. I.R.C. § 6685. A public charity must make its annual returns available for public inspection during its regular business hours at its principal office or, if the organization regularly maintains one or more regional or district offices having three or more employees, at each of its regional or district offices. An individual may make a request to inspect the organization's annual return in person or in writing. The organization must provide the individual a copy without charge other than a reasonable fee for any reproduction and mailing costs.

50. I.R.C. § 4958. A disqualified person for this purpose is any person who was, at any time during a five-year period ending on the date of the transaction, in a position to exercise substantial influence over the affairs of the charity.

51. The "taxable period" is the period beginning with the date on which the transaction occurs and ending on the earliest of (1) the date of the mailing of a notice of deficiency

with respect to the initial tax or (2) the date on which the initial tax is imposed. I.R.C. § 4958(f)(5). An excess benefit transaction is corrected by undoing the excess benefit to the extent possible and taking any additional measures necessary to place the organization in a financial position no worse than that in which it would have been had the disqualified person acted under the highest fiduciary standards. I.R.C. § 4958(f)(6).

52. An organization manager is defined as any officer, director, or trustee of a public charity or any individual having powers or responsibilities similar to those of officers, directors, or trustees regardless of title. Prop. Reg. § 53.4958-1(d)(2). Thus, a member of the board of directors of a public charity can be subject to the penalty.

53. I.R.C. § 4958(d)(2). Participation includes silence or inaction on the part of an organization manager where the manager is under a duty to speak or act. Prop. Reg. § 53.4958-1(d)(3). If a manager relies on a "reasoned legal opinion" that a transaction is not an excess benefit transaction, the manager's participation in the transaction will be due to reasonable cause and not knowing or willful. The maximum amount of tax imposed on the manager shall not exceed $10,000 for any one excess benefit transaction.

54. An individual serves as president, chief executive officer, or chief operating officer, regardless of title, if that individual has or shares ultimate responsibility for implementing decisions of the governing body or supervises management, administration, or operation of the charity.

55. An individual serves as treasurer or chief financial officer, regardless of title, if that individual has or shares ultimate responsibility for managing the charity's financial assets and has or shares authority to sign drafts or direct signing of drafts, or to authorize electronic transfer of funds, from a charity's bank accounts.

56. Treas. Reg. § 53.4958-3. The regulations refer to I.R.C. § 414(q), which set out the amount of $80,000 (adjusted for inflation). The amount later was increased to $100,000.

57. The facts and circumstances that tend to show a person has substantial influence over the affairs of a charity include, but are not limited to, the following: (1) the person founded the charity; (2) the person is a substantial contributor; (3) the person's compensation is based on revenues derived from activities of the charity; (4) the person has authority to control or determine a significant portion of the organization's capital expenditures, operating budget, or compensation for employees; (5) the person has managerial authority or serves as a key advisor to a person with managerial authority; or (6) the person owns a controlling interest in a corporation, partnership, or trust that is a disqualified person. Treas. Reg. § 53.4958(e).

58. A public charity must establish an intent to provide an economic benefit as compensation for services by reporting the benefit on Form W-2 or Form 1099. If the charity fails to provide evidence that it intended to provide an economic benefit as compensation for services when paid, any services provided by a disqualified person will not be treated as provided in consideration of the economic benefit. Treas. Reg. § 53.4958-4(c)(ii).

59. Appropriate data include compensation levels paid by similarly situated organizations, both taxable and tax exempt, for functionally comparable positions; the location of the organizations, including the availability of similar specialties in the geographic area; independent compensation surveys by nationally recognized independent firms; and actual written offers from similar institutions competing for services of the disqualified person. Treas. Reg. § 53.4958-6(d)(2).

60. Adequate documentation includes an evaluation of the individual whose compensation is being established and the basis of determining that the individual's compensation is reasonable in light of that evaluation and data.

61. Relevant information would include independent appraisals of the value of property a charity intends to purchase from, or sell or provide to, a disqualified person.

62. The regulations, Treas. Reg. § 53.4958-4(a)(3)(i), pursuant to § 4958, exempt from the definition of an excess benefit transaction an "initial contract" that provides for a "fixed payment." An "initial contract" is defined as a binding written agreement between a tax exempt organization and a person who was not a disqualified person immediately prior to entering into the contract. A "fixed payment" is defined as "an amount of cash or other property specified in the contract, or determined by a fixed formula specified in the contract, which is to be paid or transferred in exchange for the provision of specified services or property." The regulations give as an example a tax exempt organization entering into a contract to employ a chief financial officer at a salary of $200,000. Because the financial officer, as a new employee, would not be a disqualified person at the time of the contract, the contract would qualify as an "initial contract" subject to a fixed payment and § 4958 would not be applicable. However if the financial officer is promoted subsequently to chief executive officer at a salary increase of $40,000, changes in the employment relationship would constitute material changes in the initial contract so that the board will have entered into a new contract with a then disqualified person, and § 4958 would be applicable. (Treas. Reg. § 53.4958-4(a)(3)(vii), Examples 1 and 4.)

63. A private foundation, like a public charity, applies for federal tax exempt status by filing Form 1023. If a museum does not attempt to qualify as a public charity because of its few donors, it would indicate on Form 1023 that it is a private foundation. A museum that is a private foundation because of its small number of donors should attempt to qualify as a private "operating" foundation. To do so, the museum currently would complete Schedule E of Form 1023.

64. I.R.C. § 170(e)(1)(B). The Code states that the deduction is limited to the property's fair market value *less* the amount that would be a long-term capital gain if the property were sold at its fair market value. This means that a donor may deduct only the donor's tax basis in the property (generally cost less depreciation).

There is an exception for some gifts of stock. A donor may deduct the fair market value of qualified appreciated stock, which is stock for which market quotations are readily available on an established securities market. A gift of stock must be less than ten percent of the value of all outstanding stock in the corporation. The ten percent limitation applies to the aggregate amount of donations by a donor (including spouse, siblings, ancestors, and lineal descendants) to all private nonoperating foundations. I.R.C. § 170(e)(5).

Gifts to private nonoperating foundations are subject to a thirty percent (of adjusted gross income) annual limitation (twenty percent for gifts of capital gain property), whereas gifts to public charities and to private operating foundations are subject to a fifty percent limitation (thirty percent for gifts of capital gain property). In addition, gifts to private nonoperating foundations are determined after all gifts to public charities have been computed. Gifts to private nonoperating foundations can be deducted only as to the excess of the fifty percent limitation over total gifts to public charities.

65. Further discussion of the charitable contribution deduction for gifts to museums, especially artifacts and antiquities, is in Chapter 4.

66. A private foundation that distributes one hundred percent of all contributions it received during the year by the fifteenth day of the third month after the close of the foundation's taxable year also is treated in the same manner as a public charity for purposes of determining the charitable contribution deduction for donors [Treas. Reg. § 1.170A-9(g)(1)]. Private foundations maintaining a common fund wherein all contributions received

are pooled also qualify donors for the same contribution deduction benefits available to public charities [Treas. Reg. § 1.170A-9(h)(1)].

67. I.R.C. § 4940. The tax is reduced to one percent for any year in which the private foundation's qualifying distributions equal or exceed the sum of the foundation's assets times the average percentage payout for a base period plus one percent of the foundation's net investment income for the year [I.R.C. § 4940(e)]. (The tax reduction from two percent to one percent is not available if the foundation was liable during any base period for the penalty tax [pursuant to § 4942] on undistributed income.)

68. Treas. Reg. § 53.4940-1(e). Gross investment income is the gross amount of income from interest, dividends, rents, and royalties, excluding any amounts that were subject to the tax on unrelated business taxable income. Income of this category derived from assets devoted to charitable activities is included in gross investment income. Gross investment income includes net capital gain. [Treas. Reg. § 53.4940-1(d)].

69. Treas. Reg. § 53.4940-1(e). A foundation could not include administrative expenses relating to grant making, for example. Expenses that are incurred for both investment and for exempt purposes are allocated between the two. Depreciation, computed using the straight-line method, is deductible in computing net investment income. Cost depletion is also deductible. Tax exempt interest on governmental obligations and expenses incurred to produce this income are excluded from the computation [Treas. Reg. § 53.4940-1(c)(2)]. (Tax exempt interest on governmental obligations is not subject to the excise tax.)

70. The foundation manager is subject to an initial tax of 2.5 percent of the amount involved (maximum of $10,000) if the foundation manager knew the act was self-dealing and the manager willfully participated. An additional tax of fifty percent of the amount involved (maximum of $10,000) is imposed on the manager if the manager refused to agree to a part or all of the correction of the self-dealing act. "Amount involved" is the greater of the amount of money and the fair market value of other property given or the amount of money and the fair market value of other property received [Treas. Reg. § 53.4941(e)-1(b)]. In the case of payment of compensation, "amount involved" is the excess compensation (amount above a reasonable compensation) paid by the private foundation.

The correction period begins on the date of the self-dealing act and ends on the earliest of (1) the date when the act is corrected, (2) the date the IRS mails a deficiency notice of tax on the self-dealing act, or (3) the date when the initial tax is assessed [IRC § 4941(e)(1)]. Should the self-dealing act not be corrected within this period, the additional penalty tax of two hundred percent of the amount involved is imposed.

71. I.R.C. § 4941(d). For purposes of § 4941 only, a disqualified person includes government officials.

72. A lease is "without charge" even though the foundation agrees to pay for utilities, janitorial expenses, or other maintenance costs so long as payment is not made directly or indirectly to the disqualified person (the substantial contributor or the foundation manager) [Discussion in Treas. Reg. § 53.4941(d)-2(b)(2)].

73. The correction period is the earlier of the date of mailing of a notice of a tax deficiency regarding the initial tax or the date on which the initial tax was assessed.

74. Treas. Reg. § 53.4942(a)-2. The amount is not reduced by the penalty taxes imposed pursuant to I.R.C. §§ 4942–45.

75. Conversion of an asset previously not used for charitable purposes to a charitable use is a qualifying distribution. Amount of the qualifying distribution is the fair market value of the converted asset on the conversion date [Treas. Reg. § 53.4942(a)-3(a)(5)].

76. Treas. Reg. § 53.4942(a)-2(c). Any pledge of money or property to the foundation also is not included. (A functionally related business is a trade or business that is related to the foundation's exempt purposes.)

Assets used for exempt purposes include administrative assets (office equipment and supplies), real estate, physical facilities on public display (paintings and works of art), interest in a functionally related business, reasonable cash balances, and program-related investments. A reasonable cash balance is determined on an annual basis of 1.5 percent of the combined fair market value of all foundation assets used in determining minimum investment return. Any amount of cash in excess of the 1.5 percent figure that is treated as exempt purpose property must be explained on the foundation's annual return (Form 990PF).

Property that is used both for exempt and nonexempt purposes is considered as being used entirely for exempt purposes if at least ninety-five percent of total use is for exempt purposes. If less than ninety-five percent is used for exempt purposes, a reasonable allocation must be made between exempt and nonexempt uses.

77. This is the trust's minimum investment return. The ranch was not used for charitable purposes; thus, minimum investment return is five percent of its net value.

78. I.R.C. § 4942(g)(2). Generally the IRS must approve set-asides in advance.

79. The forms also are accessible through the website for GuideStar, a § 501(c)(3) organization that collects information, including annual returns (the 990 and the 990PF), relating to nonprofit organizations.

80. I.R.C. § 4943. Section 4943 does not apply to a foundation's holdings in a functionally related business or to a trade or business in which at least ninety-five percent of the gross income is derived from passive sources. Gross income from passive sources includes dividends, interest, rents from real property (and from personal property leased with real property if rents from the personal property are an incidental amount), royalties, and gains from sales of property and goods other than inventory items [Treas. Reg. § 53.4943-10(b)].

A private foundation that acquires excess business holdings other than by purchase can avoid the excise tax by disposing of the excess holding within ninety days from the date the foundation knows, or has reason to know, of the event that caused the foundation to have excess holdings. The ninety-day period is extended to include the period during which the foundation is prevented by federal or state securities laws from disposing of the holdings. If a private foundation acquires excess holding because of a gift or bequest, it has five years to dispose of the holdings before it has liability for the penalty tax [Treas. Reg. §§ 53.4943-2; 53.4943-6].

81. The correction period is the earlier of the IRS's mailing of a notice of deficiency for the initial tax or the date on which the IRS assesses the initial tax.

82. The date after the earlier of the mailing of a tax deficiency notice for the ten percent penalty, or the date on which the IRS assesses the ten percent penalty.

83. I.R.C. § 4944(b)(1). A foundation manager also may be liable for a tax on jeopardy investments. If the foundation manager participated in making a speculative investment knowing that she was jeopardizing the foundation, a five percent penalty of the amount so invested (maximum of $5,000) is imposed on the manager. A manager's participation must be willful and not due to reasonable cause. There is an additional tax of five percent (maximum of $10,000) if the manager refuses to agree to removal of part or all of the investment from jeopardy. A manager's action is due to reasonable cause if the manager relied on advice of counsel expressed in a reasoned, written legal opinion. In addition, the manager may rely on the advice of a qualified investment counselor (given in writing in accordance with

generally accepted practices) that a particular investment would provide for long- or short-term financial needs of the foundation.

84. Certain investments are scrutinized closely. Trading in securities on margin, trading in commodity futures, investments in working interests in oil and gas wells, purchase of "puts" and "calls," purchase of warrants, and selling short are considered speculative investments [Treas. Reg. § 53.4944-1(a)(2)]. The determination of whether an investment is speculative is made at the time of the investment and not subsequently on the basis of hindsight.

85. The earlier of date of mailing of a notice of deficiency as to the initial ten percent penalty tax or the date on which the ten percent tax is assessed.

86. A tax is imposed on the foundation manager of 2.5 percent of the amount involved (maximum of $5,000) if the manager knowingly and willfully agreed to the expenditure. In addition, there is a tax of fifty percent of the amount involved (maximum of $10,000) imposed on the foundation manager if the manager refused to agree to part or all of the correction. A foundation manager is subject to the tax only if the manager was authorized by the foundation to approve, or to exercise discretion in recommending approval for, foundation expenditures. Relying on the advice of counsel will protect the manager if the manager made full disclosure of the factual situation to legal counsel and had a reasoned, written legal opinion that the expenditure was not a taxable expenditure.

87. The requirement of advance approval of a private foundation's scholarship procedures is strictly enforced. If approval is obtained later, it will not be made retroactive. Expenditures made prior to IRS approval will be taxable expenditures. An application for tax exempt status on Form 1023, which details the scholarship grant program of a private foundation, will serve as a request for approval of the program [Rev. Rul. 87-77, 1987-1 C.B. 334]. If the IRS has not notified an organization that its grant procedures have been approved or disapproved within forty-five days after the organization has submitted properly a request for approval, the organization may consider its procedures approved until it receives actual notice from the IRS that its procedures are not acceptable.

88. The foundation must obtain a full and complete report from each grantee on how funds were spent. It then must make a full, detailed report with respect to the expenditures to the IRS. Each grant to a nonpublic organization must be subject to a written commitment, signed by an appropriate officer, director, or trustee of the grantee organization, that the grantee will repay any portion of the grant not used for grant purposes, will submit full and complete annual reports on the manner in which funds were spent, will make its books available to the grantor, and will not use funds for lobbying, to influence the outcome of any public election or any voter education drive, and will not undertake any activity other than a charitable one [Treas. Reg. § 53.4945-5(b)].

89. A grant will be a taxable expenditure if the grantee fails to make grant reports unless the grantor (1) awarded the grant according to expenditure responsibility requirements, (2) complied with all reporting requirements, (3) made a reasonable effort to obtain required reports, and (4) withheld any future payments on any grant until the grantee organization provided the report. Required reports are submitted with the foundation's annual return (Form 990PF).

90. I.R.C. § 4940(d). An exempt operating foundation must obtain a ruling letter from the IRS recognizing its status and must attach a copy of the ruling letter to its annual return (Form 990PF).

91. "Substantially all" is eighty-five percent or more. Because private operating foundations must make qualifying distributions for the active conduct of their exempt activities in this amount, they are not subject to the penalty tax for failure to distribute income.

92. Treas. Reg. § 53.4942(a)-2(d). Net short-term capital gains are included, but long-terms gains are not. Gross income also includes certain items called "income modifications." Income modifications include tax exempt interest and amounts received that previously were treated as qualifying distributions, such as amounts previously set aside for a specific project but not necessary for the purposes for which they were set aside.

93. Treas. Reg. § 53.4942(b)-1. Grants made to other organizations to assist those organizations in conducting activities that help accomplish their exempt purposes are "indirect" expenditures and cannot be counted in determining whether the organization had sufficient qualifying distributions.

94. Payments to individuals in the form of grants, scholarships, or other such payments are qualifying distributions made directly for the active conduct of the organization's exempt activities only if the foundation maintains some significant involvement in active programs in support of which it made the grants or scholarships. Significant involvement requires more active participation than just selecting, screening, and investigating applicants for grants.

95. Support from any one exempt organization is counted only if the foundation receives support from no fewer than five exempt organizations. Support from the general public can be counted only to the extent that total amount of support received from any one individual, trust, or corporation does not exceed one percent of the foundation's total support for the period.

96. I.R.C. § 507(a)(2). One willful and flagrant act (or failure to act) that is voluntary, conscious, and knowingly committed and that is deemed to be a gross violation of the penalty tax provisions will permit the IRS to terminate a foundation.

97. I.R.C. § 507(b)(1)(B). A private foundation giving notice to the IRS is treated as if it were a new organization with its first tax year beginning on the date of commencement of the sixty-month period. The notice must state the § 509 Code section under which the organization seeks classification.

98. I.R.C. § 6104(d). Returns for the three most recent tax years and the foundation's Form 1023 must be made available to the public during regular business hours at the foundation's principal offices. Failure to comply with a public inspection or copying request will subject the foundation to penalty provisions of § 6652(c)(1)(C),(D) of $20 per day, maximum of $10,000. Treas. Reg. § 301.6104-3(e).

A foundation may have an employee present during an inspection of the return, but it must permit the individual conducting the inspection to take notes freely [Treas. Reg. § 301.6104-3(e)]. If the individual provides photocopying equipment at the place of inspection, the foundation must permit the individual to photocopy any return at no charge. The foundation may charge a reasonable fee for providing copies.

If the district director determines that a foundation is the subject of a harassment campaign and that, as a result, requests would not be in the public interest, the foundation need not fulfill a request for copies (Treas. Reg. § 301.6104-5).

CHAPTER 4

FUNDING AND UNRELATED BUSINESS TAXABLE INCOME

> Obviously any group that has to have funding also needs to get attention to their issues.
>
> BJORN LOMBORG

> A democratic government is the only one in which those who vote for a tax can escape the obligation to pay it.
>
> ALEXIS DE TOCQUEVILLE

A museum director should be aware of opportunities for grants and be knowledgeable of laws, including tax provisions, that apply to donations and to revenue obtained through commercial ventures and investments. This chapter considers a museum's production of revenue to include funding from outside sources and through donations as well as any income generated from commercial activities and investments. The chapter reviews the tax provisions relating to donations, particularly requirements for donors to obtain a charitable contribution deduction for their museum donations, and to a museum's taxation on income obtained from "unrelated" commercial transactions.

A. FUNDING FOR MUSEUMS

1. Federal Funding

In 1965, Congress made a formal determination that museums are vital to the preservation of the cultural heritage of the United States and that they should be supported in their role as curator of the "national consciousness."[1] Congress established the National Foundation on Arts and Humanities in 1965 to develop and promote a broadly conceived national policy of support for the humanities and the arts and for those institutions that preserve the cultural heritage of the nation.[2] This agency provides for funds and services to nonprofit organizations including museums.[3] The Institute of Museum and Library Services was established within the National Foundation on Arts and Humanities to encourage and assist museums in their educational role and in carrying out their public service role of "connecting the whole of society to the cultural, historic, natural, and scientific understanding that constitutes our heritage."[4]

The National Museum and Library Service Board was created as part of the Institute of Museum and Library Services.[5] Its director is authorized, subject to policy and advice of the board, to enter into agreements and provide grants to pay a "Federal share" of the cost of supporting museums in providing learning and access to collections, information, and educational resources in a variety of formats (including exhibitions, programs, publications, and websites); in supporting the conservation and preservation of museum collections; and in the development of specialized programs for specific segments of the public, such as programs for urban neighborhoods, rural areas, Indian reservations, and other state institutions.[6] The board also provides guidance on its website for applying for grants, including for participating in grant programs through partnerships with eligible organizations.

2. Grants from Private Nonoperating Foundations

Public donations and grants can be a major source of funding. A primary but elementary method to obtain grants is to seek funding from private nonoperating foundations. As noted in Chapter 3, § 4942 of the Internal Revenue Code requires private nonoperating foundations to distribute their adjusted net income to public charities or private operating foundations to avoid a possible one hundred percent penalty tax for failure to distribute income. Thus, private nonoperating foundations, in deciding on the charities to which they will distribute their income, of necessity consider programs of the various charities. Charitable private nonoperating foundations undoubtedly would regard favorably museum projects and programs and may agree to fund museum acquisitions of which they are made aware.

As noted in Chapter 3, a private foundation must file Form 990PF annually with the IRS to report its activities for the year. A private nonoperating foundation also must provide information on Form 990PF about its grant program. The foundation must state how a charity can apply to the foundation for a grant. The foundation must indicate the form the charity must use to submit a proposal, the manner in which a charity must submit the proposal, any deadlines for proposals, the person to whom the charity must submit its grant proposal, and that person's address. A copy of Form 990PF must be filed with the state's Office of the Attorney General at the same time it is filed with the IRS; thus, these forms for all private nonoperating foundations are easily accessible.[7] A museum employee can peruse Form 990PF and obtain considerable information about grants that are available from endowed tax exempt nonprofit organizations as well as the procedure required to apply for these grants.

3. Fund-Raising Activities

Fund-raising activities can cause problems for charities. Many museums acquire funding through professional solicitors. Some states require nonprofit organizations that are engaged in solicitations within the state, to register, generally with the Secretary of State, and often to pay a solicitation fee. A few states exempt from registration some charitable groups and some exempt organizations that receive only a small amount of contributions, as well as those whose fund-raising is carried on by volunteers. Some states have required that a certain percentage of total contributions received be used for the charitable purposes for which the funds were collected. The constitutionality of statutes and ordinances requiring registration prior to solicitation often has been an issue in the courts. Courts generally have upheld statutes and ordinances that are not arbitrary or discriminatory on the theory that a municipality may reasonably regulate solicitation to protect its citizens from fraudulent appeals.[8] Some states require that contracts with professional fund-raising groups be reported. Some require professional fund-raising consultants and professional solicitors to register annually and pay a fee to the state. However, the Supreme Court ruled unconstitutional a Maryland statute prohibiting a charitable organization from paying expenses of more than twenty-five percent of the amount raised for fund-raising activities.[9] The Supreme Court was of the opinion that there is no connection between fraud and high solicitation and administrative costs.

Example 1. A state statute prohibits a professional fund-raiser from charging an "unreasonable fee." In Riley v. National Federation of Blind of North Carolina, 487 U.S. 781 (1988), the Supreme Court ruled unconstitutional a statute in North Carolina that included this prohibition. The statute provided for a three-tiered definition of an unreasonable fee. The Supreme Court held that the statute was an unconstitutional infringement on freedom of speech. The Court also ruled as unconstitutional a provision in the act requiring a professional fund-raiser to obtain an approved license prior to solicitation of any funds. The Court further ruled unconstitutional a provision in the act requiring professional fund-raisers to disclose to potential donors, before an appeal for funds, the percentage of charitable contributions collected during the previous year that actually were turned over to the charity. The Court stated that mandating speech, that a speaker would not otherwise make, "necessarily alters the content of the speech." The Supreme Court commented, however, that it did not intend to suggest that states "must sit idly by and allow their citizens to be defrauded by fund-raisers" and stated that law enforcement officers should be ready and able to enforce the law.[10] The Supreme Court was of the opinion that because a state constitutionally may require fund-raisers to disclose certain financial information to the state, it could police fund-raising activities in this manner. Although the Court agreed that this method of policing fund-raisers could be a less efficient means of preventing fraud than requiring an approved permit prior to solicitation, it decided that a state could not sacrifice speech for efficiency. According to the Supreme Court, the requirement in the North Carolina statute was an unconstitutional infringement on freedom of speech.

4. Licensing Agreements

A museum director may decide to obtain outside funds through reproducing and marketing works of art from its collection as well as by selling products generally. If a museum chooses to market products and cannot develop the objects through its own resources and personnel, it should consider entering into a contract with a reputable firm to do so. A licensing program can provide substantial revenue to a museum and, given a product of quality, can enhance the overall reputation of the museum as well as expand its cultural and educational influence.

Should a museum elect to license the production and marketing of its products, some caution is needed. The museum should investigate the firm's ability to create a product of quality, its ability to market effectively, and its financial stability and reputation. The rights and responsibilities of the museum and a firm designated to produce and/or market the museum's products should be set out carefully in a licensing agreement. The licensing agreement is a contract that authorizes a person or a firm to manufacture and market reproductions and other objects for the museum. The contract between the parties can limit the sale of the product to a specified territory or industrial area, and it can limit the manufacturer to a specific design or specified product.

In negotiating a licensing agreement for the production and/or marketing of a museum's reproductions or other objects, a museum official should consider the following. The agreement should contain clauses regarding assignability, termination, option to renew, and right of the museum to reject any product both initially and throughout the terms of the agreement. The museum should be the sole judge of whether a product has met the standards of quality established by the parties, and the licensee should be required to furnish the museum with evidence of the quality of the licensed products at periodic intervals. From the museum's standpoint, royalties from the sale of reproductions of its collections should be based upon gross sales and not upon net profit.[11] (A sample licensing agreement is included in the Appendix.)

a. Basic Principles of Contract Law

The basic fundamentals of contract law are summarized to alert the museum director to the possible consequences of licensing agreements (as well as other contracts to which the museum may negotiate and to which it may become a party).

Contract law imposes duties and obligations and bestows rights upon parties to a contract based upon terms of the contract. The parties to a contract create their rights and obligations by mutual agreement and often determine the liability for a breach of the contract. A contract then is an agreement which bestows rights and creates obligations. Its essentials are parties with capacity to contract, proper subject matter, sufficient consideration, mutuality of assent or agreement, and mutuality of obligations. The law imposes a duty on the parties to a contract to perform their agreement; this duty is the obligation of the contract. Every obligation is the counterpart of a corresponding right.

The purpose of a contract is to reduce to writing the conditions on which the minds of the parties have met and to fix their rights and duties with respect to those conditions.

Every agreement, whether written or oral, is the result of an offer and the acceptance of that offer.[12] The offer and acceptance must have the characteristics of a bargain. To be enforceable, the parties to a contract must have the legal capacity and mental competence to contract. Further, a contract must have consideration to be binding. Consideration is the price bargained for and paid for a promise to perform. It can be a benefit to the party agreeing to perform, or a loss or detriment to the party to whom the agreement is made.[13]

An ordinary contract involves two parties, the offeror and the offeree. Still, some contracts are drafted in a form wherein performance is rendered to a third party, called a third-party beneficiary. Third-party beneficiaries, who are donee or creditor beneficiaries, normally have enforceable rights under contracts executed by other parties. (Donee beneficiaries are third parties upon whom a gift is conferred by the contract. Creditor beneficiaries have a debt discharged by a contract between two other parties.)

> Example 2. A, an individual, contracted with B that A would contribute $10,000 to Museum X, B's favorite charity, if B would perform certain tasks enumerated in the contract. B performed her obligations under the contract, but A refused to pay the $10,000 to Museum X. Museum X is a donee beneficiary under the contract between A and B and, as such, has an enforceable right against A to collect the $10,000.

The duties and rights of parties to a contract are created by, and arise solely, from the contract. If any essential element of an agreement is not present, the contract is not enforceable. Because a court cannot write a contract for the parties, a court will not enforce a contract that does not contain essential terms. Further, a court will not relieve a party of obligations under a contract because the contract has become difficult to perform although a court may consider the fairness of the agreement in determining rights of the parties. A court will not enforce a contract that offends public morals or that is contrary to public policy. A court construes the terms of a contract according to the law of the location where the contract was executed unless the parties agree otherwise.

> Example 3. History Museum is located in Illinois. It intends to grant a company located in California a license to reproduce and sell its art

objects. The proposed contract specifies that the law of the state of California applies. This may cause problems for the museum should questions arise regarding interpretation of the contract. All provisions will be construed according to California law. The contract also may provide for venue in California. This means that a lawsuit filed to construe the provisions of the contract must be brought in California. The museum director should consider deleting these provisions or requiring that Illinois be substituted for California.

Contracts may be express or implied. An express contract is one wherein the intention of the parties and the terms of the agreement are expressed by the parties, in writing or orally, at the time of the agreement. Implied contracts are those contracts implied in fact or implied in law. Parties may be as firmly bound by implied contracts as by express contracts, aside from requirements of the statute of frauds, discussed below. If there is an express contract, the law will not imply some other agreement. Further, there must be some act or conduct of a party for an implied contract to arise. The essential elements of an implied contract are a benefit conferred on one party by another, recognition of the advantage by the party benefitted, and acceptance and retention of the benefit under circumstances wherein it would be inequitable for the benefited party to retain the advantage without payment of its value. A contract implied in fact is a true contract, the agreement of the parties being inferred from the circumstances, while a contract implied in law is a duty imposed by law and treated as a contract for the purposes of a remedy only.

A party who fails to perform according to the terms of a contract is in "breach" of the contract. A breach of contract is a nonperformance of a party's duty under a contract.

Discharge of performance can occur through impossibility of performance or by "accord and satisfaction." If a party to a contract enters into a different later agreement with the other party, the later agreement is called an "accord." When the party performs the duty under the subsequent agreement, he or she performs the accord; this is called "satisfaction." The satisfaction operates as a discharge of the original contract.

Example 4. Art Museum agreed to pay a stated sum of money to a party in consideration of the party making repairs to the museum building. Art Museum later offered to satisfy the sum of money owed by delivering merchandise of the same value to the other party to the agreement. The other party accepts the subsequent agreement. There is accord. When Art

Museum delivers the merchandise in satisfaction, the original agreement will be discharged.

Article 2 of the Uniform Commercial Code (U.C.C.) of the various states governs the sales and purchases of personal property. Because museum collections are personal property, the commercial code of the states would be applicable to acquisitions and to some deaccessions. A sales contract is an ordinary contract subject to the law relating to contracts; however, the U.C.C. contains a number of provisions that modify the general law of contracts. The U.C.C. adds to sales agreements much that is not expressed by the parties. It imposes obligations of good faith and permits parties to prove "extrinsic" terms. The principal modifications of the general law of contracts brought about by the U.C.C., Article 2, are summarized below.

b. Terms of Sales Agreements

The U.C.C. Article 2 permits less certainty in a contract for the sale and purchase of goods than the common law of contracts. A valid contract for sale is enforceable even though the price is not settled.[14] Conduct by both parties which recognizes the existence of a contract is sufficient to establish a sales contract regardless of whether or not the terms are established.[15] A contract for the sale of goods may be made in any manner sufficient to show agreement, including conduct by both parties that recognizes the existence of a contract.[16] An agreement is sufficient to constitute a contract for sale "even though the moment of its making is undetermined."[17] A definite and "seasonable" expression or acceptance or a written confirmation that is sent within a reasonable time operates as an acceptance even if it states terms additional to, or different from, those offered or agreed upon.[18] Acceptance of an offer to make a contract can be made in any reasonable medium.[19]

c. Statute of Frauds (Requirement That Contracts Be in Writing)

Although Article 2 of the U.C.C.[20] requires contracts for the sale of goods in excess of $5,000 to be in writing, these contracts will be enforceable even though they are not in writing if the goods are manufactured specially for the buyer and are not suitable for sale to others. If the purchaser has received and accepted the goods, a contract need not be in writing to the extent of the goods received and accepted. Further, if the person against whom enforcement is sought admits in pleadings, testimony, or otherwise in court that a contract or sale was made, the contract will be enforceable, even though not in writing, to the extent of the quantity of goods admitted.[21]

d. Rejection of Goods

The purchaser of goods may reject an entire delivery of goods if the goods fail, in any respect, to conform to the contract.[22] The buyer may reject the whole or may accept in part and reject the rest. This right of the buyer is subject to the requirement that the buyer act in good faith and observe reasonable commercial standards of fair dealing in the trade.[23] For goods to be delivered in separate lots, the buyer may reject any installment that is nonconforming if the nonconformity substantially impairs the value of that installment and cannot be cured.[24] If there is a nonconformity that impairs the value of the entire contract, there is a breach of the whole, but the buyer will reinstate the contract if he accepts a nonconforming installment without reasonable notification of cancellation.

e. Risk of Loss

The risk of loss of shipped goods generally remains with the seller until the buyer receives the goods.[25] In the absence of carrier shipment authorization, risk of loss passes to the buyer on the buyer's receipt of the goods if the seller is a merchant; otherwise, risk passes to the buyer on tender of delivery.

f. Warranties

A seller need not give a buyer an express warranty for a guarantee to attach to goods.[26] An affirmation of the value of goods or a statement purporting to be merely the seller's opinion or commendation of the goods does not create a warranty, but any description of the goods that is made a part of the basis of the bargain creates an express warranty that the goods will conform to the description. Any sample or model that is made a part of the agreement creates an express warranty that the whole of the goods will conform to the sample or model. In addition, an affirmation of fact or promise a seller makes to a buyer that relates to the goods and that becomes part of the basis of the bargain creates an express warranty that the goods will conform to the affirmation or promise. A warranty that the goods will be merchantable is implied in a contract of sale if the seller is a merchant as to the goods sold. Words in a contract negating or limiting warranty are given effect.[27] All implied warranties are excluded by expressions such as "with all faults" or "as is." (Warranties are discussed in reference to the purchase of fake artworks in Chapter 5.)

B. TAX ISSUES RELATING TO FUNDING OBTAINED THROUGH DONATIONS

As discussed in Chapter 5, museums receive substantial collections in the form of donations. Museum directors must have some knowledge of the tax law relating to gifts as donors become concerned about tax deductions for their donations. Legal requirements to complete a gift and issues relating to restrictions placed on gift property are discussed in Chapter 5. This chapter reviews the tax requirements relating to the charitable contribution deduction, includes a discussion of the benefits of deferred giving, and reviews the requirements for valuing property donations to museums.

1. Charitable Contribution Deduction

Gifts to charitable organizations that qualify under § 501(c)(3) of the Internal Revenue Code (discussion in Chapter 3) provide the donor with a charitable contribution deduction. For gifts to a museum that qualifies either as a public charity or as a private operating foundation (discussion in Chapter 3), individuals may deduct the amount of cash and the fair market value of property that would produce a long-term capital gain for tax purposes if the property were sold or exchanged. (Property that would produce a long-term capital gain if sold or exchanged is property that qualifies as a capital asset and that has been held by the donor for over a year. A capital asset is investment property, such as stocks and bonds, and property held in a personal context [rather than in a trade or business], such as a personal residence or a personal automobile.) The deduction for property that would not produce a long-term capital gain if sold is limited to the donor's tax basis in the property. (Generally, tax basis would be the donor's cost less any depreciation allowable on the property for tax purposes.) The deduction for gifts of property to private nonoperating foundations generally is limited to the donor's tax basis in the property.[28]

> Example 5. In the current year, an individual donates to History Museum, a public charity, stock that the individual purchased three years ago as an investment. The stock cost $10,000, but is worth $90,000 on the date of the gift. The individual's taxable income before deducting

a charitable contribution for the stock donation, is $400,000.[29] He can claim a charitable contribution deduction on his income tax return of $90,000, the value of the stock.

Example 6. Assume the individual in Example 5 bought the stock only five months before he donated it to the museum. Because he did not hold the stock for over a year, any gain on its sale would be a short-term capital gain. His charitable contribution deduction is limited to the $10,000 cost in the stock.

Example 7. An individual purchased the prints of prominent artists, including Rivers, Lipton, Krasner, Bayer, and Caulfield from Marlborough Gallery at approximately one-sixth of Marlborough's retail-list prices. Marlborough was disposing of some excess inventory representing the middle part of its inventory. It retained a substantial number of copies of the same prints for sale in the regular course of its business, which, over a period of years, almost certainly would have been sold at or about the retail price. The individual held the prints for sixteen months and then donated them to a museum that qualified as a public charity for tax purposes. The cost of the prints was $4,000. The individual contends the prints are worth $50,000. She deducts $50,000 on her income tax return in the year of her donation after obtaining an appraisal from the museum's curator. The IRS would permit a deduction of only $4,000 for the prints. The individual's deduction undoubtedly would be limited to the donor's cost of the prints because cost would be the best estimate of the prints' fair market value. (A further problem is that the museum's curator provided the appraisal. The donor is required to obtain an appraisal from an independent appraiser, as discussed below.)

Example 8. The individual in Example 7 also donated to the museum some Indian artifacts and eagle feathers for which she paid $1,000 two years ago. She deducted $40,000 on her tax return in the year of donation as the alleged fair market value of the artifacts and eagle feathers. The IRS probably would deny any tax deduction for the Indian artifacts and eagle parts. In Sammons v. Comm., 838 F.2d 330 (9th Cir. 1988), the taxpayers deducted $548,380 for their donation of eagle artifacts to the Museum of Native American Cultures. The IRS contended the taxpayers were not entitled to a deduction for donation of the eagle artifacts because the taxpayers could not have obtained title to the artifacts pursuant to the Bald and Golden Eagle Protection Act,[30] the Migratory Bird Treaty Act,[31] and the Endangered Species Act.[32] (These acts are discussed in Chapter 9.) Further, according to the IRS, public policy mandated that the taxpayers be denied a deduction for their contribution. The tax court determined the value of the artifacts on the date of gift to be $140,000, which was the amount the taxpayers paid for the artifacts. The Ninth Circuit Court of Appeals ruled that, although the taxpayers had violated federal law when they purchased the eagle artifacts (discussion in Chapter 9), it did not follow that they did not have title to the artifacts when they donated them to the museum. Further, the Ninth Circuit decided public policy should not prohibit a deduction because the court decided there was no evidence that allowance of the deduction would encourage the acquisition or killing of protected bird species. The Ninth Circuit permitted the deduction but limited the deduction to the taxpayers' cost in the artifacts.[33]

A deduction is not permitted for a gift of a donor's services.[34] A donor also cannot take a charitable contribution deduction for the donation of a right to use the donor's property.[35] A deduction is permitted, however, for any travel expenses incurred in donating one's service to a charity.[36]

Example 9. A donor permits a museum to use rent-free two floors of the donor's office building. Because the donor only transferred a right to use the property, the donor may not deduct the rental value.

An original work of art and a copyright interest in that work are treated as two interests in the same property. As a result, no charitable deduction is permitted for income tax purposes if the donor gives an original work of art but retains the copyright interest.[37] For estate and gift tax purposes, on the other hand, these interests are treated as separate properties;[38] thus, a charitable deduction would be permitted for estate and gift taxes even though the copyright interest was not transferred.

2. Deferred Giving

A museum director may be able to obtain substantial and valuable donations through deferred giving. A donor benefits from deferred giving because the donor who transfers a remainder interest in the donor's property during life to a charity can retain the earnings from the property for life (as well as for a second life, that of a spouse and/or a child, for example), obtain a charitable deduction for income tax purposes in the amount of the value of the remainder interest, and pass the property tax-free upon death without the necessity of probate. The property will pass to the charity immediately upon the death of the income beneficiary or beneficiaries with no probate costs and will pass free of estate tax as the estate will have a charitable deduction for the value of the property passing to the charity. (If the property is donated to a charity by will, the donor receives no income tax deduction for the transfer, only an estate tax deduction.) The benefit to the charity is that it is assured of receiving the property as the donor has made an irrevocable transfer during life. (Donations through a will can be negated because a will can be revoked or amended.) Still, transfers of gift property of less than a donor's entire interest generally will not provide a donor with a charitable contribution deduction unless the transfer is in the form of a charitable remainder annuity trust, a charitable remainder unitrust, or is a transfer to a pooled income fund.[39] Thus, a museum director must have some knowledge of the tax rules governing these types of transfers.

A deduction for a contribution to a charity of an income, remainder, or future interest in property is limited.[40] However, a deduction may be taken for a contribution of an undivided interest in personal property for a portion of a year. Still, when the fractional interest is an art object, a later contribution of the remaining interest is limited to the lesser of the value of the art object on the date of the first donation or the date of the additional contribution.[41]

> Example 10. An individual contributes a painting for which he paid $10,000 several years ago, to a museum but reserves the right to the use, possession, and enjoyment of the painting during his lifetime. The painting is worth $400,000 on the date of the gift. The donor is not entitled to a charitable contribution deduction. However, if the donor had transferred an undivided one-quarter interest in the painting, with the museum being entitled to full possession during three months of each year, the donor would be permitted a charitable contribution deduction of $100,000, which is the value of the one-quarter interest he transferred ($400,000 x 1/4 interest). A problem is that the individual would be required to "recapture" his deduction (report the $100,000 as income plus interest and a ten percent penalty on the additional tax for that reporting year) if the museum did not receive the individual's entire interest in the painting by the earlier of ten years later or the date of the donor's death.[42] Assume the donor donated the remaining three-quarters interest in the painting five years later when the painting was worth $800,000.

> The donor would be limited to an additional contribution deduction of only $300,000, the difference between the value of the painting at the time of the earlier fractional interest contribution (which was $400,000) less the amount of the deduction at that time (which was $100,000). If the painting was worth only $250,000 when the donor contributed his remaining interest, he would be entitled to a deduction of only $150,000 (the $250,000 lesser value at the time of the additional contribution less the earlier deduction of $100,000).

A donor may transfer to a charity a remainder interest in a personal residence and retain an estate in the property for life or for a term of years and be permitted an income charitable contribution deduction for the value of the remainder interest.[43] The residence would pass to the charity free of estate tax as the estate would have a charitable deduction for the value of the residence upon the donor's death. A donor also may take an income tax charitable contribution deduction for the donation of a remainder interest in a farm (and an estate tax charitable deduction) even though the donor retains a life estate or an estate for a term of years.[44]

A deduction is permitted for the value of a qualified conservation contribution if certain requirements are met. A qualified conservation contribution is the donation of a qualified real property interest to a government or a publicly supported charity exclusively for conservation purposes.[45] Conservation purposes include the protection of a relatively natural fish, wildlife, or plant habitat, or similar ecosystem.[46] The preservation of an historically important land area or a certified historic structure is a conservation purpose.[47] Although a deduction is permitted for the value of a qualified conservation interest, donors have not been very successful in taking deductions for conservation easements.

> Example 11. In Minnick v. Comm., T.C.M. 2012-345 (2012), the Tax Court ruled that a taxpayer was not entitled to a deduction for a conservation easement on land on which a bank mortgage existed because the mortgage was not subordinated to the easement when it was granted. The IRS disallowed the deductions because the conservation easement was not protected in perpetuity. Terms of the easement permitted the taxpayer to amend the easement by agreement with the charity donee. Further, the bank's mortgage was not subordinated at the time of the grant. The IRS also determined the easement was overvalued. The taxpayer contended the bank would have been willing to subordinate its

mortgage at the time the easement was granted and that he intended it to be subordinated; however, the court agreed with the IRS that intention and willingness are not what matters. Treasury Regulations[48] require a subordination agreement. The court pointed out that without a subordination agreement, the bank would have been able to seize the land in the event of default on the mortgage, and the land would then be free of the conservation easement. The court agreed with the IRS that the taxpayer should be subject to a § 6662 accuracy-related penalty tax because the taxpayer should have known about the subordination provision in the regulations.

Example 12. In Belk v. Comm., 140 T.C. No. 1, (2013), the Tax Court ruled that a conservation easement agreement, which permitted a taxpayer to change the real property subject to the conservation easement, precluded a charitable contribution deduction. The Tax Court held that I.R.C. § 170(h)(2)(C) prevented the deduction because the taxpayer did not donate an interest in real property subject to a use restriction granted in perpetuity.

Example 13. In Pollard v. Comm., T.C. Memo 2013-038 (2013), the Tax Court affirmed the IRS's disallowance of a charitable contribution deduction for a conservation easement when the IRS showed it was part of a quid pro quo arrangement by which the taxpayer granted the easement in exchange for the granting of his subdivision exemption request from a county.

An estate can take an estate tax exclusion up to $500,000 for donations of qualified conservation easements on land if the donation is made to a "qualified" public charity that is in the conservation or historic preservation field.[49]

A transfer in trust of an income interest, which is less than the donor's entire interest, does not qualify a donor for a charitable contribution deduction unless the transfer is either a guaranteed annuity interest or a unitrust interest and the donor is treated as owner of the trust (so that annual income from the trust is taxed to the donor). Income trusts (with a charitable income interest and a noncharitable remainder beneficiary), which meet the requirements to provide the donor with a charitable contribution deduction for the value of the income interest, are called charitable lead trusts.

A guaranteed annuity lead trust is an arrangement by which a determinable amount is paid periodically, but not less often than annually, for a specified term to a specified charity.[50] A unitrust interest is an irrevocable right of a charity under a trust instrument to receive a variable amount per year based upon a fixed percentage of the net fair market value, determined annually, of trust assets.[51] The deduction for a charitable contribution of a guaranteed annuity interest or of a unitrust interest is limited to the fair market value of the interest on the date of the contribution using tables set out in Treasury publications.[52] The value is computed by subtracting the present value of all interests in the transferred property, other than the guaranteed annuity or unitrust interest, from the fair market value of the transferred property.

> Example 14. An individual with a substantial increase in her taxable income for the current year transferred $100,000 to a museum in the form of a charitable lead annuity trust in which the museum was the trustee and paid itself $10,000 per year for ten years. At the end of ten years, the fund reverted to the donor. The donor had a charitable contribution deduction in the year of transfer, subject to annual percentage limitations,[53] of $61,446 ($100,000 x 0.61446).[54] The donor was taxed on income from the trust. The advantage of the gift was that it funded the donor's long-term charitable pledge to the museum and provided a substantial charitable deduction in the current year when the individual had substantially more income than in previous years or that she expected in future years.

Charitable lead trusts are also called split-interest trusts and are treated as private foundations for tax purposes (discussion of private foundations in Chapter 3). As a result, these trusts are subject to penalty taxes on certain prohibited acts (discussed in Chapter 3).

A donor may not claim a charitable contribution deduction for the value of a remainder interest placed in trust for a charity unless the trust is a charitable remainder trust or a pooled income fund. Charitable remainder trusts and pooled income funds also are called split-interest trusts and are treated as private foundations. As such, they also are subject to penalty taxes on certain prohibited acts.

A charitable remainder trust provides for a specified distribution at least annually to one or more noncharitable beneficiaries for life or for a term of years not exceeding twenty years, with an irrevocable remainder interest held for the benefit of a charity. The specified distribution to be paid at least annually must be a definite sum. For a charitable remainder annuity trust (CRAT), it cannot be less than five percent or more than fifty percent of the initial net fair market value of all property placed in the trust. For a charitable remainder unitrust (CRUT), it cannot be less than five percent or more than fifty percent of the net fair market value of trust assets valued annually. In addition, the value of the remainder interest donated to a charity must be at least ten percent of the initial net fair market value of all property placed in a charitable remainder trust and at least ten percent of the net fair market of the property of a charitable remainder unitrust as of the date property is contributed to the trust.[55]

No amount may be paid to noncharitable income beneficiaries of a charitable remainder trust other than the fixed amount provided for in the trust agreement. There may not be a power to invade, alter, amend, or revoke the trust for the beneficial use of anyone other than the public charity holding the remainder interest. Upon termination of the trust, the property must be transferred to the charity or held for its benefit and use.[56]

The present value of a charitable remainder interest that is a qualified charitable remainder trust for tax purposes is deductible for income, estate, and gift tax purposes.[57]

> Example 15. An individual transferred $100,000 to a museum in the form of a charitable remainder annuity trust in which the donor received $10,000 per year for ten years. At the end of ten years, the property became the property of the museum. The donor was entitled to a charitable contribution deduction in the year of transfer, subject to annual percentage limitations, of $38,554, computed as follows: $100,000 x 0.385543.[58] The trust was not subject to income taxation, but the donor was taxed on the annual payment of $10,000.[59]

A pooled income fund is a trust formed to pay income to one or more noncharitable beneficiaries with the remainder to a public charity. Property transferred by the donor is commingled with the property of others making similar transfers. The trust must be maintained by the donee charity (no donor or income beneficiary may be a trustee).[60] The present value of the remainder interest at the date of transfer of property to the fund is the amount of the charitable contribution deduction.[61] A museum can be the beneficiary of a pooled income fund only if it qualifies as a public charity under § 509(a)(1) of the Internal Revenue Code (discussion of § 509(a)(1) in Chapter 3).[62]

Each income beneficiary in a pooled income fund is assigned a proportionate share of the annual income earned by the fund, the share, or unit of participation, being based on the fair value of the property on the date of transfer. Fair market value of a unit in the fund is determined by fair market value of the property in the fund at that time divided by the number of units then in the fund. The value of each unit of participation will fluctuate with each new transfer of property in relation to the appreciation or depreciation in value of property in the fund, but all units always will have equal value. The share of income allocated to each unit of participation is determined by dividing the income of the fund for the year by the outstanding number of units in the fund at the end of the year. Each income interest must receive income in an amount determined by the rate of return earned by the fund for the year. When an income interest is terminated, the trustee must sever from the fund an amount equal to the value of the remainder interest upon which the income interest was based. The amount so severed either must be paid to, or retained for the use of, the designated public charity.

> Example 16. On January 5, A and B transferred property with a value of $30,000 and $60,000, respectively, to a newly created pooled income fund which was maintained by X Museum. A and B retained for themselves a life income interest, with the remainder donated to X Museum. The pooled income fund assigned an initial value of $100 to each unit of participation in the fund; thus, A received 300 units and B received 600 units. On April 1, C transferred property to the fund with a value of $22,000, retaining a life income interest and contributing the remainder to X Museum. Fair market value of property in the fund on the date of C's transfer was $99,000; consequently, A's and B's units had a value of $110 ($99,000/900). C was assigned 200 units of participation in the fund ($22,000/110).

A pooled income fund provides the donor with a charitable contribution deduction equal to the value of the remainder interest and relieves the donor of any investment responsibilities. The donor also pools his funds with that of others and obtains better investment opportunities.[63] Upon the donor's death, there is no probate cost.

> Example 17. A donor was sixty-five years of age when she transferred $100,000 to a pooled income fund maintained by a museum. The fund had been earning a ten percent return for the past four years. The donor had a charitable contribution deduction in the year of transfer, subject to annual percentage limitations, of $32,030, computed as follows: $100,000 x 0.32030.[64] The donor received income from the fund until

the donor's death at the rate of return earned by the fund for the year. Upon the donor's death, the funds became the property of the museum. Because the donor transferred a remainder interest in the property during her lifetime, the property was not in the donor's estate. Thus, there was no probate cost to the donor's estate or heirs.

3. Valuation

Because the donation of long-term capital gain property to a charity provides the donor with a charitable contribution deduction for the value of the property (discussed above), the valuation of artifacts becomes a major consideration for donors, for the IRS, and for museums. A potential donor may request a museum official to value an object prior to a donation. The ICOM Code of Ethics for Museums[65] permits a museum to provide opinions on the value of objects only pursuant to an official request from other museums or competent legal, governmental, or other responsible public authorities. The ICOM Code of Ethics states that when a museum is the beneficiary of an artifact, appraisal of the object must be undertaken independently. A museum official can utilize this provision in the ICOM Code of Ethics to justify the museum official's refusal to provide a valuation to a potential donor. Still, the official might more effectively refer to federal tax requirements, which do not permit donee appraisals for property donations. A donor cannot obtain a charitable contribution deduction for property donations (other than publicly traded stock) unless the donor obtains an appraisal from a qualified outside third-party appraiser.[66]

Congress became concerned that the value of the property might be claimed falsely or overstated for charitable contribution deductions. To alleviate this possibility and the requirement of auditing independently every charitable donation to verify the amount deducted, there are disclosure requirements for property donations. A donor may not claim a deduction for noncash gifts of more than $500 unless the donor attaches Form 8283 to the donor's tax return. The form requires the donee charity to acknowledge receipt of the gift. Further, if the claimed value of the property (except publicly traded stock) exceeds $5,000, the donor must obtain a written independent appraisal of the property.[67] The appraisal must be made no earlier than sixty days before the date of the contribution and must be received before the due date of the return on which the deduction was first claimed. A separate qualified appraisal is required for each item of property not included in a group of similar items of property.

If a donee charity, or a successor donee, disposes of property for which the donor has claimed a deduction in excess of $5,000, including stock, within three years of receipt, the charity must file Form 8282 with the IRS and furnish to the IRS, with a statement to the donor, the name of the donor, the donor's tax identification number, a description of the property, date of the contribution, amount received on disposition of the property, and date of disposition.[68]

The IRS has published guidelines for making appraisals of donated properties, such as art objects, literary manuscripts, and antiques.[69] Facts bearing on value are cost, selling price of the item, sales of comparable properties, cost of reproduction, opinion evidence, and appraisals. The weight to be given to opinion evidence depends on its origin and the thoroughness with which it is supported by experience and facts. Only where expert opinion is supported by facts having strong probative value will the opinion be given appropriate weight. The underlying facts must corroborate the opinion. If they do not, the opinion will be discounted or disregarded. The IRS requests that the following information be included in an appraisal: (1) complete description of the object, indicating size, subject matter, medium, name of the artist, approximate date of creation, and interest transferred; (2) cost, date, and manner of acquisition; (3) history of the item, including proof of authenticity; (4) photograph of a size and quality that would permit full identification of the subject matter; and (5) statement of the factors upon which the appraisal was based, such as sales of other works by the same artist, quoted prices in dealer's catalogues of the artist's works, the economic state of the art market at or around the time of valuation, record of any exhibitions at which the particular art object has been displayed, and statement as to standing of the artist in the profession and in the particular school or time period.[70]

The IRS does not accord recognition to any appraiser or group of appraisers to the extent of accepting their appraisals without question.[71] The IRS uses members of an art advisory panel to perform the public service of advising the IRS concerning values that taxpayer-donors give to particular works of art. Members of this panel are art museum directors, curators, scholars, art dealers, auction representatives, and appraisers.[72] This art advisory panel is managed by Art Appraisal Services (AAS), which provides advice and assistance to the IRS and other governmental agencies on valuation questions. Employees with the IRS must refer to the AAS donations that involve a taxpayer's appraisal of $50,000 or more for a single work of art as well as for historical memorabilia.[73]

Example 18. The IRS has ruled that the best evidence of fair market value depends on actual transactions and not on some artificially calculated estimate of value contrary to the prices at which the items changed hands in the marketplace. In Rev. Rul. 80-69, 1980-1 C.B. 55, a taxpayer-donor purchased an assortment of gems for $500x from a promoter who advised him the price was wholesale and that he would be entitled to a deduction of $1500x should he donate the gems to charity. When the taxpayer later donated the gems to a museum, the IRS ruled that his deduction would be limited to $500x.

Example 19. The Tax Court limited a deduction for gifts of African art objects to a charitable organization to the appraised value as established by the IRS in Neely v. Comm., 85 T.C. 934 (1985). The taxpayer-donor was assessed negligence penalties and additional interest for substantial underpayment of income taxes. In Lio v. Comm., 85 T.C. 56 (1985), the Tax Court limited a deduction for a limited edition lithograph donated to a charitable organization to cost of the lithograph.

Example 20. The Tax Court permitted an individual a charitable contribution deduction of $311,000 for the donation to the National Museum of American History of a gold coin, gold disk, and gold chain recovered from the Spanish galleon the *Nuestra Señora de Atocha*. In Perdue v. Comm., TC Memo 1991-478, 62 TCM 845 (1991), the Tax Court rejected the IRS's lower valuation of $74,000. It disagreed with the IRS that the numismatic market, rather than auction or museum sales markets where premiums are paid for the aura of an artifact, was the proper market to determine fair market value.

Example 21. An individual donated an alleged Charles Russell, for which he had paid $10,000 to a museum and claimed a $250,000 charitable contribution deduction on his income tax return in Doherty v. Comm., 16 F.3d 338 (9th Cir. 1994). The IRS contended the painting was worth only $100 because authenticity was in doubt. The Tax Court had permitted a deduction of $30,000. The Ninth Circuit Court of Appeals court ruled that a challenge to the authenticity of a painting would lower the fair market value at the time of the contribution even though the painting's authenticity was questioned later, after the gift was made. The Ninth Circuit agreed with the Tax Court's valuation of $30,000.

An estate's possession of an artwork that was stolen presents problems in that the IRS undoubtedly will require an estate tax valuation that does not include a discounted value because the work was stolen. A theft victim could later bring a successful claim to recover the artwork after the statute of limitations has run on a recovery of any estate tax paid on the artwork.

> Example 22. The IRS discussed the inclusion of stolen artifacts in an estate in TAM 9152005 (1991) and ruled that art objects a decedent stole during and immediately after World War II, which the decedent possessed at his death, were included in the decedent's gross estate pursuant to § 2033 of the Internal Revenue Code. The IRS further ruled that even though the artifacts were, under most circumstances, transferrable only in an illicit market, the appropriate market for establishing value included the discreet retail markets of the international network of traffickers in stolen art as well as the legitimate retail art markets consisting of international auction firms, advertised displays in antiques publications, and legitimate art and antiques dealers.[74] The IRS also ruled that the estate could not take a deduction under § 2053(a)(3) of the Code for claims brought by persons from whom the art objects were stolen.

4. Disclosure Requirements

A donor must substantiate charitable contributions in excess of $250. Because a donor is not permitted a charitable contribution deduction for gifts to a charity in excess of $250 if the donor does not have written acknowledgment of the contribution from the donee organization, a donee museum must acknowledge all donations to it in excess of $250. The written acknowledgment from the donee museum must state (1) the amount of cash and a description of property other than cash contributed, (2) whether the museum provided any goods or services in return for the contributed property, and (3) a description and good-faith estimate of the value of any goods or services provided the donor by the donee museum.[75]

Charitable organizations also must inform donors that quid pro quo contributions in excess of $75 are deductible only to the extent the contribution exceeds the value of goods or services provided the donor by the donee organization.[76] The donee organization must give the donor a written statement that informs the donee of the amount of the contribution deductible for income tax purposes and states that the deduction is limited to the excess of the amount of any money and value of any property contributed over the value of goods and services provided by the donee organization. A donee organization also must furnish a donor with a good-faith estimate of the value of the goods or services it will give the donor.[77]

C. UNRELATED BUSINESS TAXABLE INCOME

A museum that earns income through commercial activities which are unrelated to the museum's exempt purposes will be subject to income tax liability in the same manner as are taxable organizations. The theory for taxation is that an unrelated business activity distorts exempt purposes of the organization and is a form of unfair competition to taxable organizations. The fact that profits from an unrelated business are used by an exempt organization to perform its charitable functions has no bearing on whether an unrelated business activity is taxed.

A museum (or a supporting organization) that has "unrelated business taxable income" in excess of $1,000 must file Form 990T by the fifteenth day of the fifth month following the close of its year and pay tax on that income. Tax liability on unrelated business income is computed in the same manner as for a taxable entity. If the museum is incorporated, it will be taxed at corporate rates. If it is a trust, it will be taxed in the same manner as a taxable trust.[78]

A museum's taxable income is determined by computing the museum's net income from the following sources: (1) an unrelated trade or business, (2) net rentals from personalty, (3) a part of any net investment income from a controlled organization, and (4) a percentage of net income from any "debt-financed" properties.

1. Income from an Unrelated Trade or Business

A museum will be taxed on any income it derives from an "unrelated trade or business." "Unrelated business taxable income" is defined as gross income derived from any unrelated trade or business, regularly carried on, less deductions directly connected with carrying on the trade or business. An "unrelated trade or business" is one in which the conduct of transactions is not related substantially to the exercise or performance of an organization's charitable purposes.[79]

a. Not Substantially Related to a Museum's Charitable Purposes

Determining whether the activities of a museum are "substantially" related to a museum's charitable purposes necessitates an examination of the relationship between the museum's income-generating activities and the accomplishment of the museum's exempt purposes. A trade or business is related to a nonprofit organization's exempt purposes only where conduct of a venture has a causal relationship to the achievement of the organization's exempt purposes. The causal relationship must be substantial.[80]

Example 23. A museum sells reproductions of objects from the museum's collections. The sales have a causal relationship to the museum's exempt purpose. They are related to the educational purposes of the museum and will not be taxed.

Example 24. An art museum sells pottery, children's books, toys, and other gifts, especially during holidays. The sales are not related to the museum's educational purposes and will be taxed.

b. Business Regularly Carried On

A trade or business from which income is derived is taxed only if it is "regularly carried on." In determining whether a business is regularly carried on, the frequency and continuity with which activities for the production of income are conducted and the manner in which they are pursued are considered. Activities will be conducted regularly if they manifest a sequence and continuity and are pursued in a manner similar to comparable commercial activities of taxable organizations. Activities normally conducted on a year-round basis will not be regularly carried on if an exempt organization engages in the activities for only a few weeks. However, where activities are undertaken generally by a commercial business only on a seasonable basis, conduct of these activities by an exempt organization during a significant portion of the season would constitute regular conduct of the trade or business.[81]

Example 25. A museum's operation of a sandwich stand for three weeks at a state fair would not be the regular conduct of a trade or business. However, operation of a year-round business activity for one day each week, such as a museum's operation of a commercial parking lot on Saturday of each week, would constitute the regular carrying on of a trade or business.

c. Exploitation of a Museum's Exempt Function

A tax exempt organization may use an asset or facility necessary for the conduct of its exempt functions in a commercial context. Income from the added use of the assets or facility would be income from an unrelated trade or business.[82]

Example 26. A museum has a theater auditorium specially designed and equipped for showing of educational films in connection with its program of public education in the arts and sciences. The theater is used in the evenings as an ordinary motion picture theater for public entertainment. Income from operation of the theater in the evenings would be income from an unrelated trade or business.

An exempt organization may generate goodwill or a reputation that would be capable of being exploited in commercial endeavors. Unless commercial activities generated by exploiting the organization's exempt purposes contribute importantly to the accomplishment of an exempt purpose, any income from these activities is income from an unrelated trade or business.

Example 27. An art museum has an excellent reputation in the arts. It exploits its reputation by selling endorsements of various artifacts and artworks. The endorsements do not contribute importantly to the museum's accomplishment of its exempt purpose; thus, income from the endorsements would be income from an unrelated business.

2. Specific Exclusions from Unrelated Trade or Business

Certain activities are specifically excluded from the definition of an unrelated trade or business so that income from such ventures is not subject to tax. Excluded activities are (1) a trade or business in which substantially all work in carrying on the business is performed for the organization without compensation, i.e., by volunteers; (2) a trade or business carried on by a charitable organization primarily for convenience of its members, students, guests, officers, or employees; and (3) a trade or business that consists of selling donated merchandise.

3. Gift Shops

Operation of a gift shop can cause unrelated business taxable income. Sales of items in a gift shop must have a causal relationship to an organization's exempt purposes to be considered a related activity. Determination is made on an item-by-item basis. Sales of items that relate to the organization's exempt purposes would not be taxed.[83] Sales of other items that do not contribute importantly to the organization's exempt purposes would be taxed. In addition, sales of items related to a museum's exempt function that have been converted into some other object will be taxed.[84] Still, if a gift shop is managed and operated by volunteers, none of the sales will be taxed.

Example 28. An art museum sells in its gift shop reproductions of objects from its collections and greeting cards displaying printed reproductions of artworks in its collection. These sales would be from a related activity and income from the sales would not be taxed.[85] In Rev. Rul. 73-105, 1973-1 C.B. 264, the IRS ruled that sale of reproductions of objects from a museum's collections and reproductions of works related to a specific type of museum, such as artistic works for art museums and historical works for historical museums, would not be an unrelated trade or business. The card sales provide a broader segment of the public with a knowledge of the arts and of the museum and, thus, more interest in visiting the museum and sharing in its educational program.

Example 29. The art museum in Example 28 also sells scientific books and souvenir objects of the city as well as miscellaneous items, such as toothpaste, paper, pencils, cosmetics, etc. These sales are not related to the museum's exempt purposes, and income from the sales would be taxed. However, if all work in the gift shop is performed by volunteers, the sales would not be taxed. In PLR 8149054, the IRS ruled that operation of an art gallery by an exempt art center was not an unrelated trade or business because work was performed by volunteers.

Example 30. An art museum sells souvenir objects of the city and imprints its museum logo on the items. Imprinting of the logo on the item will not cause income from the sales to be exempt from taxation.[86]

Example 31. A museum that displays objects from the ocean converts the objects into jewelry to be sold in its gift shop. The sales will be taxed.[87]

Example 32. A "living museum," from which visitors could experience a semblance of daily life from a historical period and which operated an art gallery, was selling books, tapes, records, films, toys, food, and compact discs. Some of its products were sold to museums and schools. In PLR 9550003, the IRS ruled that toys, games, and food products that were related to the educational topics of the museum would not be taxed. It also ruled that engraving and gift-wrapping services which portrayed objects in the collection contributed to the museum's exempt purposes. It decided that Christmas tree gift-wrap sets and ornaments not depicting items in the museum's collections would be taxed, but it ruled that sales of souvenirs that "borrow in design" from items in the museum collections, such as key rings, shot glasses, spoons, and thimbles, would not be taxed. The IRS decided that note cards, calendars, napkins, and paper plates that depicted works in the museum collection would be exempt from taxation. However, it ruled that items that are "interpretations of museum works," such as furniture, dinnerware, silverware, jewelry, and coasters, were not related to the organization's exempt purposes and would be taxed. It decided that reproductions of artifacts in the museum's collections were related to the organization's exempt purposes and that film, batteries, ponchos, and umbrellas were sold for the convenience of visitors and would not be taxed. Sales of "contemporary products" and products sold in retail establishments, such as cigarettes, golf clothing, newspapers, prepackaged foods, and toiletries, would be taxed. The museum sold through retail, wholesale, and mail-order outlets. The IRS concluded that selling off-site would not cause sales to be taxed because the sales helped enhance the public's understanding of topics addressed in the museum and also would encourage buyers to visit the museum.

Example 33. An art museum sold items that developed a child's artistic abilities. In PLR 9720002, the IRS ruled these sales were related substantially to the museum's educational purposes but ruled that sales of other children's items, such as baby play gyms, tot blocks, fruit and vegetable playsets, and animal-shape wagons, which generally develop a child's motor skills, were not related and would be taxed.

4. Snack Bar and Cafeteria

A museum's operation of a snack bar, cafeteria, or coffee shop will not be an unrelated business activity if the operation is for the convenience of the museum's staff, members, employees, and visitors.[88]

Example 34. A museum operates a restaurant that is open to the public. It advertises the restaurant monthly in a local magazine and provides the general public access to the restaurant. In PLR 9720002, the IRS ruled, on facts similar to these, that a museum would be taxed on sales to customers who did not pay the museum admission fee.

5. Parking Lot

A museum's operation of a parking lot is not taxed if the museum is operating the parking lot for the convenience of its staff, members, employees, and visitors. If a parking lot is operated for the general public, income from its operation will be taxed.[89]

6. Travel Tours

Income from travel tours will be taxed if a museum works with a travel agency that pays the museum on a fee-per-person basis. On the other hand, study tours led by staff members that combine daily lectures and related classroom studies have been held to be educational in nature and, thus, not an unrelated trade or business.

> Example 35. History Museum develops travel tours for persons who are interested in learning of the geography and culture of the United States. One tour is a study tour to national parks and to historical monuments. The study tours are conducted by museum professionals and are open to all who agree to participate in the required study program. The study program consists of college-level courses related to the location visited by the tour and requires that certain hours be devoted to organized study, preparation of reports, and recitation by the students. The tour program is not an unrelated business, and proceeds from the tours would not be taxed.

> Example 36. A museum develops a travel tour program for its members. None of the tours include scheduled instruction or curricula related to the destinations being visited. The tour program is an unrelated trade or business, and proceeds from the tours will be taxed.

> Example 37. A scientific organization that is engaged in environmental research is exempt from federal income tax as an organization described in § 501(c)(3). The organization is engaged in a long-term study of how agricultural pesticide and fertilizer use affects the populations of various bird species. It collects data at several bases located in an important

agricultural region of a particular country. The minutes of a meeting of the organization's board of directors state that, after study, the board has determined that nonscientists can perform reliably needed data collection in the field under supervision of the organization's biologists. Board minutes reflect that the board approved offering one-week trips to the organization's bases in a particular country, where participants will assist the organization's biologists in collecting data for the study. Tour participants collect data during the same hours as the organization's biologists. Normally, data collection occurs during the early morning and evening hours, although the work schedule varies by season. Each base has rustic accommodations and few amenities, but the country is renowned for its beautiful scenery and abundant wildlife. The organization promotes the trips in its newsletter and on its Internet site and through various conservation organizations. The promotional material describes the work schedule and emphasizes the valuable contribution made by trip participants to the organization's research activities. Treas. Reg. § 1.513-7 states that based on the facts and circumstances, sponsoring trips to the organization's bases in the particular country is an activity substantially related to the organization's exempt purpose and, thus, does not constitute an unrelated trade or business within the meaning of § 513(a).

Example 38. An educational organization devoted to the study of ancient history and cultures and exempt from federal income tax as an organization described in § 501(c)(3) conducts archaeological expeditions around the world, including in a particular region in a foreign country, in connection with its educational activities. In cooperation with the national museum of this country, the educational organization recently presented an exhibit on ancient civilizations of that particular region in the foreign country, including artifacts from the collection of the national museum. The educational organization instituted a program of travel tours to the country's archaeological sites located in the particular region. The tours were proposed initially by the educational organization's staff members as a means of educating the public about ongoing field research the organization conducted. It engaged a travel agency to handle logistics, such as accommodations and transportation arrangements. In preparation for the tours, the educational organization developed educational materials relating to each archaeological site to be visited on the tour, describing in detail the layout of the site, the methods used by its researchers in exploring the site, the discoveries made at the site, and their historical significance. The educational organization also arranged special guided tours of its exhibit in that particular region of the foreign country for individuals registered for the travel tours. Two archaeologists from the educational organization (both of whom had participated in prior archaeological expeditions in the particular region of the foreign country) accompanied the tours. These experts led guided tours of each site and explained the significance of the sites to tour participants. At several of the sites, tour participants also met with a working team of archaeologists from the educational organization and the national museum, who shared their experiences. The educational organization prepared promotional materials describing the educational nature of the tours, including the daily trips to its archaeological sites and the educational background of tour leaders, and provided a recommended reading list. The promotional materials did not refer to any particular recreational or sightseeing activities. Based on the facts and circumstances, sponsoring trips to that particular region in the foreign country is an activity substantially related to the educational organization's exempt purposes. The scheduled activities, which include tours of archaeological sites led by experts, are part of a coordinated educational program designed to educate tour participants about the ancient history of that particular region in the foreign country and the educational organization's ongoing field research. In an example, with facts similar to this example, Treasury Regulations[90] stated that the educational organization's tour program did not constitute an unrelated trade or business.

7. Sale of Artworks

A museum's sale of artworks generally is taxed. An art museum's exempt function of educating the public by displaying original works of art for public appreciation is not met if the artworks are sold. Selling artworks obviously removes them from public display.[91]

Example 39. An art museum wants to give recognition to local artists. It permits the artists to exhibit and to sell their works as part of an exhibit of the works of local artists. The museum receives a commission from the sales. The IRS ruled in PLR Rul. 8634001 that, in the limited circumstances where a sales gallery is not advertised, when selection for exhibit and sale is based on criteria emphasizing quality and educational merit of the works, when works displayed are of relatively unknown artists who displayed their works locally and thereby expose area residents to a broader variety of art, and when works are selected by a committee based on quality and professionalism of the work rather than on potential for profit, the museum would not be taxed on commissions from the sale.

8. Fund-Raising Activities

Fund-raising activities are excepted from unrelated business status because they generally are not regularly carried on, are usually conducted by volunteers, and often involve the sale of donated merchandise.

9. Income from Advertising

As a general rule, proceeds from an exempt organization's sale of advertising in a periodical or other publication will constitute income from an unrelated trade or business activity involving exploitation of the organization's exempt activities. The amount of unrelated business taxable income is the sum of the net advertising income less any circulation loss.[92]

> Example 40. A museum conducts an intensive advertising solicitation campaign for a number of months. The advertising would be "regularly carried on" and the proceeds would be taxed.

> Example 41. Volunteers for a museum sell advertising over a period of two months to raise funds. Proceeds from the advertising would not be taxed because volunteers sold the ads.[93]

10. Income from Sponsorships

Income from sponsorships is taxed as income from advertising unless amounts received from the sponsorships constitute "qualified" sponsorship payments.[94] A "qualified sponsorship payment" is a payment received by a tax exempt organization from a person engaged in a trade or business when there is no substantial return benefit to the payor other than the use or "acknowledgment" of the name or logo of the payor's business.[95] To be a qualified sponsorship payment, there can be no arrangement or expectation that the payor will receive any substantial return benefit other than the use or acknowledgment of the name or logo (or product lines) of the payor's trade or business in connection with the activities of the payee charity. This use or acknowledgment does not include advertising the payor's products or services (including messages containing qualitative or comparative language, price information, or other indications of savings or value; an endorsement; or an inducement to purchase, sell, or use such products or services). In addition, a qualified payment cannot be contingent upon the level of attendance at certain events, broadcast ratings, or other factors indicating the degree of public exposure to one or more events. The payment cannot include entitlement of the payor to the use or acknowledgment of the payor's name or logo in regularly scheduled and printed material published by or on behalf of the payee charity that is not related to and primarily distributed in connection with a specific event conducted by the payee charity.

> Example 42. An art museum organizes an exhibition and receives a large payment from a corporation to help fund the exhibition. The museum recognizes the corporation's support by using the corporate name and established logo in materials publicizing the exhibition, including banners, posters, brochures, and public service announcements. The museum also hosts a dinner for the corporation's executives. The Treasury[96] stated, in an example with similar facts, that a museum's use of the corporate name and logo in connection with the exhibition constituted acknowledgment of the sponsorship and, thus, was not a substantial return benefit. However, the Treasury also stated that the dinner for corporate executives was a substantial return benefit because the value of the dinner exceeded two percent of the total payment; only that portion, if any, of the payment that exceeded the fair market value of the dinner could be a qualified sponsorship payment.

11. Trade Shows

Conventions or trade show and public entertainment activities are not treated as unrelated trades or businesses for § 501(c)(3) organizations.[97]

12. Income from Investments

As a general rule, income from investments is not unrelated business taxable income. Thus, dividends, interest, annuities, royalties, as well as gains from the sale, exchange, or other disposition of investment property, normally are not taxed.

a. Rental Income

Except for rents from debt-financed property or from property rented to controlled organizations (see discussion below), rents from real property are not taxed.[98] Rents from personal property generally are taxed.

Rents from personal property are taxed unless the personal property is leased with real property and the rents attributable to the personal property are an incidental amount of the total rents received.[99] Rents attributable to personal property are an incidental amount if rents are ten percent or less of total rents from leased property. The percentage is determined at the time the lessee first places personal property in service. In addition, rents from real property will not be excluded from unrelated business income if more than fifty percent of total rents received are attributable to personal property, determined at the time the personal property is first placed in service.[100]

If an exempt organization renders special services to lessees, payments for occupancy do not constitute rent from real property and will be taxed. Services are rendered to a lessee if they are primarily for the lessee's convenience and are other than those normally rendered in connection with the rental of property for occupancy only.[101]

> Example 43. A museum leases a theater in its building for catered parties, meetings, wedding receptions, and other such events. The museum provides bartending and other personal services at these events. Although the rent is from real property, the income generated from leasing the theater would be taxed because special services are rendered.[102]

> Example 44. A museum rents an antique tea service to a local organization for use at a reception. The income from leasing the tea service would be subject to tax. It is income from personal property.

b. Royalty Income

Royalty income is excluded from the unrelated business tax. A museum director may decide to market objects that are not related to its collection. Because the objects are not reproductions of artifacts in the museum collection, the museum will be taxed on sales of the objects. However, the museum can enter into a licensing agreement with another organization and receive royalty income from sales. A museum will generally not be taxed on royalties it receives from licensing agreements with other companies (discussion of licensing agreements above). However, the licensee must be an independent contractor and not an agent of the museum. To be royalty income, the licensee should bear the risk of loss. The licensor, the museum, should not make capital contributions or control the income. However, a museum's retention of quality control rights in the licensing arrangement will not cause the royalty income to be taxed.[103] Retaining the right to require a licensee to refrain from engaging in any activity that would affect adversely the exempt licensor's reputation also would not cause royalty income to be taxed. However, if a museum's members or staff make personal appearances to endorse products or services of the licensee, payment for services are payments for personal services and will be taxed.

Example 45. A history museum sells art objects that are not reproductions of any of the museum's collections. Income from such sales would be taxed. However, if the museum enters into a licensing agreement and has the licensee sell the objects and pay the museum a royalty on the sales, the museum will not have taxable income.

Example 46. A museum rents its member lists for a fee to other charitable organizations. In Sierra Club, Inc. v. Comm., 86 F.3d 1526 (9th Cir. 1996), the Ninth Circuit Court of Appeals decided that income from rental of member lists was "passive" and did not constitute compensation for services rendered. In Common Cause v. Comm., 112 T.C. 332 (1999) and Planned Parenthood Federation of America v. Comm., T.C. Memo 1999-206, the courts decided that an organization's master and rental lists were intangibles in which the organization had ownership rights. If an organization does not engage directly in any significant activities with regard to rental list transactions, the courts stated the income from the sale of its mailing list would be royalty income and would not be taxed.

Example 47. A museum has a joint venture for an affinity card arrangement with a credit card company wherein the museum will receive income from the credit card company when it receives payments on credit cards that depict the museum's name and logo. Courts have ruled that such affinity card income is royalty income and, thus, is not taxed.[104]

13. Income from a Controlled Organization

Although investment income generally is not taxed, a portion of interest, annuities, royalties, or rents derived from an organization controlled by a tax exempt organization will be included in unrelated business taxable income.[105] Dividends received from a controlled organization are not taxed, however.

"Control" of an organization is stock ownership of more than fifty percent, in vote or value, and ownership of more than fifty percent of the profits or capital interests of a partnership or more than fifty percent ownership of any beneficial interest in any other entities. In a nonstock organization, control means that more than fifty percent of the directors or trustees are either representatives of, or are directly or indirectly controlled by, the tax exempt organization.[106]

The amount of income that is unrelated business taxable income to the controlling organization depends on whether the controlled organization also is tax exempt or is a for-profit organization. If the controlled organization is tax exempt, the amount of business taxable income is the amount a payment to a controlling organization reduces the unrelated business taxable income of the controlled organization. If the controlled organization is a for-profit entity, the amount of taxable income is the portion of the controlled organization's taxable income that would reduce its unrelated business taxable income if it were tax exempt.

14. Income from Unrelated Debt-Financed Property

A percentage of income from a tax exempt organization's debt-financed property is taxed to prevent a for-profit organization from using the exempt status of a nonprofit organization to shield income from taxation (by buying a business through debt financing, then selling it to a tax exempt organization but subsequently leasing it back from the tax exempt organization, with the tax exempt organization paying off the purchase price debt through nontaxable rent income). Income from a tax exempt organization's debt-financed property is taxed in proportion to the amount of acquisition debt on the property. Debt-financed property is property that is not used to perform a tax exempt organization's exempt purposes and that is subject to acquisition indebtedness.[107]

The portion of income from the property that is subject to tax is called unrelated debt-financed income. Gain on the sale of debt-financed property is taxed. The amount of the taxable income is determined by multiplying net income from the property by a percentage, computed by dividing "average acquisition indebtedness" on the property by "average adjusted basis" of the property. The percentage is called the debt/basis percentage.

a. Average Acquisition Indebtedness

Acquisition indebtedness is the unpaid amount of any indebtedness incurred by an exempt organization in acquiring or improving debt-financed property.[108] Average acquisition indebtedness is the average amount of acquisition indebtedness on unrelated property for a specific year, except that for purposes of computing gain or loss on the sale of the property, it is the highest amount of acquisition indebtedness during the twelve-month period ending on the date of the sale or other disposition.

Average acquisition indebtedness is computed by determining the amount of the outstanding principal indebtedness on the first day in each calendar month during a year in which the organization has the property, adding these amounts together, and dividing the sum by the total number of months the organization held the property during the year.

Example 48. A museum purchased a building that was not used to perform its exempt purposes on June 1 of the current year. The building cost $510,000, with $300,000 of the purchase price being paid with borrowed funds. The museum made payments of $21,000 per month ($20,000 attributable to principal and $1,000 to interest) on its purchase money loan. The average acquisition indebtedness for the year is $250,000, computed as follows: Indebtedness is calculated on the first day of each calendar month the property is held. These amounts are then totaled as noted below:

July	$300,000
August	280,000
September	260,000
October	240,000
November	220,000
December	200,000
	$1,500,000

Average acquisition indebtedness is $250,000 ($1,500,000 divided by 6 months).

b. Average Adjusted Basis

Average adjusted basis of debt-financed property is the average amount of the adjusted basis (generally cost less depreciation) of the property during the portion of the year the property is held by the tax exempt organization.[109] It is the average of the adjusted basis of the property as of the first day during the taxable year the organization holds the property and the adjusted basis on the last day during a year that the organization holds the property.

Example 49. The museum in Example 48 claimed depreciation on the building of $27,000 for the year. The average adjusted basis of the building would be $506,500, computed as follows: Beginning basis (cost) of $510,000 plus ending basis of $503,000 (which is cost [$510,000] less depreciation [$27,000] divided by 2). (The average acquisition indebtedness is divided by the average adjusted basis of the property to determine the debt/basis percentage.)

c. Debt/Basis Percentage and Taxable Income

Example 50. Average acquisition indebtedness on the building the museum in Example 48 purchased was $250,000. Average adjusted basis, as computed in Example 49, was $506,500. Thus, the debt/basis percentage would be forty-nine percent (average acquisition indebtedness/average adjusted basis = $250,000/$506,500).

Example 51. Assume the museum receives net rental income of $30,000 from the building. Of this amount, $14,700 ($30,000 x 49 percent) would be debt-financed income. The $14,700 would be offset by forty-nine percent of the expenses directly incurred with respect to the building to determine the net rental income that would be taxed. Assume expenses directly incurred with respect to the building total $10,000. Of this amount, $4,900 ($10,000 x 49 percent) would be a deduction from the $14,700 so that $9,800 ($14,700 - $4,900) would be the amount of debt-financed income taxed to the museum.

NOTES

1. Pub. L. 89-209, the National Foundation on the Arts and the Humanities Act of 1965.

2. 20 U.S.C. § 953. See discussion of the selection process in the funding for art projects as it relates to an artist's freedom of expression in Chapter 7.

3. See Arts, Humanities and Museums Amendments of 1985, Pub. L. No. 99-104, 2 U.S.C.C.A.N 1055, 1058 (1985). Financial assistance was provided for professionally directed, community-based or emerging organizations, and organizations that have historic origins in, and are reflective of, the culture of a minority, inner city, rural, or tribal community.

4. 20 U.S.C. §§ 9102 and 9171.

5. 20 U.S.C. § 9105a.

6. Id. at § 9173. The federal share of the costs cannot be more than fifty percent.

7. The forms also are accessible through the website for GuideStar, which is a § 501(c)(3) organization that collects information relating to nonprofit organizations, including annual returns filed with the IRS (Form 990 and Form 990PF).

8. See, e.g., Thomas v. Collins, 323 U.S. 516 (1943); National Foundation v. City of Fort Worth, 425 F.2d 41 (5th Cir. 1969); and Stretch v. Pennsylvania Comm. on Charitable Organizations, 579 F. Supp. 172 (M.D. Pa. 1984).

9. Secretary of State of Maryland v. Joseph H. Munson Co., Inc., 467 U.S. 947 (1984). See also Schaumburg v. Citizens for a Better Environment, 444 U.S. 620 (1980).

10. In Illinois, ex rel. Madigan v. Telemarketing Associates, Inc. 538 U.S. 600 (2003), the Supreme Court ruled the Illinois Attorney General stated a valid claim against a nonprofit organization that retained at least eighty-five percent of funds it collected allegedly to aid Vietnam veterans. The nonprofit falsely stated to potential donors that a significant amount of each dollar they donated to the charity would be used for specifically identified charitable endeavors. The Court decided there clearly was fraud when one potential donor asked what percentage of her contribution would be used for fund-raising expenses and was told that ninety percent or more would go to the vets.

11. A computation of net profit depends upon accounting principles and concepts. It is subject to varied interpretations. For example, there may be a dispute as to whether depreciation is included as a deduction in arriving at net profit. If so, the method of computing depreciation—straight line, accelerated, or some other method—may also be disputable. (Accelerated depreciation generally, initially at least, will produce a much lower book net profit than would the straight-line method.) There may be alternative methods to account for other expenses and costs (and one method may produce a lower book net profit than another).

12. Restatement, Contracts 2d. § 22.

13. Id. at § 71.

14. U.C.C. § 2-204(3). Section 2-204(3) provides for the enforceability of contracts even though one or more terms is left open if the parties intended to make a contract and there is a reasonably certain basis for giving an appropriate remedy.

15. Id. at § 2-207(3).

16. Id. at § 2-204(1).

17. Id. at § 2-204(2).

18. Id. at § 2-207(1).

19. Id. at § 2-206(1).

20. Id. at § 2-201.

21. Id. at § 2-201(3).

22. Id. at § 2-601.

23. Id. at § 2-103(1)(b).

24. Id. at § 2-612.

25. Id. at § 2-509(1).

26. Id. at § 2-313.

27. Id. at § 2-316.

28. As noted in Chapter 3, there is an exception for some gifts of stock to a private nonoperating foundation. A donor may deduct the fair market value of qualified appreciated stock, which is stock for which market quotations are readily available on an established securities market. A gift of stock must be less than ten percent of the value of all outstanding stock in the corporation. The ten percent limitation applies to the aggregate amount of

donations by a donor (including spouse, siblings, ancestors, and lineal descendants) to all private nonoperating foundations. I.R.C. § 170(e)(5).

29. There is an annual limitation on gifts of long-term capital gain property to public charities and private operating foundation of thirty percent of an individual's adjusted gross income. In the example, thirty percent of $400,000 would $120,000; thus, the individual could deduct the entire $90,000 in the year of the donation. Discussion of these limitations in note 64 in Chapter 3.

30. 16 U.S.C. §§ 668–668d.

31. 16 U.S.C. §§ 703–11.

32. 16 U.S.C. §§ 1531–43.

33. See discussion in Anne-Marie Rhodes, 31 *Cardozo Arts & Entertainment Law Journal* 45 (2012) of issues relating to the estate valuation of a three-dimensional work of art by Robert Rauschenberg, a "sculptural combine" called *Canyon*, that contained a stuffed bald eagle with its wings fully extended outward from the bottom of the canvas. The *Canyon* was one of the works of art, which were valued at $800 million, in the estate of art dealer and collector Ileana Sonnabend, who died in 2007. Because selling *Canyon* would subject the seller and the purchaser to criminal prosecution under the Bald and Golden Eagle Protection Act (BGEPA) and the Migratory Bird Treaty Act, the estate contended *Canyon* had no value for estate tax purposes. However, the IRS Art Advisory Panel valued *Canyon* at $65 million. The IRS accepted this valuation because it contended the work could be sold on the illicit market and issued a deficiency notice against the estate for $29.2 million in estate taxes plus $11.7 million in penalties.

It is interesting that the IRS contended in the Sammons case, discussed in Example 8, that a donation of eagle feathers would have no value for income purposes because a purchase of the eagle parts would violate the BGEPA. The IRS contended the donor could not claim a charitable contribution deduction as the eagle feathers could not be sold, but the IRS also took the position that *Canyon*, which could not be sold because a sale would violate the BGEPA and the Migratory Bird Treaty Act, would have no discounted value for estate tax purposes because, according to the IRS, the work could be sold on the illicit market. (Further discussion of estate tax valuation of *Canyon* below at note 74.)

34. Treas. Reg. § 1.170A-1(g).

35. I.R.C. § 170(f)(3)(A).

36. The deduction for travel is permitted only if there is no significant element of personal pleasure, recreation, or vacation in the travel [I.R.C. § 170(j)]. Although expenses for meals and lodging are deductible only if they are incurred while the donor is away from home performing charitable services, a donor may deduct transportation expenses even though the donor is not away from home. The deduction for transportation expenses is the actual cost of gas and oil directly related to the use of a car in providing charitable services or a standard mileage rate (currently fourteen cents per mile).

37. I.R.C. § 170(f)(8).

38. I.R.C. §§ 2055(e)(4)(A) and 2522(c)(3)

39. I.R.C. § 170(f)(2)(B). A deduction *is* permitted for a transfer not in trust if the transfer is an undivided part of a donor's interest, is a remainder interest in a personal residence or farm, or is a remainder interest in real property to be used exclusively for conservation purposes. A contribution of a remainder interest in real property that is historically important land or a certified historic structure, or a restriction (granted in perpetuity) on the use that may be made of real property, will provide the donor with a charitable contribution deduction for the value of the remainder interest or of the value of the restriction.

40. I.R.C. § 170(f)(2)(A). A gift of a future interest in tangible personal property is complete for purposes of claiming a charitable contribution deduction only when all intervening interests and rights to actual possession or enjoyment of the property have expired.

41. I.R.C. § 170(o), which was added to the Internal Revenue Code in 2006.

42. Section 170(o) provides that a deduction for a fractional interest in artwork is limited to the lesser of the value of the interest at the time of the fractional contribution or at the time of any additional contribution. If the remaining interest is not contributed within the earlier of ten years later or the date of the donor's death, the donor must recapture the earlier deduction and pay interest and a ten percent penalty.

43. Treas. Reg. § 1.170A-7(b)(3). A personal residence for these purposes includes a vacation home or stock owned by the donor as a tenant-stockholder in a cooperative housing corporation (if the dwelling which the donor is entitled to occupy as a stockholder is used by the donor as a personal residence).

44. Treas. Reg. § 1.170A-7(b)(4). A farm for these purposes means any land used by the donor or the donor's tenant for the production of crops, fruits, or other agricultural products or for the sustenance of livestock. In determining the value of a remainder interest in a personal residence or in a farm, depreciation and depletion must be deducted [Treas. Reg. § 1.170A-12(a)(1)]. (Depreciation is computed by the straight-line method and depletion by the cost-depletion method.) The gift also must be discounted at a six percent rate. Computation of the value of a remainder interest, by taking into consideration depreciation and discount factors, is discussed in Treasury Regulations (Treas. Reg. § 1.170A-12).

45. The conservation purpose must be protected in perpetuity [I.R.C. § 170(b)(2)]. A qualified real property interest includes a remainder interest, a restriction (granted in perpetuity) on the use that may be made of the real property, and the donor's entire interest in the property other than a qualified mineral interest. For a donation of a perpetual conservation restriction, value of the restriction is the amount of the charitable contribution deduction [Treas. Reg. § 1.170A-14(b)(2)]. Value is computed by determining fair market value of the property before and after the restriction.

The preservation of land areas for outdoor recreation by the general public or for education of the general public qualifies as a conservation purpose. For example, the preservation of a water area for use of the public for boating or fishing, or a nature or hiking trail for use of the public, would qualify.

Eligible recipients of contributions of partial interests for conservation purposes are restricted to governments and publicly supported charities (discussion of these charities in Chapter 3) [I.R.C. § 170(c)(1)].

46. The preservation of a habitat or environment, which to some extent has been altered by human activity, would qualify if the fish, wildlife, or plants exist there in a relatively natural state. Conservation purposes also would include preservation of open space including farmland and forest land where preservation is for the scenic enjoyment of the general public and is pursuant to a delineated governmental conservation policy.

47. The term "historically important land area" includes independently significant land areas and historic sites, the physical or environmental features of which contribute to the historic or cultural importance and integrity of certified historic structures.

48. 26 C.F.R. § 1.170A-14.

49. I.R.C. § 2031(c). The deduction is the lesser of $500,000 or a percentage of the value of the land subject to the easement reduced by the amount of any charitable deduction claimed. The applicable percentage is forty percent reduced by two percentage points for each percentage point (or fraction thereof) by which the value of the qualified conservation

easement is less than thirty percent of the value of the land determined without regard to value of the easement. The land must be located within twenty-five miles of a metropolitan area, national park, or wilderness area, or within ten miles of an urban national forest area. Proximity to a national park or wilderness will not be sufficient if the area is not under significant development pressure. Also, the exclusion does not apply to the extent the land is debt-financed property.

50. Treas. Reg. § 1.170A-6(c)(2)(i). An amount is determinable if the exact amount that must be paid under conditions specified in the governing instrument of the trust can be determined on date of the transfer.

An income interest is not a guaranteed annuity interest if the trustee may pay any amount for a private purpose before expiration of all the charitable income interests (unless the amount for a private purpose is paid from a group of assets that are devoted exclusively to private purposes pursuant to the trust's governing instrument).

51. Treas. Reg. § 1.170A-6(c)(2)(ii). An income interest in the form of a unitrust, like a guaranteed annuity interest, is not a qualified annuity interest if the trustee may pay any amount for a private purpose before expiration of all the charitable income interests (unless the amount for the private purpose is paid from a group of assets devoted exclusively to private purposes by terms of the trust instrument).

52. Treas. Reg. § 1.170A-6(c)(3). The tables are set out at Treas. Regs. §§ 20.2031-7A and in IRS publications 1457 and 1458.

53. Annual limitations on charitable contributions are discussed in notes in Chapter 3 in conjunction with a discussion of public charities, private operating foundations, and private nonoperating foundations. Gifts to private nonoperating foundations are subject to a thirty percent (of adjusted gross income) annual limitation (twenty percent for gifts of capital gain property), whereas gifts to public charities and to private operating foundations are subject to a fifty percent limitation (thirty percent for gifts of capital gain property). In addition, gifts to private nonoperating foundations are determined after all gifts to public charities have been computed. Gifts to private nonoperating foundations can be deducted only as to the excess of the fifty percent limitation over total gifts to public charities.

54. Table B, Treas. Reg. § 20.2031-7A(d)(6), provided a valuation of 0.61446.

55. I.R.C. § 664(d)(1). The Treasury provides sample forms that can be used for transfer of a partial interest to a charity in the form of a unitrust, a charitable remainder annuity trust, or a pooled income fund which will meet requirements of the Internal Revenue Code and, thus, will provide the donor with a charitable contribution deduction for the partial interest passed to a charity. Provisions of these forms are set out at Rev. Procs. 88-53 (pooled income fund) and 2005-52, 2005-53, 2005-54, 2005-55, 2005-56, 2005-57, 2005-58, 2005-59 (CRATs and CRUTS) and provide for transfers based on a term of years or those with remainder interests for one or for more than one measuring life.

56. Treas. Reg. §§ 1.664-2(a)(6), 1.664-3(a)(4) and (6). A charitable remainder annuity trust may not have additional contributions after the initial contributions, but a unitrust may. If additional contributions are made to a unitrust after the initial contribution, the governing instrument for the unitrust must provide that the annuity payment to the non-charitable beneficiaries will be the fixed percentage (not less than five percent or more than fifty percent) of the sum of the net fair market value of assets excluding any added assets and the value of the added assets times the percentage of time the added assets have been held during the year [Treas. Reg. §§ 1.664-2(b), 1.664-3(b)]. A unitrust must require that should the trustee incorrectly determine the fair market value of the trust assets, the trustee must pay the income recipient for an overvaluation, in an amount equal to the difference. If

income of a unitrust is less than the fixed percentage of the net fair market value of assets of the fund valued for that year, the trust instrument may provide for payment of the lesser amount. This option is not available for a charitable remainder annuity trust. [Treas. Reg. §§ 1.664-2(a), 1.664-3(a)].

57. For a charitable remainder interest, consult tables set out in Treas. Regs. § 20.2031-7 and IRS Publication 1457 to determine value of the remainder interest. The present value of a remainder interest in a unitrust is computed by using tables set out in Treas. Regs. § 1.664-3(c) and IRS Publication 1458.

58. Table B, Treas. Reg. § 20.2031-7A(d)(6). A donor should consult IRS publications 1457 and 1458 or apply for a revenue ruling as to valuation.

59. Charitable remainder trusts are exempt from income tax unless they have unrelated business taxable income.

60. Treas. Reg. § 1.642(c)-5(b)(5). The governing instrument of a pooled income fund must contain certain provisions set out in Treas. Reg. § 1.642(c)-5(b). Beneficiaries of the fund and the share of income distributable to each person must be specified. Power to revoke or terminate the income interest of any designated beneficiary may be exercisable only by will of the donor. The governing instrument must direct the trustee to distribute income currently or within the first sixty-five days following the close of the taxable year in which the income is earned. (A statement must be attached to the tax return of the pooled income fund indicating the date and amount of such payments. The income beneficiaries must include these amounts in their gross income for tax purposes.) The governing instrument must provide that the income interest of any beneficiary terminates with the last regular payment made before the death of the beneficiary or must provide that payments be prorated to the date of death of the beneficiary.

An income interest may be created for the public charity that is the recipient of the remainder interest, or, in the alternative, the donor need not create a life interest in all the income from the transferred property, leaving some of the income to pass to the remainder charity. (A donor is not permitted a charitable contribution deduction for the value of an income interest of a public charity or for any amount of income paid to the charity.

61. Treas. Reg. § 1.642(c)-6. The value is determined by computing the present value of the life income interest and subtracting it from the fair market value of the entire property. Present value of the life income interest is determined by life contingency tables set out in Treas. Regs. § 1.642(c)-6(e)(6) but particularly in IRS publications. A donor may request a revenue ruling as to valuation if computation of valuation requires use of a factor not provided for in the regulations.

62. I.R.C. § 642(c)(5)(a).

63. A pooled income fund which is maintained by a charity holding the remainder interest includes funds transferred by all donors in that particular form. The fund may be invested jointly with other properties, not a part of the fund, which are held by the charity. Records must be maintained that sufficiently identify the portion of the total fund which is owned by the pooled income and the income earned by that portion [Treas. Reg. § 1.642(c)-5(b)(4)]. The fund may not be invested in tax exempt securities.

A national organization of a local public charity that was named as recipient of the remainder interest may maintain the fund on behalf of the local charity. The fact that the local organization or chapter is incorporated separately from the national organization is immaterial [Treas. Reg. § 1.642(c)-5(b)(5)].

64. Table A, Treas. Reg. § 20.2031-7A. A donor should consult IRS publications on valuation (see IRS Publication 1457).

65. ICOM Code of Ethics for Museums 5.2.

66. Treas. Reg. § 1.170A-13(c).

67. Treas. Reg. § 1.170A-13(c). The appraisal must include a description of the property, the physical condition of the property, the terms of the agreement that would restrict the donee's use of the property, and the qualifications of the appraiser. The appraiser may not accept a fee based on the amount of the appraisal.

In determining whether gifts of noncash property require an appraisal, gifts of similar items to more than one donee are aggregated. Thus, if a donor claimed a deduction of more than $5,000 for gifts of similar items to several donees, the donor would be required to obtain a written appraisal of the value of the gifts.

68. I.R.C. § 6050L. Failure to file the form can cause the charity to pay substantial penalties. I.R.C. §§ 6721, 6723. If the donor's claimed value exceeds the property's correct value based on the property's selling price, the overvaluation may subject the donor to a penalty of twenty percent to forty percent of any tax underpayment. I.R.C. § 6662.

69. Rev. Proc. 66-49, 1966-2 C.B. 1257. The IRS will provide a statement of value which can be used to substantiate the value of art for income, estate, or gift tax purposes. In Rev. Proc. 96-15, 1996-1 C.B. 627, the IRS informs taxpayers how to obtain IRS review of the taxpayer's valuation of a work of art before filing a return. It sets out procedures for requesting and obtaining a statement of value from the IRS.

70. Rev. Proc. 66-49, cited in note 69.

71. An appraisal report should contain a summary of the appraiser's qualifications, the basis upon which the appraisal was made (including any restrictions on use of the property), the date the property was valued, and the signature of the appraiser. Rev. Proc. 66-49, cited in note 69.

72. Internal Revenue Manual, I.R.M. 4.48.2.1.

73. Id. at 4.48.2.2.

74. See discussion in Anne-Marie Rhodes, 31 Cardozo Arts & Enter. L. J. 45 (2012) of issues relating to the estate valuation of a three-dimensional work of art by Robert Rauschenberg (a "sculptural combine" called *Canyon*) that contained a stuffed bald eagle with its wings fully extended outward from the bottom of a canvas. Rauschenberg apparently gave the work to the noted art dealer and collector Ileana Sonnabend; the work was in her estate when she died in 2007. According to reports, Rauschenberg created *Canyon* in 1959 after the enactment in 1940 of the Bald and Golden Eagle Protection Act (BGEPA). One of Teddy Roosevelt's Rough Riders reportedly had acquired the eagle and stuffed it prior to enactment of the BGEPA. According to reports, Rauschenberg stated he obtained the bird in 1959 from a fellow artist who had retrieved it from the trash when it was discarded after the death of the person who had originally acquired it. Pre-1940 bald eagles can be donated, but it is a violation of the BGEPA to sell a pre-1940 eagle or its parts. After learning of *Canyon* from its being loaned to museums for exhibition, federal Fish and Wildlife agents notified Sonnabend of the restrictions imposed on the work by BGEPA. Sonnabend then applied for a permit to retain the work. In valuing her estate, which included works of art valued at over $800 million, the estate contended *Canyon* had no value because it could not be legally sold. However, the IRS Art Advisory Panel decided the work was worth $65 million. The IRS accepted this value because it determined the work could be sold on the illicit market. It issued a deficiency notice against the estate of $29.2 million in taxes and $11.7 million in penalties. Presumably the estate reached a settlement agreement with the IRS which provided that the estate would not owe any estate tax on *Canyon* if the estate would donate the work to a museum. The estate then allegedly settled the issue with the IRS when it donated *Canyon* to the Museum of Modern Art.

75. I.R.C. § 170(f)(8).

76. I.R.C. § 6115(a). The term "quid pro quo contribution" is a payment a donor/payor makes to a charity partly as a contribution and partly in consideration for goods or services provided the donor/ payor by the charity.

77. Failure to meet disclosure requirements will subject the donor organization to a penalty of $10 for each contribution for which the organization failed to make a disclosure (limited to a maximum of $5,000 for any particular fund-raising event or mailing). I.R.C. § 6714. (Although museum personnel should not place a value on objects donated to the museum, in this limited context, they must place a value on the goods or services the museum renders to a donor in exchange for a donation.)

78. If a museum has unrelated business taxable income in excess of $1,000, it must make quarterly payments of estimated tax on such income. Estimated payments are made by making deposits of the tax through the Federal Tax Deposit (FTD) system in the same manner as taxable entities.

79. I.R.C. § 513(a). The term "trade or business" includes an activity performed for production of income from the sale of goods or the performance of services.

80. Treas. Reg. § 1.513-1(d). Production or distribution of goods or performance of services must contribute importantly to the accomplishment of a museum's charitable purposes. In determining whether an organization's activities contribute importantly to the accomplishment of its exempt purposes, size and extent of activities must be considered in relationship to the nature and extent of the exempt function they purport to serve.

81. Treas. Reg. § 1.513-1(c). Business activities that are intermittent are compared with the manner in which commercial activities of the same type are generally pursued by taxable organizations to determine whether they are "regularly carried on" by an exempt organization. Income producing or fund-raising activities conducted for only a short period of time ordinarily will not be treated as regularly carried on if the activities occur only sporadically. Further, the fact that activities are conducted on an annual recurring basis will not necessarily cause them to be seen as regularly conducted.

82. Treas. Reg. § 1.513-1(d). The fact that the asset or facility is needed to perform the organization's exempt functions is not material. When a tax exempt organization uses its facilities for both tax exempt purposes and also for production of unrelated business taxable income, its expenses are allocated between the two activities on some reasonable basis.

83. Rev. Rul. 73-105, 1973-1 C.B. 264.

84. PLR 8024111.

85. Rev. Rul. 73-104, 1973-1 C.B. 263.

86. Id. See also PLR 9450028.

87. PLR 8024111.

88. See Rev. Rul. 69-268, 1969-1 C.B. 160; Rev. Rul. 74-399, 1974-2 C.B. 172.

89. PLR 8735004.

90. Treas. Reg. § 1-513-7.

91. In Rev. Rul. 76-151, 1976-1 C.B. 151, the IRS stated it would deny tax exempt status to organizations whose purpose was to sell artworks of local artists, the theory being that these organizations serve the private interests of local artists.

92. Circulation income or loss is attributable to the production, distribution, or circulation of a publication including amounts realized from the sale or distribution of the readership content of a periodical [Treas. Reg. § 1.512(a)-1(f)]. Circulation income is not taxed, but a circulation loss can offset advertising income.

93. TAM 199914035.

94. I.R.C. § 513(i).

95. Id.

96. Treas. Reg. § 1.513-4(f).

97. I.R.C. § 513(d)(3).

98. Treas. Reg. § 1.512(b)-1(c)(2). If the amount of rent from real property depends in whole or in part on income or profits derived from leased property, other than an amount based on a fixed percentage of gross receipts or sales, rents will not be excluded from unrelated business income.

99. Treas. Reg. § 1.512(b)-1(c)(2)(ii)(b).

100. I.R.C. § 512(b)(3)(B).

101. The supplying of maid service would be this type of special service, but the furnishing of utilities or the cleaning of public entrances, stairways, and lobbies would not be.

102. PLR 8734007.

103. Rev. Rul. 81-178, 1982-2 C.B. 135.

104. Oregon State Univ. Alumni Ass'n v. Comm., 193 F.3d 1098 (9th Cir. 1999) and Sierra Club, Inc. v. Comm., T.C. Memo 1999-86.

105. If amounts are included as unrelated business taxable income under other code provisions, they are not treated also as unrelated business income from a controlled organization [Treas. Reg. § 1.512(b)-1(l)(5)]. However, for rent derived from a controlling organization's lease of debt-financed property to a controlled organization, the amount of rent included in unrelated business taxable income of the controlling organization first is determined under rules relating to income from a controlled organization. Only that portion of rents not taxed as income from a controlled organization will be subject to rules relating to income from debt-financed property.

106. Treas. Reg. § 1.512(b)-1(l)(4). A trustee or director is controlled if the tax exempt organization has power to remove the trustee or director and can designate a new trustee or director.

107. Treas. Reg. § 1.514(b)-1(b)(1). To the extent property is used to carry out a tax exempt organization's exempt purposes, the property is not treated as debt-financed property. Property is used for an exempt purpose if eighty-five percent or more of its use is devoted to an organization's exempt purposes. Property used for research activities and property used in a related trade or business would not be debt-financed property.

108. Any indebtedness incurred before acquisition or improvement of the property will be acquisition indebtedness if the indebtedness would not have been incurred but for acquisition or improvement of the property [I.R.C. § 514(c)]. Should an exempt organization acquire debt-financed property for an indeterminate price, initial acquisition indebtedness is the fair market value of the property on the date of acquisition less any down payment [Treas. Reg. § 1.514(a)-1(a)(4)].

If property acquired is subject to a mortgage, the outstanding principal indebtedness secured by the mortgage is treated as acquisition indebtedness even though the organization does not assume or agree to pay the indebtedness. For property acquired by gift or bequest, any outstanding mortgage will not be treated as acquisition indebtedness for the ten-year period following the date of acquisition [Treas. Reg. § 1.514(c)-1(b)]. (For property acquired by gift, this is the case if the mortgage was placed on the property more than five years before date of the gift and the donor held the property for more than five years prior to the gift.)

109. Treas. Reg. § 1.514(a)-1(a)(2). The organization must adjust the property for depreciation for the entire time the organization has held the property regardless of whether it was exempt from taxation during any of that time period.

PART II

MUSEUM COLLECTIONS

CHAPTER 5

ACQUISITIONS

Give me a museum and I'll fill it.

PABLO PICASSO

A museum has to renew its collection to be alive, but that does not mean we give on an important old work.

DAVID ROCKEFELLER

Part I (Chapters 1–4) set out laws and principles relating to governance of a museum. Part II (Chapters 5–8) summarizes laws that affect museum collections—(1) the laws associated with purchased and donated acquisitions, as well as acquisitions on loan, to include problems and issues relating to possibly unauthentic works and stolen or illegally imported objects in collections; (2) issues relating to the deaccessioning of parts of a collection; (3) laws protecting artists; and (4) copyright laws for rights retained by artists in some artworks in a collection, as well as for copyrights a museum may have in a part of its collection. Part III (Chapters 9–11) covers national and international laws that protect and preserve the natural and cultural heritage and that, in so doing, also affect the acquisition and maintenance of museum collections.

Museums acquire permanent additions to their collections by purchase or through gifts, but many also have collections on loan. The International Council of Museums (ICOM) Code of Ethics states that no object should be acquired by purchase, gift, loan, bequest, or exchange unless the acquiring museum is satisfied a valid title is held. It also states that evidence of lawful ownership in a country is not necessarily valid title.[1] When a museum acquires additions to its collection either through purchase or by gift, a museum director wants confidence that the museum has acquired good title and that its acquisitions are authentic works. A museum director also must adhere to all legal requirements for acquisitions on loan.

The Code of Ethics for Museums,[2] subscribed to by the American Alliance of Museums (AAM), recognizes that museums "make their unique contribution to the public by collecting, preserving and interpreting the things of the world." The ICOM Code of Ethics for Museums requires museums in its membership to conform to international, regional, national, and local legislation and treaty obligations,[3] and it states that the governing body of each museum should "comply with any legally binding trusts or conditions relating to any aspect of the museum, its collections and operations."[4] The ICOM Code of Ethics for Museums also states that the governing body of each museum should adopt and publish a written collections policy which addresses the acquisition, care, and use of collections.[5] Museum directors and curators must be aware of laws that apply to their museum collections to carry out these obligations.

This chapter summarizes the general laws applying to museum acquisitions and to collections on loan. It also considers issues relating to the deaccession of objects in the collection.

A. PURCHASES

A museum director needs assurance when he purchases accessions to the museum collection that the seller has legal title to the objects in question, that all acquisitions conform to representations regarding quality and origin, and that the museum will not violate any laws regulating acquisitions. A purchase of museum collections is governed by a state's commercial code and by specific federal and state acts regulating acquisitions.

Because museum collections are personalty (as distinguished from real property), Article 2 of the Uniform Commercial Code (U.C.C.), which has been enacted by the various states, governs the sales and purchases of objects in the collection. Because U.C.C. Article 2 relates to commercial transactions and is applicable to personalty in general, but not specifically to museum collections, the state statutes that incorporate U.C.C. Article 2 may not provide discrete solutions to many problems unique to the museum world. An example is the question of how a museum can obtain good title if an artifact may have been stolen. As discussed in more detail in Chapter 6, U.C.C. § 2.403(1) provides that a purchaser cannot obtain good title to property if there has been a thief in the chain of title. This principle is recognized statutory law in all states except Louisiana (discussed below and in Chapter 6). The effect of § 2.403 is that purchasers of stolen cultural property can be exposed indefinitely to claims of original owners. The sale of artworks by one who has defective title to a "purchaser in good faith" is another example. Although a thief can never pass good title, U.C.C. § 2-403(2) provides that the entrusting of possession of goods to a merchant who deals in goods of that type gives the merchant power to transfer all rights of the entrustor to a buyer in the ordinary course of business; consequently, a bailor (discussed below) can pass good title if the buyer is a purchaser "in good faith." Still, there is some question whether a purchaser of art or historical treasures can be a purchaser "in good faith" when a seller has defective title. A court may rule that to be a good-faith purchaser, a potential buyer of art and historical treasures must have investigated an artifact's provenance (which as discussed below is the history of the ownership of a work of art).

1. Authentification—Forgeries

Another example of the difficulty in applying to museum purchases state statutes that have incorporated U.C.C. Article 2 is the issue of whether an expression of the authenticity of a work is an express warranty under U.C.C. § 2-313. The possibility that a museum has accessioned a fake work of art will present a major problem for the museum. The difficulty in detecting some forgeries, as well as the lack of clarity in the law to provide redress should a purchased work not be as it was purported, present crucial concerns in the acquisition of valuable works.

> Example 1. The court, in Balog v. Center Art Gallery, Hawaii, Inc., 745 F. Supp. 1556 (D. Haw. 1990), referred to a law review article by Leonard Duboff [6] to set out in detail circumstances relating to the fabrication of paintings. The court noted that fabrication of paintings has been accomplished by several methods. A signature of a recognized painter may be added to an unsigned work, or an existing signature may be replaced with a more valuable one by painting over the original signature. As the court recognized, some fabricators complete partially finished or discarded canvases which show the marks of age, while others reproduce, and sell as genuine, copies of specific originals. Often imitators begin faked paintings and then pass them to specialists who add the finishing touches. Sometimes paintings of students of a master are sold as the

> master's product. A counterfeiter may create a copy of a specific piece and then sell it as a genuine original. The court pointed out that a pastiche is a complex form of fabrication whereby a forger excises a number of details of various different paintings of the same artist and reassembles them into a new work. The counterfeiter must be so intimate with the technique of the master as to be able to select those details, which closely resemble the master's style, that may be fabricated into a pastiche. The court noted there are many unsigned paintings, especially those of classical periods. A signature can be fixed to these unsigned paintings with varnish that grows to look more authentic with the passage of time. The court recognized that completing an unfinished or discarded canvas of an original artist is particularly attractive as a medium of forgery because the canvas itself would possess the correct age of the period, and the older, authentic portions of the work might "belie the forger's additions." It noted that students of a particular artist may have been so influenced by their master's technique that simple alterations and touch-ups would be sufficient "to disguise a work and render it a plausible product of the artist himself." The court pointed out that drawings are faked frequently. Because drawings contain fewer details than a finished product, a counterfeiter often finds them easier to produce and to pass off as originals. The court noted that there are techniques whereby paper can be aged artificially so as to simulate that which was used during the drawing's purported era. The court recognized that, when done effectively, these counterfeits are extremely difficult to detect.

Methods to detect art forgeries include available scientific tests and laboratory processes that can range from the application of ultraviolet or infrared light as a means of revealing the substructure of a painting to the use of radiocarbon dating, x-ray diffraction, thermoluminescence, obsidian hydration, examination of fission tracks, and other microscopic techniques.[7] One method employs an expert who uses accumulated experience with, and knowledge of, the technique and work of a particular artist to arrive at a judgment as to whether a painting is genuine. This obviously involves intuition and expertise.[8]

The problem of forgeries of artworks and artifacts is not addressed specifically in state statutes. The limited provisions in the Uniform Commercial Code that relate to the problem only address the issue indirectly. While U.C.C. § 2-313 provides that goods sold shall conform to any affirmation of fact or promise made by the seller, U.C.C. § 2-316 states that "implied" warranties are negated by expressions such as "with all faults" or "as is." Still,

§ 2-316 makes a negation or limitation of warranty inoperative to the extent this construction would be unreasonable. In addition, words or conduct relevant to the creation of an express warranty and words or conduct tending to negate or limit a warranty are construed wherever reasonable to be consistent with each other. The assumption is that an express warranty is not negated by a limitation of warranty whereas an implied warranty would be. All implied warranties are excluded by expressions such as "with all faults" or "as is," but presumably an express warranty, unlike an "implied" warranty, is not negated by certain expressions limiting warranty.

A seller need not give a buyer an express warranty for a guarantee to attach to goods.[9] As noted in Chapter 4, an affirmation of the value of goods or a statement purporting to be merely the seller's opinion or commendation of the goods does not create a warranty, but any description of the goods that is made a part of the basis of the bargain creates an express warranty that the goods will conform to the description. Any sample or model that is made a part of the agreement creates an express warranty that the whole of the goods will conform to the sample or model. In addition, any affirmation of fact or promise made by the seller to the buyer that relates to the goods and that becomes part of the basis of the bargain creates an express warranty that the goods will conform to the affirmation or promise. A warranty that the goods will be merchantable is implied in a contact of sale if the seller is a merchant as to the goods sold. Still, words in a contract negating or limiting warranty are given effect.[10]

There is a question whether a statement that a work is that of a specific artist or is a period piece constitutes an express warranty, which would not be negated by an expression that a sale of the work is "with all faults" or is sold "as is." For example, if a work stated to be that of a famous artist is sold "as is," would the purchaser have a cause of action to recover the purchase price if the work is not authentic? Does the sale "as is" negate any possible warranty of authenticity or does it merely refer to defects in the painting (the painting is sold subject to all defects) so that the purchaser still would have a cause of action for recovery of the purchase price should the work be found to be a forgery? The fact that an art gallery is offering a work of art for sale should inspire confidence that the work is genuine and that the listed artist is, in fact, the creator of the work. A warning to the contrary should be given special prominence to be effective. A court nonetheless could find that listing a painting as a work of a particular famous artist is not an express warranty and that any disclaimer effectively waived any implied warranties to include that of authenticity. A court also could determine that a purchaser who is a museum director or curator should have as superior a knowledge and experience in the art world as an art dealer and, thus, that a purchaser for a museum assumes the risk that a painting is not genuine.

Example 2. In Weisz v. Parke-Bernet Galleries, Inc., 67 Misc. 1077, 325 N.Y.S.2d 576 (Civ. Ct. N.Y. City 1971), rev'd, 77 Misc. 2d 80, 351 N.Y.S.2d 911 (N.Y. App. Term 1974), an individual purchased a painting listed in an auction catalogue as a work of Raoul Dufy. The purchaser later discovered the painting was a forgery and filed suit against the art gallery to recover the purchase price of the painting. The art gallery denied liability, contending that the catalogue described "conditions of sale," which included a disclaimer of warranty as to genuineness or authorship. The lower court found the art gallery liable because it decided the individual did not have superior knowledge and experience and that, as a result, the disclaimer was ineffective. However, the appellate court disagreed and ruled that a stated opinion of a seller does not give rise to an express warranty. Thus, according to the New York appellate court, the disclaimer negated any warranty as to authenticity. The appellate court held that the buyer assumed the risk that identifications could be wrong.

After the Weisz decision noted in Example 2, New York added a statute that goes beyond provisions of the Uniform Commercial Code to provide protection for art collectors.[11] The New York statute provides that a description furnished to a buyer by an art merchant which identifies a work with an author becomes a part of the basis for the bargain and creates an express warranty of the authenticity of the authorship. Such a warranty cannot be negated or limited merely because formal words such as "warranty" or "guarantee" are not used.

Example 3. In Balog v. Center Art Gallery, Hawaii, Inc., cited in Example 1, the court decided that purchasers of a number of pieces, purportedly produced by Dali, were precluded effectively, by the relatively low price of the pieces, from undertaking an extensive investigation into the veracity of the seller's claims that the works were genuine. The court ruled the seller violated the express warranties provided for in the Hawaiian Code (which incorporated the provisions of U.C.C. § 2-313). The court in Balog agreed with the lower court in Weiss (discussed in Example 2), rather than the appellate court, and thought that "the requirements of fair dealing, where there is a relationship between parties in which there is a basic inequality of knowledge, expertness, or economic power," provides a basis for a victim "to seek redress of damages based on a violation of the express warranties provided for by § 2-313." The court held that it was reasonable for the Balogs, as amateur buyers, to rely on the art dealer's representations regarding the authenticity of the artworks. The court also ruled the statute of limitations was tolled until the buyers discovered the pieces were not genuine.

There are other problems involved when there is a question of the authenticity of a work of art. There may be time limitation problems in bringing an action to rescind the sale of an artwork if the work is not determined to be a forgery until several years after its purchase. Further, it is difficult to prove a work is or is not genuine. There may be differing "expert" opinions regarding authenticity. In some cases the artist may even deny authorship of a work. In addition, an artist's heirs may contend a work attributed to the artist is a forgery. Ultimately a court decides authenticity even though a court cannot judge a work's genuineness.

As one court pointed out, in quoting a law review article by Ronald D. Spencer,[12] authentication is the process by which art experts—academic or independent art historians, museum or collection curators, art dealers, or auction house experts—attribute a work of visual art to a particular artist. One scholar quoted by this court pointed out that while questions of authenticity typically arise when someone asserts a work is a copy, they also arise where works were created in collaboration with others and where works were subsequently altered by another even when an alteration was prompted by an attempt at restoration.[13] The court[14] commented that determinations of the authenticity of artwork are complex and highly subjective assertions of fact. It declared that, because of the procedures and processes by which civil litigation is decided, courts are not equipped to deliver a meaningful declaration of authenticity. Nonetheless it recognized that courts must address issues of authenticity and often are required to issue findings as to a work's authenticity as claims are brought by sellers, purchasers, and appraisers of artworks. Still, as this court[15] observed, the relief awarded by a court only binds the parties to the transaction; it does not attempt to affect the art market generally.[16]

Provenance refers to the history of the ownership of a work of art and is important in determining authenticity. The ICOM Code of Ethics for Museums defines "provenance" as "The full history and ownership of an item from the time of its discovery or creation to the present day, through which authentic and ownership are determined." Because provenance is the source and subsequent custodial history of an artwork, a work's provenance is given weighty consideration in the process of authentication.[17]

Another means to determine authenticity is an artist's catalogue raisonné. A catalogue raisonné is a monograph or descriptive catalogue that sets out a complete list of an artist's works, describes their chronology and history, and describes the works in a manner that makes them readily identifiable. A catalogue raisonné of a particular artist would be written, after years of research, by leading experts on that artist. Still, a catalogue raisonné has limitations in proving or disproving a work's authenticity as illustrated in the following examples.

Example 4. The authenticity of an alleged Alexander Calder mobile was in question in Greenburg Gallery v. Bauman, 817 F. Supp. 167 (D.D.C. 1993), aff'd, 36 F.3d 127 (C.A.D.C. 1994). A mobile titled *Rio Nero*, which was alleged to be the work of renowned artist Alexander Calder, did not have the delicate balance required for proper hanging. Provenance of the mobile weighed heavily in favor of authenticity, but an expert on the works of Calder had contended the mobile was a forgery. The court accepted the testimony of one expert witness that the original had been misassembled and abused so that, on cursory examination, it did not exactly resemble the original photo of the mobile and, further, that the abuse had caused it to lose its delicate balance. One expert testified the "flawless provenance" of the artwork was the "best proof of authenticity." Based on testimony of these two experts, the court decided the mobile was more likely than not authentic and ruled the mobile was not a forgery.

Example 5. An art collector had two theatrical stage sets and related material that he contended were the work of Alexander Calder. The collector filed suit against a private foundation that catalogued Calder's works, seeking a declaration that the artworks he held were authentic. The Calder Foundation was formed in 1988 for the principal purpose of cataloguing all works produced by Calder and making his works available for public inspection to facilitate art education and research. All members of the foundation were related to Calder by blood or marriage. The foundation had documented more than seventeen thousand of Calder's works for publication in its catalogue raisonné. The art collector decided to sell his works and submitted documentation to the foundation for authentication and inclusion in the foundation's Calder catalogue raisonné. He contended that without a catalogue raisonné number from the foundation, his work was essentially unmarketable. Without explanation, the foundation did not include the works in the catalogue raisonné. In

Thome v. Alexander & Louisa Calder Foundation, Inc., 70 A.D.3d 88, 890 N.Y.S.2d 16 (N.Y. 2009), the court considered the collector's request. It decided that, regardless of whether the art world had accepted the foundation as the body to create an authoritative Calder catalogue raisonné, that fact alone did not give the court the right to dictate what the foundation would include in the catalogue. The court commented that a declaration of authenticity would not resolve the art collector's situation because his inability to sell his alleged Calder works was a function of the marketplace. According to the court, if buyers would not buy works unless the Calder Foundation had listed them in its catalogue raisonné, the problem lay in the art world's voluntary surrender of that ultimate authority to a single entity. The court opined that if it was immaterial to the art world that the art collector had proof his sets were built to Calder's specifications and that Calder approved of their construction, it would be immaterial to the art world that a court had pronounced the work to be "authentic." The court rationalized that the collector's problem could be solved only when buyers were willing to make their decision based upon the work and the unassailable facts about the creation, rather than permitting a foundation's decisions as to what merits inclusion in its catalogue raisonné to dictate what was worthy of purchase. The court ruled that unless the art collector could establish an independent legal right to have his work included in the catalogue, such as an enforceable contractual promise to include it, the court could not mandate its inclusion.

Example 6. An art museum bought for $15,000 a painting the curator contended was a work of Jackson Pollock. The painting would be worth $10 million if it could be authenticated. The curator submitted the painting to the Pollock-Kramer Authentication Board for authentication, but the board refused to authenticate the painting. The curator contended the board was working with major art galleries to control the market for works of Jackson Pollock by refusing to authenticate certain works and by the art galleries refusing to sell works of Jackson Pollock unless they had been authenticated by the board. Would the museum have a cause of action against the board? In Kramer v. Pollock-Kramer Foundation, 890 F. Supp. 250 (S.D.N.Y. 1995), the owner of an alleged Pollock contended that Christie's and Sotheby's together controlled one hundred percent of the Pollock auction market and that they auctioned only Pollock works authenticated by the Pollock-Kramer Authentication Board or listed in the Jackson Pollock Catalogue Raisonné. The owner of the alleged

Pollock contended that the board's refusal to authentic his painting indicated a conspiracy to control the Pollock market. The court ruled that the owner of the alleged Pollock had a "reasonable alternative" to selling his painting at auction and held that his complaint failed to support the existence of a conspiracy because it presented "no coherent theory of participation by Sotheby's or Christie's in the alleged conspiracy." The court determined that Sotheby's and Christie's must warrant authenticity of a work pursuant to § 13 of the New York Arts and Cultural Affairs Law; thus, their decision to sell only works approved by the board as genuine related to their fear of being sued for breach of warranty should a work be found to be a fraud. The court decided they were not motivated by malice or an unlawful motive.

Example 7. In Herstand & Co., Inc. v. Gertrude Stein, Inc., 211 A.D. 2d 77, 626 N.Y.S.2d 74 (N.Y. 1995), a purchaser of a Balthus drawing brought an action to rescind the contract of sale because the parties were mutually mistaken as to the drawing's genuineness. When Balthus was showed a photograph of the drawing, he denounced it as a fake and wrote "faux manifest" on the back. The court in Herstand noted that the drawing existed in 1954 and the repudiation occurred in 1990. A prominent art dealer submitted an affidavit in the case in which he opined as "self-evident" that the artist was the definitive expert on what was the artist's own work. The art dealer stated in the affidavit that when a living artist repudiates a work as a forgery or a fake, the work becomes unmerchantable and unsalable. The court agreed that there might be situations where the artist's own acceptance or rejection of a questioned work would be the "final word," but ruled that this case was not one of them. The court decided the Balthusian certifications of falsity were pure hearsay. It disagreed with the art dealer that "nothing can be imagined which would induce an artist to repudiate his own genuine work." The court concluded that "history tells us otherwise." The court noted the opinion of one expert witness that Balthus was acting from personal animus against his former wife by repudiating the authenticity of one of his works, which she possessed. The court noted that the purchaser of the drawing had not produced an expert who would state that the drawing was a fake while the seller had proffered at least one expert who asserted the drawing was genuine. The court concluded the art dealer's statement merely reflected the dealer's views with respect to the market impact of the artist's actions upon the dollar value of the drawing.

Example 8. In Boule v. Hutton Galleries, Inc. & Khidekel, 328 F.3d 84 (2nd Cir. 2003) and 320 F. Supp. 2d 132 (S.D.N.Y. 2004), French collectors, the Boules, who owned several works attributed to the Russian Supremacist artist Lazar Khidekel, sued the artist's son and daughter-in law and an art gallery that was selling the son's collection of Khidekel's art. The Boules had acquired 176 works attributed to Khidekel through nontraditional channels because it was both illegal and dangerous to acquire Russian avant-garde art prior to fall of the Soviet Union. When the Boules met with the Khidekels about the Boules' collection, the son commented that the bulk of the collection was created when Lazar was a young student, probably as early as 1920. The Khidekels later, in 1992, began an association with Hutton, a prominent dealer of art of the Russian avant-garde, and then moved to New York in 1993. The Khidekels soon entered into a consignment agreement with Hutton to facilitate the sale of their collection of Khidekel's works. In 1996, the Khidekels and Hutton sent a jointly signed letter to several art galleries repudiating the Boules' paintings. The Khidekels were quoted as stating that the paintings were not Khidekel's works. The son told one curator that the Boule collection was "not by my father, they're fakes." The Second Circuit Court of Appeals ruled the Boules had to prove Khidekel created the paintings and held that the Boules had the burden to prove the falsity of the Khidekels' statements regarding the paintings. On remand of the case to the district court, the court found that the Boules were unable to establish by a preponderance of the evidence that the Khidekels in their collection were authentic. However, the court ruled that the Boules did prove the Khidekels expressed no skepticism upon first viewing the Boule collection and that the son had signed sixteen certificates of authenticity. The court found that statements by the artist son and daughter-in-law regarding authenticity of the Boules' works did destroy the value of some of the works for which the son had provided certificates of authenticity.

Example 9. In Rosen v. Spanierman, 894 F.2d 28 (2nd Cir. 1990), the Second Circuit Court of Appeals ruled that a breach of warranty claim accrues when a purchaser buys a painting and not when she discovers the painting is inauthentic. The court commented that a painting's lack of authenticity is discoverable immediately through the trained eye of an art expert and that it is not unreasonable to expect a purchaser of valuable art to obtain a second opinion on a painting's authenticity. The purchaser brought a claim for breach of warranty of authenticity against an art gallery that had sold him a painting the art gallery expressly warranted as an original work by John Singer Sargent. The purchaser discovered the painting was not a genuine Sargent when he attempted to sell it at a Christie's auction nineteen years later. The court ruled the purchaser's claim was not timely.

Example 10. In Greenwood v. Koven, 880 F. Supp. 186 (S.D.N.Y. 1995), a seller of a painting brought an action against an auctioneer for breach of a consignment agreement and a breach of the duty of loyalty when the auctioneer investigated the authenticity of the painting the seller consigned to the auctioneer for sale. The seller owned a pastel purportedly created by Georges Braque, a prominent twentieth-century French painter. Christie's sold the alleged Braque pastel by auction for $600,000 and remitted the sale proceeds to the owner. Later, when Christie's purportedly became concerned about the authenticity of the pastel and the potential liability those concerns portended, Christie's rescinded the sale, returned the purchase price to the purchaser, and sought return of the sale proceeds from the pastel's previous owner. Koven purchased the pastel from the Rosenberg Gallery in 1948 for $1,400. After Koven consigned the painting to Christie's for sale, Christie's began its standard procedure for reviewing, cataloguing, and exhibiting the pastel prior to its sale. Two specialists in Braque examined the pastel and concluded it was an authentic Braque work. The pastel then was physically examined by a number of members in a departmental review who also determined the pastel was genuine. The purchaser of the painting raised questions about the pastel's authenticity shortly after the sale. In order to provide the purchaser with some assurances, Christie's sought documents of the pastel's provenance from Koven and the widow of the owner of the Rosenberg Gallery. Rosenberg confirmed that the Braque pastel had been purchased from the Rosenberg Gallery. Christie's then assured the purchaser of the pastel's provenance and assured her that Christie's had no doubts about the pastel's authenticity. The purchaser still was not convinced and demanded that Christie's provide her with written verification of the work's authenticity by a scholar. Christie's then contacted Claude Laurens, who held the *droit moral* for Braque. Under French law, after the death of an artist, an heir or designee by will is given authority to assert the artist's moral rights, including the right to authenticate works alleged to be created by the artist. Christie's contacted Laurens through his son Quentin and had the pastel flown to France where it could be examined by Quentin Laurens. Quentin informed Christie's that he did not believe the pastel to be the work of Braque and that he would not issue a certificate of authenticity. Christie's then rescinded the sale. Koven contended Christie's actions benefitted the purchaser rather than her. The court agreed that Christie's acted in the capacity of an agent on behalf of Koven and that an agent acts in a fiduciary capacity on behalf of its principal. However, the court stated that agency principles can be modified by contract and referred to the consignment agreement between the parties which explicitly permitted Christie's to act against Koven's interests by providing Christie's with authority to rescind the sale. The court ruled that Christie's actions in investigating authenticity of the pastel were reasonable and that Christie's did not breach a duty to Koven when it undertook to investigate authenticity of the pastel.

Example 11. In Mickle v. Christie's, Inc., 207 F. Supp. 2d 237 (S.D.N.Y. 2002), the court also ruled Christie's did not violate any fiduciary duty by cancelling a sale when questions arose regarding a painting's authenticity. The Mickles, who asserted they had no formal training in art, consigned to Christie's for auction a painting they represented to have inherited from their grandmother. The painting was an unsigned work that the Mickles attributed to the noted nineteenth-century American painter, Carl Wimar. Based on information provided by the Mickles, the opinion of an expert, and the assessments of its own staff, Christie's concluded the painting was properly attributed to Wimar. The painting sold at auction for $750,000 to the Schwarz Gallery. However, subsequent to the auction, the gallery raised doubts about attribution of the painting to Wimar allegedly based on negative reports circulating among members of the trade. The gallery then refused to pay for the painting. Christie's refused to rescind the sale; it wrote the gallery that it stood by the attribution and that the negative hearsay did not constitute grounds for rescission. During litigation, a senior curator at the National Museum of American Art examined the painting at Christie's offices and expressed his opinion that the painting was not the work of Wimar. Christie's then sent the painting to an expert selected by the gallery. After this expert informed the parties of his opinion that the painting was not by Wimar, Christie's cancelled and rescinded the sale. Christie's noted that it forfeited a commission of $122,500. The Mickles contended Christie's owned fiduciary duties to them. The court, however, found that Christie's rescission of the sale was a valid exercise of Christie's discretion and rights under the consignment agreement. The court noted that Christie's had an honest belief that it could be subjected to liability if it did not rescind the sale.

Example 12. In Krahmer v. Christie's Inc., 903 A.2d 773 and 911 A.2d 399 (C. Chan. Del, 2006), purchasers of a painting at an auction in 1986 sought to rescind the contract of sale because the painting allegedly was a fake. Christie's had offered for sale in 1986 a painting it represented to be by Frank Weston Benson. Christie's represented the painting's provenance as a "Midwestern club." The Krahmers bought the painting for $38,500. After the purchase, Christie's gave the Krahmers a nameplate which stated the painting belonged to the Detroit Club of Michigan and that the Detroit Club had purchased the painting directly from Benson. In 1990, Christie's provided the Krahmers with an updated appraisal of the painting in which it confirmed the painting's authenticity and raised its value to $85,000. In 1999, the Krahmers wrote to the Benson Catalogue Raisonné Committee to have their Benson painting listed as authentic. They then learned that another Benson painting of the same subject was in the collection of the New Britain Art Museum. The committee advised the Krahmers that there might be two finished works by Benson; the committee did not suggest that the painting might not be genuine. In 2002, the Krahmers attempted to sell the painting at Sotheby's auction house. After Sotheby's sent the painting to a restorer to assess its condition, the restorer expressed concern that the painting was not authentic. The Krahmers informed Christie's of this suspicion and the parties agreed to have the Benson Catalogue Raisonné Committee determine the painting's authenticity. The committee issued a report in 2003 that the painting was a fake. Christie's refused to rescind the 1986 sale because it stated that there was a six-year warranty of authenticity on the painting and that had expired long ago. The court found that prior to the 1986 auction, the Krahmers were given a catalogue of paintings for sale and the catalogue conspicuously informed potential buyers that there was a six-year warranty of authenticity. The Krahmers contended they were amateur art collectors who had reasonably relied on the representations of a reputable auction house that held itself out as an expert in American art. They argued that questions as to the authenticity of artwork normally do not arise until some future date. The court, however, decided that Christie's served only as a mere intermediary between the seller and the buyer. The court thought the buyers could have safeguarded their investment by verifying the painting's authenticity with an independent third-party appraisal. The court pointed out that a buyer at auction assumes a greater risk as to authenticity than a buyer who purchases directly from the artist.

2. Acquiring Good Title

With stolen art inundating the art market, many museums have encountered claims of theft victims to works in their collections. A museum director may discover a museum has defective title to one of its valuable pieces.[18] Further, requests for repatriation of cultural treasures illicitly brought into the United States often surface. These problems are difficult to resolve.

As noted in Chapter 6, in common law countries, the judicial remedies for the return/restitution of stolen cultural property are based on the common law principle, the English *nemo dat* rule,[19] which provides that one who purchases property from a thief, no matter how innocently, acquires no title in the property. Title remains with the true owner. A New York court commented that the English common law rule "stands as a bulwark against the handiwork of evil, to guard to rightful owners the fruits of their labors."[20] Later, the New York court[21] confirmed the principle basic in the law that "a thief conveys no title as against the true owner."

The common law *nemo dat* principle has been codified into express law in the United States through U.C.C. § 2.403. Thus, the principle is recognized statutory law in all states of the United States with the exception of Louisiana.[22] As explained in Chapter 6, the effect of the English common law rule, codified in the United States in U.C.C. § 2.403, is that purchasers of stolen cultural property can be exposed indefinitely in U.S. courts to conversion claims of original owners.

In the United States, a suit to recover stolen property must be brought pursuant to state property law. A lawsuit would be brought in a state court as a replevin suit or a suit for conversion unless the parties can seek jurisdiction of a federal court based on diversity of citizenship (but in which case the federal court must apply state law).

Example 13. An art museum purchased a valuable painting from an art dealer. The art dealer gave the museum a brochure listing the artworks it had for sale. On the last page of the brochure was a statement in small print that the art dealer assumed no risk, liability, or responsibility for title to its paintings. The museum did not demand evidence that the art dealer had good title to the painting. A few years after the purchase, an individual informed the museum the painting belonged to him, that it was confiscated from his home during World War II. The individual demanded that the museum return the painting to him. Should the museum return the painting? In Porter v. Wertz, 53 N.Y.2d 696, 439 N.Y.S.2d 105, 421 N.E.2d 500 (1981), the New York State Attorney General wanted a court to rule that it was a departure from reasonable commercial standards for a purchaser of a valuable painting to fail to inquire about title to a painting or to question the credentials of the seller as an art dealer. According to the State Attorney General, good faith among art merchants requires an inquiry as to the ownership of an objet d'art. The Art Dealers Association of America, on the other hand, contended that such a rule of law would cripple the art business. The court declined to rule on the good-faith question.

Example 14. In Rosenburg v. Seattle Art Museum, 42 F. Supp. 2d 1029 (W.D.Wash. 1999), the heirs of Paul Rosenberg filed a complaint against the Seattle Art Museum for return of a Matisse, valued at $2 million, which had been donated to the museum by the Estate of Bloedel. The Bloedels purchased the painting from a gallery in New York City in 1954. Heirs of Rosenberg, a Parisian art collector and gallery owner prior to World War II, alleged the painting was stolen by the Nazis and later possessed by the museum. Upon research into the provenance of the painting, the Seattle Art Museum agreed the Rosenburg heirs were the rightful owners of the painting and returned it to them. The museum then filed a third-party complaint against the gallery, which sold the painting to the Bloedels, for breach of title, fraud, and negligent misrepresentation. The court initially ruled the museum did not have standing to sue the gallery for defrauding the Bloedels. It noted that the law in the State of Washington provides that transferring ownership of personal property does not transfer thereby a claim for fraud associated with the purchase of that property. However, it agreed to hear the case after the museum obtained an assignment of the Bloedels' fraud claim from the Bloedel heirs. The case then was settled.

U.C.C. § 2-714(2) provides that a purchaser who has received goods which were not as warranted may recover the difference between the value of the goods as accepted and the value the goods would have had if they had been as warranted. This provision provides more expansive damages than a remedy consisting simply of return of the purchase price. While this provision provides protection for the innocent purchaser, there is a danger when the purchaser later sells the artwork. The defective title will not have been cured, and should the rightful owner sue the purchaser, the latter may be compelled to respond in damages for the appreciated value of the artwork. Limitation on time during which suit may be brought does not begin until the rightful owner asserts a claim to the property (in New York) or until the rightful owner should have discovered the location of the artwork (in other states).[23]

> Example 15. Art Museum purchased a Chagall painting for $250,000 from a New York gallery. The New York gallery had purchased the painting from a Parisian art gallery. In 1932, an individual purchased the painting at an auction in Belgium. When the Nazis invaded Belgium, the individual fled, leaving all his possessions, including the Chagall painting, in his apartment. When he returned six years later, the painting was gone. The German authorities had removed it and had left a receipt for it. The individual learned that Art Museum had the painting from an art book which carried a reproduction of the painting plus a statement that it was in the possession of Art Museum. The individual was successful in a suit against Art Museum for recovery of the painting. Art Museum then sued the art gallery for the value of the painting, $500,000. Assuming the art gallery is financially sound, Art Museum should recover the value of the painting, $500,000. In Menzel v. List, 24 N.Y.2d 91, 298 N.Y.S.2d 979 (1969), List, the purchaser of a Chagall from a New York gallery, in facts as above, was ordered to return the painting to Menzel, the original owner. However, the court ordered the gallery to pay List, the possessor of the Chagall, the value of the painting. The court held that List was entitled to recover the value of the painting and was not limited to the purchase price.

While state courts in the United States (with the exception of Louisiana state courts) follow the common law principle codified in U.C.C. § 2.403, which prevents a seller from conveying good title to property that, at one time, was stolen, there nonetheless can be a cut-off of the theft victim's title after a certain number of years should a court decide a theft victim did not exercise due diligence in pursuing the victim's claim. The ICOM Code of Ethics for Museums defines due diligence as "the requirement that every endeavor is made to establish the facts of a case before deciding a course of action, particularly in identifying the source and history of an item offered for acquisition or use before acquiring it." The ICOM Code states that a museum's "due diligence" in ensuring that any object offered for purchase, gift, loan, bequest, or exchange has not been illegally obtained or exported from its country of origin should establish the full history of an item since discovery or production.

As considered in Chapter 6, the question that arises in title claims is whether a theft victim's claim is precluded by the statute of limitations or the so-called equitable doctrine of laches. The effect these procedural hurdles have on a victim's claim to stolen cultural property is discussed in that chapter. While one court[24] expressed concern for an innocent purchaser when the original owner had not exercised due diligence to recover the stolen property, courts initially tilt the balance in favor of theft victims who can face difficult burdens in meeting a due diligence requirement. Several courts have recognized the extraordinary obstacles persons who suffer art looting confront in locating their property through the "labyrinth of the international art market."[25]

Many years may elapse before a theft victim can identify what has been stolen or even determine that a theft has occurred.[26] Because, as between a dispossessed owner and a good-faith purchaser of cultural property, some courts will balance the equities in favor of the dispossessed owner, current law should impose a higher standard of diligence on the purchaser. A museum director must conduct appropriate and comprehensive investigations into title to artworks and other cultural property prior to purchase to ensure good title to such works, or when title cannot be perfected, to establish a laches defense should an original owner later surface.

Both for ethical reasons and to ensure good title to valuable works, a museum must exercise due diligence in investigating the provenance or title to a work prior to purchase. An adequate due diligence investigation requires an inquiry into several categories or types of art world authorities or resources.[27] The first inquiry should be to those institutions, persons, or art world participants to whom theft victims most likely might report their losses. A second category of inquiry should be to locations where the type of work in question, if stolen, reasonably might be expected to be reintroduced into the legitimate market. A final category is to those resources that reasonably might assist an informed attempt to determine whether a particular work has been stolen.

One resource that should be consulted is an artist's catalogue raisonné, which, as noted above, is a comprehensive compilation of many of the known works of an individual artist and often includes information concerning the history of ownership and display of each work presented. Available stolen art databases, archives, or registries which should be consulted include the Art Loss Register (ALR), Recipero's TRACE Database, and the New York State Holocaust Claims Office.[28] The ALR has its office in London. TRACE is a computerized online service operated by Recipero and located in Gloucestershire, UK. The ALR was created in 1991 as a joint venture that included as partners the International Foundation for Art Research (IFAR) and several insurance companies and other art world investors in London. ALR maintains a computerized database of reportedly stolen art objects using reports of losses compiled by IFAR since 1977 from a variety of sources, including local and state police agencies, art dealers, homeowners, church committee members, museum registrars, library professionals, and periodic reports from the FBI and INTERPOL. TRACE also receives reports of stolen and missing objects from a variety of sources including a number of losses disclosed by the FBI.

B. GIFTS

Museums receive substantial collections, as well as funding, in the form of donations. Museum directors must have some knowledge of the law and tax consequences relating to property donations. Donors are concerned about tax deductions for gifts, and museum directors must be concerned that legal requirements to transfer ownership of artifacts are met. The tax provisions relating to donations were discussed in Chapter 4. This chapter covers the legal requirements to complete a gift and issues relating to restrictions placed on gift property.

1. Legal Requirements

A gift is a voluntary transfer of property from one to another without consideration. The requisites of a valid gift are an intention to make a gift, a delivery of the property given, and an acceptance by the donee.[29] A donor must have freedom of will to make a valid gift. A gift resulting from duress, fraud, or undue influence may be set aside. A donor also must have sufficient mental capacity to make a gift.[30] In addition, a donor's intention to make a gift must be clear and unmistakable and must be a present intention.[31]

Delivery of the subject of a gift must be complete and unconditional. Because a gift is transferred for no consideration, a court action is not available to enforce a gift if it has not been delivered fully. Delivery of the subject of a gift may be actual, constructive, or symbolic, but it must transfer possession to the donee and must be a present and irrevocable title. The donor must be divested of control and dominion over the property.[32]

Once a gift has been perfected by sufficient delivery and acceptance, it cannot be revoked. To substantiate its title to gifts, then, a museum must obtain and retain sufficient documentation of completed gifts. (See Appendix for a sample form for delivery and acceptance of a gift of personalty.)

> Example 16. In Herzog Foundation v. University of Bridgeport, 699 A.2d 955 (Conn. 1997), a donor sought to enforce a provision of a restricted gift to a university. The Supreme Court of Connecticut referred to the common law rule that a donor who has made a completed charitable contribution, whether in trust or as an absolute gift, has no standing to enforce terms of the gift unless the donor expressly reserved the right to do so. The Connecticut Supreme Court decided that state statutory law did not change the common law and, thus, did not grant the donor the right to enforce an unreserved restriction on the donor's completed gift. This court held that a donor's right to enforce a restriction on a completed gift is enforceable only at the instance of the Attorney General.

2. Cy Pres Doctrine

Property and funds may be given to a museum in the form of a charitable trust wherein certain restrictions are placed upon use of the trust property and funding.[33] The so-called cy pres doctrine requires that administration of a charitable trust be carried out with as close an approximation to the intent of the donor as is reasonably practicable. A charitable organization may not receive a gift for one purpose and use it for another unless a court, applying cy pres, authorizes a variation.[34] Only a court may invoke cy pres.[35] The cy pres doctrine applies, to vary the terms of a restricted gift, only if the donor indicated a "general" charitable intent; it is not applicable if a gift was made with a "specific" intent.

A museum director must administer a gift according to the directives of the donor; however, when conditions or restrictions placed upon gift property become impossible to accomplish, the director may petition a court to change or delete the restrictions under the cy pres doctrine. The alternative is that the gift will lapse.

In instances where a trust would fail because restrictions on property placed in a charitable trust make it impossible to administer the trust, a court may apply the doctrine of deviation, which is analogous to the cy pres doctrine, to ease administrative restraints the donor did not anticipate at the time of the gift.[36] The doctrine of deviation applies when the administrators of a charitable trust seek ways to accomplish the objectives of a gift or of the trust. Although deviation differs somewhat from cy pres (which applies to avoid failure of a gift), the rules are similar and often are confused. Terms subject to deviation are limited to administrative provisions of the trust, i.e., "the details of administration" which the creator of a trust "has prescribed in order to secure the more important result of obtaining for the beneficiaries the advantages" the trust creator stated he wished them to have.[37] In order to permit deviation from the administrative provisions of a trust, courts generally require the presence of two elements: (1) unforeseen and unforeseeable change in circumstances, and (2) a frustration of the trust creator's main objectives by the change assuming strict obedience to the trust creator's directions were required.[38]

> Example 17. A trust fund was established several years ago to help create and maintain Art Museum. The trustor provided in the declaration of trust that the trustees would use funds from the trust to acquire artworks. The museum was housed in a building that had been adequate when the trust fund was established. Presently, however, the museum collection has increased to the point that there is lack of space to display the entire collection. Trustees of the fund want to use some of the trust funds to finance in part a new building for the museum. The trustees would petition a court to deviate from the terms of the trust to help finance the building. In Cleveland Museum of Art v. O'Neill, 129 N.E.2d 669 (Ohio Com. Pl. 1995), trustees of a trust fund established to support work of the Cleveland Museum of Art sought a declaratory judgment in which they asked a court to interpret provisions of the trust agreement. The trust was established to help create and maintain an art museum. Funds were to be used to acquire art objects. When the museum collection had increased to the point that there was lack of space to display the entire collection, trustees wanted to use some of the trust funds to finance in part a new building. The court had no hesitancy in determining that under existing circumstances, creators of the trust would have been willing to deviate from their expressed method of financing the museum and would have permitted trust funds to be used to help finance the building. In view of changed conditions that trust creators could not have anticipated, the court reasoned the trustors would not want to see the work of the museum defeated or impaired by lack of space. According to the court, the long-range purpose of the trust would remain the same, i.e., maintenance of an outstanding museum of art. By court decree, then, trustees of the trust fund were permitted to deviate from the provisions of the trust agreement.

Example 18. A Pennsylvania court [In re The Barnes Foundation, 684 A.2d 123 (Pa. Super 1996)] noted that relief afforded by deviation is not based on mere convenience, but on the necessity of effecting a change in the situation where compliance with the trust would impair substantially accomplishment of the purposes of the trust. The Barnes Foundation had an extensive collection of works of art housed in its buildings in Merion, Pennsylvania. The trustees contended that conditions in the trust instrument establishing the foundation had become impracticable. The trustees wanted to amend the trust instrument regarding its prohibition against ever loaning, selling, or otherwise disposing of any pieces of the collection and regarding the art gallery's admission policy. The court granted the requested trust modifications.

Example 19. In Yale University v. Blumenthal, 621 A2d 1304 (Conn. 1993), a testator left his property in trust for his wife with the provision that upon her death or remarriage the net undistributed income would be paid to Yale College to be used to build a wing for the Yale Medical School for the "treatment of the sick poor." Upon death of the testator's wife, the net income was distributed to Yale. However, the amount was not sufficient to construct a new wing to the medical school. In addition, university officials stated the medical school could not limit treatment to the "sick poor." Yale sought advice from the Attorney General of the state as to whether it could use the funds to benefit the school of medicine in whatever manner it chose to further its educational purposes. It contended the restrictions in the will were "obsolete, inappropriate and impractical." Because the Attorney General could not agree with Yale on a proper utilization of the funds, Yale filed a court action seeking release from restrictions in the will. The Connecticut Supreme Court permitted removal of the restrictions.

Example 20. In Russell v. Yale University, 737 A.2d 941 (Conn. App. 1999), Connecticut courts ruled that a donor who has made a completed donation has no authority to bring an action in court to enforce the terms of the gift unless the donor expressly reserved the right to do so. (As noted above in Example 16, in Herzog Foundation, Inc. v. University of Bridgeport, 699 A.2d 995 (Conn. 1997), the Connecticut Supreme Court recognized that at common law a donor who has made a completed donation has no authority to bring an action to enforce the terms of the gift unless the donor expressly reserved the right to do so.)

Example 21. In Howard v. Administrators of Tulane Educational Fund, 986 So.2d 47 (La. 2008), the Supreme Court of Louisiana ruled differently. It decided that the heirs of a donor-testator had the right to revoke a donation for nonperformance of a conditional grant. The Louisiana Supreme Court decision is based on Louisiana statutes, which are founded on the French Civil Code. The Louisiana Court ruled that the donor's heirs, in their capacity as successors, could seek enforcement of a conditional donation. The Louisiana Supreme Court stated that a donor has the right to revoke a donation for nonperformance of conditions imposed on the donee. The court referred to the right as an extraordinary remedy, especially in the context of donations *inter vivos* (occurring during life) that are by definition irrevocable. According to the Louisiana Supreme Court, the right to revoke and, thus, to enforce a donation for nonperformance of a condition, is transmitted upon death to the donor's successors.

C. LOANS

The ICOM Code of Ethics for Museums prescribes the same stewardship requirements for collections on loan as to those obtained by purchase or by gift. It states that every effort should be made to ensure that an object has not been illegally obtained or exported from its country of origin before acquiring an object on loan and that no object should be acquired by loan unless the object's owner has good title.[39]

Loans of museum collections are subject to the law of bailments. When property is delivered for a specific purpose to another person or entity with a contract, express or implied, that the person or entity to whom such property was delivered will return or account for the property, a bailment occurs. The person or entity that delivers the property to another under circumstances wherein a bailment occurs is called a bailor; the person or entity to whom the property is delivered is called a bailee.[40]

1. Law Relating to Bailments

Courts characteristically divided bailments into one of three types: (1) those for the sole benefit of the bailor, (2) those for the sole benefit of the bailee, and (3) those for the mutual benefit of both parties.[41] Courts then would impose a particular standard of care on a bailee in caring for property entrusted to the bailee and, in determining the liability for loss or damage to the property, would consider the nature of the bailment. Where the bailment was for the mutual benefit of the bailor and bailee, the bailee would be held to the exercise of ordinary care in relation to the property and would be liable for ordinary negligence. Where the bailment was for the sole benefit of the bailor, the bailee was only bound to slight care and was liable for gross negligence. Where the bailment was for the sole benefit of the bailee, the bailee was bound to great care and was liable for slight negligence. Any deviation from the terms of the bailment rendered the bailee absolutely liable for any damages to the property while it was in the bailee's possession.

Example 22. At the request of an art museum, an individual loans the museum a valuable art collection for exhibition. The individual permits the museum to display the art collection for a period of one year without compensation to the individual. The bailment generally would be for the sole benefit of the bailee, the museum. Still, if the collection becomes more valuable as a result of the display, it may become a bailment for the mutual benefit of the individual and the museum.

Example 23. Assume the art collection in Example 22 is stolen. If the bailment is for the mutual benefit of the parties, the museum would not be liable if it exercised ordinary care to prevent theft. If the bailment is for the sole benefit of the museum, the museum probably would be liable for the value of the collection, as it would, in that case, be liable for the slightest negligence.

Example 24. In Gardini v. Museum of City of New York, 173 Misc. 791, 19 N.Y.S.2d 96 (1940), a court held a museum liable for loss of a diamond brooch that had been entrusted to the museum for exhibition purposes. The owner of the brooch had been given a written receipt for the brooch which stated the museum was not responsible for the safekeeping of articles entrusted to it for exhibition. The court held the owner of the brooch could infer the museum would exercise reasonable care in safeguarding the brooch, and the receipt did not absolve the museum from liability for gross negligence.

Example 25. In Colburn v. Washington State Art Ass'n, 80 Wash. 662, 141 P.1153 (1914), a court held that one who places an exhibit in a museum, which refuses to permit a lock on the case, assumes the risk of theft by leaving the exhibit there with the knowledge of the method by

> which it might be protected. The court held that the bailment was for the mutual benefit of the parties and the bailee museum was required to exercise only ordinary diligence to prevent theft of the articles.

A contract can change the duty of care. The parties may by contract diminish the liability of the bailee, or they may limit the amount of the bailee's liability to an agreed valuation of the bailed property. Parties to a contract are free to contract as they choose, provided their agreement is not against public policy. Thus, the parties can agree that one of the parties is exempt from liability for negligence (assuming there is equality of bargaining power between the parties). A provision waiving liability may be valid against all fault except gross negligence.

> Example 26. Assume the art collection in Example 22, which was loaned to the museum, is stolen or destroyed. Although the museum has insurance coverage, the art collection is priceless and cannot be replaced. A bailment for the sole benefit of the bailee requires extraordinary diligence and great care on the part of the bailee. Museum officials should have contracted with the owner of the collection that the museum's liability for the art collection would be limited to the museum's insurance coverage or to some other stated amount.

A bailee may be liable for conversion if the bailee appropriates bailed property to the bailee's own use, if the bailee uses the property in a manner not authorized by the bailment contract, or if the bailee sells or transfers the property. The negligence of a bailee in the care of the bailed property does not constitute a conversion, but if a bailee fails to use that degree of care that the circumstances or events demand, the bailee may be liable to the bailor in an action in conversion for the subsequent loss of the property or for its full value if the property is rendered worthless.

A bailee who has added something of value to bailed property by the bailee's labor or skill has a lien on the property for the value of the bailee's efforts unless there is a special contract to the contrary. If a bailee voluntarily parts with possession of the property before receiving compensation, the bailee's lien may be lost.

Upon termination of a bailment, the bailee is ordinarily under an absolute duty to redeliver the bailed property to the bailor in its original or altered form, or to account for the property in accordance with the contract of bailment. Where the manner or redelivery is specified, the bailee must comply strictly with the terms of redelivery or be liable in the event of loss. If the bailment contract is silent on this question, the bailee's obligation generally is regulated by the custom and usage of the business at the place where the bailment is made. If a bailee wrongfully delivers a bailor's property, the bailee is liable for conversion.

Example 27. An art investor (Price) and some German nationals brought an action against the United States for its refusal to turn over to them watercolors painted by Adolf Hitler and photographic archives the United States took from Germany during its allied occupation after World War II. The photographic archives were compiled by Heinrich Hoffmann and his son. Hoffmann, who served as a photographer in the Bavarian army, first met Hitler in 1919 and became Hitler's personal friend. Hoffmann was the only person permitted to photograph Hitler, and he accompanied Hitler everywhere on his road to power. Hoffmann's many photographs provided a record of twenty-five years of German history. The United States Army seized a portion of the Hoffmann archives in 1945. The Army also seized four watercolors painted by Hitler that Hoffmann acquired during the 1930s and 1940s. Price purchased the right to the archives and the paintings from Hoffmann's heirs and then demanded that the United States government deliver them to him. Although the federal government is immune from suit unless it consents to be sued, the Tucker Act[42] permits suit against the federal government based on an "express or implied" contract with the government. In Price v. United States, 707 F. Supp. 1465 (S.D.Tex. 1989), a federal district court awarded damages against the government. However, the Fifth Circuit Court of Appeals [69 F.3d 46 (5th Cir. 1995) and 81 F.3d 520 (5th Cir. 1996)] reversed the district court's decision and dismissed the claims. In 1998, Price, the art collector, was dismissed from the case. Then, in Hoffmann v. United States, 53 F. Supp. 2d 483 (D.C. 1999), the Hoffman heirs contended that an "implied-in-fact bailment" contract was created in 1945 between the United States government and the Hoffmanns when the Army seized the collection. They contended the United States government had a fiduciary obligation to return the bailed property. In Hoffman v. United States, 266 F. Supp. 2d 27 (D.C.D.C. 2003), the court ruled that if an implied-in-fact contract of bailment was created in 1945, any claim to the property accrued in 1949 because at that time the government refused to return the photographic archive at the request of Hoffmann's son. Because the lawsuit was filed six years after that date, the court ruled any claim was time barred.

Although a bailor fails to recover bailed property, the property remains the property of the bailor unless the bailment contract specifies otherwise. A cause of action on the part of the bailor to recover the property would not begin to run until the bailee converted the property. This rule can cause problems for museums that have objects on loan for a long period of time when the bailor has made no effort to reacquire the objects. It also presents problems for museums that earlier did not properly catalogue objects in their collection and, thus, have no evidence as to whether certain objects were acquired by gift, in which case the museum would have good title, or were loaned to the museum so that the museum would not have title to the goods.

Example 28. A state statute in Texas[43] provides a means to obtain good title to an artifact in a collection that was acquired by loan when the lender has not requested a return of the object. The statue provides that property on loan to a museum for fifteen years or more will become abandoned property if no person has made a claim for the property. The property can become property of the museum if the original lender does not respond after two years from the date the museum gives the original lender notice by a letter, which it mails to the lender's address with a proof of receipt returned to the museum, of its possession of the property. If the lender has no address, the museum must publish notice once a week for two consecutive weeks in a newspaper of general circulation in the county where the museum is located or the county in which the lender resides, if known. The statute provides that a two-year statute of limitations runs from the date the museum gives the lender notice under the statute. Should the lender not reacquire the property after the two-year period, a purchaser from the museum would acquire valid title to the property. A museum that accepts a loan for an indefinite period or for a period in excess of seven years must inform the lender in writing of the terms of this statute.

An art dealer who has been entrusted with a painting is a bailee, and, as such, can pass good title to the painting to a bona fide purchaser.[44]

Example 29. In 1930, an artist who resided in Europe, Alphonse Mucha, left some of his paintings with an art dealer in Boston. The artist later requested their return to him in Czechoslovakia. However, in 1935, upon the Muchas' return to Europe, Mucha asked the dealer to retain his paintings and return them to him at some future date. The art dealer did not return the paintings to the artist but rather suggested in a letter to Mucha that the artist's son pick up the paintings when he was in the United States. Mucha died soon thereafter without reacquiring the paintings. The art dealer later sold his business. A purchaser of some articles at the final sale took some rolled-up paintings in the basement without paying for them; thus, he was not a purchaser from the bailee art dealer. The paintings included the Mucha paintings. The individual later sold one of the Mucha paintings that Mucha had left with the art dealer. Subsequently, upon learning of the purchaser's possession of one of the paintings, Mucha's son filed suit to recover the painting. The purchaser contended the art dealer had converted the paintings, the bailed property, when he failed to return the paintings to Mucha. Because the alleged act of conversion occurred in 1935, the purchaser contended the statute of limitations had run on any claim Mucha's son might have as to his ownership of the painting. In Mucha v. King, 792 F.2d 602 (7th Cir. 1986), the Seventh Circuit Court of Appeals ruled against the purchaser. The court noted that the statute of limitations as to bailed property does not begin to run until a bailee has converted the bailed property. The court pointed out that, while the art gallery did not return the paintings to Mucha, it had written him that it would be better to have his son pick up the paintings when he came to the United States. The court ruled that this written response was not an act of conversion. Because there was no conversion of the bailed property, the Seventh Circuit held that the statute of limitations did not begin to run as against the bailor, Mucha, and that Mucha retained title to his paintings.

Because of the potential problems that can arise when a painting or a collection is on loan, a museum director should set out the terms of each loan in an agreement between the museum and the owner of the loaned object or collection. The bailment agreement should do the following: specify the objects loaned; place a value on the objects agreed upon by the parties; state the manner in which the museum is to exhibit the objects or collection on loan; set out the amount of space allotted to display the loaned collection, as well as the method of exhibition and any publicity to be given the exhibit; specify the amount of insurance required for the collection; and specify the museum's liability for any damage to, or loss of, the exhibit. By agreeing upon and placing a valuation for objects on loan and by purchasing adequate insurance based on that valuation with a specified liability, the parties can be protected should the collection be destroyed, damaged, or stolen in any context. The bailment contract also might have a provision that if the owner (bailor) does not reclaim the collection after a certain length of time, the property will become a gift to the museum. (See sample form for bailment contract in the Appendix.)

2. International Loans of Artistic Treasures

The sharing of art through loans or traveling exhibits is a means of increasing knowledge and goodwill among the various countries involved. International loans of artistic treasures have been hindered in the past by the cost of insuring these exhibitions. To solve the problem of funds to acquire international exhibitions on loan, Congress passed the Arts and Artifacts Indemnity Act[45] in 1975. Pursuant to this act, the federal government provides indemnification for museum exhibitions of works of art, including tapestries, paintings, sculptures, folk art, graphics, craft arts, manuscripts, rare documents and books, photographs, motion pictures, audio and video tapes, and other objects or artifacts that are of educational, cultural, or scientific value and that are certified by the Secretary of State or the Secretary's designee as being in the national interest.[46]

An indemnity agreement under the act, if approved, covers all eligible items while they are on exhibition in the United States or elsewhere when the display is part of an exchange of exhibitions.[47] An indemnity agreement pledges the full faith and credit of the United States to pay any amount for which the government becomes liable under the agreement.[48]

The program has fostered international cooperation through the sharing of cultural treasures. Most countries have realized that a sharing of each state's cultural treasures is feasible and represents a vital alternative to the tacit approval in the past to powerful nations looting and pilfering the artifacts of smaller, defenseless countries. The Arts and Artifacts Indemnity Act provides the means to accomplish the objective of permitting U.S. citizens to share in the cultural treasures of the world.

3. Exemption of Loans from Seizure

Artworks and other cultural property on loan have been subject to seizure because of claims of theft victims and others. As noted previously, ICOM posits that a museum should not acquire an object unless the director is satisfied the object has not been stolen or exported from its country of origin in violation of that country's laws. It specifies that the policy applies to exhibitions on loan as well as to purchases and gifts. Difficult problems surface for a museum that has an object on loan, which is later alleged to have been stolen.

Example 30. In the Matter of the Grand Jury Subpoena Duces Tecum v. Museum of Modern Art, 719 N.E.2d 897 (N.Y. 1999), an Egon Schiele painting on loan to a New York museum from the Leopold Museum in Austria was subpoenaed by the New York District Attorney's Office pursuant to a grand jury investigation into the theft of the painting during the German annexation of Austria. The museum moved to quash the subpoena on the grounds it was invalid pursuant to New York's exemption from seizure act.[49] The New York statute did not have an exception to the exemption from seizure for stolen works.[50] The highest court in New York granted the museum's motion. However, the federal government then commenced a forfeiture proceeding and seized the painting. In U.S. v. Portrait of Wally, 663 F. Supp. 2d 232 (S.D.N.Y. 2009), the federal district court decided trial was warranted on the issue of whether the possessor of the painting knew the painting was stolen when the Leopold Museum imported it into the United States for exhibition. The case was settled prior to its going to trial. The Leopold Museum agreed to pay the estate of the original owner $19 million, and the estate agreed to release the painting. As part of the settlement, the painting was displayed publicly at the Museum of Jewish Heritage before being returned to the Leopold Museum in Vienna. Further, at all future displays of the painting, the painting's true provenance, including the Nazi theft of the painting have to be noted.

There has been a significant increase in the number of museums applying to the federal government for exemption from seizure of their loan exhibitions under the Federal Immunity from Seizure Act.[51] The Department of State, which processes these applications, requires that each applicant submit a certification that the applicant has undertaken professional inquiry into the provenance of the objects. The applicant must certify that it does not know, or have reason to know, of any circumstances with respect to any of the objects in the loan that would indicate the potential for competing claims of ownership.

Example 31. In Malewicz v. City of Amsterdam, 517 F. Supp. 2d 322 (D.D.C. 2007), the surviving heirs of the Russian artist Kazimir

Malewicz brought a claim against the City of Amsterdam in which they contended the City of Amsterdam acquired Malewicz's paintings illegally. Malewicz had entrusted his paintings to friends in Germany for safe keeping during World War II. After the war, the City of Amsterdam's Stedelijk Museum acquired some of the paintings from one of the persons to whom Malewicz had entrusted them. In 2003, the Stedelijk loaned the paintings to the Guggenheim Museum in New York and the Menil Collection in Houston. The Stedelijk required the museums to obtain immunity from seizure for the paintings while they were in the United States. The Malewicz's heirs contended the Foreign Sovereign Immunities Act, 28 U.S.C. § 1602, et. seq. (discussed in Chapter 6), did not bar their claim against the City of Amsterdam because the city had carried on commercial activity in the United States in connection with the loan. The city, on the other hand, contended its presence in the United States was "isolated and transitory." The court referred to the fact that the Stedelijk knew of the heirs' adverse claims and had insisted the American museums procure a promise of immunity from the U.S. State Department. The court stated the Stedelijk's requirement that the museums obtain immunity from seizure indicated the Stedelijk did anticipate "being haled into court." The court decided that while there was a close question of whether the city's contact with the United States in connection with the loan of the paintings was "substantial," the record contained sufficient contacts to establish jurisdiction under FSIA's expropriation exception.[52]

D. NATURAL AND CULTURAL HERITAGE RESTRICTIONS

Heritage laws are discussed in Part III (laws protecting the natural heritage are discussed in Chapter 9; laws in the United States protecting the cultural heritage are summarized in Chapter 10; and international conventions protecting natural and cultural heritage are reviewed in Chapter 11). These laws also must be considered before museum officials accession objects to the museum's collections. As an example, those museums that have botanical or zoological specimens must consider laws that prohibit and may even criminalize the acquisition of specimens on threatened or endangered species lists. Museum officials may not acquire objects that are protected by the Archeological Resources Protection Act, discussed in Chapter 10, and must consult with tribal leaders before accessioning tribal artifacts that are protected by the

Native American Graves Protection and Repatriation Act, also discussed in Chapter 10. The acquisition of objects found on shipwrecks is regulated by the federal government pursuant to the Abandoned Shipwreck Act, discussed in Chapter 10. International conventions protecting heritage, which are discussed in Chapter 11, have provisions museums must consider in accessioning objects. Thus, museum officials and personnel should consult Part III as well in making decisions regarding accessions to their collections.

E. DEACCESSIONING

Deaccessioning is the procedure whereby museums sell or dispose of unwanted or less desirable pieces in their collections to provide funds for new purchases or to achieve a balanced collection. Before disposing of a part of a museum's collections, the museum director must consult state statutes regarding disposition of assets of a charitable organization and must consider restrictions on the disposition of pieces acquired by gift, as well as ethical questions regarding dispositions. The decision to deaccession vests a great deal of discretion in a museum's trustees. The trustees must consider the ultimate effect of deaccessioning upon the collection as a whole as the entire collection is dedicated to the public benefit.

The ICOM Code of Ethics for Museums contains several provisions relating to removing collections.[53] The Code states that removal of an object from a museum collection must only be undertaken with a full understanding of the significance of the item, its character, and any loss of public trust that could result from the removal.[54] The ICOM Code of Ethics, in recognizing that collections are held in public trust, states that collections may not be treated as realizable assets. It requires that compensation received from deaccessioning and disposal of objects be used solely for the benefit of the collection and usually for acquisitions to that collection.[55] The ICOM Code states that museum personnel, the governing body, or their families or close associates should not be permitted to purchase objects that have been deaccessioned from a collection for which they are responsible.[56]

> Example 32. The Illinois Art Museum had a valuable collection of musical instruments and paintings by Boucher, Delacroix, and Rubens in its collections. Museum trustees decided to sell these pieces at an auction to finance the museum's debts. In Scott v. Silverstein, 94 Ill. App. 3d 431, 418 N.E.2d 1087 (1978) and Scott v. George F. Harding Museum, 58 Ill. App. 3d 408, 374 N.E.2d 756 (1981), the Attorney General intervened and obtained a court order to prevent the auction.

The ICOM Code of Ethics for Museums emphasizes that every museum should have a policy defining authorized methods for removing an object permanently from its collections and must have complete records of all deaccessioning decisions, the objects involved, and the disposition of any deaccessioned object.[57] Museums should adopt guidelines to govern their deaccessioning procedures that generally will restrict deaccessioning to those collections that are no longer relevant and useful for the purposes and activities of the museum and when the pieces cannot be stored properly and preserved. A museum director also should make reasonable efforts to ascertain whether the museum is free to dispose of any piece from its collection. The director must observe mandatory restrictions on the disposition of any object from the museum's collection unless a court authorizes deviation.

The ICOM Code places responsibility for a decision to deaccession on the museum governing body in conjunction with the museum director and the curator of the collection concerned.[58] Museum trustees should approve the deaccessioning of pieces in a collection only upon the recommendation of the appropriate curator or a responsible authority approved by the curator, upon the approval of the museum's director, and in accordance with policies approved by the museum's board of directors. In accordance with the ICOM Code of Ethics, some museum professionals posit that any funds received from the disposal of any object from a museum's collections should be applied solely for the purchase of additions to the museum's collections.

When a museum's board of directors approves the deaccessioning of pieces in the museum's collections, the directors preferably should place the pieces with another museum or nonprofit public institution. This follows the requirement of many state statutes and Treasury Regulations[59] regarding the requirement that, to maintain tax exempt status, assets of a charitable organization must be distributed for an exempt purpose upon dissolution of the organization (discussion of tax exempt status of a museum in Chapter 3). Sales of pieces in a museum collection should be at advertised public auctions or at the public marketplace to best protect the interest, objectives, and legal status of the museum. A museum director should not give preference to, or sell privately to, museum employees, officers, members of the governing body, or their representatives.

Example 33. In Georgia O'Keeffe Foundation (Museum) v. Fisk University, 312 S.W.3d 1 (Tenn. Ct. App. 2009), a private university, to which over two hundred pieces of art owned by Georgia O'Keeffe and her late husband's estate had been gifted conditionally by the artist, sought permission to sell two of the art pieces. (The collection consisted of ninety-seven pieces from the Alfred Stieglitz estate and four paintings from Georgia O'Keeffe's personal collection.) The Georgia O'Keeffe Museum intervened and contended that any sale of the collection violated conditions of the gift and should result in the entire collection reverting to the Georgia O'Keeffe Museum as the successor-in-interest to the artist's estate. The Attorney General also intervened in the lawsuit. The court ruled that the museum, as assignee of a residuary beneficiary of an artist's estate, did not have a right of reversion of the art and that the artist's conditional gift was made with a general charitable intent. The court ruled that, without a right of reversion, the O'Keeffe Museum could not be a party to the action. The court remanded the case to the district court to determine whether cy pres relief was available. After finding that cy pres relief was available to modify the conditions imposed by donors of the artworks, the district court approved agreements whereby another museum would purchase a fifty percent interest in the art for $30 million and would thereafter share in the display and maintenance of the artwork. The district court conditioned approval of the agreements on the requirement that the university establish an endowment of $20 million from proceeds of the sale in furtherance of the donor's intent to make the art available for the citizens of Nashville, Tennessee. The Attorney General contended the district court exceeded the scope of remand and erred in determining the agreement with the museum most closely reflected the donor's intent. The university sought a review of the district court's requirement that it establish an endowment. On appeal [In re Fisk University, 392 S.W.3d 582 (Tenn. Ct. App. 2011), the appellate court determined that the university's financial condition rendered strict compliance with the terms of the gift impracticable. The court decided that O'Keeffe's motivation for the gifts to the university was to promote the study of art in Nashville and the South. The appellate court ruled that the agreement to sell a portion of the art closely approximated the donor's charitable intent but ruled that the district court lacked authority to condition approval of sale on the university's creation of an endowment.

Example 34. A question arose regarding valuable artworks in a museum funded by a municipality.[60] After the city became bankrupt, a city "emergency manager" wanted to list some of the valuable artworks in the museum's collection as possible assets available to pay the city's debts. A public outcry followed wherein concerned citizens asserted that art collections are important cultural resources that should never be treated as disposable assets. They quoted the provision in the AAM Code of Ethics for Museums,[61] which states a museum's disposal of any of its collection through sale must be solely for the advancement of the museum's mission and proceeds from a sale can only be used for acquisitions or for direct care of the collection. The state Senate then passed a bill that would prohibit a municipal museum from selling any of its artworks unless the sale was in connection with a relocation of the art collection to a comparable facility within the same municipality. The Senate bill stated that a governmental museum must adhere to the AAM Code of Ethics for Museums.

Example 35. A New York court ruled [In re Friends for Long Island's Heritage, 80 A.D.3d 223, 911 N.Y.S. 2d 412 (S. Ct., App. Div., 2nd Dept., N.Y., 2010] that in a judicial dissolution proceeding, a court could order that assets held for a limited purpose cannot be used to pay creditors. The court confirmed that New York's long-standing policy honoring donors' restrictions on the use of donated property had greater weight than the claims of creditors. The court stated that the New York Not-for-Profit Corporation Law[62] emphasizes the view that the public places greater importance on limitations on the use of a donated asset than the entity which actually holds it. The court decided that even in dissolution, the limitations on donated assets must be honored and not necessarily to the lesser extent of cy pres. The court pointed out that items in a museum collection could be lost to the public forever if they could be used to pay debts during liquidation. According to the court, to permit assets held for a specific purpose to be liquidated to pay claims of creditors would extinguish the purpose behind the gift. The court ruled that, with respect to a special collection and consistent with the doctrine of cy pres, the court could provide for sale as a single collection to an entity engaged in activities substantially similar to those of the entity in liquidation. A condition of sale would be that the purchasing entity agreed to be bound by the collection's gift agreement.

Example 36. In Vanderbilt Museum v. American Ass'n of Museums, 113 Mis. 2d 502, 449 N.Y.S.2d 399 (1982) the American Association of Museums (currently the American Alliance of Museums) suspended the accreditation of the New York Art Museum because of serious questions regarding maintenance, disposition, and distribution of museum property. The museum filed suit against the AAM contending the museum's accreditation was suspended without notice or a hearing. The court ruled that participation in a voluntary accreditation program is substantially similar to membership in a voluntary membership association. According to the court, some kind of notice and hearing often is required before a member can be suspended or expelled, at least where the association is formed for economic purposes or where the members are entitled to privileges or rights of property.

NOTES

1. ICOM Code of Ethics for Museums, 2.2.

2. Adopted in 1991, and amended in 2000, by the American Association of Museums (AAM). The name of the AAM was changed in 2012 to the American Alliance of Museums.

3. ICOM Code of Ethics for Museums, Principle 7.

4. Id.

5. Id. at 2.1.

6. Leonard Duboff, *Controlling the Artful Con: Authentication as Regulation*, 27 Hastings L. J. 973 (1976).

7. Leonard Duboff, cited in note 6.

8. Discussion in Balog v. Center Art Gallery, Hawaii, Inc., 745 F. Supp. 1556 (D. Haw. 1990). The court noted in Balog that a buyer's incentive to employ the various techniques available to authenticate a work is a function of the purported value of the potential investment.

9. U.C.C. § 2-313.

10. U.C.C. § 2-316.

11. N.Y. Arts & Cult. Aff. Law § 13.01.

12. Thome v. Alexander & Louisa Calder Foundation, Inc., 70 A.D.3d 88, 890 N.Y.S.2d 16 (N.Y. 2009), quoting Ronald D. Spencer, *The Expert versus the Object: Judging Fakes and False Attribution in the Visual Arts* (New York: Oxford Press, 2004), xi.

13. Leonard Duboff, cited in note 6 and quoted in Thome v. Alexander & Louisa Calder Foundation, Inc., cited in note 12.

14. Thome v. Alexander & Louisa Calder Foundation, Inc., cited in note 12.

15. Id.

16. The court in Thome, cited in note 12, concluded that the art collector was not entitled to a declaration of authenticity with respect to the work he claimed was created by Alexander Calder.

17. Discussion in Boule v. Hutton, 320 F. Supp.2d 132 (S.D.N.Y. 2004).

18. The ICOM Code of Ethics defines "valid title" as the "indisputable right to ownership of property, supported by full provenance of the item since discovery or production."

19. *Nemo dat quod non habe* [He who has not cannot give].

20. Menzel v. List, 267 N.Y.S.2d 804, 819 (1966).

21. Menzel v. List, 298 N.Y.S.2d 979, 246 N.E.2d 742 (N.Y. 1969).

22. Louisiana is a civil law state and does not follow the common law *nemo dat* principle. In *Dunbar v. Seger-Thomschitz*, 638 F. Supp. 2d 659 (E.D. La., 2009), aff'd, 615 F.3d 574 (5th Cir. 2010), cert. den., 131 S.Ct. 1511 (2011), a federal district court in Louisiana noted that under the Louisiana Civil Code, § 3491, ownership can be lost through possession sufficient to acquire the property through acquisitive prescription, citing All-State Credit Plan Natchitoches, Inc. v. Ratliff, 279 So.2d 660 (La. 1972).

23. Discussion of statute of limitations on suits for recovery of stolen property in Chapter 6.

24. O'Keeffe v. Snyder, 416 A.2d 862 (N.J. 1980).

25. Id. In Hoelzer v. City of Stamford, Connecticut, 933 F.2d 1131(2nd Cir. 1991), the court observed that "because [stolen] art work can be both extremely valuable and highly marketable to an underground clientele, the difficulties original owners face in recovering missing art abound."

26. For example, in Autocephalous Greek-Orthodox Church of Cyprus v. Goldberg & Feldman Fine Arts, Inc., 917 F.2d 278 (7th Cir. 1990), discussed in Chapter 6, a Greek-Orthodox church in Cyprus, in an area under the control of Turkish military forces, did not learn that its priceless Byzantine mosaics had been looted until perhaps three years after the theft had occurred.

27. In Black Hills Institute of Geological Research v. Williams, 88 F.3d 614 (8th Cir. 1996), the Eighth Circuit Court of Appeals ruled that "a party who has knowledge of facts that would cast doubt upon the transferability of title has a duty to investigate that title and a lack of caution and diligence in such situations amounts to bad faith." The court ruled that the institute's failure to investigate diligently whether a fossil found on an Indian reservation could be sold absent government approval prevented the institute from being a good faith, bona fide purchaser.

28. An artwork with a questionable provenance from 1933 to 1945 may be Holocaust looted art. Discussion of Nazi looted art in Lawrence M. Kaye, "Looted Art: What Can and Should be Done," 20 Cardozo L. Rev. 657 (1998).

29. Brown, Personal Property § 7.1. The donee has the burden of proof to show that these requirements have been met.

30. Id. at § 7.12.

31. If some essential element necessary to make a perfected gift is lacking, the donor may revoke the gift at any time before it is perfected. Id. at § 7.1.

32. Id.

33. The International Council of Museum (ICOM) stated in its 1986 Code of Professional Ethics, 3.5 (1986), that museum officials may have to reject offers of gifts that are subject to special conditions if the conditions proposed are judged to be contrary to the long-term interests of the museum and its public.

34. See Bogert & Bogert, Trusts and Trustees, § 394. Restatement (2nd) Trusts, § 399 states, "If property is given in trust to be applied to a particular charitable purpose, and it is, or becomes, impossible or impracticable or illegal to carry out the particular purpose, and if the [donor] manifested a more general intention to devote the property to charitable purposes, the trust will not fail, but the court will direct the application of the property to some charitable purpose which falls within the general charitable intention of the [donor]."

35. The basic premise for application of the cy pres doctrine is to defeat failure of a charitable donation. Bogert & Bogert, Trusts and Trustees § 394.

36. Restatement (2nd) Trusts § 381 states, "The court will direct or permit the trustee of a charitable trust to deviate from a term of the trust if it appears to the court that

compliance is impossible or illegal, or that owing to circumstances not known to the [donor] and not anticipated by him, compliance would defeat or substantially impair the accomplishment of the purposes of the trust." As noted in Chapter 1, the Uniform Prudent Management of Institutional Funds Act, which was adopted by the Uniform Laws Commission in 2006 and has been enacted by most states, provides that upon application by a charitable institution, a court may modify a restriction in a gift instrument if the restriction has become impracticable or wasteful or impairs management or investment of the fund or, because of circumstances not anticipated by the donor, modification would further the purposes of the fund. The act requires the institution to notify the Attorney General of the state and give the Attorney General an opportunity to be heard. The act also provides that if an institution determines restrictions in a gift instrument, which created a fund that is less than $25,000 and that has been in existence for a certain specified number of years, are unlawful, impracticable, impossible to achieve, or are wasteful, and the institution notifies the Attorney General of the state, the institution itself may release or modify the restrictions if it then uses assets of the fund consistent with the charitable purposes of the fund.

37. Bogert, The Law of Trust and Trustees, § 27.

38. In re The Barnes Foundation, 684 A.2d 123 (Pa. Super 1996).

39. ICOM Code of Ethics for Museums, 2.2 and 2.3.

40. Am. J. 2d Bail. § 2.

41. Thompson on Real Property § 13.07.

42. 28 U.S.C. § 1491(a).

43. Tex. Prop. Code Ann. §§ 80.00180.008.

44. See U.C.C. Article 2-403(2), which provides that the "entrusting of possession of goods to a merchant who deals in goods of that kind gives him power to transfer all rights of the entrustor to a buyer in ordinary course of business."

45. 20 U.S.C. §§ 971–77. The act is administered by the Federal Council on the Arts and Humanities. Applications for indemnity are submitted to this council. Indemnification was limited to $1.2 billion for a single international exhibition and $750 million for any single domestic exhibition. The act set a limit of $10 billion at any one time for international exhibitions and $5 billion at any one time for domestic exhibitions. 20 U.S.C. § 974.

46. 20 U.S.C. § 972(a).

47. 20 U.S.C. § 972(b)(1). Any person, nonprofit agency, institution, or government can apply for an indemnity agreement. The application must describe each item to be covered by the agreement, including an estimated value of the items. The application must set forth policies, procedures, techniques, and methods with respect to preparation for, and conduct of, the exhibition of the items, and any transportation related to the objects. If the council approves, an agreement is made between the council and the applicant whereby the credit of the United States is pledged as liability for damages to the objects on loan. Id. at § 973.

48. 20 U.S.C. § 973(c).

49. New York Arts and Cult. Aff. Law § 12.03. Discussion of theft of the Schiele paintings at Lawrence M. Kaye, "A Quick Glance at the Schiele Paintings," 10 DePaul-LCA J. Art & Ent. L. 11 (1999).

50. New York amended its antiseizure statute in 2000 so that it was not limited to "civil" proceedings (amendment to N.Y. Arts and Cult. Aff. Law § 12.03, effective in May 2000). A Texas statute, Tex. Civ. Prac. & Rem. Code § 61.081(a), prohibits a court from seizing any work of fine art "while it is en route to an exhibition, or in the possession of

the exhibitor or on display as part of the exhibition." However, the exemption from seizure does not apply if "theft of the work of art from its owner is alleged and found proven by a court."

51. 22 U.S.C. § 2459.

52. The Malewicz case is also discussed in Chapter 6 (Example 22 in that chapter).

53. ICOM Code of Ethics for Museums, 2.12 to 2.17.

54. Id. at 2.13.

55. Id. at 2.16.

56. Id. at 2.17.

57. Id. at 2.15.

58. Id. at 2.14.

59. Treas. Reg. § 1.501(c)(3)-1(b)(4).

60. Detroit city officials wanted to list valuable art treasures in the collection of the Detroit Institute of Art as assets of the city in bankruptcy proceedings involving the city.

61. Cited in note 2.

62. New York Not-for-Profit Corporation Law, § 1002-a(c)(1).

CHAPTER 6

STOLEN AND ILLEGALLY EXPORTED ARTIFACTS IN COLLECTIONS

A nation's culture resides in the hearts and in the soul of its people.
MAHATMA GANDHI

Some museums have artifacts in their collections that have questionable provenances. These artifacts may have been stolen or illegally exported from their country of origin. As noted in Chapter 5, with stolen art inundating the art market, many museum officials have encountered claims of theft victims to works in their collections and may have discovered the museum has defective title to one or more of its valuable pieces. Museum directors must be familiar with laws relating to title to artworks and historical treasures to respond correctly, both legally and ethically, to possible demands from individuals and/or countries for the return of objects in museum collections that have questionable provenances or that lack documentation.

Issues relating to a museum's lack of clear title to some artifacts in the collection often are tied to a concern to protect the cultural heritage on an international scale (discussed in more detail in Chapter 11) and, in so doing, to halt the illicit, international trade in cultural property. Cultural nationalism embraces the theory that all cultural property should remain in the country of its origin. As the populace becomes aware and acknowledges that the cultural heritage of each country is bound with, and includes, the cultural treasures of all nations, a concern for the preservation of international treasures evolves.[1] The theory maintains that a society learns of itself by studying its artistic treasures and that a nation's artistic treasures can be better investigated and understood in their original setting; thus, the principle demands the protection of international sites and artifacts. The ICOM Code of Ethics states that when a country of origin seeks the restitution of an object that can be demonstrated to have been exported or otherwise transferred in violation of the principles of international and national conventions and shown to be part of the cultural heritage of another country or people, officials of the museum concerned should, if legally free to do so, take prompt and responsible steps to cooperate in return of the object.[2]

The American Alliance of Museums (AAM)[3] Board of Directors has recognized the importance of protecting international cultural sites and artifacts and has adopted principles relating to museum collections to stem the international trade in art and antiquities. The AAM Standards Regarding Archaeological Material and Ancient Art, published in July 2008, set out criteria relating to archaeological material and ancient art to guide operations of museums that own or acquire archaeological material and ancient art originating outside the United States. The AAM recommends that museums require documentation that an object was out of its probable country of modern discovery by November 17, 1970, the date on which the 1970 UNESCO Convention on the Means of Prohibiting and Preventing the Illicit Import, Export and Transfer of Ownership of Cultural Property[4] was signed. (The 1970 UNESCO Convention is discussed in Chapter 11.) For objects exported from their country of modern discovery after November 17, 1970, the AAM recommends that museums require documentation that the objects have been, or will be, legally exported from their country of modern discovery and legally imported into the United States.

A. IMPORTATION LAWS ON ARTIFACTS FROM OTHER COUNTRIES

Currently, the United States has only two statutes regulating the importation of artifacts from other countries—the Pre-Columbian Monumental or Architectural Sculpture or Mural Act[5] and the Cultural Property Implementation Act (CPIA),[6] which ratified a part of the 1970 UNESCO Convention (summarized below but discussed in more detail in Chapter 11).

1. Pre-Columbian Monumental or Architectural Sculpture or Mural Act

The Pre-Columbian Monumental or Architectural Sculpture or Mural Act[7] was adopted in 1972 to prohibit the importation into the United States of any pre-Columbian monumental or architectural sculpture or mural from Mexico, South America, Central America, or the Caribbean unless the government of the country of origin had issued a certificate that exportation of the artifact from that country did not violate any of its laws.[8] Any objects imported into the United States in violation of the act are subject to seizure and forfeiture under customs laws of the United States.[9]

A pre-Columbian monumental or architectural sculpture or mural will be permitted entry into the United States if the importer files with the district director of customs, at the time of making entry, a certificate issued by the government of the country of origin certifying that the exportation was not in violation of the laws of that country.[10] If the importer does not have a certificate from the government of the country of origin at the time of making entry, the director of customs will store the sculpture or mural and permit the importer ninety days to produce such a certificate.[11] Otherwise the sculpture or mural is forfeited to the United States. If the country of origin presents a request in writing, the director of customs will return the sculpture or mural to that country.[12]

2. Cultural Property Implementation Act

Congress enacted the Cultural Property Implementation Act (CPIA)[13] in 1983 to implement into domestic law Articles 7(b) and 9 of the 1970 UNESCO Convention on the Means of Prohibiting and Preventing the Illicit Import, Export and Transfer of Ownership of Cultural Property. As pointed out in Chapter 11, at that time, members of Congress noted that the demand for cultural artifacts had resulted in the irremediable destruction of archaeological sites and objects and, thus, was depriving situs countries of their cultural patrimony and the world of important knowledge of the past.[14] The CPIA is an attempt to halt this pillage. A museum director must be aware of the provision of the CPIA as cultural treasures covered under the act are subject to seizure if they were imported into the United States in violation of the act.

The CPIA provides that when a participating nation makes a request to the United States for import restrictions on cultural property from that nation, because the requesting nation contends the cultural patrimony of the nation is in jeopardy from the pillage of its cultural properties, the President may enter into a bilateral agreement with that nation to apply import restrictions.[15] The import restrictions would provide that no designated archaeological or ethnological material exported from the requesting nation could be imported into the United States unless the requesting nation issued a certificate that the exportation was not in violation of that nation's laws.[16] The term "archaeological material" refers to an object of cultural significance that is at least 250 years old and has been normally discovered as a result of scientific excavation, clandestine or accidental digging, or exploration on land or under water.[17] The term "ethnological material" refers to an object that is the product of a tribal or nonindustrial society and is important to the cultural heritage of a people because of its distinctive characteristics, comparative rarity, or contribution to the knowledge of the origin, development, or history of that people.[18]

The act is not applicable to any designated archaeological or ethnological material or any article of cultural property imported into the United States that a recognized museum has purchased for value, in good faith, and without notice that the material or article was imported in violation of the act if the museum has held the material or article in the United States for a period of not less than three consecutive years. However, this saving provision applies only if (1) acquisition of the material or article was reported in a publication of the museum, any regularly published newspaper or periodical with a circulation of at least fifty thousand, or a periodical or exhibition catalogue which is concerned with the type of article or material sought to be exempted from the act; (2) the material or article has been exhibited to the public for a period or periods aggregating at least one year during the three-year period; or (3) the article or material has been catalogued and the catalogue material made available upon request to the public for at least two years during the three-year period.[19] The act is not applicable to material and articles that have been in the United States for at least twenty consecutive years if the claimant establishes that it purchased the material or article for value without knowledge or reason to believe it was imported in violation of law.

3. National Stolen Property Act

Some countries have patrimony laws that declare State ownership of all property found at a State's archaeological sites. In these States, antiquities are treated as stolen cultural property when the antiquities are taken from sites without permission from the State. For example, in its Law 117, the Egyptian government declared ownership in 1983 of all its archaeological artifacts pursuant to its Antiquities' Protection Law.[20] The 1932 Act with Respect to Antiquities in Greece provided that all antiquities belong to the State. Individuals could not acquire ownership of antiquities. After the effective date of the National Monuments Acts in 1994, the Republic of Ireland acquired ownership of all archaeological objects found in the State if the object had no known owner at the time it was found.[21] The trade in antiquities became illegal in Italy in 1939 with the enactment of the Law for the Protection of Works of Artistic and Historic Interests.[22] The Federal Act on Monuments and Archaeological, Artistic and Historic Zones in Mexico provided that historic and artistic monuments in private ownership were subject to export control.[23] In 1926 the Republic of Turkey declared in force and effect a 1906 decree that all antiquities found in or on lands in Turkey were owned by the republic. Also, in 1926, the republic adopted a Turkish Civil Code which declared that antiquities found on Turkish land were property of the republic.[24]

Although both the Pre-Columbian Monumental or Architectural Sculpture or Mural Act and CPIA provide for the forfeiture of artifacts as penalties under the acts, some courts decided that additional deterrents were needed[25] and applied the National Stolen Property Act (NSPA)[26] to punish encroachments upon legitimate and clear ownership rights to imported artifacts. The NSPA makes it a felony offense knowingly to sell or receive stolen goods in interstate or foreign commerce,[27] and courts have applied the NSPA to the illegal importation of artifacts from foreign countries that have asserted legal title to artifacts located within their boundaries, including those noted above, even though agents of these nations may never have physically possessed the artifacts.

> Example 1. In United States v. McClain, 545 F.2d 988 (5th Cir. 1977) and 593 F.2d 658 (5th Cir. 1979), the Fifth Circuit Court of Appeals upheld the conviction under the NSPA of certain individuals who sold pre-Columbian artifacts in Texas. Although there was evidence in the case that the artifacts had been illegally imported, there was no evidence as to the time or manner of importation. Still, it was clear that the defendants knew their activity was illegal under Mexican law and that the government of Mexico might claim ownership of the artifacts. On defendants' appeal of their conviction, the government successfully asserted that ownership of pre-Columbian antiquities had, by statute, been vested in the Mexican government. Thus, the appellate court agreed with the government that the artifacts were stolen within the meaning of the NSPA. The Fifth Circuit rejected the defendants' contention that the Pre-Columbian Monumental or Architectural Sculpture or Mural

Act had the effect of narrowing the NSPA so as to make it inapplicable to artifacts declared to be property of another country.

Example 2. The Second Circuit Court of Appeals later applied the NSPA to punish encroachments upon legitimate and clear State ownership rights to illegally imported artifacts from Egypt. In United States v. Schulz, 333 F.3d 395 (2nd Cir. 2003), cert. denied, 540 U.S. 1106 (2004), a well-known art dealer was convicted under NSPA for knowingly transporting stolen Egyptian antiquities. The art dealer met Jonathan Tokeley Parry (Parry), a British national, through a mutual friend in 1992. Parry showed the art dealer a photograph of an ancient sculpture of the head of Pharaoh Amenhotep III and told the art dealer he had obtained the sculpture in Egypt earlier from a man who represented himself to be a building contractor. Parry had used an Egyptian middleman named Ali Farag (Farag) to facilitate the transaction. Parry allegedly had smuggled the sculpture out of Egypt by coating it with plastic so that it would look like a cheap souvenir. He removed the plastic coating once the sculpture was in England. The art dealer allegedly offered Parry a substantial fee to serve as the agent for the sale of the Amenhotep sculpture. Parry and the art dealer then allegedly set out to create a false provenance for the sculpture so that they could sell it. They claimed it had been brought from Egypt in the 1920s and had been maintained since that time in an English private collection, which they called the Thomas Alcock Collection. They allegedly prepared fake labels for the sculpture, which were designed to appear as if they had been printed in the 1920s. Parry later sold the sculpture to the art dealer for $800,000, and the art dealer sold it to a private collector in 1992 for $1.2 million. Parry and the art dealer allegedly became partners in an effort to bring more Egyptian antiquities into the United States for resale, smuggling them out of Egypt disguised as cheap souvenirs, assigning a false provenance to them, and restoring them with 1920s techniques. Parry was arrested in Great Britain in 1994 and Farag was arrested in Egypt. Each was charged with dealing in stolen antiquities. Although Parry was arrested, he, with the art dealer, allegedly continued to obtain Egyptian antiquities. After a jury found the art dealer guilty, he was sentenced to a term of thirty-three months imprisonment. The art dealer contended the objects he had taken were not stolen within the meaning of the NSPA. He contended the objects were not owned by anyone and, thus, could not be stolen. The prosecution, on the other hand, successfully demonstrated the Egyptian government owned the antiquities pursuant to its patrimony law, Law 117, which provides that all antiquities found in Egypt after 1983 are property of the Egyptian government. The Second Circuit Court of Appeals affirmed the conviction. The Second Circuit concluded the NSPA applies to property stolen from a foreign government when that government asserts actual ownership of the property pursuant to a valid patrimony law. The court ruled that the NSPA applies to property taken in violation of a foreign patrimony law and that the CPIA is not the exclusive means of dealing with stolen artifacts and antiquities, as the art dealer had contended.

Example 3. In Peru v. Johnson, 720 F. Supp. 810 (C.D. Cal. 1989), the court decided Peru had not sufficiently stated a claim of ownership to Pre-Columbian artifacts it claimed were excavated from historical monuments in Peru. The court ruled against Peru because evidence did not indicate the country in which the artifacts were found nor the country from which they were exported. In addition, the court determined the extent of Peru's claim of ownership as part of its domestic law was uncertain. The court decided that restrictions on the export of certain artifacts were addressed to protection of the artifacts and that the restrictions did not imply ownership. The court commented that possession of the artifacts was allowed to remain in private ownership and that these objects could be transferred. The court characterized an export restriction as an exercise of the police power of the state. It stated that these restrictions do not create ownership in the state.

Example 4. The Republic of Turkey seeks recovery of artifacts in possession of the Art Museum of New York. The Republic of Turkey contends the artifacts were excavated from burial grounds in the Ushak region of Turkey and exported to the United States in contravention of Turkish law. It claims all artifacts found in Turkey belong to the Republic of Turkey. The museum contends the statute of limitations has run on any claim the Republic of Turkey might have. In Republic of Turkey v. Metropolitan Museum of Art, 762 F. Supp. 44 (S.D.N.Y. 1990), the court held that the statute of limitations had not run against the Republic of Turkey in a claim it brought against the Metropolitan Museum of Art.

A museum director who wishes to purchase a valuable artwork or an ancient artifact should contact certain organizations to determine if the artwork or artifact is listed as stolen property. These organizations include the following: (1) the FBI, which maintains a central archive of stolen art in the United States; (2) the International Criminal Police Organization (INTERPOL), which is a group of police agencies that computerize information on stolen art; (3) the International Foundation for Art Research (IFAR), which monitors trafficking in stolen art; (4) the Art Loss Register (ALR), which is located in London and which maintains a computerized database of reportedly stolen art objects; (5) the TRACE database of Recipero, which is located in Gloucestershire, UK; (6) the Art Dealers Association of America; (7) the International Council of Museums and Sites, which coordinates and develops measures and security systems for museums throughout the world; (8) Europa Nostra, which is a European organization interested in the conservation of the architectural heritage of Europe; and (9) the New York State Holocaust Claims Office. Other organizations include Christie's, Sotheby's, and Harvard University's Dumbarton Oaks Institute for Byzantine Studies, which is the leading center in the United States for the study of Byzantine art.

> Example 5. Some individuals have approached the director of Historical Museum to purchase a collection of nearly two thousand ancient Greek and Lycian silver coins. The price they have quoted to the museum is reasonable. The museum should not purchase the coins without investigating provenance of the coins. If the individuals obtained the coins illegally from Turkey, they, as well as the museum director if he decides to purchase the coins, could be prosecuted under the National Stolen Properties Act. In Republic of Turkey v. OKS Partners, 797 F. Supp. 64 (D. Mass. 1992), the Republic of Turkey sued possessors of ancient Greek and Lycian silver coins, which the Republic of Turkey maintained were unearthed in Turkey, under the Racketeering Influenced and Corrupt Organizations Act (RICO),[28] alleging as a "pattern of racketeering activity" the sale of such coins and that the sale could be in violation of the National Stolen Properties Act. The Republic of Turkey contended that under Turkish law all artifacts within Turkey's borders are Turkish property even before they are discovered.

B. RETURN/RESTITUTION OF STOLEN AND ILLEGALLY EXPORTED ARTIFACTS

In common law countries, the judicial remedies for the return/restitution of stolen cultural property are based on the common law principle *nemo dat* (discussed in Chapter 5),[29] which provides that one who purchases property from a thief, no matter how innocently, acquires no title in the property. Title remains with the true owner. The common law countries are those whose laws are based on the English common law and include Australia, Canada (except Quebec), New Zealand, England, Wales, Ireland, India (except Goa), Pakistan, South Africa, Hong Kong, and the United States (except Louisiana).

In most civil law States, a purchaser of stolen property can obtain good title after a limitations period. Countries whose legal systems are based on civil law generally permit a legal owner to recover stolen property from an innocent purchaser for a specified period of years after the theft. After that period of time, the purchaser has good title to the property.[30] As set out in Italian Civil Code,[31] the person or entity who purchases stolen property must be a "good-faith" or "innocent" purchaser for the limitations period to begin to run. However, Swiss law presumes a purchaser acts in good faith; a victim seeking to reclaim stolen property has the burden of establishing the purchaser did not act in good faith.[32]

> Example 6. In Dunbar v. Seger-Thomschitz, 638 F. Supp. 2d 659 (E.D. La. 2009), aff'd, 615 F.3d 574 (5th Cir. 2010), cert. den., 131 S.Ct.1511 (2011), a Louisiana court rejected a victim's claim when it applied the civil law principle of acquisitive prescription to award title to stolen cultural property to the purchaser-possessor. (The acquisitive prescription principle is part of the Louisiana Civil Code and is based on Roman and French civil law. Although civil law countries have acquisitive prescription provisions, Louisiana is the only state in the United States with this provision. This is because Louisiana law, unlike the law in any other state, is based on the Napoleonic Code, which embodies the civil law principles discussed above. The law in all the other states is based on the common law adopted from England and discussed above, which provides that a purchaser cannot acquire good title to purchased property if there was a thief in the chain of title.)

The taking of property by a foreign government may be valid, in which case an original owner will not have a claim for return of the property. Differing principles apply to the taking of property during war. "Booty" is "property necessary and indispensable for the conduct of war," such as food, means of transportation, and means of communication; its taking is lawful. "Pillage," or "plunder," is the taking of private property not necessary for the immediate prosecution of the war effort. Taking under these circumstances is illegal, and the original owner's title is not extinguished.

> Example 7. In Menzel v. List, 267 N.Y.S.2d 804 (1966), the court ruled that the taking of property by members of Hitler's government in World

War II was not subject to the Act of State Doctrine, which would have precluded any inquiry into the validity of the acts of the German authorities. The court noted that the Act of State Doctrine rests upon a confluence of four factors: (1) the taking must be by a foreign sovereign government; (2) the taking must be within the territorial limits of the government; (3) the foreign government must be extant and recognized by this country at the time of the suit; and (4) the taking must not be violative of a treaty obligation. The court found that a painting, to which plaintiff claimed ownership, was not seized "by a foreign sovereign government but rather by the 'Centre for National Socialist Ideological and Educational Research,' an organ of the Nazi party." Further, the location of the property was not within the jurisdiction of the German government, and the Third Reich was not recognized by the United States at the time of the trial. The court also ruled that the taking of the painting was "pillage" or "plunder" so that title of the original owner was not extinguished.

Example 8. In Konowaloff v. Metropolitan Museum of Art, 702 F.3d 140 (2nd Cir. 2013), the Second Circuit Court of Appeals agreed with the district court that the Act of State Doctrine precluded an original owner's action to obtain a painting the Russian Bolshevik regime had confiscated from his great-grandfather in 1918. The Second Circuit pointed out that, under the Act of State Doctrine, courts in the United States will not examine the validity of taking of property within a foreign country's territory even if the complaint alleges the taking violates customary international law. In response to the original owner's contention that the Act of State Doctrine should not apply because the Soviet government is no longer "extant," the court noted that the successor to the U.S.S.R. had not renounced 1918 appropriations by that government. The court observed that the current Russian government apparently was disinclined to engage in further appropriations of private property and had initiated an investigation into the 1930s art sales, but pointed out that it had not repudiated the 1918 appropriation, which was the government act that deprived the original owner his right to the painting.

I. Statute of Limitations

Although all states except Louisiana recognize the common law *nemo dat* rule that a purchaser can never obtain good title if there is a thief in the chain of title, a state's statute of limitation provisions will prescribe a maximum time limit for filing a lawsuit regarding a victim's claim for return of stolen artwork or cultural property. After the statute of limitations relating to a specific claim has expired, a court will dismiss a claimant's action. Courts decide a statute of limitations question by "balancing the equities" between the parties.[33] With the exception of New York courts[34] and possibly in California because of its statute[35] relating to a theft victim's discovery of the location of stolen historical or artistic property, courts in the United States have ruled that the statute of limitations on suits to recover stolen property begins to run when the rightful owner knew "or reasonably should know" of his or her cause of action and the identity of the possessor of the property.[36]

In New York, limitation on the time during which suit may be brought to recover stolen property does not begin until the rightful owner asserts a claim to the property and the possessor refuses to return the property.[37] Courts in New York have determined that this rule is better than the discovery rule applicable in other states because it "gives the owner relatively greater protection and places the burden of investigating the provenance of a work of art on the potential purchaser."[38] A New York court[39] referred to the discovery rule in other states in which the statute of limitations in suits to recover works of art that had been stolen begins to run from the time the true owner discovers or should have discovered the whereabouts of the stolen art. It explained that New York rejected the discovery rule because New York courts decided the rule did not provide a reasonable opportunity for individuals of foreign governments to receive notice of a possessor's acquisition of artwork and sufficient time to take action to recover a work. The court was concerned that New York would become a "haven for cultural property stolen abroad" because stolen works would be immune from recovery under limited time periods. The court concluded it was inappropriate to shift the burden to the wronged owner.

> Example 9. In O'Keeffe v. Snyder, 416 A.2d 862 (N.J. 1980), the New Jersey Supreme Court ruled the statute of limitations on a suit to recover stolen paintings begins to run when the true owner discovers, or by exercise of reasonable diligence and intelligence should have discovered, facts which form the basis of a cause of action. The court affirmed that apart from the discovery rule, the statute of limitations in replevin actions ordinarily runs against the owner of lost or stolen property from the time of the wrongful taking. However, as the court commented, this was ordinarily true absent fraud or concealment. According to the New Jersey court, where a chattel is fraudulently concealed, the general rule is the statute is tolled. The New Jersey statute of limitations[40] provided that a suit for

recovery of goods must be commenced within six years after the cause of action accrues. According to the New Jersey Supreme Court in O'Keeffe, this discovery rule avoids the harsh result of a mechanical application of the limitations statute. According to the court in O'Keeffe, the discovery rule provides that a cause of action will not accrue until the injured party discovers, or by exercise of reasonable diligence and intelligence should have discovered, facts which form the basis of a cause of action.

Example 10. In Museum of Fine Arts, Boston v. Seger-Thomschitz, 623 F. 3d 1 (1st Cir. 2010), cert. den., 131 S. Ct. 1612 (2011), the First Circuit Court of Appeals ruled the discovery rule applied to a conversion and replevin claim to recover possession of a valuable oil painting formerly owned by an Austrian-Jewish art collector, Oskar Reichel, and held by the Boston Museum of Fine Arts (MFA). Seger-Thomschitz, the sole surviving heir of Reichel, alleged Reichel was forced to sell the painting under duress after Nazi-Germany annexed Austria in 1938. The court affirmed the district court's ruling that Seger-Thomschitz's claims were time-barred. The court determined the painting had been on almost continuous display at the MFA since 1973 and decided Seger-Thomschitz, with reasonable diligence, could have discovered her claim to the painting in 2003 when she learned the Nazis had confiscated artworks from Reichel. Because she did not make a demand on the MFA until 2007, the First Circuit affirmed summary judgment on the MFA's limitations defense.

In 1983, California adopted a three-year statutory limitation period to govern accrual of causes of action for recovery of articles of historical, interpretive, scientific, or artistic significance that begins to run at "the discovery of the whereabouts of the article by the aggrieved party." Although later, in 2007, in Orkin v. Taylor (discussed below in Example 15), the Ninth Circuit Court of Appeals concluded the California discovery rule incorporates the principle of constructive notice, the Ninth Circuit, in Cassirer v. Thyssenbornemisza Collection Foundation (discussed in Example 11), ruled constitutional an amended California limitation period that provides for a six-year statute of limitation on the "actual" discovery of "works of fine arts."

Example 11. In Von Saher v. Norton Simon Museum, 578 F.3d 1016 (9th Cir. 2009), as amended by 592 F.3d 954 (9th Cir. 2010), cert. den., 131 S. Ct. 3055 (2011), the Ninth Circuit Court of Appeals ruled that a victim's cause of action in California begins to accrue when the victim discovered or reasonably could have discovered the victim's claim and the whereabouts to a stolen painting. However, in Cassirer v. Thyssen-bornemisza Collection Foundation, 737 F.3d 613 (9th Cir. 2013), the Ninth Circuit noted that Cal. Civ. Proc. § 338(c) was amended after the Von Saher decision and ruled the amended statute was not preempted by a foreign affairs doctrine and, thus, was constitutional. The Ninth Circuit approved the newly enacted provision [§ 338(c)(3)], which provides for a six-year statute of limitations for "an action for the specific recovery of a *work of fine art* brought against a museum, gallery, auctioneer, or dealer" brought before 2018. The amended provision specifies the six-year period is triggered on a victim's "actual discovery" of the identity and whereabouts of an unlawfully taken or stolen *work of fine art*.

2. Due Diligence Requirement

Initially the New Jersey Supreme Court in O'Keeffe v. Snyder, discussed in Example 9, imposed a due diligence requirement upon a theft victim as a prerequisite to proving the victim's claim to her stolen artworks. The New Jersey Supreme Court decided that it should protect an innocent purchaser from an owner who "sleeps on his rights." The court referred to the axiom that a possessor has the right to retain property except as against the true owner. The court recognized that the only imperfection on a bona fide purchaser's claim is the original owner's right to repossess the property and commented that when that imperfection is removed, the possessor should have good title for all purposes.

Although the New Jersey Supreme Court imposed a due diligence requirement on a theft victim to protect innocent purchasers of artworks, some courts in the United States referred to unfortunate results of the mandate and shifted the due diligence requirements to potential purchasers of valuable artifacts.

Example 12. In Kunstsammlungen Zu Weimar v. Elicofon, 678 F.2d 1150 (2nd Cir. 1982), the Second Circuit Court of Appeals refused to impose a due diligence requirement upon the rightful owner and ordered the return to the original owner of two priceless Albrecht Duerer portraits created around 1499 and stolen in 1945 from a castle located in Germany. The paintings were stolen in 1945 from the Kunstsammlungen zu Weimar, a German art museum, during the American occupation of the town of Weimar from a castle where they had been placed for safe keeping. Elicofon purchased the paintings in good faith in 1946 from an ex-serviceman who appeared at his New York residence and claimed he had purchased them in Germany. Some twenty years later, upon discovery of the location of the Duerer paintings, the museum demanded their return and sued when Elicofon refused to return them. Elicofon moved for summary judgment under a provision of German property law called *Ersitzung*, which permitted title to moveable property to be obtained by its good-faith acquisition and possession without notice of a defect in title for a period of ten years from the date on which the rightful owner lost possession. The court ruled Elicofon did not acquire title to the painting under *Ersitzung*. It held New York's choice of law dictated that questions relating to the validity of a transfer of personal property were governed by the law of the state where the property was located at the time of the alleged transfer. Because Elicofon purchased the painting in New York, the court ruled New York law applied. In applying New York law, wherein a good-faith purchaser does not obtain good title to stolen property, the court ruled that Elicofon did not acquire title to the painting. Elicofon expressed concerns that the court's ruling would require a bona fide purchaser to wait for a demand from the true owner before the statute of limitations would begin to run.

Example 13. In Solomon R. Guggenheim Found. v. Lubell, 569 N.E.2d 426 (N.Y. 1991), a New York court confirmed that New York courts do not impose a due diligence requirement on victims of art thefts. In Lubell, the court ruled that a museum could recover a Chagall gouache that was stolen from it in the late 1960s even though the museum had done little to learn of the gouache's whereabouts. The court decided it would be inappropriate to shift the burden to take action to the wronged owner.

Example 14. In Autocephalous Greek-Orthodox Church of Cyprus v. Goldberg, 917 F.2d 278 (7th Cir. 1992), the Seventh Circuit Court of Appeals applied Indiana law to rule for the Republic of Cyprus in its cause of action for the return of stolen Byzantine mosaics created in the early sixth century. The Seventh Circuit decided the Republic of Cyprus and the Church of Cyprus had exercised due diligence in their search to locate and recover the mosaics. An art collector, Goldberg, purchased four Byzantine mosaics, consisting of small chips of colored glass and created in the early sixth century, from an individual who said the mosaics had been purchased in Switzerland. Later the Republic of Cyprus and the Church of Cyprus claimed ownership of the mosaics. Representatives from the Republic of Cyprus told the museum director that the four Kanakaria mosaics were affixed originally to the apse of the Church of the Panagia Kanakaria in the village of Lythrankomi, Cyprus, in A.D. 530. During and after a Turkish invasion in 1974, the Republic of Cyprus and the Church of Cyprus were denied access to occupied northern Cyprus. There was much looting of churches during the invasion, and many mosaics, frescoes, and icons in the churches and national monuments were stolen or destroyed. The mosaics were removed from the apse of the church sometime between 1976 and 1979. Neither the Church of Cyprus nor the Republic of Cyprus had authorized their removal or sale. Under Indiana law, a thief cannot pass any right of ownership of stolen items to any subsequent purchasers. The Seventh Circuit ruled that because the mosaics were stolen from the rightful owner (the Church of Cyprus), the purchaser of the mosaics never obtained title to, or right of possession of, the mosaics. The court disagreed with the purchaser that the statute of limitations had run on the owners' claim. The Seventh Circuit held that the owners' cause of action did not accrue until the owners, using due diligence, knew, or were on reasonable notice of, the identity of the possessor of the mosaics. The court ordered the mosaics returned to the Church of Cyprus and the Republic of Cyprus. If the Seventh Circuit had applied the law of Switzerland, the purchaser, Goldberg, more likely would have prevailed. As noted, the *nemo dat* rule is not applicable in civil law countries such as Switzerland. In civil law countries, a bona fide purchaser can obtain good title to stolen goods after a certain period of time.

Example 15. The Ninth Circuit Court of Appeals, in Orkin v. Taylor, 487 F.3d 734 (9th Cir. 2007), seemed to have reverted to placing the due diligence requirement on the victim in applying California law. Descendants of a Jewish art collector brought suit in 2002 to recover a Van Gogh painting from the possessor of the painting. The descendants of the Jewish collector alleged their ancestor sold the painting under duress when she fled Germany in 1939. These persons were descendants of Jewish art collector Margarete Mauthner who left her possessions behind when she fled Germany for South Africa where she remained until her death in 1947. Her descendants referred to Military Government Law No. 59, which was promulgated by the Allied Forces after conclusion of World War II and which established a presumption that any transfer or relinquishment of property by a person within the period January 30, 1933, to May 8, 1945, was an act of confiscation. The possessor's father acquired the painting in 1963 at a Sotheby auction. According to the possessor, the acquisition was publicized and the painting was exhibited publicly from November 1986 until March 1987. In 1990, the painting was offered for sale through Christie's auction house in London. The Jewish heirs made demand for the painting in 2001 and contended they did not discover the basis of their claim until then. Still, the Ninth Circuit ruled their claim was time-barred. The Ninth Circuit decided the Jewish heirs could have discovered the painting's whereabouts much earlier. This court thought the possessor's acquisition of the painting was discoverable at least by 1990 when she held it out for sale at an international auction and "most probably as early as 1963" when she acquired it in a highly publicized international auction. The Ninth Circuit concluded that had the Jewish heirs investigated any of the publicly available sources, they could have discovered both their claim to the painting and its whereabouts.

Example 16. A federal district court in Louisiana, in Dunbar v. Seger-Thomschitz, 638 F. Supp. 2d 659 (E.D. La. 2009), aff'd 615 F.3d 574 (5th Cir. 2010), cert. den., 131 S.Ct. 1511 (2011), also shifted the due diligence requirement back to the victim in applying Louisiana law. The court considered § 3491 of the Louisiana Civil Code, which, according to the court (and contrary to the common law rule), provides that one who has possessed movable property for ten years acquires ownership by prescription. Neither title nor good faith is required for this prescription. The court cited O'Keeffe v. Snyder (discussed in Example 9) and noted that claimants have been found to have exercised due diligence by notifying the Art Dealers of America, the International Foundation for Art Research, UNESCO, and similar national and international organizations. The issues in Dunbar arose from an ownership claim brought by Dr. Claudia Seger-Thomschitz (Seger) against Sarah Blodgett Dunbar (Dunbar) for an Oskar Kokoschka painting entitled Portrait of a Youth. Seger was the sole heir of the Raimund Reichel estate. She alleged the painting had been confiscated by the Nazis from Reichel's ascendants in Vienna, Austria, in 1939. Prior to the painting's alleged confiscation, Raimund Reichel's father, Dr. Oskar Reichel, transferred ownership of the painting and four others to Otto Kallir-Nirenstein (Kallir) in 1938. Kallir was a Jewish art dealer whose art gallery exhibited the painting in

1924 and 1933 for possible sale at the request of the Reichel family. He was accused of dealing in stolen art as an agent of the Nazis. Sarah Reed-Platt purchased the painting from Kallir's gallery in New York in 1946 and bequeathed it to her daughter, Sarah Blodgett Dunbar. Dunbar had continuous, uninterrupted possession of the painting since she inherited it from her mother in 1973. Seger contended that Kallir did not have ownership of the painting and was not capable of transferring ownership. Although the court acknowledged there are special considerations related to stolen works of art, antiquities, or cultural property, it decided a court must consider whether a claimant used due diligence in recovering the art. The court then accepted Dunbar's adverse ownership claim and denied Seger's claim.

Example 17. The First Circuit Court of Appeals ruled that the statute of limitations barred a victim's claim to a painting the Nazis confiscated from her relative, an Austrian-Jewish art collector, in Museum of Fine Arts, Boston v. Seger-Thomschitz, 623 F.3d 1 (1st Cir. 2010), cert. den., 131 S.Ct. 1612 (2011), rehr. den., 131 S.Ct.2176 (2011). In this case, which was discussed in Example 10 with respect to the ruling of the First Circuit Court of Appeals that the statute of limitations barred the victim's claim, the First Circuit Court of Appeals also apparently reverted to placing the due diligence requirement on the victim. The First Circuit applied the law of Massachusetts rather than the law of Austria or New York, but found that under Massachusetts law, the statute of limitations precluded the victim's claim because the victim did not make a demand for the painting until more than three years after the court decided her cause of action accrued. As noted in Example 10, the First Circuit affirmed summary judgment on the Museum of Fine Art's limitations defense.

3. Laches Defense

Laches is an affirmative defense which permits a court to cut off a claim when the claimant has delayed unreasonably and inexcusably in instituting litigation and thereby has prejudiced the accused significantly.[44]

Example 18. In Vineberg v. Bissonnette, 548 F.3d 50 (1st Cir. 2008), the First Circuit Court of Appeals considered the viability of a laches defense asserted by a current possessor of a work of art in the possessor's effort to fend off an action for replevin. The case involved a claim by the heirs of Dr. Max Stern, who had inherited an art gallery in Dusseldorf, Germany. Dr. Stern, who was of Jewish ancestry and who became an object of Nazi persecution, was ordered to liquidate his gallery and its inventory. He was forced to sell works of art much below their fair market value. After his death, trustees of the Stern Foundation claimed title to a painting in the possession of Baroness Maria-Louise Bissonnette. The baroness took possession of the painting in 1959 and formally inherited it as part of her mother's estate in 1991. The Stern Foundation had filed a claim for the painting with the New York Holocaust Claims Processing Office. The court rejected a proffered laches defense. It noted that laches is an affirmative defense and an equitable defense and ruled that a successful showing of laches requires proof both that a claimant delayed prosecution of his claim and that the resulting delay prejudiced the current possessor or purchaser's substantial rights. The First Circuit accepted that the defense involves not only delay but also a party's detrimental reliance on the status quo. The court stated, "A de facto confiscation of a work of art that arose out of a notorious exercise of man's inhumanity to man now ends with the righting of that wrong through the mundane application of common law principles. The mills of justice grind slowly, but they grind exceedingly fine."

Example 19. In Museum of Fine Arts, Boston v. Seger-Thomschitz, 623 F. 3d 1 (1st Cir. 2010), cert. den., 131 S.Ct. 1612 (2011), rehr. den., 131 S. Ct. 2176 (2011), the First Circuit Court of Appeals refused to apply the doctrine of laches as a matter of federal common law to replace a rigid discovery rule limitations period. The claimant of a valuable oil painting confiscated by the Nazis after Nazi-Germany annexed Austria in 1938 contended that her case implicated important federal interests and should be governed by federal timeliness principles based in equity rather than the state's statute of limitations. However, the First Circuit refused to adopt a federal common law laches rule that would have placed the burden on the possessor to prove lack of diligence by the painting's claimant.

Example 20. In Bakalar v. Vavra, 619 F.3d 136 (2nd Cir. 2010), the Second Court of Appeals considered application of a laches defense regarding stolen artwork. That court decided initially that placing the burden of locating stolen artwork on the true owner, and foreclosing the rights of that owner to recover the owner's property if the burden is not met, would encourage illicit trafficking in stolen art. It decided that shifting of the burden onto the wronged owners was inappropriate and that a better rule placed the burden of investigating the provenance of a work of art on a potential purchaser. In Bakalar, the current possessor of a drawing by Egon Schiele sought a declaratory judgment that he was the rightful owner of the drawing. The drawing was one of 81 Schieles included in a collection of 449 artworks owned by Grunbaum, an Austrian artist. Grunbaum, who kept the collection in his Vienna apartment, was deprived of his possession of the drawing after being arrested by the Nazis. Grunbaum died in Dachau in 1941. The Nazis arrested his wife in 1942, and she died shortly thereafter in a concentration camp in Minsk. A Swiss art gallery purchased the drawing in 1956. In that same year, the Galerie St. Etienne purchased the drawing and shipped it to New York, and in 1963, sold it to Bakalar for $4,300. Bakalar filed the action seeking a declaratory judgment that he was the rightful owner of the drawing after Sotheby's withdrew a winning bid of approximately $675,000 for the drawing after Vavra and Leon Fischer challenged Bakalar's title. (An Austrian court had designated Vavra and Fischer as the legal heirs to the Grunbaum estate.) Vavra and Fischer, who were residents of the Czech Republic and New York, filed counterclaims for a declaratory judgment and replevin. The district court decided Swiss law applied. It held that under New York's choice of law rules, questions relating to the validity of a transfer of personal property are governed by the law of the state where the property is located at the time of the alleged transfer. However, the Second Circuit Court of Appeals court ruled that the district court erred in holding Swiss law, rather than New York law, applied. The appellate court opined that Swiss law placed significant hurdles to recovery of stolen art and almost "insurmountable" obstacles to recovery of artwork stolen by the Nazis from Jews and others during World War II and the years preceding it. The appellate court noted that if Swiss law applied, it was immaterial whether the drawing was stolen. It decided resolution of an ownership dispute between parties who otherwise had no connection to Switzerland did not implicate any Swiss interest simply because the drawing passed through there. The appellate court recognized the drawing was purchased in Switzerland by a Swiss art gallery but that the gallery resold it within five months to a New York art gallery. It noted that a stolen piece of artwork was delivered in New York to a New York art gallery, which sold it in New York to Bakalar. The appellate court decided a substantial part of the events or omissions giving rise to the claims in the case occurred in New York. It determined that application of New York law in the case would not have any adverse effect on the Swiss art gallery nor would it affect any Swiss citizen or Swiss interest. On remand to the district court, 819 F. Supp. 2d. 293 (S.D.N.Y. 2011), the district court ruled laches barred Vavra's and Fischer's claim. The district court decided that Vavra's and Fischer's ancestors were not diligent in pursuing their claims and stated that because Bakalar was an ordinary non-merchant purchaser of art, he had no obligation to investigate the provenance of the drawing. Upon appeal of this district court decision, the Second Circuit, 500 Fed. Appx.6 (2nd Cir. 2012), found there was no clear error in the district court's finding that laches was a bar to the victims' claims. In a New York case, In the Matter of Flauenbaum, 22 N.Y.3d 962 (Ct. App. N.Y.), the Court of Appeals of New York affirmed a ruling of a New York appellate court that a German museum's assertion of a claim to recover from a probate estate a three-thousand-year-old gold tablet, which was a part of the museum's holdings until it became missing at the end of World War II, was not barred by laches. The New York court pointed out that the estate failed to demonstrate an "essential element" of laches, namely prejudice.

4. Claims From and Against Foreign Governments

Although a current possessor of stolen cultural property may be successful in claiming good title to the stolen property through prescription in a civil law country, the original owner/victim or the victim's heirs may be successful in bringing a claim in the United States for return of the property or payment for the property's value. For example, a court may accept jurisdiction of a cause of action against a foreign government in possession of stolen cultural property by finding waiver or exemption from the foreign government's otherwise immunity from suit.

The Foreign Sovereign Immunities Act (FSIA) was enacted in 1976 to remedy problems relating to immunity for foreign governments. Pursuant to the Foreign Sovereign Immunities Act,[45] foreign States have some immunity from suit in federal courts. However, the following transactions, among some others, are exempt from immunity:[46] (1) cases in which the foreign State has waived immunity either explicitly or by implication; (2) cases in which the action is based upon a commercial activity carried on in the United States by the foreign State; (3) cases in which rights in property taken in violation of international law are in issue and property, or property for which it was exchanged, is in the United States; (4) cases in which rights in property in the United States acquired by gift or succession or rights in immovable property situated in the United States are in issue; and (5) cases in which money damages are sought against a foreign State for personal injury or death or damage or loss of property caused by the tortious act or omission of that foreign State or one of its employees while acting within the scope of office or employment.

Example 21. In Republic of Austria v. Altmann, 541 U.S. 677 (2004), the Supreme Court affirmed a decision of the Ninth Circuit Court of Appeals that U.S. courts had jurisdiction to hear a claim of a Holocaust victim as against the Republic of Austria. Maria Altmann brought a claim against the Republic of Austria for the recovery of six Gustav Klimt paintings the Nazis took from her deceased Jewish uncle, Ferdinand Bloch.[47] The Republic of Austria contended it was immune from the jurisdiction of U.S. courts under the FSIA. However, the Ninth Circuit Court of Appeals court affirmed the decision of the district court that a foreign State is not immune from the jurisdiction of U.S. courts when the issue is whether rights in property were taken in violation of international law. The Ninth Circuit decided that Austria could not expect immunity in light of its complicity in, and perpetuation of, the discriminatory expropriation of the Klimt paintings. It noted that the seizures violated both Austria's and Germany's obligations under the 1907 Hague Convention on the Laws and Customs of War on Land and that Austria's Second Republic officially repudiated all Nazi transactions in 1946. Although the U.S. Supreme Court did not endorse the reasoning of the Court of Appeals, it affirmed the Ninth Circuit's judgment because it determined that the FSIA clearly applies to conduct that occurred prior to the act's enactment in 1976.

Example 22. In Malewicz et al. v. City of Amsterdam, 517 F. Supp. 2d 322 (D.D.C. 2007), the heirs of Kazimir Malewicz filed a complaint in the U.S. District Court for the District of Columbia against the City of Amsterdam for its alleged wrongful possession of fourteen artworks of Malewicz. The district court denied the City of Amsterdam's motion to dismiss and agreed with the Malewicz heirs that the City of Amsterdam should not be immune from suit pursuant to the FSIA. The Malewicz heirs alleged that when the Nazis ascended to power and began their attacks against "degenerate art," Malewicz entrusted his works to several friends in Germany, including Hugo Haring. All the works Malewicz had brought to Berlin were shipped to a Hannover museum where they subsequently were concealed in the museum's basement. Haring later agreed with the post–World War II director of the Stedelijk for a loan of the Malewicz works to the Stedelijk. In 2003, the Stedelijk loaned the paintings to the Guggenheim Museum in New York and the Menil Collection in Houston. The Stedelijk required that the museums obtain immunity from seizure for the paintings while they were in the United States. The court thought the fact that the Stedelijk knew of the heirs' adverse claims and had insisted the American museums procure a promise of immunity from the U.S. State Department indicated the Stedelijk did anticipate "being haled into court." The court was concerned that there was a close question of whether the City of Amsterdam's contact with the United States in connection with the loan of the paintings was "substantial" but ruled that the record contained sufficient additional contacts to establish jurisdiction under the FSIA's expropriation exception. (The Malewicz heirs and the City of Amsterdam reached a settlement in 2008 whereby the City of Amsterdam returned four paintings to the Malewicz heirs.)

Example 23. In Cassirer v. Kingdom of Spain, 616 F.3d 1019 (9th Cir. 2010), cert. den., 131 S. Ct. 3057 (2011), an American citizen, Claude Cassirer, whose grandmother's Pissarro painting allegedly was confiscated in 1939 by an agent of the Nazi government in Germany because she was Jewish, filed suit to recover the painting from the Kingdom of Spain and the Thyssen-Bornemisza Collection Foundation, an instrumentality of Spain, which claimed to own the painting. Spain and the foundation moved to dismiss, asserting that sovereign immunity pursuant to the FSIA made them immune from suit in the United States courts. Cassirer relied on the "international takings" or "expropriation" exception in the FSIA that confers subject matter jurisdiction over a foreign State when "rights in property taken in violation of international law" are at issue and when the instrumentality is engaged in a commercial activity in the United States. Spain and the foundation maintained the exception was not applicable because the painting was taken in violation of international law by Germany, and not by either of them, and because the foundation was not engaged in commercial activity in the United States sufficient to trigger the exception. In 1939, Lilly Cassirer, Claude Cassirer's grandmother, decided she had to leave Germany. German Jews had been deprived of their civil rights, their property was being "Aryanized," and the Kristallnacht pogroms had taken place throughout the country. Although Lilly wished to take the painting with her, an official appraiser appointed by the Nazi government refused to permit her to take the painting out of Germany and demanded she give it to him for approximately $360. Fearing she would not otherwise be permitted to go and knowing she would not obtain the money as the funds would be paid into a blocked account, Lilly complied. The appraiser traded the painting to another art dealer who also was persecuted and fled Germany for Holland. After Germany invaded Holland, the Gestapo confiscated the painting and returned it to Germany where it was sold at auction to an anonymous purchaser in 1943. It appeared in a New York gallery in 1952 and was sold to a St. Louis collector. It was sold again in 1976 to a New York art dealer who, in turn, sold it to Baron Hans-Heinrich Thyssen-Bornemisza. Bornemisza lived in Switzerland. In 1988, Spain paid the Baron $50 million to lease his collection for ten years. Five years later Spain paid the foundation $327 million to purchase the entire collection, including the Pissarro painting. As part of the agreement, Spain provided without charge the Villahermosa Palace in Madrid to the foundation for use as the Thyssen-Bornemisza Museum. Claude Cassirer discovered the painting was on display at the museum in Madrid in 2000. He requested Spain's Minister for Education, Culture and Sports, who was chair of the foundation's board, to return the painting. The request was refused. In 2003, five members of Congress wrote the minister requesting return of the painting; this request also was refused. The Ninth Circuit Court of Appeals ruled the expropriation exception to the FSIA was applicable even though neither the Kingdom of Spain nor the foundation in possession of the painting took the painting from its owner. This court further ruled that Cassirer was not required to exhaust judicial remedies available in Germany or Spain before suing in the United States under the expropriation exception because, as the court stated, Congress had not mandated exhaustion; thus, sound judicial discretion governed. The Ninth Court found that the foundation had engaged in sufficient commercial activity in the United States to support jurisdiction pursuant to the FSIA. (The foundation had borrowed artworks from American museums, had encouraged U.S. citizens to visit the museum and had accepted entrance fees from them, had sold various items to U.S. citizens including images of the painting, and maintained a website where U.S. citizens could buy admission tickets using U.S. credit cards to view paintings on display.)

Example 24. In Orkin v. Swiss Confederation, 770 F. Supp. 2d 612 (S.D.N.Y. 2011), the court ruled that the "takings" exception of the FSIA does not apply when the property at issue passed in the first instance to a private individual and then, from the private individual, to a foreign government. According to the court, the FSIA will apply only if property initially was taken or expropriated by other sovereigns. When an acquisition is by a private individual, the court ruled there is no subject matter jurisdiction under the FSIA's "taking" clause. The property at issue, a Van Gogh pen-and-ink drawing, was sold by a German of Jewish descent to a Swiss art collector to help fund her family's escape from the Nazis. The drawing passed to the Swiss Confederation as a bequest from the art collector.

Example 25. In Rubin v. Islamic Republic of Iran, 637 F.3d 783 (7th Cir. 2011), judgment creditors, who had obtained a judgment against the Islamic Republic of Iran for injuries sustained in a suicide bombing in Israel carried out by a terrorist organization with the assistance of Iranian material support and training, attempted to enforce their judgment by seeking to execute or attach various collections of Persian artifacts in the possession of a museum and a university. Two of the collections of Persian antiquities were owned by Iran but were on long-term academic loan to the University of Chicago's Oriental Institute. One collection was owned by Chicago's Field Museum of Natural History; however, plaintiffs contested the Field Museum's title. The judgment creditors claimed Iran owned the collection because Ernst Herzfeld, from whom the Field Museum purchased the collection, allegedly stole the artifacts and smuggled them out of Iran in the 1920s and 1930s. Iran, however, did not claim ownership of the collection. Iran claimed immunity from attachment of its collections under the FSIA,[48] which provides that a foreign State's property in the United States is immune from attachment unless a specific statutory exception to immunity applies. The Seventh Circuit Court of Appeals noted that the commercial-activity exception in the FSIA[49] permits a judgment creditor to execute against property of a foreign State in the United States but only if an agency or instrumentality of the foreign State has been found to have engaged in commercial activity. It further pointed to the exception[50] that permits execution against property of a foreign State in the United States but only if that property has been used for commercial activity. The court ruled that the property of a foreign State in the United States is presumed immune from attachment, that immunity inheres in the property, and that it does not depend on an appearance or special pleading by the foreign State. Further, it ruled a court must satisfy itself that an exception to the FSIA[51] applies before it can order attachment or other execution on foreign-State property in the United States.

Example 26. In Rubin v. Islamic Republic of Iran, 709 F.3d 49 (1st Cir. 2013), the First Circuit Court of Appeals ruled that antiquities allegedly belonging to Iran that were in possession of U.S. museums were not "blocked assets" subject to attachment under the Terrorism Risk Insurance Act (TRIA).[52] Judgment creditors in the case sought to attach by trustee process various antiquities allegedly belonging to Iran following the creditors obtaining a $109 million default judgment against the Islamic Republic of Iran arising out of a suicide bombing carried out by an Iran-sponsored terrorist group. The creditors were U.S. citizens who were injured in a 1997 terrorist attack that Hamas orchestrated in Jerusalem. They sued the Islamic Republic of Iran, alleging that Iran had provided material support to Hamas and was therefore liable for the attack. They sought to collect their default judgment by attaching certain antiquities they claimed were the property of Iran but that were in the possession of two U.S. museums. The museums contended that Iran did not own the antiquities and that, even if it did, the antiquities would be immune under the FSIA. Although under certain circumstances TRIA permits the attachment of property that might otherwise be immune under the FSIA, the museums contended TRIA does not displace the traditional rule that a judgment creditor may execute only against assets that a judgment creditor owns and that the district court was correct in concluding that Iranian law did not vest title to the antiquities in Iran. The First Circuit determined that the antiquities were not "contested" assets, and, thus, they could not qualify as "blocked assets" under TRIA. TRIA defines a "blocked asset" as any asset seized or frozen by the United States under the International Emergency Economic Powers Act.[53] The First Circuit ruled that because Iran had never made a claim to, or directed transfer of, any of the antiquities at issue in the case, the antiquities were not "contested"; thus, even if the antiquities qualified as "assets of" Iran under TRIA, they would be "uncontested" assets. As a result, the court concluded the antiquities were not attachable under TRIA. The First Circuit ruled that the judgment creditors had failed to demonstrate that any of the antiquities in the museums' possession fell within the exception in TRIA that foreign sovereign property in the United States is immune from attachment and execution.

Example 27. In deCsepel et al. v. Republic of Hungary et al., 714 F.3d 591 (D.C.C. 2013), the Court of Appeals for the District of Columbia affirmed a district court's ruling that the victims' claims against the Republic of Hungary and a number of its museums for their refusal to return pieces of art confiscated from the victims' ancestor, the Baron Mor Lipot Herzog, and their alleged breach of bailment agreements entered into in World War II, fell within the FSIA's commercial activity exception. It ruled that there was a jury question whether the claims were time-barred and reversed the district court's finding of comity regarding a Hungarian judgment which dismissed claims to eleven pieces of artwork. The appellate court ruled that there was a jury question as to whether a Hungarian judgment was entitled to comity. The victims alleged that at least forty works of art were known to be in the possession of Hungarian museums and that several were openly exhibited as "From the Herzog Collection." The court pointed out that the relevant statute of limitations is the District of Columbia's three-year limitations period for claims relating to the recovery of personal property or damages for its retention. Pursuant to the statute, a bailment claim accrues when a victim demands the return of the property and the current possessor refuses, or the possessor takes some action that a reasonable person would understand to be either an act of conversion or inconsistent with a bailment. (Laws relating to bailments were discussed in Chapter 5.) The appellate court reversed the district court's granting comity to a Hungarian judgment that dismissed the Herzog family's claim to eleven pieces of artworks. The appellate court ruled that granting comity would be inappropriate if the Hungarian proceedings failed to provide an opportunity for a full and fair trial under "a system of jurisprudence likely to secure an impartial administration of justice."

In contrast to stolen property, laws in the United States have not prevented purchasers from acquiring good title to illegally exported artifacts. Courts in the United States generally have not disturbed a purchaser's possession of an illegally exported artifact if the artifact was not stolen.

Example 28. In Jeanneret v. Vichey, 693 F.2d 259 (2nd Cir. 1982), the Second Circuit Court of Appeals refused to set aside the sale of a painting that had been illegally exported from Italy. Title to a Matisse was ultimately vested in the seller of the painting, Anna Vichy. She did not obtain an export license or permit from the Italian government when the painting was brought to the Vichyes' apartment in New York. Jeanneret negotiated there to purchase the painting for approximately $230,000. The painting then was sold to Jeanneret in Geneva and was included in Jeanneret's Geneva gallery. After Jeanneret learned of the painting's illegal exportation from Italy, she sought to rescind the sale. The Second Circuit decided that possession of an art object cannot be lawfully disturbed in the United States solely because it was illegally exported from another country and rejected her claim.

Example 29. In Peru v. Johnson, 720 F. Supp. 810 (C.D. Cal. 1989), the court ruled that restrictions on the export of certain artifacts were addressed to protection of these artifacts and that these restrictions do not imply ownership. The court commented that possession of illegally exported artifacts is allowed to remain in private ownership and that these objects may be transferred. The court characterized an export restriction as an exercise of the police power of the state. It stated that export restrictions do not create ownership in the state.

Although courts have ruled that export restrictions do not prevent a purchaser of illegally exported cultural property from obtaining good title to that property, there nonetheless is a problem for persons and entities when they acquire illegally exported cultural artifacts. The country of origin may bring action, including criminal indictments, against the possessors of the property.[54] The ICOM Code of Ethics for Museums states that every effort must be made before acquisition to determine that no object offered for purchase, gift, bequest, or exchange has been illegally exported from its country of origin.[55]

C. MEDIATION TO SETTLE DISPUTES

Because of the difficulty of applying conflicting and often ill-defined laws to resolve cultural property disputes, alternative dispute resolution may be the most effective means of resolving conflicts regarding ownership and possession of cultural property. Submitting complicated issues related to ownership, possession, and repatriation of stolen and/or illegally exported cultural property to arbitration or mediation will prevent one party from becoming subject to another party's national court system, which may be unfamiliar, slow, and expensive.

In addressing the issues related to ownership of valuable cultural property, ICOM established an alternative dispute resolution mechanism in cooperation with the World Intellectual Property Organization (WIPO), a United Nations agency, to provide a more effective system for museums to resolve ownership questions relating to collections with gaps in provenance.[56] The ICOM-WIPO mediation program provides a feasible and attractive means to settle ownership questions and provides a corresponding avenue for increased protection of cultural property.[57] A mediator serves as a non-coercitive neutral facilitator. The focus of the program is to avoid the shortcomings of litigation through assisting parties to reach an agreement through direct communication and increased understanding.[58]

As one expert on the means to protect cultural property stated,[59] "[M]uch is at stake: the public's access to art in the present, respect and consideration for the individual and/or community whose past is embedded in the work of art, and the museum's ability to perform its service to society of protecting heritage for future generations."[60] Indeed, the effective utilization of a mediation process may be the only adequate method to resolve ownership controversies and also may be vital to the long-term preservation of the cultural heritage of humanity.

NOTES

1. See John Merryman, "Thinking about the Elgin Marbles," 83 Mich. L. Rev. 1881 (1985). Merryman maintains that cultural property is "important to the cultural definition and expression of a country, to shared identity and community. They tell people who they are and where they came from. In helping to preserve the identity of specific cultures, they help the world preserve texture and diversity." According to Merryman, a "people deprived of its artifacts is culturally impoverished."

2. ICOM Code of Ethics for Museums, 6.3.

3. As noted in Chapter 5, the original name of the AAM was American Association of Museums. This was its name in 2008 when the document was drafted. The name was changed to American Alliance of Museums in 2012.

4. Nov. 14, 1970, 823 U.N.T.S. 231 (1972).

5. 19 U.S.C. §§ 2091–95 (1972).

6. 19 U.S.C. §§ 2601–12 (1983).

7. Cited in note 5.

8. The act defines a pre-Columbian monumental or architectural sculpture or mural as any stone carving or wall art, or any fragment or part thereof, which is the product of a pre-Columbian Indian culture of Mexico, Central America, South America, or the Caribbean Islands. 19 U.S.C. § 2095(3). It is an immobile monument or architectural structure or part of such monument or structure, and it is subject to export control by the country of origin.

9. The act does not provide for criminal sanctions.

10. 19 C.F.R. § 12.107. Entry is also permitted if the importer presents satisfactory evidence the sculpture or mural was exported from the country of origin on or before June 1, 1973.

11. Id. at § 12.109. Satisfactory evidence that the sculpture or mural was exported from the country or origin before June 1, 1973 is also sufficient.

12. Id. at § 12.109.

13. Cited at note 6.

14. See 1982 U.S. Code Cong. & Admin. News (96 Stat.) 4908, 4100.

15. 19 U.S.C. § 2602.

16. Id. at § 2606. No article of cultural property documented as appertaining to the inventory of a museum, or a religious or secular public monument in any nation, that has been stolen from that nation or from an institution, can be imported into the United States. Id. at § 2607. Any designated archaeological or ethnological material or article of cultural property imported into the United States is subject to seizure and forfeiture.

17. Id. at § 2601.

18. Id.

19. The act also does not apply to material or articles that have been in the United States for less than ten consecutive years and that have been exhibited for not less than five years during that period in a recognized museum in the United States open to the public. It also does not apply to material and articles that have been in the United States less than ten consecutive years but in an instance wherein the country concerned has received or should have received during that period fair notice of location of the material or articles within the United States.

20. Article 6. The Antiquities Protection Law [Antiquities Protection Law (Egypt), Article 6 (Law 117)] stated all antiquities, with the exception of religious endowments (*waqfs*), are deemed to be public property.

21. No person could have possession of an archaeological object after 1994.

22. Law n.1089/39. Under this law, all archaeological objects belong to the State unless they were in private ownership prior to 1902. Further, only the State (or a private citizen by special permit) can conduct excavations.

23. Law of Archaeological Monuments, 1897, Art. 1; Law on Protection and Conservation of Monuments and Natural Beauty, 1930, Art.1; Law for Protection and Preservation of Archaeological Historic Monuments, 1934, Art.1; Federal Law Concerning Cultural Patrimony of the Nation,1970, Art. 52; and Federal law on Archaeological Artistic and Historic Monuments and Zones, 1972, Arts. 27, 55, and 96. These objects could be exported temporarily or permanently only with a permit granted by the government.

24. Turkish Civil Code, 1926, Art. 697.

25. See United States v. McClain, 593 F.2d 658 (5th Cir. 1979).

26. 18 U.S.C. §§ 2314–15.

27. Id. at § 2315.

28. 18 U.S.C. §§ 1961–68.

29. *Nemo dat quod non habet* [He who has not cannot give].

30. See Italian Civil Code, Article 1153; Spanish Civil Code, Article 464; Swiss Civil Code, Article 934; and Sweden Personal Property (Bona Fide) Acquisitions Act (1986:796).

31. Article 1153.

32. Swiss Civil Code, Article 934.

33. Discussion in Robert E. Madden, Steps to Take When Stolen Artwork Is Found in an Estate, 24 Est. P. 459, 462 (1997).

34. See Solomon R. Guggenheim Found. v. Lubell, 569 N.E.2d 426 (N.Y. 1991).

35. Cal. Civ. Proc. Code § 338. See discussion on p. 252.

36. See, e.g., O'Keeffe v. Snyder, 416 A.2d 826 (N.J. 1980).

37. See Solomon R. Guggenheim Found., cited in note 34.

38. The court in Solomon R. Guggenheim Found., cited in note 34, did state, however, that an owner's failure to exercise reasonable diligence to locate a stolen artwork would be considered in the context of another defense, laches.

39. Solomon R. Guggenheim Found., cited in note 34.

40. N.J. Stat. Ann. § 2A:14-1.

41. Cal. Civ. Proc. Code § 338.

42. Orkin v. Taylor, 487 F.3d 734 (9th Cir. 2007). Cassirer v. Thyssenbornemisza Collection Foundation, 737 F.3d 613 (9th Cir. 2013).

43. Cal. Civ. Proc. § 338(c)(3).

44. See David D. Higgins, The Application of the Doctrine of Laches in Public Interest Litigation, 56 B.U.L. Rev. 181 (1976). Unlike the statute of limitations, laches does not apply to mere delay alone, but only to delay that causes an accused harm or prejudice.

45. 28 U.S.C. § 1602-11.

46. Id. at § 1605.

47. See Altmann v. Republic of Austria, 317 F.3d 954 (9th Cir. 2002) and 327 F.3d 1246 (9th Cir. 2003).

48. 28 U.S.C. § 1609.

49. Id. at § 1610(b).

50. Id. at § 1610(a).

51. Id. at § 1609.

52. 28 U.S.C. § 1610(g). TRIA was enacted in 2002 to permit attachment in aid of execution of an FSIA judgment. The act permits claimants to impose liens on property of State sponsors of terrorism.

53. 50 U.S.C. §§ 1701–2.

54. For example, Italy brought a criminal indictment against a prior curator of a prominent U.S. museum on charges of conspiring to export looted antiquities from Italy. Although museum officials agreed to return forty ancient artifacts in its collection to Italy, Italy would not drop the criminal charges against the curator. (An Italian judge, later, in 2010, dismissed charges against the curator when he decided the statute of limitations had run on the allegations.) Greece also brought criminal action against the former curator but dropped charges when museum officials agreed to return to Greece forty artifacts in its collections. Italy has entered into agreements with several U.S. museums for return of some of the objects in their collections.

55. ICOM Code of Ethics for Museums, 2.3.

56. WIPO is an agency of the United Nations, but it is a product of the 1883 Paris Convention for the Protection of Industrial Property and the 1886 Berne Convention for the Protection of Literary and Artistic Works. A need for the international protection of intellectual property became evident as early as 1883 when the predecessor of WIPO came into existence as a means to address that need. WIPO became a specialized agency of the UN in 1974, with the mandate to administer intellectual property matters recognized by member States of the UN. It entered into a cooperation agreement with the World Trade Organization (WTO) in 1996 and, thus, expanded its role in the management of globalized trade.

A fundamental part of WIPO's activities is to promote the protection of intellectual property. It currently administers several treaties that establish internationally agreed rights and standards for their protection. While the Paris and Berne Conventions remain the "cornerstones of WIPO's treaty system," subsequent treaties have expanded the protection they offer. One example is the 1996 WIPO Copyright Treaty, which contains basic rules updating the international protection of copyright and related rights to the Internet age. WIPO attempted to simplify and harmonize procedures for obtaining and maintaining trademarks and patents in countries through the Trademark Law Treaty of 1994 and the Patent Law Treaty of 2000. Through its treaties, WIPO has provided services to simplify and reduce the cost of making individual applications or filings in all the counties in which protection for a given intellectual property right is sought.

57. Discussion at www.icom.museums. ICOM's Art and Cultural Heritage Mediation program is a joint mediation program with the World Intellectual Property Organization (WIPO). WIPO has a renowned Arbitration and Mediation Center that provides mediation expertise and facilities to combine with ICOM's art and cultural heritage expertise. Mediation is provided through a procedure adapted to the settlement of art and cultural heritage disputes or assistance in negotiations in the art and cultural heritage field, including restitution and authenticity issues. The mediation process is a voluntary procedure in which the parties have primary responsibility for resolving their disputes or reaching an agreement after negotiations.

58. ICOM issued a document that cited its policy of many years to "encourage the negotiated resolution of disputes regarding the ownership of objects in museum collections that allegedly were stolen or illegally exported from the country of origin" and articulated its position that there should be "the early settlement of such disputes through voluntary settlement procedures rather than through lengthy and expensive litigation or through political decisions." LegComm 2007—Guidance Notes on ICOM Mediation Process, *ICOM News* no. 1 (2006), available under "Statements" at www.icom/museum/html. The document provides guidance notes on the ICOM mediation process and refers to ICOM's panel of international mediators nominated "to consider issues relating to the return/restitution of cultural property in museum collections that was stolen, illegally exported, illegally confiscated, or otherwise wrongfully expropriated."

59. Boylan, P., Emeritus Professor of Heritage Policy and Management, City University, London, first chair of the Legal Affairs Committee for the International Council of Museums.

60. LegComm 2007—Guidance Notes on ICOM Mediation Process.

CHAPTER 7

ARTISTIC COLLECTIONS AND THE RIGHTS OF ARTISTS

> The true work of art is but a shadow of divine perfection.
>
> MICHELANGELO

> The art of painting is about the heart telling another heart where he found salvation.
>
> FRANCISCO GOYA

Museums have an essential role in promoting and advancing the arts. In carrying out their responsibilities to preserve and protect artworks in their collections, museum officials must be knowledgeable of laws that can both aid and impede policies and procedures they have adopted to conserve priceless museum collections. Chapter 8 considers the security copyright laws can provide for museums, as well as the limitations of the copyright laws in protecting and preserving museum collections. Museum officials also must consider the rights, both personal and economic, of the creators of their collections. The property right or economic interest of an artist, which is protected in the United States through the copyright laws, and the current copyright protection of the moral rights of certain visual artists, are discussed in Chapter 8.

This chapter serves as an introduction to laws protecting art and artists with a consideration of legal issues arising prior to, as well as outside of, copyright protection. The concept of artistic rights involves two elements—one is a personal right in an artist, called a moral right or *droit moral*; the other is a property right of an artist, sometimes referred to as the *droit de suite*. The personal right or moral right protects the personality of the artist and is a recognition that literary or artistic works are extensions of the personalities of the creators and that artists should have special protection for their works even after the works are sold or transferred. Originally an artist's personal or private right did not receive protection in the United States through the copyright laws as did the property or economic rights of an artist. Thus, artists sought protection of their personal right through other means that are discussed in this chapter.

This chapter also addresses other legal issues relating to artists, to include artistic freedom of expression, defamation of artists and their works, and the rights of privacy and publicity.

A. MORAL RIGHT

An artwork is unique in that the artist's personality exists in the artist's creation. This special aspect of an artwork provides a distinct interest or private right for artists that warrants protection long after artists' works have passed to purchasers and collectors. The moral right, or *droit moral*, is a right personal to the artist or creator and is separate and apart from the property or economic interests of the artist. It is a right that has long been recognized in some European countries and in those countries that adhere to the Berne Convention for the Protection of Literary and Artistic Works.[1] The Berne Convention and the Berne Union, consisting of at least 165 member nations, attempt to reconcile the policies of the various nations regarding international copyrights. The Berne Convention has immense significance to artists in that it has provided protection and international recognition of an artist's private right in the artist's creation. The Berne Convention specifically recognizes that the moral right should survive a transfer of ownership of an artist's work. Article 6bis of the Berne Convention provides that

> [i]ndependently of the author's economic rights and even after the transfer of the said rights the author shall have the right to claim authorship of the work and to object to any distortion, mutilation or other modification of, or other derogatory action in relation to the said work, which would be prejudicial to his honor or reputation.

The Berne Convention refers to two elements of the moral right: the right of paternity and the right of integrity of a work. Other elements of the moral right may include a right to create a work and a right to publish a work. The paternity right consists of an artist's right to be made known to the public as the creator of a work, the right to prevent another person being named as the author, and the right to prevent others from attributing wrongfully to the artist a work he has not created. The right of integrity is the right of an artist or author to prevent distortions of his work. This right prevents others from making changes to, modifying, or distorting an artist's work.

As noted in Chapter 8, the United States did not include provisions of the Berne Convention in the U.S. Copyright Act[2] until its accession to the Berne Convention in 1988. Still, ratification of the Berne Convention in 1988 did not include a ratification of Article 6bis, which provides for the artist's moral right. Later, in 1990, Congress enacted the Visual Artists Rights Act (VARA),[3] discussed in Chapter 8, to provide for a right of paternity and to protect a right of integrity for certain visual artists. Through VARA, certain visual artists now have copyright protection for a paternity right and a right of integrity that endures for the life of the artist.[4]

Although copyright law in the United States did not provide for an artist's right of paternity until VARA became affective in 1991, there was a limited recognition of the concept in some states.[5]

Example 1. In Chamberlain v. Feldman, 300 N.Y. 135, 89 N.E.2d 863 (1949), a New York court held that heirs of Mark Twain could prevent the publication of one of Mark Twain's short stories by a person who had purchased the manuscript at an auction after the author's death. The court stated that the common law copyright, or right of first publication, is a right different from that of ownership of the physical paper. The first of these rights does not necessarily pass with the second. The court stated that the separate common law copyright or control of the right to reproduce belongs to the artist or author.

Courts encountered difficulties when artists sought to protect their personal rights of integrity in their creations prior to the copyright protection provided visual artists through the enactment of VARA. Protection of an artist's right of integrity in the United States originally was only through the torts (civil wrongs) of unfair competition or libel (both discussed below).

Example 2. In Granz v. Harris, 198 F.2d 585 (2nd Cir. 1952), the Second Circuit Court of Appeals ruled that attributing authorship of abbreviated versions of an artist's musical performances to the artist would constitute the tort of unfair competition. The Second Circuit held that a contract between an artist and the purchaser of master discs carried by implication, without the necessity of an express prohibition, the duty not to sell records that made the required legend a false representation. The Second Circuit also found that the sale of abbreviated records constituted a breach of contract. In a concurring opinion in this 1952 case, Justice Frank declared that an artist is entitled to prevent the publication of a garbled version as his product. Without rejecting the doctrine of moral right, Justice Frank concurred that a court should not rest its decision on that doctrine if it is possible to rule for the artist under either a tort or contract theory.

Example 3. In Crimi v. Rutgers Presbyterian Church in the City of New York, 194 Misc. 570, 89 N.Y.S.2d 813 (1949), members of a church had commissioned an artist to paint a mural on a wall in the sanctuary of the church. A later congregation decided it did not like the mural and had it painted over when the church building was redecorated. The artist filed suit against church members to compel them to remove the obliterating paint from the mural. The New York court ruled that the artist retained no rights in the work after the artist had made an unconditional sale.[6] (It is a question whether Congress's enactment of VARA, which also provides protection for artwork incorporated in, or made a part of, a building,[7] would have prevented the obliteration of the artist's work.)

Other moral rights, including the right to publish or withhold a work from publication, have had limited recognition under the copyright law.[8] Some courts have held these rights to be a part of the right of privacy (discussed below).[9]

B. *DROIT DE SUITE*

The property or economic right of an artist or author is protected in the United States through the copyright law (discussed in Chapter 8). An artist's property right is a temporary monopoly that Congress grants an artist to prevent others from exploiting the artist's creation. This property right assures an artist she will have the exclusive right to control both the reproduction of her creation and the performance and exhibition of her work.

Some European countries enlarge upon the property right of an artist to include the *droit de suite*. The *droit de suite*, originated in France in the 1920s and currently is in general practice throughout Europe.[10] It grants an artist, or an artist's heirs, the right to collect a percentage of the price of each of an artist's works on a subsequent sale of the work. The right protects those artists who must sell works of art for economic reasons when they are virtually unknown and cannot secure fair prices. The artists are entitled to a portion of the increase in value of their artworks.

California is the only state in the United States that has recognized the *droit de suite*,[11] and there has been a challenge to the constitutionality of the California statute.[12] The California statute provides that when a work of art sells within the State of California for more than $1,000 or the seller resides in California, the seller is required to pay the artist five percent of the sales price. If the seller is unable to locate and pay the artist within ninety days, the statute requires the seller to transfer to the Arts Council an amount equal to five percent of the selling price. If the artist still cannot be located, the Arts Council is required to deposit the funds in the state treasury to be used to acquire fine art.

C. FREEDOM OF EXPRESSION

Artists' expressions may become controversial for varied reasons—some art is in the form of protest art while some art may violate community standards regarding decency and may even violate obscenity laws. Although the right of an artist to express ideas freely is guaranteed by the First Amendment, the right is not without bounds. Courts have ruled that the display of paintings and other exhibitions need not be permitted in every context. As one court reasoned, the interest of others should be considered.[13] This court thought that freedom of speech must recognize, at least within limits, the freedom not to listen.[14] Courts may afford no protection to sexually explicit artwork that might be offensive to the average person in a community. Still, courts are reluctant to become judges of the worth of art.

> Example 4. In Bleistein v. Donaldson Lithographing Co., 188 U.S. 239 (1903), Justice Holmes stated that "it would be a dangerous undertaking for persons trained only in the law to constitute themselves final judges of the worth of pictorial illustrations, outside of the narrowest and most obvious limits." Justice Holmes commented that it was doubtful whether the etchings of Goya or the paintings of Manet would have been certain of protection when they were seen for the first time.

> Example 5. In Silberman v. Georges, 91 A.D. 2d520, 456 N.Y.S.2d 395 (1982), three individuals filed a defamation action against an artist

because they thought the artist's painting, *Mugging of the Muse*, which demonstrated an apparent attempt at assassination by three males on a street, depicted them as the assassins. The court ruled the painting was "obviously allegorical" and, thus, was not defamatory. The court noted that the painting was not an accusal because it did not indicate that the three individuals actually participated in an assault. The court opined that while the picture's effect could well have caused extreme embarrassment, there was no cognizable injury.

Example 6. In Radich v. Criminal Court of New York, 385 F. Supp. 165 (S.D.N.Y. 1974), an artist was convicted in state court for exhibiting certain constructions, comparable to sculptures, that had been fashioned as expressive of protest against the Vietnam War and that prominently incorporated the American flag. The court ruled that the artist's conviction for displaying offensive sculptures deprived him of his First Amendment rights. The court ruled that a citizen is entitled to assert views that may be unpopular to the majority.

Example 7. In Piarowski v. Illinois Community College, 759 F.2d 625 (7th Cir. 1985), the president of a college ordered the chairman of the art department to remove from a public exhibit in the college three works of art that the chairman had created and was displaying. The chairman claimed the action of the president violated his rights under the First Amendment. The Seventh Circuit Court of Appeals ruled that while the artwork was obscene, it was not wholly devoid of artistic merit. The Seventh Circuit held that although the artist's status as an employee would give the college more control over his activities than that of a stranger, the college did not have unlimited control. Still, the court noted that the gallery was not a public forum as it was not open to the public. The Seventh Circuit found that the chairman's rights had not been violated.

Example 8. A state art commission rejected the placement of a portrait, which the members deemed to be offensive, in a hall at the state university. The artist filed suit against the art commission, contending that its decision in rejecting his painting was an unlawful censorship of free artistic expression. In Silvette v. Art Commission of Commonwealth of Virginia, 413 F. Supp. 1342 (E.D. Va. 1976), a court ruled that the action of the committee did not violate the First Amendment right of free artistic expression. The court decided that someone or some group must determine ultimately whether a work of art has substantial artistic and cultural significance in order to advise and counsel the recipient institution. According to the court, this duty includes the right to state the reasons thereof. The court ruled this advice and counsel does not violate the First Amendment right of free artistic expression. The court opined that an artist cannot force the acceptance of the artist's painting.

Example 9. An art instructor displayed a painting offensive to others in a corridor of a university. When university officials ordered him to remove the painting, he sued the university, contending the university had violated his First Amendment rights. In Close v. Lederle, 424 F.2d 988 (1st Cir. 1970), the First Circuit Court of Appeals ruled that the university was warranted in finding the exhibit was inappropriate given the primary use to which the corridor was put. This court held that the university could order removal of the painting to afford protection to a captive audience, some of whom were children, in that display of the painting could violate an unwilling bystander's right to privacy. Though the court stated the painting might not be regarded as obscene in a constitutional sense, its display need not be permitted in every context. The First Circuit decided the interests of others should be considered.

Example 10. In Sefick v. City of Chicago, 485 F. Supp. 644 (W.D. Ill., 1979), a faculty member, who also was an administrator of a university, wanted to exhibit sexually explicit and racially offensive artwork in one of the busiest corridors in the university. When university officials refused to permit him to exhibit the artwork in the corridor but told him to move the works to another room, he sued the university. The court noted that the university employed the faculty member in a responsible administrative, as well as an academic, position. It ruled that there was no First Amendment violation when the university simply ordered him to move the art to another room in the building.

Example 11. In Applegate v. Dumke, 25 Cal. App. 3d 304, 101 Cal. Rptr. 645 (1972), candidates for master's degrees in art at a university were required to complete a group of ten pieces of sculptures. The sculptures then were exhibited on the campus of the university. A student created nude sculptures, some of which depicted sexual and erotic acts, as his master's project. The university decided not to exhibit his work. The student then sued the university, contending that the university's refusal to exhibit the sculptures he created violated his First Amendment rights and was a breach of his contractual right to exhibit his work. The court ruled that the student had no First Amendment right to have his sculptures exhibited. The court noted that the university bulletin made no reference to an exhibit as a prerequisite to a master's degree; thus, the court held the student also had no contractual right to exhibit his work. The court decided faculty members and other students could not claim such a right.

Example 12. In Serra v. U.S. General Services Administration, 847 F.2d 1045 (2nd Cir. 1988), a sculptor sought to bar the General Services Administration (GSA) from removing his controversial sculpture from the Federal Plaza in Manhattan. The GSA commissioned the sculptor to create a work on the plaza. The contract between the parties provided that the work would be the property of the government. Some members of the public urged removal of the work because of its "unappealing aesthetic qualities." The Second Circuit Court of Appeals agreed that artwork may constitute speech for First Amendment purposes under some circumstances but concluded that the First Amendment has limited application where the artistic expression belongs to the government rather than to a private individual.

Example 13. In White v. City of Sparks, 341 F. Supp. 2d 1129 (D. Nev. 2004), the court ruled that a city ordinance, which prohibited artists from selling their art on city streets and parks without first obtaining a license, violated artists' First Amendment rights. The artist in this case earned his living as an artist by traveling throughout the United States, setting up an easel on streets and in parks, and interacting with passersby who took an interest in his work. His subject matter was nature and his paintings often included trees, mountains, animals, and birds. Many had a Native American theme that incorporated the artist's philosophy about the environment, the spirituality of the universe, and the need to protect animals. The city ordinance permitted artists to sell their paintings in the city's parks if the paintings they offered for sale conveyed a religious, political, philosophical, or ideological "message." The artist contended all paintings, photographs, prints, and sculptures are inherently expressive, thereby eliminating the need for any individualized inquiry into the expressiveness of a particular piece of artwork. Although the court declined the artist's invitation to apply a presumption of First Amendment protection to all visual artwork, it ruled the city's pre-approval scheme operated as an unconstitutional prior restraint on speech. The court pointed out that the city had not delineated any objective standards; thus, city officials could easily interpose their personal judgments in a manner inimical to the protection of First Amendment rights.

The First Amendment does not protect works that are "obscene." In Miller v. California,[15] the Supreme Court set out the following "proper" test for obscenity: (1) whether "the average person, applying contemporary community standards" would find the work, taken as a whole, appeals to the prurient interest; (2) whether the work depicts or describes in a patently offensive way, sexual conduct as specifically defined by the applicable state laws; and (3) whether the work, taken as a whole, lacks serious literary, artistic, political, or scientific value.[16] As the Supreme Court noted in Miller, obscenity is determined by applying contemporary community standards rather than national standards.

Example 14. In Pope v. Illinois, 481 U.S. 497 (1987), the Supreme Court ruled that the third or "value" prong of the tripartite test under Miller requires the trier of fact to determine whether a work, "taken as a whole, lacks serious literary, artistic, political, or scientific value" by applying a reasonable person standard rather than "contemporary community standards." The court ruled that, in deciding the value question, the ideas that a work represents need not obtain majority approval to merit protection, and that the value of a work does not vary from community to community based on the degree of local acceptance it has won. The proper inquiry should be whether the work, taken as a whole, has value to a "reasonable person."

The National Foundation on Arts and Humanities considered and rejected suggestions that funding for the arts should be denied for any project that in the experts' views would be "patently offensive to the average person and that lacked serious literary or artistic merit."[17] A committee considering the issue determined that it would be inappropriate for panelists to determine a national standard of what is patently offensive to the average person. The committee did note that rejection of the "patently offensive" language should not be construed as constituting committee support for obscenity.[18] A provision in the act establishing the National Endowment of the Arts[19] (NEA) states,

(1) artistic excellence and artistic merit are the criteria by which applications are judged, taking into consideration general standards of

decency and respect for the diverse beliefs and values of the American public; and

(2) applications are consistent with the purpose of [the] section. Such regulations and procedures shall clearly indicate that obscenity is without artistic merit, is not protected speech, and shall not be funded. Projects, productions, workshops, and programs that are determined to be obscene are prohibited from receiving financial assistance under [the] Act from the National Endowment for the Arts.

Currently then, "artistic excellence and artistic merit" are the criteria by which applications for funding from the NEA are judged, "taking into consideration general standards of decency and respect for the diverse beliefs and values of the American public."[20]

Example 15. In Finley v. National Endowment for the Arts, 524 U.S.569 (1997), the Supreme Court reversed a decision of a lower court wherein the lower court had held to be in violation of the First Amendment the provision in the act creating the NEA,[21] which stated that in judging funding applications "general standards of decency and respect for the diverse beliefs and values of the American public" must be taken into consideration. In reversing the lower court, the Supreme Court ruled that the "decency and respect" clause does not silence speakers by "threatening censorship of ideas," and does not "compromise First Amendment values." The Supreme Court commented that "Congress has wide latitude to set spending priorities" and ruled that the provision of the act "merely adds some imprecise considerations to an already subjective selection process."

Museum exhibitions also may be offensive to some members of the public. Museum directors often encounter negative public reaction to controversial exhibits. Difficult issues surface as to the deference one should give to public opinion when a director elects to provide a forum for controversial artists and issues. While a display in a museum undoubtedly would have artistic value, a museum director must be cautious regarding some art exhibitions.

Example 16. In Crowley v. Smithsonian Institution, 636 F.2d 738 (D.D.C. 1980), a history museum had an exhibit, called the Emergence of Man, that contained references to evolution. The exhibit included specimens from the museum's collection to dramatize the diversity of life on Earth, the adaptation of plant and animal life to their environments, and the way in which organisms change over time in response to environmental and other influences. The exhibit was funded partially with a federal grant. Some members of the public objected to the exhibit and were concerned that it was supported with federal funds. They contended federal funds should be committed equally to explain creation along the lines of the biblical account in Genesis. The Court of Appeals for the District of Columbia ruled that the action of officials of the Smithsonian's Museum of Natural History in presenting exhibits containing references to the theory of evolution fell within the language of the statute creating the Smithsonian "to increase and diffuse knowledge among men."[22] The court noted that the exhibit did not express implicitly or explicitly "that the evolutionary theory of the origin of man and of all plants and animal life is the only credible theory of the origin of life." The exhibits did not mention religion in general nor did it disparage religion or any religious tenet. The court concluded that an exhibit is not impermissible because its message may be repugnant to creationism. It stated that governmental financial support of a theory of the origin of life advocated by religious groups, with less than substantial support from secular research and scholarship, would be an impermissible establishment of religion. It commented that no member of the public was under a compulsion to go to the museum. Members of the public are "free to avoid the exhibits which they find offensive and may focus on the other exhibits of which there are many."

Example 17. In Cuban Museum of Arts & Culture v. City of Miami, 766 F. Supp. 1121 (S.D.Fla. 1991), a museum in Miami had leased a building from the City of Miami to house its exhibits. The museum decided to exhibit works of Cuban artists and included in the exhibit a number of works that were created either by artists who had not renounced the Castro regime or by artists who continued to live in communist Cuba. The exhibit evoked hostility and threats from members of the local Cuban community. A bomb was exploded underneath the automobile of an attorney serving as a director and vice president of the museum. Later, individuals and groups appeared before city officials and demanded that the directors be removed and supplanted with others who allegedly "were more in tune with the political goals and spirit of democracy that the local Cuban community espoused." They asked the city to investigate alleged violations of the museum's lease agreement with the city. The city then terminated the lease with the museum. The court ruled that a decision of the museum that art should be exhibited and made available to the public regardless of the political beliefs and ideology of the artists was protected constitutionally. The court decided that the decision to terminate the lease was based on the intolerant bickering among various groups and the dissension within the local community. It ruled that the city could not attempt to accomplish well-intentioned goals of bringing peace within the community by sacrificing those whose views and method of expression had caused others to respond with hostility and scorn. It held that the city's actions were an improper exercise of governmental power. The court stated that the First Amendment must assure that government does not curtail valid expression because a majority, a plurality, or any segment of its constituency wishes to prohibit or penalize that expression. It commented that it was ironic that the curtailment and punishment of expression was the result of actions taken by those who claimed to loathe governmental intolerance existing in communist Cuba.

Example 18. In Brooklyn Institute of Arts and Sciences v. City of New York, 64 F. Supp. 2d 184 (1999), a museum had a display of a "Sensation Exhibit" to which city officials objected. City officials contended the exhibit desecrated the "most personally and deeply held views of the people in society." The Mayor of New York ordered funding for the museum's operating expenses withheld until the museum removed the exhibit. The court granted the Brooklyn Institute an injunction barring the Mayor and the City of New York from withholding funds that already had been appropriated to the museum for operating expenses and maintenance. The court distinguished facts in this case from those in Finley v. National Endowment (discussed in Example 15). Funding in the Brooklyn Institute case had been appropriated prior to the exhibit, and the funds were appropriated for operating expenses rather than for supporting the project.

D. DEFAMATION

Defamation consists of the torts (civil wrongs) of libel and slander—libel is written defamation, while slander is oral. Defamation of a person tends to damage that person's reputation or to diminish esteem, respect, goodwill, or confidence in the defamed person. Libel, for example, has been statutorily defined[23] as "a defamation expressed in written or other graphic form that tends to injure a living person's reputation and thereby expose the person to public hatred, contempt, ridicule, or financial injury or to impeach any person's honesty, integrity, virtue, or reputation or to publish the natural defects of anyone and thereby expose the person to public hatred, ridicule, or financial injury." In either form, defamation is an invasion of another's reputation and good name. It is false communication that vilifies a person. To establish a cause of action for libel or slander, an injured party must prove that the challenged party made a false and defamatory communication to a third person.[24] Thus, defamation requires that something be communicated to a third person which may affect that person's opinion of the defamed party. Derogatory words and insults directed only to the injured party are not defamation.

A challenged party in a defamation lawsuit may have a defense of privilege or truth, either of which can be a complete defense. The defense of "privilege" is available in judicial proceedings (to the judge, the witnesses, parties in the case, and counsel for the parties). It is available in legislative proceedings, executive communications, and political broadcasts. Publishers have a qualified privilege. Because a communication must be "false" as well as defamatory, "truth" can be a complete defense. Still, the defense of truth can be perilous for a challenged party because the party admits the defamatory statement in utilizing the defense. The challenged party may be unable to prove the truthfulness of an injurious communication.

Only living persons may be defamed. There is no defamation of a person who is deceased unless there also is a reflection upon those still living. The theory is that while there may be liability to those living who are themselves defamed, to provide a deceased person with a right of action would interfere with historical research.

Example 19. Art Museum wants to hire a curator. It requests information from History Museum regarding one of History Museum's former employees. The director of History Museum informs the director of Art Museum orally that the former employee was shiftless, incompetent, and dishonest. The former employee has a cause of action against the director of History Museum for slander. Although truth is a defense, it may be difficult for the director of History Museum to prove the former employee indeed possesses these traits.

One may make denigrating comments about artworks that can provide a cause of action for defamation. Defamation of an artwork encompasses statements that a painting is not authentic. Further, refusal to include a work in a catalogue raisonné of an artist's work can lead to a defamation claim. As discussed in Chapter 5, a catalogue raisonné is regarded as a definitive catalogue of the works of a particular artist.[25] The preparation of catalogues raisonnés generally is undertaken by scholars who have studied an artist's work, dealers with expertise in that artist's work, an artist's estate, or some combination of these persons or entities.[26] In the art world, refusal or failure to include a work in the artist's catalogue raisonné is tantamount to a determination that the work is not authentic.[27] Inclusion of a painting in a catalogue raisonné serves to authenticate the work. Non-inclusion suggests a work is not genuine.

Example 20. In Mennella v. Schon, 979 F.2d 357 (5th Cir. 1992), a collector purchased from an art gallery a painting that allegedly was a work of the Flemish Master Sir Anthony Van Dyck and was over 300 years old. The purchase price was $400,000. The collector made a down payment on the painting but then demanded authentication so that the collector could secure a loan to pay part of the purchase price. The appraiser stated that the painting, a portrait of Princess Mary, eldest daughter of King Charles I, was one of five copies by Van Dyck. The collector became concerned that the painting might be a forgery and enlisted the aid of museum attorneys to void the sale and to recover the down payment. The collector's attorneys referred to the contract as an "agreement to purchase" rather than a sale. The art gallery, which had sold the collector the painting, then shipped the painting to an art gallery in London where it was sold for $1,400,000. Having learned of the sale, the collector contended the sale of the painting to him had been completed and that the London sale was a conversion. The court ordered the art gallery to return the down payment but did not order a return of the painting to the collector. Attorneys for the art gallery informed the collector's attorneys that the collector would be sued for defamation if he made any statements that the painting was not authentic. The court in Mennella noted that a successful defamation claim requires (1) defamatory words; (2) publication to someone other than the one defamed; (3) falsity; (4) malice, actual or implied; and (5) injury. The court decided that there was no indication the collector spoke the allegedly defamatory words or that the collector published the statements, if any, to a third party. It also found that the collector did not act with malice and that the art gallery did not suffer any injury.

Product disparagement also is an action to recover for words or conduct that tend to reflect negatively upon the condition, value, or quality of a product or property. This action, which traces its ancestry to the common law tort of slander, has been applied in cases involving statements that an artwork is inauthentic or forged. Product disparagement requires a claimant to prove falsity of a statement, publication to a third party, malice, and special damages.

> Example 21. In Kirby v. Wildenstein, 784 F. Supp. 1112 (S.D.N.Y. 1992), the owner of a painting by the nineteenth-century French artist Jean Beraud entered into a consignment agreement with Christie's for the painting to be offered for sale at Christie's 1988 auction. At the same time, the recognized expert on Jean Beraud was preparing a catalogue raisonné of the artist's works. One of the terms of the consignment agreement between the painting's owner and Christie's was that Christie's would communicate with the Beraud expert to verify that the painting would be included in the forthcoming Beraud catalogue raisonné. The Beraud expert asked Wildenstein, a world-renowned art expert and also a Beraud expert, to examine the painting. After Wildenstein scrutinized the painting, looked at both the front and the back, and observed it from various distances, Wildenstein decided the canvas had been relined and thought figures in the painting were more blurred than those of other Berauds he had seen. He concluded the painting either was "skinned" (meaning it had suffered the removal of paint through over cleaning) or that it was a copy. When the painting's owner attempted to sell the painting at auction, there were no bidders. The owner then brought a product disparagement claim against Wildenstein, contending Wildenstein made false and disparaging statements about the painting that prevented its sale and left it "burned" and otherwise devalued. The court decided the painting's owner had not proved special damages. He could not name any person who might have bid on the painting but who did not do so because of the alleged disparagement. The court also pointed out there was no evidence to demonstrate Wildenstein circulated his statements. The court ruled the painting's owner failed to demonstrate that any losses he sustained were related to the allegedly disparaging statements.

E. INVASION OF PRIVACY

An artist must consider the right of privacy (the right to be left alone) when painting a portrait or taking a photograph of an individual or individuals. Museum personnel must consider the right when displaying a possibly objectionable painting or photograph. Invasion of privacy includes an appropriation of a party's name or likeness for another's benefit or advantage. Although violation of one's right of privacy is similar to libel or slander, it is much broader. Violation of a person's right of privacy is actionable even though there is no false or defamatory communication made about the injured party. An injured party may have a cause of action for violation of the party's privacy even though the questionable communication is true.

The right of privacy is the right to be free from intrusion upon one's physical solitude or seclusion. To be an invasion of privacy, a matter must be made public that would be offensive and objectionable to a reasonable person of ordinary sensibilities. A painting or photograph taken without permission can be a violation of privacy if the painting or photograph portrays an individual in an offensive or objectionable manner.[28]

> Example 22. In Estate of Hemingway v. Random House, 296 N.Y.S.2d 772, 244 N.E.2d 250 (1968), a New York court rejected the claim of the widow of Ernest Hemingway that the publication of a biography of Hemingway, which contained lengthy quotations from the writer, violated her right of privacy.[29]

> Example 23. In Benally v. Amon Carter Museum of Western Art, 858 F.2d 618 (10th Cir. 1988), members of a Navajo tribe brought suit against a museum for releasing photographs of them. Laura Gilpin had photographed members of the tribe in native dress. Although tribal members allegedly gave Gilpin permission to take the photographs, they had not authorized the photographs' publication or public exhibition. One photograph of Benally, a Navajo woman, and her child, titled *Navajo Madonna*, became part of Gilpin's collection. It later was published on a postcard, in three books, in magazines, and was exhibited at least thirty-five times throughout the United States. Gilpin's photographic collection was bequeathed to the museum upon Gilpin's death. Museum officials spent considerable time in Santa Fe, New Mexico, transferring and cataloguing the negatives for use in the museum and producing a documentary film about Gilpin and her work. After Gilpin's death, the museum provided copies of photographs from the Gilpin Collection, including *Navajo Madonna*, to several magazines in which the photographs were reproduced. Tribal members sued the museum, contending they were unaware the photographs had been exhibited and published and objected to the reproduction because of traditional Navajo belief that publication of photographs can have bad effects on persons in the photographs.

The museum contended that, because it was a nonprofit organization, its activities in New Mexico could not be characterized as "transacting business"; thus, the New Mexico court did not have jurisdiction over it. The Tenth Circuit Court of Appeals concluded the museum's activities in New Mexico in soliciting the devise of the Gilpin Collection, negotiating the terms of the collection's maintenance and exhibition, traveling to New Mexico to take possession of the collection, and invoking the benefits of New Mexico's laws of testamentary disposition were significant to the jurisdictional inquiry. The Tenth Circuit concluded these activities manifested a purposeful intent to conduct business in New Mexico and ruled it had jurisdiction to hear the case. The parties later settled the case before the court could rule on the question of whether the museum violated tribal members' rights of privacy based on their special objections to the photographs.

As noted, to take and publish a photograph or paint a portrait of an individual that would be objectionable to a "reasonable person of ordinary sensibilities" is an invasion of the individual's privacy. The photograph of Benally and her child, discussed in Example 23, would not have been objectionable to a person with "ordinary" sensibilities in that it was a beautiful and unique photograph. However, the photography would be objectionable to Benally because of her particular culture. There is a question of whether the concept of a "reasonable person of ordinary' sensibilities" should be enlarged to consider the culture or religion of an individual who objects to having a photograph or painting of herself. If so, publishing the *Navajo Madonna* photograph would have violated Benally's right of privacy. Benally shared the Navajo belief that taking one's photograph produced harmful results.

The right of privacy is a personal one. It does not extend to members of the complaining party's family unless the privacy of the family members also is invaded. Further, the right of privacy is not assignable and does not survive death.[30]

Example 24. A historical museum wants to display the letters of a famous person to his mistress. If the famous person is still living, the museum may violate the person's right of privacy by displaying the letters without consent (unless the person's status as a public figure makes disclosure in the public interest). The museum also might be subject to possible liability if its officials fail to secure the consent of the famous person's mistress. If the persons are no longer living, there can be no invasion of privacy action as a cause of action because violation of one's right of privacy does not survive death. Thus, the museum would be protected so long as the rights of privacy of living persons also are not invaded.

F. RIGHT OF PUBLICITY

The right of publicity is a form of the right of privacy. The right is of recent origin and developed to protect the commercial interest of famous persons in their identities. The right has been defined as the inherent right of every person to control the commercial use of his identity.[31] While the right to privacy protects a person from depiction in an unfavorable light, the right of publicity protects one's pecuniary interest in the commercial use of one's likeness.[32]

The right of publicity is an economic right. It is a right to control and profit from the commercial use of one's name or likeness. The theory of the right is that a celebrity's identity can be valuable in the promotion of products and that the celebrity has an interest which may be protected from unauthorized commercial exploitation of that identity.[33] The right is not a right of censorship, but rather a right to prevent others from misappropriating the economic value generated by a celebrity's fame through the merchandising of the "name, voice, signature, photograph, or likeness" of the celebrity.[34] The right of publicity then assumes that the famous have an exclusive legal right during lifetime to control and profit from the commercial use of their names and personalities. Courts have ruled that the appropriation of another's name and likeness without consent—whether in a photograph or a sculpture—for financial gain violates a public figure's right of publicity.[35] The unauthorized use of a photograph can be a violation of a right of publicity as well as the right of privacy.

Example 25. In Haelan Laboratories, Inc. v. Topps Chewing Gum, Inc., 202 F.2d 866 (2nd Cir. 1953), the Second Circuit Court of Appeals ruled that "in addition to and independent of 'a right of privacy, a person' has a right in the publicity value of his photograph, i.e., the right to grant the exclusive privilege of publishing his picture, and that such a grant validly may be made 'in gross,' i.e., without an accompanying transfer of a business or anything else."

While the right of publicity can provide a cause of action against an artist who appropriates another's likeness without consent, the right of publicity also may provide economic protection to an artist should the artist's name or product be used in any unauthorized manner. Copyright laws (discussion in Chapter 8) protect an artist's expression of an idea in a tangible form, i.e., a painting or a sculpture, whereas the availability of protection under a right of publicity is not limited to a tangible medium of expression.

Example 26. A museum has several works of Picasso in its collection. It is planning a special exhibition and plans to sell shirts with a likeness of Picasso. The heirs of Picasso have threatened to sue the museum, contending that it has no legal right to sell the shirts. The heirs may have a legal right of publicity in the likeness of Picasso that the museum cannot exploit.

Example 27. The Supreme Court recognized the right of publicity in Zacchini v. Scripps-Howard Broadcasting, 433 U.S. 562 (1977). In that case a performer in a "human cannonball" act brought an action against a television broadcasting company to recover damages allegedly suffered when, against his wishes, the broadcasting company videotaped his entire performance and played the videotape on a television news program. The court decided that the broadcast of a film of the performer's entire act posed a substantial threat to the economic value of that performance. According to the Supreme Court, the performer's act was the product of his own talents and energy, the end result of much time, effort, and expense, and that much of its economic value lay in the right of exclusive control over publicity given the performance. As the Court stated, if the public can see the act free on television, it will be less willing to pay to see it.

The Zacchini case is the only decision by the Supreme Court on the right of publicity, and the right has not been recognized in all the states. Some states have recognized the right through case law, however, and some by statute as well. For example, Texas statutory law[36] establishes a statutory property right in the use of an individual's name, voice, signature, photograph, or likeness after the death of the individual, if the same had commercial value at the time of the individual's death or came to have commercial value after that time. This property right may be registered with the Texas Secretary of State. Persons, other than certain heirs of the deceased, may not use the deceased individual's name, voice, signature, photograph, or likeness in any manner including the advertising or selling of merchandise, goods or services, except for certain permitted media uses.[37] California[38] made the right a property right that was freely transferable or descendible. Its statute authorized recovery of damages by any living person whose name, photograph, or likeness had been used for commercial purposes without the person's consent and provided that the statutory right of publicity was descendible to that person's heirs.

> Example 28. In Carson v. Here's Johnny Portable Toilets, Inc., 698 F.2d 831 (6th Cir. 1983), an entertainer sued a corporation that rented and sold "Here's Johnny" portable toilets. The Sixth Court of Appeals ruled the corporation invaded the entertainer's right of publicity by its intentional appropriation of his identity for commercial exploitation even though the corporation did not use his name or likeness. In a dissenting opinion in Carson, Justice Kennedy expressed concern about a court recognizing a right of publicity. Justice Kennedy noted that protection under a right of publicity creates a common-law monopoly that removes items, works, and acts from the public domain, whereas federal policy favors free enterprise. According to Justice Kennedy, protection under a right of publicity confers a monopoly on the protected individual that is potentially broader, offers fewer protections, and potentially competes with the federal statutory monopolies—the copyright, trademark, and patent laws. As Justice Kennedy pointed out, under the federal acts, notice to the public of the right is required, whereas under the right of publicity the public is unaware of the right claimed by the owner.

Because the right of publicity has the potential of censoring significant expression by suppressing alternative versions of celebrity images, an artist who has created a work that includes an image of a famous person and who is faced with a right of publicity challenge to her work, may assert an affirmative defense that her work is protected by the First Amendment.[39] Courts have ruled that a state's interest in preventing an "outright misappropriation" of intellectual property not covered under federal copyright must be balanced with the interest in free expression according to the relative importance of the interests at stake;[40] thus, courts must distinguish between those forms of artistic expression protected by the First Amendment and those that must "give way to the right of publicity." One court stated that any test must incorporate the principle that the right of publicity cannot, consistent with the First Amendment, be a right to control a celebrity's image by censoring disagreeable portrayals. The court opined that when a celebrity "thrusts himself or herself forward into the limelight, the First Amendment dictates that the right to comment on, parody, lampoon, and make other expressive uses of the celebrity image must be given broad scope."[41] This court reasoned that an artist faced with a right of publicity challenge to her work should have an affirmative defense that the artist's work is protected by the First Amendment if it has significant transformative elements or that the value of the work does not derive primarily from the celebrity's fame.[42]

Example 29. In Cardtoons, L.C. v. Major League Baseball Players Assoc., 95 F.3d 959 (10th Cir. 1996), the Tenth Circuit Court of Appeals held a sports artist's right of free expression outweighed a baseball player's right of publicity. The artist featured readily identifiable caricatures of major league baseball players with a humorous commentary about their careers on the back. The cards ridiculed the players using a variety of themes. In balancing the players' property rights with the artist's First Amendment rights, the Tenth Circuit commented on the pervasive presence of celebrities in the media, sports, and entertainment and ruled that the trading cards were expressions protected by the First Amendment.

Example 30. In Comedy III Productions, Inc. v. Saderup, Inc., 21 P.3d 797 (Cal. 2001), an artist with over twenty-five years of experience in making charcoal drawings of celebrities sold lithographs and T-shirts bearing a likeness of "The Three Stooges" reproduced from a charcoal drawing he had made. The holder of all rights in "The Three Stooges" sought damages against the artist for violation of its publicity rights in the former three-man comedy act. The Supreme Court of California ruled that depictions of celebrities that amounted to little more than the appropriation of the celebrity's economic value are not protected under the First Amendment. Still, the court decided that a work that contains significant transformative elements is not only worthy of First Amendment protection but also is less likely of interfering with the economic interest protected by the right of publicity. In this context, the court stated that First Amendment protection of a work outweighs whatever interest the state may have in enforcing the right of publicity. In determining whether a work is sufficiently transformative, the California court looked to whether the marketability and economic value of the challenged work derived primarily from the fame of the celebrity depicted. If not, according to the court, there generally would be no actionable right of publicity. If the value of the work comes principally from some cause other than the fame of the celebrity—for example, from the creativity, skill, and reputation of the artist—the California court thought it could be presumed that sufficient transformative elements were present to warrant First Amendment protection. Still, if the work related principally to the fame of the celebrity depicted, the court stated it would not necessarily follow that the work was without First Amendment protection. It could still be a transformative work. However, in considering whether the artist's work depicting "The Three Stooges" had any significant transformative or creative contribution, the California court decided the marketability and economic value of the work derived primarily from the fame of the celebrities the artist portrayed. In applying the transformative standard, the court found no transformative elements in the artist's work that required First Amendment protection and ruled that the artist could continue to depict "The Three Stooges" only with consent of the holder of the right of publicity for "The Three Stooges."

Example 31. In ETW Corp. v. Jireh Publishing, Inc., 332 F.3d 915 (6th Cir. 2001), a sports artist created a painting titled *The Masters of Augusta*, which commemorated Tiger Woods's victory at the Masters Tournament in Augusta, Georgia, in 1997. At that event, Woods became the youngest player ever to win the Masters Tournament, while setting a 72-hole record for the tournament and a record 12-stroke margin of victory. In the foreground of the artist's painting were three views of Woods in different poses. Woods's licensing agent filed suit against the artist alleging a violation of Woods's right of publicity. The Sixth Circuit Court of Appeals noted what it termed "an inherent tension" between the right of publicity and the right of freedom of expression under the First Amendment and noted that the tension becomes "particularly acute" when the person seeking to enforce the right is a famous person whose exploits, activities, accomplishments, and personal life are subject to constant scrutiny and comment in the public media. The Sixth Circuit found that the transformative elements of Woods's victory at the 1997 Masters Tournament, "with all the trappings of that tournament in full view, including the Augusta clubhouse, the leader board, images of Woods's caddy, and his final round partner's caddy," were sufficient to bring the artist's work within the protection of the First Amendment. The Sixth Circuit commented that the Masters Tournament is probably the world's most famous golf tournament and Woods's victory in the 1997 tournament was a historic event in the world of sports. The Sixth Circuit ruled the artist's work did not violate Woods's right of publicity.

Example 32. In Hart v. Electronic Arts, Inc., 717 F.3d 141 (3rd Cir. 2013), a former college football player contended a video game developer violated his right of publicity when it appropriated his likeness for use in the NCAA Football series of video games. The video game developer used the player's image in the promotion of NCAA Football by showing him throwing a pass with actual footage from Rutgers University's Bowl Game against Arizona University in 2009. The Third Circuit Court of Appeals noted, as being self-evident, that video games are protected as expressive speech under the First Amendment. The video game developer contended the First Amendment shielded it from liability from a right of publicity violation because NCAA Football is a protected work. In balancing the interests of the parties, the Third Circuit noted the varying approaches courts had taken in attempting to strike a balance between the competing interests in the right of publicity and the First Amendment. In determining whether the interest in safeguarding the rights of publicity overpowered the interest in safeguarding free expression, the Third Circuit looked to the decision of the California Supreme Court in Comedy III Prods., Inc. v. Saderup, discussed in Example 30. The Third Circuit noted that the transformative use test was first articulated by the California Supreme Court in Comedy III Prods., Inc. The Third Circuit also considered the Sixth Circuit's decision in ETW Corp. v. Jireh Publishing, Inc., discussed in Example 31. The Third Circuit concluded that the transformative use test appeared to strike the best balance between interests protected by the right of publicity and interests protected by the First Amendment. It ruled that the photograph of the player in the game's montage was shielded by the First Amendment, but remanded the case back to the district court for a determination of whether the entire work was sufficiently transformative to escape the player's right of publicity. It ruled that only the player's likeness in the photograph was protected by the First Amendment and that the district court should determine whether his overall claim surmounted First Amendment protection.

Courts had been divided on whether a right of publicity survives death, but apparently most courts now would agree the right of publicity survives death of its owner and is inheritable and devisable.[43] States that have statutorily recognized a right of publicity permit a postmortem right of publicity. The majority of the states limit the right to fifty years or less, while some have permitted it for much longer periods after the death of the celebrity.[44]

Example 33. In Hebrew University of Jerusalem v. General Motors, 903 F. Supp. 2d 932 (C.D. Cal, 2012), a purported holder of a postmortem right to publicize the image of Albert Einstein filed an action against an alleged infringer who used an image of Einstein in an advertisement for a vehicle it sold. The court noted that a slight majority of states with statutory rights of publicity limited the right's postmortem duration to fifty years or less. The court thought that an open-ended right of publicity, or even a postmortem duration longer than fifty years, raised considerable First Amendment concerns and created a potentially infinite curb on expression. The court opined that "overprotecting intellectual property is as harmful as underprotecting it." The court ruled that a maximum duration of fifty years appropriately reflected the balance between a meaningful enforcement of the right of publicity after a famous individual's death and the public's interest in free expression. Because this case was not filed until 2010 and the court determined that 2005 would have been the last year the holder of the postmortem right to publicize the image of Albert Einstein could sue to enforce any right of publicity it might have inherited from Einstein, the court dismissed the case.

G. UNFAIR COMPETITION

An artist may have a cause of action for unfair competition if the artist's work is presented in a distorted form or false description or endorsement.[45] False attribution of authorship or the unauthorized disclosure of an author's or artist's name also can constitute the tort of unfair competition.[46]

Example 34. In Eden Toys, Inc. v. Florelee Undergarment Company, Inc., 697 F.2d 27 (2nd Cir. 1982), the Second Circuit Court of Appeals ruled that Florelee had made a false designation of origin of a character on its nightshirts that resembled the "Paddington Bear," or a false description, and that it had violated the Lanham Act.

The federal statute called the Lanham Trademark Act[47] has become an important weapon for artists seeking to protect their reputations and the integrity of their works. This act prohibits the use of a false designation of origin, or any false description or representation in connection with any goods or services that are introduced into commerce. False endorsement occurs when a celebrity's identity is connected with a product or service in a manner in which consumers are likely to be misled about the celebrity's sponsorship or approval of the product of service.[48] The elements of a Lanham Act false endorsement claim are similar to the elements of a right of publicity claim.[49] One court opined that the act generally should be construed to apply to artistic works only where the public interest in avoiding consumer confusion outweighs the public interest in free expression.[50]

Example 35. Assume a museum obtains permission from an artist to show a tape of the artist's works. The museum staff would like to edit the tape to remove two objectionable paintings and to redact a small part of another painting the museum director thinks would be objectionable to sensitive members of the public. If the staff does remove portions of the tape and redacts a modest portion of a particular painting without permission from the artist, would the museum be liable to the artist under the tort of unfair competition? In Gilliam v. American Broadcasting Companies, 538 F.2d 14 (2nd Cir. 1976), the Second Circuit Court of Appeals recognized that relief has been granted for misrepresentation of an artist's work by relying on the law of unfair competition. The court noted that the tort of unfair competition can be used to vindicate an author's personal right to prevent presentation of the artist's works to the public in a distorted form. In Gilliam, a group of British writers and performers known as "Monty Python" sought an injunction to restrain American Broadcasting Companies from broadcasting edited versions of three separate programs originally written and performed by "Monty Python." The court held that the excising impaired the integrity of the original work. The court found a violation of the Lanham Act,[51] which is the federal counterpart to unfair competition. The court stated that this act is violated if a representation of a product, although technically true, creates a false impression of the product's origin. Thus, an obligation to mention the name of the author carries the implied duty, as a matter of contract, not to make such changes in the work that would render the credit line a false attribution of authorship.

Example 36. In Boule v. Hutton Galleries, Inc. & Khidekel, 328 F.3d 84 (2nd Cir. 2003) and 320 F. Supp. 2d 132 (S.D.N.Y. 2004), French collectors, the Boules, who owned several works attributed to the Russian Supremacist artist Lazar Khidekel, sued the artist's son and daughter-in-law and an art gallery that was selling the son's collection of Khidekel's art. The Boules contended that statements made by Hutton Galleries and the Khidekels that disparaged the authenticity of their collection violated the Lanham Act. The Khidekels were quoted in an *ARTnews* article expressing their opinion that the Boules' paintings were not Khidekel's works. The Second Circuit Court of Appeals stated that a claimant under the Lanham Act has the burden of proving that a statement is false and was made in commercial advertising or promotion. The Second Circuit ruled the Boules had to prove Khidekel created the paintings and that the Boules had the burden to prove the falsity of the Khidekels' statements regarding the paintings. The Second Circuit decided the Khidekels' statements were not commercial speech and found there was no violation of the Lanham Act. The Second Circuit commented that the Khidekels' statements in *ARTnews* contributed to the reporters' discussion of an issue of public importance—fraud in the art market—and was protected by the First Amendment.

Example 37. In Navarra v. Marlborough Gallery, Inc., 820 F. Supp. 2d 477 (S.D.N.Y. 2011), a private, high-end art gallery owner, who marketed ceramics by Chu, a renowned, Paris-based artist, brought a Lanham Act violation claim against a competitor, Marlborough Gallery, that commissioned vases hand-painted by Chu. The gallery owner, Navarra, also alleged Marlborough engaged in a systematic campaign to achieve monopoly power in a global market for the sale of Chu's ceramics and asserted a violation of the Sherman Act. Navarra contended Marlborough was behind an advertisement in an arts journal that warned readers the Navarra-commissioned ceramics were not genuine. The court found that the Navarra-commissioned ceramics were not original works of art. Each plate was a "reproduction" of a unique, original work by Chu and each sold for approximately $2,100. The court also found that the Marlborough-commissioned vases were original, unique works of art and that they retailed for approximately $280,000 each. The court ruled that the Navarro-commissioned plates were not "reasonably interchangeable" with the Marlborough-commissioned vases. It determined that the relevant market Navarro proposed for purposes of the Sherman Act was implausible and found no Sherman Act violation. The court decided that Navarra could offer no more than speculation that any of the allegedly false and defamatory statements about him were attributable to Marlborough. The court found the statements were not commercial speech and ruled there was no Lanham Act violation.

Example 38. In University of Alabama Board of Trustees v. New Life Art, Inc., 683 F.3d 1266 (11th Cir. 2012), the Eleventh Circuit Court of Appeals ruled an artist's use of a university's trademarks in paintings, prints, and calendars did not violate the Lanham Act. The artist painted famous football scenes involving the University of Alabama. The paintings featured realistic portrayals of the university's uniforms, including helmets, jerseys, and crimson-and-white colors. The artist reproduced his paintings as prints and calendars, as well as on mugs and other articles. The university contended the artist needed permission to depict its uniforms because they were trademarks. The court stated it would construe the Lanham Act narrowly when deciding whether an artistically expressive work infringes a trademark. The court opined that in the context of allegedly misleading titles using a celebrity's name, the act is not applicable unless the title has no artistic relevance to the underlying work whatsoever, or if it has some artistic relevance, unless the title explicitly misleads as to the source of the work. The court stated the risk of misunderstanding, not engendered by an overt claim in the title, is so outweighed by the interests in artistic expression as to preclude application of the Lanham Act.

NOTES

1. 828 U.N.T.S. 222. The Berne Convention for the Protection of Literary and Artistic Works includes a provision that recognizes a moral right in an artist. The Berne Convention, which has been in existence for over a hundred years, symbolizes international protection for authors and artists.

2. Pub. L. 94-553 (1976), Title 17 of the U.S. Code.

3. Pub. L. 101-650 (1990), codified at 17 U.S.C. § 106A. The Visual Artists Rights Act of 1990 added § 106A to the Copyright Act to provide for a right of paternity and a right of integrity for certain defined visual artists.

4. 17 U.S.C. § 106A. Discussion of the right and the definition of a "visual artist" for this purpose in Chapter 8.

5. The right also was recognized under the tort of unfair competition or as a violation of one's right of privacy or right of publicity. Discussion of rights of privacy and publicity at notes 28–43 and accompanying text.

6. Section 113, added to the Copyright Act by VARA for works of visual art incorporated in, or made a part of, a building, now might have prevented church members from removing the mural. See further discussion in Chapter 8.

7. 17 U.S.C. § 113, discussed in Chapter 8.

8. See 17 U.S.C. § 106(3). The right to distribute copies of a copyrighted work gives the copyright holder the right to control the first public publication of his work.

9. Discussion of right of privacy at notes 28 and 29 and accompanying text.

10. See discussion of the *droit de suite* in Notices, Library of Congress, 77 FR 58175-01, 2012 WL 4086675. The notice points out that resale royalty rights are optional under the Berne Convention for the Protection of Literary and Artistic Works (discussed in note 1 and accompanying text) and that these rights are not part of current U.S. copyright law. The notice refers to the fact that there can only be one sale at a time under U.S. copyright law and that only the initial sale will inure to the benefit of an artist or sculptor.

11. See Cal. Civ. Code § 986. The Visual Artists Rights Act did not include a property right in an artist; thus, the Copyright Act probably does not preempt a state statute that provides for a right to resale royalty. [See H.R. Rep. No. 101-514, 101st Cong. 2d Sess. 21, Pub. L. No. 101-650, 104 Stat. 4089 (1990)]. Still, there was an allegation in Estate of Graham v. Sotheby's Inc., 860 F. Supp. 2d 1117 (S.C. Cal. 2012) that the Copyright Act does preempt the California statute.

12. In Estate of Graham v. Sotheby's Inc., cited in note 11, a federal district court ruled that the California resale royalty right statute violated the commerce clause of the U.S. Constitution because, according to the district court, it regulated sales occurring wholly outside of California. Currently, pursuant to a request from Congress, the U.S. Copyright Office is undertaking an inquiry to review how current copyright law affects and supports visual artists and how a federal resale royalty right for visual artists would affect current and future practices of groups or individuals involved in the creation, licensing, sale, exhibition, dissemination, and preservation of works of visual art. (Discussion in Notices, Library of Congress, cited in note 10.) The Library of Congress notice pointed out that California developed its state law on resale royalties in part as a result of the indignation expressed by many within the art community when Robert Rauschenberg's 1958 painting *Thaw* was originally sold for $900 and then resold fifteen years later for $85,000 without compensation to the artist. The notice referred to a 1992 Copyright Office report which had concluded there was insufficient economic and copyright policy justification for enacting royalty right or *droit de suite* legislation in the United States. However, as discussed in the notice, since 1992, the number of foreign countries with resale royalty legislation has increased from thirty-six to more than sixty. In 2001, the notice reported that the EU had adopted a directive in 2001, which generally required member states to implement harmonized resale royalty legislation by 2006. Further, the notice pointed to many countries outside the EU that had statutes providing artists with resale royalties.

The notice set out provisions of a bill titled Equity for Visual Artists Act of 2011, which was introduced into Congress in 2011 to provide for a resale royalty right. (The European directive covers all "original works of art," whereas the California statute protects "works of fine art." The 2011 bill would govern works of "visual art.") The U.S. Copyright Office was asked to consider how a resale royalty right would affect the first sale doctrine of the U.S. Copyright Act (17 U.S.C. § 109), which, as the Copyright Office pointed out, is a fundamental tenet of U.S. copyright law. The Copyright Office also expressed concern that other exceptions and limitations that support the dissemination of works of art to the public would be affected adversely by a resale royalty right.

13. Close v. Lederle, 424 F.2d 988 (1st Cir. 1970). See also Silvette v. Art Comm. of Commonwealth of Va., 413 F. Supp. 1342 (E.D. Va. 1976).

14. Close v. Lederle, cited in note 13.

15. 413 U.S. 15 (1973).

16. The Supreme Court in Miller offered examples of definitions that might appear in a state statute for purposes of regulation: patently offensive representations or descriptions of ultimate sexual acts, normal or perverted, actual or simulated, and patently offensive representations or descriptions of masturbation, excretory functions, and lewd exhibition of the genitals. The court did acknowledge that no one would be subject to prosecution for the sale or exposure of obscene materials unless those materials "depict or describe patently offensive 'hard core' sexual conduct specifically defined by the regulating state law, as written or construed."

17. See Pub. L. No. 99-104, 2 U.S.C.C.A.N. 1055 (1985). Some of the concerns were that such a provision would be overly broad and would not reflect the Supreme Court's decision in Miller v. California, discussed in notes 15 and 16 and accompanying text.

18. See 2 U.S.C.C.A.N. 1071-2. The committee expressed its intent that panels reviewing and recommending applications for funding through the National Foundation on Arts and Humanities should not recommend grants for applications that lacked serious literary or artistic merit. The statute declares that "obscenity is without artistic merit, is not protected speech, and shall not be funded." Projects, productions, workshops, and programs that are determined to be obscene are prohibited from receiving financial aid from the National Endowment for the Arts.

19. 20 U.S.C. § 954(d).

20. Id. A temporary independent commission was established in 1989 to review grant-making procedures and to consider standards for publicly funded art. [See Pub. L. No. 101-121, 103 Stat. 741 (1989)]. The 1989 statute provided that none of the funds appropriated for the NEA could be used to promote, disseminate, or produce materials that in the judgment of the committee could be considered obscene, including sexual exploitation of children, and that, when taken as a whole, did not have serious literary, artistic, political, or scientific value. The temporary commission was established to review grant-making procedures of the NEA and to consider whether the standard for publicly funded art should be different than the standard for privately funded art.

21. 20 U.S.C. § 954(d)(1).

22. 20 U.S.C. § 41. Discussion in Chapter 1 of this language, which was taken from James Smithson's will wherein he bequeathed his estate to the United States to create the Smithsonian Institution.

23. See, e.g., Tex. Civ. Prac. & Rem. Code § 73.001.

24. Restatement (2d) Torts § 558.

25. Discussion in Kirby v. Wildenstein, 784 F. Supp. 1112 (S.D.N.Y. 1992).

26. Discussion in Thome v. Alexander & Louisa Calder Foundation, 70 A.D. 3d 88, 890 N.Y.S.2d 16 (2009), quoting Michael Findlay, "The Catalogue Raisonné," in *The Expert Versus the Object: Judging Fakes and False Attribution in the Visual Arts*, Ronald D. Spencer, ed. (New York: Oxford University Press, 2004).

27. Discussion in Thome v. Alexander & Louisa Calder Foundation, cited in note 26. Discussion of the acquisition of works that are not authentic in Chapter 5.

28. Eavesdropping upon private conversations, unwanted telephone calls, compulsory blood tests, and illegal searches have been listed as possible violations of privacy. Discussion in Prosser and Keeton on Torts, § 117. In National Bank of Commerce v. Shaklee Corp., 503 F. Supp. 533 (W.D. Tex. 1980), a Texas court held that misappropriation of one's name and likeness for commercial purposes was an invasion of privacy.

29. The New York court referred to her status as a public figure. The court stated that because she was a public figure, she would be required to show the publisher published the item with knowledge of its falsity or in reckless disregard of the truth.

30. Restatement (2d) Torts § 652I.

31. See discussion in McCarthy on Publicity and Privacy, § 1.3.

32. The right of publicity was first recognized in Haelan Laboratories, Inc. v. Topps' Chewing Gum, Inc., 202 F.2d 866 (2nd Cir. 1953). The right of publicity differs from the right of privacy (the right to be left alone) in that it provides a person the ability to control use of his identity in commerce. See treatment in Cardtoons v. Major League Baseball Players Ass'n, 95 F.3d 959 (10th Cir. 1996), which is discussed in Example 29.

33. Memphis Development Foundation v. Factors, Etc., Inc., 616 F.2d 956 (6th Cir. 1980).

34. See Comedy III Productions, Inc. v. Saderup, Inc., 21 P.3ed 797 (Cal. 2001), which is discussed in Example 30.

35. Martin Luther King, Jr., Center for Social Change v. American Heritage Products, Inc., 694 F.2d 674 (11th Cir. 1983).

36. Tex. Prop. Code §§ 26.001–26.015.

37. A person who uses a deceased individual's name, voice, signature, photograph, or likeness in a manner not authorized by the statute will be liable to damages in the amount of any profits from the unauthorized use and attorney's fees.

38. Cal. Civ. Code § 3344.

39. Discussion in Comedy III Productions, Inc. v. Saderup, Inc., cited in note 34. The authors of Restatement (2nd) of Torts, § 652 note at comment "c" that the right of publicity "is fundamentally constrained by the public and constitutional interest in freedom of expression." The authors comment that "use of a person's identity primarily for the purpose of communicating information or expressing ideas is not generally actionable as a violation of the person's right of publicity."

40. Discussion in Comedy III Productions, cited in note 34.

41. Id.

42. Id.

43. A few courts earlier ruled that the right of publicity did not survive death. The courts in Memphis Development Foundation v. Factors, Etc. Inc., 616 F.2d 956 (6th Cir. 1980) and Sinkler v. Goldsmith, 623 F. Supp. 727 (D. Ariz. 1985), ruled that the right of publicity did not survive the death of the owner. However, even some earlier courts found the right did survive death. See Factors Etc. v. Pro Arts, Inc., 579 F.2d 215 (2nd Cir. 1978) and Martin Luther King, Jr. Center for Social Change v. American Heritage Products, Inc., 694 F.2d 674 (11th Cir. 1984).

44. Virginia had granted the right for twenty years after death (Va. Code Ann. §§ 8.01-40); Pennsylvania for thirty years (Pa. C.S.A. § 8316); Florida for forty years (Fla. Stat. Ann. § 540.08); Illinois, Kentucky, Nevada, and Texas for fifty years (Ill. Comp. Stat. § 1075/30; Ky. Rev. Stat. § 391.170; Nev. Rev. Stat. § 597.790; Tex. Prop. Code § 16.012). Ohio had permitted a postmortem right of publicity for sixty years (Ohio Rev. Code Ann. § 2741.02); California for seventy years (Cal. Civ. Code § 3344.1); and Indiana and Oklahoma for one hundred years (Ind. Code Ann. § 32-36-1-8; 12 Okla. Stat. Ann. § 1448). Washington had permitted the right for seventy-five years when the celebrity's persona had commercial value (Wash. Rev. Code Ann. §§ 63.60.010–63.60.040); and Tennessee, indefinitely so long as the persona had commercial value (Tenn. Code Ann. §§ 47-25-1102 to 1104).

45. In Jaeger v. American Pictures, 330 F. Supp. 274 (S.D.N.Y. 1971), the court stated that a work which bears an author's name but severely garbles, distorts, or mutilates the work provides the author with a cause of action under the tort of unfair competition.

46. Unfair competition and false advertising is a violation of the Lanham Act, 15 U.S.C. § 1125.

47. Id.

48. Discussion in ETW Corp. v. Jireh Publishing, Inc., 332 F.3d 915 (6th Cir. 2001). As the Sixth Circuit Court of Appeals noted, courts have recognized false endorsement claims under the act where a celebrity's image or persona is used in association with a product so as to imply the celebrity endorses the product.

49. Discussion in ETW Corp. cited in note 48.

50. Id.

51. Cited in note 46.

CHAPTER 8

COPYRIGHT LAWS

Great art picks up where nature ends.

MARC CHAGALL

An artist is not paid for his labor but for his vision.

JAMES WHISTLER

A museum director must be aware of basic provisions of the federal copyright act because a director often is confronted with issues and controversies involving copyright issues. As noted in Chapter 7, the property right of an artist and the moral rights of certain visual artists are protected in the United States through the copyright law.[1] A museum director must be cognizant of the copyright interests of artists, or artists' heirs, in those works in the museum collection that are not in the public domain. The director also must know what rights the museum has in works in the collection where the copyright may have been transferred to, or acquired initially by, the museum. With the shift in the economy to the information age, museums can provide, but also market, a valuable information asset via the Internet in the form of digital images of works in their collections. As museums respond to the global demand for cultural information and transform works in their collections to digital form for transmission to a worldwide audience, museum directors must tailor critical copyright issues to a cyberspace environment.

Copyright law in the United States was modified by the Copyright Act of 1976,[2] which became effective January 1, 1978. Under prior law, the right of an artist or author to his creation had common law protection, which continued indefinitely until the work was made available to the public. Protection was regulated by the states. The Copyright Act of 1976 brought in a single system of statutory protection for all copyrightable works whether published or unpublished. Pursuant to the 1976 act, the federal government has preempted the field; state provisions on copyright law are not effective.[3]

This chapter summarizes the principal provisions of the copyright act to set out any property rights museums may have in pieces in their collections as well as the property and moral rights of artists. It also summarizes provisions in the act that both protect and obstruct a museum's right to use and exhibit copyrighted works in a museum collection.

A. SOURCES AND EXTENT OF COPYRIGHT PROTECTION

Copyright protection applies to an original work of "authorship" fixed in any tangible medium of expression and comes into existence (inheres) at the moment of creation of an original work. A copyright notice is not required to secure the copyright. Property rights of an artist or author are protected for the artist's or author's life plus seventy years after death.[4]

Works of authorship subject to copyright include literary works;[5] musical works (including any accompanying words); dramatic works (including any accompanying music); pantomimes and choreographic works; pictorial, graphic, and sculptural works; motion pictures and other audiovisual works; sound recordings; and architectural works.[6] Copyright protection does not extend to ideas, procedures, processes, systems, methods of operation, concepts, principles, or discoveries.[7]

The owner, or co-owners, of a work is the source of copyright ownership. Although this generally would be, and undoubtedly should be, the creator or creators of a work, an artwork deemed to be a "work made for hire" disqualifies the creator of the work for copyright protection. A "work made for hire" includes a "work prepared by an employee within the scope of employment" and certain categories of commissioned works, which are produced as a result of a special order.[8] If an artist prepares a work within the artist's scope of employment, the artist's employer is considered to be the source of copyright ownership and is regarded as the initial owner of the copyright unless there is an agreement to the contrary.[9] Commissioned works are "works made for hire" only if there is an express agreement in writing signed by the parties stating that the work is to be considered a work made for hire.[10]

Example 1. An employee of a museum prepares a work of art while she is employed by the museum and during her working hours. The museum would own the copyright in the work unless the museum and the employee agreed otherwise in a written agreement.

Example 2. A museum director commissioned a person to prepare a work of art for a museum. The museum would own the copyright in the work only if there was a written agreement to that effect.

Example 3. In Community for Creative Non-Violence v. Reid, 490 U.S. 730 (1980), the Supreme Court found that a nonprofit organization which commissioned a sculptor to produce a sculpture of contemporary homeless persons as a display dramatizing the plight of the homeless was not the "employer" of the sculptor and, thus, the sculpture was not a "work made for hire." Members of the nonprofit organization, which was dedicated to eliminating homelessness in the United States, decided the organization should participate in the annual Christmastime Pageant of Peace in Washington, D.C., by sponsoring a display to dramatize the plight of the homeless. The sculptor conceived the idea for the nature of the display: a sculpture of a modern Nativity scene in which, in lieu of the traditional Holy Family, the two adult figures and the infant would appear as contemporary homeless people huddled on a street-side steam grate. The legend for the pedestal was "And still there is no room at the inn." A member and trustee of the nonprofit organization later decided to take the sculpture on a tour of several cities to raise money for the homeless. The sculptor objected because he thought the design material in the sculpture was not strong enough to withstand the ambitious itinerary and refused to return the work to the nonprofit organization. The Court determined that the sculptor was an independent contractor and ruled that because there was no written agreement, the sculpture was not a work made for hire. Thus, the nonprofit organization was not deemed to be the creator of the work; the sculptor held the copyright in the work. The Court did state that the nonprofit organization could be a joint author of the sculpture if its ideas and concepts were embodied in the work. In that event, the nonprofit organization and the sculptor could be co-owners of the copyright in the work.

Section 106 of the Copyright Act grants a copyright owner the exclusive right to reproduce a copyrighted work [106(1)], to prepare derivative works [106(2)], to distribute a work publicly [106(3)], to perform a copyrighted work publicly [106(4)], and to display a copyrighted work publicly [106(5)].[11] These rights are divisible and are often referred to as a "bundle" of rights. Still, once a work is sold, the exclusive right to distribute the work is terminated. A copyright owner cannot in that event control future disposition of sold copies of the work.[12] When an artist sells his work, the artist also loses the display right in the work. The artist does not lose the right to reproduce the work, however. In addition, one who has merely rented a work or who has a work on loan does not acquire a display right.

The divisibility of the "bundle" of rights held by a copyright owner is of relevance to a museum director regarding works in a museum collection. Generally, a museum may not transfer the right to display a work on loan to a museum without permission from the copyright owner.[13] Even though a museum has purchased a work of art so that some part of the copyright has been transferred, the artist may not have transferred the divisible right of reproduction.[14] If an artist has retained a copyright in a work that is part of a collection and that is not in the public domain (or if the artist has not transferred the divisible rights of reproduction and the right to prepare derivative works), the artist (or the artist's heirs) would have the exclusive right to make reproductions or prepare derivative works from the original work.[15] Thus, a museum may not be authorized to reproduce those works in its collection that are not in the public domain. A museum must secure permission from those artists (or from the artists' heirs) who retained rights in their works prior to preparing images of works not in the public domain. Engaging in or authorizing a reproduction or preparation of a derivative work and the public distribution of a copyrighted work without the copyright owner's permission is copyright infringement.[16] The extension of copyright protection to life plus seventy years excluded many more artists' works from the public domain and can limit reproductions of some historical documents as well.

> Example 4. A museum purchases a painting from an artist. The artist does not transfer the artist's rights to make reproductions or to prepare derivative works when she transfers other rights in her copyright to the museum. The museum has the right to display the painting and the right to sell the work, but it may not make reproductions of the work without permission from the artist.

> Example 5. A museum has a painting on loan from a person other than the artist. If the lender does not own the painting, the lender may not have display rights and, in that event, may not transfer display rights to

the museum. The museum must secure permission from the owner of the painting to display the work.

Example 6. In Franklin Mint Corp. v. National Wildlife Art Exchange, 575 F.2d 62 (3rd Cir. 1978), the artist Albert Earl Gilbert painted a watercolor of cardinals called *Cardinals on Apple Blossom* for the incorporator of the National Wildlife Exchange. Gilbert sold the painting and the copyright to National Wildlife. Later Gilbert agreed to paint a series of watercolor wildlife pictures, including one of cardinals, for Franklin Mint. One of his paintings, *The Cardinal*, resembled *Cardinals on Apple Blossom* and had been painted using some of the same source material. National Wildlife sued the artist, contending that he had infringed National Wildlife's copyright in the painting *Cardinals on Apple Blossom*. Gilbert demonstrated in court that he could paint the scene from memory by painting it again in the courtroom. The Third Circuit decided there are tendencies of some painters to return to certain basic themes and stated that these basic themes may be copied time and time again. The Third Circuit also recognized that while a copyright on a painting of a particular scene prevents that painting from being copied, the original scene may be copied.[17] The Third Circuit in Franklin Mint commented that an artist who produces a rendition with photograph-like clarity and accuracy may be hard pressed to prove unlawful copying by another who uses the same subject matter and same technique. The Third Circuit Court of Appeals ruled that there was no copyright infringement.

A copyright in a contribution is separate and distinct from a copyright in the collective work as a whole, and in the absence of an express transfer, the owner of a collective work obtains only certain limited rights to each contribution.[18] Thus, in the absence of an express transfer, the author of a separate individual article that appears in a collection retains all rights in the article except the right to reproduce and distribute the contribution as part of the collective work.[19]

Example 7. An author submits an article for publication to a literary magazine published by a museum. Unless the author transfers his copyright in the article, the museum would have a copyright only in the collective work.

Example 8. A museum has a copyright in a collective work, a periodical that is mailed monthly to its members. The work contains several articles, the rights to which the museum plans to license for electronic distribution. The museum would have a problem in doing this. In New York v. Tasini, 533 U.S. 483 (2001), the Supreme Court ruled that, in the absence of a transfer of copyright or any rights thereunder in the individual works of a collective-work, a publisher may not license individual works because the publisher would not hold rights in the individual articles. In Tasini, freelance authors of articles previously published in periodicals brought a copyright infringement action against publishers and owners of electronic databases after the articles were made available on the databases. The Supreme Court noted that the Copyright Act permits a freelancer to benefit from demand for a freelance article standing alone or in a new collection and that, after authorizing initial publication, the freelancer may also sell the article to others. The Court commented that the Copyright Act "would scarcely preserve the author's copyright in a contribution" if a print publisher could reproduce or distribute discrete copies of the contribution in isolation or within new collective works without the author's permission. The Court commented that the publisher of the periodical could have obtained rights to license the individual articles by contracting expressly for electronic-licensing rights when it accepted articles for publication in its collective work.

A transfer of a copyright holder's exclusive rights is not valid unless the transfer is in writing and is signed by the copyright owner or the owner's authorized agent.[20] A transfer of a right on a nonexclusive basis does not require a writing. A copyright holder generally transfers copyright ownership by contract. The contract can be recorded in the U.S. Copyright Office.[21] Although recordation is not required to validate a transfer between parties, it does provide certain legal advantages and may be required to validate the transfer as against third parties. An author or artist, or the author's or artist's heirs, can terminate a transfer of a copyright at any time during a five-year period beginning at the end of thirty-five years from the date of the transfer.[22] An author or artist would complete the termination by serving an advance notice in writing upon the holder of the copyright.

B. ORIGINAL WORK OF AUTHORSHIP

A work must have an element of "originality" to be protected."[23] Copyright protection does not extend to ideas underlying a work or to the functional or factual aspects of a work. Courts have recognized that works of fiction receive greater protection than works that have strong factual elements, such as historical or biographical works[24] or works that have strong functional elements.[25] Still, works that are merely compilations of fact may be copyrightable.[26] A compilation is entitled to copyright protection if its selection and arrangement of data is original.[27] Copyright protection does not extend to "sweat of the brow" compilations because, as the Supreme Court has ruled, granting copyright protection to "sweat of the brow" works would distort basic copyright principles by creating a "monopoly in public domain materials without the necessary justification of protecting and encouraging the creation of 'writings' by 'authors.'"[28]

Copyright is limited for a derivative work. As one court ruled, a derivative work "must be substantially different from the underlying work to be copyrightable."[29] Copyright protection is limited for a photograph.[30] A photographer cannot copyright the subject matter of a photograph. To be copyrightable, preparation of the photograph must involve an element of originality. Further, just as ideas are not copyrightable, expressions commonly associated with, or that naturally flow from, certain themes and subjects, are not copyrightable.[31]

Example 9. In Gracen v. Bradford Exchange, 698 F.2d 300 (7th Cir. 1983), the Seventh Circuit Court of Appeals considered the originality requirement for a painting derived from a photograph. An artist made a painting of Dorothy from the movie *The Wizard of Oz* (for which MGM had a copyright) from photographs and her recollections of the movie. She submitted the painting to the copyright holder's licensee pursuant to competition for a contract to produce a series of paintings about *The Wizard of Oz* to be used on collectors' plates. The artist won the competition but refused the contract and displayed a photograph of the painting and other drawings to persons whom she was soliciting for artistic commissions. The person who later then signed a contract with MGM to do the series of collectors' plates was given the artist's painting to help him in doing his painting of Dorothy. The artist contended this person's painting of Dorothy was a "piratical copy" of her painting. She brought copyright infringement action against this person, MGM, and the manufacturer of the plates. The district court ruled that the artist could not copyright her painting and drawings because they were not original and that she infringed MGM's copyright. The Seventh Circuit Court of Appeals ruled that while the artist had a license from MGM to make a derivative work and, thus, did not infringe MGM's copyright, she could not copyright her painting. The Seventh Circuit decided that the purpose of the term "original" is "not to guide aesthetic judgment but to assure a sufficiently gross difference between the underlying and the derivative work to avoid entangling subsequent artists depicting the underlying work in copyright problems." The appellate court stated that a copyright owner would naturally be reluctant to authorize a licensee to take out a copyright on derivatives because a copyright in the derivative would impede the licensor in making the licensor's own derivative works or in licensing others to do so. As the Seventh Circuit stated, if the requirement of originality is interpreted too liberally it would inhibit rather than promote the creation of derivative works by giving the first creator a considerable power to interfere with the creation of subsequent derivative works from the same underlying work. The Seventh Circuit ruled that a derivative work must be substantially different from the underlying work to be copyrightable. This appellate court agreed that artistic originality is not the same as the legal concept of originality in the Copyright Act. As the Seventh Circuit reasoned, when a painter paints from life, no court will hold the artist's painting not to be copyrightable in that it is an exact photographic likeness. The appellate court pointed out that the artist's painting of Dorothy was from a photograph and, thus, ruled it was not an original derivative work within the meaning of the Copyright Act.

Example 10. In Woods v. Bourne, 60 F.3d 978 (2nd Cir. 1995), the Second Circuit Court of Appeals also addressed the issue of copyright protection for a derivative work. The case involved conflicting claims to royalties generated by various uses of the song "When the Red, Red, Robin Comes Bob, Bob, Bobbin' Along." The claimants, heirs of song composer Harry Woods, contended they had the right to royalties from the song generated during an extended renewal term of the original copyright. The alleged infringers contended they were entitled to the royalties because all the later uses of the song were attributable to their derivative works. The district court ruled for the claimants because it found that no versions of the song were sufficiently original to qualify as derivative works. The Second Circuit commented that to obtain copyright protection for a derivative work "there must be at least some substantial variation [from the underlying work], not merely a trivial variation." The Second Circuit ruled that for a work to qualify as a derivative work, it must be independently copyrightable. The original aspects "must be more than trivial." The appellate court noted the opinion in Gracen regarding the originality requirements for a painting derived from a photograph. The Second

Circuit decided that to determine whether a work is sufficiently original to be a derivative work, a judge must make findings of fact based upon a comparison of the original with the later work. According to the Second Circuit, the judge must then apply the legal standard of originality to the facts to determine whether the standard has been met. The Second Circuit agreed with the district court that there was no sufficient originality for the later works to qualify as derivative works.

Example 11. In Rogers v. Koons, 960 F.2d 302 (2nd Cir. 1991), a photographer who had created a black-and-white photograph titled *Puppies* sued a sculptor for copyright infringement. The sculptor created a work, the *String of Puppies*, by copying from a notecard of *Puppies*. The photographer had selected the light, location, and bench on which the puppies' owners were seated, and he had arranged the small dogs for the photograph. He made *Puppies* part of his catalogue of images available for further use, from which he made a living. The photographer used the *Puppies* photograph as part of an exhibit a number of times. He sold a signed print to a private collector and licensed it for use in an anthology. The Second Court of Appeals ruled that the sculptor infringed the photographer's copyright. In answering the sculptor's claim that a photograph is not an original work of authorship, the court noted that the elements of originality in a photograph include posing the subjects, lighting, angle, selection of film and camera, evoking a desired expression, and almost any other variant involved. The Second Circuit commented that substantial similarity that is a violation of the Copyright Act does not require literally identical copying of every detail.

Example 12. In Leigh v. Warner Bros., 212 F.3d 1210 (11th Cir. 2000), the Eleventh Circuit Court of Appeals considered copyright issues related to a photographer who had been hired to take a photograph that would appear on the cover of an upcoming edition of the novel *Midnight in the Garden of Good and Evil: A Savannah Story*. The photograph used was that of a sculpture of Savannah's Bonaventure Cemetery known as "the Bird Girl." The film based on the book, also titled *Midnight in the Garden of Good and Evil*, included a replica of the Bird Girl and was prepared by Warner Bros. The Eleventh Circuit agreed that the photographer's copyright did not cover the appearance of the statue itself or the association of the statue with the *Midnight* story. The Eleventh Circuit ruled that the photographer was not entitled to copyright protection for his choice of subject matter. The court stated that even though association of the statue with the book was under the photographer's control, this element was one over which the photographer exercised no creative control. The Eleventh Circuit decided this association was merely the photographer's idea, which the photographer could not copyright. The Eleventh Circuit did think that the Warner Bros. promotional single-frame images could be substantially similar to some aspects of the photographer's work that was protected by copyright. The Eleventh Circuit noted that elements protected by the photographer's copyright were the lighting, shading, timing, angle, and film and the overall combination of these protected elements as well as the mood they conveyed.

Example 13. In Harney v. Sony Pictures Television, Inc., 704 F.3d 173 (1st Cir. 2013), the First Circuit Court of Appeals refused to expand a photographer's copyright protection because of events that occurred after the photograph was taken and ruled that a recreated photograph used in a movie did not infringe the photographer's copyright. The First Circuit noted that copying another's work does not invariably constitute copyright infringement. It stated that the copying must be sufficiently "extensive that it renders the infringing and copyrighted works 'substantially similar.'" The court further stated that it is permissible to mimic the non-copyrightable elements of a copyrighted work because copyright protection extends only to those components of a work that are original to the author and commented that a work sufficiently 'original' to be copyrighted may nonetheless contain unoriginal elements. The First Circuit decided that inquiry into substantial similarity embraces two different types of scrutiny. A court initially dissects the earlier work to separate its original expressive elements from the unprotected content. The two works then must be compared holistically to determine if they are "substantially similar," but the court gives weight only to the protected aspects of the work as determined through the dissection. The First Circuit ruled the two works are substantially similar if an "ordinary observer, unless he set out to detect the disparities, would be disposed to overlook them, and regard their aesthetic appeal as the same." The First Circuit stated the determination of substantial similarity is ordinarily assigned to the fact finder. This court determined that the division between protected and unprotected elements of a photograph can be likened to the separation drawn by copyright law between protected expression and unprotected ideas. The First Circuit stated that subject matter a photographer did not create can be viewed as "fact" that, like ideas, is not entitled to copyright protection. According to the First Circuit, the exclusion of facts from copyright protection arises from the constitutional requirement of "originality." This court explained that facts are not original in the constitutional sense because they do not owe their origin to an act of authorship. According to the First Circuit, because facts are discovered, rather than created, they are "part of the public domain available to every person." The court then stated that compilations of facts ordinarily are entitled to copyright protection. The First Circuit decided that where neither the subject matter of the earlier work nor its arrangement are attributable to the photographer, the court must look closely to identify the expressive choices in the photographer's work that qualify as original. The First Circuit found that while it was undisputed the movie copied the photo, the movie adaptation of the photo did not infringe the photographer's copyright in his work.

A court[32] that addressed the question of whether photographic transparencies are copyrightable, decided that while the "overwhelming majority" of photographs would "reflect at least the modest amount of originality required for copyright protection . . . 'slavish copying,' although doubtless requiring technical skill and effort, does not qualify." The court decided that a "change of medium alone is not sufficient to render" a product "original and copyrightable."[33] The court concluded that reproducing works in a collection in the form of photographic transparencies, which then are converted to digital form, without more, would not add the required element of originality to make the reproduction copyrightable. One court explained that, while "the requisite level of creativity is extremely low," still, "without some creative spark," the "labor that goes into independently creating (as opposed to simply reproducing) a work is insufficient to bring that work within the scope of copyright."[34] Because the industriousness of a collection is not relevant to a determination of copyrightability and because a finding of creativity is subjective, a court's recognition of a developer's labor may override any finding of creativity.

A digital image would be a derivative work. Having concluded that a copyright in a derivative work is "thin,"[35] courts have ruled that copyright in a derivative work only extends to original material contributed by the author of the derivative work, as distinguished from preexisting material used in the work.[36] Thus, there will be a substantial element of uncopyrightable material in a digital image of an underlying public domain work. The issue is the degree of originality required for photographic transparencies to provide a museum some copyright protection in its digital images of public domain works.

The digital images of artworks, which one court held were not copyrightable, were substantially exact reproductions of public domain works albeit in a different medium. The court did acknowledge that copies in a new medium are copyrightable where, "as often but not always is the case," the copies do contain some identifiable original contribution.[37] Thus, if a museum adds some element of originality to photographic transparencies of public domain works in its collections, the original element would be copyrightable. Perhaps including a narrative of the artist's life and/or a description of the subject of the work would provide some originality to make a digital image copyrightable.

Example 14. In Bridgeman Art Library v. Corel Corp., 25 F. Supp.2d 421 (S.D.N.Y. 1998), Bridgeman claimed to have exclusive rights in photographic transparencies of a substantial number of well-known works of art located in museums around the world. Bridgeman transformed the transparencies into digital images in which it also claimed exclusive rights. Bridgeman had acquired rights to market reproductions of public domain works of art owned by museums and other collections which it obtained from the owners of the underlying works or from freelance photographers it hired. Bridgeman maintained a library of the reproductions in the form of large-format color transparencies and digital files. The photographer claimed a copyright in the photographs and then would assign it to Bridgeman. Bridgeman would attach a color correction strip to each transparency to ensure that the image was a genuine reflection of the original work as it existed in the circumstances in which it was photographed. Bridgeman distributed its images as transparencies and as digital files on CD-ROM. The high-resolution transparencies were made available to clients through licensing arrangements. Corel was a Canadian corporation that marketed computer software products. It had a set of CD-ROMs that contained 700 digital reproductions of well-known paintings by European masters. Bridgeman contended that Corel had infringed its rights in approximately 120 of its images. It claimed that its transparencies of the public domain works, from which it prepared its digital images, were the only authorized transparencies of some of the works. The court concluded that the images were copied from the underlying works without any avoidable addition, alteration, or transformation. The court decided that although designing technology to produce exact reproductions of documents requires much engineering talent, it did not make the reproductions copyrightable. It ruled that Bridgeman's images lacked sufficient originality to be copyrightable.

Because computers provide the best method to transmit digital images of cultural property, the recognition of computer programs as copyrightable material and caselaw defining the perimeters of copyright protection for computer programs provide some guidance in determining the perimeters for copyright protection for digital images that contain some elements of originality. Computer programs are recognized as copyrightable literary works and data compilation that constitute intellectual creations. The Copyright Act was amended in 1980 to extend copyright protection to computer programs.[38]

The pre-electronic rule that copyright protection applies to an original work of authorship fixed in any tangible medium of expression has been construed to embrace technological devices. A work is "fixed" in a tangible medium of expression when its embodiment in a copy "is sufficiently permanent or stable to permit it to be perceived, reproduced, or otherwise communicated for a period of more than transitory duration."[39] Section 101 of the Copyright Act defines "copies" as material objects "in which a work is fixed by any method now known or later developed, and from which the work can be perceived, reproduced, or otherwise communicated, either directly or with the aid of a machine or device." As one court noted, this definition was intended to clarify that a work stored on a disk or tape can be a copy of a copyrighted work even if it cannot be perceived by human senses without technological aid.[40]

C. ARTISTS' MORAL RIGHT

As noted in Chapter 7, the Berne Convention for the Protection of Literary and Artistic Works[41] provides for a moral right in artists. Congress ratified accession to the Berne Convention in 1988, but it did not adopt, at that time, the concept of an artist's moral right.[42] Later, in 1990, Congress enacted the Visual Artists Rights Act (VARA)[43] to amend the Copyright Act and thereby grant certain visual artists a statutory right of attribution and a right of integrity.[44] An artist's moral right provided by VARA may also restrict the display rights of a possessor of the work.[45]

The moral right of a visual artist is protected in the United States only for the life of the artist; however, most countries that are parties to the Berne Convention protect the moral right for the life of the artist plus fifty years after death (except for states in the European Union that have extended protection for seventy years after death).[46]

An artist's right of integrity is the right of the artist to prevent distortions of her work. Thus, in the United States a visual artist has the right to prevent any intentional distortion, mutilation, or other modification of his work that would be prejudicial to the artist's honor or reputation. An artist can prevent any destruction of a work of recognized stature. Any intentional or grossly negligent destruction of the work is a violation of the right.[47]

An artist's moral right applies to a work of visual art that has been incorporated in or made a part of a building in a way that removing the work from the building would cause the destruction, distortion, mutilation, or other modification of the work.[48] If a visual artist consented in a written agreement, signed by the owner of the building and the artist and specifying that installation of the artist's work could subject the work to destruction, distortion, or mutilation by reason of its removal, the artist would not have a moral right in the work.

Example 15. A building owner contracted with an artist for the artist to design, create, and install a sculpture and other permanent installations to the entry of the building. The contract provided that the artist would retain a copyright in his work. During the time the artist was preparing the work, the building owner decided she did not like the artist's work and ordered the artist to discontinue preparing the work and to vacate the building. The artist refused and contended the building owner would violate his rights under VARA by ordering removal of his work. In Carter v. Helmsly-Spear, Inc., 861 F. Supp. 303 (S.D.N.Y. 1994), aff'd in part, vacated in part, rev'd in part, 71 F.3d 77 (2nd Cir. 1995), a district court noted that VARA prevents the destruction of a work of "recognized stature" placed on a building. The district court set out a test to determine whether a work is protected. An artist must show that the visual art in question has "stature," i.e., is viewed as meritorious and that this "stature" is "recognized" by art experts, other members of the artistic community, or by some cross-section of society. The artist would be required to call expert witnesses to testify as to the "stature" of the work. Still, the Second Circuit Court of Appeals did not consider the "stature" of the work in deciding whether it was protected by VARA. It ruled in Helmsly that the building owner could terminate the work of the three artists because it decided the artists were employees, rather than independent contractors, and, thus, their creation was a "work made for hire" in which the building owner had the copyright. The Second Circuit court refused to rule on whether a statement in the contract between the artists and the building owner, stating that the artists retained the copyright, made them independent contractors. The Second Circuit pointed out the artists were paid a weekly salary and were furnished their supplies. Thus, the Second Court found their agreement with the building owner to be outside the scope of VARA's protection. The Second Circuit apparently balanced the rights of the parties and thought protection of the building owner's rights outweighed the artist's and the public's interest in protecting a work of art incorporated in, and made a part of, the building.

Example 16. In Martin v. City of Indianapolis, 192 F.3d 608 (7th Cir. 1999), a city demolished an outdoor stainless steel sculpture as part of an urban renewal project. The artist sued the city under VARA. The Seventh Circuit Court of Appeals ruled the artist had a right under VARA that would prevent the city from destroying the work. The Seventh Circuit noted the phrase in VARA of a work of "recognized stature" was not defined. It adopted the test set out by the district court in Carter v. Helmsly discussed in Example 15. The Seventh Circuit in Martin decided that because there was no written waiver by the artist of his moral right, he had retained that right and the city was liable in damages because it destroyed his work. A dissenting judge expressed concern that "to avoid being a perpetual curator of a piece of visual art that has lost (or perhaps never had) its luster, a recipient [of art] must obtain at the outset a waiver of an artist's rights under VARA." The dissenting judge admonished municipalities that, before awarding building permits for erection of a sculpture, they would be well advised to obtain a written waiver of an artist's rights, for "if not, once destroyed, art of questionable value may acquire minimum worth of $20,000 under VARA."

Example 17. The First Circuit Court of Appeals addressed the question of whether unfinished works are entitled to protection under VARA in Massachusetts Museum of Contemporary Art Foundation, Inc. v. Buchel, 593 F.3d 38 (1st Cir. 2010). A museum, which opened in 1999 as a center for the creation and display of contemporary art, contracted with an artist, Christoph Buchel, for the artist to complete for exhibition at the museum a football-field-sized art installation titled *Training Ground for Democracy*. The parties agreed that after the installation was finished and after the public exhibition period had concluded, the museum would not contest Buchel's sole title to any copyright in the completed work. After tensions developed between Buchel and the museum regarding the work and members of the museum staff continued work on the installation, the museum sued Buchel, seeking a declaration that it was entitled to represent to the public the materials and partial constructions assembled in connection with the exhibit Buchel planned. Buchel counterclaimed and contended that VARA prohibited the museum from publicly displaying his unfinished work. The First Circuit Court of Appeals agreed with Buchel that VARA applied with equal force to incomplete artistic endeavors that otherwise would be subject to the act. The First Circuit recognized that the moral right protects the personality and creative energy which an artist contributes to his work and that this convergence between artist and artwork "does not await the final brush stroke or the placement of the last element in a complex installation." The First Circuit also thought the museum may have violated the artist's display rights by violating his moral rights.

Example 18. Assume an artist painted a mural on a building in 1970 at the request of the then owner of the building. The building owner "accepted and paid for" the work in 1971. The original owner of the building sells the building in 2014, and the new owner wants to paint over the mural. The artist, as well as several members of the public, object. Framers of the Visual Artists Rights Act (VARA), which now is codified at 17 U.S.C. §§ 106A and 113 and which became effective in 1991, noted that destruction of works of art "has a detrimental effect on the artist's reputation and . . . also represents a loss to society." However, VARA does not cover works of visual art created before the effective date of the act if "title" has been transferred from the artist prior to that date. The term "title" has a different application with respect to works of art. An artist has the bundle of rights in her creation that are set out in § 106 of the Copyright Act and noted above. There is a question whether the fact that the artist's work was "accepted and paid for" constituted a transfer of "title" to the work. An artist retains "rights" (to make reproductions and derivative works) in the artist's creation even though the work is sold if the artist does not transfer all her bundle of rights. Thus, "title" to the work may not have been transferred and the artist may have a protected moral right in the work. The new building owner may have a problem pursuant to § 113 of the Copyright Act if the owner paints over the mural.

For works of contemporary artists in the United States for whom the moral rights exists only for life of an artist, but for modern artists in most other countries that are parties to the Berne Convention and presumably for all artists in countries that protect the moral right in perpetuity, a computer user's augmentation or alteration of an image of an artist's work may violate the artist's moral right.[49] This imaging also may violate an artist's right of privacy and right of publicity.[50]

D. FAIR USE OF COPYRIGHTED WORKS

The "fair use" of a copyrighted work is a use of a copyrighted work that is not an infringement of the copyright.[51] Fair use is the use of a copyrighted work by reproduction for criticism, comment, news reporting, teaching (including multiple copies for classroom use), scholarship, or research.[52] Fair use most often is defined as the "privilege in others than the owner of a copyright to use the copyrighted material in a reasonable manner" without the copyright owner's consent, notwithstanding the monopoly granted to the copyright owner.[53]

In determining whether a use of copyrighted material is a fair use, the following factors are considered:[54] (1) the purpose and character of the use, including whether the use is of a commercial nature or is for nonprofit educational purposes; (2) the nature of the copyrighted work; (3) the amount and substantiality of the portion used in relation to the copyrighted work as a whole; and (4) the effect of the use upon the potential market for, or value of, the copyrighted work.

Example 19. In Wright v. Warner Books Inc., 953 F.2d 731 (2nd Cir. 1991), the Second Circuit Court of Appeals ruled that an author's sparing use of creative expression from unpublished letters and journals of a late author constituted fair use and was a defense to the charge of infringement as a matter of law. The court noted that the book did not exploit the literary value of the letters and journals nor did it diminish their marketability. The court decided that use of portions of the letters and journals was *de minimis* and beyond the protection of the Copyright Act.

Example 20. A critical inquiry is whether an allegedly infringing work "merely supersedes" the original work or, as the Second Circuit Court of Appeals ruled in Castle Rock Entertainment, Inc. v. Carol Publishing Group, 150 F.3d 132 (2nd Cir. 1998), "instead adds something new, with a further purpose or different character, altering the first with . . . new meaning or message." In Castle Rock Entertainment, the issue was whether a book, *The Seinfeld Aptitude Test*, which was a trivia quiz book devoted to testing readers' recollection of scenes and events from the television series *Seinfeld*, infringed the copyright in *Seinfeld* and, if so, if the infringement constituted fair use. The Second Circuit ruled that the publisher of the book unlawfully copied from *Seinfeld* and held that the copying was not fair use. The Second Circuit reasoned that the inquiry should be a consideration of whether the new work is "transformative." According to the Second Circuit, if the secondary use added value to the original or "transformed the original in the creation of new information, new aesthetics, new insights and understanding," the fair use doctrine protected the work. This court opined that "this is the very type of activity that the fair use doctrine intends to protect for the enrichment of society" and commented that the "more transformative the secondary use, the less likelihood that the secondary use substitutes for the original." The Second Circuit decided that "by the very nature" of transformative endeavors, persons other than the copyright holder would be "better equipped" and could more likely fill "market and intellectual niches." Still, the Second Circuit determined that any transformative purpose in the book *The Seinfeld Aptitude Test* was slight to nonexistent.

Example 21. In Cariou v. Prince, 714 F.3d 694 (2nd Cir. 2013), a photographer brought a copyright infringement action against a well-known appropriation artist, a gallery, and a gallery owner based on their use of the photographer's copyrighted photographs of Rastafarians and Jamaican landscapes in paintings the artist made that were marketed and sold by the gallery and its owner. The Second Circuit Court of Appeals disagreed with the district court (that had ruled the gallery and the artist were not entitled to the defense of fair use). The Second Circuit decided that twenty-five of the artist's thirty paintings were transformative as a matter of law and, thus, constituted fair use of the copyrighted photographs. The Second Circuit observed that these paintings manifested an entirely different aesthetic from the photographs. It thought the images had a different character from the photographs and "employed new aesthetics with creative and communicative results" distinct from the photographs. The Second Circuit stated that the more transformative a new work, the less will be the significance of other factors, like commercialism, that may weigh against a finding of fair use. The Second Circuit remanded to the district court a determination of whether the gallery and artist were entitled to a fair use defense with respect to the remaining five paintings.

A small degree of copying can preclude a defense of fair use if the copying is the essential part of the copyrighted work. No more of a work may be copied than is necessary for the particular use.[55] Fair use permits the photocopying of a complete work in some instances. It permits library photocopying in proper circumstances, which include an evaluation of all the applicable criteria and the facts of the particular case.[56] The reproduction of copyrighted material for purposes of classroom teaching can constitute fair use, but a finding of a non-profit educational purpose does not compel automatically a finding of fair use.

The question of how much copying for classroom use is permissible was of major concern to Congress and, although it did not include a provision in the Copyright Act on the subject, it did approve a set of guidelines with respect to it.[57] These guidelines represent minimum standards of fair use; they are not binding. The guidelines indicate that multiple copies for classroom use are permissible if three tests are met: brevity, spontaneity, and cumulative effect.[58] Spontaneity assumes that the copying was made as a result of a decision to use a work so close in time to its need that it would be unreasonable to expect a timely reply to a request for permission. Cumulative effect requires that the copied material be for only one course.

There is a presumption that every commercial use of copyrighted material is not fair use, and, as some courts have observed, the likelihood that future market harm exists is "implicit in the presumption that every commercial use is presumptively unfair."[59] Parody can provide a fair use defense, but copying for scholarly use without limits does not.

> Example 22. In Campbell v. Acuff & Rose Music, Inc., 510 U.S. 569 (1994), the Supreme Court concluded that parody, like other comment and criticism, may qualify as fair use. It decided that parody can qualify regardless of whether it is published or performed for profit. The Supreme Court decided that parody must mimic an original to make its point and that a copied work must, at least in part, be an object of parody.

> Example 23. In American Geophysical Union v. Texaco Inc., 60 F.3d 913 (2nd Cir. 1995), the Second Circuit Court of Appeals considered issues governing the photocopying of entire journal articles for a scientist's own use, either in a laboratory or as part of a personal file assisting that scientist's particular inquiries. The alleged infringer in Texaco was a chemical engineer employer at a corporate research facility who stayed abreast of developments in his field by reviewing specialized scientific and technical journals. He photocopied individual journal articles in the belief that

doing so would facilitate his current or future professional research. The Second Circuit ruled that his copying was not fair use.

Example 24. In Princeton Univ. Press v. Michigan Document Services, 99 F.3d 1381 (6th Cir. 1996), the Sixth Circuit Court of Appeals ruled that a commercial copy shop violated the Copyright Act when it reproduced substantial segments of copyrighted works of scholarship, bound the copies in "course packs," and sold the "course packs" for a fee to students for their use in fulfilling reading assignments of professors.

Section 117 of the Copyright Act provides that an "owner" of a copy of a computer program may make another copy or adaptation of the computer program provided the new copy or adaptation is used only "as an essential step in the utilization of the computer program in conjunction with a machine."[60] Users of the Internet would not be owners of digital images exhibited on the Web; thus, this provision would not permit downloading of the images. Given the commercial context in which Internet users view digital images, it may be difficult to fit copying of copyrighted digital works for personal use into a "fair use" or "personal use" exception.

E. FIRST SALE DOCTRINE

Section 106 of the Copyright Act, which grants a copyright owner the exclusive rights listed above, is limited by §§ 107 through 120 of the act. One of these limitations is § 109(a), which expressly permits a purchaser of a copyrighted work the authority to sell that work. Section 106(3) gives a copyright holder the exclusive right to distribute copies of his work by sale or other transfer; however, § 109(a) states that, notwithstanding the provisions of § 106(3), the owner of a particular copy "lawfully made," or any person authorized by the owner, is entitled to sell or otherwise dispose of possession of the copy without authority of the copyright owner. This "first sale" provision grants protection to a buyer who resells purchased copyrighted material.[61] After the first sale of a copyrighted work, any subsequent purchaser becomes an owner of that work and also can resell it. As an example, the purchaser of a book, once sold by authority of the copyright owner, may sell the book again, but the purchaser cannot publish a new edition of the book. The first sale doctrine does not apply to a person who possesses a copy of a copyrighted work without owning it, such as a lessee or a licensee.[62]

There has been a question of whether there is a geographical limitation on the "first sale" doctrine. Section 602 of the Copyright Act gives a copyright owner the right to prohibit the unauthorized importation of copies. It states that importation, without authority of a copyright owner, of works acquired outside the United States is an infringement of the exclusive right to distribute copies of the work. Courts had to address the issue of whether § 602 also was limited by §§ 107 through 120 of the act; thus, the question confronting the courts was whether the "first sale" doctrine was applicable to imported copies. The Supreme Court addressed this issue in 1998 with respect to a work initially manufactured in the United States, sold abroad, and then resold in the United States. The Court held the first sale doctrine is applicable to imported copies.[63] The Court did not address applicability of the doctrine to a work produced abroad and then sold in the United States until 2013 when it ruled that the doctrine also applies to works produced abroad and then sold in the United States.[64]

Example 25. In Kirtsaeng v. John Wiley & Sons, Inc., 133 S. Ct. 1351 (2013), a citizen of Thailand moved to the United States to study mathematics. He asked friends and family in Thailand to buy foreign edition English-language textbooks in Thai book shops, where they sold at low prices, and mail them to him in the United States. He then sold the books in the United States at a profit. His defense to an infringement suit by the books' publisher was that his books were "lawfully made" and acquired legitimately and that the first sale doctrine of § 109(a) of the Copyright Act permitted importation and resale without the copyright owner's further permission. The Supreme Court agreed and ruled that the first sale doctrine applies to copies of copyrighted works lawfully made abroad. The Court decided § 109 favored the seller's position; the Court noted that the section said nothing about geography. The Court found that both historical and contemporary statutory context indicated that Congress did not have geography in mind when writing the present version of § 109(a). The Court stated that a nongeographical reading also is supported by the canon of statutory interpretation that "when a statute covers an issue previously governed by the common law," it is presumed that "Congress intended to retain the substance of the common law. It noted that the common-law "first sale" doctrine made no geographical distinctions. The Court opined that a geographical interpretation of the "first sale" doctrine would likely require libraries to obtain permission before circulating the many books in their collections that were printed overseas.

F. MEANS TO SECURE COPYRIGHT PROTECTION

As noted previously, copyright protection inheres at the moment of creation of an original work, and a copyright notice is not required to secure the copyright. Still, under copyright law prior to the 1976 Copyright Act, publication without a statutory notice caused a work to fall into the public domain.[65] Pursuant to the 1976 Copyright Act, a work became part of the public domain if the copyright owner had authorized publication of the work without a notice of copyright and failed to register a claim for copyright in the U.S. Copyright Office within five years of publication without the notice. Distribution of only a relatively small number of copies without the notice did not cause the copyright to be lost if efforts were made to add the notice later. The Berne Convention Implementation Act of 1988 amended the Copyright Act to provide that a notice "may" be placed on all publicly distributed copies of a work.[66] Thus, since 1988, copyright notice is not mandatory. Still, while current language of the Copyright Act removes the requirement of a notice, it is best to affix a notice. If a notice of copyright is placed on a published copy of a work, an infringer cannot mitigate damages based on a claim of innocent infringement.[67]

Example 26. A Picasso maquette was given by Picasso to the Public Building Commission of Chicago. The maquette was displayed without a statutory notice of copyright. In Letter Edged in Black Press, Inc. v. Public Building Commission, 320 F. Supp. 1303 (N.D. Ill. 1970), a case decided prior to enactment of the Copyright Act of 1976, a court ruled that the Public Building Commission of Chicago lost statutory protection for the maquette. The court ruled the common law copyright protection was lost when the maquette was displayed without copyright notice. The court held that the maquette then fell into the public domain. Under current provision of the Copyright Act, the Public Building Commission would not lose its copyright protection. Placing a copyright notice on a work is not mandatory. However, failure to place a notice of copyright may permit an infringer to reduce damages based upon the infringer's allegation that she was an innocent infringer.

Example 27. A museum wants to display on the Internet a photograph that was created in 1960. Presumably the museum need not seek permission of the photographer if the photograph does not have a copyright notice because in 1960 a copyright notice was mandatory. Thus, the photograph would be public domain material. If the photograph were created in 1978, a lack of notice also undoubtedly would mean that the photograph was in the public domain because, although the 1976 Copyright Act provided that a work published without a notice would not be in the public domain if only a few copies were distributed without the notice, the creator was required to register the work and to make efforts to place the notice on the work later. If the photograph was created after 1988, the museum cannot assume the photographer is not claiming copyright ownership solely because the photograph has no copyright notice.

Example 28. As noted previously, the Berne Convention does not require a copyright notice for original works. The French artist Pierre-Auguste Renoir and one of his assistants, Richard Guino, created eleven sculptures between 1913 and 1917. They were first published in France in 1917 under Renoir's name but without a copyright notice. In 1973 Guino obtained a determination from a French court that he was a coauthor. He was awarded a one-half interest in the sculptures. Renoir and Guino signed an agreement that the Guino family would control production and reproductions of the sculptures. The Societe Civile Succession Richard Guino registered a copyright in the sculptures with the U.S. Copyright Office in 1984. The registration represented that the sculptures either were first published in England in 1983 or unpublished. Still, the sculptures would be in the public domain in the United States because they had been published without a copyright notice prior to 1976. However, because the Berne Convention does not require notice, the sculptures had copyright protection in France. In 2003, the heirs of Pierre-Auguste Renoir sold some of his sculpture reproductions to the owner of an art gallery in Arizona; the gallery owner then later sold the reproductions. The Societe filed a copyright infringement complaint against the owner of the art gallery. The Societe contended the gallery and the Renoir heirs had engaged in reproduction activities in 2003 that infringed the Societe's copyright in the sculptures. It contended the sculptures were protected by 17 U.S.C. § 104A even though the works lacked a proper copyright notice. Renoir's heirs and the owner of the art gallery contended the sculptures were in the public domain and to remove them from the public domain because they were foreign works violated their First Amendment rights. In Society Civile Succession Guino v. Renoir, 549 F.3d 1182 (9th Cir. 2008), the Ninth Circuit Court of Appeals ruled the art gallery and the Renoir heirs infringed the Societe's copyright in the sculptures. In Golan et al. v. Holder et al., 132 S. Ct. 873 (2012), the Supreme Court ruled that the Uruguay Round Agreements Act (URAA) § 514, which now grants copyright protection to works protected in their country of origin even though they are in the public domain in the United States, is constitutional. The Court referred to the Berne Convention and noted that Berne is the principal accord governing international copyright relations. The Court cited Article 18 of Berne, which requires countries to protect works of other member states unless a work's copyright term has expired in either the country where protection was claimed or in the country of origin. It noted that, despite Article 18, when the United States joined Berne in 1989, it did not protect any foreign works that had never been protected in the United States. In 1994, however, the World Trade Organization stated it would enforce the Agreement on Trade-related Aspects of Intellectual Property Rights, which mandated implementation of Berne's first twenty-one articles. The Supreme Court referred to Congress's response by enacting § 514 of the URAA. The Court ruled that § 514 does not exceed Congress's authority under the Copyright Clause. It noted that the text of the Copyright Clause does not exclude application of copyright protection to works in the public domain. The Court also referred to historical practice, which it decided corroborated its reading of the Copyright Clause as permitting the protection of previously unprotected works. It ruled that the First Amendment does not inhibit the restoration authorized by § 514. The Supreme Court concluded that the First Amendment does not render public domain works untouchable by Congress and ruled in Golan v. Holder that Congress can protect works that have previously been in the public domain.

Although copyright protection occurs at the moment of creation of an original work and a copyright notice is not required to secure the copyright, the owner of a work should place a notice on all visually perceptible copies that are distributed to the public to alert the public the owner is claiming copyright ownership. The required elements for notice are (1) the symbol ©, the word "Copyright," or the abbreviation "Copr."; (2) the year of first publication of the work; and (3) the name of the owner of the copyright in the work, an abbreviation by which the name can be recognized, or a generally known alternative designation of the owner.[68]

A notice of copyright should be affixed to copies of works in such a manner and location as to give reasonable notice of the copyright claim. The

Register of Copyrights prescribed by regulation-specific methods of affixation and position of the notice on various types of work.[69] For two-dimensional pictorial, graphic, or sculptural works, a notice can be placed on either the front or the back of the work or on a permanent mounting, matting, or framing. For three-dimensional works, a label on any visible portion, including a permanent base, is sufficient.

Within three months after a work has been published with a copyright notice in the United States, the copyright owner must deposit two copies of the work with the Library of Congress.[70] Registration of published or unpublished works, which is separate from depositing a work with the Library of Congress, is permissive. Registration can occur at any time during the copyright term.[71] An author or artist can register a claim by depositing copies of his work with the Copyright Office with a completed application form and a fee.

While copyright occurs automatically (inheres) at the moment it is created without regard to whether the copyright ever is registered, registration has been required to initiate an action for copyright infringement.[72] Whether filing an application for registration is sufficient to support the initial filing of a claim of infringement was not clear. While some courts had held that an action for infringement could not be asserted unless the certificate of registration had been issued, the Supreme Court apparently disagrees.[73] A certificate of registration made within five years of creation of a work constitutes prima facie evidence of the validity of a copyright and of the facts stated in the certificate.[74] Thereafter, a court has discretion as to what weight it will give the certificate.

If infringement occurs after registration, the copyright owner is entitled to extraordinary remedies of attorney's fees and statutory damages.[75] If an infringement suit occurs before registration, the owner is entitled only to an injunction and actual damages.[76]

A creator of an original work may obtain application forms for registration from the U.S. Copyright Office. There are five application forms: Form TX (for nondramatic literary works), Form PA (for works of the performing arts), Form VA (for works of the visual arts), Form SR (for sound recordings), and Form RE (for renewal of registration).

G. LIABILITY FOR INFRINGING COPYRIGHTED WORKS

In a copyright infringement suit, a copyright owner must prove ownership of a copyright in a work and copying of the work by the alleged infringer.[77] The copyright owner must demonstrate the alleged infringer used the owner's work as a "model" or "inspiration." The copyright owner must show that the alleged infringer's work is "substantially similar" to the copyright owner's work.[78] There is "substantial similarity" between an original and a copied work when it is obvious that the alleged copy was appropriated from the copyrighted work.[79] One court[80] stated that if one holds a copyright in digital images, "similarity would be judged only with respect to those elements materially altering or embellishing the underlying works, the public domain paintings."

Similarity can be both literal and nonliteral. Literal similarity occurs when an alleged infringer copies an actual segment of a copyrighted work. Nonliteral similarity involves copying the "fundamental essence or structure" of a work.[81]

H. APPLICATION OF COPYRIGHT LAWS IN A DIGITAL ENVIRONMENT

If a computer user downloads an artist's work and subsequently alters the work, the user may have violated the artist's moral right. The dilemma is that an Internet user can modify or distort digital images easily. Prevention is virtually impossible.[82] Because copyright laws are not effective to protect an artist's moral right from digital image downloading, encryption technology should be used to block access to digital images of artworks that are subject to artists' moral rights.[83] A museum exhibiting works in its collections through digital images on the Internet should protect the moral rights of the artists in their works by some means of blocking the otherwise unrestrained downloading of the images.[84]

There are other problems relating to digital imaging of works in a museum collection. It often is difficult to identify an Internet infringer or locate the point of an infringing act for Internet users. Copyright holders have brought infringement suits against operators of computer bulletin board services and Internet access providers. Internet service providers may be liable for direct infringement because of their role in copying material when they receive, transmit, and store postings that their customers make if their customers, in this process, are making copies of wrongfully posted copyrighted material. Direct infringement does not require intent or any particular state of mind, but a provider would be an innocent infringer and only subject to nominal damages if the provider was unaware of any infringement. Further, pursuant to amendments to the Copyright Act by the Digital Millennium Act of 1998,[85] a service provider can avoid liability if the service provider did not know an activity on the system or network was infringing.[86]

In addition to the problem of a copyright owner identifying an Internet infringer and locating the point of an infringing act, a copyright holder also must confront the difficult problem of determining the proper forum and choice of law for an infringement claim.

> Example 29. An artist who resides in the United States created a painting that is copyrighted under the U.S. Copyright Act. While the painting was on loan to a museum in France, a French artist copied the painting and sold his copied painting in France. The creator of the original work learns of the copy. She wants to sue the French artist for copyright infringement. The artist must decide whether to bring an infringement action in the United States or in France.

The principle of "national treatment," which provides that authors and artists should enjoy in other countries the same protection for their works as those countries grant their own authors and artists, developed pursuant to Article V(2) of the Berne Convention and the Universal Copyright Convention. Most courts in the United States have ruled that the principle implicates a "rule of territoriality." According to the Ninth Circuit Court of Appeals, this rule specifies that the applicable law in an infringement action would be the copyright law of the state in which the infringement occurred, not that of the country of which the author is a national.[87] However, the Second Circuit of Appeals disagrees.[88] According to the Second Circuit, the principle of national treatment does not express any choice of law rule. Rather, according to the Second Circuit, it "simply requires that the country in which protection is claimed must treat foreign and domestic authors alike."[89] The Second Circuit explained that, because copyright is a form of property, a court should decide which law governs copyright infringement by determining the interest of the parties based "on the law of the state with 'the most significant relationship' to the property and the parties."[90]

I. PROTECTION AND LIABILITY OUTSIDE COPYRIGHT LAWS

The summary in this chapter of copyright provisions should suggest to the reader that the extent of copyright protection often is difficult to determine conclusively and that protection is limited. Creators of works sometimes find better protection in other sources of the law, such as those discussed in Chapter 7.

The right of privacy and right of publicity, discussed in Chapter 7, grant state law protections, as well as corresponding liabilities, outside the copyright law. Still, unlike copyright protection, which supposedly provides uniformity through a federal law that preempts often inconsistent state provisions, the scope of the right of privacy and publicity developed from the common law and are subject to variable definitions under state laws.[91]

Some aspects of an artist's work may be protected through an unfair competition right of action, and some museums have sought trademark protections for their collections. As pointed out below, a problem with seeking protection outside the copyright law is that a court may decide the copyright laws have preempted these claims.

As noted below, for protection of "sweat of the brow" creations, such as digital images of public domain works in a museum collection, a contractual arrangement between a museum and the users of the images may provide protection for the museum that is unattainable through copyright law.

1. Right of Publicity

While copyright laws protect an artist's expression of an idea in a tangible form, i.e., a painting or a sculpture, the right of publicity protects against an unauthorized use of a celebrity's name or image, as noted in Chapter 7. The availability of protection under a right of publicity is not limited to a tangible medium of expression.[92] As discussed in Chapter 7, protection under a right of publicity creates a common law monopoly that effectively removes some works from the public domain.[93] Further, famous artists may find protection from unauthorized use of their names with their works through the right of publicity.

Because the right of publicity may provide economic protection to an artist should the artist's name or product be used in any unauthorized manner, a possible violation of this somewhat ill-defined right must be considered in preparing digital reproductions of collections.

2. Unfair Competition

Unfair competition issues surface if an artist's work is presented in a distorted form as noted in Chapter 7. There is a violation under the Lanham Act[94] if a representation of a product, although technically true, creates a false impression of the product's origin.

Some courts have addressed the issue of whether a false copyright notice is actionable under the Lanham Act as a false designation of origin.[95] A few courts have ruled that placing a copyright notice on an infringing product can be a false designation of origin actionable under the Lanham Act.[96] This possibility presents a caveat to a museum should it place a copyright notice on digital images of works in its collections if the images have no original element.

3. Trademarks

One court[97] considered whether one could make a trademark or comparable use of a copyrighted image, which would serve as a trademark, that would provide a cause of action under the Lanham Act. This might be a possibility if the images bears trademarks or service marks of a museum. If the images are copyrightable and are associated with the museum, copying of the images could be a violation of the Lanham Act. On the other hand, if the images are exact reproductions of public domain works, albeit in a different medium, the images may not be copyrightable. In Bridgeman Art Library v. Corel Corp.,[98] a federal district court in New York pointed out that an image could be used "in a manner that would engender confusion as to the copyright holder's association with or sponsorship of a product for which the image appeared." In that event, the New York federal district court concluded "there might be a violation of the Lanham Act in a different context."[99]

> Example 30. After a museum registered the words "The Rock & Roll Hall of Fame" as its service mark with the United States Patent and Trademark Office, a world-famous architect designed a facility for the Rock & Roll Hall of Fame Museum. Officials with the museum stated that the museum building design was a unique and inherently distinctive symbol of the freedom, youthful energy, rebellion, and movement of rock and roll music. A photographer began marketing and distributing posters featuring a photograph of the museum against a colorful sunset. The words "Rock N' Roll, Hall of Fame" appeared on a border underneath the photograph. In Rock & Roll Hall of Fame and Museum, Inc. v. Gentile Productions, 71 F. Supp. 2d 755 (N.D. Ohio 1999), the museum brought an action against the photographer in which it contended the photographer's poster infringed upon its registered service marks. The court decided that the museum did not use their building design as a trademark. It found that consumers did not believe the building was a trademark or that the photograph in the poster functioned as a trademark. The court viewed the photograph as a photo of a well-known public landmark and dismissed the case. (As noted in Chapter 10 in discussing the

Architectural Works Protection Act, architectural works are protected by § 102 of the Copyright Act; however, pursuant to § 120(a) of the Copyright Act, a photograph of a building with copyrighted design is not an infringement of the copyright.)

4. Misappropriation

The doctrine of unfair competition by misappropriation was established by the Supreme Court in an early case in which it ruled that misappropriation "is the act of converting to one's own use and profit the product of another's labor."[100] A state law misappropriation claim generally includes the following elements:[101] (1) a person or entity generates or collects information at some cost or expense; (2) the value of the information is highly time-sensitive; (3) the unauthorized use of the information is in direct competition with the product or service offered by the creator of the information; and (4) the ability of other parties to "free-ride" on the efforts of the creator of the information so reduces the incentive to produce the product or service that its existence or quality is threatened substantially or so little profitable as to cut off the service in effect by rendering the cost prohibitive in comparison with the return. The Fifth Circuit Court of Appeals commented that while federal copyright law "focuses on the value of creativity, state misappropriation law is specifically designed to protect the *labor*—the so-called 'sweat equity' that goes into creating a work."[102]

The difficulty in seeking protection of a "sweat of the brow" creation embodied in a reproduced work under a misappropriation doctrine is that such an action may be preempted by the Copyright Act. One court concluded that, despite "the seemingly divergent purposes of federal copyright law and state misappropriation law," the rights protected under these laws are equivalent and, thus, a state misappropriation claim is preempted by the Copyright Act.[103]

State law actions under unfair competition or misappropriation claims are preempted by the Copyright Act if two elements are present. The rights asserted under state law must be rights that are equivalent to those protected by the Copyright Act. In addition, the work involved must fall within the "subject matter" of the Copyright Act.[104] One court dismissed an unfair competition claim because the court decided the claim was based solely on rights equivalent to those protected by the federal copyright law.[105] Another court dismissed a misappropriation claim because, according to that court, it was preempted by the Copyright Act.[106] The court rejected a "partial preemption doctrine."[107]

5. Trade Dress

A museum or artist may find protection for its works by demonstrating a trade dress violation. There may be a violation of the Lanham Act[108] if another artist or entity markets an artwork or other product similar to, or that appears to imitate, the museum's or the complaining artist's work so that there is confusion for the consumer with respect to the two works.

Example 31. Romm Art Creations, the world-wide distributor of Tarkay posters, became concerned that Simcha International was selling posters, which bore the signature "Patricia," that closely resembled the Tarkay posters produced from the artist's collection known as "Women and Cafes." Itzchak Tarkay is an Israeli artist of international renown. He gave an exclusive right to reproduce some of his original artworks as posters to Givon Prints. Givon, in turn, licensed Romm Art to distribute and sell the posters. The "Women and Cafes" series, as a result of widespread attribution and advertising, became recognized by the trade and by consumers as "Tarkays." Romm sued Simcha, alleging trade dress infringement under the Lanham Act and unfair competition acts from its alleged sale and reproductions of the Tarkay works through its series of "Patricia" paintings. In Romm Art Creations, Ltd. v. Simcha International, Inc., 786 F. Supp. 1126 (E.D.N.H. 1992), Romm contended that the "Patricia" series were "slavishly similar and entirely derivative" of the Tarkay "Women and Cafes" collection. The court decided there was a likelihood of confusion from Simcha's trade dress. The court considered the strength of the Tarkay trade dress, the similarity of the two trade dresses, the directly competitive nature of the products offered, the inference of Simcha's intentional copying, and the lack of deliberate and measured consumer product selection in a gallery or poster shop. It found a violation of the Lanham Act.

One court[109] criticized the Romm Art Creation decision noted in Example 31 and referred to a "debate over the use of trademark law to protect the rights of artists in their visual style." It thought the better rule appeared to be that protection an artist receives against infringement of his work arises under copyright law, not the Lanham Act. This court declared that trade dress law does not protect an idea, a concept, or a generalized type of appearance and that the court in Romm Art Creations misapplied the Lanham Act to artistic style, which, according to this court, cannot receive trade dress protection. The court noted references to the Romm Art decision as being "a perfect example of a failed claim for copyright infringement masquerading as one for unfair competition." It opined that the court in Romm Art Creations, by improperly applying the Lanham Act to a copyright claim, circumvented copyright law's prohibition on the protection of ideas.

J. LICENSING OF DIGITAL IMAGES

A "sweat of the brow" creation that is not protected by the copyright laws may have protection through contract law. If a museum has not added the originality required to obtain a copyright in digital images of public domain works in its collection, it may be able to obtain exclusive rights to its "sweat of the brow" skills in making reproductions by licensing the dissemination of the images. A museum that makes reproductions of its public domain works through photographic transparencies would authorize others to use the reproductions, or exclude access to such reproductions, by an access contract or a license. An access contract would permit online and Internet services while a license would permit access to and downloading of software into a licensee's system and the continuing right to use the software after it is downloaded.[110] A license of digital images defines the product, distinguishes between single use and network use, consumer use and commercial use, and between private use and the right to public display.[111]

> Example 32. The Seventh Circuit Court of Appeals ruled, in ProCD, Inc. v. Zeidenberg, 86 F.3d 1447 (7th Cir. 1996), that purchasers of computer software are bound by the software's shrink-wrap licenses as a matter of contract law. The Seventh Circuit decided that the Copyright Act does not prevent shrinkwrap licenses from being enforceable. The court decided that shrink-wrap licenses facilitate distributions of object code "while concealing the source code (the point of a clause forbidding disassembly)" and "serve the same procompetitive functions as does the law of trade secrets." It noted that these licenses may provide other benefits for consumers, such as the right to make extra copies, the right to use the software on multiple computers, and the right to incorporate the software into the user's products. The court decided that "whether a particular license is generous or restrictive," a contract is not equivalent to the exclusive rights within the scope of copyright law and, thus, may be enforced. As the Seventh Circuit[112] ruled, rights created by contract are not equivalent to the exclusive rights within the general scope of

> copyright. The Seventh Circuit referred to a copyright as a "right against the world" and stated that while "silence means a ban on copying," contracts, on the other hand, affect only their parties; strangers may do as they please. The Seventh Circuit noted that contracts do not create "exclusive rights." According to Seventh Circuit, a licensee is restricted by a license agreement and is subject to contract law while copyright infringement is beyond the scope of a license.

Some courts have criticized the Seventh Circuit's decision in ProCD, discussed in Example 32. One court[113] stated that a claim against an alleged infringer who is not a party to a license agreement must be a claim under the copyright law rather than the law of contracts. Some of the criticism of the ProCD decision is that a shrinkwrap license is an end-user agreement; it cannot be reviewed at the time of purchase of a software package. While a consumer does not have the opportunity to examine the purchased product prior to signing a shrinkwrap license agreement, a purchaser of a museum's digital images would sign an access contract after viewing the product. The person signing an access contract should not have the concerns that exist with respect to a shrinkwrap license.

The Uniform Laws Commission adopted the Uniform Computer Information Transactions Act in 1999. One purpose of the uniform act was to reduce the uncertainty as to the validity of shrinkwrap licenses. Drafters of the act[114] noted that, while the new digital environment had increased the risk of unfair copying, licensing contracts to market digital images provided producers of cultural information a means to enforce exclusivity and, thus, to limit use of this information. The drafters[115] pointed out that many access contracts do not depend on intellectual property rights. The owner of a computer system has a fundamental right to exclude others from access to its system, and, thus, can condition the terms by which it permits access.

A museum director might consider preserving the museum's interests and "sweat of the brow" work in its digital images through a license or an access contract, which also can bring in additional revenue for the museum.

NOTES

1. The act is set out at 17 U.S.C. §§ 101–810. Sections 106A and 113 provide some protection for a visual artist's moral rights. The Visual Artists Rights Act of 1990 (VARA) amended the Copyright Act to provide certain visual artists the rights of attribution and integrity. Section 106A creates a right of attribution that extends not only to an artist's right to be identified as the creator of a work or to prevent use of the artist's name in an

improper identification but also to the right to publish anonymously or under a pseudonym. Section 106A also establishes a right of integrity that provides some visual artists the right to prevent certain modifications of their work, including distortions, mutilations, and destruction. However, modifications are prohibited only if they are prejudicial to an artist's reputation or honor and if they are intentional or the result of a negligent act or omission. The rights of attribution and integrity are granted to the artist, not to the copyright owner (unless, of course, the artist is also the copyright owner because the work has not been sold or title transferred).

2. Pub. 94-553, Title 17 to the U.S. Code.

3. 17 U.S.C. § 301(a).

4. 17 U.S.C. § 301(a). Prior to the effective date of the Copyright Extension Act of 1998 (CTEA), protection was for life plus 50 years. The Copyright Extension Act, Pub. L. 105-109, extended copyright protection 20 years to harmonize U.S. copyright law with the extended coverage adopted by the European Union. See "EU Directive," Article 1, 93/90 EEC of October 29, 1993, OLJ 290. The Supreme Court upheld the CTEA's extension of copyright right protection by 20 years for existing copyrights in Eldred v. Ashcroft, 537 U.S. 186 (2003). In the case of joint ownership, the 70 years are measured from the date of death of the last surviving author. For works made for hire, discussed in notes 8–10 and accompanying text, the term is 95 years from the first publication or 120 years from creation, whichever is shorter. For unpublished works in existence on January 1, 1978, the duration of the copyright generally will be computed in the same manner as for new works: life plus 70 years or 95 or 120 years for works for hire. Works that were copyrighted before 1978 and, thus, had been published by January 1, 1978, were eligible for copyright renewal for a term of 67 years. See 17 U.S.C. § 304. Pursuant to the CTEA, copyright in its renewal term will have a copyright term of 95 years from the date copyright was secured originally. Prior to the Copyright Act of 1976, statutory copyright protection began on the date of publication (or the date of registration in unpublished form) and continued for 28 years from that date. A copyright was subject to renewal for a second 28 years, making a total potential term of 56 years.

The Copyright Act of 1976 extended copyright protection to an author's life plus 50 years. The Copyright Term Extension Act of 1998, which extended copyright protection to an author's life plus 70 years, did *not* provide that works that were in the public domain on the date of enactment of the act became copyrighted works. The act only extended the term of the copyright for works that were not in the public domain on the date of its enactment.

5. Literary works are defined in 17 U.S.C. § 101 as "works, other than audiovisual works, expressed in words, numbers, or other verbal or numerical symbols or indicia, regardless of the nature of the material objects, such as books, periodicals, manuscripts, phonorecords, film, tapes, disks, or cards, in which they are embodied."

6. 17 U.S.C. § 102(a). Works of the federal government are not subject to copyright protection. 17 U.S.C. § 105.

7. 17 U.S.C. § 102(b).

8. 17 U.S.C. § 101. Moral rights protection under 17 U.S.C. § 106A, discussed in notes 41 to 49 and accompanying text, does not extend to a work made for hire. In Community for Creative Non-Violence v. Reid, 490 U.S. 730 (1980), the Supreme Court ruled that the term "employee" refers to a hired party in a conventional employment relationship. The Court stated that a determination of whether a hired party is an employee is made by considering the hiring party's right to control the manner and means by which the hired

party accomplishes the project. Other relevant facts to the inquiry include the location of the work, the duration of the relationship between the parties, whether the hiring party has the right to assign additional projects to the hired party, the extent of the hired party's discretion over when and how long to work, the method of payment, and the tax treatment of the hired party. The Court decided that the extent of control the hiring party exercises over the details of the product is not dispositive.

9. 17 U.S.C. § 201(b). According to one author, the Copyright Act has a "callous disregard for the paternity right of creative persons." See Treece, "American Law Analogues of the Author's 'Moral Right,'" Am. J. Com. L. 494 (1968). Treece asserted that the work-made-for-hire arrangement "severs completely the relation between the creator and ownership of the work."

10. Community for Creative Non-Violence v. Reid, cited in note 8. The Supreme Court ruled that, if an artist is an independent contractor, there must be a written agreement for the artist's work to be a "work for hire."

11. 17 U.S.C. § 106.

12. Section 109 of the Copyright Act grants the owner of a copy the right to sell or otherwise dispose of the copy without authority of the copyright owner.

13. Only the owner of an art object has the exclusive right to display the object. Thus, only the owner could authorize someone else to display the work. If a museum has a work on loan and is not the owner of the work, it could not authorize another to display the work without consent from the owner.

14. A copyright owner's exclusive rights, set out at 17 U.S.C. § 106, include the right to reproduce the copyrighted work. This right is divisible from the right to distribute, the right to display, and the right to prepare derivative works. Sale of a painting, for example, would not transfer the right of reproduction to the purchaser unless the transfer specifically includes the right.

15. In Mirage Editions, Inc. v. Albuquerque A.R.T. Co., 856 F.2d 1341 (9th Cir. 1988), the Ninth Circuit Court of Appeals ruled that sale of a copyrighted work without a specific transfer by the copyright holder of the exclusive right to prepare derivative works does not transfer that right to the purchaser. The derivative works right remains unimpaired with the copyright holder.

16. 17 U.S.C. § 501. An infringer is liable for either the copyright owner's actual damages and any additional profits of the infringer, or statutory damages. If an artist has retained reproduction rights, a cultural institution should obtain a licensing agreement from the artist or the artist's heirs to reproduce the works.

17. In Bleistein v. Donaldson Lithographing Co., 188 U.S. 239 (1903), the Supreme Court held that pictorial illustrations are within the protection of the copyright law. The Supreme Court noted that while a copy of an original scene may not be copied, the original scene may be copied.

18. 17 U.S.C. § 201(c).

19. Pursuant to § 201(c), a publisher can reprint an article from one edition of an encyclopedia in a later revision of it, but cannot revise the contribution itself or include it in a new anthology or an entirely different collective work. In New York v. Tasini, 533 U.S. 483 (2001), the Supreme Court ruled that a question regarding § 201(c) is not whether a user can assemble a revision of a collective work from a database, but rather whether a database itself perceptibly presents an author's contribution as part of a revision of the collective work.

20. 17 U.S.C. § 204.

21. 17 U.S.C. § 205.

22. 17 U.S.C. § 203.

23. 17 U.S.C. § 102(b). In Feist Publications v. Rural Tel. Service, 499 U.S. 340 (1991), the Supreme Court commented that the "sine qua non of copyright is originality." In Modern Pub., a Div. of Unisystems v. Landoll, Inc., 841 F. Supp. 129 (S.D.N.Y. 1994), the court commented that a relatively modest amount of originality suffices for copyright protection.

24. See Maxtone-Graham v. Burtchaell, 803 F.2d 1253 (2nd Cir., 1986), cert. denied, 481 U.S. 1059 (1987). In Robinson v. Random House, 877 F. Supp. 830 (S.D.N.Y. 1995), the court ruled that a historical fact is not copyrightable. It stated that no biographer holds a monopoly in a story of a subject's life. According to the court, because the retelling of history proceeds in certain chronological order, there can be no copyright on the sequence of a story's element. Still, while there is no copyright in the order of presentation of facts, nor in their selection, the court did hold that the expression of historical facts is protected.

25. See Baker v. Selden, 101 U.S. 99 (1879). An accounting textbook is an example.

26. The Supreme Court commented, in Feist Publications, cited in note 23, that in a compilation, the author's choices as to selection and arrangement, if these choices are made independently and entail a minimal degree of creativity, are sufficiently original that Congress may protect the compilations through copyright laws. The Court noted, however, that this type of copyright protection is subject to an important limitation. Copyright protection extends only to those components of the work that are original to the author.

27. In Feist, cited in note 23, the Supreme Court ruled that copyright protection would attach to a compilation if the compilation is (1) the collection and assembly of preexisting material, facts, or data; (2) the selection, coordination, or arrangement of those materials; and (3) the creation, by virtue of the selection, coordination, or arrangement, of an original work of authorship. The Court in Feist stated that a compiler's choices as to selectivity, coordination, or arrangement, made independently by the compiler, are entitled to copyright.

28. Feist Publications, cited in note 23. The Supreme Court discussed in Feist, the "sweat of the brow" theory used by some previous courts interpreting the Copyright Act of 1909 to protect factual compilations. As the Supreme Court noted, the underlying theory was that "copyright was a reward for the hard work that went into compiling facts." The Supreme Court in Feist rejected the theory and commented that some earlier courts erroneously concluded that authors were precluded absolutely from saving time and effort by relying on facts contained in prior works.

29. Gracen v. Bradford Exchange, 698 F.2d 300 (7th Cir. 1983).

30. Still, in Rogers v. Koons, 960 F.2d 302 (2nd Cir. 1991), the court ruled that a photograph can be an "original work of authorship" protected by the Copyright Act.

31. As discussed in Leigh v. Warner Bros, 10 F. Supp. 2d 1371 (S.D.Ga. 1998) and 212 F.3d 1210 (11th Cir. 2000), this concept, which is known as *scènes à faire*, recognizes that certain expressions lack enough originality to justify copyright protection.

32. Bridgeman Art Library v. Corel, 36 F. Supp. 2d 191 (S.D.N.Y. 1999).

33. The court, in Bridgeman, cited in note 32, set out three situations in which "there is room for originality" in photographs.

> (1) There may be originality which does not depend on creation of the scene or object to be photographed or anything remarkable about its capture and which resides in such speculates as angle of shot, light and shade, exposure, effects achieved by means of filters, developing techniques, etc. (2) There may be creation of the scene or subject to be

photographed. (3) A person may create a worthwhile photograph by being at the right place at the right time. According to the court, the merit of the photograph consists of the photographer's capturing and recording a scene unlikely to recur.

34. Alcatel USA, Inc. v. DGI Technologies, Inc., 166 F.3d 772 (5th Cir. 1999). In Warren Publishing, Inc. v. U.S., 115 F.3d 1509 (11th Cir. 1997), the Eleventh Circuit Court of Appeals commented that a compiler's choices as to selection, coordination, or arrangement are the only portions of a compilation that "arguably are even entitled to copyright protection." The court noted that an analysis of a compiler's acts of selection are relevant only to determine whether the compiler exercised any individual judgment that is equivalent to creativity.

35. See Feist, cited in note 23. The Court stated in Feist that notwithstanding a valid copyright, a subsequent compiler would remain "free to use the facts contained in another's publication to aid in preparing a competing work, so long as the competing work does not feature the same selection and arrangement."

36. 17 U.S.C. § 103(b). It does not imply any exclusive right in the preexisting material. Further, the copyright is "independent of, and does not affect or enlarge the scope, duration, ownership, or subsistence of, any copyright protection in the preexisting material." 17 U.S.C § 103(b). As the Supreme Court stated in Feist, cited in note 23, copyright protection would extend only to the original elements contributed by the author. Thus, a museum could obtain a copyright for its digital images only with respect to those elements materially altering or embellishing the underlying works.

37. Bridgeman Art Library v. Corel, cited in note 32.

38. Pub L 96-517, § 10, codified at 17 U.S. C. §§ 101 and 117. Congress adopted changes recommended by the National Commission on New Technological Uses of Copyrighted Works (CONTU). Computer software is subject to copyright protection as a "literary work." 17 U.S.C. §§ 101, 102(a)(1). A computer program has been defined as "a set of statements or instructions to be used directly or indirectly in a computer in order to bring about a certain result." 17 U.S.C. § 101. In Bernstein v. U.S. Dept. of State, 922 F. Supp. 1426 (N.D. Cal. 1996), aff'd, 176 F.3d 1132 (9th Cir. 1999), op. w/drawn, 192 F.3d 1308 (9th Cir. 1999), the Ninth Circuit Court of Appeals concluded that this statutory language supported the conclusion that copyright protection extends both to source code and object code. The Ninth Circuit noted that source code is essentially a set of instructions used indirectly in a computer because, as the court commented, it first must be translated into object code to achieve the desired result.

39. 17 U.S.C. § 101.

40. Matthew Bender & Company, Inc. v. West Publishing Co. 158 F.3d 693 (2nd Cir. 1998). The Second Circuit Court of Appeals in Matthew Bender concluded that CD-ROM discs were copies. It stated that CD-ROM discs could infringe a copyright even if the information embedded upon them was not perceptible without the aid of a CD-ROM player. In Mai Systems v. Peak Computer, Inc. 991 F.2d 511, 518 (9th Cir. 1993), the Ninth Circuit Court of Appeals ruled that the loading of copyrighted software into RAM (Random Access Memory) created a "copy" of that software.

41. 828 U.N.T.S. 222. The Berne Convention, which was first accepted in Berne, Switzerland, in 1886, symbolizes international protection for authors and artists. The Berne Union, consisting of at least 165 member nations, attempts to reconcile the policies of the various nations regarding international copyrights. The Universal Copyright Convention

also seeks to protect the rights of authors and artists through international copyright protection. The Universal Copyright Convention was signed at Geneva, Switzerland, in 1952, by forty nations including the United States.

42. The Berne Convention Implementation Act of 1988, Pub. L. No. 100-568, provided that U.S. adherence to the Berne Convention did not expand or reduce any right of an artist of a work to claim authorship of a work or "to object to any distortion, mutilation, or other modification of, or other derogatory action in relation to," a work that would prejudice the artist's honor or reputation. Thus, when the United States initially became a member of the Berne Convention, it did not adopt the concept of an artist's moral right.

43. Pub. L. 106-650 (1990), codified at 17 U.S.C. § 106A.

44. Only the creator of a work of visual art has the rights conferred by 17 U.S.C. § 106A. A "work of visual art" is defined in the Copyright Act, 17 U.S.C. § 101, as

> a painting, drawing, print, or sculpture, existing in a single copy, in a limited edition of 200 copies or fewer that are signed and consecutively numbered by the author, or, in the case of a sculpture, in multiple cast, carved, or fabricated sculptures of two hundred or fewer that are numbered consecutively by the author and bear the signature or other identifying mark of the author; or . . . a still photographic image produced for exhibition purposes only, existing in a single copy that is signed by the author, or in a limited edition of 200 copies or fewer that are signed and consecutively numbered by the author. A work of visual art does not include . . . a poster, map, globe, chart, motion picture or other audiovisual work, book, magazine, or electronic publication.

Some state statutes have provided for a moral right for artists. See, e.g., Cal. Civ. Code § 987; Me. Stat. tit. 27, § 303; and N.Y. Arts & Cultural Aff. Law § 14.03. However, these state provisions were preempted by the Federal Copyright Act and, thus, are ineffective as to some works of visual artists. See 17 U.S.C. § 301(f)(1). Section 301(f)(1) states that all legal or equitable rights that are equivalent to any rights conferred by § 106A with respect to works of visual art are governed exclusively by §§ 106A and 113(d). The provision specifically states that "no person is entitled to any such right or equivalent right in any work of visual art under the common law or statutes of any State."

45. 17 U.S.C. § 106A(e). Transfer of ownership of any copy of a work of visual art is not a waiver of the artist's moral right. Although an artist may waive a moral right in the artist's work by an express agreement in writing, an artist may not transfer the right.

46. In France and Poland the moral right has been perpetual. Article L.121-1 of the French Code on Intellectual Property has provided that the right is perpetual, inalienable, and imprescriptible. Further, the right has been transmissible to an artist's heir and could be granted by will to a third party. See also Article 16 of the Act of 4 February 1994 on Copyright and Neighbouring Rights (Poland). The EC directive for member countries of the EU would harmonize the author's right at seventy years after death of the artist or seventy years after a work was made available to the public. EC Directive N 93/98 dated October 29, 1993.

47. 17 U.S.C. § 106A. The modification of a work of visual art which is the result of the passage of time, the inherent nature of the materials, or the result of conservation or of public presentation is not a distortion, mutilation, or other modification.

48. 17 U.S.C. § 113(d). If the owner of a building wishes to remove a work of visual art that is a part of the building, the artist's rights apply unless the owner has made a diligent, good-faith attempt without success to notify the artist of the owner's intended action

affecting the work, or the owner provided the notice in writing and the artist notified failed, within ninety days after receiving the notice, either to remove the work or to pay for its removal. 17 U.S.C. § 113(d). The owner of a building has made a diligent, good-faith attempt to locate the artist if the owner has sent notice by registered mail to the artist at the artist's most recent address that was recorded with the Register of Copyrights. (The Register of Copyrights has a system of records whereby any visual artist, whose work has been incorporated in, or made a part of, a building, may record the artist's identity and address with the Copyright Office.)

49. Although in the United States the moral right extends only for an artist's life, in most other countries that are parties to the Berne Convention, the moral right is maintained until the extinction of the artist's economic rights.

50. Discussion of right of privacy and right of publicity in Chapter 7.

51. 17 U.S.C. § 107.

52. Id. In Sony Corp. of America v. Universal City Studios, Inc., 464 U.S. 417 (1984), the Supreme Court stated that copyright protection never has conferred upon a copyright owner complete control over all possible uses of the copyright owner's work. As the Court noted, any individual may reproduce a copyrighted work for a "fair use"; the copyright owner does not possess the exclusive right to such a use.

53. Discussion in Marcus v. Rowley, 695 F.2d 1171 (9th Cir. 1983).

54. 17 U.S.C. § 107.

55. In Marcus v. Rowley, cited in note 53, the Ninth Circuit Court of Appeals found a violation of the copyright act when a school teacher copied almost fifty percent of the claimant's teaching materials into a booklet which she prepared for her classes. She used the booklet for three school years. The court ruled that fair use does not cover such extensive use of copyrighted material.

56. A library or archive that provides reproducing equipment must display a notice next to the equipment that the making of copies may be subject to copyright law. See 17 U.S.C. § 108.

57. In drafting the 1976 Copyright Act, the Copyright Committee recognized that there is a need for greater certainty and protection for teachers concerning limited copying. See Notes of Committee on the Judiciary, H.R. No. 1476, 94th Cong., 2d Sess. 5, reprinted in 1976 U.S.C.C.A.N. 5659, 5674. In order to meet that need, § 504(c) of the act was amended to provide teachers and other nonprofit users of copyrighted material with broad insulation against unwarranted liability for infringement.

58. Section 504, which provides remedies for infringement, provides that if an infringer believed and "had reasonable grounds for believing his or her use of the copyrighted work was a fair use," the court must remit statutory damages if the infringer is "an employee or agent of a nonprofit educational institution, library, or archives itself" and was acting within the scope of employment when the infringing act occurred.

59. See Sony Corp. v. Universal City Studios, Inc., 464 U.S. 417 (1984); Cable/Home Communications Corp., 902 F.2d 829 (11th Cir. 1990); and Playboy Enterprises, Inc. v. Frena, 839 F. Supp. 1552 (M.D. Fla. 1993). In Princeton Univ. Press v. Michigan Document Services, 99 F.3d 1381 (6th Cir. 1996), the Sixth Court of Appeals ruled that the burden of proof is on the copyright holder to show market effect if the use is a noncommercial one. On the other hand, it held that the burden of proof is on the alleged infringer if the challenged use is of a commercial nature.

60. Congress created the National Commission on New Technological Uses of Copyrighted Works (CONTU) to recommend revisions to the Copyright Act to reflect advances

in computer technology. CONTU proposed a version of § 117 identical to the one enacted except that it recommended that the section provide it would not be copyright infringement for a rightful possessor of a copy of a computer program to make another copy or adaptation of that program. Congress substituted the words "owner of a copy" for "possessor of a copy." See Pub. L. 96-517, 96th Cong., 2d Sess. (1980). Discussion in DSC Communications Corp. v. Pulse Communications, 170 F.3d 1354 (Fed. Cir. 1999). The Federal Circuit Court of Appeals in DSC Communications pointed out that restrictions in a licensing agreement that limits a licensee's right to transfer copies of software or the right to disclose details of the software to third parties is inconsistent with a right to transfer copies to third parties. The court held a licensee subject to such licensing restrictions was not an "owner" under § 117 of the Copyright Act.

61. The "first sale" doctrine provides that once the owner of a copyright consents to the sale of copies of his work, the copyright holder may not exercise the distribution right as to those copies. As the Eleventh Circuit Court of Appeals noted in Allison v. Vintage Sports Plaques, 136 F.3d 1443 (11th Cir. 1998), any other rule would extend the copyright monopoly so far as to permit a copyright holder to control the disposition of "lawfully obtained tangible personal property."

62. Discussion in Apple, Inc. v. Psystar Corp., 658 F.3d 1150 (9th Cir. 2011).

63. Quality Kind Distributors, Inc. v. L'Anza Research International, Inc., 523 U.S. 135 (1998).

64. Kirtsaeng v. John Wiley & Sons, Inc., 133 S. Ct. 1351 (2013).

65. Once a work goes into the public domain, there is no copyright protection. A work in the public domain may be copied.

66. 17 U.S.C. § 401(a).

67. 17 U.S.C. § 401(d).

68. 17 U.S.C. § 401(b). The notice would be as follows: © 2014 Jane Doe. In order for a work to be protected under the Universal Copyright Convention, the notice must contain the letter *C* enclosed in a circle, together with the date and name of the owner. The year may be omitted for pictorial, graphic, or sculptural works where the work is reproduced in greeting cards, stationery, dolls, jewelry, or other such articles.

Copyright Office Circular 38 contains general information about international copyright protection for U.S. authors. Circular 38 explains use of the phrase "All Rights Reserved" that often follows the copyright notice. The term provides some advantages for copyright protection for U.S. authors in South American countries that are parties to the Buenos Aires Convention of 1920 though not members of the Universal Copyright Convention.

69. 17 U.S.C. § 401(c).

70. 17 U.S.C. § 407(a). The Register of Copyrights may exempt by regulation any categories of works from the deposit requirements. See 17 U.S.C. § 407(c). At any time after publication of a work, the Register of Copyrights may make written demand for the required deposit on any of the persons obligated to make the deposit. Unless deposit then is made within three months after demand is received, the person on whom the demand was made is liable for a fine of not more than $250 for each work plus the retail price of the copies demanded. If the person willfully or repeatedly fails to comply with the demand, the fine can be $2,500. See 17 U.S.C. § 407.

71. 17 U.S.C. § 408.

72. 17 U.S.C. § 411(a). In Hass Studio v. Palm Press, Inc. 164 F.3d 110 (2nd Cir. 1999), the Second Circuit Court of Appeals dismissed a copyright infringement claim and awarded

sanctions when the copyright was not registered prior to filing the claim. The complaint based its claim of copyright ownership on the fact that it was awaiting registration from the Register of Copyrights. The Register of Copyrights later rejected the copyright application.

73. See Fonar Corp. v. Comenick, 105 F.3d 99 (2nd Cir. 1997) and M.G.B. Homes, Inc. v. Ameron Homes, Inc. 903 F.2d 1486 (11th Cir. 1990). The Eleventh Circuit Court of Appeals ruled, in M.G.B. Homes, that the registration requirement is a jurisdictional prerequisite to an infringement suit. The Supreme Court disagreed in Reed Elservier, Inc. v. Muchnick, 559 U.S. 154 (2010). The Supreme Court ruled in Muchnick that § 411(a)'s registration requirement is a precondition to filing a claim but does not restrict a federal court's subject matter jurisdiction. In Muchnick, a district court had certified a class action and approved settlement for freelance authors who had contracted with publishers to author works for publication in print media but had retained copyrights in those works. The authors sued the publishers for copyright infringement when the publishers made electronic reproductions of their works. The class action involved both authors who had registered their works and authors who had not. The Court ruled the district court had jurisdiction to approve the settlement. Registration is not a prerequisite to an infringement action where a work's country of origin is a Berne Convention country outside the United States.

74. 17 U.S.C. § 410(c). As the court noted in Autoskill, Inc. v. National Educ. Support Sys. Inc., 994 F.2d 1476 (11th Cir. 1993), cert. denied, 510 U.S. 916 (1993), once a party produces a registration certificate, the burden of disputing the validity of the copyright shifts to the other party.

In Modern Publishing v. Landoll, Inc., 841 F. Supp. 129 (S.D.N.Y. 1994), the court commented that the certificate establishes a presumption of originality in the registered work as only original works of authorship are entitled to copyright protection.

75. 17 U.S.C. § 412.

76. Id. This provision excepts actions under 17 U.S.C. § 106A with respect to an artist's moral rights.

77. Section 504 sets out a copyright infringer's liability as either the copyright owner's actual damages and the infringer's additional profits or statutory damages in a sum not less than $750 or more than $30,000 as the court considers just. A court can increase statutory damages to $100,000 for a willful offense but also may reduce damages to $200 for an innocent infringer. Section 505 permits a court to include recovery of costs of suit and reasonable attorney's fees for a prevailing party. Section 506 provides that a person who willfully infringes a copyright for purposes of commercial advantage or private financial gain can be subjected to criminal fines. This provision does not apply to a infringement of a visual artist's moral rights set out in § 106A.

78. 3 Nimmer on Copyright §§ 13.01(B) and 13.03, discussed in Castle Rock Entertainment, Inc., v. Carol Publishing Group, 150 F.3d 132 (2nd Cir.1998). In Modern Pub., a Div. of Unisystems v. Landoll, Inc., 841 F. Supp. 129 (S.D.N.Y. 1994), the court ruled that copying may be proved by proof of the alleged infringer's access to the protected work and a substantial similarity between the works so that copying may be inferred.

79. Discussion in Castle Rock Entertainment, Inc., v. Carol Publishing Group, cited in note 78.

80. Bridgeman Art Library v. Corel, cited in note 32.

81. 3 Nimmer on Copyright § 13.03, discussed in Castle Rock Entertainment, Inc., which is cited in note 78. The emphasis in literal similarity is on the quantity of the copying.

For nonliteral similarity, courts determine whether the two works are similar in ideas or expression.

82. Software packages which permit a computer user to use a mouse to enlarge, shrink, move, distort, or smudge downloaded digital images are available.

83. One method to resolve barriers related to copyright protection on the Internet is the technology created to block or track infringing uses. An example is a "flickering screen" from which text cannot be saved or printed, and cryptography. Encryption involves running a readable message known as "plaintext" through a computer program that translates the message according to an equation or algorithm into unreadable "ciphertext." Decryption is the translation back to plaintext when the message is received by someone with an appropriate "key." The message is both encrypted and decrypted by common keys.

84. The Digital Millennium Copyright Act added Chapter 12 to the U.S. Copyright Act to provide, that, at the end of the two-year period beginning on the date of the enactment of Chapter 12, persons may not circumvent a technological measure that effectively controls access to a work subject to copyright protection. Section 1201(a) states that

> no person shall manufacture, import, offer to the public, or otherwise traffic in any technology, product, service, device, component, or part thereof that . . . is designed primarily or produced for the purpose of circumventing a technological measure that effectively controls access to a protected work . . . [and that] has only limited commercially significant purpose or use other than to circumvent a technological measure that effectively controls access to a [protected] work.

The Digital Millennium Copyright Act of 1998 implemented the 1996 World Intellectual Property Organization Copyright, Performances and Phonograms Treaty (WIPO). Pub. L. 105-304, 105th Cong. 2d Sess. The WIPO treaty is a special agreement within the meaning of Article 20 of the Berne Convention which provides that countries which are parties to the Berne Convention reserve the right to enter into special agreements among themselves in so far as the agreements grant authors and artists more extensive rights than those granted by the Berne Convention or contain provisions that are contrary to the convention. WIPO is an agency of the UN, but it is a product of the 1883 Paris Convention for the Protection of Industrial Property and the 1886 Berne Convention for the Protection of Literary and Artistic Works. A need for the international protection of intellectual property became evident as early as 1883 when the predecessor of WIPO came into existence as a means to address that need. WIPO became a specialized agency of the UN in 1974, with the mandate to administer intellectual property matters recognized by member States of the UN. It entered into a cooperation agreement with the World Trade Organization (WTO) in 1996 and, thus, expanded its role in the management of globalized trade.

A fundamental part of WIPO's activities is to promote the protection of intellectual property. It currently administers several treaties that establish internationally agreed rights and standards for their protection. While the Paris and Berne Conventions remain the "cornerstones of WIPO's treaty system," subsequent treaties have expanded the protection they offer. One example is the 1996 WIPO Copyright Treaty, which contains basic rules updating the international protection of copyright and related rights to the Internet age. WIPO attempted to simplify and harmonize procedures for obtaining and maintaining trademarks and patents in countries through the Trademark Law Treaty of 1994 and the Patent Law Treaty of 2000. Through its treaties, WIPO has provided services to simplify and reduce the cost of making individual applications or filings in all the counties in which protection for a given intellectual property right is sought.

85. Pub. L. 105-304 (1998), 17 U.S.C. § 512.

86. The Digital Millennium Copyright Act of 1998 amended the U.S. Copyright Act, 17 U.S.C. § 512(a), to provide that a service provider will not be liable for damages for copyright infringement by reason of the provider's "transmitting, routing, or providing connections" for material through a system or network controlled or operating by the service provider, or "by reason of the intermediate and transient storage of that material" under the following circumstances:

> (1) transmission of the material was initiated by or at the direction of a person other than the service provider; (2) transmission, routing, provision of connections, or storage is carried out through an automatic technical process without selection of the material by the service provider; (3) the service provider did not select the recipients of the material except as an automatic response to the request of another person; (4) no copy of the material made by the service provider in the course of such intermediate or transient storage was maintained on the system or network in a manner ordinarily accessible to anyone other than anticipated recipients, and no such copy is maintained on the system or network in a manner ordinarily accessible to such anticipated recipients for a longer period than is reasonably necessary for the transmission, routing, or provision of connections . . . (5) the material is transmitted through the system or network without modification of its content.

Pursuant to § 512(b), a service provider also is not liable under the act "if the material was made available online by a person other than the service provider . . . the material is transmitted from that person . . . through the system or network . . . at the direction of that other person; and . . . the storage was carried out through an automatic technical process for the purpose of making the material available to users of the system or network who, after the material is transmitted, request access to the material." Section 512(c) provides that a service provider is not liable for copyright infringement "by reason of the storage at the direction of a user of material that resides on a system or network controlled or operated by or for the service provider, if the service provider" (1) "does not have actual knowledge that the material or an activity using the material on the system or network is infringing . . . in the absence of such actual knowledge, is not aware of facts or circumstances from which infringing activity is apparent; or . . . upon obtaining such knowledge or awareness, acts expeditiously to remove, or disable access to, the material"; (2) if the service provider "does not receive a financial benefit directly attributable to the infringing activity in a case in which the service provider has the right and ability to control such activity"; and (3) if the service provider, "upon notification of claimed infringement . . . responds expeditiously to remove, or disable access to, the material that is claimed to be infringing or to be the subject of infringing activity." Pursuant to § 512(d), the same exceptions to liability apply to a service provider "referring or linking users to an online location containing infringing material or infringing activity, by using information location tools, including a directory, index, reference, pointer, or hypertext link."

87. See, e.g., Subafilms Ltd. v. MGM-Pathe Communications Co., 24 F.3d 1088 (9th Cir. 1994), cert. denied, 115 S. Ct. 512 (1994) and Creative Technology, Ltd. v. Aztech System PTE, Ltd., 61 F.3d 696 (9th Cir. 1995).

88. See Itar-Tass Russian News Agency v. Russian Kurrier, Inc., 153 F.3d 82 (2nd Cir. 1998). According to the Second Circuit in Itar, the Berne Convention cannot be the source of law because it is not self-executing. Further, according to the Second Circuit, because the U.S. Copyright Act has no choice of law provision, the matter is left to federal common law. The Second Circuit decided that the result would be that the applicable law would not necessarily be the same for each element of a copyright claim.

89. Id.

90. The Second Circuit in Itar, cited in note 88, set out as relevant factors, the nationality of the authors, the place of initial publication, and the country of origin as determined under the Berne Convention.

91. Discussion in Chapter 7.

92. Allison v. Vintage Sports Plaques, 136 F.3d 1443 (11th Cir. 1998). Because the right of publicity protects against an unauthorized use of an image, a celebrity could control when, and if, his image could be distributed. However, in Allison, the Eleventh Circuit Court of Appeals ruled that the first-sale doctrine applies to the right of publicity. As the Eleventh Circuit stated in Allison, a holding that the first-sale doctrine limits the right of publicity would not eliminate completely a celebrity's control over the use of his name or image. A celebrity would continue to enjoy the right to license the use of his image in the first instance, and, thus, would enjoy the power when, or if, his image would be distributed.

93. In Carson v. Here's Johnny Portable Toilets, 698 F.2d 831 (6th Cir. 1983), discussed in Example 28 in Chapter 7, Justice Kennedy expressed concern, in a dissenting opinion, that a right of publicity creates a monopoly to the protected individual that is potentially broader that the copyright law. Another problem, according to Justice Kennedy, is that the public generally is unaware of the claimed right. In Uhlaender v. Henricksen, 316 F. Supp. 1277 (D. Minn. 1970), the court stated that the right of publicity protects pecuniary, rather than emotional, interests.

94. 15 U.S.C. § 1125. Discussion of Lanham Act in Chapter 7.

95. In Lipton v. Nature Co., 71 F.3d 464 (2nd Cir. 1995), the Second Circuit Court of Appeals ruled that alleged infringing parties did infringe a claimaint's copyright in a book of animal terms by creating a line of merchandise that utilized these terms. The merchandise bore copyright notices in the infringing parties' names. The district court had concluded that the copyright notices the infringing parties placed on their infringing merchandise constituted false designations of origin with the meaning of § 43(a) of the Lanham Act. However, the Second Circuit reversed, deciding that a false copyright notice alone could not constitute a false designation of origin under the Lanham Act. See also Kerr v. New Yorker Magazine, Inc., 36 F. Supp. 2d 32 (S.D.N.Y. 1999).

96. See, e.g., Manufacturers Techs., Inc. v. Cams, Inc., 706 F. Supp. 984 (D. Conn. 1989); and Sunset Lamp Corp. v. Alsy Corp., 698 F. Supp. 1164 (S.D.N.Y. 1988).

97. Bridgeman Art Library v. Corel Corp., 25 F. Supp. 2d 421 (S.D.N.Y. 1998).

98. Id.

99. Id.

100. International News Service v. Associated Press, 248 U.S. 215 (1918).

101. Discussion in National Basketball Ass'n v. Motorola, Inc., 105 F.3d 841 (2nd Cir. 1997).

102. Alcatel USA, Inc. v. DGI Technologies, Inc., 166 F.3d 772 (5th Cir. 1999). The Fifth Circuit Court of Appeals in Alcatel USA, set out elements of the claim under Texas law: (1) the creation of a product through extensive time, labor, skill, and money; (2) the use of that product in competition with the creator, thereby giving the user a special competitive

advantage because the user was burdened with little or none of the expense incurred by the creator of the product; and (3) commercial damage to the creator of the product.

103. Alcatel, USA, Inc., cited in note 102. In DSC Communications Corp. v. Pulse Communications, 170 F.3d 1354 (Fed. Cir. 1999), the Federal Circuit Court of Appeals ruled that a trade-secret misappropriation under Virginia law is not preempted by § 301 of the Copyright Act because it "requires 'misappropriation' of information, either by a person who used improper means or by a person who knew or had reason to know that the information was derived through improper means or from or through a person who owed a duty not to reveal it, or by accident or mistake."

104. 17 U.S.C. § 301(a). See T.B. Harms Co. v. Eliscer, 339 F.2d 823 (2nd Cir. 1964), cert. denied, 381 U.S. 15 (1965), in which the Second Circuit Court of Appeals held that an action arises under the Copyright Act if, and only if, the complaint is for a remedy expressly granted by the act, or requires construction of the act, or presents a case where the distinctive policy of the act requires that federal principles control disposition of the claim.

105. Kodadek v. ViaCom International, Inc., 152 F.3d 1209 (9th Cir. 1998). See also Alcatel USA., cited in note 102, wherein the Fifth Circuit Court of Appeals ruled that an action for misappropriation under Texas common law of unfair competition was preempted because, according to the court, misappropriation does not require any element beyond those required for copyright infringement.

In Wendt v. Host International, Inc., 125 F.3d 806 (9th Cir. 1997), the Ninth Circuit Court of Appeals stated that a right of publicity claim is not preempted by the federal copyright act if the claim contains elements that are different from copyright infringement, but if all a claimant is seeking is to prevent a party from exhibiting a copyrighted work, the claimant is "making a claim equivalent to an exclusive right within the general scope of copyright."

In Baltimore Orioles, Inc. v. Major League Baseball Players, Ass'n, 805 F.2d 662 (7th Cir. 1986), the Seventh Circuit Court of Appeals ruled that a challenge to a television broadcast of live games without consent as a right of publicity violation was preempted.

106. National Basketball Ass'n v. Motorola, Inc., cited in note 101.

107. The Second Circuit Court of Appeals in National Basketball Ass'n, cited in note 101, decided that § 301 of the Copyright Act bars state law misappropriation claims with respect to uncopyrightable as well as copyrightable elements. It determined that adoption of a partial preemption doctrine would "expand significantly the reach of state law claims and render the preemption intended by Congress unworkable." It was of the opinion that public domain material should not be protected by permitting state law to grant exclusive rights in that material. Thus, according to the Second Circuit, the "subject matter of copyright" that is preempted by § 301 must include all works of a "type" covered by the Copyright Act if the works are not protected directly by the act.

108. Cited in note 94.

109. Leigh v. Warner Bros., 10 F. Supp. 2d 1371 (S.D.Ga. 1998), aff'd in part, rev. in part, and remanded, 212 F.3d 1210 (11th Cir. 2000).

110. See discussion in reporter's notes to Uniform Computer Transactions Act, Uniform Laws Commission, 1999, p. 21.

111. Discussion in ProCD, Inc. v. Zeidenberg, 86 F.3d 1447 (7th Cir. 1996).

112. Id.

113. Microsoft Corp. v. Harmony Computers & Electronics, 846 F. Supp. 208 (E.D.N.Y. 1994).

114. Reporter's Notes at § 105.

115. Reporter's Notes at § 102.

PART III

HERITAGE

CHAPTER 9

NATURAL HERITAGE PROTECTION

> Here is your country. Cherish these natural wonders. Cherish the natural resources. Cherish the history and romance as a sacred heritage, for your children, and your children's children. Do not let selfish or greedy interests skin your country of its beauty, its riches, or its romance.
>
> THEODORE ROOSEVELT

> The nation behaves well if it treats its natural resources as assets which it must turn over to the next generation increased, and not impaired, in value.
>
> THEODORE ROOSEVELT

Copyright laws provide an important legal resource for museums as they seek to protect and preserve their artistic collections and correspondingly to provide for a cultural legacy in artworks for present and future generations. Still, as noted in Chapter 8, copyright laws are limited in their application. Museum officials must look to, and have a knowledge of, other laws, both national and international, that protect artistic and other cultural treasures to procure guidance in preserving the artistic and cultural objects in their collections. Indeed the code of ethics adopted by the International Council of Museums (ICOM)[1] requires its member museums to conform to all national and local laws, and to respect the legislation of other States, that impact their operations.[2]

Part III (Chapters 9–11) of this text summarizes laws, both national and international, that protect the natural and cultural heritage. Chapters 9 and 10 examine the national and some state laws that are important for the protection of (1) the natural heritage (Chapter 9), and (2) the cultural heritage (Chapter 10). Chapter 9 includes a brief summary of the international convention for the protection of the natural heritage, and Chapter 11 reviews international conventions that seek international protection of the cultural and natural heritage.

A. LAWS PROTECTING THE NATURAL HERITAGE

As natural history museums seek to protect and preserve the natural heritage and for those museums that collect biological, zoological, and geological specimens, laws protecting wildlife and natural resources become important to museum personnel. Numerous statutes and regulations curb the misuse of natural resources and wildlife. The ICOM Code of Ethics for Museums[3] states that museums should not acquire biological or geological specimens that have been collected, sold, or otherwise transferred in contravention of local, national, regional, or international law or treaty relating to wildlife protection or natural history conservation. The ICOM Code of Ethics[4] also affirms that museums which have collections that include live botanical or zoological specimens should give special consideration to the natural and social environment from which these specimens were derived as well as any local, national, regional, or international law or treaty relating to wildlife protection or natural history conservation.[5]

1. The Convention on International Trade in Endangered Species of Wild Fauna and Flora

The Convention on International Trade in Endangered Species of Wild Fauna and Flora (CITES)[6] was drafted to ensure that the international trade in plants and animals did not threaten the survival of the wild. The Preamble to CITES states that "international co-operation is essential for the protection of certain species of wild fauna and flora against over-exploitation through international trade." The Convention governs and monitors the external trade in many species of animals and plants through import and export permit requirements from or to a foreign country to ensure the global protection and survival of wildlife and plants. CITES assigns different levels of protection to different species; these species are divided into three appendices to the Convention. Appendix 1 provides the highest level of protection for the most critically endangered species. CITES places an absolute ban on international trade in Appendix 1 species for "primarily commercial purposes."[7]

At least 176 countries have ratified CITES. The United States implemented the convention in 1973 through enactment of the Endangered Species Act (ESA; discussed below).[8] The ESA authorizes the Secretary of the Interior to promulgate CITES-based regulations;[9] and the Department of the Interior has issued regulations that mirror the language of CITES.[10] An import permit from the United States and a valid foreign export permit issued by the country of origin are required to import into the United States from a foreign country any wildlife or plant listed in the appendices to the Convention. To be a valid foreign document, export permits from a foreign country must be signed by a management authority from a country that is a party to the Convention. For export from countries that are not parties to the Convention, special documents in the form of an import-export permit and a letter from the proper authority are required. A U.S. export permit is required to export wildlife and plants from the United States.

Example 1. In United States v. Place, 693 F.3d 219 (1st Cir. 2012), an individual was convicted in a jury trial in Massachusetts for charges related to the illegal trafficking of sperm-whale teeth and narwhal tusks in violation of CITES as implemented by the ESA and regulations authorized by the ESA. The individual had sold various antiques, artifacts, and Nantucket-related paraphernalia for decades from a shop on Nantucket island and over the Internet. An apparently lucrative element of the individual's business was selling scrimshawed narwhal tusks and sperm-whale teeth (teeth carved with images and designs) to wealthy Nantucket tourists eager for a piece of the island's whaling history. He also sold uninscribed, or "raw," teeth to local scrimshanders-artisans who would then carve designs into the teeth. He frequently obtained tusks and teeth—both scrimshawed and raw—over the Internet and sold them for a substantial profit. The sperm whale is listed in CITES Appendix 1. The First Circuit Court of Appeals noted that international trade in sperm-whale teeth and narwhal tusks requires an export permit, that international trade in sperm-whale teeth requires an additional import permit, and that the species cannot be obtained primarily for commercial purposes. The individual contended he did not know that his trafficking was illegal; he stated he thought that old, scrimshawed, and native teeth were exempt from regulation. The First Circuit determined there was substantial evidence that the individual knew his conduct was illegal, and the court upheld his conviction.

Example 2. In Marcum v. Salazar, 694 F.3d 123 (D.C. Cir. 2012), applicants for permits from the U.S. Fish and Wildlife Service (FWS) to import hunting trophies taken from elephant hunts in Zambia filed a lawsuit claiming that the FWS had unlawfully denied their permit requests. Each applicant had killed at least one elephant in Zambia for sport and then applied for an import permit to import the trophy into the United States. The District of Columbia Circuit Court of Appeals dismissed their appeal.

Example 3. In Conservation Force v. Salazar, 699 F.3d 538 (D.C. Cir. 2012), the District of Columbia Court of Appeals ruled that the FWS's delay in processing for nearly nine years applications for permits to import Canadian wood bison as hunting trophies did not constitute a violation of the ESA under the ESA's citizen-suit provision. Organizations and individuals that supported sustainable hunting of Canadian wood bison brought an action against the Secretary of the Interior and the FWS for its delay in processing their applications and requested recovery of their attorney's fees. The appellate court stated that the delay by the FWS in processing the applications was an instance of agency delay on a matter not subject to firm time constraints. At the time the individuals applied for permits, the Canadian wood bison was classified as "endangered" under the ESA. Later, in 2012, the wood bison was reclassified from endangered to threatened status. On remand of the case directing the FWS to reconsider its denial of the application to import trophies of the Canadian wood bison that were taken legally in Canada, the district court, in Conservation Force v. Salazar, 915 F. Supp. 2d 1 (D.D.C. 2013), pointed out that although importation of threatened species is, like the import of endangered species, generally prohibited under the ESA, a person seeking to import a threatened species has more options. The court noted the wood bison is listed in Appendix 2 of CITES and a Canadian export permit would satisfy the requisite showing of CITES. The court refused to relieve the FWS from the court's remand.

Example 4. In United States v. Long Cove Seafood, Inc., 582 F.2d 159 (2nd Cir. 1978), an individual took wildlife in violation of state conservation laws. The federal government filed charges against the individual under the National Stolen Property act (NSPA; discussion in Chapter 6 of the NSPA and its application of the taking of cultural property found in a country that has declared ownership in artifacts). The Second Circuit Court of Appeals decided that the State of New York had not asserted a true ownership interest in wildlife that would provide for a conviction under the NSPA. The appellate court noted that property rights to wildlife are obtained by reducing them to possession. It refused to accept the government's broad definition of "stolen" property and ruled that wild fish, birds, and animals are, as a general rule, owned by no one. Thus, the Second Circuit refused to convict the individual under the NSPA.

2. Migratory Bird Treaty Act

The Migratory Bird Treaty Act (MBTA),[11] which was enacted in 1918, makes it unlawful to pursue, capture, kill, purchase, transport, import, or carry a migratory bird (or any part of a migratory bird or a nest or egg of this bird) that is included in the terms of the conventions between the United States and Great Britain, between the United States and the United Mexican States, between the United States and Japan, and between the United States and the (former) Union of Soviet Socialist Republics. The Secretary of the Interior may determine when, and to what extent, it is compatible with the convention to permit hunting, taking, killing, and sale of migratory birds. The temperature, distribution, abundance, economic value, and breeding habits of the migratory flight of the birds must be considered. The act makes it unlawful to ship or transport from one state to another a bird (or a part of a bird or a nest or egg of a bird) that was captured or killed contrary to the laws of a state or contrary to the laws of Canada.[12]

Example 5. In United States v. Tawahongva, 456 F. Supp. 2d 1120 (D. Ariz. 2006), the court upheld the conviction of a member of the Hopi tribe under the MBTA for failing to obtain a permit prior to taking golden eagles. The FWS searched a fenced area behind a Hopi tribe member's residence, within the boundaries of the Hopi reservation, and seized two live golden eagles. The court ruled that the MBTA did not violate the tribe member's right to the free exercise of his religion.

3. Marine Mammal Protection Act

The Marine Mammal Protection Act,[13] which was enacted in 1972, provided for a moratorium on the taking and importation of marine mammals and marine mammal products. Prior to Congress enacting the ESA, Congress determined that certain species and population stocks of marine mammals were in danger of extinction as a result of individuals' activities.[14] Congress determined that marine mammals are resources of great international significance, aesthetic and recreational as well as economic. Congress decided these mammals should be protected and encouraged to develop to the greatest extent feasible, commensurate with sound policies of resource management, and that the primary objective of their management should be to maintain the health and stability of the marine ecosystem. A marine mammal is any mammal that is adapted morphologically to the marine environment or that primarily inhabits the marine environment.[15] No part of a marine mammal may be taken or imported without a permit.[16] No person or vessel may take a marine mammal in waters or lands under the jurisdiction of the United States or use a port or harbor for a purpose in any manner connected with the taking or importation of marine mammals, or marine-mammal products, without a permit.[17]

The act does not apply to any Native American, Aleut, or Eskimo who resides in Alaska and who dwells on the coast of the North Pacific Ocean or the Arctic Ocean if the taking is for subsistence purposes or is for purposes of creating and selling authentic native articles of handicrafts and clothing.[18]

4. Endangered Species Act

The Endangered Species Act (ESA)[19] serves as the means by which the United States meets its responsibilities to CITES. Congress determined that certain species of fish, wildlife, and plants in the United States have been rendered extinct as a consequence of economic growth and development untempered by adequate concern and conservation and that other species of fish, wildlife, and plants have been so depleted in numbers that they were in danger of, or threatened with, extinction.[20] It enacted the ESA in 1973 to provide a means to conserve the ecosystems on which endangered and threatened species depend and to initiate a program for the protection of affected species.[21] The act authorizes the Secretary of the Interior to determine which species are endangered or threatened and specifies that the list be set forth in the regulations.[22] Endangered or threatened species may not be possessed, sold, carried, transported, imported, or taken without a permit.

Permits may be issued to acquire endangered or threatened species for scientific purposes or to enhance the propagation or survival of affected species.[23]

Example 6. In United States v. Species of Wildlife Consisting of Fully Mounted Leopard, 404 F. Supp. 1298 (E.D.N.Y. 1975), an individual purchased stuffed animals from the Republic of Kenya, Africa, pursuant to a contract dated August 1, 1972, and imported the stuffed animals into the United States on February 26, 1973. One was a leopard slain prior to March 30, 1972, the date on which leopards were placed on the endangered species list. The FWS seized the stuffed leopard upon its importation into the United States, and the individual was fined $5,000. The court held that there was no exemption from the ESA because the contract for purchase of the animal was entered into after leopards were placed on the endangered list. However, the individual was assessed a fine of only $10 because the animal was killed prior to March 30, 1972, and, thus, prior to the effective date of the ESA. The court did uphold forfeiture of the animal.

Example 7. In United States v. Kepler, 531 F.2d 797 (6th Cir. 1976), an individual was convicted for illegally transporting animals in interstate commerce. The individual had transported a leopard and a cougar from Florida to a zoo in Kentucky; he had not applied for a permit. The court upheld his conviction under the ESA. The defendant had claimed an exemption from the act for animals held in a controlled environment, but the court noted that the exemption does not apply if the animals are held in the course of commercial activity.

Example 8. The Army Corps of Engineers proposed a project at the site of a harbor where the FWS had not designated a critical habitat for the akoko, an endangered plant that grew at the site. Environmental groups filed suit to require the FWS to designate a habitat. The Ninth Circuit Court of Appeals noted in Enos v. Marsh, 769 F.2d 1363 (9th Cir. 1985), that the ESA requires federal agencies to ensure their actions are not likely to jeopardize the continued existence of an endangered or threatened species or result in the destruction or adverse modification of the critical habitat of a species. The Ninth Circuit ruled that because the plant was found in a nonnative habitat and because biological and physical features essential to its existence were unknown, the plant's habitat was incapable of being determined. Thus, the court held that the FWS was not required to designate a critical habitat for the akoko.

There is a three-step process to ensure compliance with the requirements of the ESA when a federal project is being considered: (1) a federal agency proposing to take action must inquire of the FWS whether a species that is listed or proposed to be listed may be present in the area of the proposed action; (2) if an endangered or threatened species is present, the agency must prepare a biological assessment to determine whether the species is likely to be affected by the action; and (3) if the assessment determines that the endangered species or threatened species is likely to be adversely affected, the agency must formally consult with the FWS. After initiation of the consultation, the federal agency must not make any irreversible commitment of resources that would foreclose an alternative action that would not jeopardize the existence of the endangered species. The formal consultation results in the issuance of a biological opinion by the FWS. If the proposed action would jeopardize the species, the action may not go forward unless the FWS can suggest an alternative.

Example 9. Environmental groups were concerned that an endangered species in a foreign country was in danger of extinction. They wanted to conserve the ecosystem for the species and were concerned about action of a federal agency in that country that could destroy the ecosystem. The Secretary of the Interior had promulgated a rule interpreting the ESA as being applicable only to actions within the United States or on the high seas. In Lujan v. Defenders of Wildlife, 504 U.S. 555 (1992), the environmental groups filed suit to challenge the rule. The Secretary of the Interior contended that the environmental groups did not have "standing" (right to sue) to challenge the rule because they had not demonstrated they had suffered an injury in fact (discussion of standing to sue in Chapter 1). The Supreme Court agreed in Lujan that environmental groups did not have standing to challenge the rule promulgated by the Secretary of the Interior, which interpreted the ESA as being applicable only to actions within the United States or on the high seas. Although one Justice concurred in the majority opinion because he was of the opinion the ESA does not apply to activities in foreign countries, this Justice thought a person who has visited the critical habitat of an endangered species has a professional interest in preserving the species and its habitat and that interest is sufficient to confer standing.

Example 10. An owner of livestock set a trap for grizzly bears because the bears had been attacking his livestock on a nightly basis. When a grizzly bear was killed as a result of the trap, the livestock owner was penalized under the ESA. In Christy v. Hodel, 847 F.2d 1324 (9th Cir. 1988), the Ninth Circuit Court of Appeals rejected the livestock owner's argument that destruction of his private property by protected wildlife constituted a governmental taking of his property. The court also ruled that the livestock owner did not have a fundamental right to kill the grizzly bear in order to protect his livestock.

The ESA is not applicable to the taking of an endangered species by a Native American, Aleut, or Eskimo who is an Alaskan native residing in Alaska or any nonnative permanent resident of an Alaskan native village if the taking is primarily for subsistence purposes.[24] Nonedible byproducts of species taken under this exception may be sold in interstate commerce when made into authentic native articles of handicrafts and clothing. The exemption does not apply to any nonnative resident of an Alaskan native village found by the Secretary of the Interior not to be dependent primarily upon the taking of fish and wildlife for consumption or for the creation and sale of authentic native articles of handicrafts and clothing.

Example 11. In United States v. Nuesca, 945 F.2d 254 (9th Cir. 1991), the Ninth Circuit Court of Appeals addressed the issue of whether a Native Hawaiian could be convicted under the ESA. A Native Hawaiian was convicted under the ESA for taking green sea turtles and an Hawaiian monk seal. The Native Hawaiian contended there was an equal protection violation because the act exempted native Alaskans but not native Hawaiians. However, the Ninth Circuit affirmed the conviction of the Native Hawaiian, rejecting his claim that the act violated the equal protection clause.

5. Lacey Act

The Lacey Act[25] makes it unlawful to import, export, transport, sell, receive, or purchase wild mammals, wild birds, or fish in violation of a federal law, regulation, or treaty or wild mammals, wild birds, or fish that the Secretary of the Interior determines by regulation to be injurious to human beings or to agriculture, horticulture, forestry, or wildlife within the United States. The act also makes it unlawful to trap, capture, or willfully disturb or kill a bird, fish, or wild animal of any kind on lands or waters set apart or reserved as sanctuaries, refuges, or breeding grounds for these birds, fish, or animals. The act prohibits the shipping in interstate commerce of wild animals unless they are marked plainly with names and addresses of the shipper and consignee and with an accurate statement indicating the contents of the package.[26] A person who violates the Lacey Act is subject to both civil and criminal penalties.[27] Further, any wildlife imported, exported, transported, sold, received, acquired, or purchased in violation of the act is subject to forfeiture.[28]

The Lacey Act has two levels of criminality. A person who transports, buys, or sells wildlife in knowing violation of any law, treaty, or regulation, including CITES, the ESA, and CITES regulations, is guilty of a felony. A person who transports, buys, or sells wildlife that the person should have known violated a law, treaty, or regulation is guilty of a misdemeanor.[29]

6. Bald and Golden Eagle Protection Act

The Bald and Golden Eagle Protection Act (BGEPA),[30] which was enacted in 1940, provides that the bald eagle, commonly known as the American eagle, and any golden eagle, may not be taken, possessed, sold, purchased, transported, exported, or imported at any time or in any manner. The prohibitions extend to any part of an eagle, including its nest or eggs, and apply whether the eagle is dead or alive. (The Migratory Bird Treaty Act, discussed above, also prohibits the possession and taking golden eagles except as authorized by law.) The bald or golden eagle may be taken or possessed for scientific or exhibition purposes in public museums, scientific societies, and zoological parks, but a permit must be obtained from the Secretary of the Interior.[31]

> Example 12. In U.S. v. Smith, 29 F.3d 270 (7th Cir. 1994), the Seventh Circuit Court of Appeals ruled that scienter (intent) is not required for a criminal conviction. The Seventh Circuit affirmed the conviction of an individual who received eagle feathers in the mail from a friend in Canada's Vancouver Island. The individual planned to use the feathers in a macrame project, but she testified she knew she was not supposed to possess eagle feathers. The feathers were discovered by U.S. Customs. The court ruled federal agents are not restricted by the Fourth Amendment restriction on search and seizures when they conduct routine searches.

Many Native American tribes point to the BGEPA as a federal act that interferes with their religious practices. They contend it violates the American

Indian Religious Freedom Act (AIRFA) as well as their First Amendment rights and rights provided them by various treaties (AIRFA is discussed in Chapter 10).

The U.S. Department of the Interior, through its FWS, currently will issue permits to take and possess eagle parts for religious purposes but only to members of federally recognized Indian tribes that are eligible to receive services from the United States Bureau of Indian Affairs.[32] Members of recognized Indian entities can obtain permits to take, possess, or transport dead eagle parts for religious activities, but permits are not granted to obtain live eagles or live eggs of eagles.[33] Application for a permit must state the name of the tribe and the name of the tribal religious ceremony for which eagles are required.

Dead eagle parts and feathers currently are sent to the national Eagle Repository in Commerce City, Colorado (the repository was previously in Pocatello, Idaho). The repository receives eagles and eagle parts and distributes them to permit holders on a first-come first-served basis. However, demand generally exceeds supply and applicants have had to wait up to three years for an eagle carcass and six to nine months for loose feathers.[34]

Example 13. In United States v. Abeyta, 632 F. Supp. 1301 (D.N. M. 1986), a resident and member of the Isleta Pueblo and a member of the Katsina Society (a religious society that engages in traditional ceremonial practices deeply rooted in ancient Pueblo religion), took parts of a golden eagle to procure its feathers for use in a religious ceremony of the Katsina Society. It is a tradition and lore of the Katsina Society to require ceremonial use of eagle feathers and parts. According to members of the Katsina Society, the eagle is a primary messenger to the spirit world and the ceremonial use of its feathers permits the living to communicate with the spirit world beyond. There is a procedure established by the Secretary of the Interior to obtain eagle feathers and eagle parts from a repository established by the FWS. The court acknowledged the importance of protecting and preserving the golden eagle even though it was not listed as an endangered species but held that the administrative apparatus erected to accommodate Native Americans' religious needs (the repository) was offensive and ineffectual. The tribal member in this case did not avail himself of the procedure. When the Department of the Interior filed a violation notice charging the individual with knowing possession of parts of a golden eagle without a permit, he asserted his right to take parts of the eagle under the Treaty of Guadalupe Hidalgo and the First Amendment. Although the federal district court ruled in Abeyta that the taking was a lawful and protected expression of religious liberty secured by the Treaty of Guadalupe Hidalgo and by the First Amendment, the Supreme Court held in U.S. v. Dion, 476 U.S. 734 (1986), that the BGEPA is read as abrogating the rights of Native Americans to take bald and golden eagles pursuant to treaties with the United States. The Supreme Court ruled that Congress specifically intended to prohibit Native Americans from hunting bald or golden eagles except pursuant to a permit. Thus, according to the Supreme Court, any treaty rights of the Native Americans were abrogated.

Example 14. In U.S. v. Thirty-Eight Golden Eagles or Eagle Parts, 649 F. Supp. 269 (D. Nevada, 1986), the government sought the forfeiture of eagles and eagle parts obtained from a member of the Red Lake Bank of Chippewa Indians for allegedly violating the Eagle Protection Act. The court ruled that the act did not violate the tribe member's free exercise rights or AIRFA. It further held that the tribe member failed to establish a violation of a treaty between the Red Lake Bank of Chippewa Indians and the United States.

Example 15. In U.S. v. Hardman, 297 F.3d 1116 (10th Cir. 2002), the Tenth Circuit Court of Appeals ruled that excluding sincere practitioners of Native American religions who were not members of federally recognized tribes from applying for a permit for possession of eagle feathers would violate the Religious Freedom Restoration Act (RFRA)[35] unless the government can show that limiting permits for eagle feathers to members of federally recognized tribes is the least restrictive means of advancing the government's interests in preserving eagle populations and protection of Native American culture. [The Supreme Court ruled in Lyng v. Northwest Indian Center Protective Assoc., 485 U.S. 439 (1988), discussed in Chapter 10, that AIRFA does not provide for a private right of action; thus, tribes have sought protection for their sacred sites through the RFRA.] Under the RFRA, the government cannot substantially burden a person's exercise of religion unless the government demonstrates that the burden to the person is in furtherance of a compelling governmental interest and is the least restrictive means of furthering that compelling interest.

Example 16. In United States v. Friday, 525 F.3d 938 (10th Cir. 2008), a member of the Northern Arapaho Tribe of Wyoming was charged with violating the BGEPA after he shot a bald eagle without a permit for use in a Sun Dance. The Tenth Circuit Court of Appeals decided that the government has tried to accommodate Native American religions while still achieving its compelling interests. The Tenth Circuit commented that "while that accommodation may be more burdensome than the Northern Arapaho would prefer, and may sometimes subordinate their interests to other policies not of their choosing, the law can only accommodate religion." The Tenth Circuit decided that "it cannot wholly exempt religion from the reach of the law."

Example 17. In United States v. Vasquez-Ramos, 531 F.3d 987 (9th Cir. 2008), two Native Americans who were not members of federally recognized Indian tribes were indicted for possessing feathers and talons of bald and golden eagles without a permit in violation of the BGEPA. The Ninth Circuit Court of Appeals ruled that the BGEPA does not violate the RFRA. The Ninth Circuit stated that the defendants could not complain their rights under the RFRA were violated by the government's refusal to expand the government's eagle collection and distribution practices.

Example 18. In United States v. Wilgus, 638 F.3d 1274 (10th Cir. 2011), the Tenth Circuit Court of Appeals ruled that the government's eagle-feather protection scheme was the least restrictive means of furthering the government's compelling interests in protecting eagles and Native American religions and that it does not violate the RFRA. The Tenth Circuit decided that the government's compelling interests in protecting eagles and in protecting the religion of federally recognized tribes, and not in preserving Native American religion generally, were balanced and advanced in the least restrictive manner by the government's criminalization of possession of eagle feathers without a permit, which is available only to members of recognized tribes.

Example 19. An individual donated eagle artifacts to a museum of Native American cultures and claimed a charitable contribution deduction for the fair market value of the artifacts. The IRS denied the deduction and contended that the individual violated the BGEPA and the ESA when he purchased the eagle parts. In Sammons v. Comm., 838 F.2d 330 (9th Cir. 1988), the Ninth Circuit Court of Appeals ruled that donors of eagle artifacts could deduct the cost of the artifacts but not the fair market value. The Ninth Circuit decided that even though the donors may have made an illegal contract when they purchased the eagle artifacts, they had sufficient ownership interest in the artifacts to donate them to a museum. The court determined that the donors should not be denied a deduction based upon public policy by deciding that permitting a deduction for contribution of the eagle parts to a museum would not frustrate severely or immediately national or state policy. According to the Ninth Circuit, permitting a deduction, but only for the cost of the artifacts, would not encourage necessarily the acquisition or killing of protected bird species.[36]

7. Free-Roaming Horse and Burro Act

Congress has declared that wild free-roaming horses and burros are living symbols of the historic and pioneer spirit of the West. According to Congress, they contribute to the diversity of life forms within the nation and enrich the lives of the American people. Because Congress determined that these horses and burros were fast disappearing from the American scene, Congress adopted a policy of protecting wild free-roaming horses and burros from capture, branding, harassment, or death. The Free-Roaming Horse and Burro Act[37] prescribes criminal penalties for the removal, or the conversion to private use, of wild free-roaming horses or burros on public lands without authority from the Secretary of the Interior or the Secretary of Agriculture.[38]

All wild free-roaming horses and burros are under the jurisdiction of the Secretary of the Interior for the purpose of management and protection. The Secretary may cause excess wild free-roaming horses and burros to be captured humanely and removed for private maintenance and care if the Secretary determines an adoption demand exists by qualified individuals and determines the individuals will provide humane treatment and care.

Example 20. In United States v. Tomlinson, 475 F. Supp. 1531 (D. Wyo. 1983), the court found that the defendants captured wild horses under a "shroud of secrecy" and removed them from public lands without giving notice to, or receiving consent from, the Secretary of the Interior. The court noted that the defendants sold the horses to a slaughterhouse for commercial purposes. The defendants had been charged with removing wild and free-roaming horses from federal public lands and with the interstate transportation of stolen property under the National Stolen Property Act (NSPA). The NPSA made the offense a felony whereas the Wild Free-Roaming Horses and Burros Act provided punishment of only imprisonment for no more than one year. The court decided the Wild and Free-Roaming Horses and Burros Act indicates the United States has asserted a true ownership interest in wild horses and burros present on federal public lands. The court determined the act supersedes the common law that wild fish, birds, and animals are owned by no one and distinguished the court's ruling in United States v. Long Cove Seafood, Inc., discussed in Example 4, wherein the Second Circuit Court of Appeals refused to convict an individual under the NSPA. The court ruled in Tomlinson that the individuals who took the wild horses could be indicted under the NSPA.

B. REQUIRED PERMITS

Permits must be obtained both to import and to transport certain plants and wildlife.[39] For injurious wildlife, endangered species, marine mammals, or migratory birds imported into the United States, a completed Declaration for Importation of Fish or Wildlife (Form 3-177) must be filed by the importer with the district director of customs at the port of entry.[40] All wildlife imported into the United States must be cleared by an FWS office.[41] Wildlife must be imported into the United States only at designated ports of entry.[42] However, the director of the Bureau of Sport Fisheries and Wildlife can issue a permit authorizing a scientist to import wildlife for scientific purposes at other ports of entry.[43] Wildlife also may be imported at other ports of entry in order to minimize deterioration or loss.[44]

No duty is required for importation of natural history articles but an institutional form (Customs Form 3325) or a bond (Customs Form 301) may be required.[45] Specimens of archaeology, mineralogy, or natural history (including specimens of botany or zoology other than live zoological specimens) imported for a public or private scientific collection for exhibition or other educational or scientific use, and not for sale or other commercial use, are duty free.[46] The common and scientific name of the specimens must be listed as well as the name and address of the importer and the name of the carrier.[47] If the laws or regulations of the country of origin restrict the possession or transportation of wildlife, the importer may be required to produce foreign documentation showing that those laws have not been violated. This documentation must be in the form of original permits from the foreign country or copies of any importing contracts or agreements.[48] While an import-export license is required for any person engaged in a business as an importer or exporter of wildlife, public museums, or other public scientific or educational institutions, importing or exporting wildlife for research or educational purposes, and not for resale, are exempt from the license requirement.[49] However, records must be maintained that fully and correctly disclose each importation or exportation of wildlife and the subsequent disposition of the wildlife. Duly authorized FWS officers must have access at reasonable times, upon notice, to the museum premises to examine the inventory of imported wildlife and the required records. An import-export permit (Form 3-200) must be obtained from the U.S. Department of the Interior, Director of Fish and Wildlife.

A customs officer may refuse clearance of imported wildlife for the following reasons: a federal law or regulation has been violated; the correct identity of the wildlife has not been established; required foreign documentation is not authentic; or the importer has filed an incomplete declaration of importation.

A permit is required to collect scientific specimens.[50] Applications are submitted to the FWS using Form 3-200. The application should indicate the common and scientific names of the species to be covered by the permit; the number, age, and sex of the species; and the activity to be authorized. The application should describe the institution and the facilities where the wildlife will be used or displayed and housed. The resume of the person who will care for wildlife should be included. A full statement of the reasons why the applicant should obtain the permit should be included.[51] Copies of all contracts and agreements pursuant to the activities to be authorized must be attached. For endangered species, the permittee must submit a written report to the director of the FWS of her activities pursuant to the permit not later than ten days after completion of the activity. The death or escape of any living wildlife covered by the permit must be reported immediately to the office of the FWS. The carcass of any dead wildlife covered by the permit must be stored in a manner that will preserve its use as a scientific specimen.[52] The holder of a permit must carry it at all times while in the field. Reports may be required to be filed regarding activities conducted under the permit. Written documentation of all taking, possession, transportation, sale, purchase, exportation, or importation of wildlife pursuant to the permit must be retained for five years after the date of the issuance of the permit.[53]

Packages containing wild animals or birds cannot be shipped in interstate commerce unless they are plainly marked with the names and addresses of the shipper and consignee and with an accurate statement indicating the contents of the package.[54] "Marking permits" can be obtained from the FWS to permit shipping across the United States by marking each package with the label.

Because states also are authorized to make and enforce laws and regulations regarding the taking and/or possession of wildlife, state laws and regulations must be consulted as well.[55]

NOTES

1. International Council of Museums (ICOM) Code of Ethics for Museums (2013). As noted previously, the ICOM Code of Professional Ethics was adopted unanimously by the General Assembly of ICOM in 1986. It was amended in 2001 and retitled ICOM Code of Ethics for Museums in 2004.

2. ICOM Code of Ethics for Museums, cited in note 1, at 7.1.

3. Id. at 2.6.

4. Id. at 2.7.

5. There are criminal sanctions, as well as civil penalties, in the United States for obtaining or possessing certain wildlife without proper permits. See 18 U.S.C. §§ 41–42; 16 U.S.C. §§ 705–6; 16 U.S. C. § 1375, 16 U.S.C. § 1540, and 16 U.S.C. § 3373. States have varying laws and regulations. A museum seeking scientific specimens must consult both local laws and federal laws regarding the particular specimens sought. Discussion of required permits at notes 39–55 and accompanying text.

See "Acceptable Field Methods in Mammalogy: Preliminary Guidelines Approved by the American Society of Mammalogists," American Society of Mammalogists, *Journal of Mammalogy*, 1987, for guidelines on acceptable field methods in mammalogy.

6. 27 U.S.T. 1087 (March 3, 1973). Text available at www.unesco.org.

7. Id., Article III(3)(c).

8. 16 U.S.C. §§ 1531–40. Implementing Provisions of the Endangered Species Act at 16 U.S.C. §§ 1537A and 1538(c)(1).

9. Id. at § 1537.

10. 50 C.F.R. §§ 23.1–23.92.

11. 16 U.S.C. §§ 703–12.

12. 16 U.S.C. § 705. An employee of the Department of the Interior authorized to enforce the provisions of the act has authority to arrest any person committing a violation of the act. It is a felony offense to violate the act. 16 U.S.C. §§ 706, 707.

13. 16 U.S.C. §§ 1361–1407.

14. Id. at § 1361.

15. Id. at § 1362(5).

16. Id. at § 1371. This includes the raw, dressed, or dyed fur or skin. Permits may be issued for taking and importation for purposes of scientific research and for public display if the taking or importation is reviewed first by the Marine Mammal Commission.

17. Id. at. § 1372. Any person who violates the act may be assessed a civil penalty of not more than $10,000 for each violation. Id. at § 1375. Any person who knowingly violates the act is subject to criminal penalties including a fine of up to $20,000 for each violation and/or imprisonment for up to a year.

18. Id. at § 1371(b). Only authentic native articles of handicrafts and clothing may be sold in interstate commerce.

19. Cited in note 8.

20. 16 U.S.C. § 1531(a).

21. Section 1538 of the act exempted from its coverage any fish or wildlife that was held in captivity or in a controlled environment on December 28, 1973, or the date of the publication in the Federal Register of a final regulation adding the fish or wildlife species to the list of endangered species. The act did not apply to raptors or their progeny legally held in captivity or in a controlled environment on November 10, 1978, until the time the raptor or progeny was returned intentionally to a wild state.

22. 16 U.S.C. § 1533. A list of species on the endangered list are set out in federal regulations at 50 C.F.R. § 17.11(h).

23. 16 U.S.C. § 1539. Each application for a permit is published in the Federal Register, thereby inviting views or arguments regarding the application.

24. Id. at § 1539(e).

25. 18 U.S.C. § 41 and 16 U.S.C. § 3371–78.

26. 16 U.S.C. § 3372(b). The Lacey Act makes it unlawful to transport a wild animal or bird to the United States under inhumane or unhealthful conditions. 18 U.S.C. § 42(c).

27. The act provided for civil penalties of $10,000 for a violation of the act and criminal penalties of a fine up to $20,000 and five years imprisonment. 16 U.S.C. § 3373.

28. Id. at § 3374.

29. Id. at § 3373(d)(1)-(2)

30. 16 U.S.C. § 668.

31. Id. at. § 668a. An employee of the Department of the Interior who was authorized to enforce the act could arrest any person in possession without a permit of any part of a bald or golden eagle.

32. See 50 C.F.R. § 22.22. The tribes are recognized and listed under the Federally Recognized Tribal List of 1994, 25 U.S.C. § 479a-1. An applicant for a permit to obtain eagles or eagle parts for use in a religious ceremony must attach a certification of enrollment in a federally recognized Indian tribe.

33. 50 C.F.R. § 22.22.

34. Discussion in U.S. v. Hardman, 297 F.3d 1116 (10th Cir. 2002). To accommodate the religious practice of the Hopi, the Fish and Wildlife Service has promulgated regulations permitting Hopi lawfully to obtain and possess golden eagles for their religious use.

35. 42 U.S.C. § 2000bb.

36. See discussion in Anne-Marie Rhodes, 31 Cardozo Arts & Enter. L.J. 45 (2012) of issues relating to the estate valuation of a three-dimensional work of art by Robert Rauschenberg, a "sculptural combine" called *Canyon*, that contained a stuffed bald eagle with its wings fully extended outward from the bottom of the canvas. *Canyon* was one of the works of art, which were valued at $800 million, in the estate of art dealer and collector Ileana Sonnabend, who died in 2007. Because selling *Canyon* would subject the seller and the purchaser to criminal prosecution under the BGEPA and the Migratory Bird Treaty Act, the estate contended *Canyon* had no value for estate tax purposes. However, the IRS Art Advisory Panel valued *Canyon* at $65 million. The IRS accepted this valuation because it contended the work could be sold on the illicit market and issued a deficiency notice against the estate for $29.2 million in estate taxes plus $11.7 million in penalties. (The estate purportedly settled the case with the IRS through an agreement whereby the IRS would eliminate the estate tax and penalties after the estate donated *Canyon* to a museum.)

It is interesting that the IRS contended in the Sammons case, discussed in Example 19, that a donation of eagle feathers would have no value for income purposes because a purchase of the eagle parts would violate the BGEPA. The IRS contended the donor could not claim a charitable contribution deduction as the eagle feathers could not be sold, but the IRS also took the position that *Canyon*, which could not be sold because a sale would violate the BGEPA and the Migratory Bird Treaty Act, would have no discounted value for estate tax purposes because, according to the IRS, the work could be sold on the illicit market. (Further discussion of income and estate tax valuations of donations of eagle feathers or artworks containing eagle feathers in Chapter 4.)

37. 16 U.S.C. § 1331–40.

38. Any person who willfully removed or attempted to remove a wild, free-roaming horse or burro from public lands without authority from the Secretary, or converted a wild free-roaming horse or burro to private use without authority, or maliciously caused the death or harassment of any wild, free-roaming horse or burro was subject to a fine of not more than $2,000 and/or imprisonment. Id. at § 1338.

39. See 50 C.F.R. §§ 13.1,13.11, 13.12, 14.16, and 14.61. Procedures for obtaining permits are set out in these regulations and also on the website of the Fish and Wildlife Service.

40. 50 C.F.R. §§ 16.15, 14.31, and 14.61. See also 19 C.F.R. § 12.26.

41. 50 C.F.R. § 14.52.

42. 50 C.F.R. § 14.11, 14.12, and 14.16. The designated ports of entry arc Anchorage, Houston, Los Angeles, San Francisco, Miami, Honolulu, Chicago, Louisville, Memphis, New Orleans, New York, Seattle, Dallas/Fort Worth, Portland, Baltimore, Boston, and Atlanta. 50 C.F.R. § 14.12.

43. See 50 C.F.R. § 14.31.

44. 50 C.F.R. § 14.32.

45. See 19 C.F.R. § 10.49 and 10.75.

46. If a museum transferred the duty-free specimens within a five-year period, the museum should write U.S. Customs in Washington, D.C., for forms to use in applying for a transfer.

47. 50 C.F.R. § 14.31. For animals imported into the United States (except for those imported from Canada or Mexico), an import permit also must be secured from the U.S. Department of Agriculture. This department regulates care of live animals under the Animal Welfare Act. 7 U.S.C. § 2131. For live animals and endangered species, Form 65 must be filed with the U.S. Department of Agriculture. State permits also must be obtained for those animals listed on the federal list of rare and endangered species. For those specimens capable of carrying human disease, a permit must be obtained from the Surgeon General through the Department of Health and Human Services. Plants require additional registration through the Department of Agriculture. Marine animals must have additional registration with the Department of Commerce (National Marine Fisheries Service).

48. 50 C.F.R. § 14.52(c).

49. 50 C.F.R. §§ 14.91 and 14.92(b)(3).

50. 50 C.F.R. §§ 13.11, 17.22, and 17.32. For live animals, a permit must be secured from the Department of Agriculture; for animals capable of carrying human disease, a permit is required from the Department of Health and Human Services. For collection of scientific specimens on National Wildlife Refuges, application for a research proposal should be submitted to the refuge manager detailing the scientific work. For collection of scientific specimens in a national park, a written permit must be obtained from the superintendent, and the research proposal must be described. Permits are issued only to persons officially representing reputable scientific or educational institutions.

51. See 50 C.F.R. § 17.22.

52. Often permits are required from other agencies. For example, importation of certain birds, including parrots, require a permit from the Public Health Service (19 C.F.R. §§ 12.24 and § 12.26). Certain fowl, wild ruminants, and plant pests require a permit from the Department of Agriculture, Animal and Plant Health Inspection Service (19 C.F.R. §§ 12.14 and 12.26). Wildlife and birds imported from Mexico must be accompanied by a Mexican export permit (19 C.F.R. §§ 12.26). Importation of fowl from Canada requires a certificate issued by a Canadian government veterinarian (19 C.F.R. § 12.26).

53. 50 C.F.R. § 13.46.

54. 16 U.S.C. § 3372(b). Annual reports for collected species must be filed using Form 3-202.

55. Id. at. § 3378. For most states, one should consult the state game and fish division to obtain information on procedures to comply with state requirements. Either a permit or a hunting license usually is required.

CHAPTER 10

LAWS IN THE UNITED STATES PROTECTING CULTURAL HERITAGE

> A people without the knowledge of their past history, origin and culture is like a tree without roots.
>
> MARCUS HARVEY

> Without memory, there is no culture. Without memory, there would be no civilization, no society, no future.
>
> ELIE WIESEL

The United States has been dilatory in its efforts to preserve and to protect artistic, archaeological, and anthropological resources. As one court observed, the United States has had a "short cultural memory."[1] Still, Congress became apprehensive early in the twentieth century that historical treasures in the United States were in jeopardy and that many had been destroyed without consideration of their value. The impetus to enact legislation to preserve historical treasures within the boundaries of the United States was precipitated by two concerns. One was the recognition that, in recent years, large numbers of historic structures, landmarks, and areas had been destroyed "without adequate consideration of either the values represented therein or the possibility of preserving the destroyed properties for use in economically productive ways."[2] The second concern was the "widely shared belief that structures with special historic, cultural, or architectural significance enhance the qualify of life for all."[3] The enactment of historical preservation statutes resulted from recognition that historical treasures not only "represent the lessons of the past and embody precious features of our heritage, they serve as examples of quality for today."[4] There then evolved widespread concern that historical treasures be protected and preserved with Congress establishing a partnership with the individual states to encourage or require the preservation of buildings and areas with historic importance.[5] Further, the National Trust for Historical Preservation in the United States[6] was chartered in 1949 as a private, nonprofit organization to receive donations of sites, buildings, and objects significant in U.S. history and culture and to preserve and administer them for the public benefit.[7]

This chapter summarizes in the order of their enactment the statutes Congress has adopted to protect and preserve those historical treasures that are important in the history and culture of the United States.

A. ANTIQUITIES ACT OF 1906

The first attempt by Congress to save historic treasures within the United States was its enactment of the Antiquities Act of 1906.[8] The act provides penalties for destroying or damaging any historic ruins on public lands.[9] It prohibits the appropriation, injury, or destruction of any historic or prehistoric ruin or monument, or any object of antiquity on lands owned or controlled by the federal government.[10] Congress enacted the act in response to vandalism that occurred at the Casa Grande ruins in Arizona, but the act also represented an attempt to preserve Mount Vernon in Virginia.[11]

The Antiquities Act is limited in its application in that it subjects a person to penalties for the appropriation of any "ruin," "monument," or "object of antiquity."[12] The definition of these terms is not clear and becomes a problem in applying the act.

> Example 1. An individual appropriated face masks found in a cave on the San Carlos Indian Reservation. These masks were later identified by a San Carlos medicine man as having been made recently by another medicine man and having been used by the Apache Indians in religious ceremonies. After the religious ceremonies, the artifacts were traditionally deposited in remote places on the reservation for religious reasons and never were allowed to leave the reservation. The individual was convicted

in a federal district court under the Antiquities Act of 1906 for appropriating objects of antiquity from government land. According to a professor of anthropology who testified in the case, an "object of antiquity" can include an object that was made just yesterday if it relates to religious or social tradition of long standing. The individual appealed his conviction, contending the term "object of antiquity" is unclear in its meaning and that the Antiquities Act of 1906 is void for vagueness. In United States v. Diaz, 499 F.2d 113 (9th Cir. 1974), the Ninth Circuit Court of Appeals reversed the decision of the federal district court because it reasoned that a person must be able to know with reasonable certainty those objects he may not take. The court noted that the word "antiquity" can refer not only to the age of an object but also to the use for which the object was made and to which it was put, subjects which, the court decided, would not likely be of common knowledge. The appellate court declared the Antiquities Act to be unconstitutionally vague.

Example 2. Another individual was convicted of a violation of the Antiquities Act of 1906 for excavating a prehistoric Mimbres ruin at an archaeological site that was inhabited about A.D. 1000–1250. The individual appealed the conviction, contending the Antiquities Act of 1906 is vague and, thus, unconstitutional. In United States v. Smyer, 596 F.2d 939 (10th Cir. 1979), the Tenth Circuit Court of Appeals court upheld the conviction. It distinguished United States v. Diaz, discussed in Example 1, and noted that the Diaz case involved newly created artifacts. According to the Tenth Circuit in Smyer, a person of ordinary intelligence should know that one may not excavate a prehistoric Indian burial ground and appropriate artifacts that are 800–900 years old. The court ruled that, as the law had been applied to the prosecution of the defendants for taking artifacts from ancient sites for commercial motives, the act was not unconstitutionally vague.

B. HISTORIC SITES ACT

The Antiquities Act of 1906 became more effective when Congress enacted the Historic Sites Act in 1935.[13] The Historic Sites Act declared it a national policy "to preserve for public use historic sites, buildings, and objects of national significance for the inspiration and benefit of the people of the United States."[14] The Secretary of the Interior was authorized to restore, reconstruct, and maintain historic sites and properties and to establish and maintain museums for these purposes.[15] The Secretary was also given the power to contract and to enter into cooperative agreements with the states, municipal subdivisions, private organizations, and individuals, to protect, preserve, maintain, or operate any historic or archeologic building, site, object, or property connected with a public use.[16]

> Example 3. The Secretary of Interior has determined that certain land in the city of St. Louis, Missouri, possesses exceptional value as an historic site. Through the city of St. Louis, and pursuant to the Historic Sites Act, the Secretary institutes condemnation proceedings to acquire the land. The owner of the land challenges the acquisition, contending that the Historic Sites Act does not authorize the condemnation of property. In Barnidge v. United States, 101 F.2d 295 (8th Cir. 1939), the Eighth Circuit Court of Appeal ruled that the federal government may acquire by eminent domain, or otherwise, sites of national historic significance for the purposes declared in the Historic Sites Act and preserve them to commemorate and illustrate the nation's history. The court noted that the Historic Sites Act authorizes the Secretary of the Interior to acquire property for the purposes of the act and that another federal statute[17] grants the federal government condemnation power to acquire real estate for public use.[18]

C. NATIONAL HISTORICAL PRESERVATION ACT

Congress declared, in 1966, that "the spirit and direction of the nation are founded upon and reflected in its historic heritage" and that "preservation of this irreplaceable heritage is in the public interest so that its vital legacy . . . will be maintained and enriched for future generations of Americans."[19] The National Historic Preservation Act (NHPA)[20] was enacted in 1966 to provide for the maintenance and expansion of a National Register of districts, sites, buildings, structures, and objects significant in United States history, architecture, archaeology, and culture.[21] The act also provides for matching grants-in-aid to the National Trust for the purpose of preserving historical properties for the public benefit. The act requires the head of any federal agency, having direct or indirect jurisdiction over a proposed federal, or federally assisted, undertaking in any state, to consider the effect of the undertaking on any district, site, building, structure, or object included, or eligible to be included, in the National Register. The agency must make the determination prior to approval of the expenditure of any federal funds on the undertaking or prior to the issuance of a license to proceed with a federally assisted project.[22]

The NHPA was amended in 1980 to provide better guidance for the national historic preservation program at the federal, state, and local levels.[23] At that time, Congress pointed out that a partnership had developed among the federal government, the several states, and the private sector to protect the nation's historic resources. It noted that the small movement at the turn of the twentieth century to save a few historic treasures had grown immensely.[24]

The 1980 amendments to the NHPA also compelled the Secretary of the Interior to direct and coordinate U.S. participation in the 1972 UNESCO Convention Concerning the Protection of the World Cultural and Natural Heritage (discussed in Chapter 11).[25] As noted in Chapter 11, the 1972 UNESCO Convention established an intergovernmental committee, the World Heritage Committee, to provide international assistance in the protection of cultural property. The World Heritage Committee maintains an inventory of property forming part of the cultural and natural heritage of a country. From this list, it establishes a World Heritage List. The Secretary of the Interior nominates properties of international significance to the World Heritage Committee for inclusion on the World Heritage List. Only property determined to be of national significance can be nominated.

> Example 4. Penn Central Transportation Company owns a building called the Terminal, which has been designated as one of New York City's most famous buildings. Penn Central wanted to tear down a portion of the Terminal and construct an office building on its top. When the City of New York refused to grant permission, Penn Central sued the City of New York and alleged that restrictions the city placed on its property constituted a "taking" of its property without due process of law. In Penn Central Transportation Co. v. City of New York, 438 U.S. 104 (1978), the Supreme Court decided the New York law did not interfere in any manner with present uses of the Terminal and ruled that Penn Central was not entitled to compensation for the law's restriction in its use of the Terminal. The Supreme Court likened the Landmarks Preservation Law of the City of New York to zoning laws that substantially relate to the promotion of the general welfare but require no payment to the property owner due to a diminution in property value brought about by the application of the law to the owner's property. The Court ruled that the Terminal's designation as a landmark not only permitted the owner to continue to use the property but assumed that the owner would do so precisely as it had for the past sixty-five years—the building would remain a railroad terminal containing office space and concessions.

Example 5. In Mayes v. City of Dallas, 747 F.2d 323 (5th Cir. 1984), the property owner of a home within a historic preservation district wanted to change the property's exterior features. The owner wanted to paint the brick home and to construct a walkway with pylons across the front lawn. A city preservation regulation required prior approval for any exterior changes. The Fifth Circuit Court of Appeals ruled that the owner could not change the property's exterior without prior approval from city authorities. The Fifth Circuit held that a municipality has the constitutional power to regulate use of private property in the interest of historic preservation and cited the Penn Central decision discussed in Example 4. The Fifth Circuit ruled in Mayes that the city ordinance satisfied due process criteria.

Example 6. When a group of investors wanted to erect a riverfront park in the historical district of New Orleans, the Vieux Carre sought an injunction to arrest construction of the park. In Vieux Carre Property Owners, Residents & Associates, Inc. v. Brown, 875 F.2d 453 (5th Cir. 1989), cert. denied, 493 U.S. 1020 (1990), the Fifth Circuit Court of Appeals cited Citizens Committee for Hudson Valley v. Volpe, 425 F.2d 97 (2nd Cir. 1970), cert. denied, 400 U.S. 949 (1970), in which the Second Circuit Court of Appeals had ruled that an interest in widely shared aesthetic and environmental concerns falls within the zone of interest to be protected by the NHPA. However, the Fifth Circuit in Vieux Carre decided that the local project was only subject to a federal permit and did not require a historical impact review under the NHPA. The Fifth Circuit held that nationwide permits authorizing "truly inconsequential projects" were not "triggering 'licenses'" under the NHPA[26] and, thus, these activities escaped the historical review requirements of the NHPA. The Fifth Circuit did rule that the Vieux Carre was within the zone of interests sought to be protected by the NHPA.[27]

Example 7. In St. Bartholomew's Church v. City of New York, 914 F.2d 348 (2nd Cir. 1990), cert. denied, 111 S. Ct. 1103 (1991), church members of a historic church wanted to erect a commercial office tower on a church building to expand the church's ministerial and charitable activities. When the city refused to permit the construction, church members sued the city because they contended the city's landmarks law as applied to them violated their free exercise of religion. The Second Circuit Court of Appeals ruled that a city's landmarks law does not violate a church's free exercise.

The Second Circuit decided church members failed to prove they could not continue their religious practices in the church's existing facilities. The Second Circuit determined that although a landmarks law might "freeze" church property in its existing use and prevent a church from expanding or altering its activities, the Supreme Court's decision in Penn Central (discussed in Example 4) explicitly permitted these restrictions.

Example 8. In First Covenant Church v. City of Seattle, 840 P.2d 174 (Wash. 1992), the Supreme Court of Washington ruled that a city's landmarks preservation ordinance did violate a church's right to free exercise of religion under the First Amendment. The Supreme Court of Washington distinguished the St. Bartholomew's Church decision, discussed in Example 7, because St. Bartholomew's sought an exception for an adjacent building, not for its house of worship. In addition, the Washington court found that the Second Circuit in St. Bartholomew's did not consider the constitutionality of a liturgy-based religious exemption. The court noted that St. Bartholomew's had accepted designation as a landmark without objection, whereas the First Covenant Church had continuously objected to this designation. Further, the First Covenant Church claimed the landmark designation reduced the value of its principal asset by almost one-half.

D. NATIONAL ENVIRONMENTAL POLICY ACT

The National Environmental Policy Act (NEPA),[28] enacted in 1969, requires that environmental and cultural values be considered along with economic and technological values when proposed federal projects are assessed.[29] The act provides that the federal government must use all practicable means to improve and coordinate federal plans, functions, programs, and resources "to the end that the nation may preserve important historic, cultural, and natural aspects of the national heritage."[30] If proposed major federal action "significantly affect[s] the qualify of the human environment," the appropriate governmental agency must prepare an environmental impact statement.[31] An environmental impact statement (EIS) is a detailed statement of the environmental impact of (1) a proposed federal action, (2) any adverse environmental effects that cannot be avoided should the proposal be implemented, (3) alternatives to the proposed action, (4) the relationship between local short-term uses of the environment and the maintenance and enhancement of long-term productivity, and (5) any irreversible and irretrievable commitments of resources that would be involved in the proposed action should it be implemented.[32]

NEPA followed enactment of the Reservoir Act,[33] which was adopted to provide for the preservation of historical and archaeological data that might otherwise be lost or destroyed as a result of flooding or other alterations of the terrain caused by a federal construction project or a federally licensed activity or program.[34] The Reservoir Act requires a federal agency to provide information to the Secretary of the Interior whenever it finds, or is notified in writing by an appropriate historical or archaeological authority, that its activities in conjunction with a federal construction project or federally licensed project or program may cause irreparable loss or destruction of significant scientific or prehistorical data. The Secretary of the Interior is then required to investigate the areas affected.

The interrelationship between NEPA and the NHPA on federally funded projects that impact historic structures can become an issue. NEPA requires federal agencies to "preserve important historic and cultural aspects of the nation's heritage."[35] Compliance with the NHPA does not assure compliance with NEPA. Each act mandates "separate and distinct procedures, both of which must be complied with when historic buildings are affected."[36] Both acts essentially create obligations that are chiefly procedural in nature and both have the goal of generating information about the impact of federal actions on the environment. While there are similarities between the goals and demands of the two acts, each act must be taken on its own terms.[37] The demolition of a building listed in the National Register may be viewed as a "major" federal action.[38] Still, this "consideration is interwoven with the requirement that the challenged action must significantly affect the quality of the human environment."[39] One court concluded that because the impact on the physical environment of the demolition of an historic building is a social concern, NEPA was not applicable.[40]

Example 9. The U.S. Army Corps of Engineers issued a permit for the placement of riprap (large boulders to stabilize shore banks from erosion) without taking required measures to protect the cultural and archaeological resources of an area. The Corps may have violated both the NHPA and NEPA. A federal agency must examine the effects of its actions on property eligible to be included in the National Register. Further, eligible property is not limited to property that has been formally determined to be eligible. In Colorado River Indian Tribes v. Marsh, 605 F. Supp.

2425 (C.D. Cal. 1985), the court pointed out that NEPA requires a federal agency to prepare an EIS if a proposed project will degrade some environmental factor. If an agency determines the statement need not be prepared, a court may review the reasonableness of the agency's determination. If the determination is found unreasonable, the court will order that an EIS be prepared. The court noted that courts are split on whether the action must be "major." In Colorado River Indian Tribes, the court looked at the reasonableness of the agency's determination without considering whether "major" federal action occurred.

E. ARCHAEOLOGICAL RESOURCES PROTECTION ACT

The Archaeological Resources Protection Act of 1979 (ARPA)[41] enlarges upon the Antiquities Act of 1906 and was enacted to protect archaeological resources and sites located on public and Native American lands.[42] The act prohibits the sale, purchase, transport, exchange, or receipt of any archaeological resources removed without permission from public or Indian land after 1979.[43] ARPA is more explicit as to its coverage than is the Antiquities Act. For example, unlike the Antiquities Act, which does not define "ruin" or "object of antiquity," ARPA specifically defines an "archaeological resource" that is protected by the act. An "archaeological resource" protected under the act is any material remains of past human life or activities that is of archaeological interest and that is at least a hundred years of age.[44]

Museum directors must be especially concerned as to acquisitions of historical treasures found in the United States that are at least a hundred years of age. As noted above, the act covers the receipt or purchase, as well as the sale, of any archaeological resource removed from federal or Native American land. Still, under the act, the Secretary of the Interior may promulgate regulations providing for (1) the exchange between universities, museums, or other scientific or educational institutions of archaeological resources removed from public lands and Indian lands; and (2) the ultimate disposition of resources removed pursuant to the act.[45]

F. ARCHITECTURAL WORKS COPYRIGHT PROTECTION ACT

The Architectural Works Copyright Protection Act[46] was enacted in 1990 as "result of the United States adherence to the Berne Convention for the

Protection of Literary and Artistic Works."[47] In adopting the act, Congress determined that architecture is a form of artistic expression that "performs a significant societal purpose, domestically and internationally."[48] The act provides protection through the Copyright Act for "works of architecture," i.e., the "constructed design of buildings."[49] An architectural work that is protected by the Copyright Act is the design of a building as embodied in any tangible medium of expression, including a building, architectural plans, or drawings. Still, state and local landmarks, historic preservation, zoning, or building codes relating to protected architectural works are not preempted by the Copyright Act.[50]

The Copyright Act[51] permits the unauthorized "making, distributing, or public display of pictures, paintings, photographs, or other pictorial representations" of an architectural work if the building in which the work is embodied is located in or is ordinarily visible from a public place. Thus, the Copyright Act provides a limitation on the copyright owner's right to prepare derivative works from an architectural work. The Copyright Act[52] permits the owner of a building embodying a protected architectural work to "make or authorize the making of alterations to [the] building" and to "destroy or authorize the destruction" of the building without the copyright owner's consent.

G. NATIONAL FILM PRESERVATION ACT

Congress did not recognize a moral right for film producers in motion pictures when it enacted the Visual Artists Rights Act (VARA) in 1990. Still, Congress has acknowledged that motion pictures "are an indigenous American art form that has been emulated through the world . . . [that] certain motion pictures represent an enduring part of our Nation's historical and cultural heritage," and that certain films should be included as a part of the national cultural heritage.[53] Congress determined that it was appropriate and necessary for the government to recognize motion pictures as significant American art forms deserving of protection, and, consequently, it sought to preserve certain designated films through its adoption of the National Film Preservation Act of 1988[54] and 1992.[55]

The National Film Preservation Act established a National Film Registry for the purpose of maintaining and preserving films that are culturally, historically, or aesthetically significant.[56] The Librarian of Congress provides these films with a seal to indicate that they have been included in the National Film Registry.

H. VISUAL ARTISTS RIGHTS ACT

When delegates from the United States met with copyright experts from several Berne nations in Geneva in 1987 to discuss the United States joining the Berne Convention, the consensus was that adoption of a moral right in artists was not necessary for compliance with Berne standards.[57] As noted in Chapter 8, the United States joined the Berne Convention in 1988, but it did not, at that time, amend the Copyright Act to include moral rights in artists. The Berne Convention Implementation Act did not expand or reduce any right of an artist to claim authorship of a work or to object to a distortion, mutilation or other modification of, or other derogatory action in relation to, a work that would prejudice the artist's honor or reputation.

Artists lobbied Congress extensively for a recognition of their moral rights and, in 1990, did secure an amendment to the Copyright Act to provide for a moral right for visual artists.[58] As discussed in Chapter 8, the Visual Artists Rights Act (VARA) was passed in 1990[59] as an amendment to the Copyright Act to provide for a moral right for visual artists.

In enacting VARA, Congress related that the act was of the utmost importance to professional artists who build their future on the integrity and authenticity of art in public and private collections and to the public in preserving its cultural legacy.[60] It noted that the act would prevent distortions of works that would "cheat the public of an accurate account of the culture of our time."[61] Congress reflected that the act would mitigate against destruction of these creations and would protect their historical legacy.

I. PRESERVATION OF AMERICA'S HERITAGE ABROAD

In 1985, Congress established the Commission for the Preservation of America's Heritage Abroad[62] in order to preserve and protect cemeteries, monuments, and historic buildings associated with the foreign heritage of U.S. citizens. The commission was charged with the duty of identifying and publishing a list of those cemeteries, monuments, and historic buildings located abroad that are associated with the foreign heritage of U.S. citizens from eastern and central Europe and of encouraging the preservation and protection of these structures. In cooperation with the Department of State, the commission was to obtain assurances from foreign governments that the cemeteries, monuments, and buildings it identified would be preserved and protected.

J. TAX INCENTIVES FOR HISTORIC PRESERVATION

Some provisions of the Internal Revenue Code, which grant tax benefits for preserving historic structures, have further encouraged rehabilitation of historic structures. As discussed in Chapter 3, a landowner is permitted a charitable contribution deduction for grants of remainder interests in real property, or for restrictions in perpetuity on the use to be made of real property, if the landowner donates these interests to charities for historic preservation of the land or structures.[63] A taxpayer may also take a credit against income tax liability for costs of restoring or renovating the interior or exterior of a building to preserve the historic structure of the building if the building is used in the taxpayer's trade or business or in an investment venture.[64]

The tax credit, which is granted taxpayers who rehabilitate historic structures for use in their businesses or as investments, applies to expenses incurred in the "substantial" rehabilitation of a historic building. To qualify as a "historic" building, a building must have been built before 1936. A building is "substantially rehabilitated" if rehabilitation expenditures during the first twenty-four months exceed the greater of the adjusted basis of the property (generally cost less depreciation), or $5,000.[65] The credit is ten percent of the cost of restoring or renovating the interior or exterior of the building or, if the building is a certified historic structure, the credit is twenty percent.[66] At least fifty percent of the existing external walls must be retained in place as external walls and at least seventy-five percent of the existing external walls must be retained in place as internal or external walls. Further, at least seventy-five percent of the existing internal structural framework of the building must be retained in place.[67]

> Example 10. An individual purchases a building that is a certified historic structure, for $38,000, and expends $50,000 in 2014 to rehabilitate the building. The individual begins using the building as his office on December 10, 2014. Because the building is a certified historic structure, he may reduce his tax liability in 2014 in the amount of $10,000, by claiming a credit of twenty percent of the $50,000 rehabilitation costs ($50,000 x 20 percent). He would reduce the rehabilitation expenses by the amount of the credit ($50,000 - $10,000) and add the remaining cost ($40,000) to the remaining $38,000 initial cost of the building. The individual then would depreciate the recomputed $78,000 cost he would have in the building ($40,000 + $38,000) by using the straight-line depreciation method over a period of thirty-nine years (with a

mid-month convention in the year of acquisition).[68] In 2015, he would have a depreciation deduction of $2,000 ($78,000 divided by 39).

K. SUNKEN TREASURES

Because admiralty principles determine ownership of sunken vessels, historical preservation laws have not protected sunken treasures. The means to protect underwater treasures, as well as questions of title to sunken ships and to the artifacts found on these vessels, surfaced after individuals and governments acquired means to locate and excavate these vessels. As archaeologists and governments became concerned about the protection and preservation of the underwater cultural heritage and the lack of laws to protect underwater treasures, they enlisted assistance from the international community to protect sunken vessels and artifacts found on these vessels. A recognition that all States must accept responsibility for protecting and preserving the underwater cultural heritage, and preventing its commercial exploitation, led to the enactment of the Convention on the Protection of the Underwater Cultural Heritage in 2011. This convention and the international efforts to protect and preserve underwater cultural heritage are discussed in Chapter 11. This Chapter 10 reviews below historical preservation laws in the United States that seek to protect the underwater cultural heritage and case law that has addressed issues of ownership and possession of sunken treasures.

1. Law of Finds and Law of Salvage

There has been complex litigation involving the issue of ownership of shipwrecks and ship artifacts. The public originally encouraged the "hardy and adventurous mariner" to engage in "laborious and sometimes dangerous enterprises" to locate and excavate these wrecks.[69] Ownerships of these vessels was determined by the law of admiralty. Courts decided questions of title to sunken and abandoned shipwrecks by applying the law of finds and the law of salvage.[70] The law of salvage assumes the property is owned and has not been abandoned. The law of finds, on the other hand, determines title to abandoned property.[71]

Courts in the United States have applied the law of finds, rather than the law of salvage, in cases involving ancient shipwrecks where no owner is likely to come forward.[72] Title to recovered treasure vests either in the sovereign or in the finder. The English common law of finds is that title to abandoned property found on the seas is "the prerogative of the crown."[73] The law in the

United States, however, is that title to the property rests in the finder unless there is "legislative exercise of the sovereign prerogative."[74] The federal government had used the Antiquities Act of 1906 and the Archaeological Protection Act to exercise this "sovereign prerogative" and, thus, to assert title to ancient vessels which had sunk near the U.S. coast.

Example 11. In Treasure Salvors, Inc. v. Unidentified Wrecked & Abandoned Sailing Vessel, 569 F.2d 330 (5th Cir. 1978) the United States asserted title under the Antiquities Act to a Spanish galleon, the *Nuestra Señora de Atocha*, that sunk off the coast of Florida in 1622. The Fifth Circuit Court of Appeals noted that by its terms the Antiquities Act applied only to lands owned and controlled by the federal government. Because the wreck of the vessel rested on the continental shelf, it was outside the territorial waters of the United States. The Fifth Circuit applied the law of finds to award title to the vessel to Treasure Salvors.

Example 12. In Klein v. Unidentified Wrecked & Abandoned Sailing Vessel, 758 F.2d 1511 (11th Cir. 1985), the United States asserted title under the Antiquities Act and the Archaeological Protection Act to an eighteenth-century English ship, the *Fowey*, that was shipwrecked off the coast of a national park system known as Biscayne National Monument. The remains of the *Fowey* were within government territory. Klein discovered the vessel in 1978 while he was sport diving. After he removed several artifacts from the vessel, the government obtained an injunction to prevent any further salvage efforts on his part. The Eleventh Circuit Court of Appeals ruled that the United States had title to the ship. The Eleventh Circuit explained that, while the law of finds applied, there were two exceptions to the rule that a finder acquires title over the owner of the land on which the property was found. This court declared that the owner of the land is awarded title to abandoned property if the property is embedded in the soil, or if the owner of the land has constructive possession because the property is not considered to be lost. The Eleventh Circuit decided that the United States had title under both exceptions. The vessel was embedded in the soil, and it was not considered to be lost. In Klein, the Eleventh Circuit explained that a salvor is entitled to a salvage award if three conditions are met: (1) a maritime peril existed from which the ship could not have been rescued without the salvor's assistance; (2) the salvor's act was voluntary; and (3) the act was successful in saving or helping to save at least part of the property at risk.

An assessment of Biscayne National Monument, prepared for the Park Service, had listed the eighteenth-century wreck. Because the shipwreck had already been inventoried, the Eleventh Circuit held that it was not lost. This court did not grant Klein a salvage award because, according to the court, his "unauthorized disturbance of one of the oldest shipwrecks in the Park and his unscientific removal of the artifacts did more to create a marine peril than to prevent one."

Example 13. In Martha's Vineyard Scuba Headquarters, Inc. v. Unidentified, Wrecked & Abandoned Steam Vessel, 833 F.2d 1059 (1st Cir. 1987), the First Circuit Court of Appeals observed that, to maintain a salvor's franchise to the exclusion of the efforts of other salvors, the salvage operation must be "(1) undertaken with due diligence, (2) ongoing, and (3) clothed with some prospect of success."

Example 14. In Columbus-America Discovery v. Atlantic Mut. Ins., 974 F.2d 450 (4th Cir. 1992), the Fourth Circuit Court of Appeals noted six "main ingredients" admiralty courts use when fixing an award for salvage: (1) the labor expended by the sailors in rendering the salvage service; (2) the promptitude, skill, and energy displayed in rendering the service and saving the property; (3) the value of the property employed by the salvors in rendering the service, and the danger to which the property was exposed; (4) the risk incurred by the salvors in securing the property from the impending peril; (5) the value of the property saved; and (6) the degree of danger from which the property was rescued.

Congress eventually decided admiralty principles were not "well-suited to the preservation of historic and other shipwrecks" that may have considerable cultural value.[75] In addition, many states had recognized that historic shipwrecks are cultural resources needing greater protection and had enacted legislation to protect these resources for the public. To eliminate the confusion over the ownership of, and the responsibility for, historic shipwrecks in state waters, Congress enacted the Abandoned Shipwreck Act[76] in 1988 to protect underwater archaeological treasures in state waters.[77]

2. Abandoned Shipwreck Act

Congress noted that when it adopted the Submerged Lands Act,[78] and thereby transferred ownership to the states of all natural resources and submerged lands out to a distance of three miles,[79] it had not specified whether the states also owned nonnatural objects, such as shipwrecks that rested on or within submerged lands.[80] Congress explained that notwithstanding this lack of clarity, numerous states had enacted legislation that pertained to the management of abandoned or historic shipwrecks in state waters. Still, state courts had only limited success in enforcing these statues, and some courts held that state regulation was preempted by admiralty principles.[81] These courts applied either the law of finds or the law of salvage to adjudicate the disputes before them.[82] The Abandoned Shipwreck Act (ASA) was Congress's answer to the problem. To protect these archaeological resources, the act claims federal ownership of certain shipwrecks and simultaneously transfers title to these wrecks to the states for administration, management, and regulation.[83] It recognizes that historic shipwrecks "that contain both historic information and tangible artifacts are subject to salvage operations, with resultant loss of historical information and artifacts to the public."[84]

The ASA provides states with the "responsibility for management of a broad range of living and nonliving resources in State waters and submerged lands"[85] including "abandoned shipwrecks, which have been deserted and to which the owner has relinquished ownership rights."[86] The act awards the United States title to any abandoned shipwreck that is embedded in a state's submerged lands, but the United States then transfers title back to the state.[87] The act specifies that the law of salvage and the law of finds do not apply to abandoned shipwrecks embedded in a state's submerged lands.[88]

> Example 15. A salvor finds a sunken ship while scuba diving off the coast of Texas. She removes several of the artifacts from the ship and sells them. She is then sued by the State of Texas and the United States, both entities claiming title to the ship. The United States plans to transfer the artifacts to the Smithsonian. Officials of the State of Texas want the artifacts placed in the State Historical Museum. The salvor, on the other hand, contends she is the owner of the ship, and all the artifacts found with it, because she discovered the ship. In addressing the question of who has title to the shipwreck and its artifacts, the ASA would award the United States title to the shipwreck because it was embedded in the state's submerged lands, but the act then requires the United States to transfer title back to the State of Texas. Because of the ASA, the law of finds and the law of salvage do not apply. The salvor would not have title to the ship and its artifacts and would not be entitled to a salvage award.[89]

Example 16. In Sea Hunt, Inc. and Commonwealth of Virginia v. The Unidentified Shipwrecked Vessel or Vessels and Kingdom of Spain, 221 F.3d 634 (4th Cir. 2000), cert denied, 531 U.S. 1144 (2001), the Fourth Circuit Court of Appeals considered title to two vessels commissioned into the Spanish Navy, the *La Galga*, a fifty-gun frigate placed in service in 1732, and the *Juno*, a thirty-four-gun frigate commissioned in 1790. The ships were lost off the shores of present-day Virginia in 1750 and 1802. The *La Galga* left Havana in 1750 to escort a convoy of merchant ships to Spain. It encountered a hurricane near Bermuda and eventually sank off the coast of the Maryland/Virginia border. The *Juno* set sail from Veracruz bound for Spain in 1802. It was beset by a ferocious storm and began taking on water. At least 413 sailors, soldiers, and civilians perished in its sinking. The wrecks were discovered after the State of Virginia issued a salvage company, Sea Hunt, Inc., permits to conduct salvage operations. Sea Hunt spent about a million dollars in conducting remote sensing, survey, diving, and identification operations, which it contended resulted in locating the remains of the wrecks. Virginia asserted ownership over the shipwrecks pursuant to the ASA, but Spain filed a claim of ownership pursuant to the 1902 Treaty of Friendship and General Relations between the United States and Spain. The reciprocal immunities established by the treaty protect U.S. shipwrecks and military gravesites. Under terms of the treaty, Spanish vessels, like those belonging to the United States, may be abandoned only by express acts. The United States had defended Spain's ownership of the vessels. It contended that protection of the sacred sites of other nations assists in preventing the disturbance and exploitation of its sites and that Spain's interest was rooted in customary international law. In addressing the question of ownership of the wrecks, the court held that the Kingdom of Spain had not expressly abandoned the ships and ruled that both vessels remained the property of Spain. The court noted that the ASA is applicable only if a shipwreck is "abandoned" and that a shipwreck is abandoned only where an owner has relinquished ownership rights. It determined from the legislative history of the ASA that sovereign vessels are treated differently from privately owned ones. The court agreed that an inference of abandonment is permitted, but "only when no owner appears." The court denied Sea Hunt a salvage award because Sea Hunt knew the vessels were Spanish ships and that Spain might make a claim of ownership and decline salvage. It recognized that the owner of a vessel can refuse unwanted salvage.

Example 17. The issue of ownership by the U.S. government as to its submerged military planes was addressed in Int'l Recovery v. Unidentified Wrecked and Abandoned Aircraft. 218 F.3d 1255 (11th Cir. 2000), cert. denied, 531 U.S. 1144 (2001). A torpedo bomber crashed off the Florida coast during a training flight in 1943. The plane was built in 1938 and flew "neutrality patrol" in the central Atlantic until it was assigned in mid-1941 to the aircraft carrier *Yorktown* operating in the Pacific. In 1942, the plane participated in the Battles of Midway and the Coral Sea. During the Battle of the Coral Sea, torpedo bombers sank the Japanese aircraft carrier *Shoho* and badly damaged the carrier *Shokaku*. After overhauling the bomber in question, the Navy used the plane for training in Miami. During a torpedo attack instruction flight in 1943, the bomber crashed in deep international waters approximately eight miles east of Miami Beach. The Navy "struck" the plane from the inventory of active aircraft in 1943 and had taken no steps to locate or salvage the plane since that time. In 1990, a group searching for Spanish galleons located the bomber and offered to sell the location to the National Museum of Naval Aviation. The United States claimed ownership of the bomber and rejected salvage operations. The Eleventh Circuit Court of Appeals ruled that the United States had not abandoned its ownership of the plane. It decided that the government holds its interests in trust for all the people and should not be "deprived of those interests by the ordinary court rules designed particularly for private disputes over individually owned pieces of property." The Eleventh Circuit stated that "officers who have no authority at all to dispose of Government property cannot by their conduct cause the Government to lose its valuable property rights by their acquiescence, laches, or failure to act." This appellate court determined that the ASA did not apply because the plane was not a shipwreck and because it was not embedded in a state's submerged lands. The court decided that whether or not the salvor would be entitled to a salvage award depended on whether the United States had rejected the salvor's efforts, and, if it had rejected salvage, when it did so.

Some states have enacted recent legislation pursuant to the ASA to recognize their role in preserving sunken treasures. For example, South Carolina attempted to resolve the conflict between encouraging and rewarding appropriate and beneficial endeavors of salvors with the state's concern that historic treasures from sunken ships may be lost as a result of some salvage operations. The South Carolina Underwater Antiquities Act[90] provides that the state has title to all submerged antiquities.[91] The South Carolina Institute of Archaeology and Anthropology is designated as the custodian of all archaeological materials. A person requesting to conduct operations in the course of which submerged antiquities may be removed must apply to the institute for a license. However, the disposition of recovered submerged historic property includes a division with the licensee, i.e., the salvor.[92]

The State of Georgia claims title to, and the exclusive right to regulate the investigating, surveying, and recovery of, all submerged cultural resources, defined as all prehistoric and historic sites, ruins, artifacts, treasure, shipwrecks or vessels, and their cargo or tackle, which have remained on the bottom for more than fifty years, and similar sites and objects found in the Atlantic Ocean within the three-mile territorial limit of the state or within its navigable waters.[93] The Department of Natural Resources is the custodian of all submerged cultural resources.[94] Persons desiring to conduct an investigation, a survey, or recovery operations must apply to the department if submerged cultural resources may be endangered, removed, or destroyed.[95] The department will grant a permit if the department determines the public interest and the preservation and protection of submerged cultural resources will be served by permitting these operations. However, the permittee may not retain any recovered submerged cultural resources unless the department determines the resources have no significant historical, archeological, or monetary value or are of such limited historical, archeological, or monetary value as to be reasonable compensation for the efforts of the permittee in furthering the public interest through recovery of the cultural resources.[96]

Massachusetts asserts title to underwater archaeological resources within its inland or coastal waters that have historical value. It only claims title if the underwater resources have remained unclaimed for a hundred years or more.[97] A board of underwater archaeological resources has the duty and responsibility to encourage the discovery and reporting of, and to protect and preserve, historical, scientific, and archaeological information about underwater archaeological resources located within the state's inland and coastal waters.[98] The board may grant permits to qualified persons, organizations, or corporations for the orderly salvage or removal of underwater archaeological resources.[99]

L. NATIVE AMERICAN ARTIFACTS

During the early part of the nineteenth century, the excavation and removal of contents of Native American graves for reasons of profit or curiosity became a common practice. Countless Indian burial sites were desecrated, and thousands of Native American human remains and funerary objects were sold or transferred and then housed in museums in the United States.[100]

Native American tribes have recognized sovereignty along with state and foreign governments.[101] The Indian Reorganization Act of 1934 (IRA)[102] authorizes the Secretary of the Interior to take land in trust for individual Indians and for federally recognized Indian tribes.[103] Congress may preempt the operation of state law with respect to Indian trust land.[104]

Example 18. A Native American sold the rights to excavate on his land to the Black Hills Institute of Geological Research. The land, located within the boundaries of the Cheyenne River Sioux Indian Reservation, was held by the federal government in trust for the Native American. During excavation, researchers from the institute uncovered mammoth remains and ten tons of bones from a *Tyrannosaurus rex* that were 65 million years old. The fossil was the largest and most complete *Tyrannosaurus rex* skeleton known to man. The institute paid the Native American $5,000 for the fossil and moved it to the Black Hills Museum of Natural History for public display and research. Later, upon order of the U.S. Attorney for South Dakota, federal officers seized the fossil based on the researchers having violated the Antiquities Act, which bans the removal of antiquities from federal lands. The Black Hill Institute filed suit against the federal government, contending that it had title to the fossil. The federal government asserted it had ownership of the fossil as trustee for the Native American. The government claimed the fossil is an ingredient of the land and, as such, is land. It insisted the Native American could not sell land held in trust for him unless he obtained prior approval from the Secretary of the Interior. (The Indian Reorganization Act[105] prohibits the sale of Indian land unless approved by the Secretary of the Interior.) In Black Hills Institute v. S.D. School of Mines & Tech., 12 F.3d 737 (8th Cir. 1993),[106] the Eighth Circuit Court of Appeals agreed the federal government held the fossil in trust for the Native American. The institute originally filed suit against the Department of Justice contending that, after seizure of the bones, the federal government stored this priceless treasure under inadequate circumstances. The Eighth Circuit ordered the South Dakota School of Mines and Technology to serve as custodian of the fossil until ownership could be determined. The Black Hills Institute and the Black Hills Museum of Natural History Foundation, Inc. then filed a complaint in the nature of a quiet title action to assert permanent ownership of the fossil. The court, however, decided the federal government had ownership of the bones. In Black Hills Institute of Geological Research v. Williams, 88 F.3d 614 (8th Cir. 1996), the Eighth Circuit imposed a due diligence requirement on Black Hills as the purchaser of Indian artifacts. It held that a party who has knowledge of facts that would cast doubt upon the transferability of title to the artifacts has a duty to investigate the title. It ruled that a lack of caution and diligence amounts to bad faith. The court then held that Black Hills Institute's failure to investigate diligently whether a fossil found on the Indian reservation could be sold absent governmental approval prevented the institute from being a good-faith, bona fide purchaser.

Because Indian lands are controlled by the federal government, the Antiquities Act of 1906[107] also prohibits the destruction or appropriation of Indian ruins and antiquities. However, as noted above, the act is limited in its protection of Indian artifacts in that it subjects a person to penalties for the appropriation of any "ruin," "monument," or "object of antiquity," and the definition of these terms is not clear.

Amendments to the National Historic Preservation Act (NHPA) in 1980, 1992, and 1994 included provisions requiring the Secretary to establish a program and promulgate regulations to assist Indian tribes in preserving their particular historic properties.[108] The NHPA now mandates the Secretary of the Interior to foster communication and cooperation between Indian tribes and state historic preservation officers in the administration of the national historic preservation program to ensure that all types of historic properties and all public interests in these properties are given due consideration. A tribe can assume all or any part of the functions of a state historic preservation officer with respect to tribal lands if the tribe's chief governing authority so requests and the tribe designates a tribal preservation officer to administer the tribal historic preservation program through appointment by the tribe's chief governing authority. Properties of traditional religious and cultural importance to an Indian tribe or Native Hawaiian organization may be determined to be eligible for inclusion in the National Register.

The NHPA has provided Indian tribes additional benefits in that the NHPA is interrelated with the National Environmental Protection Act (NEPA),[109] and, thus, has brought required tribal input into major federal projects. Under § 106 of the NHPA, the Advisory Council on Historic Preservation (ACHP), a federal agency created by Congress pursuant to the NHPA, must be given a reasonable opportunity to comment on the effect of federally assisted projects on historic properties. This would include properties of traditional religious and cultural tribal importance.[110] Thus, pursuant to NEPA and the NHPA, parties to a major federal project must invite the participation of affected federal, state, and local agencies, but also any affected Indian tribe, in federal projects that affect historical properties or cultures.[111]

1. American Indian Religious Freedom Act

A concern among Native American tribes that Congress and the general public were not respecting their religious practices freedoms and that the Antiquities Act was apparently ineffective in protecting Indian artifacts and ruins[112] led tribes to continue a program to lobby Congress to recognize their special cultures and religious practices. Congress responded to these pressure groups seventy-two years after it had enacted the 1906 Antiquities Act. In 1978, Congress enacted the American Indian Religious Freedom Act (AIRFA)[113] to protect and preserve the traditional religious rights of American Indians. The act requires the federal government to protect and preserve for Native Americans their inherent right of freedom to believe in and exercise their traditional religions. Various federal departments, agencies, and other instrumentalities responsible for administering relevant laws are to evaluate their policies and procedures in consultation with native traditional religious leaders in order to determine appropriate changes necessary to protect and preserve Native American religious cultural rights and practices.

While AIRFA led to a change in some governmental policies, it did not provide the protections Native Americans demanded. For example, Native Americans were not successful in citing AIRFA as authority for their right to retain their native cultural resources.[114] Although Native Americans contended the act authorized them to obtain the return of Indian religious artifacts and human remains that were a part of museum collections, the act only has application to federal agencies and does not call for the return of Native American objects and human remains.[115] Further, courts had ruled that the act was merely a statement of the federal government's policy that it will recognize the religious beliefs of Native Americans as well as the religious beliefs of others.[116]

> Example 19. In Lyng v. Northwest Indian Center Protective Association, 485 U.S. 439 (1988), a logging company and the United States Forest Service wanted to construct six miles of paved road to the Blue Creek Unit of the Six Rivers National Forest. The road would provide access to Chimney Rock, which is the sacred high country to the Yurok, Karok,

> and Tolowa Indians. These tribes used the area for religious rites and for the training of medical and spiritual practitioners. The tribes sought a court injunction to prevent construction of the road. The Supreme Court ruled that construction of the road would not unlawfully burden the tribes' exercise of religion under AIRFA. The Supreme Court ruled that the logging company had the right to build the road and that AIRFA was nothing more than a restatement of the First Amendment to guarantee religious freedom for all U.S. citizens. The Court noted that the government had taken numerous steps to minimize the immediate impact that construction of the road would have on the tribes' religious activities—such as choosing the route that best protected sites of specific rituals from adverse audible intrusions, and planning steps to reduce the visual impact of the road on the surrounding country.

Amendments to AIRFA in 1994 provided somewhat more recognition of Indian cultures. These amendments were applied in a 1999 case[117] to prevent rock climbers from challenging the Secretary of the Interior's approval of a plan that would prevent rock climbing on Devil's Tower during the month of June when Indians engage in their Sun Dance and other religious ceremonies.

2. Archaeological Resources Protection Act and National Historic Preservation Act

The Archaeological Resources Protection Act (ARPA; discussed above)[118] has provided some protection to Native American tribes in their attempts to preserve their cultural treasures because the act requires a permit to excavate upon public or Indian lands,[119] and a person can procure a permit to excavate on Indian lands only by the consent of the tribe.[120] Although archaeological resources protected by ARPA are artifacts that are at least a hundred years of age and thus would not include religious objects of recent origin such as the Indian masks in U.S. Diaz (discussed above in Example 1), the requirement of a permit from a Native American tribe to excavate upon Indian land has halted much of the taking of Native American artifacts and religious objects from Indian lands.[121] By requiring a permit from a Native American tribe to excavate on tribal land, ARPA provides added protection for Native American tribes in their attempts to protect their cultural and funerary objects. In addition, another statute makes a person who willfully steals or converts for personal use or for the use of another any property belonging to, or in the custody of, an Indian tribal organization subject to criminal prosecution.[122]

As noted above, the Secretary of the Interior may promulgate regulations providing for (1) the exchange between universities, museums, or other scientific or educational institutions of archaeological resources removed from public lands and Indian lands, and (2) the ultimate disposition of resources removed pursuant to the act.[123] Any exchange of resources removed from Native American lands is subject to the consent of the tribe that has jurisdiction over the land.

Example 20. In United States v. Austin, 902 F.2d 743 (9th Cir.1989), cert. denied, 498 U.S. 874 (1990), defendants had been indicted under ARPA for excavating a Native American archaeological site. The defendants contended the act was unconstitutionally overbroad and vague. The Ninth Circuit Court of Appeals ruled that ARPA was not unconstitutional.

Amendments to the National Historic Preservation Act (NHPA) in 1980, 1992, and 1994 included provisions requiring the Secretary of the Interior to establish a program and promulgate regulations to assist Indian tribes in preserving their particular historic properties.[124] The NHPA now mandates the Secretary of the Interior to foster communication and cooperation between Indian tribes and state historic preservation officers in the administration of the national historic preservation program to ensure that all types of historic properties and all public interests in these properties are given due consideration. A tribe can assume all or any part of the functions of a state historic preservation officer with respect to tribal lands if the tribe's chief governing authority so requests and the tribe designates a tribal preservation officer to administer the tribal historic preservation program through appointment by the tribe's chief governing authority. Properties of traditional religious and cultural importance to an Indian tribe or Native Hawaiian organization may be determined to be eligible for inclusion in the National Register.[125]

The NHPA has provided Indian tribes additional benefits in that the NHPA is interrelated with NEPA[126] and, thus, has brought required tribal input into major federal projects. As noted previously, NEPA mandates a federal agency to take a hard look at the environmental consequences of a major federal action before taking any steps. This includes a federal project that involves property of cultural tribal importance. The Ninth Circuit Court of Appeals[127] has stated that both acts are designed to ensure that a federal agency will "stop, look, and listen" before moving ahead. Thus, pursuant to NEPA and the NHPA, parties to a major federal project must invite the participation of affected federal, state, and local agencies, but also any affected Indian tribe, in federal projects that affect historical properties or cultures.[128]

3. Native American Graves Protection and Repatriation Act

The Supreme Court's adverse interpretation of AIRFA in 1988 in the landmark case of Lyng v. Northwest Indian Center Protective Assoc., discussed above in Example 19, made the Indian tribes realize they needed more governmental protection for their funerary and cultural objects. In 1988, a Senate Select Committee on Indian Affairs held a hearing regarding legislation that would provide a process for the repatriation of Native American remains.[129] This panel was split on what to do about human remains that are not culturally identifiable and debated the proper treatment of these remains. Some thought there should be a system developed for repatriation while others believed scientific and educational needs should predominate.[130] The panel did decide federal legislation was needed. As a result of the panel's findings and after further lobbying by Indian tribes, the Native American Graves Protection and Repatriation Act (NAGPRA)[131] was enacted in 1990 and became effective in 1991.

When NAGPRA became effective in 1991, Native American tribes obtained the legislation they long judged necessary to secure their religious and funerary objects. This act required federal agencies and museums that had possession or control over collections of Native American human remains and associated funerary objects to compile an inventory of these items and, to the extent possible, based on information possessed by the entities, to identify the geographical and cultural affiliation of the items.[132] Museums were required to complete the inventories in consultation with tribal governments and Native Hawaiian organization officials and traditional religious leaders within a five-year period from the act's enactment.[133] Museums were also required to supply documentation of existing records for the purpose of determining the geographical origin, cultural affiliation, and basic facts surrounding the acquisition and accession of Native American human remains and associated funerary objects.[134] If a cultural affiliation of Native American human remains and associated funerary objects was established with a particular tribe, then, upon the request of a known lineal descendant of the Native American or the tribe, the museum was required to return the remains and associated funerary objects expeditiously to the tribe unless the museum could show a right of possession to the objects.[135] A "right of possession" is possession obtained with the voluntary consent of an individual or group that had authority of alienation.[136] The original acquisition of Native American human remains and associated funerary objects excavated, exhumed, or otherwise obtained with full knowledge and full consent of the next of kin or the official governing body of the appropriate culturally affiliated Indian tribe is deemed to give a right of possession to those remains.

> Example 21. A member of a museum's board of directors had in his possession a hunting spear that was handed down to him by him ancestors. The last chief of one of the major tribes gave the spear to his great-great-grandfather over a hundred and fifty years ago to seal a friendship between his great-great-grandfather and the chief. The board member donated the spear to the museum a few years ago. Recently, members of the tribe have asked the museum to repatriate the spear to the tribe. Must the museum return the spear to the tribe? The museum will not be required to repatriate the spear if it can demonstrate a right of possession in the board member. The board member can show a right of possession by providing documentation that the chief had authority of alienation (the spear belonged to the chief) and that the chief voluntarily donated the spear to his great-great-grandfather.

A review committee, established pursuant to NAGPRA,[137] is responsible for compiling an inventory of culturally unidentifiable human remains that are in the possession or control of federal agencies and museums and for recommending specific actions for developing a process for disposition of these remains. This committee is responsible for monitoring the inventory and identification process to ensure a fair and objective consideration and assessment of all available relevant information and evidence. It makes recommendations, if appropriate, regarding future care of cultural items that are to be repatriated. The committee consults with Indian tribes and Native Hawaiian organizations and museums on matter affecting the tribes or organizations and consults with the Secretary of the Interior in the development of regulations to carry out NAGPRA provisions. Upon request from a tribe, the review committee will review and make findings related to the identity or cultural affiliation of cultural items or the return of the items. The committee is charged with facilitating the resolution of any disputes among Indian tribes, Native Hawaiian organizations, or lineal descendants and federal agencies and museums relating to the return of the items.

Example 22. In U.S. v. Kramer, 168 F.3d 1196 (9th Cir. 1999), the Ninth Circuit Court of Appeals court pointed out that while Congress enacted NAGPRA to protect cultural patrimony and to repatriate cultural objects held or controlled by federal agencies and museums, the act also applies to individual traders in Native American artifacts.[138] The court referred to § 4 of NAGPRA, which amended Title 18 of the U.S. Code to criminalize the trafficking in Native American human remains and cultural items. Congress "gave teeth" to the act through criminalizing trafficking in Native American human remains and cultural items in an effort to eliminate the profit incentive perceived to be a motivating force behind the plundering of these items. As the Ninth Circuit noted, this provision makes it unlawful knowingly to sell, purchase, use for profit, or transport for sale or profit any Native American cultural item obtained in violation of NAGPRA.

Example 23. In U.S. v. Tidwell, 191 F.3d 976 (9th Cir. 1999), an individual was convicted for trafficking in Native American cultural items and for unlawfully removing archeological resources from Indian lands. The individual, Tidwell, attempted to sell eleven Hopi masks, also called Kwaatsi or Kachina, and a set of priest robes from the Pueblo of Acoma. These artifacts had been taken from the Hopi reservation. A federal agent purchased three of the religious Hopi masks from Tidwell and two others were found when the agent searched Tidwell's properties. The court found that Tidwell knowingly traded in these items and rejected his vagueness challenge to NAGPRA.

Example 24. In Bonnichsen v. United States, 969 F. Supp. 614 and 628 (D. Ore. 1997), 217 F. Supp.2d 1166 (D. Nevada 2002), 357 F.3d 962 (9th Cir. 2004), and 367 F.3d 864 (9th Cir. 2004), a set of human remains, believed to be over 9,000 years old, was discovered in 1996 near Kennewick, Washington, along the bank of the Columbia River, by a spectator watching a boat race from the shoreline. A local anthropologist applied for a permit to excavate the skeleton. The U.S. Army Corps of Engineers decided the remains were subject to NAGPRA and, thus, transferred the remains to an Indian tribe for reburial. The Corps disallowed scientific study of the remains. Scientists contended the discovery of "Kennewick Man" was of great historical and anthropological significance and wanted to study the remains. They filed suit against the U.S. Army Corps of

Engineers to enforce what they contended was a legal right to study the remains. Others who joined in the case were the Asatru, members of the Asatru Folk Assembly, which is a legally recognized church that represents Asatru, a major indigenous, pre-Christian, European religion. They contended the man was actually one of their ancestors and was not related to present-day Native Americans at all but rather to Europeans. The Ninth Circuit instructed the Corps to consider whether there was more than one wave of ancient migration to the Americas, or if there were subpopulations of early Americans and whether NAGPRA applies to remains or cultural objects from a population that failed to survive and that is not related directly to modern Native Americans. It also instructed the Corps to determine whether NAGPRA requires either expressly or implicitly a biological connection between the remains and a contemporary Native American tribe, whether there must be a cultural affiliation between the remains and a contemporary Native American tribe, and, if so, how that affiliation can be established if no cultural objects are found with the remains. The court directed the Corps to determine whether there is evidence of a link, either biological or cultural, between the remains and a modern Native American tribe or to any other ethnic or cultural group including those of Europe, Asia, and the Pacific Islands. The district court determined that substantial evidence did not support a determination that the remains were Native American within the meaning of NAGPRA and ruled for the scientists. This decision was affirmed upon appeal by the Ninth Circuit Court of Appeals, 367 F.3d 864 (9th Cir. 2004). The Ninth Circuit ruled that human remains must bear some relationship to a presently existing tribe, people, or culture to be "Native American" within the meaning of NAGPRA. The Ninth Circuit decided that no reasonable person could conclude from the record that Kennewick Man is "Native American" under NAGPRA.

Example 25. In determining affiliation with a current Native American group, the court in Fallon Paiute-Shoshone Tribe v. United States, 455 F. Supp. 2d 1207 (D. Nev. 2006), held to be arbitrary and capricious a determination by the Bureau of Land Management (BLM) that ancient human remains found in a cave adjacent to tribal land were not affiliated with any modern-day Native American tribes. The court noted that after a finding of nonaffiliation, interested Native American tribes are permitted to provide their own evidence, both scientific and cultural, in their attempt to demonstrate affiliation. The remains were found in

1940 during an excavation near Fallon, Nevada, in a place known as Spirit Cave. The most important find in the excavation was the well-preserved, partially mummified body of a man now known as the "Spirit Cave Man." The find was removed from the cave and analyzed. Upon initial review, it was believed that the Spirit Cave Man remains were between 1,500 and 2,000 years old. However, as part of the inventory and identification process required after NAGPRA was enacted, radiocarbon dating was authorized on the remains. The dating was completed in 1994 or 1995 and showed that the initial estimate for the age of the bones was flawed significantly. The remains were, in fact, nearly 10,000 years old and, accordingly, were a significant scientific find. The scientific community made several requests to study the remains after the discovery of their age. Around this time, a tribe began making inquiries about repatriation of the remains. In 1996, the tribe requested that the BLM temporarily inter the remains and cease all testing. The tribe believed it was the caretaker of the Spirit Cave Man remains and that disturbing the burial site of a deceased, such as the Spirit Cave Man, carried negative repercussions. The tribe contended that, once the BLM had retained its experts, the BLM shut it out of the decision-making process. The court ruled that NAGPRA required the BLM to consider fully and fairly the tribe's evidence and to uphold or reverse its determination of nonaffiliation based on a reasoned and coherent discussion of the evidence and its reasons for believing or disbelieving affiliation. Because this did not occur, the court ruled that the BLM's determination was arbitrary and capricious. The court did state, however, that its order should not be read to mandate a finding of affiliation.

Through its enactment of NAGPRA, Congress agreed with Native Americans that museums should repatriate Native American artifacts in their collections to provide the tribes with artifacts that should become a part of a special Native American heritage. Still, many scientists have been concerned that this legislation, which requires the repatriation of Indian artifacts, would impinge upon scientific research. The Bonnichsen case, discussed in Example 24, illustrates the continuing conflict between most Native Americans, who demand repatriation and subsequent burial of ancient human remains, and scientists and others who think the study of ancient remains should prevail over Indian religious beliefs that may require the burial of these remains.

The decisions in the Bonnichsen and in the Fallon Paniute-Shoshone Tribe case illustrate the conflicting, often incompatible considerations that can occur in legitimate efforts to protect and preserve a cultural heritage that includes several differing cultures. However, while the controversy between scientists and Native Americans, with respect to the discovery and repatriation of human remains found in the United States, will continue, a recognition and preservation of a distinct Native American culture, and the involvement of the museum community in this effort, undoubtedly has broadened the public's understanding and appreciation of the historical heritage of the United States generally, a heritage that includes and encompasses a special and distinctive Native American history.

4. International Implications of Native American Graves Protection and Repatriation Act

The enactment of NAGPRA has had international recognition. NAGPRA actually set a precedent with museums on an international level to encourage the repatriation of cultural objects to indigenous communities. The UNIDROIT Convention on Stolen or Illegally Exported Cultural Objects (discussed in Chapter 11), which was completed in Rome in 1995,[139] has similar repatriation requirements to those of NAGPRA and on an international directive. The UNIDROIT Convention also addresses claims for restitution of sacred and communally important cultural objects that belong to, and are used by, tribal or indigenous communities.

Although the 1995 UNIDROIT Convention endorses the repatriation of cultural property on an international scale, the repatriation requirements set out in the 1995 UNIDROIT Convention, which are discussed in Chapter 11, are less precise than those in NAGPRA (which sanctions the complete and unequivocal repatriation of Native American cultural and funerary objects to affiliated tribes). Still, Congress has rejected any efforts to point to NAGPRA as congressional endorsement for the repatriation of other artworks and/or antiquities. In enacting NAGPRA, Congress stated that the act "reflects the unique relationship between the Federal government and Indian tribes and Native Hawaiian organizations and should not be construed to establish a precedent with respect to any other individual, organization, or foreign government."[140]

The United States has not ratified the 1995 UNIDROIT Convention for similar concerns that had caused many persons, including those in the museum community, to reject and initially oppose the enactment of NAGPRA. However, some have contended that congressional ratification of the 1995 UNIDROIT Convention would make a statement to the international art and antiquities community, similar to the one Congress made to Native

Americans in 1990 when it enacted NAGPRA, that the United States recognizes and respects the property, history, and cultures of others. Ratification of the UNIDROIT Convention could have the affirmative effect of assisting art- and archaeologically-rich countries in protecting their cultural patrimony from the illicit international art and antiquities market. The international conventions that seek to protect the cultural heritage from this illicit market are discussed in the next chapter.

NOTES

1. Autocephalous Greek-Orthodox Church v. Goldberg & Feldman Fine Arts, Inc., 917 F.2d 278 (7th Cir. 1990).

2. Discussion in Penn Central Transportation Co. v. City of New York, 438 U.S. 104 (1978).

3. Id.

4. Id.

5. See, e.g., Ariz. Rev. Stat. Ann. §§ 41-861 to 41-866; Cal. Pub. Res. Code §§ 5020.1-5029.5; Conn. Gen. Stat. Ann. §§ 7-147a to 7-147y; Mass. Ann. Laws, ch. 9, §§ 26-28; N.Y. Parks, Rec. & Hist. Preservation Law §§ 3.01-.23; 37 Pa. C.S.A. §§ 101 et. seq.

The State of Florida has declared that the "rich and unique heritage of historic properties in [the] state, representing more than 10,000 years of human presence, is an important legacy to be valued and conserved for present and future generations." Fla. Stat. Ann. § 267.061(l)(a). This statute provides that the "destruction of these nonrenewable historical resources will engender a significant loss of the state's quality of life, economy, and cultural environment."

In Maine, the Maine Historic Preservation Commission was established to implement the policy of the state "to preserve the architectural, historic and environmental heritage of the people of the State and to develop and promote the cultural, educational, and economic benefits of these resources." 27 M.R.S.A. § 501.

In Pennsylvania, the legislature made a finding that the "irreplaceable historical, architectural, archaeological and cultural heritage of [the] Commonwealth should be preserved and protected for the benefit of all the people, including future generations." 37 Pa. C.S.A. § 102. The Pennsylvania statutes provide that the preservation and protection of historic resources are deemed to promote the public health, prosperity, and general welfare. It states that the rapid social and economic development of "contemporary society threatens to destroy the remaining vestiges of our historic heritage."

6. 16 U.S.C. §§ 468–468d.

7. Id. at § 468. The activities of the National Trust fall under the direction of a board of trustees composed of the Attorney General of the United States, the Secretary of the Interior, the director of the National Gallery of Art (Smithsonian Institution), and six U.S. citizens.

8. 16 U.S.C. §§ 431–33.

9. Id. at § 433. Under the act, permits are required to excavate upon federal property. These permits are granted by the Secretary of the Interior, the Secretary of Agriculture, and the Secretary of the Army and are issued only to reputable institutions for scientific or historic preservation purposes.

10. A person who excavates on federal lands without permission of the department of the federal government having jurisdiction over the land will be fined and may be subject to imprisonment. Id. at § 433.

11. The act authorizes the President to set aside historic places, landmarks, and structures, as well as other lands of scientific value, as national monuments.

12. 16 U.S.C. § 433.

13. 16 U.S.C. §§ 461–67.

14. Id. at § 461.

15. Id. at § 462(f).

16. Id. at § 462(e).

17. 40 U.S.C. § 257.

18. In United States v. 16.92 Acres of Land, 670 F.2d 1369 (7th Cir), cert. denied, 459 U.S. 824 (1982), the Seventh Circuit Court of Appeals ruled that the federal government has condemnation powers under various federal statutes pursuant to 40 U.S.C. § 257. The court ruled that a federal statute need not specifically include condemnation as a permissible method of property acquisition. According to the court, unless a statute excludes condemnation as a method of property acquisition, the federal government has this right.

19. 16 U.S.C. § 470.

20. 16 U.S.C. §§ 470a to 470w-6.

21. To obtain a listing in the National Register, nominations are made on National Register Nomination Form NPS 10-900 with accompanying continuation sheets. The form must be completed in accord with the requirements and guidance listed in the NPS publication "How to Complete National Register Forms." See 36 C.F.R. § 60.3(i). Forms are obtained from the State Historic Preservation office. The criteria applied to evaluate property for the National Register were set out in 36 C.F.R. § 60.4. Qualifying property included buildings, sites, and objects

> that are associated with events that have made a significant contribution to the broad patterns of [U.S.] history; that are associated with the lives of persons significant in [that history]; or that embody the distinctive characteristics of a type, period, or method of construction . . . that represent the work of a master . . . that possess high artistic values, that represent a significant and distinguishable entity whose components may lack individual distinction, or that have yielded, or may be likely to yield, information important in prehistory or history.

22. Id. at § 470f. The Advisory Council on Historic Preservation adopted procedures concerning an agency's commenting responsibility. If a federal agency complied with this procedure, it could adopt any course of action it believed to be appropriate. 36 C.F.R. § 60.2.

23. The 1980 act, 16 U.S.C. §§ 470a-1, 470d, 470w-5, provided for a loan insurance program to establish a national museum of the building arts. The insured loan program was added to stimulate private investments in the preservation of properties included in the National Register. Historic properties were often viewed as high-risk investments, and nonprofit organizations interested in saving historic structures often had difficulty qualifying for loans. Most of the loans that could be insured under the act would be for acquisition and development projects.

24. See National Historic Preservation Act Amendments of 1980, Pub. L. No. 96-515, 1980 U.S. Code Cong. & Admin. News 6380.

25. 16 U.S.C. § 470a-1(a). The Secretary of the Interior acts in cooperation with the Secretary of State, the Smithsonian Institution, and the Advisory Council on Historic Preservation.

The 1980 act, 16 U.S.C. §§ 470a-1, 470d, 470w-5, provided for procedures for implementing the 1972 UNESCO World Heritage Convention discussed in Chapter 11. The U.S. Senate approved the 1972 convention in 1973 but implementing legislation was not enacted until 1980.

26. 16 U.S.C. § 470f.

27. See Boarhead Corp. v. Erikson, 923 F.2d 1011 (3rd Cir. 1991), in which the owner of a farm whose title was traced from a grant to William Penn and which had been used as the burial grounds of Native Americans complained that the Environmental Protection Agency had decided to conduct precleaning-up activities on the farm without complying with the National Historic Preservation Act.

28. 42 U.S.C. §§ 4331–70a.

29. Id. at §§ 4331–32.

30. Id. at § 4331(b)(4).

31. Id. at § 4332(2)(C). The NEPA mandates a federal agency to take a hard look at the environmental consequences of a major federal action before taking any action. It requires federal agencies to analyze, to the fullest extent possible, the potential environmental impact of "major Federal actions that significantly affect quality of the human environment." Id. at § 4332(2)(c). To meet this requirement, the NEPA requires that federal agencies prepare an environmental impact statement (EIS) before undertaking any major federal actions that may affect significantly the quality of the human environment.

32. An EIS is more than just a disclosure document. It must be used by federal officials in conjunction with other relevant material to plan actions and to make decisions.

33. 16 U.S.C. §§ 469–469c-1.

34. Id. at § 469i.

35. Discussion in Preservation Coalition, Inc. v. Pierce, 667 F.2d 851 (9th Cir. 1982).

36. Id.

37. Id. The Ninth Circuit Court of Appeals, in Preservation Coalition, cited in note 35, stated that both acts are designed to ensure that a federal agency "stop, look, and listen" before moving ahead. The court recognized that the NEPA "requires federal agencies to make detailed reports on major federal actions significantly affecting the quality of human environment," but decided that the federal action in the disputed transaction was not major.

38. See Committee to Save the Fox Building v. Birmingham Branch of Federal Reserve Bank of Atlanta, 497 F. Supp. 504 (N.D. Ala. 1980).

39. Id.

40. Id.

41. 16 U.S.C. §§ 470aa-70mm.

42. Id. at § 470aa(b). The purpose of the act is to "secure for the present and future benefit of the American people, the protection of archaeological resources and sites located on public and Indian lands." The act was also intended "to foster increased cooperation and exchange of information between governmental authorities, the professional archaeological community, and private individuals having collections of archaeological resources" obtained before October 31, 1979.

In United States v. Austin, 902 F.2d 743 (9th Cir.), cert. denied, 498 U.S. 874 (1990), defendants indicted under the Archaeological Resources Protection Act for excavating a

Native American archaeological site alleged that the act was unconstitutionally overbroad and vague. The court ruled that the act was not unconstitutional.

43. 16 U.S.C. § 470ee(a). The act also prohibits the excavation, removal, damage, or alteration of any archaeological resource. The act provides for the issuance of permits to excavate upon public or Indian lands. Id. at § 470cc. Persons receiving permits under the Archaeological Resources Protection Act need not also obtain permits under the Antiquities Act. Native American tribes or their members need not obtain a permit under either act for the excavation or removal of any archaeological resource located on their lands if tribal law regulates the excavation and removal of archaeological resources. Under the Archaeological Resources Protection Act, the Secretary of the Interior may promulgate regulations providing for (1) the exchange between universities, museums, or other scientific or educational institutions of archaeological resources removed from public lands and Indian lands, and (2) the ultimate disposition of resources removed pursuant to the act. 16 U.S.C. § 170dd. Any exchange of resources removed from Native American lands is subject to the consent of the tribe that has jurisdiction over the land. A violator is subject to a fine of $10,000 and/or imprisonment of not more than one year or, if the value of the object is more than $500, to a fine of $20,000 and/or imprisonment of not more than two years. Id. at § 470ee(d). A second violation causes the penalty to be a fine of as much as $100,000 and/or imprisonment for as long as five years.

44. 16 U.S.C. § 470bb(l).

45. Id. at § 470dd.

46. 17 U.S.C. §§ 101, 102(a)(8).

47. H.R. Rep. No. 735, 101st Cong., 2d Sess. 8 (1990), reprinted in 1990 U.S.C.C.A.N. 6941.

48. Pub. L. No. 101-650, 1990 U.S.C.C.A.N. (101 Stat.) 6936.

49. Id. at 6942.

50. 17 U.S.C. § 301(b)(4).

51. Id. at § 120(a).

52. Id. at § 120(b).

53. 2 U.S.C. § 178 (1988). (The 1988 National Film Preservation Act was repealed in 1992 and reenacted as an amendment to the Copyright Act.) Copyright Act amendment at 17 U.S.C. § 101, 102(a)(6).

54. 2 U.S.C. § 178. This act was repealed in 1992 by the National Film Preservation Act of 1992, Pub. L. No. 102-307, 102 Stat. 307 (1992).

55. Pub. L. No. 102-307, 102 Stat. 307 (1992). This act amended the Copyright Act and repealed the 1988 act.

56. Former 2 U.S.C. § 178 was repealed in 1992 as noted in note 53.

57. Discussion at 1988 U.S.C.C.A.N. 3715. Discussion of artists' moral rights in Chapters 7 and 8.

58. 17 U.S.C. § 106A was added to the Copyright Act as a result of the Visual Artist Rights Act of 1990 (VARA) as noted in Chapter 8.

59. Pub. L. 101-650, 101st Cong., 2d Sess. 21.

60. 1990 U.S.C.C.A.N. 6916.

61. Id.

62. 16 U.S.C. § 469j.

63. I.R.C. § 170(f)(3)(B), 170(h). The amount of the deduction is the value of the restriction or remainder interest.

64. IRC §§ 46, 47; Treas. Reg. § 1.46-1(q)(iii).

65. Id. at § 47(c)(1); Treas. Reg. § 1.48-12(b)(2).

66. Id. at § 47(a); Treas. Reg. § 1.46-1(q). A certified historic structure is a building that is listed in the National Register or is located in a registered historic district and has been certified by the Secretary of the Interior as being of historic significance to the district. A registered historic district is one listed in the National Register or one designated under the statute of a state (or local government), but only if the Secretary of the Interior certifies that the statute contains criteria that achieve the purpose of preserving historically significant buildings and if the district meets substantially all the requirements for districts to be listed in the National Register. IRC § 47(c)(3); Treas. Reg. § 1.48-12(d).

67. I.R.C. § 47(c)(1)(A)(ii); Treas. Reg. § 1.48-12(b)(3).

68. A mid-month convention provides for a depreciation deduction of one-half a month for the month the building is placed in use.

69. See discussion in Commonwealth v. Maritime Underwater Surveys, Inc., 531 N.E.2d 549 (Mass. 1988). Maritime claimed title to the pirate ship *Whydah*, which capsized in 1717 during a storm off the Cape Cod coast. The ship was "laden with plundered cargo."

70. See, e.g., Treasure Salvors, Inc. v. Unidentified Wrecked & Abandoned Sailing Vessel, 569 F.2d 330 (5th Cir. 1978).

71. Id.

72. See. e.g., Maritime Underwater Surveys, cited in note 69 and Treasure Salvors, Inc. v. Unidentified Wrecked & Abandoned Vessel, 569 F.2d 330 (5th Cir. 1978).

73. Maritime Underwater Surveys, cited in note 69.

74. Id.

75. H.R. Rep. No. 514 (II), 100th Cong. 2d Sess.4 (1988), reprinted in 1988 U.S. Code Cong. & Admin. News 377.

76. Pub. L. No. 100-298, § 2, 102 Stat. 432 (1988), codified at 43 U.S.C. §§ 2101–6 (1988).

77. H.R. Rep. No. 514 (II), cited in note 75.

78. 43 U.S.C. §§ 1301–15 (1988). The Submerged Lands Act, or Outer Continental Shelf Deep Water Royalty Relief Act, vests title in the United States to the lands and natural resources under the navigable waters extending three miles from a coastal state's respective coastline, but it also recognizes a coastal state's title to and ownership of the lands and navigable waters in the offshore seabed. The act transfers title and development rights in natural resources to the states without disturbing the sovereignty of the federal government over the marginal sea. In United States v. Main, 420 U.S. 515 (1975), the Supreme Court held that the Submerged Lands Act grants the United States paramount rights to the seabed located beyond the three-mile limit.

79. 43 U.S.C. § 1311 (1988). This is the case except in Texas, Puerto Rico, and the west coast of Florida, where it is three marine leagues or nine statute miles. 43 U.S.C. § 1301(b).

80. H.R. Rep. No. 514 (II), cited in note 75, 1988 U.S. Code Cong. & Admin. News, 371.

81. See, e.g., Cobb Coin Co., Inc. v. Unidentified, Wrecked & Abandoned Sailing Vessel, 525 F. Supp. 186 (S.D.Fla. 1981).

82. See Zych v. Unidentified, Wrecked & Abandoned Vessel, 941 F.2d 525 (7th Cir. 1991).

83. The Abandoned Shipwreck Act is an exercise of the federal government's "recognized sovereign prerogative to assert title to abandoned shipwrecks that lie within the waters of the United States" and is "also consistent with the recognized exception from the

law of finds for shipwrecks embedded in submerged lands of a state." H.R. Rep. No. 514 (II), cited in note 75 at 1988 U.S. Code Cong, & Admin. News, 365, 366.

84. H.R. Rep. No. 514 (II), cited in note 75, reprinted in 1988 U.S. Code Cong. & Admin. News, 365, 366.

85. 43 U.S.C. § 2101(a).

86. Id. at § 2101(b).

87. Id. at § 2105. However, the act provides that any abandoned shipwreck in or on the public lands of the United States is the property of the U.S. government. Any abandoned shipwreck in or on Indian lands is the property of the Native American tribe owning these lands.

88. Id. at § 2106(a). The act specifically states that it does not change the law relating to shipwrecks other than to those embedded in submerged lands of a state or embedded in coralline formations protected by a state on submerged lands of a state.

89. Prior to the Abandoned Shipwreck Act, states began to assert title to shipwrecks embedded in state lands. See Texas Antiquities Code § 191.091, which designated as state archaeological landmarks sunken or abandoned pre-twentieth-century ships and wrecks of vessels embedded in land belonging to the State of Texas.

In Subaqueous Exploration v. Unidentified, Wrecked Vessel, 577 F. Supp. 597 (D. Md. 1983), a salvage company brought an action seeking title to three abandoned vessels believed to be the *Santa Roselea*, the *Royal George*, and the *San Lorenzo de Escoral* that sank in the Atlantic Ocean approximately two hundred years ago. The vessels had been seized by the U.S. marshal for Maryland. The court found the vessels were within the territorial jurisdiction of Maryland. Under § 2-309 of Maryland's Natural Resources Act, any object or material of historical or archaeological value or interest found on archaeological sites or land owned or controlled by the state, was the property of the state.

90. S.C. Code Ann. §§ 54-7-610 to 54-7-850.

91. Id. at § 54-7-730.

92. Id. at §§ 54-7-640, 650, 770(6). A licensed salvor will receive at least fifty percent of the artifacts in value or in-kind.

93. Code of Ga. § 12-3-80.

94. Id. at 12-3-81.

95. Id. at § 12-3-82.

96. Id. This provision compared favorably to the South Carolina statute wherein a salvor could receive at least fifty percent of the artifacts in kind. Any person who fails to obtain a required permit or who intentionally destroys or removes any underwater cultural resource is guilty of a misdemeanor. Id. at § 12-3-83.

97. Mass. Gen. Laws, 6 § 180.

98. Id. at §§ 179 and 180.

99. Id. at § 180.

100. These activities were at their peak during the nineteenth century and the early part of the twentieth century. In 1868, the U.S. Surgeon General issued an order to all Army field offices to send him Indian skeletons. This action, along with an attitude that accepted the desecration of hundreds of thousands of Native American human remains and funerary objects, permitted Indian funerary objects and human remains to be sold or housed in museums and educational institutions around the country. For many years, Indian tribes attempted to have the remains and funerary objects returned to them. This effort touched off often heated debates on the rights of the Indians versus the importance to museums of

the retention of these funerary objects and remains in their collections as well as the scientific value of the objects and remains.

101. Article 1, Section 8, of the U.S. Constitution gives Congress the power to regulate commerce "with foreign nations and among the several states, and with the Indian tribes."

102. 25 U.S.C. § 465.

103. Section 465 states, "Title to any lands or rights acquired pursuant to this Act . . . shall be taken in the name of the United States in trust for the Indian tribe or individual Indian for which the land is acquired." In Carcieri v. Salazar, 555 U.S. 379 (2009), the Supreme Court ruled that the Secretary of the Interior's authority under the Indian Reorganization Act (IRA) to take land into trust for Indians is limited to Indian tribes that were under federal jurisdiction when the IRA was enacted. The Narragansett tribe was not recognized as a tribe until 1983. The Narrangansetts' ongoing efforts to gain recognition from the U.S. government finally succeeded in 1983. In granting formal recognition, the Bureau of Indian Affairs (BIA) determined that the "the Narrangansett community and its predecessors have existed autonomously since first contact, despite undergoing many modifications." 48 Fed. Reg. 6177-8. The BIA referred to the tribe's documented history dating from 1614.

104. Discussion in New Mexico v. Mescalero Apache Tribe, 462 U.S. 324 (1983). In Shivwits Band of Paiute Indians v. Utah State Department of Transportation, 428 F.3d 966 (10th Cir. 2005), the Tenth Circuit Court of Appeals balanced federal, tribal, and state interests against one another and concluded that permitting a state to exercise control over Indian land would "threaten Congress' overriding objective of encouraging tribal self-government and economic development." An Indian tribe leased land it had placed in trust with the federal government to an advertising enterprise for construction of outdoor billboards. The State of Utah opposed construction of the billboard. The court denied the state the right to prevent the construction.

105. Cited in note 102.

106. See also Black Hills Institute v. Dept. of Justice, 967 F.2d 1237 (8th Cir. 1992); and Black Hills Institute v. U.S. Dept., 978 F.2d 1043 (8th Cir. 1992).

107. 16 U.S.C. § 433.

108. 16 U.S.C. § 470a(d). See also 16 U.S.C. § 470-1.

109. Discussed at notes 28–40 and accompanying text.

110. 42 U.S.C. § 4332(c) and 16 U.S.C. § 470-1.

111. Tribes were very concerned about the Ninth Circuit's decision in Navajo Nation v. U.S. Forest Service, 535 F.3d 1058 (9th Cir. 2008) cert. den., 129 S. Ct. 2763 (2009). The Ninth Circuit Court of Appeals ruled that the government-approved use of artificial snow for skiing on a portion of a public mountain sacred in the religion of at least thirteen tribes did not violate the NEPA or the NHPA.

112. See discussion above, specifically Example 1, which summarizes United States v. Diaz, 499 F.2d 113 (9th Cir. 1974),

113. 42 U.S.C. § 1996.

114. In addition, the act did not include a provision that museums return religious artifacts belonging to Native American tribes.

115. Pursuant to the act, the Zuni earlier had negotiated unsuccessfully with the Smithsonian Institution to return certain of their artifacts which they alleged were stolen from their reservation at the turn of the century. Some Native Americans thought the Smithsonian had an obligation to return these artifacts inasmuch as the Smithsonian is completely

federally subsidized. Some contended museums partially financed by the federal government and those with tax exempt status also should return Indian artifacts.

116. See, e.g., Lyng v. Northwest Indian Cemetery Protective Ass'n, 485 U.S. 439 (1988); Wilson v. Block, 708 F.2d 735 (D.C. Cir), cert. denied, 464 U.S. 956 (1983); United States v. Top Sky, 547 F.2d 483 (9th Cir. 1976); and Crow v. Gullett, 541 F. Supp. 785 (D.C.S.D. 1982), aff'd 706 F.2d 856 (8th Cir. 1983). The Supreme ruled in Lyng that AIRFA does not provide a private right of action or any judicially enforceable individual rights.

117. Bear Lodge Multiple Use Ass'n. v. Babbitt, 175 F.3d 814 (10th Cir. 1999), cert. den. 529 U.S. 1037 (2000).

118. Discussed in notes 41-45 and accompanying text.

119. 16 U.S.C. § 470cc. A person receiving a permit under ARPA need not also obtain permits under the Antiquities Act of 1906. Further, tribe members were not required to obtain a permit under either ARPA or the Antiquities Act of 1906 for the excavation or removal of an archaeological resource located on their lands if tribal law regulates the excavation and removal of archaeological resources.

120. Id. at. § 470cc(c).

121. In addition, a person who willfully steals or converts for personal use or for the use of another, any property belonging to, or in the custody of, an Indian tribal organization is subject to criminal prosecution under 18 U.S.C. § 1163.

122. 18 U.S.C. § 1163.

123. 16 U.S.C. § 170dd.

124. 16 U.S.C. § 470a(d). See also 16 U.S.C. § 470-1.

125. Id.

126. Cited in note 28.

127. Preservation Coalition, Inc. v. Pierce, 667 F.2d 851, 859 (9th Cir. 1982).

128. As pointed out in note 111, tribes are very concerned about the Ninth Circuit Court of Appeal's decision in Navajo Nation v. U.S. Forest Service, also cited in note 111. When the Ninth Circuit ruled that the government-approved use of artificial snow for skiing on a portion of a public mountain sacred in the religion of at last thirteen tribes did not violate NEPA or the NHPA, tribes were concerned that these statutes were not providing them adequate protection.

129. Discussion in 7 U.S.C.C.A.N. 4369, P.L. 101-601 (1990).

130. Id. at 4370.

131. 25 U.S.C. §§ 3001–13.

132. Id. at § 3003(a). Those museums that receive Federal funds and have possession of, or control over, Native American cultural items are subject to the act. The Smithsonian, however, is exempt from the act. Still, the National Museum of the American Indian Act, 20 U.S.C. § 80q, enacted in 1989, required the Smithsonian to return human remains and funerary objects to Native American tribes. Id. at § 80q-9. This act established a museum within the Smithsonian to collect, preserve, and exhibit Native American objects. The act also provided for Native American research and study programs. Id. at § 80q-1.

133. 25 U.S.C. § 3003(b). The act provided that the intentional removal or excavation of Native American cultural items from federal or tribal lands for purposes of discovery, study, or removal was permitted only if the items were excavated or removed pursuant to a permit under the ARPA [25 U.S.C. § 3002(e)].

134. Id. at § 3003(b). Those museums that failed to comply with the act could be subject to civil penalties. Id. at § 3007.

135. Id. at § 3005(a)(1) and (c). If a museum does not have a right of possession or cannot prove it has a right of possession, the museum must return the objects. The act provides that a museum will not be liable for claims from an aggrieved party for claims for breach of fiduciary duty or good faith if the museum repatriates in good faith. Id. at § 3005(f).

136. 25 U.S.C. § 3001(13). As pointed out, if a known lineal descendant or an Indian tribe or Native Hawaiian organization requests the return of Native American associated funerary objects, sacred objects, or objects of cultural patrimony, the agency or museum must return the objects unless it can prove it has a right of possession to the objects. 25 U.S. § 3005(c).

137. Id. at § 3006.

138. See 25 U.S.C. § 3001(3)(D), which defines "cultural patrimony" as an object having "ongoing historical, traditional, or cultural importance" central to a Native American group or culture that "cannot be alienated, appropriated, or conveyed by any *individual regardless* of whether the individual is a member of the Indian tribe or Native Hawaiian organization" and the object was "considered inalienable by such Native American group at the time the object was separated from the group" (emphasis added).

139. 34 I.L.M. 1330 (June 24, 1995).

140. 25 U.S.C. § 3010.

CHAPTER 11

INTERNATIONAL CULTURAL HERITAGE PROTECTION

> Cultural property might be included among the natural resources of a nation over which permanent sovereignty is claimed.
>
> EMMANUEL ROUCOUNAS

> Without culture, and the relative freedom it implies, society, even when perfect, is but a jungle. That is why any authentic creation is a gift to the future.
>
> ALBERT CAMUS

This final chapter reviews the international conventions for the protection of the cultural heritage of humanity.[1] As noted throughout this text, museums have a dominate role in protecting the world's historic and cultural property, structures, and monuments.[2] To fulfill properly this essential function, museum directors not only must be aware of national and state laws that protect cultural property in their collections, they also must be knowledgeable of international conventions that protect the cultural heritage on an international scale. Perhaps a discussion of the importance of protecting cultural property would have best begun with a consideration of the provisions of these international treaties. However, a discussion of the international conventions was saved for last to provide an international perspective and recognition that international laws must be in place and must be observed and that international concern must exist if the cultural heritage of humanity is to be protected and preserved.

The five principal conventions that seek international protection of the cultural heritage of humanity are (1) the 1954 Hague Convention for the Protection of Cultural Property in the Event of Armed Conflict;[3] (2) the Convention on the Means of Prohibiting and Preventing the Illicit Import, Export and Transfer of Ownership of Cultural Property, adopted by the United Nations Educational, Scientific, and Cultural Organization (UNESCO) in 1970;[4] (3) the 1972 UNESCO Convention for the Protection of the World Cultural and Natural Heritage;[5] (4) the UNIDROIT Convention on Stolen or Illegally Exported Cultural Objects, which was completed in Rome in 1995;[6] and (5) the 2011 UNESCO Convention on the Protection of the Underwater Cultural Heritage.[7] The ICOM Code of Ethics for Museums requires its members to acknowledge these international conventions as a standard in interpreting its code of ethics.[8] The United States has ratified some of the provisions of three of the five international treaties protecting the cultural heritage: the 1954 Hague Convention, the 1970 UNESCO Convention, and the 1972 UNESCO Convention. The United States has not ratified the UNIDROIT Convention or the Convention on the Protection of the Underwater Cultural Heritage.

The 1970 UNESCO Convention on the Means of Prohibiting and Preventing the Illicit Import, Export and Transfer of Ownership of Cultural Property, which encompasses the international protection of cultural property and the return/restitution of stolen and/or illegally exported art and antiquities through regulation of international trade in cultural property, is the most authoritative international agreement on the protection of cultural property. It provides for State Parties' recognition of States' export and import restrictions on art and antiquities. The 1970 UNESCO Convention was adopted first principally by source States (those rich in archeological artifacts) while market States (those with major art and antiquities markets) were slow to implement the convention. The United States was the first market State to become a signatory to the 1970 UNESCO Convention when, in 1983, it enacted implementing legislation to adopt into domestic law Articles 7(b) and 9 of the convention.[9] The convention has acquired renewed authoritative international status as most market States now have ratified the convention, including the United Kingdom, Switzerland, Japan, Germany, Canada, and Australia.

The 1954 Hague Convention was the first convention to consider the protection of cultural property during armed conflict. Its Preamble provides that "damage to cultural property belonging to any people whatsoever means damage to the cultural heritage of all mankind," since, as the Preamble states, "each people makes its contribution to the culture of the world."[10] The Preamble to the 1970 UNESCO Convention declares that "cultural property constitutes one of the basic elements of civilization and national culture and . . . its interchange increases the knowledge of the civilization of man, enriches the cultural life of all people, and inspires mutual respect and appreciation among nations." Parties to the recent UNIDROIT Convention avowed that they were

> convinced of the fundamental importance of the protection of cultural heritage and of cultural exchanges for promoting and understanding between peoples, and the dissemination of culture for the well-being of humanity and the progress of civilisation.[11]

The value attached to cultural property mandates acknowledgment of its significance and the need for protection of this special property both by law and by public awareness. International conventions protecting cultural property assume that the collective efforts of all nations and peoples are required to protect and preserve the cultural heritage of humanity.

In 1978, in its Recommendations for the Protection of Movable Cultural Property, UNESCO endorsed the international exchange of cultural property but urged museums and similar institutions to reinforce the prevention of risks to movable cultural property by a comprehensive system of practical security measures and technical installations to ensure that all cultural property is kept, exhibited, and transported in such a manner as to protect it from all elements likely to damage or destroy it, including, in particular, heat, light, humidity, pollution, various chemical and biological agents, vibration, and shock.[12] Member States agreed to facilitate the protection of collections belonging to private organizations or individuals by inviting the owners to make inventories of their collections, to communicate the inventories to the official services responsible for the protection of the cultural heritage, and to grant access to competent official curators and technicians in order to study and advise on safeguarding measures. Member States endeavor to provide for the proper protection and presentation of cultural property in religious buildings and archaeological sites.[13] Member States must encourage competent authorities at national, regional, or local levels to provide children, young people, and adults with the means of acquiring knowledge and respect for movable cultural property and should draw the attention of the public at large by every possible means to the significance and importance of cultural property—but without stressing the purely commercial value of such property—and the opportunities available to them for participating in activities undertaken by competent authorities to protect cultural property.[14]

A. CONVENTION DEFINITIONS OF CULTURAL PROPERTY

A resolution of what to include in a list of "cultural property" is complex. While some properties leave little doubt as to their cultural significance, others may cause problems in being included in such a catalogue. Still, a proper classification is crucial for nations to preserve and protect this property and, in some instances, to agree to return cultural property with universal value to the countries of origin.

Article 1 of the 1954 Hague Convention for the Protection of Cultural Property in the Event of Armed Conflict includes in the definition of the term "cultural property"

> (a) movable or immovable property of great importance to the cultural heritage of every people, such as monuments of architecture, art or history, whether religious or secular; archaeological sites; groups of buildings which, as a whole, are of historical or artistic interest; works of art; manuscripts, books and other objects of artistic, historical or archaeological interest; as well as scientific collections and important collections of books or archives or of reproductions of the property defined above;
> (b) buildings whose main and effective purpose is to preserve or exhibit the movable cultural property defined in sub-paragraph (a) such as museums, large libraries and depositories of archives, and refuges intended to shelter, in the event of armed conflict, . . . movable cultural property . . .
> (c) centres containing a large amount of cultural property . . . to be known as "centres containing monuments."

Article 1 of the 1970 UNESCO Convention sets out a detailed list of property which it designates as "cultural property." This same list was annexed to the UNIDROIT Convention as the type of property that meets the definitional standards of "cultural property."[15] The 1970 UNESCO Convention defines "cultural property" as

> property which, on religious or secular grounds, is specifically designated by each State as being of importance for archaeology, prehistory, history, literature, art or science and which belongs to the following categories:
>
> (a) Rare collections and specimens of fauna, flora, minerals and anatomy, and objects of paleontological interest;
> (b) property relating to history, including the history of science and technology and military and social history, to the life of national leaders, thinkers, scientists and artists and to events of national importance;
> (c) products of archaeological excavations (including regular and clandestine) or of archaeological discoveries;
> (d) elements of artistic or historical monuments or archaeological sites which have been dismembered;
> (e) antiquities more than one hundred years old, such as inscriptions, coins and engraved seals;
> (f) objects of ethnological interest;
> (g) property of artistic interest, such as:
>   (i) pictures, paintings and drawings produced entirely by hand on any support and in any material(excluding industrial designs and manufactured articles decorated by hand);
>   (ii) original works of statuary art and sculpture in any material;
>   (iii) original engravings, prints and lithographs;
>   (iv) original artistic assemblages and montages in any material;
> (h) rare manuscripts and incunabula, old books, documents and publications of special interest(historical, artistic, scientific, literary, etc.) singly or in collections;
> (i) postage, revenue and similar stamps, singly or in collections;
> (j) archives, including sound, photographic and cinematographic archives;
> (k) articles of furniture more than one hundred years old and old musical instruments.

Article 1 of the 1972 UNESCO Convention defines "cultural property" as monuments that include "architectural works, works of monumental sculpture and painting, elements or structures of archaeological nature, inscriptions, cave dwellings, groups of buildings, and sites, including archaeological sites, which are of outstanding universal value from the point of view of history, art or science." Article 1 of the 1972 UNESCO Convention adds a definition of "natural heritage." The following are considered natural heritage:

> *natural features* consisting of physical and biological formations or groups of such formations, which are of outstanding universal value from the aesthetic or scientific point of view;
>
> *geological and physiographical formations* and precisely delineated areas which constitute the habitat of threatened species of animals and plants of outstanding universal value from the point of view of science or conservation;
>
> *natural sites* or precisely delineated natural areas of outstanding universal value from the point of view of science, conservation or natural beauty.

The Annex to the 1995 UNIDROIT Convention defines "cultural objects" in accordance with Article 1 of the 1970 UNESCO Convention (see above).

Article 1 of the 2001 UNESCO Convention on the Protection of the Underwater Cultural Heritage defines "underwater cultural heritage" as

> all traces of human existence having a cultural, historical or archaeological character which have been partially or totally under water, periodically or continuously, for at least 100 years such as:
>
> (i) sites, structures, buildings, artefacts and human remains, together with their archaeological and natural context;
> (ii) vessels, aircraft, other vehicles or any part thereof, their cargo or other contents, together with their archaeological and natural context; and
> (iii) objects of prehistoric character.

Legislation in some countries refer to protected cultural property as "monuments of cultural and historical value," "objects of artistic and historical interest," "ancient monuments," "national monuments," "historic monuments," "archaeological monuments and objects," and sometimes simply as "antiquities."[16] This general terminology alone, without definition, can prove troublesome to courts attempting to enforce the law.[17] For example, courts in the United States have encountered problems in enforcing provisions of the Antiquities Act of 1906.[18] The Antiquities Act of 1906 provides penalties for destroying or damaging any historic "ruin," "monument," or "object of antiquity" located on public lands in the United States.[19] As noted in Chapter 10, one U.S. appellate court reversed the conviction of an individual under the act because the court decided these terms were unconstitutionally vague.[20]

One problem with terminology that limits cultural property to antiquities, archaeological objects, and historical properties is that works of many modern artists should also be characterized as important cultural property. In enacting the Visual Artists Rights Act (VARA)[21] as an amendment to the U.S. Copyright Act (discussed in Chapters 7 and 8),[22] Congress referred to art as a part of our cultural legacy.[23] Congress commented that VARA would prevent distortions of works that "cheat the public of an accurate account of the culture of our time."[24] As noted in Chapter 8, the U.S. Congress provided for a moral right for contemporary visual artists to mitigate against destruction of artistic creations and to protect their historical legacy. The creator of a work of visual art has the right to prevent any intentional distortion, mutilation, or other modification of her work.[25] Still, because in the United States the moral right endures only for the life of the visual artist,[26] international conventions can provide added protection for contemporary artistic treasures that should also be part of the cultural heritage of humanity.

B. 1954 HAGUE CONVENTION FOR THE PROTECTION OF CULTURAL PROPERTY IN THE EVENT OF ARMED CONFLICT

Although concern for the protection of cultural property evolved in the mid-nineteenth century,[27] the first significant international legislation to protect cultural property was the 1954 Hague Convention for the Protection of Cultural Property in the Event of Armed Conflict. The Hague Convention seeks to protect cultural property during wartime. It prohibits the destruction or seizure of cultural property during armed conflict, whether international or civil in nature, and during a period of belligerent occupation, but it also applies to peacetime international trafficking in cultural property unlawfully seized during an armed conflict.[28]

The Preamble to the 1954 Hague Convention recognizes cultural property has suffered grave damage during armed conflicts and states that "damage to cultural property belonging to any people whatsoever means damage to the cultural heritage of all mankind," because "each people makes its contribution to the culture of the world." The Preamble was the first in its statement that "heritage should receive international protection."

As stated in Article 4(1), (3), parties to the 1954 Hague Convention must prohibit the destruction or misappropriation of cultural property in the event of armed conflict, but under Articles 3 and 4(4), (5), parties also must protect cultural property during peacetime, both cultural property within the party's territory and cultural property unlawfully seized during an armed conflict.

1. Protection of Cultural Property during Armed Conflict

Special protection is granted to cultural property by its entry in the "International Register of Cultural Property under Special Protection."[29] The register, which is maintained by the director-general of UNESCO, is sub-divided into three paragraphs headed "Refuges," "Centres containing Monuments," and "Other Immovable Cultural Property."[30] Each contracting party agreed to take into its custody cultural property imported into its territory from any occupied territory and agreed to return the cultural property at the close of hostilities.[31] Centers containing monuments and other immovable cultural property of very great importance may be placed under special protection if they are situated at an adequate distance from any large industrial center or from any important military objective constituting a vulnerable point and are not used for military purposes.[32]

At the request of a contracting party, Articles 12 and 13 permit special protection for transport that is exclusively engaged in the transfer of cultural property, whether within a territory or to another territory. Parties to the convention must refrain from any act of hostility directed against transport of property.

Article 40 requires a party to the convention to take into its custody cultural property imported into its territory directly or indirectly from any occupied territory. This article requires the party to return at the end of hostilities, to competent authorities of the territory from which it came, cultural property deposited with it for the purpose of protecting the property against dangers of an armed conflict. At the close of hostilities, a party to the convention also must undertake to return cultural property in its territory to the competent authorities of the territory previously occupied if the property was exported in contravention of the Hague Convention. Article 40 states that this property "shall never be retained as war reparations." Article 11 provides for withdrawal of immunity of cultural property in exceptional cases of unavoidable military necessity but only for such time as that necessity continues. Article 28 provides for penal or disciplinary sanctions against persons, of whatever nationality, who commit, or order to be committed, a breach of the convention.

2. Blue Shield

Articles 6 and 16 provide that cultural property may bear a distinctive emblem (a blue shield) during military conflict to facilitate its recognition.[33] The emblem may be displayed on flags or armlets or it may be painted on an object or represented in any other appropriate form.[34] Article 17 provides that the emblem repeated three times is used as a means of identification of immovable cultural property under special protection, the transport of cultural property, and improvised refuges.[35] Cultural property being transported under special protection is immune from seizure or capture.[36] The distinctive emblem is used alone only as a means of identification of cultural property not under special protection, persons responsible for the duties of control, personnel engaged in the protection of cultural property, and those carrying a special identity card bearing the distinctive emblem.[37]

3. International Committee of the Blue Shield

The International Committee of the Blue Shield (ICBS) was formed by four nongovernmental organizations: the International Council on Archives (ICA) located in Paris, France; the International Council of Museums (ICOM); the International Council on Monuments and Sites (ICOMOS); and the International Federation of Library Associations and Institutions (IFLA). The ICBS works in partnership with other international organizations to protect world cultural heritage that is threatened by natural and man-made disasters. It responds to emergency situations that may threaten cultural heritage and facilitates international responses to threats or emergencies. It provides training of experts at national and regional levels and works toward the protection and safeguarding of cultural heritage against flood, fire, and natural disasters.

Many national committees have been organized under the ICBS to promote the ratification and implementation of the Hague Convention by national governments. The Association of National Committees of the Blue Shield (ANCBS), which is located in the Hague, Netherlands, coordinates endeavors of the national committees regarding the strategic and operational guidelines adopted by the ICBS.

The U.S. Committee of the Blue Shield, which is the U.S. affiliate of this global network, is one of these national committees. It coordinates efforts with the military, national and local governments, and different cultural property professions to protect cultural property worldwide during armed conflict.

4. Protocols to the 1954 Hague Convention

There are two protocols to the 1954 Hague Convention. The First Protocol requires a party to prevent exportation of cultural property from a territory occupied by it and to pay indemnity to holders in good faith for any cultural property taken in contravention of the convention. The Second 1999 Protocol compels nations to curtail theft and vandalism of artifacts, to preserve cultural property when occupying foreign territory, and to avoid targeting and use of cultural sites for military purposes. The Second Protocol furnishes enhanced protection for specifically identified cultural property and legislates criminal responsibility for any property subject to enhanced protection that is the object of attack; for using cultural property in support of military action; for extensive destruction to cultural property; and for theft, pillage, or misappropriation of cultural property. The protocol provides for prosecution through proceedings in accordance with domestic law or, if applicable, with rules of international law. The 1999 Protocol states that a waiver of the convention's provisions on the basis of military necessity applies only so long as cultural property has, by its function, been made into a military objective and there is no feasible alternative to obtain similar military advantage. It assigns the decision to waive the convention requirements to the commanding officer.

The Second Protocol agreed in 1999 to give a new impetus to the ICBS's role and that of its affiliate organizations. It recognizes the ICBS as an advisory international organization to the intergovernmental Committee for the Protection of Cultural Property in the Event of Armed Conflict.

C. 1970 UNESCO CONVENTION ON THE MEANS OF PROHIBITING AND PREVENTING THE ILLICIT IMPORT, EXPORT AND TRANSFER OF OWNERSHIP OF CULTURAL PROPERTY

The 1970 UNESCO Convention on the Means of Prohibiting and Preventing the Illicit Import, Export and Transfer of Ownership of Cultural Property is the second and the most authoritative international agreement to address means to protect cultural property. Language in the 1954 Hague Convention and the 1970 UNESCO Convention addresses the concept of a "common heritage of humanity" to which everyone, of whatever nationality, should have free access.[38] Both conventions reflect a widespread concern that this common heritage could be obliterated by destruction as well as by theft and the illicit import and export of cultural properties.

The 1970 Convention provides a framework for cooperation among nations to prevent the pillage of archaeological and ethnological material and focuses on private conduct primarily during peacetime. It was enacted after the international community became concerned in the 1960s about the importation into various countries of artifacts unlawfully obtained from a country of origin.[39] The international concern about the increasingly illegal international trade in priceless art and antiquities that led to the drafting of the 1970 international agreement by the General Conference of UNESCO prompted parties to the convention to agree to oppose all illicit import, export, and transfer of ownership of cultural property with whatever means at their disposal. At the meeting of the General Conference in Paris in 1970, the several nations in attendance recognized that the illicit trade in cultural property of various nations had become a primary cause of the impoverishment of the cultural heritage of originating countries. It was concluded that international cooperation constituted one of the most efficient means of protecting each country's cultural property against the dangers resulting from the illicit transfer of such properties.[40]

An objective of the 1970 Convention is to preserve ethnological material in its societal context and to protect knowledge obtained from an informed and scientific retrieval and study of archaeological objects. Parties to the 1970 UNESCO Convention must keep an up-to-date list of important public and private cultural property whose export would constitute an appreciable impoverishment of the national cultural heritage. They must contribute to the formation of laws and regulations designed to secure the protection of the cultural heritage; promote the development of scientific and technical institutions required to ensure the preservation and presentation of cultural property; organize the supervision of archaeological excavations; take educational measures to stimulate and develop respect for the cultural heritage of all nations; and see that appropriate publicity is given to the disappearance of any items of cultural property.[41] Parties to the convention must introduce an appropriate certificate in which an exporting State would specify that the export of the cultural property in question was authorized. The certificate must accompany all items of cultural property legally exported.[42] Exportation without the certificate is prohibited.

Parties to the convention agree to take necessary measures to prevent museums and similar institutions within their territories from acquiring cultural property originating in another Party State if the property was illegally exported after the effective date of the convention. Parties agree to prohibit the import of cultural property stolen from a museum or religious or secular public monument. Further, pursuant to Article 7 of the convention, at the request of a Party State of origin, parties to the convention must take appropriate steps to recover and return any cultural property imported after entry into force of the convention provided that an innocent purchaser or a person with valid title to the property must be paid just compensation.[43]

Article 10 of the convention requires parties to the convention to agree to restrict by education, information, and vigilance movement of cultural property illegally removed from a party nation and to require antique dealers to maintain a register recording the origin of each item of cultural property, names and addresses of the supplier, and the description and price of each item sold. In addition, parties to the convention agree to inform the purchaser of cultural property of export prohibitions to which this property may be subject. Parties also agree to create and develop in the public mind a realization of the value of cultural property and the threat to the cultural heritage created by theft, clandestine excavations, and illicit exports.[44] Parties to the convention recognize the right of each party to the convention to classify and declare certain cultural property as inalienable and, thus, prohibit this specific cultural property from exportation under any circumstances.[45]

I. Guidelines of the American Association of Art Museum Directors and the American Alliance of Museums

The current significant impact of the 1970 UNESCO Convention on the international trade in art and antiquities is evidenced by guidelines promulgated by the American Association of Art Museum Directors (AAMD; the AAMD is a membership organization representing over 180 directors of major art museums in the United States, Canada, and Mexico). In June 2008, the AAMD published its "2008 Report on the Acquisition of Archaeological Materials and Ancient Art" wherein the AAMD recognized the 1970 UNESCO Convention "as providing the most pertinent threshold date for the application of more rigorous standards to the acquisition of archeological material and ancient art." The AAMD issued new guidelines for its member institutions and recommended that museums should not acquire a work unless provenance research substantiates the work was removed from the probable country of modern discovery before 1970 or was legally exported from its probable country of modern discovery after 1970. The AAMD expressed its position that museums should "go beyond the letter of the law" in considering acquisitions of art and antiquities and ensure that their acquisitions are "responsible and ethical as well as legal."

Not only has the "2008 Report on the Acquisition of Archaeological Materials and Ancient Art," which sets out guidelines for its AAMD member institutions, affected appreciably the international trade in art and antiquities in the United States, a document promulgated by the American Alliance of Museums (AAM)[46] Board of Directors also recognizes the importance of the 1970 UNESCO Convention in the United States in governing the international trade in art and antiquities. The AAM "Standards Regarding Archaeological Material and Ancient Art," published in July 2008, sets out standards relating to archaeological material and ancient art to guide operations of museums that own or acquire archaeological material and ancient art originating outside the United States. The AAM recommends that museums require documentation that an object was out of its probable country of modern discovery by November 17, 1970, the date on which the 1970 UNESCO Convention was signed. For objects exported from their country of modern discovery after November 17, 1970, the AAM recommends that museums require documentation the objects have been or will be legally exported from their country of modern discovery and legally imported into the United States.

The 2008 AAMD Guidelines and the 2008 AAM Standards address due diligence requirements for a purchaser of valuable cultural property to obtain good title to the property. They caution indirectly that no purchaser should acquire a work unless provenance research substantiates the work was removed from the probable country of modern discovery before 1970 or was legally exported from its probable country of modern discovery after 1970. (The 2008 AAMD Guidelines and the AAM Standards do not provide guidelines for museums relating to acquisitions of stolen and/or illegally exported artifacts that were out of their country of modern discovery prior to November 17, 1970.)

2. Provisional Adoption by the United States

The United States adopted only two provisions of the 1970 UNESCO Convention, Articles 7(b) and 9. It agreed to take steps contemplated by Article 7(b) for the return of covered stolen cultural property without payment of compensation except to the extent required by the Constitution of the United States for those State Parties that agreed to do the same for U.S. institutions. Pursuant to Article 9, the President can enter into a bilateral agreement with a State Party to apply import restrictions on archaeological and ethnological materials that are subject to plunder from that State. The United States declined to implement Article 10 because it thought the regulation of antiquities dealers should be best left to state and local governments.

The U.S. Congress enacted the Cultural Property Implementation Act (CPIA)[47] in 1982 (effective 1983), to implement into domestic law Articles 7(b) and 9 of the 1970 UNESCO Convention. After Congress enacted the CPIA, President Reagan delegated presidential responsibilities under the statute to the Secretary of the State, the Secretary of the Treasury, and the Director of the United States Information Agency.[48] The Secretary of State was responsible for negotiating Article 9 agreements and developing reports for the Congress. The Secretary of the Treasury was responsible for imposing emergency import restrictions and suspending non-emergency imports restrictions and publishing notice of Article 9 requests. In 2003, President George W. Bush withdrew CPIA authority that had been delegated to the Secretary of the Treasury and transferred that authority to the Secretary of Homeland Security.[49] The authority of the Secretary of Homeland Security under CPIA is delegated to Customs and Border Protection.

Article 7(b) of the 1970 UNESCO Convention prohibits importation into the United States of stolen cultural property that is documented in the inventory of another State Party. (A State Party is any country that has joined the 1970 UNESCO Convention.) As noted previously, pursuant to Article 9, the President can enter into a bilateral agreement with a State Party to apply import restrictions on archaeological and ethnological materials that are subject to plunder from that State. When the President has entered into a bilateral agreement with a requesting State Party, the President applies import restrictions curbing the importation of designated archaeological or ethnological material exported from that nation (unless the requesting nation has issued a certificate that an exportation was not in violation of that nation's laws).

When the President receives a request from a State Party to the 1970 UNESCO Convention that the United States impose measures under Article 9 of the 1970 Convention to protect the requesting country's cultural patrimony, the President must (1) publish notification of the request in the Federal Register and (2) submit this information to the Cultural Property Advisory Committee (CPAC).[50] The CPAC was established pursuant to the CPIA to advise the President (or the President's designee) on appropriate U.S. action in response to requests from State Parties for assistance in protection of their cultural heritage.[51]

The CPAC reviews requests to the United States to enter into bilateral agreements and provides its findings and recommendations to the Department of State. It advises the State Department's Undersecretary for Educational and Cultural Affairs on the import restriction requests from foreign governments. Its recommendations are considered prior to a decision, but the

CPAC has no final authority to approve or deny import restrictions. If the department's Bureau of Educational and Cultural Affairs enters into a memorandum of understanding (MOU) with a foreign country on import restrictions wherein its import restrictions differ from the CPAC's recommendation, the department must file a report with Congress that indicates how and why the import restrictions differ from the CPAC's recommendations.[52] The Cultural Heritage Center, through the Assistant Secretary of State for Education and Cultural Affairs, provides technical and administrative support for the CPAC. Meetings of the CPAC may be convened to review a new request from a foreign government, to consider a proposal to extend an existing agreement, or to conduct reviews of existing agreements. The committee consists of eleven members appointed by the President to renewable three-year terms. Two members represent the interests of museums; three members are experts in archaeology, anthropology, ethnology, or related fields; three members are experts in the international sale of cultural property; and three members represent the interests of the general public.

If the President enters into any agreement with a requesting State to implement Article 9 of the 1970 UNESCO Convention, the Article 9 agreement must designate the archaeological or ethnological material that will be protected by import restrictions.[53] After the agreement enters into force, the CPIA requires the Secretary of the Treasury to promulgate the list of the archaeological or ethnological material of the State Party covered by the agreement. The CPIA grants the Secretary of Treasury authority to determine how import restrictions will be enforced on the archaeological or ethnological objects that appear on the designated list. The regulations governing enforcement of import restrictions[54] are enforced by appropriate customs officers.

After the Secretary of the Treasury promulgates a list of the designated materials, the CIPA makes it unlawful to import any designated archaeological or ethnological material that is exported from a State Party unless the State Party issues a certification or other documentation certifying the exportation was not in violation of the laws of the State Party.[55]

In 2013, the United States had entered into bilateral agreements with sixteen States: Belize, Bolivia, Cambodia, Canada, China, Columbia, Cyprus, El Salvador, Greece, Guatemala, Honduras, Iraq, Italy, Mali, Nicaragua, and Peru.

Example 1. In United States v. An Original Manuscript, 1999 WL 97894 (S.D.N.Y. 1999), in a forfeiture action brought by the federal government, pursuant to a provision in the Cultural Property Implementation

Act (CPIA),[56] regarding a manuscript dated November 19, 1778, and bearing the signature of Junipero Serra that once was property of the national archives of Mexico, the court granted summary judgment for the United States. The claimant to the manuscript purchased it for $16,000 cash from a Mexico City book, coin, and manuscript dealer who had bought it at a flea market for $300 to $400 cash. The claimant's attorney incorporated into the bill of sale a statement that the manuscript was part of the Sanchez-Flores Collection between 1925 and 1972. In 1996, the claimant consigned the manuscript to Sotheby's for auction at an estimated price range of $20,000 to $30,000. The Mexican National Archives asserted a claim to the manuscript and requested its return. The court noted that the United States had acceded to the 1970 UNESCO Convention and formally ratified it in 1983 through enactment of the CPIA,[57] which focuses primarily on implementation of Articles 7(b) and 9 of the 1970 UNESCO Convention. The court ruled that the United States has the initial burden of proof, but it decided that to establish a prima facie case for forfeiture, the government need only demonstrate probable cause. Once the government established probable cause for forfeiture, the court held the burden of proof shifted to the claimant to establish by a preponderance of the evidence the property was not subject to forfeiture, or to establish any applicable affirmative defense. The court referred to the section of the CPIA[58] which states the government must prove an article was stolen after the effective date of the act or after the date of entry into force of the convention, whichever is later. It noted the effective date of the act was ninety days after January 12, 1983, and the convention was ratified by Mexico on or about April 1, 1973. Thus, according to the court, the government had to prove the manuscript was stolen after the later date, approximately April 12, 1983. The court determined the evidence showed the manuscript was contained in the Mexican National Archives microfilm records as of September 1993 and, thus, decided the manuscript was stolen after 1983. The court ruled the government had met its burden of establishing there was probable cause to believe the seized manuscript was the same one that had been reported as stolen from the Mexican National Archives. The court found that the claimant had been "willfully blind" to the suspicious nature of the manuscript transaction. While the court noted that the CPIA[59] provides for compensation for claimants who can establish they hold good title or are innocent purchasers, it found the claimant was not an innocent purchaser and denied him compensation.

Example 2. The bilateral agreements the United States has with Bolivia and Peru pursuant to the CPIA were reviewed in United States v. Eighteenth Century Peruvian Oil on Canvas Painting of the *Doble Trinidad*, 597 F. Supp.2d 618 (E.D.Va 2009). In this case, the court ruled that two paintings were properly seized and administratively forfeited under the CPIA regardless of whether they originated in Bolivia or Peru. (A citizen of Bolivia brought two paintings into the United States from Bolivia that included *Doble Trinidad*. The paintings were cut from their frames, rolled up, and packed in cardboard cylinders and brought into the United States via Miami International and Reagan Washington National airports. The claimant gave the paintings to Hugo Borda to take to an art gallery. The gallery informed Borda the paintings needed to be restored. After the restoration, the gallery retained the paintings to sell on consignment. A prerequisite to sale was documentation of the claimant's ownership. When the claimant was unable to provide official documentation, the gallery sent the paintings to an art dealer who observed they were representative of the Cuzco School of Art and had been cut crudely from their frames. The art dealer concluded the paintings were stolen and contacted the FBI. The FBI sent digital images of the paintings to the National Institute of Culture in Lima, Peru. An expert there concluded the paintings belonged to the Peruvian cultural patrimony and that they were subject to forfeiture under the CPIA. The court found the 1970 UNESCO Convention and a 1997 Memorandum of Understanding between the United States and Peru, as well as the 2002 and 2007 Extensions of the Memorandum ("Peru MOU") were agreements under the CPIA.[60] The court determined that the CPIA made it illegal to import into the United States the Colonial-era painting *Doble Trinidad*, which was produced in Peru by indigenous people and used for religious evangelism among these people. The court concluded the painting was important to the cultural heritage of these people and that it was without documentation from Peru certifying that its exportation from Peru did not violate Peruvian law. The court ruled the government initially has the burden to show that the CPIA applies but that after that is accomplished, the CPIA[61] places the burden of proof in the remainder of the action on the claimant. The court found the government had satisfied its initial burden. It also found the claimant had exported the paintings from their country of origin without the documentation required by the CPIA.[62] Consequently, the court ruled the paintings were subject to forfeiture under the CPIA.

Example 3. In Ancient Coin Collectors Guild v. U.S. Department of State, 641 F.3d 504 (D.C. Cir. 2011), Coin Collectors Guilds had brought an action challenging the Department of State's refusal to turn over documents relating to their Freedom of Information Act (FOIA) requests for information relating to import restriction on ancient coins from Cyprus, Italy, and China. The CPIA established that information discussed in closed meetings of the Cultural Property Advisory Committee (CPAC) is not subject to disclosure under the Federal Advisory Committee Act, which makes FOIA standards applicable to advisory committees.[63] The district court had ruled the State Department properly withheld the disputed information. The Court of Appeals for the District of Columbia affirmed in part, reversed in part, and remanded. This appellate court held the guilds failed to show information was withheld improperly pursuant to the exemption for information classified as secret by executive order.[64] It ruled the department properly withheld requested documents dealing with import restrictions pursuant to the exemption for matters specifically exempted from disclosure by statute. The appellate court approved the state's withholding of factual summaries pursuant to the exemption for inter-agency or intra-agency memorandums or letters but ruled that the state failed to establish information contained in private individuals' e-mails was exempted from disclosure. It further ruled the state failed to establish the adequacy of its search with respect to employees' archived e-mails and backup tapes.

Example 4. In Ancient Coin Collectors Guild v. U.S. Customs and Border Protection, 801 F. Supp. 2d 383 (D. Md. 2011), the guild filed an action to test the legality of import restrictions on certain ancient Cypriot and Chinese coins after customs officials seized twenty-three ancient Cypriot and Chinese coins the guild had purchased from a coin dealer in London and had imported to the United States. The invoice that accompanied the Cypriot and Chinese coins, which the guild purchased in London, stated the coins were minted in Cyprus or China, that each coin had no recorded provenance, and that for each the "find spot" was unknown. The guild imported the coins via a flight from London to Baltimore. Customs detained the coins for alleged violations of the CPIA and its regulations.[65] The guild challenged the actions of Customs and the State Department. The court ruled that the purchase invoice for the coins was sufficient to satisfy the government's burden of showing the coins were among those on the designated lists for China and

Cyprus. The burden then shifted to the guild to demonstrate the coins were legally importable. Because the guild expressly disclaimed any ability to make this showing, the court dismissed its claim.

3. Application of Convention Requirements in Other Countries

Courts in other countries have encountered interesting legal issues relating to the 1970 UNESCO Convention.

Example 5. In applying concepts of the 1970 UNESCO Convention in a suit for return/restitution of stolen cultural property, a Canadian court had to address the question of whether there is a legal problem relating to a lawsuit being brought in a country which had not ratified the 1970 Convention specifically to avoid provisions of the convention. In Union of India v. Bumper Development Corp. Ltd. [1996] L.L Pr. 78, a Canadian art lover and philanthropist, on behalf of a corporation which he controlled, in good faith purchased from a London dealer an Indian temple bronze known as a "Nataraja." The purchaser applied for export permits, which the United Kingdom granted. While the bronze was undergoing restoration work at the British Museum, it was seized by the Metropolitan Police who believed (it transpired wrongly) that the bronze had been stolen from a Swiss art collector. After the purchaser sued the police for return of the bronze, the Indian High Commission alleged the bronze had been stolen from land belonging to a ruined temple in Tamil Nadu. A trial resulted on the question whether India had a better title to the bronze than the purchaser. Although India's evidence was contradictory to provenance of the bronze and there was a possibility the Indian witnesses had been coached, the court found for the ruined temple and awarded it damages and costs. The court of appeals dismissed the purchaser's appeal, and a petition for leave to appeal to the House of Lords was refused. The bronze was returned to India. The purchaser contended India made a conscious decision not to pursue its claim for the return to India of the Nataraja in Alberta, Canada, where the purchaser's corporation was incorporated, to avoid any application of the 1970 UNESCO Convention and the equities that underlie that international agreement. (At the time of the lawsuit, the UK was not a signatory to the 1970 Convention.) The convention would have imposed upon India the obligation of paying the purchaser compensation for losing the Nataraja if the purchaser was found to be an innocent purchaser. Canada contacted India with respect to the purchaser's claim for compensation for its loss of the bronze, but India never responded to Canada. India sought to have its judgment against the purchaser for damages and costs recognized and enforced in Canada. The defense was that the judgment was contrary to Canadian public policy and the purchaser was entitled to be compensated for loss of the bronze. The purchaser argued the judgment was unenforceable as obtained by fraud and counterclaimed for $3 million as compensation for loss of the bronze under the 1970 UNESCO Convention. Both India and Canada were signatories to the 1970 UNESCO Convention. The court noted that pursuant to Canada adopting the 1970 Convention, the Attorney General of Canada could institute an action in a Canadian court for the recovery of property of the reciprocating State and that where it was established the person in control of cultural property was a bona fide purchaser for value of the cultural property and had no knowledge the property had been exported illegally from the reciprocating State, the Canadian court could fix an amount as the court considered just in the circumstances to be paid as compensation. Subject to the payment of the fixed compensation, Canada could order return of the cultural property to the reciprocating State. The Canadian court recognized that the English courts had determined the purchaser to have been an innocent purchaser, but the Canadian court commented that "just compensation" is payable only to an innocent purchaser by the requesting State in circumstances in which the foreign cultural property had been imported into the importing State. The Canadian court found no evidence that the bronze was imported into, or sent to, Canada. Rather it found that the bronze was returned to India from England. Further, the Canadian court found that the Union of India had never made a request for return or the recovery of the bronze either to the United Kingdom or to Canada. Thus, the Canadian court decided the 1970 Convention had no application to the action. The court ruled that Canada had undertaken a duty to India by becoming a signatory of the 1970 UNESCO Convention. The Canadian court found there were reasons for India to have pursued its claim in England other than the fact that, at the time of the lawsuit, the UK was not a signatory to the 1970 Convention. The bronze was in England at the time India filed its claim in England. The Indian claimants had a better legal title under the common law. The Canadian court decided India's election to take action in England did not give rise to any right in the purchaser to claim compensation from India in Canadian courts. The court rejected the purchaser's defense of public policy to refuse recognition and enforcement of foreign judgments. The court stated that in private international law, invocation of policy to refuse recognition of foreign judgments should be kept within narrow limits. The Canadian court noted the decision of the English courts was based on its finding that the ruined temple in India had a title to the bronze superior to that of the purchaser. Thus, the court awarded to the ruined temple the damages awarded by the English court of appeal. The court refused to award the purchaser compensation as an innocent purchaser.

Example 6. In Iran v. Barakat Galleries, Ltd. [2009] Q.B. 22 [2007] EWCA Civ. 1374, Iran asserted ownership of antiquities almost 5,000 years old, which were held by a London gallery that traded in ancient art and antiquities from around the world. The gallery owner claimed to have purchased the antiquities in France, Germany, and Switzerland under laws the owner alleged gave him good title to the artifacts. However, the English court recognized and enforced Iran's title to the objects. The English court decided the antiquities had been excavated and unlawfully removed from Iran even though the Iranian government never possessed the objects. The English court cited the 1970 UNESCO Convention and noted that the UK ratified the convention in 2002. It ruled that Iran had an immediate right to possession under the law of Iran and that the Iranian law, of itself, would suffice to find a claim by Iran for conversion in the English courts. The English court also cited the decision United States v. Schulz,[66] wherein a U.S. court had held an art collector criminally responsible under the U.S. National Stolen Properties Act[67] for taking artifacts unlawfully from Egypt. The English court noted that the U.S. court ruled in that case that an Egyptian patrimony law made the Egyptian government owner of the antiquities. (The Schultz case and the National Stolen Properties Act are discussed in Chapter 6.)

Example 7. In Beyeler v. Italy (33202/96) No. 1 (2001) 33 E.H.R.R. 52, a Swiss art collector had purchased a painting, *Portrait of a Young Peasant* by Vincent Van Gogh, in 1977, for 600 million lire, or 310,000 euros. The art collector bought the painting through an intermediary, a Rome antiques dealer, who applied for an export license for the painting from Italian authorities. However, the art collector waited six years, until 1983, before he declared his purchase to Italy. He intended to sell the painting to the Peggy Guggenheim Collection in Venice for 2.1 million euros. The Italian authorities refused to issue a license. They contended the painting's export would be detrimental to its national cultural heritage. Although Italian authorities claimed title to the painting under the 1970 UNESCO Convention, the European Court of Human Rights observed that Article 4 of the 1970 Convention only accords priority in certain circumstances to ties between works of art and their country of origin. (Obviously, Italy is not the country of origin of a Van Gogh painting.) The European Court noted that the issue in the case did not concern the return of a work of art to the country of origin and that, in relation to works of art lawfully in a territory and belonging to the cultural heritage of all nations, it was legitimate for a State to take measures to facilitate, in the most effective manner, the wide public access to them in the interest of the universal culture. The European Court did recognize that the Italian Minister of Culture had a right of preemption but determined the Minister could have bought the painting in 1983 when the collector stated his intent to sell the painting. Italian authorities did not inform the collector Italy wanted to buy the painting until 1988. At that time, Italian authorities wanted to pay the collector his original purchase price. The European Court noted that the Italian Ministry of Culture acquired the painting in 1988 at well below its market value and that, under its Law no. 1089,[68] it could have intervened in 1983. The European Court ruled that Italian authorities, in delaying five years to exercise their right of preemption, had violated Article 42 of the European Convention on Human Rights. The court awarded the collector/applicant damage compensation of 1.3 million euros. However, the collector/applicant challenged the award as being inadequate. In Beyeler v. Italy (33202/96) (No. 2) (2003) 36 E.H.R.R. 5, the European Court of Human Rights upheld the amount of the award, noting that it was over 420 percent of the collector's original purchase price and, thus, was sufficient.

Example 8. In Sehgal v. Union of India, 2005 WL 2205380, [2005] F.S.R. 39 (India High Court, 21 Feb. 2005), the High Court of India considered a dispute between a sculptor and the Indian government regarding a bronze mural sculpture, which the sculptor, Amar Nath Sehgal, built as a result of a commission from the Central Public Works Department. The mural was placed in the "Vigyan Bhawan," a building conceived to be a hub of international and national conferences. Sehgal alleged the sculpture acquired the status of a national treasure because it represented an essential part of Indian Art heritage. When the Indian government removed the mural from public view, Sehgal contended his rights were violated under Indian copyright law as well as cultural property law. The Indian court pointed out that cultural property from developing countries was the focus of a highly lucrative international trade in art. It noted that its negative feature was illicit export from countries of origin and referred to the 1970 UNESCO Convention, of which India was a signatory. The Indian court thought it should be the obligation of the State to honor declarations of the conventions to which it is a signatory. It interpreted India's Copyright Act of 1957 to include destruction of a work of art as being an extreme form of mutilation. The court commented that reducing the volume of an author's creative corpus affected the artist's reputation prejudicially and was actionable under § 57 of the India Copyright Act. The court ruled that, notwithstanding copyright in the mural was vested in India, India violated the sculptor's moral right of integrity in the mural and also violated the integrity of the work in relation to the cultural heritage of the nation. The Indian court was of the opinion the mural was too precious to be reduced to scrap and to languish in the warehouse of the Government of India. It ruled the sculptor had a right to recreate the work, a right to receive the broken-up mural, and a right to be compensated for loss of reputation, honor, and mental injury due to the government's offending acts. The Indian court praised the sculptor's counsel who, according to the High Court of India, argued the matter virtually on first principles and enriched the court with material to understand "the profound" issues raised in the suit. The High Court of India thought the issues required a synthesis of artists' personal rights vis-a-vis the cultural rights of the nation.

D. 1972 UNESCO CONVENTION FOR THE PROTECTION OF THE WORLD CULTURAL AND NATURAL HERITAGE

The 1972 UNESCO Convention for the Protection of the World Cultural and Natural Heritage addresses the need for international protection of cultural property.[69] It recognizes that a "heritage of all nations of the world" often remains incomplete at the national level and places the responsibility squarely upon the international community to provide "collective assistance" to individual countries in protecting their cultural properties that have universal value.[70] The purpose of the 1972 UNESCO Convention is to preserve movable cultural property, to include buildings and monuments, but also natural sites, such as geological formations and habitats of endangered species of animals and plants. The 1972 UNESCO Convention was enacted to establish "an effective system of collective protection of . . . cultural and natural heritage of outstanding universal value, organized on a permanent basis and in accordance with modern scientific methods."[71]

1. World Heritage Committee and World Heritage List

The 1972 UNESCO Convention established an Intergovernmental Committee for the Protection of the Cultural and Natural Heritage of Outstanding Universal Value, called the World Heritage Committee.[72] Each Party State to the convention submits to the World Heritage Committee an inventory of property forming part of the cultural and natural heritage situated in its territory. The World Heritage Commission must publish, under the title "World Heritage List," an up-to-date list of properties forming part of the cultural heritage and natural heritage.[73] From this list, the World Heritage Committee establishes its World Heritage List.[74] The World Heritage Committee also assembles, from the World Heritage List, the "List of World Heritage in Danger." This list consists of properties for which major operations are necessary and for which assistance has been requested.[75] The World Heritage Committee receives and studies requests for international assistance with respect to property forming part of the cultural or natural heritage to secure the protection, conservation, presentation, or rehabilitation of this property.[76]

2. World Heritage Fund

The 1972 UNESCO Convention established a fund for the protection of cultural property of outstanding universal value, called the World Heritage Fund,[77] but it also encouraged the establishment of national, public, and private foundations whose purposes would be to invite donations for the protection of the cultural and natural heritage. The World Heritage Committee may also provide international assistance to national or regional centres for the training of staff and specialists at all levels in the field of identification, protection, conservation, presentation, and rehabilitation of the cultural and natural heritage. Part of the cost of necessary work is borne by the international community, but the State benefiting from international assistance bears a substantial share of the cost unless its resources will not permit its contribution.[78]

E. 1995 UNIDROIT CONVENTION ON STOLEN OR ILLEGALLY EXPORTED CULTURAL OBJECTS

The UNIDROIT Convention on Stolen or Illegally Exported Cultural Objects[79] is a more controversial international convention in that it endorses the repatriation of cultural property. The Diplomatic Conference for the Adoption of a UNIDROIT Convention on Stolen or Illegally Exported Cultural Objects met in Rome in June 1995 with "the objective of improving the preservation and protection of the cultural heritage in the interest of all."[80] Drafters of the convention recognized that problems regarding the preservation of cultural property remained because, as the drafters noted, the illicit trade in cultural objects, the pillage of archaeological sites, and the looting and destruction of cultural property during military combat, continue.[81] They were conscious that a process was needed still to enhance international cultural cooperation and to provide and maintain a proper role for legal trading and inter-State agreements for cultural exchanges.

Parties to the UNIDROIT Convention were convinced of the fundamental importance of the protection of cultural heritage and of cultural exchanges for promoting and understanding between peoples. They considered the dissemination of culture to be for the well-being of humanity and the progress of civilization. A delegation from the United States was involved in drafting the 1995 UNIDROIT Convention, but opposition to the convention from art dealers, collectors, and some museums prevented the United States from ratifying the convention.

> Example 9. In Iran v. Berend [2007] EWHC 132 (QB), 2007 WL 261173, Iran sought to recover a Persepolis fragment it alleged was part of its national monument. Berend claimed she acquired title to the fragment after her agent purchased it at a New York auction in 1974. She claimed good title under French law because the fragment was delivered to her in Paris. Her seller had obtained an export license from the French government. The English court decided that English conflict of laws dictated that French law governed the question of title and that, under French law, Berend had good title. The English court referred to the 1970 UNESCO Convention and the 1995 UNIDROIT Convention on the International Return of Stolen or Illegally Exported Cultural Property and noted that, pursuant to these conventions, title to national treasures and works of art would be determined in accordance with the law of the place of origin of the treasures. However, the English court

decided that neither of these conventions applied because, according to the English court, neither was a part of French law in 1974. The court commented that France had been reluctant to make the conventions part of its laws because of the repercussions for public and private collections. (France ratified the 1970 UNESCO Convention in 1997.) The English court ruled Berend acquired title under French law at the moment of transfer in 1974.

1. Return of Stolen Cultural Property

Article 3(1) of the UNIDROIT Convention mandates the return of a stolen cultural object to the original owner. Further, Article 3(2) provides that any cultural object that was excavated unlawfully, or excavated lawfully but retained unlawfully, is deemed to be stolen, when consistent with the law of the State where the excavation took place. In addition, pursuant to Article 5, a party nation to the UNIDROIT Convention may demand that a court of another Party State to the convention order the return of a cultural object illegally exported from territory of the requesting nation. A cultural object that was exported temporarily under a permit for purposes such as exhibition, research, or restoration, but that is not returned in accordance with the permit, is deemed to have been exported illegally. Article 5 requires

> the court or other competent authority of the State addressed shall order the return of an illegally exported cultural object if the requesting State establishes that the removal of the object from its territory significantly impairs one or more of the following interests: (a) the physical preservation of the object or of its context; (b) the integrity of a complex object; (c) the preservation of information of, for example, a scientific or historical character; (d) the traditional or ritual use of the object by a tribal or indigenous community, or establishers that the object is of significant cultural importance for the requesting State.

2. Time Limitations for Restitution

Article 3 of the 1995 UNIDROIT Convention prescribes time limitations on claims for restitution but does not require due diligence on the part of claimants. Article 3(3) requires "any claim for restitution to be brought within a period of three years from the time the claimant knew of the location of the cultural object and the identity of its possessor, and in any case within a period of fifty years from time of the theft," but Article 3(4) provides that any "cultural object forming an integral part of an identified monument or archaeological site, or belonging to a public collection, shall not be subject to time limitations other than a period of three years from the time when the claimant knew the location of the cultural object and the identity of its possessor." Article 3(5) permits each nation to "declare that a claim is subject to a time limitation of 75 years or such longer period as is provided in its law." The convention provides that a "claim for restitution of a cultural object displaced from a monument, archaeological site or public collection . . . is also subject to that time limitation."

Article 3(7) includes as a "public collection" (not subject to time limitations other than the three-year limitation period) "inventoried or otherwise identified cultural objects owned by" religious institutions and other institutions established for "an essentially cultural, educational or scientific purpose" and recognized by a nation as serving the public interest. Pursuant to Article 3(8), claims "for restitution of a sacred or communally important cultural object belonging to and used by a tribal or indigenous community . . . as part of that community's traditional or ritual use shall be subject to the time limitation applicable to public collections."

3. Innocent Purchaser and Due Diligence Requirement

The notion of an innocent purchaser has relevance under the UNIDROIT Convention with respect to the issue of whether a current possessor of stolen or illegally exported cultural objects is entitled to compensation. Article 4(1) provides for compensation to a "possessor of a stolen cultural object" who is required to return the object if the possessor "neither knew nor ought reasonably to have known that the object was stolen" and can prove "due diligence when acquiring the object." Article 4(2) provides that "reasonable efforts shall be made to have the person who transferred the cultural object to the possessor, or any prior transferor, pay the compensation where to do so would be consistent with the law of the State in which the claim was brought."

Further, "in determining whether a possessor exercised due diligence," Article 4(4) provides that the following circumstances regarding the acquisition must be considered:

> the character of the parties, the price paid, whether the possessor consulted any reasonably accessible register of stolen cultural objects, and any other relevant information and documentation which it could reasonably

have obtained, and whether the possessor consulted accessible agencies or took any other step that a reasonable person would have taken in the circumstances.

In determining whether a "possessor knew or ought reasonably to have known that the cultural object had been illegally exported," Article 6(2) requires a party to consider "the absence of an export certificate required under the law of the requesting State."

4. Effective Date for Repatriation of Cultural Objects

Although the UNIDROIT Convention dictates the repatriation of cultural objects, provisions of the convention only apply prospectively. Article 10(1) states that required restitution under the UNIDROIT Convention does not apply to cultural objects stolen before the convention was in force in a country in which a claim is brought or, pursuant to Article 10(2), to cultural objects illegally exported before the convention was in force in the requesting country as well as the country in which the claim is brought. The UNIDROIT Convention provides for the return of all stolen or illegally exported cultural property, albeit only from the effective date of the convention in the country in which a claim is brought; however, Article 8(1) provides that a claim for restitution of stolen or illegally exported cultural objects may be brought before the courts of the country in which the cultural object is located.

Pursuant to Article 10(3), the convention does not in any way legitimize any illegal transaction that occurred before the convention was in force nor does it limit the right of any country or person to make a claim under remedies available outside the framework of the convention for the restitution or return of a cultural object stolen or illegally exported before the effective date of the convention.

F. 2001 CONVENTION FOR THE PROTECTION OF THE UNDERWATER CULTURAL HERITAGE

A press release from the General Conference of UNESCO in 2001 cited estimates by commercial salvors that there were approximately "three million undiscovered shipwrecks scattered across the world's oceans."[82] The press release referred to sunken cities, such as the trading town and pirate stronghold of Port Royal in Jamaica, which disappeared beneath the waves after an earthquake in 1692, and remnants of ancient civilizations, including the

Lighthouse of Alexandria in Egypt, and Neolithic villages being discovered under the Black Sea, which some believe could help explain Noah's great flood. The release expressed the concern of many that these "treasures of cultural heritage are under serious threat" because "no site or shipwreck is now out of bounds for treasure hunters."[83] New technologies, which have become much less expensive, have made deep-water wrecks easily accessible.[84]

Technological advances have made access to shipwrecks in deep waters much less difficult. Currently, cameras can transmit a video presence of ship artifacts, and robotic devices can permit archaeologists to study and analyze sunken objects prior to excavation. The sea is able to preserve antiquities and provide society with considerable knowledge about ancient civilizations. As a past president of the International Scientific Committee on Protection of the Cultural Underwater Heritage of the International Council on Monuments and Sites (ICOMOS) commented, "Shipwrecks can last thousands of years underwater as valid and fruitful archaeological sites."[85]

The application of admiralty law to a claim regarding derelict property "would lead to an award either of outright ownership of the recovered goods (applying the law of finds) or of entitlement to an appropriate salvage award."[86] As noted in Chapter 10, the law of finds, which "developed originally at common law and [was] then incorporated into admiralty, gives legal force to the venerable maxim 'finders-keepers.'"[87] The law of finds designates the finder, who takes possession of lost and abandoned property and who exercises dominion and control over the property, as the owner of the property. The law of salvage, on the other hand, is an ancient maritime doctrine "meant to encourage the rescue of imperiled or derelict marine property by providing a liberal reward to those who recover property on or in navigable waters."[88] Admiralty courts do not view compensation as salvage merely as pay but as a reward given for perilous services and as an inducement to search for maritime wrecks.[89]

Archaeologists and governmental experts concerned about protection and preservation of underwater cultural heritage have recognized that application to sunken vessels of the admiralty principles of the law of finds and law of salvage has been ineffective to protect these ships or their treasures. They have recognized that rules and procedures must be established to provide a legal regime wherein nations will exercise their "sovereign prerogative" and assume a duty to protect and preserve underwater antiquities.

One expert on international laws for the protection of underwater artifacts[90] opined that public international law to preserve underwater cultural heritage has been "weak" inasmuch as "freedom of the seas" has been the controlling principle.[91] He referred to the Third United Nations Convention on the Law of the Sea (UNCLOS III), which was completed in 1982 but not signed by the United Nations Conference until 1994, as the first global document to address the issue and commented that "plunder and spoilation of heritage have been more the rule than the exception."[92]

The 1982 Convention on the Law of the Sea, UNCLOS III, expanded the international maritime law of nations through its establishment of a legal order for the seas and oceans to facilitate international communication and the peaceful uses of the seas and oceans. The convention also provided for the conservation of living resources and the study, protection, and preservation of the marine environment. However, while UNCLOS III also recognized a need to protect underwater antiquities, it did not establish a means to do so. Further, it only granted a State the right to protect underwater cultural heritage to its contiguous zone (discussed below).[93] The UNESCO Convention on the Protection of the Underwater Cultural Heritage, on the other hand, sets out explicit procedures to protect underwater sites and extends a State's responsibility for protecting these sites to the continental shelf or to the edge of a State's exclusive economic zone (EEZ),[94] which is defined in Part 5 of UNCLOS III (discussed below).

1. Law of the Sea

The Third United Nations Conference on the Law of the Sea (UNCLOS III), which was adopted in 1982 and came into force in 1994, defines the regimes of the sea.[95] They are the territorial sea (an area that does not exceed twelve nautical miles from a State's coastline); the contiguous zone (an area twelve miles contiguous to and seaward of the territorial sea, or twenty-four miles from a coastal State's baseline[96]); the EEZ (an area that cannot extend beyond two hundred nautical miles from the baselines from which the breadth of the territorial sea is measured); the continental shelf (an area that extends beyond a State's territorial sea to the outer edge of the continental margin, or to a distance of two hundred nautical miles from the baselines from which the breadth of the territorial sea is measured); and the high seas (defined in Article 86 of UNCLOS III as all parts of the sea not included in the exclusive economic zone, in the territorial sea, in the internal waters of a State, or in the archipelagic waters of an archipelagic State.[97])

In establishing the regimes of the sea, UNCLOS III defined the rights of States within each zone. Article 2 of UNCLOS III provides that the sovereignty of a coastal State extends, beyond its land territory and internal waters, to an adjacent belt of sea, described as the territorial sea. This sovereignty, however, is subject to the right of innocent passage for foreign ships.[98] Article 3 of UNCLOS III states that every State has the right to establish the breadth of its territorial sea up to a limit not exceeding twelve nautical miles, measured from baselines determined in accordance with the convention. Article 33 describes the zone contiguous to a State's territorial sea (called the contiguous zone) and provides that a coastal State may exercise within this zone the control necessary to prevent infringement of its customs, fiscal, immigration or sanitary laws, and regulations within its territorial sea as well as punish infringement of laws and regulations committed within its territorial sea. The EEZ, which is the area beyond and adjacent to the territorial sea,[99] cannot extend beyond two hundred nautical miles from the baselines from which the breadth of the territorial sea is measured,[100] but the continental shelf of a coastal State also comprises the seabed and subsoil of the submarine areas that extend beyond a State's territorial sea to the outer edge of the continental margin, and also to a distance of two hundred nautical miles from the baselines from which the breadth of the territorial sea is measured (where the outer edge of the continental margin does not extend up to that distance).[101]

Two experts on the law of the sea[102] declared that there now are two distinct legal bases for coastal State rights in relation to the seabed: the first is the continental shelf and the second is the two-hundred-mile EEZ.[103] As these experts pointed out, under UNCLOS III, the minimum breadth of the continental shelf is two hundred miles and, thus, not less than the EEZ.[104] They confirmed that a continental shelf need not be claimed, but stated an EEZ always must be claimed.[105]

Although the United States has not ratified UNCLOS III,[106] Congress has declared that the natural resources of the subsoil and seabed of the continental shelf beneath the high seas, but contiguous to the coasts of the United States, are subject to the jurisdiction and control of the United States.[107]

Under UNCLOS III, a coastal State has sovereign rights over all natural resources of its EEZ, including the seabed resources,[108] but the convention does not address sufficiently a State's rights over, or the need to protect, underwater cultural property.[109] Although UNCLOS III has been identified as "the first global instrument to establish minimum rules of protection" for underwater cultural property[110] inasmuch as it imposes a duty on nations to protect historical and archaeological objects found at sea,[111] the convention addresses only indirectly the rights of the States to protect underwater cultural property. Article 149 of the convention does require States to preserve and dispose of underwater cultural property "for the benefit of mankind as a whole." Further,

Article 303 prohibits the removal from the contiguous zone (the area out to twenty-four nautical miles off-shore) of "objects of an archaeological nature and historical nature" without approval of the coastal State.[112] In addition, Article 303 prescribes a duty in nations to protect objects of "archaeological and historical nature" found at sea and to cooperate for this purpose. Still, Article 303 also states that nothing in the article affects the law of salvage or other rules or admiralty or the rights of identifiable owners.[113]

UNCLOS III states that no State may validly purport to subject any part of the high seas to its sovereignty.[114] All States have the right to sail ships on the high seas.[115] It follows that questions will develop as to the jurisdiction of a court to decide rights to shipwrecks located on the high seas.

Example 10. In R.M.S. *Titanic*, Inc. v. Haver, 171 F.3d 943 (4th Cir. 1999), cert. denied, 528 U.S. 825 (1999), the Fourth Circuit Court of Appeals applied admiralty principles to determine salvage rights to a shipwreck located on the high seas. The Fourth Circuit had to determine whether any laws govern activities in the high seas to determine title to artifacts on the RMS *Titanic*, which sank in the North Atlantic Ocean off the Newfoundland coast in April 1912. In 1985, a French/American expedition discovered the wreck's remains at a depth of approximately 12,000 feet. In 1987, Titanic Ventures, which is an American private corporation, and the Institute of France for the Research and Exploration of the Sea, a French governmental organization, conducted a joint salvage operation that recovered 1,800 artifacts from the wreck site. Titanic Ventures originally was awarded exclusive salvage rights to the *Titanic*, but this status was terminated in 1993. Later, in 1994, the district court in the Eastern District of Virginia awarded exclusive salvage rights, as well as ownership of recovered artifacts, to RMS Titanic, Inc. (RMST), a Florida private corporation and the successor to Titanic Ventures. (Titanic Ventures is the largest shareholder in RMST.) In 1996, the Virginia district court entered an injunction protecting the salvage rights of RMST against any person in the world "having notice" of its order. In 1998, the Virginia district court reaffirmed its order as to new parties who had contended they had no notice of the order—an individual, Haver, and Deep Ocean Expeditions (DOE), a British Virgin Islands corporation with its principal place of business of the Isle of Man in Great Britain. (DOE's principal resided in Germany.) DOE had begun to market tours to the wreck site for members of the public to view and to photograph the wreck. Haver was one of the persons on the tour. RMST had sought to prevent the tours. Haver and DOE appealed the decision of the district court, which had enjoined their activities. The Fourth Circuit Court of Appeals considered the authority of a U.S. court to regulate the salvage rights of a wreck that lay in international waters. The Fourth Circuit noted that any analysis regarding the authority of a U.S. court to adjudicate salvage rights in shipwrecks in international waters required inquiry first into several fundamental principles of admiralty: (1) the nature and scope of admiralty jurisdiction; (2) the applicability of salvage law as part of the common law of maritime nations, i.e., the *jus gentium*; and (3) the reach of an admiralty court's in rem jurisdiction. The court noted that nations have applied the body of admiralty law for more than 3,000 years. It commented that admiralty laws do not arise under the Constitution or the laws of the United States but rather "are as old as navigation itself." The court acknowledged that this body of admiralty law constitutes a part of the continuing maritime tradition of the law of nations—the *jus gentium*. According to the Fourth Circuit, this nonnational or international maritime law has provided "an established network of rules and distinctions that are practically suited to the necessities of the seas." The Fourth Circuit opined that this "body of maritime law has the force of law, not from extraterritorial reach of national laws, nor from abdication of its sovereign powers by any nation, but from acceptance by common consent of civilized communities of rules designed to foster amicable and workable commercial relations." Thus, the Fourth Circuit thought that, because federal courts have acquiesced in the *jus gentium* governing maritime affairs, a court can "speak" through its "own national sovereignty and thereby recognize and acquiesce in the time-honored principles of the common law of the seas." The Fourth Circuit commented that the exercise of admiralty jurisdiction had never been limited to controversies arising solely within the territorial waters of the United States, but rather issues arising on the high seas had traditionally been brought to courts of admiralty. The court concluded that because the admiralty jurisdiction of U.S. courts was not limited by the nationality of ships, sailors, or seas involved and because the principles of the law of salvage were part of the *jus gentium*, U.S. courts could, and have, adjudicated salvage claims involving foreign vessels, alien salvors, and salvage operations on the high seas. The Fourth Circuit decided that where both persons and property are beyond a nation's zone of exclusive legal power, a court's ability to adjudicate rights "is limited, but not meaningless." Thus, the Fourth Circuit concluded that while the *jus gentium* "is easy to define and declare," its enforcement must depend on persons or property involved "coming into the zone of power of participating nations." Although the district court had applied principles of the *jus gentium* to award RMST exclusive salvage rights in the *Titanic*, the question facing the court was how a court of admiralty could enforce these salvage rights with respect to property that does not lie within its jurisdiction (or in fact within the jurisdiction of any admiralty court). Still, while the Fourth Circuit conceded that "no nation has sovereignty over the high seas," the court noted that the high seas are not left without enforceable law. The court concluded that the law of salvage as shared by the nations as part of the *jus gentium* applies to the high seas and that it could enforce those rights "to the extent generally recognized on a non-exclusive basis." According to the Fourth Circuit, "shared rights to the high seas may be exercised by all nations, and the assertion by any nation of exclusive sovereignty over a portion would interfere with those rights." The Fourth Circuit was concerned that if it should recognize an "absolute limit to the district court's power that would preclude it, or essentially any other admiralty court, from exercising judicial power over wrecks in international waters," it would be "abdicating the order created by the *jus gentium* and would return the high seas to a state of lawlessness never experienced." Thus, the Fourth Circuit affirmed the district court's injunctions as they enjoined parties and persons from conducting salvage operations of the *Titanic* and interfering with the salvage operations of RMST. Still, it reversed the district court insofar as that court had prohibited the "visiting, viewing, searching, surveying, photographing, and obtaining images of the wreck or the wreck site" so long as these activities did not interfere with any salvage effort or with RMST's salvage rights.

2. International Convention on Protection of Underwater Cultural Property

Concern for the protection and preservation of the underwater cultural heritage and the lack of laws to protect underwater treasures, including the limitations in UNCLOS III relating to protection of underwater cultural property, led to the enactment of the Convention on the Protection of the Underwater Cultural Heritage in 2011. This convention provides for a comprehensive legal framework for the preservation, protection, and management of underwater cultural heritage. Drafters acknowledged the importance of underwater cultural heritage and recognized that all States must accept responsibility for protecting and preserving this heritage and preventing its commercial exploitation. In its resolution, parties to the Convention on the Protection of the Underwater Cultural Heritage recognize underwater cultural heritage as "an integral part of the cultural heritage of humanity and a particularly important element in the history of peoples, nations, and their relations with each other concerning their common heritage." The resolution notes the importance of protecting and preserving the underwater cultural heritage and the responsibility of all States and considers that "survey, excavation and protection of underwater cultural heritage" necessitates the availability and application of special scientific methods and the use of suitable techniques and equipment.

The Preamble to the Convention on the Protection of the Underwater Cultural Heritage acknowledges the importance of underwater cultural heritage "as an integral part of the cultural heritage of humanity and a particularly important element in the history of peoples, nations, and their relations with each other concerning their common heritage." The Preamble expresses an awareness that increasing commercial exploitation of underwater cultural heritage and activities "aimed at the sale, acquisition or barter of underwater cultural heritage" has threatened that heritage. It expresses a belief that "cooperation among States, international organizations, scientific institutions, professional organizations, archaeologists, divers, other interested parties and the public at large is essential for the protection of underwater cultural heritage."

Article 2 requires State Parties to cooperate in the protection of underwater cultural heritage for the benefit of humanity. Recovered underwater cultural heritage must be deposited, conserved, and managed in a manner that ensures its long-term preservation. Pursuant to Article 4, any activity relating to underwater cultural heritage to which the convention applies is not "subject to the law of salvage or law of finds unless it . . . is authorized by competent authorities . . . is in full conformity with the Convention . . . and ensures that any recovery of the underwater cultural heritage achieves its maximum protection." Article 6 encourages State Parties "to enter into bilateral, regional or other multilateral agreements . . . for the preservation of underwater cultural heritage."

Article 7 gives State Parties "the exclusive right to regulate and authorize activities directed at underwater cultural heritage in their internal waters, archipelagic waters and territorial sea." Article 8 provides that State Parties "may regulate and authorize activities directed at underwater cultural heritage within their contiguous zone." Article 9 gives all State Parties "a responsibility to protect underwater cultural heritage in the exclusive economic zone and on the continental shelf." Article 21 requires member parties to "cooperate in the provision of training in underwater archaeology, in techniques for the conservation of underwater cultural heritage, and on agreed terms in the transfer or technology relating to underwater cultural heritage." It recognizes the need to codify and develop rules relating to the protection and preservation of underwater cultural heritage and expresses the value of public education to contribute to "awareness, appreciation and protection of that heritage." Article 20 requires each member party to "take all practicable measures to raise public awareness regarding the value and significance of underwater cultural heritage and the importance of protecting it." The convention expresses concern for the increasing commercial exploitation of underwater cultural heritage, and in particular certain activities directed to the "sale, acquisition or barter of underwater treasures."

The Annex to the Convention sets out rules concerning activities directed at underwater cultural heritage. It prescribes a discipline for underwater archaeology.

As of 2013, Australia, Canada, China, Germany, Japan, the United States, and the UK were market States that had not ratified the UNESCO Convention on the Protection of the Underwater Cultural Heritage. France ratified the Convention in 2013.

3. Bilateral Agreements

Bilateral agreements are one means to resolve issues between individual countries relating to the protection of underwater cultural heritage. Article 6 of the UNESCO Convention on the Protection of Underwater Cultural Heritage encourages States to enter into bilateral agreements for the preservation of underwater cultural heritage. One such agreement is a bilateral treaty between the United States and the Government of the French Republic regarding the wreck of the CSS *Alabama*, which is located in France's territorial waters approximately seven nautical miles off the coast of Cherbourg in northwest France.

> Example 11. The CSS *Alabama*, a Confederate sloop-of-war, operated as a raider during the American Civil War to disrupt U.S. merchant shipping in the North Atlantic, the West Indies, and the East Indies. In 1864, it was sunk in battle by the USS *Kearsarge*, outside the Cherbourg harbor. France and the United States had a bilateral treaty that established a scientific committee, composed of representatives from each of the party's governments, to review measures related to scientific activities

or any project concerning development of the wreck. The agreement acknowledged the French government's prior establishment of a "zone of protection" around the wreck. In addition, the French authorities were authorized to take conservation measures to protect the wreck.

NOTES

1. The concept of a cultural heritage for all humanity evolved from ideals set out in the preambles to the two important international conventions of protection of the cultural heritage: the 1954 Hague Convention for the Protection of Cultural Property in the Event of Armed Conflict and the 1970 UNESCO Convention on the Means of Prohibiting and Preventing the Illicit Import, Export and Transfer of Ownership of Cultural Property, both of which are discussed in this chapter. Texts of these conventions can be found at www.unesco.org.

2. Principle 2 of the ICOM Code of Ethics for Museums (2013) states that museums have the duty to acquire, preserve, and promote their collections as a contribution to safeguarding the natural, cultural, and scientific heritage. It further states that museum collections are a significant public inheritance, have a special position in law, and are protected by international legislation.

3. May 14, 1954, 249 U.N.T.S. 215 (1956). Text available at www.unesco.org.

4. November 14, 1970, 823 U.N.T.S. 231 (1972). Text available at www.unesco.org.

5. November 16, 1972, 1037 U.N.T.S. 151 (1977). Text available at www.unesco.org.

6. June 24, 1995. 34 I.L.M. 1330. Text available at www.unidroit.org.

7. November 2, 2001, 41 I.L.M. 37. Text available at www.unesco.org.

8. ICOM Code of Ethics, cited in note 2, at 7.2. ICOM also requires a museum to acknowledge the 1973 Convention on International Trade in Endangered Species of Wild Fauna and Flora. (Text available at www.unesco.org.) This convention is discussed in Chapter 9.

9. 1970 UNESCO Convention cited in note 4. Text of the provisions available at www.unesco.org.

10. Preamble, Hague Convention, cited in note 3.

11. Appendix to UNIDROIT Convention on Stolen or Illegally Exported Cultural Objects, cited in note 6.

12. Recommendations for the Protection of Movable Cultural Property I, UNESCO (1978), Articles 10 and 12.

13. Id., Articles 14 and 15.

14. Id., Article 17.

15. See lists in the conventions, the full texts of which are available at www.unesco.org and www.unidroit.org.

16. Decree-Law No. 4874 of the Praesidium of the People's Assembly of September 23, 1971, Albania, protected "monuments of cultural value" or objects under the protection of the State. Decree 81-84 of May 30, 1984, Law on the Protection of the Cultural Heritage of the Nation, Honduras, protects "monuments" and "sites." The Act Concerning the Protection of Monuments of June 14, 1977, Liechtenstein, protected "monuments." Law No. 167 on the Protection of Cultural Monuments of the Mongolian People's Republic sanctioned by edict of the Presidium of the Great People's Khural of the MPR on October 12,

1970, protected "cultural monuments." The Antiquities Act 1975, New Zealand, protected "antiquities." The Act Concerning the Cultural Heritage 1979, Norway, protected "all ancient and historic monuments." The Antiquities Ordinance No. 9 of July 15, 1940, Sri Lanka, protected "antiquities." And the National Museums and Monuments of Zimbabwe Act, Ch. 313 of 1972, protected "national monuments, ancient monuments and relics."

17. Most nations provide definitions of these terms. For example, the Code for the Protection of Antiquities in Afghanistan 1958 stated that "antiquities" includes all artistic relics and monuments erected before the reign of Emperor Ahmad Shah Baba (1748 A.D.). The Bahrain Antiquities Ordinance 1970 defined an "antiquity" as any object which was constructed, shaped, inscribed, erected, excavated or otherwise produced or modified by human agency before A.D. 1780. The Antiquities Act 1968–1976, for Bangladesh, defined an "antiquity" as any ancient (more than one hundred years old) product of human activity or any object declared by the government to be an antiquity. The Antiquities Law 1935 as amended 1964 and 1973, for Cyprus, defined "antiquities" as objects produced, sculptured, inscribed, painted, or generally made in Cyprus before 1850. The Antiquities Proclamation No. 229 of 1966, for Ethiopia, defined an "antiquity" as any product of human activity, or any object of historical or archaeological interest, having its origin prior to 1850 E.C. The Monuments and Relics Act 1974, Gambia, defined "monument" as an ancient monument or antiquity, any area of land containing objects of archaeological interest, an old tree, an old building, or any other object of archaeological, ethnological, historical, or other scientific interest. The Antiquities and Monuments Act 1983, for Kenya, defined a "monument" as an immovable structure built before 1895 (unless specifically excluded from inclusion by declaration of the minister).

18. Discussion in Chapter 10.

19. 16 U.S.C. § 433.

20. United States v. Diaz, 499 F.2d 113 (9th Cir. 1974), discussed in Chapter 10. The court noted that the word "antiquity" can refer not only to the age of an object but also to the use for which the object was made and to which it was put, subjects which, the court decided, would not likely be of common knowledge. The court declared that a person must be able to know with reasonable certainty those objects he may not take. Still, in United States v. Smyer, 596 F.2d 939 (10th Cir. 1979), another appellate court refused to declare the Antiquities Act unconstitutional with respect to the prosecution of an individual who excavated a prehistoric Mimbres ruin at an archaeological site which was inhabited about A.D. 1000–1250. The court in Smyer decided that a person of ordinary intelligence should know that one may not excavate a prehistoric Indian burial ground or appropriate artifacts that are 800–900 years old.

21. Pub. L. No. 101-650, § 603(a), 104 Stat. 5128 (1990).

22. 17 U.S.C. § 106A.

23. 1990 U.S.C.C.A.N. (104 Stat.) 6915, 6916.

24. Id.

25. Pursuant to § 106A of the Copyright Act (16 U.S.C. § 106A), any intentional distortion, mutilation, or modification of a work is a violation of the right. An artist can prevent any destruction of a work of recognized stature.

26. See 17 U.S.C. § 106A.

27. Discussion in John Henry Merryman, "Two Ways of Thinking about Cultural Property," 80 Amer. J. Int'l. L. 831 (1986). Merryman discussed the work of Francis Lieber, a German émigré professor at Columbia College in New York, who argued for protection of cultural property during combat. As Merryman pointed out, the Lieber Code was the first

attempt to provide a set of principles governing the conduct of belligerents in enemy territory. Further discussion in Hays Parks, "Protection of Cultural Property from the Effects of War," Chapter 3, *The Law of Cultural Property and Natural Heritage*, Phelan, ed. (Kalos Kapp Press, 1998). Parks stated, p. 3-3, that codification of the law of war for the protection of cultural property rests principally with Dr. Francis Lieber. Parks noted that the Lieber Code recognized all cultural property as protected from intentional damage or seizure absent "military necessity." See also Patty Gerstenblith, "Protecting Cultural Property in Armed Conflict: Looking Back, Looking Forward," 7 Cardozo Pub. L. Pol'y & Ethics J. 677 (2008).

28. 1954 Hague Convention, Articles 3 and 4.

29. Regulations for the Execution of the Convention for the Protection of Cultural Property in the Event of Armed Conflict, Article 12, provides for the preparation of an International Register of Cultural Property under Special Protection.

30. Regulations for the Execution of the Convention for the Protection of Cultural Property in the Event of Armed Conflict, Article 20, 249 U.N.T.S. 270.

31. Id., Article 17. Transport exclusively engaged in the transfer of cultural property, whether within a territory or to another territory, may, at the request of a contracting party, take place under special protection. Articles 12 and 13. Parties to the convention must refrain from any act of hostility directed against transport.

32. Id., Article 8. A center containing monuments is deemed to be used for military purpose whenever it is used for the movement of military personnel or material, even in transit, but the guarding of cultural property by police force is not deemed to be use for military purposes.

33. Article 16. The Blue Shield, referred to as the cultural equivalent of the Red Cross, is the symbol specified for marking protected cultural property in the event of armed conflict. The shield consists of a royal-blue square, one of the angles of which forms the point of the shield, and of a royal-blue triangle above the square, the space on either side being taken up by a white triangle.

34. Regulations for the Execution of the Convention for the Protection of Cultural Property in the Event of Armed Conflict, Article 20, 249 U.N.T.S. 270.

35. Id., Article 17. Transport exclusively engaged in the transfer of cultural property, whether within a territory or to another territory, may, at the request of a contracting party, take place under special protection. [Articles 12 and 13] Parties to the Convention must refrain from any act of hostility directed against transport.

36. Id., Article 14.

37. Id. The use of the distinctive emblem in any other cases during an armed conflict and the use for any purpose whatever of a sign resembling the distinctive emblem is forbidden. The special identity card shall state the surname and first names, the date of birth, the title or rank, and the function of the holder. It must bear a photograph of the holder as well as the holder's signature or fingerprints, or both, and must bear the embossed stamp of the competent authorities. [Regulations for the Execution of the Convention for the Protection of Cultural Property in the Event of Armed Conflict, Article 21(2)].

38. Important works discussing a common heritage of humanity, a fundamental conception of an international law of cultural property, and other issues relating to the international protection of cultural property include: P. Bator, "The International Trade in Art," 34 Stan. L. Rev. 275 (1982); Symposium on International Art, 15 N.Y. Univ. J. Int'l. L. & Pol. 757 (1983); L. Prott & P. O'Keeffe, Law and the Cultural Heritage (1984); John Henry Merryman, "Two Ways of Thinking About Cultural Property," cited in note 27; Merryman

& Elsen, Law, Ethics and the Visual Arts (1987); Neil Bordie and Colin Renfrew, "Looting and the World's Archaeological Heritage," 34 Ann. Rev. Anth. 343 (2005); Jennifer Anglim Kreder, "The Revolution in U.S. Museums Concerning the Ethics of Acquiring Antiquities," 64 Univ. Miami L. Rev. 997 (2010); Richard M. Leventhal and Brian I. Daniels, "Orphaned Objects, Ethical Standards and the Acquisition of Antiquities," 23 DePaul J. of Art, Tech. and Intel. Prop. L. 339 (2013).

39. Discussion in 1982 U.S.C.C.A.N. 4101 with reference to Cultural Property Implementation Act, Pub. L. 97-446 (96 Stat.), implementing part of the 1970 UNESCO Convention.

40. Pub. L. No. 97-446, 1982 U.S.C.C.A.N. (96 Stat. 4098-4101, 4106).

41. Id., Article 5.

42. Id., Article 6.

43. Id., Article 7.

44. Id., Article 10.

45. Id., Article 13. Each Party State is to prevent by all appropriate means transfers of ownership of cultural property likely to promote the illicit import or export of this property and is to admit actions for recovery of lost or stolen items of cultural property brought by or on behalf of the rightful owners.

46. The original name of the AAM was American Association of Museums, and was its name in 2008 when the document was drafted. The name was changed to American Alliance of Museums in 2012.

47. 19 U.S.C. §§ 2601 et seq.

48. Exec. Order No. 12,555, 51 Fed. Reg. 8475 (1986).

49. Exec. Order No. 13,296 § 44, 68 Fed. Reg. 10,618, 10,627 (2003).

50. 19 U.S.C. § 2602.

51. Id. at § 2605.

52. Id. at § 2602(g)(2).

53. Id. at § 2601(7).

54. Codified at 19 C.F.R. §§ 12.104–12.104j.

55. 19 U.S.C. § 2606(a).

56. § 2609.

57. Cited in note 47.

58. § 2607.

59. § 2609.

60. Specifically 19 U.S.C. § 2602.

61. 19 U.S.C. § 1615.

62. 19 U.S.C. § 2606(a).

63. The state withheld documents pursuant to 19 U.S.C. § 2605(h) and (i)(1).

64. Exemption 1, 5 U.S.C. § 552(b)(1).

65. 19 U.S.C. § 2606 and 19 C.F.R. § 12.104.

66. 333 F.3d 395 (2nd Cir. 2003). The Schultz case is discussed in Example 2 in Chapter 6.

67. 18 U.S.C. §§ 1214 et seq.

68. Law No. 1089 of 1939, § 61(2).

69. Article 5 requires parties to the convention to "foster the establishment or development of national or regional centres for training in the protection, conservation and presentation of the cultural and natural heritage and to encourage scientific research in this field." Article 6 notes that parties to the convention recognize that the cultural and natural

heritage of outstanding universal value "constitutes a world heritage for whose protection it is the duty of the international community as a whole to cooperate." Parties to the convention agree to give their help to the identification, protection, conservation and preservation of such heritage. Article 7 affirms that "international protection of the world cultural and natural heritage" means the "international co-operation and assistance designed to support" individual nations "in their efforts to conserve and identify that heritage."

70. Preamble to Convention for the Protection of the World Cultural and Natural Heritage, cited in note 5.

71. Id.

72. Id., Article 8.

73. Id., Article 11(2).

74. Id., Article 11(2). See list at http://whc.unesco,http://whc.unesco.org/en/list.

75. Id., Article 11(4). The list must contain an estimate of the cost of such operations. It may include only

> property forming part of the cultural and natural heritage as is threatened by serious and specific dangers, such as the threat of disappearance caused by accelerated deterioration, large-scale public or private projects or rapid urban or tourist development projects; destruction caused by changes in the use or ownership of the land; major alterations due to unknown causes; abandonment for any reason whatsoever; the outbreak or the threat of an armed conflict; calamities and cataclysms; serious fires, earthquakes, landslides; volcanic eruptions; changes in water level, floods and tidal waves.

76. Id., Article 13. The Committee determines action to be taken with regard to requests and an order of priorities. It takes into consideration

> the respective importance for the world cultural and natural heritage of the property requiring protection, the need to give international assistance to the property most representative of a natural environment or of the genius and the history of the peoples of the world, the urgency of the work to be done, the resources available to the States on whose territory the threatened property is situated and in particular the extent to which they are able to safeguard such property by their own means.

77. Id., Article 15.

78. Id., Articles 22–26.

79. Cited in note 6.

80. Appendix to UNIDROIT Convention, cited in note 6.

81. Id.

82. Press Release, October 29, 2001, www.unesco.org/bpi/eng/unescopress/2201/01-118e.shtml. The release referred to the Northern Shipwrecks Database, which contains 65,000 ship-loss records for North American alone from A.D. 1500 to present, and the *Dictionary of Disasters at Sea* by Charles Hocking, which lists 12,542 sailing ships and war vessels lost between 1824 and 1962. The release pointed out that the Museum of Archaeology in Lisbon has listed some 850 ships that have gone to the bottom of the seas surrounding the Azores since 1522.

83. Id.

84. Id., quoting Lyndel Prott, then director of UNESCO's Cultural Heritage Division.

85. Robert Grenier in UNESCO Press Release, October 29, 2001, cited in note 82. Robert Grenier worked closely with UNESCO on the Convention for the Protection of Underwater Cultural Heritage. Grenier stated that serious damage to shipwrecks would occur well within the first century of immersion. According to Grenier, after that initial period "the degradation can be more or less stopped or slowed down until the site reaches an equilibrium and stabilizes itself for centuries."

86. Discussion in Maritime Underwater Surveys, 531 N.E.2d 2d 551 (quoting Cobb Coin Co., Inc. v. Unidentified, Wrecked & Abandoned Sailing Vessel, 525 F. Supp. 186 (S.D.Fla. 1981).

87. Discussion in Zych v. Unidentified, Wrecked & Abandoned Vessel, 941 F.2d 525 (7th Cir. 1991).

88. Id.

89. Discussion in Maritime Underwater Surveys, cited in note 86 (quoting The Blackwall, 77 U.S. (10 Wall.) 1, 14 (1869).

90. James A. R. Nafziger, "International Legal Protection of the Underwater Cultural Heritage," Chapter 2, Law of Cultural Property, Phelan, Edson, and Mayfield (eds.), pp. 2–5.

91. Id.

92. Id., pp. 2–6.

93. See Third United Nations Conference on the Law of the Sea (UNCLOS III), Article 303(2), which refers to Article 33 of the Convention. Article 33 defines, and sets out a State's rights in, its contiguous zone.

94. Discussion of contiguous zone and EEZ below at notes 96–112 and accompanying text.

95. The first United Nations Conference on the Law of the Sea (UNCLOS I) was held at Geneva in 1958. However, because the convention did not establish the breadth of the territorial sea, a second conference, UNCLOS II, was convened in 1960 to discuss the problem. Discussion in Churchill and Lowe, *The Law of the Sea*, 3rd ed., Juris Publishing, Manchester University Press, 1999, p. 15.

96. Article 5 of UNCLOS III establishes the normal baseline for measuring the breadth of the territorial sea as the low-water line along the coast. Article 8 states that waters on the landward side of the baseline of the territorial sea form part of the internal waters of the sea.

97. Article 46 of UNCLOS III defines an archipelagic State as "a group of islands, interconnecting waters and other natural features which are so closely interrelated that these islands, waters and other natural features form an intrinsic geographical, economic and political entity."

98. Article 17 of UNCLOS III grants ships of all States the right of innocent passage through the territorial sea.

99. Article 55 of UNCLOS III.

100. Id., Article 57.

101. Article 76(1) of UNCLOS III.

102. Churchill and Lowe, in *Law of the Sea*, cited in note 95.

103. Id., p. 145.

104. Id.

105. Id.

106. The United States signed the United Nations Convention in 1994, but the Senate has not provided the necessary advice and consent for ratification of the convention.

107. Congress enacted the Outer Continental Shelf Lands Act, 43 U.S.C. § 1331 et. seq., in 1953 to "implement" Congressional view "that the United States has paramount rights to the seabed." The act states that the subsoil and seabed of the outer continental shelf "appertain to the United States and are subject to its jurisdiction, control, and power of disposition." Discussion in U.S. v. Maine, 420 U.S. 515 (1975). The Supreme Court recognized in U.S. v. Maine that the act expressed Congressional intent to extend the jurisdiction and control of the United States to its outer continental shelf. The Court stated that the Submerged Lands Act of 1953, 43 U.S.C. §§ 1301–15, and the Outer Continental Shelf Lands Act of 1953, confirmed that paramount rights to the offshore seabed inhere in the United States as an incident of national sovereignty.

108. Article 56, UNCLOS III.

109. Articles 149 and 303 of UNCLOS III provide for some protection of underwater cultural property; these provisions are limited in their application as discussed in notes 110–12 and accompanying text.

110. James A. R. Nafziger, cited in note 90, pp. 2–6. Nafziger commented that although the "rules of protection are very general, somewhat ambiguous, and applicable only to treaty parties, they do at least provide a basis for a more effective regime." Id. at 2-7.

111. Article 303, UNCLOS III. Article 149 states that "all objects of an archaeological and *historical nature* found in the Area shall be preserved or disposed of for the benefit of mankind as a whole, particular regard being paid to the preferential rights of the State or country of origin, or the State of cultural origin, or the State of historical and archaeological origin" (emphasis added). Article 303 prescribes that "States have the duty to protect objects of an archaeological and *historical nature* found at sea and shall cooperate for this purpose" (emphasis added). An expert on international laws protecting underwater cultural heritage, James A. R. Nafziger, opined that Articles 149 and 303 "share an ambiguity." He referred to the term "historical nature" used to denote those objects that should be protected and questioned how this related to objects of "historical significance" or "historical value." For example, he noted that the term "historical" could "be read to refer *only* to pre-modern objects" and, thus, the convention leaves open the question whether more modern objects are covered. He concluded, "UNCLOS needs further clarification and elaboration to be of much use, by itself, in protecting the underwater cultural heritage." Discussion in James A. R. Nafziger, cited in note 90, pp. 2–9.

112. See discussion in James A.R. Nafziger, cited in note 90, pp. 2–7. As Nafziger noted, although Article 56 of UNCLOS III grants a coastal State sovereign rights over all natural resources of its EEZ, including the seabed resources, it does not grant the state sovereignty over nonnatural objects. Thus, States have no control over submerged shipwrecks and underwater sites. Further, a coastal state has rights and responsibilities under UNCLOS III for sunken treasures only to the edge of the contiguous zone, or twenty-four miles from its internal waters. (See Article 303, UNCLOS III, which states that "to control traffic in such objects, the coastal State may, in applying article 33" (which defines, and sets out a state's authority over, its contiguous zone), presume that the removal of these objects from the seabed in that State's contiguous zone without the state's approval would "result in an infringement within" the state's "territory or territorial sea of the laws and regulations" set out in article 33.

113. Id., pp. 2–8.

114. Article 89, UNCLOS III.

115. Id., Article 90.

APPENDIX

A. CONFLICT OF INTEREST POLICY FOR ______________ MUSEUM[1]

ARTICLE I

Purpose

The purpose of this conflict of interest policy is to protect the interest of ______________ Museum, hereinafter referred to as "Museum," when it is contemplating entering into a transaction or arrangement that might benefit the private interest of an officer, director, or employee of Museum or might result in an excess benefit transaction. This policy is intended to supplement but not replace any applicable state and federal laws governing conflict of interests applicable to nonprofit and charitable organizations.

ARTICLE II

Definitions

1. Interested Person

Any director, principal officer, or member of a committee with governing board delegated powers, who has a direct or indirect financial interest, as defined below, is an interested person.

2. Financial Interest

A person has a financial interest if the person has, directly or indirectly, through business, investment, or family:

a. An ownership or investment interest in any entity with which Museum has a transaction or arrangement, or

b. A compensation arrangement with Museum or with any entity or individual with which Museum has a transaction or arrangement, or

c. A potential ownership or investment interest in, or compensation arrangement with, any entity or individual with which Museum is negotiating a transaction or arrangement.

Compensation includes direct and indirect remuneration as well as gifts or favors that are not insubstantial.

A financial interest is not necessarily a conflict of interest. Under Article III, Section 2, a person who has a financial interest may have a conflict of interest only if the appropriate governing board or committee decides that a conflict of interest exists.

ARTICLE III

Procedures

1. Duty to Disclose

In connection with any actual or possible conflict of interest, an interested person must disclose the existence of the financial interest and be given the opportunity to disclose all material facts to the directors and members of committees with governing board delegated powers considering the proposed transaction or arrangement.

2. Determining Whether a Conflict of Interest Exists

After disclosure of the financial interest and all material facts, and after any discussion with the interested person, the interested person shall leave the governing board or committee meeting while the determination of a conflict of interest is discussed and voted upon by the remaining Museum board or committee members. The remaining board or committee members shall decide if a conflict of interest exists.

3. Procedures for Addressing the Conflict of Interest

a. An interested person may make a presentation at the governing board or committee meeting, but after the presentation, he/she shall leave the meeting during the discussion of, and the vote on, the transaction or arrangement involving the possible conflict of interest.

b. The chairperson of the governing board or committee shall, if appropriate, appoint a disinterested person or committee to investigate alternatives to the proposed transaction or arrangement.

c. After exercising due diligence, the governing board of committee shall determine whether Museum can obtain with reasonable efforts a more advantageous transaction or arrangement from a person or entity that would not give rise to a conflict of interest.

d. If a more advantageous transaction or arrangement is not reasonably possible under circumstances not producing a conflict of interest, the governing board or committee shall determine by a majority vote of the disinterested directors whether the transaction or arrangement is in the best interest of Museum, for its own benefit, and whether it is fair and reasonable, and in conformity with the above determination, it shall make its decision as to whether to enter into the transaction or arrangement.

4. Violations of the Conflicts of Interest Policy

a. If the governing board or committee has reasonable cause to believe a member has failed to disclose actual or possible conflicts of interest, it shall inform the member of the basis for its belief and afford the member an opportunity to explain the alleged failure to disclose.

b. If, after hearing the member's response and after making further investigation as warranted by the circumstances, the governing board or committee determines the member has failed to disclose an actual or possible conflict of interest, it shall take appropriate disciplinary and corrective action.

ARTICLE IV

Records of Proceedings

The minutes of the governing board and all committees with board delegated powers shall contain:

a. The names of the persons who disclosed or otherwise were found to have a financial interest in connection with an actual or possible conflict of interest, the nature of the financial interest, any action taken to determine whether a conflict of interest was present, and the governing board's or committee's decision as to whether a conflict of interest in fact existed.

b. The names of the persons who were present for discussion and votes relating to the transaction or arrangement, the content of the discussion, including any alternatives to the proposed transaction or arrangement, and a record of any votes taken in connection with the proceedings.

ARTICLE V

Compensation

a. A voting member of the governing board who receives compensation, directly or indirectly, from Museum for services is precluded from voting on matters pertaining to the member's compensation.

b. A voting member of any committee whose jurisdiction includes compensation matters and who receives compensation, directly or indirectly, from Museum for services is precluded from voting on matters pertaining to that member's compensation.

c. No voting member of the governing board of any committee whose jurisdiction includes compensation matters and who receives compensation, directly or indirectly, from Museum, either individually or collectively, is prohibited from providing information to any committee regarding compensation.

ARTICLE VI

Gifts, Loans, or Other Personal Benefits

Museum directors, officials, employees, and other interested persons must not accept gifts, loans, or other personal benefits that may be offered to them in connection with their duties for Museum. Occasionally professional courtesy may include the giving and receiving of gifts, but this must always take place in the name of Museum.

ARTICLE VII

Outside Employment or Business Interests

Museum directors, officials, employees, and other interested persons, although entitled to a measure of personal independence, must realize that no private business or professional interest can be wholly separated from Museum. They should not undertake other paid employment or accept outside commissions that are in conflict or may be viewed as being in conflict, with the interests of Museum.

ARTICLE VIII

Dealing in Natural or Cultural Heritage

Museum directors, officials, employees, and other interested persons should not participate directly or indirectly in dealing (buying or selling for profit) in the natural or cultural heritage.

ARTICLE IX

Interaction with Dealers

Museum directors, officials, employees, and other interested persons should not accept any gift, hospitality, or any form of reward from a dealer, auctioneer, or other person as an inducement to purchase or dispose of museum items, or to take or refrain from taking official action. Further, Museum directors, officials, employees, and other interested persons should not recommend a particular dealer, auctioneer, or appraiser to a member of the public.

ARTICLE X

Private Collecting

Museum directors, officials, employees, and other interested persons should not compete with Museum either in the acquisition of objects or in any personal collecting activity. An agreement between Museum directors, officials, employees, and other interested persons and Museum's governing body concerning any private collecting must be formulated and scrupulously followed.

ARTICLE XI

Use of the Museum's Name and Logo

Museum's name or its logo may not be used to promote or endorse any for-profit operation or product.

ARTICLE XII

Annual Statements

Each director, principal officer, and member or a committee with Museum's governing board delegated power shall annually sign a statement which affirms that person

a. Has received a copy of the conflicts of interest policy,

b. Has read and understands the policy,

c. Has agreed to comply with the policy, and

d. Understands Museum is charitable and in order to maintain its federal tax exemption it must engage primarily in activities that accomplish one or more of its tax exempt purposes.

ARTICLE XIII

Periodic Reviews

To ensure Museum operates in a manner consistent with charitable purposes and does not engage in activities that could jeopardize its tax exempt status, periodic reviews shall be conducted. The periodic reviews shall, at a minimum, include the following subjects:

a. Whether compensation arrangements and benefits are reasonable, based on competent survey information, and the result of arm's length bargaining.

b. Whether partnerships, joint ventures, and arrangements with management organizations conform to Museum's written policies, are properly recorded, reflect reasonable investment or payments for goods and services, further charitable purposes, do not use Museum's name or logo improperly, and do not result in inurement, impermissible private benefit, or an excess benefit transaction.

c. Whether Museum officials and employees have adhered to Museum's policies on refraining from personal involvement in the acquisition of objects in any personal collecting activity and have ensured Museum has not participated directly or indirectly in dealing illicitly in the natural or cultural heritage.

ARTICLE XIV

Use of Outside Experts

When conducting the periodic reviews as provided for in Article XIII, Museum may, but need not, use outside advisors. If outside experts are used, their use shall not relieve the governing board of its responsibility for ensuring periodic reviews are conducted.

____

Chair of Board of Directors (Trustee) of ____________ Museum

Dated ______________

B. AGREEMENT TO HOLD HARMLESS

I, ____________, agree to assume full responsibility for my safety while participating in a travel tour of ____________ arranged by __________ Museum. I hereby release ________ Museum, its officials, employees, and agents from any and all claims or actions resulting from any injury that may occur to me while I am participating in this travel tour. I agree to reimburse ______________ Museum for any damages it is compelled to pay, arising from any claim, demand, action, or cause of action, on my behalf as a result of this travel tour.

____________ ____________ ____________________________

Date Participant

____

Parent or Guardian if Participant is under Eighteen Years of Age

C. LICENSING AGREEMENT

This Licensing Agreement is made and entered into this _____ day of ______________, 20____, by and between ______________ Museum, a nonprofit corporation of the State of ___________, having an address at ___________________________, hereinafter referred as "Licensor," and ____________________, a corporation of the State of ______________, having an address at ________________________________, hereinafter referred to as "Licensee."

Whereas, Licensor asserts and warrants that it is the owner of all right, title, and interest in and to _________________, hereinafter called Product.

Whereas, Licensee desires to acquire an exclusive license to make, use, and sell reproductions of Product in the following territory: ____________________. Now, therefore, in consideration of the mutual covenants, conditions and limitations hereinafter set forth, the Parties hereto agree as follows:

1. Licensor grants to Licensee permission to manufacture, distribute, advertise, and market Product, which shall consist of the following ________________________________. The license herein granted to the Licensee by Licensor shall be executed only in the following territory: ______________________________.

2. Licensee agrees to pay Licensor as royalties or license fees, ____ percent (____) of Licensee's gross selling price of Product. Royalties paid on sales which are not accepted by the customer shall be credited against further royalty payments to be made. All costs incurred in the manufacturing and promoting of Product shall be the obligation of Licensee. Royalties shall not be reduced by costs incurred by Licensee for manufacturing and promoting of Product.

3. On or before the first days of March and September of each year, Licensee shall render a report to Licensor indicating the quantity of Products sold by Licensee during the preceding six months' period ending on the last days of December and June of each year, and with each of said reports, Licensee shall make payment to Licensor of the royalty which shall be due and payable in accordance with paragraph 2. At all times, Licensor or its duly authorized agent or attorney shall have access to the books of Licensee insofar as the books shall be pertinent to the subject matter of this agreement, and Licensor shall have the right to have a representative present when any examination of the books of Licensee shall be made.

4. Licensor will furnish Licensee in writing standards of quality for Product, and Licensee agrees to meet the standards of quality established by Licensor. Licensee recognizes the substantial value of the goodwill associated with Product and acknowledges that all rights therein and goodwill pertaining thereto belong exclusively to Licensor. Licensee acknowledges that if the Product manufactured and sold were of inferior quality in design, material, or workmanship, the reputation and goodwill of Licensor would be impaired. Accordingly, Licensee warrants that the licensed Product shall be of high quality. Licensor shall be the sole judge of whether or not Licensee has met or is meeting the standards of quality so established. Licensee agrees to deliver a specimen of the product to Licensor for inspection, and the written approval of the Licensor's designated employee as to the design standards of workmanship, quality of presentation, and intrinsic merit of the product shall be necessary before Licensee begins sales of the product. Licensor shall have the right to withhold approval, but Licensor is deemed to have approved the product unless Licensee is notified to the contrary within two weeks of receipt of the specimen of the product. At periodic intervals beginning with the date of this Agreement, Licensee agrees to send Licensor evidence of the continued quality of the product, for the approval of Licensor.

5. Licensee agrees to supply Licensor free of charge with __________ specimens of Product not later than the first day of issue to the public.

6. Licensee shall not make use of the name of the Licensor in any respect without prior written consent of Licensor. Licensee acknowledges it is not an agent of Licensor and agrees it will not in any manner represent itself as such in the course of the License.

7. All artwork and designs involving Product, or any reproduction thereof, shall be, and remain, the property of Licensor, and Licensor shall be entitled to use the same and to license their use by others.

8. Licensor grants this license on the express condition that the prices, terms, and conditions of sale for use or sale of licensed products shall be no more favorable to the customer than those which from time to time Licensor establishes and maintains for its own sales of similar or competing products. Licensee shall be notified of all such prices, terms, and conditions of sale fixed by Licensor.

9. Licensor assumes no liability to Licensor or third parties with respect to the licensed products manufactured or sold by Licensee. Licensee agrees to indemnify Licensor against all actions, claims, costs, damages, and expenses which Licensor may sustain as a result of the use or reproduction by Licensee

of any trademark, copyright, patent, method, or device in connection with the product. Licensee will secure at its own cost an adequate policy of product liability insurance covering Licensor as well as Licensee and will furnish a copy of the certificate to Licensor.

10. The license herein granted shall not be assignable or transferable in any manner whatsoever by Licensee.

11. This agreement shall terminate in the event of the bankruptcy or insolvency of Licensee. In any event, this agreement shall terminate on ____________________; however, Licensor has the option to renew this agreement for another _____ year period.

12. If either party fails to observe or perform any term of this Agreement, the nondefaulting party shall have the right to elect to terminate this agreement if the default is not cured within thirty (30) days after the nondefaulting party shall have given the defaulting party written notice specifying the default. In this regard, if Licensee fails to produce Product for sale by ______________________, Licensor has the option to terminate this agreement. In the event of termination for failure to produce Product for sale by __________________, all development costs shall be the obligation of Licensee.

13. This agreement shall be governed by and construed and enforced in accordance with, and subject to, the laws of the State of _________________.

Licensee:	Licensor:
__________________________	______________________ Museum
By________________________	By__________________________

D. FORM FOR GIFT OF PERSONALTY

I, __________________, of __________________, State of _____________, own the items described below. I desire to give the described property to ________________ Museum, whose address is ___________________________ __________, State of _______________.

To carry out this purpose, I do hereby give and deliver to ___________________ Museum the property described as follows:____.

I distinctly understand and declare that it is my purpose and intention to vest all incidents of absolute ownership of the property in ___________________________ Museum as of this date.

Dated: ____________________.

____

_______________________ Donor

ACCEPTANCE

The property above described donated to ____________________ Museum is hereby accepted by ____________________ Museum.

____________________ Museum

By ________________________

(Official Title)

Dated: _______________

E. BAILMENT LOAN CONTRACT[2]

By this agreement, made and entered into by and between ___________, hereinafter called Bailor, and _____________ Museum, hereinafter called Bailee, the Bailor, for and in consideration of the sum of _________ Dollars, paid by Bailee to Bailor, the receipt of which is hereby acknowledged, loans to Bailee the following described property:

1. Article (Artifact)

   Value to Owner ____

   Condition ____

2. Article (Artifact)

   Value to Owner ____

   Condition ____

   subject to the terms and conditions hereinafter set forth.

1. Delivery of the property on loan shall be made to Bailee at _____________. Acceptance or retention by Bailee of the above described property shall constitute acknowledgment that the property was received in good order and repair.

2. The term of this bailment shall commence on __________ and shall terminate on ___________.

3. The loaned property shall at all times during this bailment remain and be the sole and exclusive property of Bailor, and Bailee shall have no right of property therein. Bailee shall not transfer or deliver the loaned property to any other person or entity without prior written consent or instruction of Bailor, and Bailee may not assign this agreement or the bailment hereby granted either by its own act or by operation of law.

4. Bailee agrees to exhibit the above described loaned property in the following manner and at the specified times: ____________________________

____

____

____.

5. The amount of space allotted to display of the bailed property is _________________. Bailee is to determine and control the method of exhibition and any publicity given the exhibition.

6. The loaned property shall remain in Bailee's possession for the time specified in this agreement, but Bailee may withdraw the property from exhibition under the following circumstances: ______________________________ ______________________________________.

7. Bailee binds itself to keep and maintain the property with proper care so that the loaned property shall not be injured, ordinary wear and tear excepted. Bailee shall not be liable for damage or loss caused by war, confiscation, order of any government or public authority, or discoloration from natural or inherent causes or by any and all causes beyond Bailee's control.

8. Bailee will protect the loaned property by insurance against loss by fire and theft, payable to Bailor to the full amount of the valuation declared by Bailor and so noted opposite each article (artifact) listed herein (on page 1 of this contract). Bailee shall not be liable for any loss or damage to the loaned property in excess of the value declared by Bailor, and set out in this contract, at the time of signing this contract, and if a valuation is not declared, the liability of Bailee as to all articles (artifacts) hereby loaned shall be limited to ________________ Dollars.

9. All shipping and packaging costs for the bailed property will be paid by ___________.

10. On the expiration of the term of this bailment, Bailee shall redeliver the property hereby loaned to Bailor, in accordance with the terms and conditions set forth in this agreement. The delivery of the loaned property to a common carrier, or to any address directed by Bailor or Bailor's representative, shall be considered delivery to Bailor.

11. If, after reasonable efforts, Bailee is unable to return the work within ninety days after termination of this agreement, Bailee shall have the right to place the work in storage and to charge regular storage fees and insurance and to have a lien for such fees and costs. If Bailor does not reclaim the property after five years, the property shall become a gift to Bailee.

12. On termination of this bailment in any manner, Bailor or its agents are hereby authorized to enter upon Bailee's premises and to remove and take possession of the loaned property. Bailor may inspect the property before taking possession or accepting delivery, and if the inspection establishes that any part of the property is not in the condition required above, Bailee will do all that is necessary to place the property in the required condition.

13. Bailor and Bailee agree that no modification of this agreement shall be binding unless the modification shall be in writing duly accepted and executed by both parties.

Dated ________________

____

________________________________ Bailor

________________________________ Museum

________________________________ Bailee

NOTES

1. Taken in part from Sample Conflict of Interest Policy provided by the Internal Revenue Service as an Appendix to its instructions to Form 1023 and from the Conflicts of Interest Sections of the International Council of Museums (ICOM) Code of Ethics for Museums.

2. See 17 Texas Form § 17:14 (Bancroft-Whitney Co.) A bailment contract should specify the bailed property and its value and limit the museum's liability to that stated value. Space allotted to the bailed property and the method of exhibition and amount of publicity given the exhibit should be set out in the contract. The designation of bailed property that is not claimed by the bailor after a designated period of time as a gift to the museum can clarify the status of property left on loan indefinitely.

INDEX

ABOUT THE AUTHOR

Marilyn E. Phelan, J.D. (with honors), University of Texas School of Law, Ph.D., Texas Tech University, was the recipient of the Paul Whitfield Horn Professor of Law at Texas Tech University, which is one of the highest honors Texas Tech University can bestow on its professors. Phelan also has served as a professor of museum science at Texas Tech University. She is a certified public accountant and is certified by the Texas Board of Legal Specialization as a specialist in tax law. She was given a YWCA Woman of Excellence award and was named a Super Lawyer by *Texas Monthly*. In 2011, the American Bar Association Section of Business Law, Nonprofit Committee, awarded her the ABA Outstanding Nonprofit Academic Award for contributions and achievements in the field of nonprofit law.

www.ingramcontent.com/pod-product-compliance
Ingram Content Group UK Ltd.
Pitfield, Milton Keynes, MK11 3LW, UK
UKHW020905190926
475560UK00010B/193

9 780759 124349